EXPERIMENTAL SOCIAL PSYCHOLOGY

C

EXPERIMENTAL SOCIAL PSYCHOLOGY

Judson Mills EDITOR
University of Missouri

The Macmillan Company
Collier-Macmillan Limited, London

First Printing

Library of Congress catalog card number: 69–13571

THE MACMILLAN COMPANY
COLLIER-MACMILLAN CANADA, LTD., TORONTO, ONTARIO

PRINTED IN THE UNITED STATES OF AMERICA

To Leon Festinger

PREFACE

My main purpose in editing this book was to produce a work that will show what has been and what can be accomplished with the experimental method in social psychology. I hope that the book will make clear the value of the experimental method for the development of theoretical principles in social psychology. As social psychologists have tried to understand the phenomena of their subject, they have become increasingly interested in testing general explanatory principles and have turned more and more to the experimental method because of its great power in testing theoretical ideas.

Even though it has come to be increasingly recognized as the best method to use in investigating basic hypotheses, the experimental method is still not exploited as much as it might be in social psychology. The failure to use the experimental method when it could be used seems to be due to a lack of understanding of the nature of experiments. Partly, this seems to stem from a confusion between experimental investigations and laboratory investigations. I try to clarify the difference between experimental and laboratory studies in Chapter 15.

Somewhat ironically, the failure to appreciate the power of the experimental method seems to have occurred as an indirect consequence of this very power. Because of its great power, the experimental method has enormous prestige in science. As a result of the prestige associated with the term *experiment*, the feeling has developed that to describe a study as nonexperimental is to condemn it as unscientific. This is, of course, incorrect. There are many important scientific investigations that are not experiments, in which there is no manipulation of variables by the investigators. In fact, there are whole areas of science in which experimental work is not possible. The classic example is astronomy.

Because of the mistaken impression that nonexperimental studies are necessarily unscientific, the term *experiment* has sometimes been used very loosely to refer to any study that is conducted systematically enough to yield scientifically valuable results. The unfortunate consequence has been to blur the distinction between experimental and nonexperimental studies. Naturally enough, this tendency has occurred most frequently among those who have been concerned with problems that are impossible or difficult to study experimentally. The blurring of the difference between experimental and nonexperimental studies has made it more difficult for social psychologists to appreciate the advantages that can be gained from doing experiments. As a result, nonexperimental studies have sometimes been done to investigate social psychological problems that could be studied experimentally.

In addition to showing the value of the experimental method in social psychology, I hope that the book will help to clarify what experimental social psychology is and to resolve the issue of whether it will become a distinct area of specialization within psychology. In the past few years there have been a number of signs that it is becoming a clearly identified area of specialization. A new journal entitled *Experimental Social Psychology* has been founded, and a Society of Experimental Social Psychology has been formed. More and more psychologists who a few years ago would have identified themselves simply as social psychologists have come to consider themselves as experimental social psychologists. I hope that the book will help those of us who regard ourselves as experimental social psychologists to define what our field is.

In planning the book, I tried to choose the topics for the different sections so as to encompass the major areas of experimental research in social psychology at the present time. My choice of titles for the sections was of necessity somewhat arbitrary. Other experimental social psychologists would probably not make exactly the same choices. Disagreement about what the important problems are is to be expected in an area that is growing very rapidly. An indication of the rapid growth of experimental social psychology is the fact that almost all of the experiments cited in this book were published within the past twenty years and a majority within the past ten years. A tidy classification of the area would be premature at this time and might even hamper theoretical advances that would link previously unrelated phenomena.

I asked people who are actively engaged in research to write about the current state of knowledge concerning the different topics. Although I made suggestions, it was left to the individual authors to decide what should be discussed in their particular sections. I asked that they include only experimental studies—that is, studies in which the independent variables were manipulated. They were encouraged to be selective and were not asked to include every experiment but only those that made important contributions.

My original goal of including all of the important experiments in social psychology in one section or another has most probably not been achieved. The necessity of focusing on the important theoretical issues in order to make the experimental results meaningful by putting them into a theoretical context has meant that inevitably some very good experiments have been left out because they did not deal with any of the particular issues discussed.

Having a number of persons write different sections of a book has the disadvantage that the book may be somewhat lacking in unity of style and approach and that the level of analysis may vary from one part to another. However, I feel that there is a greater advantage to be gained from having the research in an area discussed by a person with a specialized knowledge of the area. Someone who is actively engaged in research is able to analyze the work in his area in a much more penetrating and sophisticated way. With a field that is expanding as rapidly as experimental social psychology, virtually superhuman effort would be required for one person to adequately digest and interpret all the relevant research.

Although the book deals with many of the most important problems in social psychology, the coverage is not the same as that of an introductory textbook in social psychology, nor is the book intended as a text for introductory courses. It assumes a basic familiarity with social psychology. The hope is rather that it will prove useful in advanced courses dealing with experimental social psychology. In addition to furnishing students with an understanding of the important issues that have concerned experimenters in social psychology, hopefully it will also provide a stimulus to researchers by highlighting gaps and inconsistencies in the research literature.

The dedication of this book to Leon Festinger is an attempt to acknowledge my personal debt to him and also to indicate the contribution he has made to experimental social psychology. More than any other person, he has been responsible for the development of the field. His work, which combines penetrating theoretical insight and incisive experimental design, has set the standard for research in the area and has provided a great stimulus for theoretically relevant experimental work.

J. M.

CONTENTS

PART

IV

Interdependence in Groups
Eugene Burnstein   **307**

PART

V

The Experimental Method
Judson Mills   **407**

Index

PART

I

Interpersonal Attraction, Hostility, and Perception

Dana Bramel

State University of New York at Stony Brook

1

Attraction Toward
Those Who Reward Us

The focus of these first three chapters is on attitudes—the evaluative dimensions of liking and disliking, the dispositions of approach and avoidance. In the final chapter in the section, the emphasis is on interpersonal perception—the ways in which people develop beliefs about the characteristics of other people. Of course attitudes and beliefs, however analytically distinguishable, are closely related. But the distinction does provide a defensible basis for organizing an otherwise overwhelming quantity of experimental data.

Precise operational definitions of attitudinal concepts such as liking, hostility, avoidance, and aggression are hard to come by in the literature of social psychology. In most of the experiments discussed in this section of the book attitudinal dispositions have been operationalized as pencil marks on a verbal scale, and usually the subject is led to believe that the mark he makes will have no further consequences and is confidential. This constitutes a dilution of Moreno's (1934) original stricture that the most valid response can be pried out of the subject only by promising him that his mark on the page will determine who his roommate or teammate will be. If our goal is to discover with whom the subject would like to associate in context X, task Y, or interaction Z, then Moreno is very probably correct. However, a person can conceal his true feelings even on a measure that commits him to interaction with the person he chooses. Sometimes, for example, person A might choose B, not because he likes B best, but rather because he fears that no one else will choose B and that B will feel hurt when he discovers it.

What is the best way to measure liking and disliking? One possibility is the anonymous reward-or-punishment technique. If we truly like someone, it pleases us to see him happy and hurts us to see him suffer. If we dislike him, our reaction is just the opposite. If this is so, then the person should be expected to give to those he likes the things he believes they want, and to those he dislikes, the things he believes they do not want (or at least withhold the things they want). That is, the person should be motivated to make his friend happy and his enemy unhappy. But perhaps he would try to convert his enemy into a friend by sending him gifts. To prevent this source of invalidity in the measure, the "gift" must be anonymous. This inhibits the subject from employing reward or punishment giving as a strategy for gaining anything but the pleasure or displeasure of observing or imagining the recipient's reaction to what he gets. Yet other problems remain. The person may send a reward to B, not because he especially likes B, but rather because he believes that B needs it more than A does. This is the same problem that came up in connection with Moreno's sociometric technique. Perhaps the only solution to this is to choose the type of reward–punishment dimension carefully and ensure that subjects in different experimental conditions do not perceive differential need for the reward in the target person.

A number of experiments have used measures of this sort. For example, subjects are asked to rate a research assistant confidentially, and they are under the impression that the ratings will actually be used by the powers that be to determine whether or not to continue to employ the assistant. This seems a fairly valid (on the face of it) way to measure the benevolence–malevolence of the subject's reaction to the assistant, although it also contains a strong indication of the subject's degree of respect for the assistant's competence in addition to reflecting the amount of his affection for the assistant. It is rare in psychology to find a measure that taps a single dimension and *only* that dimension. Any indicator inevitably is influenced by a number of factors. The important thing is to choose an indicator and an experimental design that effectively balance out the irrelevant factors so that differences between experimental conditions can be attributed to differences in the liking–disliking variable.

The preceding brief discussion conveys, hopefully, some idea of what this section of the book is about. We will be concerned with the *attitudes* that people have toward each other. The attitude dimension is one of evaluation, of good–bad, like–dislike, approach–avoid. It is helpful to distinguish it from the concept of *belief* (cf. Fishbein and Raven, 1962). A belief is a statement, proposition, or expectation that some entity (for example, a person) possesses a given characteristic, or attribute. Such a proposition can be considered, for analytical purposes, independently of the evaluative dimension. Thus, a person might have the *belief* that warfare reduces population, causes inflation, reduces the suicide rate, sells newspapers, and makes many people either very rich or very poor. These propositions about the characteristics of the situation in time of war may be accepted by the person with varying degrees of certainty, and they are all, in principle, capable of being empirically tested for their truth or falsity. A person holding these particular beliefs may or may not have a positive *attitude* toward war. That depends in large part upon whether he *approves of* or *likes* the various characteristics he attributes to war. An attitude is an evaluation of approval or disapproval and is not strictly capable of being called true or false. The attribution of specific, in principle verifiable, characteristics to persons is discussed in detail in Chapter 4.

In the first two chapters we deal with the stimulus characteristics of the target person—that is, the person toward whom the attitude is directed. The target person presents a certain set of characteristics, which may be perceived with varying degrees of accuracy by the observer. These stimuli include everything from personal appearance to verbal behavior to actions of aggression or benevolence. Anything about the target person is capable of arousing an attitude toward him in the observer.

In the present chapter we shall discuss a number of target-person characteristics that are likely to be pleasant and rewarding to the observer. The result, following a simple hedonistic rule that is seldom (if ever) violated, is that such a person evokes a positive attitude. In the next chapter we focus upon some of the more punishing aspects of interpersonal interaction. There we examine what happens when another person blocks our progress toward a goal or somehow injures our self-esteem. What happens to the resulting hostility, and how does it become reduced (if it does)? In the third chapter the focus moves away from the stimulus characteristics of the target person (B) and shifts to the consequences of A's action toward B. Are A's attitudes toward B affected by the ways in which A acts toward him?

The Effects of Physical Proximity and Interaction

In the absence of beliefs about the characteristics of person X, group X, or category of persons X, it is probably unusual to hold a strongly positive or negative attitude toward X. Objects about which we feel we know nothing rarely inspire us with love or hate. It *may* be possible under rather unusual circumstances. Rosenberg (1960), for example, reports some success in implanting attitudes under hypnosis without giving the subjects any information about the target of the attitudes. Note also that rather weak attitudes may exist toward groups about which a person knows nothing except that they are strangers or foreigners. The classic study by Hartley (1946) indicated that American subjects who had a generally favorable or unfavorable attitude toward foreigners in general would, if asked, make consistently positive or negative attitude statements

toward fictitious nationalities about whom they had no specific information whatsoever. Even without such specific information, however, these
subjects certainly believed that "Wallonians, Pireneans, and Daniereans"
were not like typical home-town Americans. In other words, the subjects
had *some*, although minimal, cognitions about their characteristics, if only
that these foreigners must surely be different from them in many ways.

It follows that strong attitudes are likely to be associated with having
something more than minimal information (whether true or false) about
the target. One good way to get information about somebody is to be
geographically close to him. The closer you are physically to someone,
the more likely it is that you will have strong attitudes toward that person.
Since you can sometimes be physically very close to someone but never
see him or interact with him (as is the case with some urban apartment
dwellers), obviously proximity is not always enough. But, other things
being equal, it helps.

Note that the hypothesis being developed here states that *both* strong
positive *and* strong negative attitudes are more likely toward targets
close by than those far away, simply because strong attitudes require
information of some sort. For the moment let us ignore the possibility
that *too much* information may actually inhibit the development of strong
attitudes. Given the foregoing hypothesis, it is interesting to find that most
of the empirical studies of the relation between proximity and attitudes
have focused upon the occurrence of *positive* attitudes. Correlational
studies of the relation between closeness of residence and probability of
selecting someone as a marriage partner (for example, Bossard, 1932)
show the expected results; but how about the probability of selecting
someone to beat up or rob? This example is perhaps ill chosen, because
beating up and robbing are more likely to be punished if the targets
know their attacker and can thus retaliate against him. What we really
need, then, are more direct measures of attitude, uncontaminated by
some of the powerful incentives affecting overtly benevolent or malevolent acts.

Of course, we can guess with considerable confidence what the results
of any such empirical investigations would be. If you bring together two
people who behave in punishing ways toward each other, the effect of
the proximity will be to produce negative attitudes (see, for example,
the data presented in the next chapter). If they reward each other, they
will probably develop positive attitudes toward each other. In a sense,
then, proximity by itself is probably not the most powerful variable. The
important thing is not so much having information about someone (which
is facilitated by being nearby), but rather the specific nature of that information. On contact, you can discover whether a man is a devil or a

saint, and your attitude will be affected accordingly. Without contact, you are less likely to discover these things about him.

Does this mean that proximity is a completely "empty" variable in that it has no relation to the *direction* in which subsequent attitudes develop? This is a question that has not received much empirical scrutiny. In order to test for the effects of proximity uncontaminated by the specific kind of information that is transmitted about the person, the following sort of design might be called for. All subjects in the experiment could be given a controlled amount of information about someone who was previously completely unknown to them. The independent variable would be manipulated by telling some subjects that they will be interacting with this stranger at a future time, whereas the other subjects are not told that they will ever meet the stranger. Then attitudes toward the stranger are measured. This would be a step in the direction of testing for the effect simply of knowing that you will be interacting with someone, independent of having any special knowledge about him. Such an experiment has in fact been carried out by Darley and Berscheid (1967). They started with Heider's (1958) idea that when a person feels that he and someone else are somehow part of a perceptual unit (or gestalt), there is a tendency for liking to result. The college-girl subjects in this experiment were asked to participate in continuing two-person discussion groups to talk about their own sexual behavior and standards. The experimenter gave the subject two folders of personality information allegedly describing two strangers to the subject. These two sets of descriptions had been pretested to ensure that they produced approximately equal degrees of liking (or, rather, neutrality). Before reading through the folders, the subject was told that one or the other stranger had been "randomly" selected to be her discussion partner. Knowing this, the subject's task was to read through the folders for about five minutes each and then to make some ratings of the two girls. The rationale given for this was that someone unconnected with the research on sexual behavior had asked that this rating procedure be inserted as part of a study of "interpersonal judgment." The design was counterbalanced so that half the subjects believed that girl *A* would be their discussion partner, and half expected to be with girl *B*. Dependent measures included questions such as, "How probable is it that you would like this girl?" The results indicated clearly that the subjects expressed more liking for the girl who had been "randomly selected" to be their discussion partner.

Mirels and Mills (1964) performed a similar experiment. They told the subjects (all female) that each would be paired with some unknown classmate in a future problem-solving task. All subjects then privately read a questionnaire allegedly filled in by another female student. Half were told this person was to be their future partner, and half were told it was not their partner. Within each of these two sets of subjects, half read a questionnaire designed to imply that the target person was unpleasant, whereas half saw a more neutral set of responses. The dependent variables were the subjects' ratings of the pleasantness and competence of the target person. When judging the person who gave socially undesirable answers, subjects were more favorable toward her when they expected a future task interaction than when no meeting was likely. The ratings of the more neutral person were unaffected by the expectation of future interaction.

In a similar experiment in which subjects anticipated a cooperative interaction with another person, Lerner, Dillehay, and Sherer (1967) found rather mixed effects. On adjective rating scales the initially *less* attractive of two potential partners became more attractive, but attitude toward the initially *more* attractive person did not change. This fits well with the results of Mirels and Mills, cited above, who used the same kind of attitude measure. However, on a social-distance measure asking subjects, for example, how much they would like to get to know their partner personally, this difference did not emerge. The initially *more* attractive person became even more attractive, while attitude toward the less attractive partner did not change. In the face of these apparent inconsistencies, it seems premature to attempt to specify the particular conditions under which anticipated cooperative interaction leads to increased attraction.

What other processes could generate a relationship between proximity and attitude? If people had a general tendency to assume that someone they don't know is different from them, and if they generally exaggerated these differences, then, on the average, the more you learned about someone the more you would find that he is not as different as you thought. Since there is no strong evidence that people habitually assume more dissimilarity than truly exists, we cannot say whether proximity will typically increase liking on this basis. (Stotland, Cottrell, and Laing [1960] do present some evidence that interaction, at least initially, leads to increased attribution of similarity between oneself and the other person.) We might expect, however, that in those particular instances where dissimilarity *is* exaggerated, increased information about the stranger is likely to produce a more favorable attitude. In their study of white women living in racially integrated and segregated housing projects, Deutsch and Collins (1951) suggested this as a possibility. A white person who has never been in close contact with blacks may discover in an integrated apartment building that blacks are not as different as he had thought. As we know that perceived similarity of belief and attitude generates liking, proximity will often lead to increased liking if it allows similarity to be discovered.

Another possible mediating process relating proximity to liking is that information produces predictability. If people like someone better the more his behavior is predictable, then the more information, the more predictability, and the greater the liking. This relationship undoubtedly has an upper limit. Some people are so predictable as to be very boring.

Similarity in Beliefs and Attitudes

It is refreshing to deal with a topic that not only has been carefully researched but that also brings forth wide agreement within the field of social psychology. Why is agreement refreshing? That is one way to phrase the question with which this section is concerned.

To begin with, there is ample evidence that subjects in experiments say they like people whom the experimenter leads them to believe agree with their beliefs and attitudes; they are less favorable toward people who seem to disagree with them (Aronson and Worchel, 1966; Byrne, 1961a, 1961b, 1962; Byrne and Griffitt, 1966; Byrne and Clore, 1966; Byrne and McGraw, 1964; Byrne and Nelson, 1964, 1965; Byrne, Nelson, and Reeves, 1966; Byrne and Rhamey, 1965; Byrne and Wong, 1962; Emerson, 1954; Rokeach, 1960; Schachter, 1951; Smith, 1957; Stein, Hardyck, and Smith, 1965; Triandis, 1961; Worchel and Schuster, 1966). Triandis, Loh, and Levine (1966) and Berkowitz and Goranson (1964) report two of the few nonconfirmatory studies. In a very convincing, but not experimental, study in a more "real life" setting, Newcomb (1961) has presented ample evidence to document the same point. He measured the beliefs and attitudes of university students before they arrived on campus and found that their attitudes toward each other after they had lived in the same dormitory for awhile were strongly correlated with initial similarity in orientation toward a wide variety of things ranging from black-white marriages to chess and baseball. In experimental studies in which the manipulated agreement between the subject and the stranger was varied across a large number of values (from zero to 100 per cent), Byrne and Clore (1966), Byrne and Nelson (1965), and Byrne, Nelson, and Reeves (1966) found a linear positive relation between agreement and expressed liking for the stranger.

Although these studies are rather convincing in their consistency and the strength of the findings, there is a weakness in the designs that makes explanation of the obtained relationships somewhat ambiguous. Consider the following example: Imagine a person who believes that capital punishment is a very undesirable social institution. When you confront this person with a stranger who is perceived to favor capital punishment, you find typically that the stranger is not liked. Is he disliked because he is *different* from the subject, or because he holds a *specific* belief? If our subject has learned that people who favor capital punishment are to be shunned because they possess all kinds of unpleasant, even immoral, attributes, then perhaps his disliking for the stranger is traceable to specific training concerning people who hold this specific belief. On the other hand, perhaps he dislikes the stranger because perceiving the difference between their attitudes shakes his confidence in his own attitude and makes him feel that perhaps he has been wrong to oppose capital punishment and to participate in demonstrations to that effect. If people find it unpleasant to have their beliefs and attitudes questioned, or to be told in effect that the goals to which they are committed are wrong-headed, then perhaps there is a tendency to dislike the person who introduces this cognitive dissonance (Festinger, 1957). To put these two interpretations of the liking and similarity data in simple terms, the issue is this: Do we dislike the disagreeing person because we have been trained to believe and feel that people with that particular point of view are immoral and stupid? Or do we dislike the person because any point of view different from our own punishes us because it shakes our confidence in our own correctness and questions the validity of our own commitments? When a stranger disagrees with us, are we responding to the *relationship* (the difference between our positions) or to a particular stimulus (his attitude) that we have in the past been trained to consider evil?

The research we have considered has uniformly confounded these two interpretations. How could they be separately tested? One way would be to take a group of subjects with similar opinions on a certain issue. Half the subjects would then be subjected to an effective manipulation that changes their opinions, while the others are left unchanged. Both groups are then exposed to a stranger who holds the opinion that all subjects initially agreed with. If the group of subjects whose opinions are now different from the stranger's dislike him more than do those who agree with him, one might argue that an explanation in terms of past training to dislike people with that opinion cannot account for the results.

Relevant to the question of why we dislike those who disagree with us, several studies have attempted to test the idea that we respond most favorably to an agreeing person when our confidence in our own opinion has been previously shaken. Worchel and McCormick (1963) found more liking for an agreeing person when the subject was uncertain rather than certain about his own point of view. Gerard and Greenbaum (1962) found an increase in liking for a stooge who supported the subjects when their confidence in their own judgments was especially low. Worchel and Schuster (1966) led each subject to believe he was a member of a five-man group in which all were working privately on the same "human-relations" problem in different experimental cubicles. After the subject had made his decision about the problem, he passed it along, with supporting written reasons, to the others in the "group." He then received, one by one, the written decisions of the four other persons. Different subjects received different patterns of agreement and disagreement in the set of four serial messages. Some found that the others all agreed with them; some found that the first one agreed but that the rest disagreed; the remainder discovered that the first three disagreed and the last agreed with them. The dependent measure asked the subject to rate each of the imaginary group members on degree of "liking to work with him" on a problem-solving task in the near future. The agreeing fourth man was liked significantly more when preceded by three who disagreed with the subject than when the first three had supported his own point of view. Although other interpretations of the data are possible, these results are certainly consistent with the hypothesis.

Byrne, Nelson, and Reeves (1966) predicted that subjects would care more about whether others agreed with them on unverifiable (policy, value, and taste) issues than on issues that could be settled by reference to the nearest encyclopedia or newspaper. Their results indicated that liking for a stranger was more affected by proportion of agreement on matters of value and preference than on matters of fact. This does not necessarily mean that people are more *uncertain* about the validity of their preferences (attitudes) than of their beliefs (empirically verifiable propositions). In fact, Crutchfield (1955) has presented some data indicating that people are more yielding to social pressure in matters of fact than in matters of value. The explanation for the findings of Byrne et al. probably lies elsewhere. Perhaps people believe attitudes to be more indicative of a person's motives, and thus of his goodness and badness; beliefs seem more indicative of a man's intelligence and competence. Intuitively, it appears that we like or dislike others more as a function of their perceived motivations than of their perceived abilities. Provided that our fate is not in the hands of a man, are we not more irked by his bad intentions than by his poor abilities? For the first, we feel disgust and a desire to punish; for the second, we are more likely to feel pity and even a desire to help.

If we are inclined to dislike a person who shakes our confidence in our own judgment, then heretics and renegades may arouse considerable hostility from members of the group with which they originally agreed. We often expect people with different backgrounds, values, and group memberships to disagree with us, especially on matters of attitude (as contrasted with matters of fact). When this expectation is confirmed in any given instance, our confidence is not particularly shaken. We are able very quickly to explain the disagreement and derogate the source of it; we are not caught off our guard. The situation is different when someone who was believed or expected to be firmly on our side is suddenly perceived to differ from us (the heretic) or even to have deserted our side and joined the ideological enemy (the renegade). Such a person shakes our confidence severely; one reason probably is that the heresy or apostasy calls into question either one's most deeply held values or the validity of the attitudes originally felt to be directly derived from those values. When someone originally committed to our side deserts the cause, something appears to be seriously out of joint. It is unexpected, and the deviant cannot be so easily derogated. Further, such deviation may threaten the survival of the group, either by internal confusion (the heretic) or by giving substantial direct aid to the enemy (the renegade).

An experiment by Iwao (1963) tested the effects of "heresy." The subjects, divinity-school students, heard criticism of the motives and values of their own group. The source of the criticism was allegedly either another divinity student (ingroup member) or a law student (outgroup member), always acted by the same stooge. After hearing the strong criticism, the subject was asked to make a (private) rating of attitude toward the source. The results were striking. The divinity-school subjects said they had "more in common" with the law student, as a partner, and rated him more likable, pleasant, and warm. Apparently the heretic aroused hostility, whereas disagreement from the law student came as no great surprise to the subjects.

Singer, Radloff, and Wark (1963) report a related experiment that involved a "heretic" who disagreed with the group concerning basic procedures in a problem-solving task. Because he also clearly prevented the group from succeeding, his disagreement had consequences over and above the shaking of group confidence in its attitudes. In any case, the heretic did reap dislike for his deviation. The renegade, who deserted the group in midstream, stating he wanted to join the other competing team, ended up more disliked by far than the regular members of the "enemy" team. Part of the hostility was perhaps due to the fact that he was obviously a very competent person who would no doubt help the enemy win the contest. Hence his defection had a number of punishing consequences.

Attraction and Similarity in Attitude Toward Ourselves

Do we like people who agree with us about our own attributes, and who have the same attitude toward ourselves that we have? No one will be surprised to hear that, in general, most people appreciate people who seem to like them more than people who seem to dislike them. This proposition has received support from a myriad of experiments (for example, Aronson and Linder, 1965; Aronson and Worchel, 1966; Berkowitz and Macaulay, 1961; Byrne and Griffitt, 1966; Byrne and Rhamey, 1965; Dickoff, 1961; Dittes, 1959; Dittes and Kelley, 1956; Harvey, 1962; Harvey and Clapp, 1965; Harvey, Kelley, and Shapiro, 1957; Howard and Berkowitz, 1958; Jones, 1964; Jones, Gergen, and Davis, 1962; Pepinsky, Hemphill, and Shevitz, 1958; Pepitone and Wilpizeski, 1960; Snoek, 1962; Walster and Walster, 1963).

What about people who *dislike* themselves or attribute undesirable characteristics to themselves? If you have such attitudes and beliefs about yourself, how do you react to a person who seems to like you and claims that you do not possess those undesirable attributes? If we are to be consistent with the statement that people having attitudes and beliefs similar to our own are liked, must we predict that, other things being equal, the self-derogating individual likes better those who derogate him than those who praise him? Such an outcome would probably surprise most people, and it is not likely to stand up under empirical testing. The reason is that people—even those who dislike themselves—probably prefer to be liked than disliked by the important persons in their environment. We should tentatively rephrase the prediction concerning similarity as follows: A person who dislikes you will be liked more by you if you also dislike yourself than if you like yourself. Similarly, if a person likes you very much, you should therefore like him in direct proportion to how much you like yourself. The general rule, covering the preceding two statements, would be as follows: Holding constant person A's attitude toward person B, B should like A more the more similar their attitudes toward B. This still seems unsatisfactory. Since the person who dislikes himself is more in need of help from others to raise his self-esteem, perhaps it follows that he will feel more warmth for someone who likes him than would the person who already thinks well of himself and does not need the affection of others. A test of the similarity hypothesis therefore requires that all combinations of high and low self-esteem and the receipt of liking or disliking from the other person be examined. The prediction from the hypothesis that attitude similarity is important would be that low–self-esteem people would differ less in their resultant liking for the affectionate and hostile others than would the high–self-esteem people. The low–self-esteem person has reason to like the affectionate other because it helps to raise self-esteem (Dittes, 1959); and there may be reason to like the uncomplimentary person because of agreement concerning the person's self. High–self-esteem people would have no reason to like the person who dislikes them, and they would like the affectionate person both because of similarity in attitude and perhaps because this affection helps to maintain a high level of self-esteem.

A fully experimental test of this hypothesis would involve temporarily manipulating the self-esteem of subjects in such a way that some were convinced they were very fine and some were convinced they were very unattractive. Each subject would then be exposed to convincing evidence that a stranger either liked them or disliked them on the basis of a controlled amount of contact. The closest approximation to this design is an experiment by Walster (1965). Unfortunately for us, only two of the crucial four cells of the ideal design were represented. Prior to the self-esteem manipulation, a male stooge "accidentally" met each female subject, struck up a conversation with her, and ended up asking her for a date. After the stooge had left, the experimenter gave the subject falsified results from a battery of personality tests taken earlier. Half of the subjects were encouraged to think they were wonderfully well adjusted, whereas the other half were made to doubt whether they would ever succeed at anything. Each subject was then asked to make some ratings of various people, including the stooge who had pretended to find her so attractive. The subjects with low self-esteem expressed more favorable attitudes toward the stooge than did those with high self-esteem. Fascinating as this experiment is, it does not really help us to answer the question with which we started. There is no way to establish in advance the relative power of the two opposing forces we have been discussing. Although the high–self-esteem subjects presumably find themselves in agreement with the stooge concerning their attractiveness, the low–self-esteem subjects certainly have reason to be grateful to the stooge for helping them to regain a more favorable attitude toward themselves. In order to preserve our hypothesis about the role of similarity, we would have to predict that a stooge who pretended to *dislike* the subject would be *much* more attractive to girls with low than with high self-esteem.

A line of reasoning similar to the foregoing has been presented by Deutsch and Solomon (1959), who describe an experiment that comes close to meeting our requirements, although it does not deal with globally defined self-esteem. Subjects were induced to believe that they had performed well or poorly on two intellectual tasks. They then received evaluative comments from other persons concerning their performance and their desirability as teammates. Although there was a general tendency to like best the evaluator who praised and liked the subject, this was less frequent among failing than among successful subjects, consistent with the similarity hypothesis. A similarly designed experiment by Wilson (1965) produced further confirmatory results. Subjects who were induced to decide irrevocably to withdraw from a competition were inclined to dislike a partner who later told them that their ability was really high and that they therefore should have continued in the contest.

Contrary results are reported by Jones, Hester, Farina, and Davis (1959). They asked their subjects privately to predict the reactions of a stranger who was evaluating them. The stranger always sent a derogatory evaluation to the subject. It was found that the more favorably the subject predicted she would be rated, the more favorably she rated the derogating stranger. This contradicts the similarity hypothesis quite strikingly. However, it cannot be considered conclusive, because there is no convincing evidence that the predictions made by subjects about how they would be evaluated bore any strong relation to their actual self-esteem. The stranger was perceived to have almost no basis upon which to make her judgment, so the subject may not have expected any high degree of accuracy. If you are asked to predict the first impression you will make upon someone watching through a window, you may not predict that he will correctly evaluate your true worth. This is especially problematical in this particular experiment, because all subjects were told that one of the strangers who was watching and evaluating her was a very maladjusted person.

Jones (1964) suggests that the person who is *not firmly convinced* that he possesses a certain weakness, or undesirable characteristic, will not find it reinforcing to hear someone claim that in fact the weakness is very evident. It does seem plausible that a person only dimly aware of a fault will resent the person who reminds him of it more than would the person who is fully convinced that the flaw is there. Bramel (1962) has shown that a person who has been prepared for receiving derogatory information about himself by a prior manipulation lowering his self-esteem is less defensive about the new bad trait than are subjects whose self-esteem had been initially raised above its usual level.

When we move from the other's *attitudes* (favorable–unfavorable) toward you to the more neutral realm of his *beliefs* about whether or not you possess certain characteristics, the relation between similarity and liking may be easier to demonstrate. If you are right-handed and a stranger claims, after watching you write a letter by hand, that you are left-handed, you are bound to consider that person either unintelligent, not paying attention, or deliberately lying. In any case, your evaluation of him is likely not to be especially high, unless perhaps his response is interpreted as betraying a good sense of humor. To the extent that intelligent and truthful people are liked, the more incorrect someone's judgment about you is perceived to be, the less you will be inclined to like him. Jones (1964) reports several experiments that show, for example, that the suspicion that a person is lying in order to increase his attractiveness makes him relatively disliked. The flatterer is the classic case in point.

For a full and insightful discussion of the more subtle factors involved in flattery and related matters, the reader is referred to Jones's book *Ingratiation* (1964).

Although there is much evidence that people are attracted to those who are similar to them, some writers have questioned the universality of this statement. Concerning similarity in beliefs and attitudes regarding objects, persons, and events in the environment, the data are quite clear cut. Does the rule also apply to similarities in personality dimensions such as dominance–submission, introversion–extraversion, honesty, anxiety, intelligence, orality–anality–genitality, and masculinity–femininity? Understandably, there have not been many experimental studies of this issue. It is difficult to manipulate either the subject's own personality or that of the stimulus persons to whom he is exposed. A host of correlational studies have been done, and the results are highly mixed and confusing.

Restricting ourselves to experimental studies, we find that few are available for discussion. It would be especially interesting to test the "complementary needs" hypothesis of Winch (1952). Will a person who itches but cannot scratch like a person who scratches but does not itch? Will men like women? Will the dominant prefer to associate with the submissive, and vice versa? The idea seems eminently plausible. We find that no fully experimental studies have been reported. A number of studies have been done, however, in which subjects of different personalities are systematically exposed to other persons who are similar or different in certain dimensions (for example, Altrocci, 1959; Rychlak, 1965; Hoffman and Maier, 1966). These researchers manipulated neither the subject's personality nor that of the stimulus persons. Thus we can never be certain that other variables correlated with the personality dimensions are really randomized and irrelevant to the final results.

Further Studies of Attitudes Toward Friendly and Hostile Others

Walster and Walster (1963) reasoned that one explanation for the tendency to like and choose to affiliate with people who are similar to us is that those people often like us. We support their beliefs and attitudes just as they support ours. Their tendency to like us should thus make us like them all the more. Not only do they increase our confidence in our own beliefs and attitudes, they also give us affection. If this is true, then probably people *anticipate* that they will be liked by strangers who are similar to them. Walster and Walster showed that the more subjects were induced to be concerned about how much a discussion group would like them, the more they expressed a preference for being in a group of people similar in background to themselves. McWhirter and Jecker (1967) manipulated the extent to which a stranger appeared to agree with the subject on a set of questionnaire attitude items. The greater the perceived agreement, the more the average subject expected to be liked by the stranger. In a similar study, Bechtel and Rosenfeld (1966) found that students expect not to be liked by other students of either higher or lower social status than what they believe to be their own.

Given the overwhelming evidence that people generally prefer those who like and praise them to those who dislike them, does it follow that the best way to make someone like you is to feed him a constant stream of friendly, supportive information? Aronson and Linder (1965) doubted that this was true. They designed an experiment in which each subject participated in a series of seven separate brief interactions with a stooge during a single experimental session. After each brief interaction, in which the subject and the stooge conversed about various topics, the subject was given a chance to overhear the stooge and the experimenter talking in an adjoining room. The situation was neatly designed so that the subject was certain that the stooge did not know she (the subject) was listening in on the conversation. Because the experimenter told the subject that the stooge was instructed to form an impression of her, it seemed quite natural to the subject that what she overheard was a series of evaluations the stooge was (supposedly confidentially) making of her. Four different patterns of evaluations were prepared and subjects were randomly assigned to each of these conditions. In the negative–positive condition the confederate expressed a negative impression of the subject during the first three interviews with the experimenter. She described her as being a dull conversationalist, a rather ordinary person, not very intelligent, and so on. During the fourth session the stooge began to change her mind about the subject. The stooge's expressed attitude became more favorable with each successive meeting, until, in the seventh interview, it was entirely positive. In the positive–positive condition the stooge's stated opinions were invariably positive. During the seventh interview her statements were precisely the same as those in the seventh meeting of the negative–positive condition. In the negative–negative condition the stooge expressed invariably negative feelings about the subject throughout the seven interviews. The positive–negative condition was the mirror image of the negative–positive condition. The stooge began by stating that the subject seemed interesting, intelligent, and likeable, but by the seventh session she described the subject as dull, ordinary, and so on. Because in all cases the subject was assured that the stooge had no idea she was overhearing the evaluations, the subjects probably believed the evaluations were frank statements of the stooge's true feelings.

The dependent measure of the subject's final attitude toward the stooge was taken by another person who was ignorant of the subject's experimental condition. She was asked to rate how much she liked the stooge on a scale running from +10 (like her extremely), through 0 (indifferent), to −10 (dislike her extremely). The results are presented in Table 1-1.

TABLE 1-1.   *Attitude Toward Confederate as Function of Content and Sequence of Her Expressed Attitudes Toward the Subject* (From Aronson and Linder, 1965)

Expressed Attitudes of Confederate Toward Subject	Mean Liking for Confederate
Negative–positive	+7.67
Positive–positive	+6.42
Negative–negative	+2.52
Positive–negative	+0.87

Note: Higher scores indicate greater liking.

With the exception of the last two means every mean was significantly different from every other.

It is clear from these data that how much you like a person after a series of interactions is not a simple function of the number of nice things that person says about you. The stooge was liked best at the end when her *initial* evaluations of the subject had been distinctly negative and then gave way to increasingly positive ratings. An interesting finding was that, although subjects liked the negative–positive stooge better than the positive–positive one, they actually rated her *less* friendly, nice, and warm. Indeed, the positive–positive stooge *was* friendlier, nicer, and warmer. Apparently that is not the only way to be well liked, contrary to what some popular writers on such matters have claimed. Aronson and Linder present additional evidence and argument to the effect that the subjects who liked the negative–positive stooge best were precisely the ones who were most upset when they heard the initial negative evaluations of themselves. It seems likely that the later positive statements by this stooge were all the more valuable and gratifying to the subject because they served to reduce the anxiety aroused by the prior negative statements. Aronson and Linder suggest that rewards received from unexpected sources have more value and impact than those received from people whom we expect to say nice things about us.

Threat to a Group and Intermember Attraction

According to Karl Marx (quoted in Coser, 1956, p. 35), "The separate individuals form a class only insofar as they have to carry on a common battle against another class; otherwise they are on hostile terms with each other as competitors." Speaking to the same point, Georg Simmel wrote:

> The group in a state of peace can permit antagonistic members within it to live with one another in an undecided situation because each of them can go his own way and can avoid collisions. A state of conflict, however, pulls the members so tightly together and subjects them to such uniform impulse that they either must get completely along with, or completely repel, one another. This is the reason why war with the outside is sometimes the last chance for a state ridden with inner antagonisms to overcome these antagonisms, or else to break up definitely. (Quoted in Coser, 1956, p. 87.)

It is clear that Simmel was not claiming that an outside threat to a group always increases the cohesiveness of the group. Other factors are also likely to be important, not least of which is that the group must have something more than a minimum level of integration when the threat is applied. Otherwise, it may "break up definitely." It is fascinating to test this hypothesis against historical data, as Coser (1956) and others have done. The principle has obviously been exploited by leaders of nations from time immemorial. Whether or not an external threat really exists, it may be useful to claim that it does. Consider this statement by a high official of the People's Republic of China, made shortly after the United States had made a gesture toward reconciliation: "The enemy is indeed most hateful and harmful to us, but we must see that its existence has also beneficial effect on us. To have a ferocious enemy like U.S. imperialism glowering at us and threatening us day and night will make us Chinese people always bear in mind the danger of war while living in peace, and redouble our vigilance; will keep us always on alert and sharpen our fighting spirit" (*New York Times*, March 14, 1966).

Let us explore some of the possibly important variables relevant to Simmel's hypothesis. A number of writers have claimed that hostility aroused toward persons against whom aggression would be inappropriate might be displaced onto disliked persons or groups. Adorno et al. (1950) and many others in the psychoanalytic tradition have argued that hostility toward outgroups is often a displacement of aggression that would be punished if directed at ingroup members. It seems to follow, then, that aggressive acts toward ingroup members could be reduced in frequency and strength if convenient, salient, and safe outgroup targets were available. If Berkowitz (1962) is correct in arguing that we select for displacement targets that are already disliked, then it follows that groups that have salient enemies (that is, who are conceived to be threatening) will have appropriate displacement targets and can more easily "take out their aggressions" on outsiders than insiders. Having enemies, then, may be one way to reduce the level of intragroup aggression. Lorenz (1965) makes a similar interpretation of the behavior of various lower animals.

Another possible determinant of the relationship is more in line with gestalt psychological principles. A given external threat to a category of persons may change the perceptions of those persons regarding the similarities among them. Those who are faced with the same danger automatically share a common fate. The threat serves to define an important dimension of similarity. As it has been established in other contexts that similarity usually enhances liking, it follows that the feeling, "we are all in the same boat," should produce an increase in interpersonal attraction among the actually threatened set of persons.

Another possibility is that the sudden emergency of an external threat to a group may distract the members' attention from what now appear by contrast to be petty animosities among themselves. This seems plausible at least in regard to those animosities and differences that are not directly related to the nature of the threat. Some directly relevant disagreements, on the other hand, might become accentuated in importance. A noncommunist nation believing itself threatened by attack from a communist nation might become extremely intolerant of those citizens who profess or appear to profess agreement with communist ideology.

If the threat does not appear so overwhelming as to spell certain doom for the group, group members may be pulled together in anticipation of cooperating to defeat the enemy. Peripheral group members who previously had no important role in the group and who may have been relatively isolated from other members may suddenly find themselves pulled into cooperative action as a concerted effort is made to protect the group. If cooperative action increases interpersonal attraction, then threats that seem not too great should lead to increased attraction. (cf. Deutsch, 1949; Sherif, Harvey, White, Hood, and Sherif, 1961). Again, some exceptions come to mind. Group members who are perceived by the others to be more a liability than an asset in the struggle (for example, the weak or incompetent) may not participate in the affectionate largess that is spread among the able-bodied.

The expenditure of effort to protect the group through cooperative or self-sacrificing acts may lead to an increased evaluation of the group as a means of self-justification (dissonance reduction). To the extent that the group members do things that are costly to themselves but benefit the group as a whole, they may need to justify to themselves why they are enduring the costs. An experiment by Aronson and Mills (1959) showed that people will often convince themselves that a group is very attractive if they have voluntarily undergone a difficult experience in order to join the group.

Having glanced at a few of the potentially important psychological variables that may mediate the threat and cohesiveness relationship, let us see whether the data are consistent with the reasoning. One of the earliest experimental tests was reported by Wright (1943), who found that pairs of young children who were prevented from playing with attractive toys became more cooperative between themselves after the frustration manipulation than before. Feshbach and Singer (1956) attempted to arouse anxiety in subjects by asking them to imagine various kinds of catastrophe that might befall them. They measured attitudes toward minority groups after presenting the threatening material. The interesting finding was that attitudes toward these groups became more favorable when the imagined threat was of the sort that would affect the whole community (e.g., floods, or hurricanes) but not when the threat was "personal" in the sense that it affected people in a less unified way (for example, mental illness). Raising the issue of a future atomic war (presumably a "shared" threat), however, did not have any strong effect. Mulder and Stemerding (1963) performed a dramatic field experiment to test the relation between threat and cohesiveness. They called meetings of groups of small grocers in some towns in Holland and told them that a large supermarket organization was considering locating a store in their community. The probability of this alleged economic threat was said to be either 10 per cent (low) or 80 per cent (high). After presenting this false information, the experimenters took questionnaire measures of the desire of the grocers to have further community meetings. High-threat subjects indicated a greater desire for more meetings. Unfortunately, no other measures of interpersonal attraction were reported.

In a laboratory experiment Burnstein and MacRae (1962) assembled five-man groups, each containing a black confederate. The four white college student subjects in some groups were high in antiblack prejudice and those in others were low. Half of the groups were told they had performed well, and half poorly, as a group. Private ratings of the black member after the praise-versus-threat manipulation revealed that he was more liked and respected (relative to other members) after threat to the group; but this effect was significant only among antiblack subjects. Given the possibility that scapegoating could presumably have been directed at the black member as a means of explaining the group's failure, the results for the prejudiced subjects are quite surprising and should stimulate further research into the phenomenon.

A number of studies have placed groups of subjects in competition with one another in order to determine whether threat of this sort has effects upon within-group attitudes. Wilson and Miller (1961), Wilson, Chun, and Kayatani (1965), and Singer, Radloff, and Wark (1963) found increased favorableness toward teammates following competition, but unfortunately did not include a noncompetitive control condition. Using such a control, Myers (1962) found that three-man rifle teams who competed in round-robin fashion against each other over a five-week period showed more increases in internal cohesiveness than did similar teams competing only against an objective and unchanging standard criterion. Other studies of competitive settings (for example, Bass and Dunteman, 1963; Blake and Mouton, 1962) have generally found similar effects of threat on cohesiveness. Julian, Bishop, and Fiedler (1966) found that competitive teams increased in their tendency to respect the ability of their teammates (relative to control teams), but no strong effects were found on evaluations not related to task ability. Harvey (1956) found that groups of subjects made higher private evaluations of their own group when in the presence of a hostile rather than a nonhostile outgroup. This study also reports an interesting effect on the status structure of the group. Although groups competing with hostile others increased their evaluations of their own group members, they increased the ratings of their previously high-status members more than of the initially low-status members. This is reminiscent of Hamblin's (1958) and Mulder and Stemerding's (1963) finding that a more polarized and autocratic status hierarchy tends to emerge in groups under stress.

Hamblin assembled three-person groups to play a modified shuffleboard game in which the rules for success were initially unclear. After the groups had learned the system, the rules were suddenly changed secretly so that the players found their previous techniques no longer worked. Control groups continued without any rule-change "crisis." Observation of the influence structure within each group before and after the beginning of the confusion about rules revealed that in crisis groups one person was likely to become relatively more dominating in making strategy decisions. Differentiation of degree of dominance was significantly less in control groups. In times of crisis, however, a dominating person who failed to lead the group to success was likely to be replaced by another "take charge guy."

Certainly the most dramatic (but not most carefully controlled) tests of the hypothesis relating threat and cohesiveness have been carried out by Sherif et al. (1961). These were field experiments (but without control groups) carried out in summer camps that were designed to serve as field laboratories for the study of conflict and cooperation. Shortly after they arrived at the camp, the boys were divided into two groups by the experimenters in such a way that the groups contained the same proportion of friends and strangers. A period of cooperative activities within each group (relatively isolated from the other group) then followed, in order that a structure of status and attitudes within the groups could emerge. By dexterous behind-the-scenes manipulation the experimenters then arranged things so that the two groups came into competition with each other. A series of competitive games and contests began, in which the group achieving the highest cumulative point total would win a handsome set of pocket knives. During these activities, within-group solidarity and intergroup hostility began to build up. What had started as the good sportsmanship of the postgame cheer for the other team, "2–4–6–8, who do we appreciate," eventually changed to "2–4–6–8, who do we appreci*hate*." When it became clear to one of the groups that it was losing in the cumulative competition, some internal bickering developed, indicating that when threat reaches the point of completely blocking the group goals, it may no longer serve to unify the group.

In order to fan the fires of intergroup hostility, the experimenters next planned a party that followed the end of the contest. The refreshments were placed on the table before the two groups arrived. Half were crushed and unappetizing, while half were whole and delectable. The Red Devils arrived first and, not surprisingly, took the good half of the refreshments. When the Bull Dogs arrived and saw what had happened, they immediately protested, to which the Red Devils replied, "First come, first served." Hostile insults were exchanged. The next morning the Red Devils deliberately dirtied their breakfast table to make K.P. duty more difficult for the Bull Dogs. At the next meal the situation had polarized completely as the groups began throwing food at each other. Having accomplished their purpose, the experimenters intervened and broke up the fight. In this particular experiment several techniques for reducing the intergroup hostility were tried, including cooperative camp duties, campfires, birthday parties, and athletic events emphasizing individual rather than group competition. However, the only strategy that seemed very effective was to have the group as a whole compete against an *outside* camp in a softball game in which the best players from among the Bull Dogs and Red Devils were chosen by the camp as a whole to compete against the outsiders. In effect, when the camp as a whole was threatened by another camp, the two originally hostile groups became a larger ingroup.

Sherif and his colleagues were not satisfied with this as a technique for reducing intergroup hostility, because it was achieved at the price of introducing a new hostility toward another group. In a later experiment in a very similar setting, a somewhat different technique was tried. Intergroup hostility was generated much as it had been in the earlier studies, and the expected ingroup cohesiveness developed on schedule. Then the experimenters planned several situations in which the members of both groups would have the same goals. In one such stratagem the camp water supply was shut off and the boys all worked simultaneously to follow the water line and find the trouble. In another, the boys all had to contribute money to rent a popular movie to be shown at the camp. One of the most effective of these techniques involving goals common to all members was one that required truly cooperative and coordinated effort on the part of all the boys. On an overnight camping trip to a remote spot, the decrepit old camp truck was about to leave to get food for the hungry boys at midday. As planned, it would not start. A large rope, previously used in intergroup tug-of-war contests, was lying nearby, and one of the boys suggested, "Let's get 'our' tug-of-war rope and have a tug-of-war against the truck." Members in both groups voiced approval of the plan. It took considerable effort to pull the truck, and a rhythmic chant of "Heave, heave" arose as the boys coordinated their pulling. Finally the old machine started, and there was jubilation in the camp. When the truck returned with the food, an unusual thing happened. The two groups, who ordinarily took their own quantities of food and prepared it separately, spontaneously prepared it together. As Sherif points out, it required a number of these cooperative activities toward a common goal before the intergroup hostility was reduced to a low level. Nevertheless, this kind of integrated struggle against a common enemy or threat was the only activity that was impressively effective in reducing intergroup hostility in these experiments.

Let us consider, finally, another possible interpretation of the often observed association between shared threat (or stress) and interpersonal attraction. In an interesting series of experiments Schachter (1959) found that subjects who expected shortly to receive, individually, strong electric shocks, were more motivated to await the shock together with each other than were subjects not expecting strong shocks. When other subjects were given an opportunity to wait together with persons who were not in the same anxiety arousing situation, no such differential affiliation tendency was found between subjects who expected shock and those who did not. It seemed that the threat of physical pain drew the potential victims together. Schachter summarized the results by saying that "misery loves *miserable* company." There was, however, a rather disturbing and quite unexpected qualification that had to be added to an otherwise neat package of data. The increased affiliation under threat occurred only among subjects who were the first born in their family! This peculiar finding has turned up in several further experiments, but is not as yet fully understood. The interested reader should consult Schachter (1959), Zimbardo and Formica (1963), and Ring, Lipinski, and Braginsky (1965) for further discussion of the birth-order variable. We shall try to ignore it in the following discussion. The basic finding of increased affiliation in the anticipation of stress has been replicated by a number of experimenters, for example, Darley and Aronson (1966), Gerard and Rabbie (1961), Sarnoff and Zimbardo (1961), and Zimbardo and Formica (1963).

If we wish to take the desire to be with someone as an indication of liking for that person, we may conclude that a shared threat of this sort produces interpersonal liking in many subjects. However, it is of interest to push the question further. What mediates this effect? Does the frightened subject anticipate certain reinforcing consequences of being with the other person, or is the effect traceable simply to a gestalt-like perception of unity and similarity? What kinds of incentives might the subject have for choosing to wait with someone else in the same boat? First, of course, there are the possibilities of direct threat reduction. Together, perhaps the subjects could figure out how to escape from the experiment; or perhaps they could find out techniques for reducing the pain (such as biting on a bullet). Plausible as these motives may be, Schachter found that affiliation was desired even when such direct types of aid from others could not reasonably be anticipated by his experimental subjects.

He argued, with indirect supporting evidence, that two other motives were plausible in this particular experimental situation. First, subjects might have learned (in other similar settings) that other people in the same boat often help to reduce the unpleasant emotion of fear, even though no strategies for escape or pain reduction are communicated. Second, subjects might be motivated to evaluate their own reactions to this novel situation; they may have learned in the past that this can be done effectively by finding out how the others are reacting and comparing their own feelings with the others who are facing the same threat. This idea is an extension of a theory originally stated by Festinger (1954), who claimed that people have a need to evaluate themselves, and that clear, stable self-evaluations can sometimes be achieved only by comparing oneself with others who are similar to us in certain relevant respects.

Consider first the hypothesis that subjects in these experiments anticipate that their fear will be reduced by the presence of other people also awaiting shock. How can the idea be tested? One might *ask* the subjects, as Sarnoff and Zimbardo (1961) did. They found some evidence that subjects anticipated that being with others would reduce their fear. Another approach is to observe what actually happens when threatened subjects are put together in the same room. If fear tends to decrease more when subjects are together than when alone, one could argue that past experience with this phenomenon can account for the increased affiliation motive in fearful subjects. Several experiments are relevant to this issue. Using the threat of a painful injection, Wrightsman (1960) gave questionnaire measures of "uneasiness" both before and after his subjects waited alone or together. He found, consistent with Schachter's data, that the effect was present only for first-born and only subjects. They showed a significantly greater decrease in anxiety in "together" than "alone" conditions. Wrightsman did not report any measures of interpersonal attraction, and we must mention that Ring, Lipinski, and Braginsky (1965) failed to replicate Wrightsman's results. In a recent study Latané, Eckman, and Joy (1966) induced subjects to submit to a series of fairly painful shocks in the presence of another subject who either received the same series simultaneously or received no shocks at all. Asked privately how much they liked the other person, first-born subjects reported more liking for the other person when that person also received shocks. If the subject herself was not shocked, it didn't make any difference whether the other person was shocked or not. Surprisingly, however, subjects who received shock reported privately shortly afterward that the shocks had been more "disturbing," "awful," and "unpleasant" when *both* received them than when only one received them. The authors interpreted this to mean that, in this situation, the presence of another person receiving shock does *not* make the pain less severe. If this result turns out to apply also to other unpleasant situations, what, then, produces the greater liking for a person enduring the same unpleasantness that you are?

This brings us to the second hypothesis suggested by Schachter. Perhaps the other person in the same leaky boat helps us to evaluate what our feelings are and how appropriate they are in this particular situation. If uncertainty about our own reaction is disturbing, then another person can benefit us by helping us define our own feelings. There is a risk involved, however. We may, in comparing our reactions with theirs, discover that ours are inappropriate, hence undesirable and threatening to our self-esteem. For example, we might discover that we are cowardly, because no one else seems nervous. These may be situations in which the person avoids the company of others for fear that they will provide unwanted information about himself. Not only do we want to have an accurate evaluation of ourselves, we also probably want a *favorable* self-evaluation. We can't always have both. Some experiments (for example, Sarnoff and Zimbardo, 1961; Hakmiller, 1966) have shown that there are such circumstances in which subjects actually avoid the opportunity to compare themselves with certain other people. In the experiments that arouse the anticipation or experience of physical pain, however, most subjects probably do not expect comparison with others to reveal unpleasant information about themselves. Nevertheless, it remains a possibility that makes predictions about the reinforcing or punishing value of social comparison difficult in this setting. Indirect evidence that a motive to compare one's own reactions with those of other persons has been aroused in frightening situations is presented by Gerard and Rabbie (1961), Gerard (1963),

Rabbie (1963), Zimbardo and Formica (1963), and Darley and Aronson (1966). More direct confirmation of the hypothesis comes from the experiment by Latané, Eckman, and Joy (1966). They found that subjects who received electric shocks simultaneously paid close attention to each other's emotional reactions and used this information in evaluating their own reactions, more so than did subjects who were not both being shocked. This is certainly consistent with the hypothesis that the greater liking between shared-shock subjects in this study was mediated by their serving social comparison functions for each other.

Miscellaneous Rewards That Affect Interpersonal Attraction

Few would dispute that we like people who behave in ways we like, prefer, find rewarding. The empirical problem is to establish what things are rewarding and what are not. Thus far we have discussed a number of such services that one person can perform for another. In this section we shall discuss briefly a miscellaneous set of conditions affecting attraction, all of which have received some degree of experimental study.

Reactions to Receiving Gifts

Several studies (Berkowitz and Daniels, 1963; Goranson and Berkowitz, 1966; Kleiner, 1960; Lerner and Matthews, 1967; Myers, 1962; Solomon, 1960; Wilson and Miller, 1961) indicate, not surprisingly, that people who give help on a task or who otherwise reward the subject are therefore liked; those who hinder task success are relatively disliked (Burnstein and Worchel, 1962; Lerner, 1965). The exceptions to this rule are perhaps more interesting. Thibaut and Riecken (1955) have shown that a person who complies with your request for help will be liked more if his compliance appears to be his free choice than if you believe he has been forced to help you. If he appears to help you voluntarily, you are probably more likely to attribute generosity to him or to assume that he likes you. If you believe that he seeks to gain your favor by helping you, then you will not be inclined to like him (Jones, 1964).

How do people react to the offer of aid from an enemy or a competitor? The men of Troy would have been well advised to beware Greeks bearing gifts. Kiesler (1966) reports a relevant experiment. Pairs of subjects were explicitly instructed that they were either to cooperate as a team or to be in direct competition with each other. Following a number of trials, the subject's partner appeared either to offer to share his winnings or not to do so. The first hypothesis was that the offer to share would be accepted gratefully from a member of one's own team but would be resented when coming from a competitor. The results did not support this prediction. However, as predicted, the *refusal* to share money was much more resented when coming from the team member than from the competitor.

Although no one is surprised to find a general tendency to like people who give us what we want, it is more controversial to assert that people who are merely present, but not responsible for our receiving what we want, will be liked. Lott and Lott (1960) report an experiment that seems to support this idea. Using a Hullian conditioning argument they predicted that any stimuli (for example, other persons) present when a person consumes a reward will subsequently elicit some fraction of this reinforcing goal response. This conditioning might then be detected by standard measures of attitude toward the persons who happened to be present (and perceived) at the time. This hypothesis is interesting because it says nothing about the rewarded person's inferring that the other people in any way caused the reward to be given. No one would be surprised to find that people like those who are *perceived* to reward them. But the Hullian argument (in this context) makes no assumption about this cognitive process of attributing responsibility. If people could be shown to like any stimulus present, even though cognitively attributing no causal efficacy to the stimulus, the demonstration would perhaps surprise the common-sensical "man on the street." From the point of view of the slightly more sophisticated psychologist, there is no great mystery here. There is no reason to assume that people always make a fine discrimination between events that are truly causally related and those that are not. Nor does it seem necessary to assume that the *cognition* (or perception) of cause and effect must always be present for rewards to have an impact upon subsequent behavior. The human information-processing system has enough inefficiency in other tasks to suggest that here, also, there will be no perfect correlation between the learning of emotional (attitudinal) reactions and the presence of cause–effect inferences. The reader interested in exploring this issue in a domain other than interpersonal attraction should consult the debate over the role of awareness and "correlated hypotheses" in research on verbal conditioning (cf. Insko and Oakes, 1966).

The experiment by Lott and Lott (1960) deals with this issue only indirectly. Three-person groups of same-sex elementary school children were formed so that the members of any one group contained no close friends. Each group then played a rocket-ship game in which the children took turns leading the three rocket ships through specified danger zones on an imaginary (cardboard) trip to a planet. The experimenter secretly controlled the success of each child in getting to the planet safely. Success was rewarded at the end of a series of trials with the gift of a model car for each successful trip. Half the children (chosen at random) made four successful trips (out of six possible), while half made none (their ship was symbolically "blown up" at some point in every game). The number of successful children per group was varied from zero to three. After all groups had finished, the classroom teacher administered a sociometric test asking each child privately which two children he would like to take on a holiday to a nearby star. The results indicated that rewarded children chose proportionately more of their own game-group members than did nonrewarded children. Unfortunately, no data were reported concerning the possibility that the rewarded children felt their teammates had helped them to win. As in any experiment, there are alternative explanations of the reported data. It is possible, for example, that the non-rewarded subjects may have displaced their frustration-produced hostility onto their rewarded game-mates, thus reducing their tendency to choose them. Nevertheless, the data are consistent also with the Hullian derivation. In a later study, James and Lott (1964) replicated the basic finding. Elementary-school subjects who received a nickel in each of six plays of the rocket game chose their own group members more frequently than did those who were successful in three or zero games. Curiously, the "three nickels" and "zero nickels" groups were virtually identical to each other in their choice patterns.

Since no attempt was made in these experiments to measure cognitions about cause-and-effect relations between one's success–failure and the presence (or behavior) of other people, we cannot conclude anything about the role of such cognitions. In any case the experiments do show that humans (at least young ones) do not make a perfect discrimination between stimuli that are necessary conditions for reward and those that are merely present but not causally relevant. Again, this comes as no surprise. Consider, as an illustration, the great pains taken by the scientist to distinguish the truly causal from the merely correlated factors! No one can discriminate the two with accuracy unless he can run the necessary control conditions, varying the presence–absence of the variable in question. It follows that a certain amount of "error" must frequently be present in people's cognitions about cause–effect relationships.

Effect of the Ability of the Target Person on Attitudes

According to Homans (1961) a man of high ability will receive high liking only if he is willing to put his ability to the service of others. Although this is probably true, it does not follow that ability and liking received are unrelated. A few experiments indicate that one's stated liking for another person can be affected by information concerning his abilities, in the absence of any other information about him (cf. Stotland and

Hillmer, 1962). This seems to be true to some extent even when the subject has no reason to expect that the other person's level of ability will be used either to help or hinder the subject's own task performance (cf. Iverson, 1964; Stotland and Hillmer, 1962; Stotland and Dunn, 1962). To the extent that the subject does expect some gain from association with a person of high ability, we would anticipate a stronger effect upon liking.

There is probably a limit to the positive relation between liking and ability. People of extremely high ability may appear to have other characteristics that render them less likable. We may admire and respect such people, but an element of fear or hostility may be aroused at the same time. They may appear inhuman; or the observer may feel that such persons would not like *him* because of his own relative inferiority. To the extent that a person of great ability also gives off cues implying that he is "just folks" and possesses some of the minor imperfections that everyone else has also, he will probably be liked more. Aronson, Willerman, and Floyd (1966) tested this idea in an ingenious experiment. Each college-student subject listened to a tape recording purportedly of another student who was a candidate for a university team in an intelligence competition. Half the subjects heard this candidate answer very difficult knowledge questions in an extraordinarily brilliant manner. The other half heard the same voice incompetently failing to answer even simple questions. For half of the subjects hearing each of the two tapes, the tape ended with the candidate sipping a cup of coffee after completing his answers. For the other half of the subjects, just as the questioner was handing the cup of coffee to the candidate, there was heard a great clatter and commotion as the candidate spilled the coffee over his suit and exclaimed, "Oh my goodness, I've spilled coffee all over my new suit!" The dependent measures included ratings of how much the subject liked the candidate. As expected, there was a tendency to like the intelligent candidate more than the unintelligent one. However, the effect of the spilled cup of coffee was quite different in the two cases. When the stupid candidate spilled it, he was liked even less than when he didn't. When the brilliant fellow committed the blunder, he was liked slightly *more* than when he didn't. This finding dovetails with one reported by Jones, Gergen, and Jones (1963). They found that securely high-status persons, when told to make themselves well-liked, tended to "advertise" their minor imperfections when interacting with subordinates. This was less true of low-status persons in the relationship.

To the extent that person A is in competition with someone (B) of high ability, the higher the competitor's ability, the more likely that A will fail in the competition. Hence, in such a setting we might expect some hostility toward B. In general, it seems plausible that the more another man's ability is expected to help you realize your own goals, the more you will like him. The more he is likely to use his ability to block your goals, the less you will like him.

The apparent status of a target person often affects how his behavior is interpreted. If he boasts and derogates incompetent persons, the observer will consider this acceptable from a high-status speaker but less so from a low-status one (Iverson, 1964). Similarly, Deutsch (1961) has shown that observers attribute better motives to high-status than low-status persons emitting the same verbal behavior criticizing another person. There seems to be a presumption that high-status persons have more admirable motives for performing a given act. An interesting discussion of related issues is contained in an article by Hollander (1958). However, there are probably severe limits on this generalization. Once the observer concludes that the stimulus person's behavior is morally or factually *unjustified,* the resulting change in attitude may be greater toward the high-status than low-status norm violator. In some circumstances we probably have higher standards of conduct in judging the behavior of higher-status persons (cf. the concept of "noblesse oblige"). Unfortunately, there is very little evidence relevant to this hypothesis.

Power and Liking

A number of writers (for example, Bales, 1958; Brehm, 1966; Homans, 1961; Homans and Schneider, 1955; Whyte, 1948; Zander, Cohen, and Stotland, 1959) have reasoned that there is a tendency to dislike someone who exerts power over us (that is, who is able to restrict our freedom of action, to induce us to do things we do not like to do). This hypothesis provides a convenient transition between the effects of another's status as a stimulus variable and the discussion of frustration and aggression in the next chapter. To the extent that the powerful person uses his power to induce us to do unpleasant (punishing) things, a certain amount of hostility is very likely. This is dealt with at length in the next chapter.

In the present context it is of interest to consider whether attitudes are affected by the other's power, even though the power has not been used or has not been used in a punishing manner. Since the behavior of powerful persons potentially has great importance for our own fate, one would anticipate, clearly, that lower-power persons would watch the powerful very closely. Wheeler (1964) reports an experiment designed to test this hypothesis. Subjects participated individually in a twenty-minute conversation with a person who would allegedly be "chairman" of a discussion group the subject was about to join. All subjects were informed that they could earn credit points in their psychology course as a function of the quality of their contribution to the (future) discussion. The "chairman" told half that he had no control over the number of credits the subject would receive. In the high-power condition he said it was entirely his decision and would "depend upon my mood." The dependent variable was the amount of information about the chairman correctly recalled by the subject when tested by another experimenter shortly after the twenty-minute conversation. Subjects exposed to the high-power manipulation recalled significantly more details describing the chairman.

That people are motivated to maintain accurate cognitions about powerful persons is further supported by an experiment by Wittreich and Radcliffe (1956). Each subject was fitted with a special type of spectacles that, by substitution of lenses, could be made to distort the visual appearance of viewed objects. While the subject was looking at a stimulus person, the experimenter systematically inserted a series of increasingly distorting lenses and asked the subject to report the first moment at which distortion was experienced by him. The characteristics of the stimulus person were varied on the dimension of apparent power over the low-status military-recruit subjects. Stooges wore either officer or recruit uniforms. The results were that distortion was reported earlier in the lens series when viewing a lower-power stimulus person.

In spite of these experiments it would be a mistake to infer that cognitions about powerful persons are always veridical. Certain kinds of cognitive distortion may be especially likely in observing such persons. For example, people would usually like to think that powerful persons are benevolent toward them. Such benevolence is of course less important in the case of people who have no power to affect your fate. Pepitone (1950) conducted a very elaborate and interesting experiment designed to throw light on this question. High-school subjects were given a chance to acquire coveted tickets to a university basketball game. They were told that their success was contingent on their ability to answer some questions about sports. These questions were asked by a three-man committee of adults connected with the physical-education department. In one condition of the experiment these three men were introduced to the subject as varying in power to decide concerning the tickets. After the interview, but before the subject knew the outcome, he was asked in a different context (by a different experimenter) to rate the committee members. Although, objectively, the behaviors of the three men were equated in their apparent liking for the subject, the more powerful the committee member, the more the subject believed the man liked him. In other conditions, in which the apparent power was equated but the men behaved in ways varying in friendliness, subjects attributed more power (in decision making) to the friendlier judges. Both of these effects are interpretable as showing wish-fulfilling distortion tendencies in cognitions about the judges.

CHAPTER
2

The Arousal and Reduction of Hostility

The first major contribution to the question of the effects of punishment on interpersonal attitudes was made by Dollard, Doob, Miller, Mowrer, and Sears in their thin but meaty volume, *Frustration and Aggression* (1939). Their definitions and hypotheses are still widely, but not unanimously (cf. Buss, 1966), accepted. It seems appropriate to start the discussion here. Dollard et al. defined frustration as an "interference with the occurrence of an instigated goal-response at its proper time in the behavior sequence." In other words, a frustration is an event that prevents or delays an organism from reaching its goal once progress toward the goal has begun. Aggression was defined as "an act whose goal-response is injury to an organism (or organism surrogate)." In other words, a person is aggressing if he intends to produce injury (or deliver punishment of some kind). Having defined their terms, the authors proceeded to marshal arguments and evidence to support the hypothesis that frustration is the necessary and sufficient condition for aggression. This very strong statement was shortly revised by Miller (1941), who claimed that although aggression always presupposes frustration, sometimes frustration would not produce observable aggressive responses. That is, aggression may be inhibited by fear and thus not be the most probable response in every frustrating situation.

In order to test the hypothesis relating frustration and aggression, it is necessary to block a person's progress toward a goal and observe what he does, in a situation in which cues arousing fear are minimal. In order to establish that an act is motivated by an intention to produce harm or suffering (that is, deliver noxious stimulation), it is necessary to show that the person systematically selects those acts that have produced these effects in his past experience or that are followed by cues indicating that the target of the acts finds the acts punishing. Just as one might test for the role of hunger as a motivator by checking to see whether the behavior in question tends to cease after the organism has consumed a big meal (is satiated), so one can test whether an act is motivated by a desire to hurt by noting whether it tends to cease after the person receives evidence that the target is in pain. Of course there is always some ambiguity remaining, because no act reflects the effects of only one causal variable. For example, the act of spanking a child could perhaps be shown to vary as a function of the intent to cause pain, but it simultaneously reflects the effects of other motives as well. In practice, psychologists who have studied aggression have rarely felt it necessary to demonstrate that their measures of aggression are valid. Often there is considerable face validity; sometimes there is not even that. A glance at the experimental literature reveals that hardly more care has been exercised in operationally defining frustration. It is typically assumed that subjects want certain things, and then the experimenter systematically prevents the subjects from getting them. Relatively few studies with human subjects have established in advance that the subjects are making responses leading toward a specified goal.

Having made these comments about the lack of care in operationalizing the concepts of frustration and aggression, let us be less compulsive and forge ahead anyway. Granting that the methods have been a little crude, is it nevertheless possible to make some tentatively supported statements about the relation between frustration and aggression? Experimental studies in which the subjects have relatively little reason to fear retaliation from the target of potential attack have generally shown differences in the predicted direction between frustrated and nonfrustrated conditions. Although not all subjects show the expected effect, enough of them do— enough to be detected consistently by statistical tests of significance (for example, Berkowitz, 1965; Berkowitz and Geen, 1966; Berkowitz and Holmes, 1960; Berkowitz and Rawlings, 1963; Hamblin, 1958; Hamblin, Bridger, Day, and Yancey, 1963; Hokanson, 1961; Horwitz, 1958). In an experiment in which the amount of interference with goal-directed activity (frustration) was carefully varied over a wide range of points, Hamblin et al. (1963) found a monotonic positive relation between frustration and aggression directed toward the frustrater.

It must be admitted that, as Buss (1966) points out, almost all of the experiments that have found increased aggression have used a particular type of instigating manipulation—namely, an interpersonal attack upon the subject. The frustrater typically insults the subject, delivers electric shock to him, or deprives him of an expected reward in an arbitrary and hostile manner. These are rather complex manipulations, and they involve more than is necessary to prevent the subject from reaching a desired goal. It has been quite clearly established that attacks of this sort upon adult American subjects do produce considerable aggression when there is no fear of retaliation. However, Buss (1966) and Epstein and Taylor (1967) present data that show very little aggression when the subject's desire to succeed on a task is thwarted by the apparently nonhostile behavior of a peer. Although the possibility that subjects feared retaliation from the victim was not ruled out, these data do suggest that more careful specification of exactly what is meant by *frustration* is called for in this research domain.

Displacement of Aggression

If psychologists interested in aggression were primarily concerned with testing the basic frustration–aggression hypothesis, undoubtedly more attention would have been given to operationalizing the various meanings of the concept of frustration. As it happens, the bulk of experimental work has focused upon the *direction* of aggression and the effects of making overt and vicarious aggressive acts. That is, experimenters have not worried very much about the technicalities of defining the antecedents of anger and aggressive tendencies. Rather, they have sought to find operations that would reliably produce aggressive tendencies so that they could then study how these dispositions would be expressed overtly and what factors might reduce their strength. Modern psychology's fascination with the irrational side of man's nature shows itself here, for there is more interest in the *displacement* of aggression than in direct aggression toward the frustrater or attacker. The general research strategy has been to choose some relatively sure-fire technique for arousing anger, and then to measure displaced aggression and the effects of various stimuli introduced after the initial anger arousal. Of course, displaced aggression is interesting for other reasons than its irrational character. Social psychologists tend to be much concerned with practical social problems, and the possibility that intergroup hostility and discrimination are nourished by displaced aggression has long been recognized.

Aggression is said to be displaced when it is directed toward someone or something that was in no way responsible for the frustration or attack suffered by the aggressor. In practice it is often difficult to demonstrate whether or not a given target of aggression is totally innocent of blame. Consequently, it is probably more appropriate to ask simply, "What determines the target of aggression?" In that way we avoid facing the difficult (and somewhat irrelevant) issue of the degree of innocence of the victim.

The authors of *Frustration and Aggression* argued that the most probable target for aggression is the frustrating agent itself. One might amend this slightly by saying it is the agent perceived to be the frustrater. What is the rationale for this relatively untested assumption? In the first place, aggression against the frustrater is probably more consistently reinforced than is aggression directed elsewhere. It may serve not only to remove the interference or loss suffered by the person but also to deter the frustrater from interfering in the future. Further, if the frustrating event involved a threat to the person's status or self-esteem, then he can help to restore his position by demonstrating his power to punish the frustrater. Further, there are disadvantages to aggressing against people who are not believed to be responsible for the original frustration or attack. The audience for such a displaced, and therefore morally unjustified, aggressive act is likely to disapprove and to punish the aggressor; and he may punish himself via feeling of guilt. A final possible reason why the frustrater becomes the prime target for aggression is that he tends to be nearby when the frustration occurs. If an aggressive act is more likely to occur at the time and place of the frustrating event, then persons and objects at the scene of the crime are likely to feel the brunt of the attack.

The preceding arguments, although plausible on the surface, undoubtedly oversimplify the issues involved. Consider the case in which the person who is frustrated is typically of low power relative to his frustraters. The child, for example, is often punished for aggressing against the parent-frustrater. Is it really true that the bulk of learning experiences are such that aggression against the perceived frustrater is more often rewarded than punished? Is not the person of low power more often rewarded for displacement than for retaliation against the frustrater? It is certainly questionable whether the child is typically reinforced for aggression against the parent-frustrater. However, it may also be true that displaced aggression has few rewards to offer. Further clarification of these issues is certainly in order. Nevertheless, it does appear to be intuitively true that most adults, if given a choice among various targets not differing in their perceived likelihood of retaliating against the aggressor, would prefer to injure their perceived frustrater more than anyone else.

If the perceived frustrater is the prime target, what are the conditions favoring displacement of aggression? The first obvious answer is that displacement is more likely when the frustrater is not available or is unknown. The much more frequently tested answer is that displacement occurs when the person is afraid to aggress against the frustrater. There are several possible sources of such inhibition. The person may fear retaliation from the frustrater or punishment from the audience or agents of authority (for example, police or parents). (Such inhibition of aggression is shown in an experiment by Cohen [1958]). Or he may anticipate guilt feelings for aggressing against a socially inappropriate target (for example, striking a much weaker person). These inhibitions might produce either displacement to another target or displacement to another, less preferred, aggressive response. Rather than punch his frustrater in the nose, a person might instead secretly place a burning cross on his lawn, reduce his status in the community by circulating vile rumors about him, or stick a needle through the heart of a doll made in the frustrater's image. Displacement to a different type of response has received very little experimental attention; suffice it to say that no one doubts that it occurs.

What determines the selection of a target other than the perceived frustrater? The early experiments on displacement of aggression made no attempt to manipulate the stimulus characteristics of potential targets. The researchers simply asked the question, "Will displacement occur toward person or group X?" Some more recent studies have improved upon this design by varying the target's characteristics along an explicitly chosen dimension. Let us look first at the earlier work.

The classic experiment explicitly testing for displacement was done by Miller and Bugelski (1948). This study used what was probably one of the most effective anger-arousing techniques reported in the experimental literature. The subjects were young men in the Civilian Conservation Corps who were working on a natural conservation project in a rather isolated area. One of their few diversions was to attend a regular once-a-week movie and lottery at the nearest movie house. The conniving psychologists chose one such night for the experiment. After dinner, but before the appointed time to leave for the movie, the researchers were given permission to have the men take some very difficult tests. Included in the first part were some items intended to measure attitudes toward certain national groups, including Mexicans and Japanese. As the usual time for departure approached, and then passed, the tests kept coming. When it was clear that the movie had been missed, the subjects again encountered some questions about their attitudes toward Mexicans and Japanese. By this time they were probably quite angry and hostile toward the experimenters, but there were inhibitions against making direct attacks. The questionnaire results indicated that attitudes expressed toward the foreigners were more unfavorable after the frustration than before. Since no control group was run under nonfrustrating conditions, one can only tentatively conclude that the displacement hypothesis has our increased confidence.

Later studies gave rather mixed results. Stagner and Congdon (1955) attempted to produce anger and hostility in college-student subjects by inducing them to fail on a set of tasks. Control subjects were given less failure experience. Pre- and post-measures of attitudes toward minority groups failed to show a significant effect of the frustration manipulations.

Cowen, Landes, and Schaet (1959) attempted to frustrate subjects by scoffing at their inability to solve actually impossible puzzles. They found that the frustration manipulation increased hostility toward blacks as indicated on an attitude questionnaire.

Anyone committed to the displacement hypothesis might immediately point out that this technique of producing hostility and aggression toward the environment appears much less effective than the one used by Miller and Bugelski. College students in experiments used to be (and probably still are; cf. Milgram, [1963]) notoriously submissive. When they are told by a professor that they have failed a test in a scientific setting, many of them become intropunitive, blaming themselves for the failure to reach the goal. If the self is perceived to be responsible for the frustration, then aggression is likely to be directed inward. Under these conditions, as Epstein (1965) has pointed out, neither direct nor displaced aggression against persons in the environment is very likely. One can question various aspects of these studies. For several reasons—lack of control groups, inadequate frustration manipulations, and very indirect measures of aggression—we are something less than certain about the status of the displacement notion up to this point in the review of experimental data. It is time to look for some theoretical guidance as to the precise conditions under which various displacement phenomena might be detected.

Certainly the most ambitious theory, or model, was the one proposed by Miller (1948). Although it turned out to have some weaknesses, it was an important step in the right direction. Let us take a close look at it. The basic elements of Miller's model of displaced aggression came from an unlikely place—the behavior of rats in a straight alley. One group of hungry rats was given training in which food could always be obtained by running from the start box to the goal box at the end of the alley. When the response had become well learned, the experimenters measured how strongly the rat would pull against a spring attached to a harness as a function of the distance from the goal box containing the food. It was found that the closer the animal got to the food, the harder he would pull against the resisting spring. If one plotted the strength of pull as a function of nearness to the goal, an increasing gradient was revealed, as shown schematically in Figure 2-1. A second group of rats was given a very different kind of training in the same alley. Instead of receiving food in the goal box, they received a strong electric shock. For this group, after they were forced to receive several such shocks, the same kind of harness and spring hookup was used, but this time to measure pull in the opposite direction. How hard would the animals pull away from the place where they had been shocked, as a function of their distance from that place? Again plotting the points graphically, an avoidance

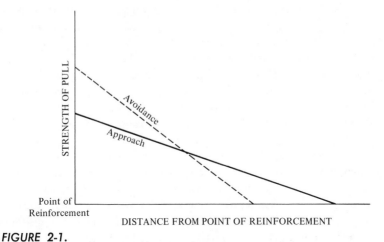

FIGURE 2-1.

Relation Between Distance from Point of Reinforcement (Food or Shock) and Strength of Pull by Rats

gradient was generated (the dashed line in Figure 2-1). It was found to be steeper than the approach gradient of the animals who were fed at the goal box. That is, for every unit of distance moving away from the goal, the avoidance tendency dropped off more precipitously than the approach tendency. By varying the amount of hunger or the strength of the electric shock, it was possible to raise or lower either gradient. However, the avoidance gradient always seemed to be the steeper of the two. The next step was to see what would happen if a new group of hungry rats were first trained to find food in the end box and then were given a series of shocks on subsequent trials when they entered the end box. If the gradients of approach and avoidance established separately on the original animals could be hypothesized to act *simultaneously* in this new group of rats, some interesting predictions would result. The rat would be in a state of conflict at some point in the alley. If the two hypothetical gradients should cross at some distance from the end box, then the tendency to approach would dominate near the start box, but the closer the animal got to the end box, the stronger would become the avoidance tendency. In fact, the rat might not approach beyond the point at which the gradients cross, for the avoidance tendency is stronger than the approach tendency at all points closer to the end box. The results of the test were essentially as predicted. The rats placed in the start box usually started down the alley, slowed down, and vacillated back and forth somewhere in the midsection of the alley. They rarely reached the end box. This behavior seemed fairly well accounted for by the model, with its two hypothetical co-acting gradients, of which the avoidance (fear) gradient was the steeper. Clearly, if the approach gradient were the steeper, the organism would either go all the way to the end or would not even get started down the runway.

Miller's next creative step was to generalize the model by substituting a different abscissa. Perhaps the same basic gradients would be found when stimulus similarity was substituted for spatial distance. Thus the strength of responses learned in reaction to a given stimulus might also drop off monotonically as the organism is presented with stimuli more and more dissimilar to the original training stimulus. Certainly the well-substantiated phenomenon of stimulus generalization would seem to predict that the more dissimilarity between a test stimulus and the original training stimulus, the less likely the organism is to make the original conditioned response. The most controversial issue involved, however, concerns the relative slopes of the approach and avoidance gradients. Will the fear gradient drop off the more rapidly of the two even when we change the test dimension from distance to similarity?

It is not necessary for us to explore here the intricacies of the animal research directed at testing this hypothesis (cf. Miller, 1959). Let us return to our central issue—namely, how can this model be applied to predicting the displacement of aggression in humans? Unfortunately, Miller has never published a systematic extension of the model to human aggression. Instead, he and his associates (Dollard and Miller, 1950; Murray and Berkun, 1955) have applied it to other instances of displacement in human behavior. For example, aspects of repression have been analyzed using the model. The extension to aggression has been made by others (for example, Bandura and Walters, 1963; Berkowitz, 1962; Whiting and Child, 1953). Because Berkowitz (1962, Chapter 5) has come closer than anyone else to experimentally testing the model, we shall examine his version of the extended Miller model while keeping in mind that Miller would not necessarily have made an extension in the same way.

Consider Figure 2–2, which is similar to Figure 2–1. Along the abscissa (stimulus dissimilarity) four points have been marked, indicating persons A, B, C, and D. Person A is the frustrater or attacker (or is perceived to be so), while B, C, and D are others with increasing dissimilarity to A. The question is this: Given that a person is angered by A, what determines the target of the subsequent aggressive response? The strength of the aggression tendency is indicated hypothetically by the solid line, while the fear or avoidance tendency is shown with steeper slope (dashed line). As drawn, the tendency to attack A is weaker than the conflicting fear response. Thus the person in this depicted situation is unlikely to aggress against A. The probability of an aggressive response is predicted to be greatest where the aggression gradient most exceeds the fear gradient in strength. One of the interesting predictions from the model

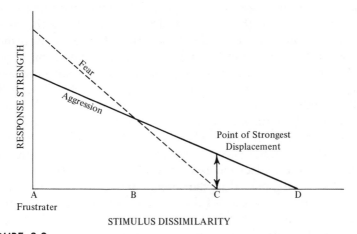

FIGURE 2-2.

Predicting the Target of Displacement of Aggression as a Function of Similarity Between Potential Targets and the Frustrater

is that displaced aggression is likely to be directed toward persons of intermediate similarity to the original frustrater. If the gradients are assumed to be linear (which Miller does not claim), the model predicts maximum aggression toward the person located at the point where the fear gradient meets the abscissa (that is, someone who arouses no fear at all). If the gradients are conceived to be monotonic but not linear, this latter prediction does not follow so inevitably.

Let us look critically at the proposed gradients. The shape of the approach (aggression) gradient seems to follow roughly from several considerations. First, as discussed earlier, there is reason to believe that the maximum strength of the aggression tendency is directed toward the perceived frustrater. Second, the well-established tendency for a response elicited by a given stimulus to be elicited less strongly by stimuli of decreasing similarity seems to predict a roughly monotonic decrease in aggressive response to persons of less and less similarity to the frustrater. In order to test for the shape of the function, it would be necessary to provide subjects with the opportunity to aggress toward targets of varying similarity to the frustrater but not differing in their tendency to arouse fear in the subjects. Such an experimental test, holding the level of fear constant, has, strangely, not been reported. A correlational study by Murney (1955) gave confirmatory results.

The fear, or avoidance, gradient runs into much more serious difficulties. According to the model (Figure 2-2) the frustrated person is most afraid of aggressing against the frustrater (point A on the abscissa), and his aggression anxiety decreases as he contemplates attacking persons of increasing dissimilarity to the frustrater. This is stated to be the case regardless of the absolute magnitude of the gradient. That is, even though fear of the frustrater may not be sufficient to inhibit aggression, it is still depicted as exceeding fear of other persons. What is the rationale for expecting fear of the frustrater to be the greatest? Recalling Miller's original rat studies, we can see how this assumption arose. The animals were shocked only in the end box. They had never received any punishment in other parts of the alley. Therefore, their fear was greatest in the end box. Is the frustrated person's fear of the frustrater really analogous to the rat's fear of the place where he has been shocked? Not necessarily. Some frustraters are powerful, dangerous, and fear-inspiring, whereas others are not. If your neighbor's dog knocks over your garbage can and strews the contents all over your yard, are you more inhibited about throwing a rock at him (direct) than at his master (displaced)? On the average, no. It seems we are often frustrated by agents that are not especially frightening. Although we can readily believe that the desire to attack the frustrater is generally higher than the desire to attack other people, is there a compelling reason why fear of the frustrater should generally exceed fear of other potential targets of aggression? One could argue that there is a slight positive correlation between the ability of people to frustrate you and their ability to retaliate against you if you were to attack them, but the mere *act* of frustrating you does not by itself seem capable of inspiring fear of retaliation in the same way that this act inspires anger and hostility (the approach tendency in the model). In the rat studies, the animals were taught that one and the same place, the end box, was the prime source of both reward (food) and punishment (shock). The human who is frustrated by someone does not necessarily then come automatically to fear the frustrater unless the frustrater reveals at that moment a power to punish that the frustrated person did not previously know he possessed. You become hostile toward someone *because* he has frustrated you; it is much less clear why you should come to fear aggressing against him *because* he has frustrated you. One possibility is that fear is aroused by the aggression tendency itself, such that the greater the hostility the greater the fear (Sears, Maccoby, and Levin, 1957). A test would require measuring the amount of punishment subjects anticipate in return for aggressive acts, real or imagined, directed toward various potential targets, including the frustrater.

In view of the lack of experimental tests, it is surprising that the extended Miller model is so often referred to as an account of displacement of aggression. The explanation, however, is not difficult to find. First, the model comes from an impressive background of animal research and has been used with some success in a few correlational studies (for example, Whiting and Child, 1953; Wright, 1954). Second, when applied to certain select situations, the model's apparent faults are concealed. Most writers (for example, Bandura and Walters, 1963; Whiting and Child, 1953; Mednick, 1964) attempt to apply the model to the situation of the child vis-à-vis his parents as frustraters. Because, for the child, the parents are the prime source both of reward and punishment, the constellation of variables approximates more closely the situation confronting the rats who have been both fed and shocked in the same end box. In this setting the model seems, at least superficially, to apply. Just as the rat approaches only part way to the end box, so the child inhibits his aggression toward the parent and may express it elsewhere. The fit, to repeat, has not been carefully tested even in this context. However, it is possible that, for the child, the more dissimilar a potential target is to the parent, the less the child fears aggressing against it. If there is such a fear gradient as a function of stimulus similarity, it would remain to be established whether its slope is steeper than that of the gradient for aggressive tendencies.

Although Berkowitz, in his excellent volume, *Aggression* (1962), seems to favor the extended Miller model, it is noteworthy that his own research on displacement has ignored the hypothetical fear gradient associated with the stimulus (Berkowitz, 1959; Berkowitz and Holmes, 1959, 1960; Berkowitz and Green, 1962) and has concentrated exclusively upon the approach (aggression) gradient. That is, he has not incorporated into his designs or discussions of data any notions about frustraters who are not only most hated but also most feared. On the contrary, in his discussion of selection of a target (1962, p. 152) he argues that a group becomes a displaced target in part *because* it is feared. The feared group elicits dislike and thus is said to appear similar to the disliked frustrater such that aggression generalizes strongly to this group. The important contribution of some of these studies is the attention they give to the heretofore rather neglected issue of defining the relevant similarity dimension to be used in predicting the generalization of aggressive tendencies.

When a person has been angered, what is likely to be the most relevant similarity dimension that might predict the direction of a displaced response? If we assume that the frustrater becomes disliked when he attacks the person, perhaps other people who are disliked (previous to the frustration) then appear similar to the frustrater. This plausible suggestion has been made persuasively by Berkowitz, and fortunately he has some data to support it. His general experimental design (Berkowitz and Holmes, 1959, 1960; Berkowitz and Green, 1962) manipulates the subject's degree of liking for potential targets before the crucial frustration manipulation is delivered to the subject. Then it is possible to measure the subject's tendency later to aggress against the potential targets when he is given a convenient opportunity to do so. The earlier experiments in the series provided moderate, but not overwhelming, support for the hypothesis that displacement of aggression occurs more strongly the more the substitute target was initially disliked.

Let us look more closely at the most carefully designed of the experiments, the one by Berkowitz and Green (1962). The subjects, male college students, were assembled two at a time along with a third student who was secretly a confederate of the experimenter. The two subjects, working independently, were given the task of designing a "novel, imaginative, and creative" floor plan for a house. When each had finished his plan, the experimenter claimed he was exchanging the plans so that each could evaluate the other's creative work. Shortly thereafter each subject received an evaluation, presumably sent by the other subject. Consistent with the instructions that this was a test of creativity under mild stress (anticipation of electric shock), the means of communicating the evaluation was by the delivery of electric shocks. The experimenter had explained that one shock meant "very creative," and the more shocks sent the worse the evaluation. Half of the subjects received only one shock, which would presumably elicit an initial liking for the other person; the other half received six shocks, intended to induce an initial dislike for him. Next, each subject worked independently on an additional test of creativity. While working, half of the subjects in each of the above groups were criticized and insulted by the experimenter over an intercom system, whereas the other half were treated in a friendlier manner. A questionnaire was inserted at this point, giving the subject an opportunity to rate the experimenter's behavior on a form supposedly to be sent to the "Chairman of the Department." The commendable purpose of this, of course, was to check on the effectiveness of the frustration manipulation. It revealed that subjects who were insulted by the experimenter indeed gave him a more unfavorable evaluation. Such a measure is, however, rather risky in an experiment on displacement of aggression. Given a chance to aggress against the experimenter directly, subjects might no longer be sufficiently angry to displace aggression onto other targets.

In the final part of the experiment the two subjects and the confederate were brought together for five minutes to assemble a footbridge from materials in the room. Separated once again, a final measure of attitudes toward the other subject and the confederate was taken. Unfortunately, this measure was not a direct indicator of aggression, since his answers on the questionnaire were not expected by the subject to be communicated to the other persons. Since the experimenter's confederate behaved in a neutral manner toward the subject, it was expected that frustration of the subject by the experimenter would not produce displacement onto

TABLE 2-1.   *Displacement of Hostility As a Function of Insult and Initial Attitude Toward Available Target Person (Mean Hostility Toward the Other Subject)* (From Berkowitz and Green, 1962)

Initial Dislike for Other Subject (S Got 6 Shocks)		Initial Liking (or Neutrality) for Other Subject (S Got 1 Shock)	
Insulted by Experimenter	*Not Insulted by Experimenter*	*Insulted by Experimenter*	*Not Insulted by Experimenter*
8.4	6.4	6.2	5.8

Note: Higher score indicates more hostility.

the confederate. The results were consistent with this prediction. The mean ratings subjects made of the other subject in each condition are presented in Table 2–1. It can be seen that the experience of having been insulted by the experimenter made subjects more hostile toward the person they already disliked, but did not appreciably affect their attitudes concerning the person toward whom they were initially more favorably disposed.

An experiment by Weatherley (1961) provides slight additional support for Berkowitz's hypothesis. Weatherly measured the subjects' attitudes toward Jews before the experiment, and selected only those who were at the two extreme ends of the scale. Half of the subjects were then insulted by the experimenter and half were treated in a neutral manner. The dependent measure of displacement was a fantasy test in which the subject had to make up stories about pictured people who had Jewish and non-Jewish sounding names. The trend of Weatherley's data suggests the possibility that subjects who strongly dislike Jews would be most likely to displace further aggression onto them when frustrated and unable to attack the frustrater directly.

An interesting experiment by Weiss and Fine (1956) can also be interpreted to be consistent with the Berkowitz position. Half of the college-student subjects were insulted and angered by the experimenter, and half were treated in a complimentary manner. Within each of these conditions some subjects were asked to read paragraphs advocating punitive treatment for juvenile delinquents, while others read control material. The dependent measure was the tendency to agree with statements recommending punitiveness toward the delinquents. The findings were that frustration increased punitiveness only of those subjects given the punitive material to read. This appears to be a definite displacement phenomenon, since the juvenile delinquents were not responsible for the frustration of the subjects. The interesting fit with Berkowitz's data is that the displacement was strongest when subjects read material tending to elicit (even under control conditions) hostility toward a potential target. Although Kaufmann and Feshbach (1963) later disputed the generality of these findings, their experiment did not unambiguously support their case.

As a final example of displacement of aggression, consider the experiment by Burnstein and Worchel (1962). Male subjects in groups of three to five were assembled to discuss a case history of a juvenile delinquent. One of the members was an accomplice of the experimenters. In the frustration conditions this person continually interrupted the discussion and thereby prevented the group from achieving the required consensus within the limited time available. In some groups his behavior seemed completely arbitrary in its unjustified obstructionism. In others, he pretended to be partially deaf and seemed to be trying without success to get his hearing aid to work. In both cases he prevented the group from fulfilling the task requirements. This person was disliked in both of these frustration conditions. However, when his interference appeared due primarily to his hearing defect, the others displaced some of their hostility onto the experimenter and onto themselves, apparently because of inhibitions about the social propriety of blaming a handicapped person.

Let us summarize the present state of experimentally derived knowledge about the displacement of aggression toward targets other than the perceived frustrater or attacker. First, no one seems to doubt that displacement occurs. Second, as to the exact determinants of target selection, Berkowitz's interpretation of the Miller-type generalization of aggressive tendencies is the most convincing, both in plausibility and in empirical support. Perhaps Berkowitz's hypothesis that displacement tends to be directed at disliked persons and groups can help to account for the often-observed tendency for an angered but aggression-inhibiting person suddenly to blow up when some relatively innocent person happens to add a small additional frustration. The explosion is often far out of proportion to the immediate cause. Does the unfortunate perpetrator of the small frustrating event reap the whirlwind because he suddenly becomes perceptually more similar to the original frustrater? Perhaps the theory of Schachter and Singer (1962) can help to illuminate such incidents as well. Could it be that the person who has inhibited his aggressive tendencies toward the original frustrater has perhaps ceased to rehearse the appropriate labels for his aroused state, so that in a way he does not know why he feels as he does? Then some small, by itself barely annoying incident occurs. It is possible that our angry, but inadequately self-labelled, friend now comes to perceive the basically innocent annoyer as the cause of his angry feelings. He then lashes out in a manner more proportionate to his emotional state than to the trespass of the startled victim.

Much more could be said, and much more remains to be discovered, about additional determinants of target selection. It is to be expected, for example, that aggressive dispositions toward displaced targets can be inhibited by fear, just as aggression toward the frustrater so often is. It appears, however, that the particular picture to be painted of the pattern of such inhibitions may be different from the one suggested by Miller's conflict model.

The Consequences of Performing Aggressive Acts

What happens to a person's interpersonal attitudes and behavior as a consequence of his having intentionally punished someone? If the punishment successfully removes a frustrating agent, or restores injured self-esteem, or ensures that a frustrater will cease his aversive behavior, perhaps its goal could be said to have been reached. Or, perhaps its goal has been reached, at least in part, simply by successfully delivering noxious stimuli to a frustrater, even though the original frustrating state of affairs continues, as claimed by Berkowitz (1962). According to certain psychoanalysts, including Freud, the goal of an aggressive act is simply the making of it. They claim that pent-up aggressive energy is drained off merely by performing the act, regardless of the effect upon the target (if indeed there *is* a target), and this draining off of tension is said to be pleasurable.

All these notions about the goals or effects of aggressive acts are related to the fascinating question of catharsis. Most generally, catharsis refers to the reduction in drive, emotion, or motivation as a result of performing an act (overtly or in fantasy). In some versions, the feedback from the consequences of the act upon the environment are considered important; in other versions (including the psychoanalytic), they are not. A considerable amount of experimental research has been concerned with testing various aspects of this question. Let us first try to define the problems; then, hopefully, we shall find some data to throw light upon them.

Part of the problem has been one of definition. In this chapter we have adopted a widely accepted definition of aggression—namely, we refer to those acts that are intended to deliver punishment to some target. This is essentially the usage of Dollard et al. in *Frustration and Aggression,* and is accepted by such authorities as Berkowitz (1962), Bandura and Walters (1963), and Feshbach (1964). Although agreement about definitions is helpful for communication, it is difficult to show that one is more or less correct than any other. If one chooses a different definition of aggression, then one studies somewhat different phenomena. Buss (1961), for example, prefers to define aggression as the delivery of noxious stimuli to someone. He thus prefers not to include the attribute of intentionality. For him a motorist's act of hitting a pedestrian is a case of aggression whether it was intentional or accidental. Before calling it aggression, Dollard et al. would want further information. Did the driver know the victim? Did he make plans to be there at that particular time? Was he angry? If he had missed the pedestrian, would he have made another pass at him?

This last question is one of the crucial parts of the operational definition of aggression advocated in this chapter. A good way to decide whether a person has an intention or goal to do something is to observe what happens when the particular end state fails to be achieved. If a person has an intent to injure someone, then if one act fails to produce injury another is likely to follow. On the other hand, if the desired amount of injury is achieved, the person should tend to stop delivering the punishment—at least in this particular situation. Thus we are saying that a major criterion, technically, for deciding whether an intention to deliver X amount of punishment exists is to observe what the person does when he receives information that that amount of punishment has been successfully delivered to the target. If he intended it, he should tend not to deliver any more punishment in this situation at this time. Of course, if the intention is successfully carried out, the aggressive behavior is reinforced and would be even more likely to recur on some *future* occasion when the aggressive feelings or intentions are again aroused. However, in the period of time immediately following the delivery of the desired amount of punishment, one would expect a reduction in the probability of aggression if additional aggression-instigating stimuli are not introduced. This is essentially an instance of satiation. Just as the person who has consumed his fill of food or water is unlikely to seek more (at that moment), so the person who has successfully delivered the desired amount of punishment would be expected to cease aggressing toward the target.

It is of course difficult to establish in advance what "the desired amount of punishment" is. If the tormentor is perceived to suffer just a bit because of something the victim does, this may fail to satiate the desire to punish and have the opposite effect—namely, increase the probability of the immediate repetition of the response. Thus a victim who would be satiated by delivering ten units of pain to his enemy might increase his rate of pressing a one-unit shock button up to the point where about ten units have been delivered. Feshbach, Stiles, and Bitter (1967) have indeed shown that an insulted subject will increase the rate of emitting a response that delivers a moderate electric shock to the enemy. In this experiment female subjects were asked to observe their tormentor secretly through a one-way screen. While observing, each was to make sentences starting with personal pronouns of her own choice. Every time "we" or "they" was incorporated in a sentence, the disliked person appeared to receive a shock shortly thereafter. Although subjects seemed on later questioning to have been completely unaware of this contingency, those who had been insulted showed an increase over trials in the emission of these pronouns. A plausible interpretation is that it was pleasant (at least reinforcing) to see the enemy suffer, but that his suffering was so slight that the desire to see him in pain was not quickly satiated.

What does this have to do with catharsis? If by "catharsis" we mean a decrease in aggressive behavior toward target X after the person has succeeded in injuring him in the desired amount, then it should be clear that this follows by definition from the concept of aggression. Catharsis, in this sense, simply means a drop in aggressiveness toward X following the successful delivery of punishment to X. According to our definition of aggression, there is no intent to injure *unless* one can (in principle) show such a catharsis effect! Thus if there is no such thing as catharsis in this sense, then there is probably no such thing as aggression as we have defined it. One would expect, then, that a notion so integral to the very definition of aggression would have been demonstrated repeatedly and would be quite noncontroversial. Strangely, this is not so.

As Berkowitz (1962) has pointed out, a catharsis-like effect may simply be due to the arousal of guilt-produced inhibition of aggression. The aggressor may feel guilty about what he has done and hence stops doing it. Or, an aggressor may cease if he fears retaliation from the target. In order to avoid contaminating our results with the guilt and fear variables, it is necessary to design an experiment either without guilt and fear or in which the effects of these can be separately assessed. To my knowledge, such an adequately designed experiment has never been done. The design seems to require first the eliciting of probably aggressive acts from subjects in a situation in which they are not inhibited about punishing the target. Some of the subjects would receive information that the target suffered from the attack, some would perhaps receive no information about the effect of the attack, and some might be told that the target was enjoying the attack. Dependent measures of aggression, hostility, and tension remaining at the end of the session would then be taken. Unfortunately, the requirements are not as simple as they at first appear. Clearly the outcome may depend very heavily upon how much the target is injured. If he were to drop dead when the subject only delivered what he thought was a moderate electric shock, one can imagine that the subject might feel terribly guilty and would bend over backward to help the bereaved family with the funeral expenses. The main problem with the experiment is that it is so difficult to guarantee that guilt is absent. And, on the other hand, if the target were to laugh and giggle on receipt of the supposedly punishing act, it seems plausible that the subject's anger and hostility would be much increased, facilitating further acts believed to be noxious for the target.

Let us take a somewhat different perspective on the same problem. Because catharsis as defined here is actually part of the defining problem for the concept of aggression, what we are really trying to do is to use the catharsis effect as an indicator that purposive aggressive tendencies have actually been aroused in a given situation. Conceived in this way, one would be less interested in demonstrating the existence of catharsis per se than in using the catharsis effect to demonstrate the intent to injure— that is, aggressive intent. But if guilt could follow punishment-delivering acts *even though the person had no intent to injure the target,* the resulting inhibition of future punishing acts might be mistakenly attributed to a catharsis process and interpreted to mean that the original acts had been intentional. We do suspect that people sometimes feel guilty even though they apparently had no intention to injure.

It is perhaps partly because of this thorny guilt problem that experimenters have not used catharsis as an indicator of aggressive intent. And the difficulty of demonstrating intent probably explains why some people (for example, Buss, 1961) have chosen to leave intent out of their definition of aggression. Perhaps that is the best solution. Or, there may be easier ways to demonstrate an intent to injure. One might try asking the subject whether he wants to hurt the target, for example. What experimenters have generally done is to use arousal manipulations that almost everyone agrees seem to produce such intent to punish, and they let it go at that.

Let us look at some experiments in which we have some reason to believe aggressive intent was produced. Do they in general find a pattern of results consistent with the catharsis hypothesis? Note that we have argued that a catharsis-like effect could be generated by guilt and fear reactions. That means that unless such reactions can be guaranteed to be absent, the evidence of a reduction in the delivery of punishment is ambiguous. Strangely, we discover that a number of experiments find, on the contrary, that if a subject delivers punishing responses to a target at time 1, he is even more likely to repeat it shortly afterward, at time 2! Such data, on the face of it, are very damaging to the catharsis hypothesis, and such data are by no means rare.

Let us look first at some early research that was thought to demonstrate catharsis effects. In one of the earliest studies Thibaut (1950) found some evidence that frustrated subjects who were able to express their hostility openly toward a perceived frustrater ended up less hostile toward the frustrater than did those who did not express their hostility openly. Thibaut and Coules (1952) found that subjects who had a chance to strike back verbally at someone who had insulted them were later less hostile toward that person than were subjects not given such a chance. However, they suggested that this difference might reflect not so much a *reduction* in hostility in "strike back" subjects as an *increase* in hostility among subjects who had been prevented from retaliating against their attacker. Further, content analysis of subjects' verbal behavior showed that those given the chance to retaliate actually made very few hostile statements at that time. Catharsis, then, seems an unlikely explanation for their results.

Pepitone and Reichling (1955) created two-person groups of strangers in the laboratory; in half of the pairs the two were induced to like each other, while in the other pairs mild disliking or neutrality was induced. Each pair was then strongly insulted by the experimenter. When the experimenter was out of the room, it was possible for hidden observers to record the amount of hostility expressed toward him by the members of the insulted pair. More open verbal hostility was expressed by the pairs who liked each other than by those who did not. For our purposes, the interesting finding has to do with subsequent ratings made of the absent experimenter. The high-liking pairs, who expressed the most hostility immediately after the experimenter left, ended up liking the experimenter better than did the low-liking pairs. Since the original hostility expression could not hit its absent target, however, this experiment is not directly relevant to the question of *injuring* the attacker. Rather, it seems to provide some support for the idea that merely expressing hostility (without hurting the target) tends to reduce hostility. Guilt unfortunately remains as a possible interpretation of the results.

The more recent research has generally treated the catharsis hypothesis unkindly. DeCharms and Wilkins (1963) designed an experiment in which male subjects were insulted by a self-assured and egotistical stooge over an intercom system. Some subjects were given a good opportunity to retaliate verbally, while others were not. Most of the subjects who had the chance did in fact make hostile statements, whereas the others made almost none. No feedback was given to the subjects as to how the stooge reacted to the hostile remarks. The dependent measures were ratings the subject made of the stooge, with the understanding that the ratings would be sent directly to the stooge. Thus, the opportunity for further verbal aggression was made available. The results indicated that subjects earlier given the chance to attack were subsequently *more* likely to criticize the stooge than were those initially not given a chance to attack. The expression of hostility apparently increased rather than decreased the probability of punitive responses occurring only a few minutes later. How can the catharsis hypothesis be maintained in the face of data of this sort? DeCharms and Wilkins provide a plausible answer—namely, that the subjects who criticized the stooge immediately after he had insulted them had no way of knowing whether they had succeeded in punishing him. This lack of feedback might have constituted an additional frustration, which then increased later aggressiveness. For all the subjects knew, the stooge might have been singing, "Sticks and stones may break my bones but words will never hurt me!"

This is not to say that catharsis is likely to occur *only* when the subject observes clear evidence that his target has been punished. Probably there are some responses that are certain enough to produce suffering so that all the subject needs is confidence that the noxious stimuli actually reached the target. Take electric shock, for example. If the subject is certain that he is delivering a strong electric shock to his target, he can be reasonably certain the target person is hurt, even though he doesn't hear the cries of pain. He could reason that unless the target is a masochist, the shocks are punishing. In the DeCharms and Wilkins study, we are not told how violent the subjects' verbal behavior was, but we can make a guess that subjects were not sure the verbal attack really hurt the target. Berkowitz (1966) performed a relevant experiment using electric shock. Each subject first received eight shocks from a confederate who appeared to be merely another subject. This annoyed the average subject, but each was informed that he would have no opportunity to deliver shocks to the confederate. Then the experimenter pretended to half of the subjects that he'd made a mistake and that they *would* have such an opportunity after all. These subjects proceeded to give as many shocks (up to ten) as they wished; on the average they gave 4.2. Shortly after, all subjects— both those who had had the opportunity to give shocks and those who had not—were given a final chance to shock the confederate. A simple catharsis hypothesis would seem to predict that the subjects who had had the prior opportunity to deliver shocks would give fewer at the next opportunity than would those who had never hurt their tormentor. The results offered no support for this prediction. There was no difference between these groups in the amount of shock delivered at the last occasion.

Finally, an experiment by Kahn (1966) also failed to support the catharsis hypothesis. Subjects were first angered by an insulting experimenter, who left the room immediately thereafter. A second experimenter then entered. With half of the subjects he made no effort to induce the subject to tell him about the first experimenter's insulting behavior. With the other subjects he probed until he got the full story, and he promised the subject that the first experimenter's supervisor would reprimand him the next day without revealing the source of the complaint. Shortly thereafter the subject was given a "confidential" form on which he could rate his liking for the first experimenter. Because this form was not to be shown to the first experimenter, the measure is not technically tapping direct aggression; it is more appropriately called an indicator of hostility.

The results on this measure showed more hostility in the group who had earlier expressed their anger than in the group who had not been encouraged to do so. As in most of these experiments, there are plausible explanations for the results. It is possible, for example, that the very warm and supportive second experimenter simply succeeded in persuading the subject that the other fellow really was deserving of punishment.

None of the studies of angered subjects that have measured changes in the tendency to deliver punishment following an initial delivery of punishment by the subject himself has convincingly shown a cathartic reduction. Some, such as the DeCharms and Wilkins, and Kahn studies already discussed, have even obtained significant results in the opposite direction. All of the studies have serious flaws from the point of view of testing the catharsis hypothesis unequivocally. How could a more crucial test be designed? Here is a tentative solution: If the goal of the person is to punish the target, is it necessary that he perform the act himself? Perhaps the goal could be partly reached simply by *observing* the target receive punishment. If a person has the intention to punish, it seems plausible that his motivation to deliver further punishment could be reduced by showing him that the target person has already received (or is about to receive) an appropriate dose of punishment, even though the dose is delivered by someone else. It seems that a situation of this type could be arranged in such a way that the angered observer would feel very little guilt as he watches his frustrater suffer by someone else's hand, or even accidentally. Although young children are reported to feel guilty even when objectively they have played no causal role in someone's misfortune, adults are probably better able to discriminate between events for which they are partly responsible and those for which they are not. The design of such an experiment requires simply that some subjects be angered by the experimenter and some treated in a neutral fashion. Then some of each group of subjects observe the experimenter suffer, while perhaps others observe him neither suffering nor enjoying. The basic dependent variable would be the amount of punishment the subjects deliver to the experimenter at some later time. Even though the subject has not himself been responsible for the experimenter's plight, it would be surprising if this situation failed to demonstrate a catharsis effect. Wouldn't your tendency to aggress against someone who insulted you be reduced if, as he walked away, you saw him slip on a banana peel and fall flat on his face?

The first published experiment that approximates this kind of test of the catharsis idea is reported by Berkowitz, Green, and Macaulay (1962). Subjects were either angered by receiving six electric shocks from a stooge, or they received only one shock. Each subject was then told how well the stooge had performed on a test of creativity. The relevant dependent measure for our purposes was a measure of the subject's mood at the end of the experiment. Considering only those subjects who had very little opportunity to aggress against the stooge, the mood results are consistent with the catharsis hypothesis. Angered subjects felt much better when they heard the stooge had done poorly than when told he had done well. Nonangered subjects felt better when the stooge had done well than when he had done poorly. If the subjects imagined that doing poorly was punishing for the stooge, the implication is that hostile tension can be reduced by hearing that your attacker is suffering.

An experiment by Bramel, Taub, and Blum (1968) provides a fairly clear test of the idea that hostility toward someone can be reduced simply by observing him suffer, even though the observer had no part whatsoever in making him suffer. The frustrater, a fellow college student of the subjects, claimed he was just temporarily filling in for the regular experimenter. With half of the subjects he behaved in a very insulting way, which clearly produced strong hostility. With the others he behaved in a neutral manner. For all subjects he pretended to be in a hurry to get somewhere else, and he left as soon as the second experimenter arrived. She entered, carrying a single reel of recording tape, and expressed surprise at seeing the "substitute" experimenter. Previous instructions had prepared the subject to expect to listen to one of a set of tape recordings reproducing "actual" experimental studies of the effects of drugs on emotional states. He knew that the persons on the tapes were student volunteers responding, under the influence of drugs, to various standard stimuli. The second experimenter proceeded to take the reel of tape from its box. Appearing nonplussed and disorganized, she stammered that a blunder had been made. The person on this tape was the "substitute experimenter" himself! The cause of the error was obvious, since the second experimenter had "not been told" about the substitution. She decided to go ahead and play the tape anyway, even though it might "bias the results if a subject knew personally the drug volunteer on the tape." The subject, left alone in the room, then listened to a tape that had been randomly selected for him. Some of them heard the "substitute experimenter" suffering miserably for about twelve minutes, supposedly under the influence of a nausea–depression–anxiety drug. Others heard the same person allegedly experiencing the effects of a "neutralizing" drug that prevents *any* strong emotions. On this tape virtually no affect was expressed. The dependent variables included ratings of liking for the person on the tape and a measure of aggression that allowed the subject to make "confidential" ratings of the experimenters "so that the Psychology Department could evaluate their performance as research assistants."

The results were consistent with a catharsis prediction. Relative to control subjects who were never insulted by the "substitute experimenter," angered subjects rated the person more favorably after hearing him suffer than after hearing the neutral tape. Ratings of the second experimenter, who behaved neutrally toward all subjects, showed no such effect, as predicted. It is interesting that the suffering of the volunteer on the tape effectively reduced hostility even though the suffering had supposedly occurred months before the insulting interaction with the subject. It is certainly unlikely that the subjects in this experiment felt any guilt regarding the past misery of the "substitute experimenter." It is also unlikely that they attributed his insulting behavior to this previous experience, given the time gap and the "fact" that his insulting behavior seemed adequately explained by his annoyance at having to "fill in" and being late for an important appointment.

Note that in this experiment the suffering of the person on the tape was not the result of any aggression toward him. He had simply volunteered in a study of drug effects and had swallowed what the scientists gave him. Thus there was no aggressor in the scene. We may find that catharsis effects are less evident when a person observes a scene in which the suffering is produced by *aggressive attacks from another person.* Further, such effects would probably be even further attenuated when the victim in the scene is someone *other than* the subject's own frustrater. After you have been frustrated by person A, does it comfort you to see person B attack person C? Some people have argued that catharsis will occur even here. This is a fascinating issue, which has important implications.

The Effects Upon an Angered Person of Observing Someone Else Aggressing

Stretching back historically at least as far as Aristotle and Plato, the debate concerning the cathartic versus arousing effects of observing scenes involving strong emotions is still going on. If those great philosophers were still alive today, they would probably be surprised to find that the matter has not yet been completely resolved. First we shall take a brief glance at what they had to say about it, and then we can discuss the recent data in proper perspective.

Plato (*The Republic*, Chapter 38): Few, I believe, are capable of reflecting that to enter into another's feelings must have an effect on our own: The emotions of pity our sympathy has strengthened will not be easy to restrain when we are suffering ourselves. . . . Does not the same principle apply to humour as well as to pathos? . . . There is in you an impulse to play the clown, which you have held in restraint from a reasonable fear of being set down as a buffoon; but now you have given it rein, and by encouraging its

impudence at the theater you may be unconsciously carried away into playing the comedian in your private life. Similar effects are produced by poetic
representations of love and anger and all those desires and feelings of
pleasure or pain which accompany our every action. It waters the growth of
passions which should be allowed to wither away and sets them up in control,
although the goodness and happiness of our lives depend on their being held
in subjection.

Aristotle (*The Poetics,* Section 6): Tragedy, then, is an imitation of an action
that is serious, complete, and of a certain magnitude; in language embellished
with each kind of artistic ornament, the several kinds being found in separate
parts of the play; in the form of action, not of narrative; through pity and
fear effecting the proper purgation [catharsis] of these emotions.

One recognizes Aristotle to be the advocate of a catharsis hypothesis. The
practical relevance of these issues has received a great deal of attention.
Whereas Plato and Aristotle were concerned about the effects of music and
dramatic poetry, the modern focus is upon movies, television, comic books,
newspapers, prize fights, and capital punishment. How is an angered
person affected by witnessing aggression performed by other people, real
and fictional?

A number of experiments have employed the following general design:
A subject is angered by the experimenter or a stooge. Then he is exposed
to a scene (presented in any of a variety of media) in which one person
aggresses against another, or in which there is mutual aggression. The
dependent variable is a measure of the subject's tendency to aggress
against the person who originally angered him. In some studies (for
example, Rosenbaum and deCharms, 1960; deCharms and Wilkins, 1963;
Wheeler and Caggiula, 1966; Wheeler and Smith, 1967) the person
attacked in the scene is the very person who frustrated the subject. In
others (for example, Feshbach, 1961; Berkowitz and Rawlings, 1963;
Berkowitz, 1965; Hartmann, 1965) the scene does not include the subject's
frustrater.

Only one of these experiments would provide any real comfort for
Aristotle, and that is the one by Feshbach (1961). Half of his subjects
were insulted and angered by the experimenter, while the rest were
treated in a neutral manner. Half of each group then saw an effectively
staged prize-fight sequence from a movie, whereas the others saw a less
aggressive movie about the spread of rumors. The dependent measure
asked the subjects to make confidential ratings of the experimenter for
the benefit of the Psychology Department's evaluation of experiments.
The results indicated that viewing the fight film apparently decreased the
aggressiveness of the angered subjects, whereas viewing the more neutral
film did not.

Having thus rested quietly lo these many years, Aristotle was to turn over in his grave more than once when further data began to come off the presses. In an experiment very similar to Feshbach's, Berkowitz and Rawlings (1963) set out to explore conditions that might be expected to increase or decrease catharsis effects. They reasoned that catharsis might be most likely when the observer could identify with the victorious prize fighter. Perhaps by "putting himself in the shoes" of the attractive aggressor, by aggressing vicariously, the observer would become less angry and would subsequently show a reduced tendency to attack his own frustrater (the experimenter). In order to facilitate the tendency to identify with the aggressor (the winner of the fight), some subjects were told that the victim in the movie (Kirk Douglas) was a scoundrel who really deserved to be beaten up. Other subjects were told that the loser was a fine fellow who didn't deserve such a fate. Before seeing the movie, half of the subjects were treated in an insulting and badgering manner by the graduate-student experimenter, while the other half were treated neutrally. A second experimenter showed the movie (describing the aggression against Kirk Douglas as either justified or unjustified) and handed out the questionnaire measure of attitudes toward the first experimenter. Since the subjects were not led to believe that their ratings of the first experimenter would be communicated to him, we do not have here a direct measure of aggression. Rather, it is a measure of residual hostility toward the experimenter. The results indicated that initially angered subjects who saw "justified" aggression against the evil Kirk Douglas were more hostile toward the insulting experimenter than were angered subjects who saw a sympathetically described Kirk Douglas take the same beating. It seems, then, that those subjects who were encouraged to identify with the aggressor actually ended up more hostile than those who were discouraged from putting themselves in the aggressor's shoes. Thus, identification with the aggressor, far from facilitating the catharsis effect, seems to have prevented it!

What happens if we compare angered subjects who saw the aggressive movie with those who did not? Ignoring the "justified" versus "unjustified" variable, was there any over-all effect of seeing the movie? Berkowitz and Rawlings did not include a nonaggressive-film control group, but, happily, Berkowitz, Corwin, and Heironimus (1963) did. They showed some of their angered and nonangered subjects an equal-length film about English canal boats. Their results, using a very similar design to that of Berkowitz and Rawlings, showed that the aggressiveness of angered subjects toward their frustrater was enhanced by seeing the fight film (relative to angered subjects who saw the canal boats film). Ratings of the experimenter made by subjects who were not angered by him were unaffected by the type of film they watched. Berkowitz and his colleagues (1965, 1966; Geen and Berkowitz, 1966) report several additional experiments in which Kirk Douglas's beating is again portrayed as justified. In these experiments there was again a *slight* tendency for more aggression following the fight film than following a control film for angered, but not for nonangered subjects. Thus a version of the catharsis hypothesis takes it on the chin once again.

Hartmann (1965) did an experiment similar to those of Berkowitz et al., using male juvenile delinquents as subjects. Half of the subjects were angered by receiving an insulting evaluation from an unseen stooge of about the same age as the subjects (13–16 years); the remaining subjects heard a mildly favorable evaluation. Each subject was then shown a movie of a basketball game involving two players of about the subjects' age. For one third of the boys the movie depicted an active but nonaggressive game; for another third the game ended in a fight, and the camera focused almost entirely upon the swinging fists and kicking feet of the more aggressive and dominant boy; for the remaining subjects the game also ended in a fight, but this time the camera focused upon the cringes and grimaces of the boy who was the victim of the aggressor. The dependent variable was the amount of electric shock the subject later delivered to the stooge who had originally evaluated him. The rationale justifying the shock apparatus was that this was a study of learning as a function of punishment for wrong answers. The subject was free to choose the magnitude and duration of shock to deliver for each (programmed) wrong answer of the stooge, who was supposedly hooked up to electrodes in the next room. The results were only partially consistent with the findings of Berkowitz and his associates. Consider first the subjects who saw the movie focusing upon the aggressive behavior of the bully. In this condition, the angered subjects later delivered slightly *less* shock than did the nonangered subjects (not statistically significant). This is consistent with a catharsis hypothesis. However, the results for the subjects who saw primarily the pain cues expressed by the victim in the movie were not in the same direction. Seeing this movie increased the aggressiveness of the angered subjects but not that of the nonangered subjects. The results in this condition certainly throw further doubt upon an unqualified catharsis hypothesis.

Considering the findings of the Berkowitz et al. studies and the somewhat mixed pattern of Hartmann's data, is it time to conclude that Aristotle's belief in a catharsis through observing other people's emotional behavior must be discarded? What might Aristotle say, other than to express his disbelief that anyone could consider watching a Hollywood film (or worse) comparable to watching Sophocles' *Oedipus Rex?*

Someone who wishes to argue in favor of catharsis through observing aggression would probably answer the question in the following way. He might say that although catharsis processes often occur under such circumstances, their effects are obscured, or masked, by the presence of other processes that tend to facilitate later aggression. A fair test of the catharsis hypothesis would then require either eliminating or controlling these other factors. Suffice it to say that the data already presented suggest that *if* catharsis processes were present but masked in these studies, such processes apparently were not terribly powerful. As Bandura points out:

> These findings are perhaps not too surprising since it is highly improbable that even advocates of vicarious drive reduction would recommend community-sponsored programs in which sexually aroused adolescents are shown libidinous movies at drive-in theaters, famished persons are presented displays of gourmands dining on culinary treats, and assaultive gangs are regularly shown films of assailants flogging their antagonists, as a means of reducing sexual behavior, hunger pangs and aggression, respectively. Such procedures would undoubtedly have strong instigative rather than reductive consequences. (1965, p. 27)

Before leaving this fascinating topic, let us examine some experiments that take a rather different approach to the vicarious-catharsis hypothesis. It is certainly true that the evidence thus far accumulated shows very little reduction in aggression in an observer who sees an aggressive scene depicting persons *who have no real relation to his own frustrating situation*. What would happen if the observer witnessed a scene in which someone attacks *the very person who frustrated the observer?* We have already described the experiment by Bramel, Taub, and Blum (1968), in which a catharsis effect was shown among subjects who observed their frustrater suffer. But there was no aggressor responsible for the suffering. The victim had volunteered in a scientific study of drug effects; no one was trying to injure him. Hence, there was no aggressor to be imitated or identified with. In the present context, in contrast, we are not simply going to tell the subject that his frustrater is suffering; rather, we are going to let the subject listen in while someone verbally attacks the frustrater. The observer hears an attack upon his frustrater, and he may or may not be given further information about the effectiveness of this attack in punishing the frustrater. How does this affect the subject's subsequent tendency to punish his frustrater? On the face of it, it certainly appears more likely there will be a reduction in aggression in this kind of situation than in those used by Feshbach (1961), Berkowitz et al. (1963), Berkowitz (1965), and Hartmann (1965). If the subject's goal is to have his *frustrater* punished, then perhaps his hostility will be reduced even if it is someone else who carries out the aggression in his place.

The previously discussed experiment by deCharms and Wilkins (1963) contained some conditions relevant to this question. The technique of arousing anger was to have a stooge call the subject an "egotistical deceitful liar," and so on, over an intercom system. The subjects in the relevant conditions did not have a chance to reply to the attack. Some of them were then allowed to listen in as another stooge (who appeared to be another subject, and who had not been attacked by the first stooge) verbally attacked the first stooge. These subjects heard the second stooge call the first "fantastic," a "bastard" who "ought to live in a jungle." The second stooge did not mention the naïve subject in his attack. Other angered subjects (controls) heard nothing, having been instructed that it was the second stooge's turn to talk to the first. Thus we have angered subjects who either hear their attacker attacked for a minute and a half, or who hear nothing. The dependent measure of aggression was a set of paper-and-pencil evaluations the subject made of the insulting first stooge. The subject was led to believe that these evaluations would be sent directly to this stooge. Analysis of these ratings indicated that much more hostility was expressed by the subjects who heard their frustrater attacked than by those who heard nothing. Once again catharsis proves to be an elusive phenomenon! But wait, maybe the trouble was that the subject didn't know whether his frustrater was really hurt by the second stooge's attack. Perhaps the catharsis can occur only if it is clear to the angered person that his enemy has really been effectively punished.

A very similar experiment by Wheeler and Caggiula (1966) was designed to throw some light on this possible explanation. This one attempted to anger subjects by having them listen over an intercom to a stooge who uttered very distasteful opinions about almost sacred institutions of American life. In one condition a second stooge then responded to these opinions by attacking the first stooge in very strong language (much of it unprintable). In a control condition he made no aggressive attack upon the first stooge. The naïve subject then got a chance to enter the fray. The dependent variable was the amount of violently hostile language used by the subject against the stooge with the vile opinions. Replicating deCharms and Wilkins (1963), these experimenters also found that subjects were more violently aggressive after hearing someone attack their frustrater than after hearing no such aggression (replicated by Wheeler and Smith, 1967). One of the variations in the design is especially interesting. In one condition, after the second stooge attacked the first stooge, the first stooge recanted, saying that his opinion was indeed probably incorrect. This is one of the few experiments in which there was some feedback to the angered subject concerning the effectiveness of an aggressive act. The results in this condition were only mildly supportive of the catharsis hypothesis. The *first* time the heretical stooge recanted, there was some evidence (although not statistically significant) that the angered subject's aggressiveness was reduced toward him. However, the experiment then continued for five more trials, on each of which the stooge uttered another socially undesirable opinion, was attacked by a second stooge, and then admitted his error. By the end of this series, those subjects who heard a repeatedly repentent stooge were aggressing against him just as strongly as were those who heard him stick dogmatically to his errors. Perhaps after a while the subject no longer took the retractions seriously, since the unpleasant fellow always snapped right back on the next trial with an equally obnoxious opinion on some new topic.

Finally, Berkowitz and Geen (1966) and Geen and Berkowitz (1966) have reported some experiments in which they have manipulated the perceived similarity between a frustrater of the subject and a character in an aggressive boxing movie. In the Berkowitz and Geen (1966) experiment, for example, subjects were first angered or not angered by a confederate of the experimenters. Then the subjects watched either a film in which Kirk Douglas is pummeled or a film of the first four-minute mile race. Some subjects were told that the confederate's name was the same ("Kirk") as that of the victim in the film, whereas others were told his name ("Bob") was different from that in the film. The subjects who saw Kirk Douglas beaten up were told he deserved every bit of it because he was a scoundrel in the story. The dependent measure was the number of painful electric shocks the subject was willing to deliver to the confederate (located in another room) after seeing the movie. If the reader can assimilate all of the variables packed into this paragraph, he is ready to look at a summary of the findings, which is presented in Table 2-2. Angered subjects who saw the fight film were most likely to shock the confederate with the same name as Douglas. If the confederate had a different name, seeing the aggressive film had no significant effect on subsequent aggression.

Several tentative conclusions can be drawn from these studies by Berkowitz and Geen. First, there is no evidence that hostility toward the

TABLE 2-2. *Mean Number of Shocks Given to Confederate After Subject Had Watched Movie* (from Berkowitz and Geen, 1966)

Confederate's Name	Aggressive Film		Track Film	
	Angered	*Nonangered*	*Angered*	*Nonangered*
Kirk	6.09	1.73	4.18	1.54
Bob	4.55	1.45	4.00	1.64

frustrating confederate is reduced by seeing someone with a similar name (Kirk Douglas) beaten up. On the contrary, aggressiveness toward the confederate was *increased* after seeing the fight film. Hence, no strong support is given to the possibility that catharsis can occur if you see someone *similar* to your frustrater injured. However, the degree of manipulated similarity was not great in these studies (only a first or last name). Second, these studies do not demonstrate that the *aggressiveness* of the fight movie is a critical variable. Recall that this film seems to increase aggression among angered subjects only if these two conditions hold: Douglas is described as a scoundrel, and the confederate has a similar name. The explanation, then, may be that the name of the confederate (for example, "Kirk") and his frustrating behavior remind the subject of the evil Kirk Douglas, thus increasing his hostile motivation. When the confederate is not frustrating, he does not arouse this additional dislike. The fact that Douglas is beaten up may have nothing to do with this effect. In fact, it may even serve to weaken the effect by reducing the subject's hostility toward the unfortunate fellow. This is a speculation that remains to be tested. In an earlier experiment, Berkowitz (1965, experiment II) presents data that show no effect on aggression whatsoever of the role similarity between the confederate (sometimes a boxer) and the evil Kirk Douglas. Hence, even the conclusion from the Berkowitz and Geen studies must remain tentative.

Having reached the end (for this discussion) of a rather long series of studies concerned with the catharsis of aggression, we can summarize the state of experimentally based knowledge about the process. It is clear that few carefully controlled experiments have shown any decrease in aggressiveness resulting from any of the following prior events: (1) the subject overtly attacks the antagonist; (2) the subject observes someone else attacking his (the subject's) antagonist; (3) the subject observes someone else attacking a person who had nothing to do with arousing the subject's anger. The experiment by Bramel, Taub, and Blum (1968) did show a catharsis effect when *no aggressor was responsible for the frustrater's suffering*. However, no one has as yet reported a completely fair test of the following hypothesis: The subject's hostility will be reduced if he observes *someone else actually injuring* his (the subject's) enemy. Although the Wheeler and Caggiula (1966) study comes closest to providing this essential test (with results weakly supporting the catharsis hypothesis), there remain several sources of ambiguity in the design.

If observing others aggressing reduces the observer's aggressive motivation through a catharsis process, the process is apparently not sufficiently powerful to show itself in a clear reduction in overt aggression. Giving feedback that the subject's frustrater has actually been injured is probably necessary. Even then, however, other forces operate to *increase* aggression in the observer. These include tendencies to imitate (cf. the work of Bandura [1965] and his associates) and tendencies for the observer's *inhibitions* about aggression to be reduced by observing someone else behaving in an uninhibited and unpunished fashion (cf. Wheeler, 1966).

There are yet other versions of the catharsis hypothesis, but little space here in which to discuss them in detail. Does the performance of *any* very active response (such as running around the block) serve to reduce the hostility and aggressiveness of an angered person? Such actions certainly tire him out, but no one seems to have published any definitive tests of the effects on aggressiveness. Does fantasy aggression (such as telling an aggressive story, or hearing an aggressive joke) reduce aggressiveness? The interested reader should consult the article by Singer (1968) for a discussion of the still rather uncertain status of this hypothesis.

3

How Behavior Toward Others Affects Attitudes Toward Them

The focus in this chapter is not so much upon the stimulus characteristics of other people and how these characteristics affect our attitudes toward them. Rather, we consider now the intriguing possibility that a person's liking or disliking for other people may be affected by his own behavior toward them. If you are induced in some way to do a good deed for a person, will you come to like him more as a result? If, for some reason, you hurt a person, will you convince yourself that he is really unattractive and deserving of the punishment he received? Since this latter question has stimulated the greater amount of fruitful research, we shall deal with it first.

The alert reader has already noticed that this hypothesis seems to contradict the catharsis hypothesis discussed earlier. Whereas the catharsis notion predicts a *decrease* in hostility following the delivery of punishment to the victim, the present discussion suggests that people sometimes have *increased* hostility following such action. In our discussion of the various forms of the catharsis hypothesis, we concluded that there was very little support for the version claiming decreased aggression after the angered person has delivered a dose of punishment to his frustrater. One reason for this may be that other factors, such as dissonance and guilt, may confound the issue. The following pages deal with these factors. An integration of the opposing predictions and the conditions under which they are likely to hold true will be presented after an exploration of the roles of dissonance and guilt.

Before starting to thread our way through the data, it will be useful to point out some theoretical guidelines. The orientation that has been most productively applied to this issue is Festinger's (1957) theory of cognitive dissonance. According to this theory, it makes a person uncomfortable to find himself behaving in a way that seems inconsistent with information he has about himself and his environment. If person *A* chooses to behave in a way that he believes injures person *B,* it will make him uncomfortable to think that *B* is a friend of his and that he, *A,* is a gentle and considerate person. Further, if he believes these things, he will be even more disturbed if he believes that he acted freely, of his own volition; and it will be even worse the more severe he believes the injury to *B* to be. All of these thoughts, or cognitions, are considerations that ordinarily would have deterred person *A* from acting as he did (or at least he *thinks* they would inhibit his tendency to perform such acts). In the usual course of things, person *A* avoids hurting his friends, especially when he has a choice; and certainly the greater the injury likely to be caused, the more he usually avoids acting in such a way. When a person with *A*'s cognitive world performs an injurious act under these circumstances, he probably experiences unpleasant feelings whenever he thinks about these things that are inconsistent with what he has done.

There are actually two sources of unpleasantness in this situation (Bramel, 1968). The first is that the person finds himself behaving in a way that is inconsistent with his expectations about himself. Because he doesn't usually choose voluntarily to hurt his friends, he is shocked to see himself doing exactly that. The second source of discomfort occurs because the person is doing something he considers to be morally wrong and hence deserving of punishment. This, of course, is the phenomenon commonly known as guilt. Guilt feelings are aroused when we act in a way that violates moral (ethical) standards and that was punished in the past. The concept *dissonance* probably includes both of these sources of unpleasantness.

If a person feels dissonance after he has delivered some punishing stimulus to another person, he will probably try to reduce these feelings by whatever techniques have worked in the past and are available and convenient in the present situation. How might he do it? Here, as elsewhere, human cognition turns out to show great ingenuity. Some of the dissonance-reduction techniques that are theoretically possible are the following (supporting experiments are indicated):

1. The person can convince himself that the injury he has caused is very slight (Brock and Buss, 1962) or nonexistent.
2. The person can convince himself that he really had no choice about how to act; thus, he can feel that he was not really responsible for what happened (Brock and Buss, 1962; 1964).
3. The person can resolve to repair the damage he has caused and thus believe that he can undo the dissonant act (Davis and Jones, 1960; Pallak, 1966).
4. The person might make his behavior more consistent with his self-concept by believing that he is a cruel or careless person. Although self-

devaluation may reduce cognitive inconsistency by making the behavior appear more consistent with other beliefs the person has, it does not necessarily serve as an effective means of reducing the guilt component of the unpleasant subjective state. Self-devaluation might actually increase guilt feelings. Unfortunately, conceptual and experimental refinements have not reached the point where this issue can be easily resolved.

5. The person might convince himself that his injurious act has other consequences that are positive and beneficial. For example, he can justify what he has done by claiming that it is necessary for science or that it will make the world safe for democracy. This prediction has received only weak experimental support.

6. He can convince himself that the victim of the punishment deserved to be punished. This might take the form of attributing undesirable characteristics to the victim (Davis and Jones, 1960; Lerner and Matthews, 1967; Pallak, 1966; Perry, 1965; Ross, 1965) or of a feeling of disliking for the victim (Davidson, 1964; Glass, 1964; Gumpert and Festinger, 1962; Pallak, 1966; Perry, 1965; Ross, 1965).

Let us take a closer look at two of the experiments concerned with these issues. Davis and Jones (1960) instructed their male college-student subjects that they were taking part in an experiment on first-impression formation, and that their task was to judge "another subject in the next room." They were first allowed to listen to the stranger (actually a voice recorded on tape) answer some questions about his background, his interests, and how he would respond to certain moral dilemmas. The subject heard the experimenter on the tape instructing the stranger that the person listening in (the true subject) would later read to the stranger his "honest" evaluation of him. The next task for the subject was to read an evaluation of the stranger to him over the intercom system. However, rather than read his own true evaluation, he was induced to read a quite negative set of comments. The rationale presented to the subject was that this experiment was also studying how people react to very positive or very negative evaluations of themselves. Half of the subjects were simply told that the schedule indicated they were to read the negative evaluation. They apparently had no choice in the matter. The other half of the subjects received the following coaxing from the experimenter:

> As far as I am concerned, you may read either of these evaluations; but I would like to ask a favor of you. Surprisingly enough, most of my recent subjects have been choosing to read the flattering evaluation of their person, so that I have not been getting much information about the effect of a negative evaluation on people. If you feel able, I'd like to ask you to read the negative evaluation of your partner. Do you think that you'll be able to do this for me? (p. 404)

Since approximately 10 per cent of the subjects given a choice actually refused to read the negative evaluation, it does seem likely that even the yielding subjects felt in some way personally responsible for their act. Half of the subjects in the choice and no-choice conditions were led to believe that they would have a chance to talk to the stranger after the experiment, and that the experimenter would explain to him that the evaluation read "was not your true opinion of him." The other half of the subjects were told that the stranger would never be told the truth and that no subsequent interaction between them would occur. The dependent variable was the amount of change in evaluation of the stranger from before to after reading the derogatory script to him.

The results indicated that the reading of the script affected the attitudes only of those subjects who were given a choice about reading it and who at the same time believed that they would never interact with the stranger again. These subjects became more negative toward the stranger. The results seem consistent with dissonance theory. Theoretically, dissonance is greater when the person feels that he freely chose to perform the injurious act (Brehm and Cohen, 1962). Subjects who anticipated that the stranger would be told immediately that the evaluation was not true probably felt that the amount of injury they had caused was relatively slight. One would indeed expect that dissonance would be less in this situation the less the perceived injury caused. Further, the subjects who expected to meet and talk to the stranger may have resolved to act sympathetically and thus to undo the damage temporarily caused. In summary, then, Davis and Jones found the most derogation of the stranger in the condition where, according to theory, the most dissonance was aroused.

If a person has been induced to say derogatory things about a person he moderately likes, dissonance can be reduced very neatly by believing that the derogatory description really fits the unfortunate fellow. A number of other experiments have tested a somewhat less plausible prediction. In these studies the subject is induced to deliver painful electric shocks to someone else. Reducing dissonance in this kind of situation by derogating the victim does not seem intuitively as likely as the derogation in the Davis and Jones experiment. Nevertheless, to the extent that subjects believe it more fitting to shock someone they dislike than someone they like, it follows that they can reduce dissonance by convincing themselves they really dislike the victim. An experiment by Glass (1964) provides a neat demonstration of this phenomenon. As in the Davis and Jones experiment, half of the subjects were made to feel that they had a choice whether or not to deliver 100-volt shocks to the other person (a confederate of the experimenter); the remaining subjects were simply told what they were to do. The second manipulated variable was the subject's level of general self-esteem. Prior to being introduced to the "learning" task in which they delivered shocks for the confederate's errors, each subject was given the falsified results of a series of personality tests he himself had taken previously. Half of the subjects were led to believe that they possessed great maturity, leadership qualities, intelligence, and interpersonal sensitivity. The remaining subjects were told that they were immature, weak, not very bright, and insensitive to others. In order to ensure that a large amount of dissonance would be aroused by delivery of shock to the gasping confederate, two further procedures were employed. First, Glass selected for the experiment only subjects who had at a previous time indicated that they were opposed to the use of electric shock in experiments on human subjects. Second, each subject was himself given a rather painful 40-volt shock in order to make it clear that 100 volts would really hurt the other person.

The dependent measures were sociometric items such as "Would you admit Mr. _____ into your circle of close friends?" They indicated that a significant amount of derogation of the victim occurred only among high (manipulated) self-esteem subjects who were given a choice about delivering the shock. Subjects in the other three conditions showed no appreciable changes from before to after giving the shocks. Again the results are on the whole consistent with dissonance theory. Those subjects who were given no choice did not derogate the victim, because they already had a good amount of justification for what they were doing— they were more or less forced to do it. Hence they would not find their behavior inappropriate. Subjects with low self-esteem (who had just been told that they were about as attractive as Pandora's box) probably experienced relatively little inconsistency between their beliefs about themselves and their knowledge that they were now delivering painful shocks to another human being. Thus, dissonance was only really strong for the subjects who were led to think very well of themselves and who felt personally responsible for what they were doing (that is, they had a choice). The results are interesting also from the point of view of distinguishing between the effects of guilt and of other components of dissonance. Presumably even the low–self-esteem subjects felt that giving shocks was inconsistent with their moral principles (opposition to use of shock on humans). If so, they should have experienced guilt when they assented ("freely") to the giving of shocks. If such guilt ordinarily leads to derogation of the victim, it is surprising that no such difference was found among low–self-esteem subjects in the choice and no-choice conditions.

Although it is true that dissonance can theoretically be reduced by derogating the victim, it does not necessarily follow that this particular cognitive process will occur in every person in every such situation. It may not even be true that the greater the dissonance, the greater the tendency to select any given strategy of dissonance reduction. It is possible that a reduction strategy effective at one level of dissonance magnitude may not be so effective (relative to other strategies) at another level. Arguing in support of this complicating issue, Ross (1965) has presented some data consistent with the hypothesis that the rank-order preference for different channels of dissonance reduction is different at different magnitudes of dissonance. His prediction was that subjects who are only slightly or moderately dissonant about having caused pain in another may try to make reparation to the victim by helping him or by thinking highly of him. When dissonance becomes so great that adequate reparation is impossible (for example, if the victim dies), derogation of the victim becomes the preferred means of dissonance reduction. Although Ross's results emerged in the predicted pattern, there remained some ambiguity as to whether the various experimental conditions actually differed *only* in magnitude of dissonance.

Two more precisely controlled experiments directed to the same issue have been conducted (Walster, Walster, Abrahams, & Brown, 1966; Walster and Prestholdt, 1966). The reasoning guiding these studies was similar to that suggested by Ross (1965). To the person who harms another, *no* reparation or compensation to the victim may be preferable to performing a reparative act that is insufficient to make up for the injury produced. The very performance of the reparative act may involve an admission of responsibility for the harm and the discomforting realization that full compensation is impossible. Having experienced this unpleasant consequence in the past, the perpetrator of an injustice may choose to make no compensation rather than make an inadequate one. Under circumstances that deter the tendency to make reparation, the harm-doer may prefer simply to justify what he has done. Since adequate reparation is most difficult when the amount of injury is great, the prediction was that subjects would attempt to make reparation only if the amount of injury they had caused was relatively slight. Consider the experiment by Walster and Prestholdt (1966). The subjects were students of social work who believed they had been assigned to work on a case involving a widow and her young daughter. They were then given certain information about the case without ever actually meeting the (fictitious) clients. Before hearing a taped report of the actual caseworker, half of the subjects were warned that this caseworker, although basically reliable, had incorrectly reported a crucial incident involving the widow and daughter. The other subjects were not told this important fact until *after* they had heard the tape and written up their own interpretation of the situation. All subjects listened to a tape that, if taken at face value, would lead them to evaluate the daughter too negatively and the mother too positively. This, of course, happened most often to the subjects who had not been warned that the tape was inaccurate. Half of each group of subjects were then led to believe that their written interpretation of the mother and daughter would be sent directly to the caseworker "actually" currently involved in the case; the remaining subjects were told that they could keep their reports or throw them away. By this clever stratagem, subjects who had not been warned about the tape and who expected their apparently biased reports actually to influence the social worker's policy toward the family found themselves committed to an act that would unjustly harm the daughter and unjustly benefit the mother. Control subjects either were not tricked into making unjust evaluations or did not expect their evaluations to have any direct impact upon the mother and daughter. The results, considered as a whole, were consistent with the hypothesis. Subjects who had misjudged the family and believed that their misjudgments would actually affect the family tended to justify their judgments by bringing their final attitudes toward the family into line with what they had written earlier. Those who had misjudged but never sent their judgments to the "real" caseworker made final attitudinal "reparation" by reversing their initial misjudgments.

An especially interesting aspect of this study, however, was the finding that the self-justification and reparation processes were most clearly shown in the ratings of the mother rather than the daughter. The mother had been initially misjudged in a *too favorable* direction. Those subjects committed to this misjudgment (sent to caseworker) ended up more favorable toward the mother than did controls. Those not committed ended up *less* favorable toward her than did controls. Although the attitude data concerning the daughter were in the predicted direction, they were much less strong. This experiment constitutes one of the few successful tests of the hypothesis that dissonance aroused by benefitting someone too much (more than they "deserve") will result in an increasingly favorable attitude toward that person. This prediction seems roughly parallel to the more familiar and well-documented finding that people justify undeservedly punishing acts by derogating the victim. It seems plausible, then, that a person who is induced (and feels responsible) to benefit someone he doesn't like will come to like that person more as a means of justifying his dissonant behavior. This hypothesis was suggested by Deutsch and Collins (1951) in order to help account for their finding of an increased liking for blacks by whites living in an integrated housing project, and was later discussed speculatively by Festinger (1957) and Brehm and Cohen (1962).

A second experiment reporting such an effect was done by Jecker and Landy (1966). Each subject participated in a concept-formation task in which he won a sum of money. The experimenter behaved in a cold and distant manner during the session. At the end of the task, one-third of the subjects were told the following: "I was wondering if you would do me a favor. The funds for this experiment have run out and I am using my own money to finish the experiment. As a favor to me, would you mind returning the money you won?" If the subject hesitated, the experimenter said, "I can't make you return the money, but I wish you would as a favor to me." Few subjects refused. Another third of the sample were asked by a secretary to return the money, because "The money Mr. Boyd is using comes from the Psychology Department's research fund, which is running extremely low." The remaining subjects were never asked to return their winnings. All subjects were asked by the secretary to fill out a questionnaire evaluating their feelings about the experiment, including their liking for the experimenter. Those who were induced to "do a favor" for the experimenter liked him more than did those who were cajoled into returning the money to the "Psychology Department." Of course the dissonance-reduction hypothesis is not the only possible interpretation of this result. One could argue that subjects who were asked by the experimenter to return the money liked him more because this request, along with the information that he was using his own funds in the pursuit of science, made the experimenter appear more dependent and "human" than his prior behavior had indicated.

There is one other experiment containing a fairly clear test of the "like those you have chosen to benefit" hypothesis. Lerner and Simmons (1966) asked subjects in groups to observe a student who appeared to be receiving electric shocks in a "learning experiment." After watching a series of trials, some groups were told they could vote, by private ballot, to decide whether the "victim" should continue with the shock experiment or should be shifted to a more rewarding schedule. All subjects voted to stop the shocks. Other subjects were given no such opportunity to affect the fate of the victim. The present hypothesis predicts that ratings of the victim will be more favorable among those given a chance (and using it) to help her than among subjects not given this opportunity. No such differences were found.

Subjects in another condition not only voted to stop the shocks but also were told by the experimenter that the group had decided that the shocks were to stop. In this condition, then, the subjects had the additional information that most of the group had voted against shock and that the shocks would therefore be stopped. These subjects rated the victim significantly more favorably than did those not given a vote and those voting without feedback as to the outcome. In this experiment it appears that the mere decision to help the victim was not sufficient to produce enhanced attractiveness. The belief that one's act actually leads to help may be necessary to produce a changed evaluation. Unfortunately, this experiment includes a confounding factor that makes the interpretation ambiguous. The group showing the increased attraction to the victim had an additional piece of information that could by itself produce the effect —namely, they believed that most of the others in their group also voted to stop the shocks. This apparent sympathy with the victim might lead the subject to think the others found her attractive. This could influence the subject's attitude even in the absence of any vote on her part.

Although several experiments give support to the "like those you have chosen to benefit" hypothesis, the data are not as unambiguous as one would like. Further, some experimenters have failed to detect such an effect. There are several plausible explanations for the fact that deroga-tion-following-harming is more reliably demonstrated than is praising-following-helping. In the case of delivering punishment the dissonance includes a large guilt component if the subject feels responsible for hurting a liked person. This behavior is likely to appear (to the actor) both unexpected and immoral. Since both unexpectedness and guilt can be reduced by believing the victim deserved what he got, derogation is a likely way to dispel the unpleasantness. Although the actor could re-duce the unexpectedness by lowering his expectation about himself (low-ering his self-esteem), this would by itself be unpleasant and would probably not reduce the guilt feelings. Derogation of the victim is much more satisfactory. By contrast, consider the cognitive world of the person who finds himself benefitting a person he dislikes. This act is perhaps unexpected, but is probably not guilt arousing (unless by acting in this way we deprive a more worthy person of benefit). The guilt is low, es-pecially if the person has been taught to "love thine enemy," "do unto others," and so on. Hence the total quantity of discomfort is lower here than in the case of hurting a friend. Further, the discomfort can be neatly reduced by convincing oneself that one is a prince—a big-hearted fel-low who is not above helping even an enemy. This self-flattering resolu-tion does not require any change in attitude toward the recipient of the aid. If this reasoning is sound, it could account for the weakness of the tendency to praise those we help. In the Walster and Prestholdt study the clear tendency to praise the mother (who was benefitted more than she appeared to deserve) may have been motivated partly by guilt, since helping the mother might very well hurt the daughter. That is, this particular situation may have aroused more guilt than is typically the case.

A cathartic reduction in hostility toward the victim of punishment has rarely been observed in experiments in which the subject himself delivers the punishment. The studies of Ross (1965) and Walster and Prestholdt (1966) suggested that subjects who initially intended to hurt, or felt hostile toward, the other person, *but never actually hurt that person,* became less hostile as a result. This phenomenon is difficult to interpret in catharsis terms because no injury was done to the target person. In our earlier discussion of catharsis, we stated that reduced hostility would be expected most clearly when the subject observes his tormenter suffering. Very few experiments have provided this unambiguous feedback to the subject. In the most clear-cut demonstration of a catharsis effect (Bramel, Taub, and Blum, 1968), the subject himself never aggressed against his frustrater. Rather, he simply observed the man suffering. A number of the experiments discussed in this chapter seem to meet the feedback-regarding-suffering requirement for a test of the catharsis hypothesis. Do they qualify in other respects? In general, they do not. The catharsis hypothesis can be expected to hold only if the person delivering the punishment *intends* (has as his goal) to hurt the target person. Only then would we expect tension reduction following feedback that the victim has been hurt. In most of the experiments involving dissonance and guilt arousal, subjects have been pressured by the experimenter into giving shocks or reading notes to people *they initially neither dislike nor wish to hurt.* Thus there is neither hostility to be reduced nor a goal of injury to be reached. In the Walster and Prestholdt (1966) experiment the subjects who found that their negative evaluation of the daughter would be used by the social worker involved in the case probably were much disturbed by this unexpected delivery of punishment, even though they disliked the daughter; that is, they had no intention to hurt her *that* much. In short, the dissonance and guilt aroused in these experiments existed precisely because the subjects *did not* intend the magnitude of punishment they were pressured or tricked into delivering. In order to justify their inappropriate and unethical behavior, they often convinced themselves the victim really deserved the punishment he received. It appears, then, that the conditions that increase the probability of dissonance are the very ones that might decrease the likelihood of catharsis. It might be argued, for example, that the more angry a person is prior to punishing someone, the less is the dissonance but the greater the possibility of catharsis. The more the person believes himself justified in his anger and aggression, the less the dissonance and the more likely that a cathartic reduction in hostility will occur.

Is Liking Affected by Suffering for Something?

Thus far we have examined situations in which a person acts in a way that directly harms or helps another person; and we have focused upon the cognitive changes by which the actor can justify his behavior. There is a related type of situation in which a person finds himself enduring some kind of unpleasantness in order to achieve or maintain membership in a group. Will he justify this "self sacrifice" by convincing himself that membership in this group is very desirable and that the group is attractive enough to warrant the sacrifice? If a group requires its potential new members to undergo some unpleasant experiences before attaining full membership, perhaps one result is that the new members become very committed to a high evaluation of the group, thus contributing to the survival of those groups that employ such initiation procedures (providing they don't scare away all the potential applicants!).

Just as the person who endures some costs in the process of helping another may justify his behavior by believing he likes the recipient, so a person who endures costs in order to become associated with someone may increase his evaluation of the new group. Aronson and Mills (1959) derived this prediction from dissonance theory. Once the initiate has undergone the unpleasantness, anything about the group that appears unattractive is inconsistent with his having sweated it out to become a member. The knowledge that you have (voluntarily) accepted pain implies, for most people, that the reward (membership) will be high. If the group turns out to be (at first sight) less good than expected, dissonance is aroused. One way to reduce it is to convince oneself that the group's excellence compensates for the unpleasantness of the initiation.

Aronson and Mills induced their college-women subjects to volunteer to join a group engaging in a series of discussions of the psychology of sex. The subjects were randomly assigned to three experimental conditions: a severe initiation, a mild initiation, and no initiation. In the severe and mild conditions each subject was told that in order to gain admission to the group, she would be required to demonstrate that she was sophisticated enough to participate freely and frankly in a sexually oriented discussion. An "embarrassment test" was then administered in which the subject read aloud some sexually relevant material in the presence of the male experimenter. He explained that he would judge from her performance whether or not she qualified for admission to the group. In the severe condition the test consisted of reciting a number of obscene words plus some lurid sexual passages from contemporary novels. In the mild condition subjects recited a short list of rather genteel words with sexual connotations. Subjects in the no-initiation condition were allowed to enter the group without any "embarrassment test." Each subject, having been told she would now be admitted to the group, listened in on what she believed to be a live discussion in progress by the group she had just joined. What she heard (on tape) was in fact a rather dull, banal, and irrelevant discussion of the secondary sex behavior of lower animals. The participants spoke haltingly, inarticulately, and unenthusiastically. Immediately after listening to the tape each subject rated the discussion and the group members on evaluative scales.

The results were consistent with prediction. The group was rated more favorably by the severe-initiation subjects than by the others. This finding has been replicated several times in somewhat different contexts (Gerard and Mathewson, 1966; Schopler and Bateson, 1962) and seems to be quite reliable. It is particularly interesting because it seems contrary to a very plausible "common sense" notion. The subjects in the severe-initiation condition presumably came to expect the group discussion to be both intriguing and useful. After all, we usually expect that the harder it is to get something, the more valuable it will be (note the expected correlation between financial cost and value received). If the severe-initiation subjects expected more than did the other subjects, and then everyone received the same objectively uninteresting "reward," why didn't the severe subjects show a big "disappointment" effect? Why didn't they say, "Compared to what I expected, this group is abysmally lousy!"? From the point of view of dissonance theory, this may indeed have been the subjects' *first* reaction; in fact, this is an important component of dissonance—the discomfort produced by events that contrast sharply with expectation. This immediate feeling of disappointment, containing an element of dissonance, could be reduced in several ways. The subject might convince herself that she had had no high expectation—that really the group is no worse than she had expected, which wasn't much. But, given the very embarrassing initiation, it is difficult for subjects to revise their expectation in retrospect. Thus it is more likely that they will distort their perception of the group, convincing themselves that their high expectations were pretty well confirmed. Dissonance is usually reduced by cognitive changes in those elements that are least resistant to change. It was probably easier for Aronson and Mills's subjects to invent various attractive aspects of the group than to deny that they had expected the group to be a good one. The safest interpretation would be that both dissonance reduction techniques occurred in this experiment, but that at least a substantial number of subjects "chose" to distort their thinking about the group's quality.

4

Determinants of Beliefs About Other People

In his influential pioneering work on the formation of attitudes and beliefs concerning other persons, Asch (1946) argued that the observer attempts to integrate the available information into a unified impression of the target person. Consider why this should be so. Because the people around us are so important in facilitating or blocking the achievement of our own goals, it is very useful to be able to predict their behavior. Such prediction, of course, requires that we make a generalization about the person whose behavior we wish to predict. We make the assumption that, in some new situation, he will behave in a manner that is systematically related to the way he behaved in some comparable past situation. If we could not find some consistency in a man's behavior from situation to situation, we could not plan our own strategy in interacting with him. Such a person would be very disturbing to us. In fact, he would not be a "person" at all (see the discussion in Campbell, 1958). Although he might appear physically to be the same as he appeared before, "his" behavior has no unity; there are no traits that can be ascribed to him except "inconsistent." Being unpredictable, he has no "personality" in the usual sense of the term. Fortunately, such a being does not exist. However, it is instructive to attempt to imagine our reaction to it if it did; it would soon be killed or at least locked up for the rest of its life. Even if, miraculously, it committed no crime, the rest of us would be horrified to interact with it.

This point helps to show how important to us it is to be able to predict other people's behavior. In doing so we formulate verbal concepts that help us to code in memory the information we have about those around us. When we are about to interact with, or behave toward, some person, we can refer to the concepts we have formulated about him as a guide to eliciting the desired responses from him. If he is "Machiavellian" we conceal our weaknesses; if "altruistic" we do not. If "intelligent" we ask for advice; if "dangerous" we avoid him. The more success we have in formulating a few general trait names or descriptive phrases that organize a lot of separate bits of information we have about him, the better we will remember and predict.

Although the incentive for forming an impression of a unifying and simplifying sort seems evident, many questions arise as to exactly how observers integrate the discrete bits of information they receive about the target person. Is it possible to formulate some general rules about how observers combine, weight, and draw inferences from the various clues they receive about the personality of another person?

The Order in Which Information Is Received

In a stimulating series of experiments Asch (1946) gave subjects lists of adjectives allegedly describing real persons. The subject's task was to give his impression of the person by writing a sketch or by selecting further adjectives that seemed to fit the person described. Consider the following example, in which the same set of six adjectives describing a single person is read to two groups of subjects (A and B), but in opposite order: *Group A:* intelligent, industrious, impulsive, critical, stubborn, envious; *Group B:* envious, stubborn, critical, impulsive, industrious, intelligent. Series A begins with generally positive qualities, and then ends on a more negative note, whereas the reverse is true for series B. Comparisons of the final impressions formed from many such lists revealed that subjects usually had more favorable impressions from lists where the attractive traits came early rather than late. Clearly the information presented early was somehow having more impact than the information that arrived later. The folk notion of the prime importance of first impressions seemed to be vindicated.

When data indicate that the material presented early has more impact on the final impression than does the material presented later, one calls the pattern a "primacy effect." A "recency effect" is the opposite. The primacy effect shown by Asch has since been found repeatedly in studies that present subjects with a closely spaced sequence of separate verbal descriptions of a "person" and ask them to form an impression at the end of the series (cf. Anderson, 1965b; Anderson and Barrios, 1961; Anderson and Hubert, 1963; Bossart and DiVesta, 1966; Briscoe, Woodyard and Shaw, 1967; Dinnerstein, 1957; Luchins, 1957a, 1958; Stewart, 1965). Although a few experiments of this type have failed to find significant primacy effects, especially with short lists of adjectives (Anderson and Barrios, 1961; Podell and Podell, 1963), significant recency effects are very rare.

There is as yet no unanimously agreed upon explanation for this primacy effect. Asch suggested that the person forms a quick impression on the basis of the early information and then interprets the later material in a manner that fits in with the general quality of the initial impression. Because the meaning of verbal material (especially adjective trait names) is ambiguous, the subjects in these experiments could select the particular interpretation of a later word that fits best with the impression already formed. As G. B. Shaw's Don Juan said of the Devil's friends:

> They are not prosperous: they are only rich. They are not loyal, they are only servile; not dutiful, only sheepish; not public spirited, only patriotic; not courageous, only domineering; not self-controlled, only obtuse; not self-respecting, only vain; not kind, only sentimental; not social, only gregarious; not considerate, only polite; not intelligent, only opinionated; not progressive, only factious; not imaginative, only superstitious; not just, only vindictive; not generous, only propitiatory; not disciplined, only cowed; and not truthful at all: liars every one of them, to the very backbone of their souls . . . beauty, purity, respectability, religion, morality, art, patriotism, bravery, and the rest are nothing but words which I or anyone else can turn inside out like a glove. (*Man and Superman*, 1935, pp. 642–643)

That the meaning of a word can be affected by the context within which it is presented seems hardly to require experimental demonstration. Suffice it to say that there are some experiments presenting evidence entirely consistent with this view (cf. Anderson and Lampel, 1965, and Anderson, 1966).

Granting that words can be turned "inside out like a glove," it remains necessary to explain why people are more likely to do this to the later than to the earlier words in a series; or, more precisely, why the meaning of the later words is adapted to fit the earlier ones rather than the reverse (or rather than a word in any position having an equal chance to modify the meaning of each of the others). Perhaps, once an impression is formed at the beginning of the series, it is less effortful to adapt the new information into the existing pattern than to upset the pattern and strive to build a new one. An impression based upon several adjectives may be so resistant to change that integration is more simply achieved by "distorting" each new isolated element as it arrives.

Other researchers have disputed Asch's theory that the primacy effect is simply due to the tendency for later information to be perceived in a biased way so as to fit into the prior impression. Anderson and his colleagues (Anderson, 1965b; Anderson and Hubert, 1963; Stewart, 1965) prefer the hypothesis that the subject simply pays less attention to the later information in the series. Anderson and Hubert (1963) reasoned that if this were true, primacy effects would disappear among subjects motivated to pay close attention to all of the adjectives in a series. They manipulated attention by telling one group of subjects that a test of recall of the adjectives would be given at the end of each list. Subjects in this condition showed no primacy effect, whereas subjects who were not specially motivated to recall showed the typical primacy pattern. However, not all of the data supported their interpretation. One group of subjects was tested for recall of the adjectives, but without any prior warning that such a test would be given. These subjects, of course, showed the standard primacy effect; but, they recalled the late adjectives much better than the early ones—as strongly, in fact, as the subjects who had been warned about the recall test. If the primacy effect is due to decreasing attention to later information, then it is surprising that subjects showing a primacy effect recall the later information better than the early and middle information.

There are several other reasons that should make one hesitant about rejecting Asch's theory in the face of the Anderson and Hubert data. The recall instructions (given prior to the list of adjectives) might well have interfered with the subjects' ability to form a unified impression. Some might have adopted a strategy of rote recall so as to do well on the test, thus tending to give up on the impression-formation task. If many subjects stopped trying to "make sense" out of the set of adjectives, no early, directing impression (in Asch's sense) would emerge to produce shifts in meaning of the later information. Finally, one wonders why Anderson's proposed decrease in attention occurs (if it does). Perhaps it occurs precisely because it becomes too effortful for the subject to integrate the late information into the dominating impression. That is, following Asch, perhaps the subject either distorts the meaning of the late information or simply tries to ignore it if it appears inconsistent with the impression already formed. One could accept the attention hypothesis and the "directed impression" hypothesis without contradiction; both distortion and ignoring are potentially useful ways to resolve inconsistency between impression and new information.

Another attempt to provide support for the decreasing-attention hypothesis has been made by Stewart (1965). As in most of the studies in this area, subjects were read lists of adjectives purportedly describing a person. When instructed to rate the favorableness of their impression at the *end* of each set, subjects showed the usual primacy effect. However, when told to describe their impression after each successive adjective within a set of four, six, or eight, the ratings at the end of the set showed no primacy effect whatsoever. Following Anderson, Stewart interpreted this to mean that instructions to respond after each adjective induce subjects to give equal attention to the entire list. If the primacy effect were due to decreasing attention, then it indeed follows that this technique should reduce the effect markedly; and it does. Although this experiment seems to present the most convincing evidence to date against Asch's change-in-meaning hypothesis, it is itself not free from ambiguity. The instructions given to subjects in the condition that showed no primacy effect are described by Stewart as follows: ". . . each successive response should be based on all the information accumulated up to that point and, as a consequence, the subject should change his response when this seemed called for." If subjects interpreted this to mean that the experimenter wanted them to change their over-all impression with each successive adjective, then the instructions were virtually a directive *not* to let the first impression dominate interpretation of the later adjectives. Thus Asch might argue that the experiment reveals no more than the fact that subjects told not to show a primacy effect will be able to follow the instructions successfully. It is well known that when subjects are instructed explicitly to beware of clinging to their first impressions, primacy effects tend to disappear (Luchins, 1957b; 1958). This suggests that people are less biased by the early information in situations where they expect that contradictory information is likely to follow later on (as, for example, in political campaigns, debates, and trials in courts of law).

Unfortunately for the Asch hypothesis, there are yet other experiments that seem (at least superficially) to present counterevidence. Luchins (1957a and b; 1958) did a series of experiments in which subjects were presented with two paragraphs describing a boy named Jim. One paragraph presented him as an introverted person (I), whereas the other, taken by itself, made Jim appear extraverted (E). To test for order effects it is necessary to give the two paragraphs in the EI sequence to some subjects and in the IE sequence to others. One can then compare final impressions from the two sets of subjects. If Jim appears more extraverted to EI subjects, and more introverted to IE subjects, a primacy effect is revealed. When the two paragraphs were presented without a temporal break, Luchins found primacy effects regularly. However, he found that primacy could be significantly reduced by increasing the temporal interval between the two paragraphs and by giving the subjects irrelevant tasks to do in the interval. In the face of this evidence Asch could readily reply that the time and tasks allowed the initial impression to be forgotten, so that it was no longer strong enough to affect interpretation of the new information.

However, one of Luchins' experiments poses more difficulty. In this one (1958) the temporal break between paragraphs was filled by a questionnaire asking subjects their impressions of Jim on the basis of the first paragraph of information. This took around fifteen minutes to complete. Then the second paragraph was presented and followed by a new copy of the same questionnaire. The results showed a tremendously strong recency effect. In fact, *IE* subjects ended up describing Jim as more extraverted than did control subjects who read only the *E* paragraph! Clearly, subjects were not interpreting the second paragraph so as to fit it in with the first. On the contrary, it seems more accurate to suggest that the *E* paragraph appeared even more *E*-like when it followed the *I* paragraph than when it was alone! Why did his subjects show such a striking recency effect? Interviews with the subjects afterward revealed that the filling out of the intervening impression questionnaire had made it very difficult for them to perceive the two paragraphs as describing the same person. In effect, it is as if many of them gave up on the task of forming a unified impression of a single personality. Why would the intervening questionnaire have this effect? Perhaps the fifteen minutes of focused thought produced such a clear-cut impression of Jim that the difference of content in the second paragraph was especially noticeable. This could plausibly lead subjects to the hypothesis that the second paragraph didn't really describe the same person. Hence, when asked to describe their impression of the "person you've just read about," they described the man in the second paragraph. An experiment by Briscoe, Woodyard, and Shaw (1967) used similar kinds of material and also found a final recency effect when subjects had to rate the person first, in between the two paragraphs.

It should be evident that the Luchins and the Briscoe, Woodyard, and Shaw experiments definitely require some modification or elaboration of the Asch hypothesis. One might say that the inconsistency between early and late information can be reduced by believing the later information is really consistent (Asch), by ignoring the later information (Anderson, et al.), or by believing that the later information describes someone else (Luchins). This last reaction may be most likely to occur when conditions make the contrast particularly salient—as when the initial impression is strong and subjectively certain and is then confronted with material of very different meaning (as established in a control group).

Finally, there are two more experiments that pose new problems for the Asch or consistency-maintenance theories. The results in the two experiments are similar, so it will suffice to describe one of them (Walster, Walster, et al., 1966); the other (Walster and Prestholdt, 1966) has been discussed in an earlier chapter. In these experiments a target person is first described by one observer and then by another. The subject reads or hears both views of the person and then gives his impression of him. The two sources of information are not equally authoritative, however. One observer is nonexpert; the other appears to be highly authoritative concerning the target person. Regardless of the order of presentation, the authoritative observer always explicitly contradicts the nonexpert by showing that the nonexpert had badly misinterpreted the motives directing the target person's ambiguous behavior. Thus the subject hears a very authoritative source in first or second position contradict the impression presented by a nonexpert observer. The results are very interesting; they show strong recency effects. That is, the information in the second position has more impact than that in the first position. One would not be very surprised by data showing neither primacy nor recency in this situation. One could argue that subjects would tend to disregard the nonexpert observer and base their impression solely upon the information supplied by the authoritative one. But the obtained recency effect is more difficult to explain. When the authoritative person comes first, one would expect subjects to disregard the following nonexpert information. When the nonexpert comes first, subjects would tend to accept it (not knowing an expert is to follow); would this not lead them to discredit the expert slightly so as to maintain at least part of their initial impression? This would produce a primacy effect, and it obviously is not what happened in this experiment. Perceptual contrast may afford an explanation. When the authoritative information comes first, the subject accepts it and ignores the later information. When the authoritative information comes second, it appears in stark contrast to an already formed impression (cf. Luchins, 1958, discussed above) and hence has even more impact than if it had appeared first. The over-all result would be a recency effect.

Walster and her associates prefer a different explanation, which is also plausible. They suggest that the subjects who are exposed to the authoritative contradiction in the second position feel guilty or indignant about their earlier mistaken impression and attempt to make up for their error by reversing to the other extreme of the attitude dimension. Thus, if you feel guilty about having judged the target person initially too harshly, you can symbolically make up for the injustice by thinking more highly of him than you would have done in the *absence* of the initial bad impression. It should be mentioned, parenthetically, that Walster and Prestholdt (1966) found that such overcompensation reactions did not occur when subjects believed their initial impression had actually helped or harmed the target person. Under those circumstances, argue the authors, guilt or indignation is more effectively reduced by believing that your initial impression had been justified.

We have seen that primacy effects are most reliable in situations that allow the subjects to maintain the belief that each piece of information is a reasonably accurate description of the *same person*. When the information is presented so that items vary strikingly in authoritativeness, or so that there are interruptions or warnings about the arrival of contradicting information, less primacy is found. Anything that encourages the subject to think that more than one person is being described decreases the probability that he will attempt to mold later information into a fit with the developing impression. If this is true, then experiments that explicitly present subjects with descriptions or behavior samples of *different* persons might show that, for example, the impression of the second person presented is displaced away from the impression of the first (contrast effect). Thus, if two men differ in their apparent joviality when seen temporally separated, they should appear even more different when seen together. Holmes and Berkowitz (1961) report an experiment of this kind. Subjects first listened to a tape-recorded interview dominated by a male "psychologist in the college administration." For half of the subjects his role was nonsupportive and belligerent; for the others, he sounded more friendly. Next, subjects heard a shorter tape, either of a male student or a second male psychologist speaking in a rather neutral manner. Their task was to describe the person on this second tape. The results generally revealed a contrast effect in ratings of this person. That is, he was rated more favorably when following the belligerent first tape than when following the friendly tape. Levy (1960) found a similar effect when asking subjects to rate persons whose photographs were shown in sets of three. On the basis of preratings made of the photographs individually, Levy assembled them so that two photos in each set were homogeneous in pre-rating and differed in varying manipulated amounts from the third photo. The more extreme the difference between the pair and the third, the more extreme the rating of the third; that is, relative to its rating in isolation, its rating in context was displaced away from that of the pair.

Contrast effects of this sort have been found also in experiments that present subjects with opinion statements and ask them to judge the characteristics of the speaker. Consistent with some earlier quasiexperimental work of Manis (1960; 1961), Berkowitz and Goranson (1964) induced subjects to dislike a person (A) who then expressed an opinion at a later time that disagreed strongly with each subject's own opinion. These subjects rated A's basic position as even more extremely disagreeing than it "actually" was. Subjects induced to like the source of the opinion did not show this contrast effect. A plausible explanation is that it is painful to disagree with someone you like, so disagreement tends to be minimized. Disagreement with someone you dislike is not necessarily unpleasant and may even be satisfying. Manis (1961) has suggested that one way to discredit a disliked or low-prestige communicator is to attribute an absurdly extreme position to him. Once you have converted your ideological opponent into a straw man, he presents no problem to the stability of your own beliefs and attitudes. Consistent with this, Jones and Kohler (1958) showed that subjects were very good at learning the "obviously specious" arguments used by their ideological opponents, but not so good at learning their opponents' more persuasive arguments. Of course, attributing "straw man" attitudes to an opponent is not the only way to discredit him. Attribution of incompetence and evil intentions may occur as well, as shown, for example, by Pilisuk (1962), and by Feather and Jeffries (1967).

Other Determinants of How Separate Pieces of Information Are Integrated

There are of course other factors than the order of presentation of information that affect the character of the final impression one has of another person. The meaning of a bit of information affects the direction of the final impression to a certain extent independent of the order of presentation. Asch (1946) showed, for example, that the words *warm* and *cold*, when included individually in otherwise identical lists of adjectives, produced markedly different impressions. Mensh and Wishner (1947) and Wishner (1960) replicated this finding in similarly designed experiments. In a more realistic setting, Kelley (1950) told students in a classroom that a new instructor was about to come in to conduct a discussion and that the academic department wanted to know how the class reacted to him. Brief typed sketches were distributed to the subjects. Half of these described the new man as "rather warm," while half said he was "rather cold"; in both sketches he was also called industrious, critical, practical, and determined. The information was said to have been contributed by "people who know him." After the discussion period led by the new instructor, all subjects filled out an anonymous questionnaire concerning him. Those who had read the "warm" preinformation gave the man generally more favorable ratings than did the "cold" group, in agreement with Asch's findings. Kelley asked the subjects to rate the man's "personality" rather than concrete aspects of his classroom behavior. Hence it is not possible to conclude with certainty that impressions of his *classroom behavior* were actually influenced by the initial information.

Asch found that inserting one or the other of certain polar opposite traits (such as warm and cold) had much more impact upon check-list descriptions of the person described than did other polar traits (such as polite and blunt). He concluded that some traits are more "central" in organizing an impression than are others. Wishner (1960) attempted to operationalize Asch's rather vague concept of centrality of a trait. He hypothesized that a trait may play a central organizing role if the experimental subjects believe that someone possessing that trait is likely also to possess traits A, B, C, and so on. The more strong implications a trait name has in the cognitive worlds of the subjects, the more likely that its inclusion in a list will have an impact upon the final impression formed.

The more clear implications, or meaning, a trait name has by itself, the more difference it makes whether the list includes it or its opposite. Wishner found, in support of this reasoning, that the more clear implications a trait has in isolation, the more its inclusion in a list affects the nature of the final impression.

Several experiments have shown that subjects have difficulty in integrating lists that contain terms that imply the opposite of each other for the person who hears them. Haire and Grunes (1950) gave one group of college student subjects a list of seven words and phrases describing a man who "works in a factory." A second group read the same list except that the word "intelligent" was added near the end. The sketches subsequently written by the first group were fairly unanimous in characterizing the factory worker as an unintelligent "typical American Joe." It was apparent that "factory worker" was highly associated with "unintelligent" in the cognitive worlds of most of these subjects. It is to be expected, then, that the introduction of "intelligent" in the second list would produce some cognitive dissonance. In fact, these subjects did show evidence of trying to resolve an inconsistency. Some "promoted" the worker to foreman, whereas others denied that he was intelligent. In a similar experiment Pepitone and Hayden (1955) told subjects that a certain man was a member of each of a set of six voluntary social organizations. Five of these were manifestly conservative upper socioeconomic groups, such as the National Association of Manufacturers. The sixth group was the Communist Party for one group of subjects and the Socialist Party for the others. Content analysis of the sketches written to describe the man indicated that subjects had more difficulty integrating the Communist Party than the Socialist Party into their impressions, presumably because the contrasting implications were more extreme in the list containing the Communist Party.

Bruner and Perlmutter (1957) attempted to make predictions about the impact of a trait name or social category name in the process of forming an impression of someone. They were interested in the dimension of "category differentiation." They reasoned that the more familiar one is with members of a certain category (for example, nationality or occupational group), the less certain one is that any given member will possess any specific characteristic—that is, the more contact you have had, the more differentiated the category appears and the less they "all look alike." This hypothesis is probably not true in regard to the effects of the increase from zero to "some" information, since with zero information the observer is likely to be quite uncertain about group characteristics. However, it seems plausible as a description of the relation between amount of information and equivocality of category implication as amount of information increases above some medium level. The hypothesis is then that, within limits, the more contact you have had with members of a certain category, the less likely you are to be confident about drawing inferences solely from this category membership.

Bruner and Perlmutter tested the proposition by presenting brief written descriptions of persons to three different nationality groups of subjects —American, French, and German. After choosing adjectives describing their impressions of each person, subjects were asked to indicate what aspect of the initial information had determined each aspect of the resulting impression. The results, consistent with the hypothesis, revealed clearly that the nationality of a stimulus person carried much more weight if he was a foreigner than if he was a compatriot of the subject. For example, American subjects seemed to rely more heavily on the knowledge that the described person was French or German than on the knowledge that he was an American, even though in all other respects the information presented to the subjects was identical. The experimenters also found that college students put less weight on knowing the person to be a university professor than on knowing him to be a businessman. It would be interesting to see this experiment replicated so that the amount of experience subjects have with a given social category is manipulated within the experiment itself.

That the impact of trait implications is not restricted to the use of verbal stimulus material is shown by the results of an experiment by Stritch and Secord (1955). They found that artist-produced alterations in specific parts of photographs of human faces markedly changed subjects' judgments of other, unaltered, parts of the faces. For example, photo *1A* differs from *1B* only in that the hair is neater in *1A*; subjects who see *1A* rate the man's skin to be more smooth than do subjects who see *1B*.

Predicting Global Evaluation from a Knowledge of Evaluation of the Separate Elements

What is the relation between the evaluation of the whole and the evaluations of each of the components separately and in isolation? Can we predict the perceived beauty of a face from a knowledge of the beauty of each of the parts viewed independently? Obviously there are problems with this, not the least of which being that the spatial and temporal arrangements of the parts are very important and are not derivable from observing the parts in isolation. A face may be composed of admirable eyes, nose, and mouth, but if they are arranged as a cubist painter might do it, the result can be bizarre. The importance of order of presentation in impression formation has already been discussed; it is clear that the final impression cannot be completely predicted merely from a knowledge of the independent evaluations of each adjective in isolation.

Nevertheless, it would be interesting to discover a combination rule that would yield a good approximation to the value of the final global impression. A number of psychologists have attempted to derive such a rule. Two formulations have received enough experimental attention to merit discussion here. One, proposed by Anderson (1962), claims that the final impression of a series of adjectives describing a person can be well predicted from a calculation of the *average* evaluations the subject has of each of the adjectives in the set measured separately. According to one version of this averaging theory (Anderson, 1965a), one can assume that the subject has an impression of the target person after the nth adjective has been presented; the effect of adjective $n + 1$ is to move the impression in its direction—that is, some kind of compromise is made, such that the impression after adjective $n + 1$ is closer to the value of that adjective than it was prior to its occurrence (unless the value of adjective $n + 1$ is exactly equal to the value of the impression existing after presentation of adjective n). The competing theory, proposed by Triandis and Fishbein (1963), claims that the effect of adjective $n + 1$ depends upon whether it, by itself, tends to elicit a positive, negative, or neutral evaluative response. If its value is on the same side of neutral as is the impression existing after adjective n, adjective $n + 1$ increases the polarization of the impression; if on the opposite side of neutral, the polarization of the impression is decreased and may even be reversed. Their theory predicts, then, that a positive adjective will make the impression more positive, a negative will make it more negative, and a neutral adjective will leave the impression unaffected. The effect of each new piece of information is usually to add or subtract from the polarization of the existing impression; hence this is called a *summation* theory.

Both averaging (Anderson) and summation (Triandis and Fishbein) theories agree that a negative adjective makes a positive impression less positive, and that a positive adjective makes a negative impression less negative (although they would disagree as to the amounts of change produced). Disagreement is clearest in regard to predicting the effect of an adjective that is on the same side of neutral as the existing impression at the moment of the new arrival. According to Triandis and Fishbein, the effect is to polarize the impression even more (away from the neutral point), regardless of whether the new adjective is itself more or less polarized than the existing impression. According to Anderson, the impression will become more polarized if the new adjective is itself more polarized, but *less polarized* if the new adjective is itself less polarized than the existing impression.

Fishbein and Hunter (1964) presented subjects with varying-length lists of adjectives describing a certain "Mr. A." All of the adjectives had been independently rated by other subjects from a comparable sample as being on the positive side of the evaluative scale. The list presented to each subject contained either one, two, four, or eight adjectives. Each successive adjective had been independently rated as less positive than any preceding adjective in the list. The subject's impression of Mr. A on an evaluative scale was measured at the end of the list. It is clear that the summation theory must predict that the longer the list, the more positive the over-all impression produced (because all adjectives were positive). The data showed a significant trend in the predicted direction, although the two-adjective list did not produce a more positive impression than the one-adjective presentation.

Fishbein and Hunter argued that an averaging theory would predict that the impression would become *less* positive as successively less positive (but still above neutral) adjectives were added to the list. At first sight this interpretation of averaging theory seems justified. However, Anderson's version of the theory requires that one further specification be met. It is necessary to show that the momentary impression existing after adjective n in the Fishbein and Hunter experiment was actually higher (more positive) than the independently rated value of adjective $n + 1$ in isolation. If so, then Anderson's theory would be invalidated by the obtained *increase* in the positiveness of the impression. But if the momentary impression happened to be lower than the independently scaled value of adjective $n + 1$, Anderson's theory would agree with that of Fishbein and Hunter in predicting that this adjective would increase the positiveness of the impression. What is needed, then, is to present a list of, say, three adjectives to one group; to a second group present the same list of three, but with a fourth, less polarized adjective added to the end. The three-adjective group provides the measure of the momentary impression existing at the end of the three adjectives. Suppose that the impression created by the three is higher than the separately measured value of the fourth. If the fourth results in a more positive impression, then the averaging theory would have great difficulty in accounting for the results. Note that a crucial test requires that the relation between the momentary value of the existing impression and the independently established value of the next adjective must be known before the averaging theory can make a clear prediction.

Anderson (1965b) has presented some data that, although not predicted unequivocally by his own theory, are certainly damaging to the summation theory. Independently rated adjectives were combined in lists of two and four. All adjectives in any one list were on the same side of the neutral point. It was found that two highly polarized (positive or negative) adjectives produced a more polarized impression than did a set containing the same two along with two less polarized adjectives. Similar results are reported in three experiments by Hendrick (1967). A simple summation theory would seem to predict the opposite. However, other researchers have frequently found results contrary to Anderson's and Hendrick's—namely, that as one adds further adjectives on the same side of neutral as the preceding ones, the impression becomes more polarized. These studies (L. R. Anderson and Fishbein, 1965; Fishbein and Hunter, 1964; Podell and Amster, 1966) are of course consistent with the summation theory but do not invalidate N. H. Anderson's averaging formulation because they do not demonstrate that the momentary impression is actually higher than the independently scaled value of the next adjective. One must conclude that the empirical resolution of this debate has not yet been reported.

Several other experiments, using different kinds of serially presented information about the target person or group, are relevant to the current discussion. Willis (1960) asked one sample of subjects to rate the attractiveness, individually, of photographed students in a yearbook. Other subjects were then shown sets of two or three such photographs selected systematically on the basis of the judges' earlier ratings of them. The final ratings of "attractiveness" of the set were compared with the mean scale value of the individually prejudged photographs in the set. The global judgments were more polarized than the mean prejudged values. Sets of three were evaluated more extremely than sets of two. The more homogeneous the set members in prejudged value, the more the set judgment exceed the mean in polarization. This result, although consistent with summation theory, is not necessarily inconsistent with an averaging theory if one assumes a less polarized "initial impression" existing prior to viewing the photographs.

Similar results are reported by Weiss (1963). Subjects were asked to read attitude and opinion statements allegedly made by a target person. On the basis of preratings of the statements taken individually, sets of three were assembled with varying degrees of internal homogeneity of viewpoint expressed toward capital punishment. The task was to judge the global attitude of the target person toward capital punishment. Homogeneous sets produced ratings that exceeded the mean polarization of the items taken individually. In fact, the global rating usually exceeded in polarization even the most polarized item in the set (also found by Manis, Gleason, and Dawes, 1966). Such a finding provides some difficulties for an averaging theory.

There is some evidence that the more polarized pieces of information in a relatively homogeneous set of adjectives or opinion statements carry more weight in influencing the final impression than do the less polarized elements. Weiss's (1963) data are consistent with this, and more direct evidence in support of this is reported by Podell and Podell (1963) and Manis, Gleason, and Dawes (1966). The latter experiment is an especially well-designed investigation that succeeds in avoiding some of the measurement problems in this research area (especially the untested assumption that rating scales have psychologically equal intervals along their entire extent). Using explicitly ordinal data, these researchers showed that the more extreme attitude statements in sets of two or three had most impact upon the final ratings, but that this was true only in sets of relatively homogeneous (consistent) statements.

Finally, an interesting application of averaging and summation predictions has been made by Hastorf, Osgood, and Ono (1966). Subjects were asked to view photographs in a stereoscope (which allows presentation of a different picture to each eye simultaneously). The photographs represented various different emotional expressions posed by an actor. In the initial series two identical pictures were simultaneously viewed and rated with adjectives by the subjects. Then varying combinations (for example, "rage" and "glee") were viewed and rated. Most subjects reported that the pair appeared fused into a single face. Ratings made of the emotional state of the fused image turned out to be a compromise between the independently prerated values of the pictures, supporting an averaging as opposed to a summation prediction.

Although present evidence does not allow a clear-cut evaluation of the relative merits of summation and averaging theories, it is apparent that both require refinement in order to fit all of the relevant data. An aspect that has received relatively little attention is the relation between the separate pieces of information about the target person. A given trait name or opinion statement has implications about the other traits or statements in the list. It seems likely that a piece of information that is almost identical in meaning to some other element in the list will have less impact than a less redundant item would have.

Inferring Motives, Abilities, Beliefs, and Habits from a Person's Overt Behavior

Having observed a man's acts, most people seem willing to make some statements about the man's past experiences, motives, abilities, and enduring patterns of thinking and behaving. How are such inferences arrived at? In the language of Jones and Davis (1965), how does the observer infer dispositions from perceived acts? Although we must restrict ourselves here to a rather small number of relevant experiments, an interesting discussion of many additional hypotheses can be found in Heider's book *The Psychology of Interpersonal Relations* (1958).

The attribution of characteristics to other people is often affected by perception of the circumstances surrounding their acts. Consider, for example, how an observer decides whether a speaker or a writer really believes what he is saying. It is well known that a man's actual beliefs and attitudes about a particular topic are only one set of the potential determinants of his verbal behavior. People sometimes lie or reveal only part of what they believe the truth to be. Several experiments have shown that observers are more confident in predicting the true beliefs of a speaker when he appears to have little to gain by lying.

In addition to replicating the Steiner and Field (1960) finding that an assigned speech is less revealing about a speaker's true attitudes than is a freely chosen position, Jones and Harris (1967) carried the reasoning a step further. They suggested that the apparent presence or absence of choice on the speaker's part will be taken into account most when the position advocated is unpopular (rarely encountered). A speaker defending the widely accepted point of view will be perceived to believe what he is saying regardless of whether he volunteered to defend it or was assigned the job in a debate setting. The observer makes the reasonable assumption that if nearly everyone believes in the position advocated, the speaker probably does also. When an unpopular point of view is presented, however, the observer will assume that only the man who volunteers really accepts the position advocated. Subjects who read a speech praising or maligning Fidel Castro of Cuba showed the predicted pattern of estimates of the speaker's true point of view.

Jones, Davis, and Gergen (1961) had subjects listen to a tape-recorded job interview. They were instructed that the interviewer had been told in advance to convince the interviewer that he (the applicant) was well suited for the job of being either an astronaut or a submariner. The interviewee also appeared to know what personality characteristics would be looked for in an applicant—"inner directedness" for astronauts and "other directedness" for submariners. Each subject heard an interviewee applying for one job or the other. Half of the subjects heard the applicant answer questions in a distinctly "inner-directed" way, and half in an "other-directed" way. Thus, for half of the subjects, the interviewee behaved as he had been instructed to—that is, to appear well suited to the job; the remaining subjects heard him responding in a way contrary to the intent of the instructions. The interviewee who answered in a manner inappropriate to his assigned role was judged to be more "candid" and to be revealing his true feelings. The subjects generally reported that they had a clearer idea of this interviewee's real personality. Apparently a person who says something contrary to the demands of his role and who appears to be sacrificing certain salient rewards in the situation (here, the approval of those who instructed the interviewee to "get the job") may appear to be more honest.

One might make the further prediction that such a person will be perceived to hold his beliefs more strongly or to be more opposed to lying. If this is so, then he might be more persuasive. Clear support for this prediction comes from the experiment by Walster, Aronson, and Abrahams (1966). A person advocating a position apparently harmful to his own immediate welfare was not only rated more honest but was also significantly more persuasive than when the speaker stood to gain personally from the widespread acceptance of his stated position. Similar results are reported by Mills and Jellison (1967). They found that a speaker was rated less sincere and more cynical and opportunistic when a standard speech was presented to an audience expected to approve it than to an audience the speaker expected would *not* approve of the position advocated. Again, the more an observer believes the speaker could be motivated to lie (in order to gain some reward or escape some punishment), the less he is inclined to attribute sincerity to the speaker and to be persuaded by what he hears.

Jones, Jones, and Gergen (1963) found, similarly, that if B agrees with A's prior statement on an issue, less sincerity is attributed to B by an observer the more B is perceived to desire A to like him. B is also liked less by the observer when he agrees under these circumstances. A series of related experiments making the same general point has been reported by Bem (1965; 1967). His subjects are typically told to think about some specific person who agrees to say or write a statement advocating a particular point of view. The more money the observed person is offered for assenting to make the requested statement, the less he is perceived to agree with the statement. In view of the consistency of all of these experiments, one is tempted to extrapolate as follows: People who risk punishment by stating a position (either verbally or by other means) will be perceived to be more sincere and will therefore be more effective in gaining acceptance of what they assert. Of course sincerity is not sufficient grounds for believing what a man says. To the extent that the advocate risks extreme punishment, he may be perceived as sincere but insane; out of touch with "reality," his persuasiveness is slight.

Inferences about a man's motives have been studied in other situations as well. Imagine a person, A, who appears to be influential and of high status; if he is observed to grant the explicit request of a lower-status person, the observer is not likely to conclude that A felt coerced into compliance. Rather, it is more plausible to believe that he had some motive other than fear. Thibaut and Riecken (1955) performed two experiments in which observers rated a complying person who appeared to be of either high or low status relative to the person making the request. Observers tended to attribute benevolence more to the high- than the low-status complier. Comparable results are reported by Heider (1967) in an experiment in which A is portrayed as either more or less powerful (status, money, strength, and so on) than B. Whether A was perceived to benefit or harm B affected observers' attribution of good or bad personal qualities to A most when A exceeded B in power. The actions of the powerful person, then, are perceived as reflecting his enduring traits rather than the result of coercion emanating from other persons or the nonpersonal environment.

Strickland (1958) developed a related hypothesis. Imagine two men, A and B, working under a supervisor, and suppose that it is convenient for the supervisor to "drop in" and check the progress of A (and he does so), but not of B. Assume that A and B turn in equally good work at the end of the day. Which worker will the supervisor perceive as being trustworthy and capable of working independently? Strickland's experiment showed that the answer is worker B, who had not been under periodic surveillance. Plausibly, the supervisor may assume that A's output was determined by the fear that the supervisor would "drop in" again. If so, A could not necessarily be trusted to work so well on his own. During the latter half of this experiment, it was made equally convenient for the supervisor to monitor either A or B. He typically checked up on A more than B.

DeCharms, Carpenter, and Kuperman (1965) explored a further determinant of attribution of motives to an actor. They reasoned that a person, A, who complies with the request of B, whom A likes and respects, will be perceived as feeling more free than when A dislikes B and complies. Subjects read short vignettes describing some person who is persuaded by a liked or disliked agent. For example, an Army private agrees to stand extra guard duty at the request of his commanding officer, who offers an incentive of a few added days on leave. The private who is described as liking the officer was perceived by most subjects as feeling more free and uncompelled than the private who dislikes the officer. Possibly subjects assume that some implicit threat of punishment is present when A dislikes B, whereas A may be perceived as simply wanting to please a liked B. It is interesting that even though incentives for compliance can be readily imagined in both situations, the person potentially seen as wanting to please is considered more free than the one who possibly wants to avoid threatened punishment. If this correctly describes the reasoning of the subjects, it suggests a curious asymmetry in the average person's thinking about freedom, coercion, and determinism. Further research might fruitfully explore this possibility—that a sense of subjective freedom is attributed more to people seeking positive incentives than to those seeking to avoid punishment.

How Information About Oneself Affects Beliefs About Other People

Projection

When a person receives information about his own personality, thoughts, feelings, or behavior, significant changes in his beliefs about other people sometimes occur as a result. If the information implies that he has more of the characteristic than he had previously believed, the effect could be either to increase or decrease the amount of this characteristic he believes other people to possess. If a perceived increase in his own possession leads to an *increase* in the amount he attributes to others, we say that he is projecting the characteristic. If it leads to a decrease in the amount he attributes to others, we do not have a commonly accepted name for what has happened. Researchers have been more interested in projection than its reverse.

The concept of projection actually covers several different processes. The one that has received the most attention from theorists and experimenters is what might be called "defensive projection." The hypothesis is that people often successfully reduce subjective unpleasantness by thinking that other people possess the very thing that disturbs them. If *A* feels ashamed or guilty because of information that he possesses too much of an undesirable characteristic, *X*, he may find it comforting to attribute large amounts of *X* to other people.

This projection might help to reduce his unpleasant emotional state in a number of alternative ways. Let us speculate about a few of these, most of which were suggested in scattered places in the writings of Sigmund Freud (cf. Freud, 1924; Fenichel, 1945). Perhaps, by focusing his attention upon the faults (real or imagined) of other people, the anxious Mr. *A* successfully avoids thinking about his own faults. Perhaps Mr. *A* can help himself deny possession of *X* by showing his moral indignation at the supposed presence of *X* in Mr. *B*. Thus, for example, a person trying to hide (even from himself) his desire to read pornographic literature might actively campaign to "clean up the magazine stands!" Better yet, he could volunteer his own personal services to read the questionable material and help decide which were acceptable for the public and which not. In this way, he not only affirms his own purity but also provides a morally acceptable way to enjoy the very activity he condemns. More generally, the person who projects his own unacceptable characteristics onto other people may thereby allow himself to participate in the illicit behavior vicariously without taking the blame. Is it possible for example, that the person obsessed with fears of being sexually attacked may be able in this way to engage in fantasies that might otherwise arouse guilt feelings?

Another way in which attribution of X to others may be comforting is that it may facilitate the reevaluation of the trait by the person who projects it. Thus, if Mr. A can believe that many people possess X, then X ceases to appear deviant. To the extent that a person's moral standards are tempered by observation of the behavior of others and a conception of what is humanly possible, the more common (the less deviant) a given trait, the less moral opprobrium attaches to it. Alternatively, even if projection of the trait onto other people does not make it appear any the less odious in its extreme forms, the projector may at least gain comfort in thinking that he is no worse than average on this particular dimension.

These speculations, although increasing our confidence that such anxiety-reducing processes exist, are of course no substitute for solid experimental data. These data, which are surveyed below, indicate clearly that in some circumstances the probability that person A will attribute X to person B can be increased by telling A that he himself possesses X. The major problem in interpreting some of these experiments is that projection can plausibly be explained without assuming the presence of any unpleasant emotional states—whether they be called anxiety, shame, guilt, or dissonance. Consider the following hypothetical example: A psychologist gives a rather mysterious paper-and-pencil test to a group of college students. When they have finished the test booklet, he tells them that the test measures a personality dimension known as "impedance," and that this dimension is unrelated to intelligence. The booklets are then "scored," and each subject is given privately one of two scores, randomly allocated. Half of the subjects find that they have scored 30, and half 70, on a 100-point scale. Each person is then asked to predict the score of the student sitting next to him—a person he does not know. What are the mean attributions likely to be? It seems plausible to expect that those with a score of 70 will predict numerically higher scores than will those whose scores appear to be 30. This, clearly, would demonstrate projection, since the more the subject appears to possess the trait, the more of it he attributes to other persons. Was anxiety aroused by the score and reduced by the projection? It seems unlikely that much anxiety was aroused by receiving a score on a meaningless dimension—especially when the subject has no idea whether it is preferable to be high or low in "impedance." What seems more likely is that the subject is simply doing the best he can to solve the problem the experimenter has given him. In the first place, he may not care what the other person's score is; but if asked, he is willing to hazard a guess. How ought he to estimate the other's score? Practically the only relevant information available is his own score (especially if the test booklet gave little clue to the nature of "impedance"). The most rational guess of the average person would be that another person picked at random would have the same score that he has. In the absence of information, the best prediction is the average score; because the average person would assume his score is near the middle of the distribution, he predicts that others tend to concentrate in that part of the scale as well. One might plausibly make the additional prediction that subjects who are induced to believe the target person is similar to them in *other* respects will assume him similar on "impedance" as well. Stotland, Zander, and Natsoulas (1961) present data consistent with this hypothesis.

This example serves to make the point that projection can very plausibly occur in the absence of any significant amount of anxiety associated with the characteristic in question. This is especially cogent in situations in which subjects are *instructed* to rate other people—that is, where the experimenter provides an incentive for problem solving. Without such an incentive, subjects might not even think about whether or not others possess the trait. This suggests that one indicator of the presence of defensive motives may be the tendency of the person to attribute the trait to others "spontaneously," even without being asked for an opinion. Unfortunately, no well-controlled experiments using this indicator have been reported. Without some kind of indicator of anxiety or defensiveness, it is difficult to decide whether the projection shown in certain experiments is of the defensive variety. In discussing the research it will not always be possible to come to a conclusion on this issue.

Murstein (1956) gave Rorschach tests to college students who had previously rated themselves as to their general friendliness–hostility. Half of the subjects were told that the Rorschach revealed them to be very hostile, while half were told that it indicated very little hostility. The examiner, who had given the evaluations in a neutral and professional manner, was then rated by the subject on an allegedly anonymous questionnaire. Only one category of subjects showed an unusual tendency to attribute hostility to the examiner. These were the ones who initially rated themselves as friendly and were then told they were basically hostile. If one reasons that these are precisely the subjects one would expect to be most disturbed by the Rorschach interpretation, then it is plausible to argue that the attribution of hostility represents defensive projection in the experiment. An alternative interpretation of the data is also plausible. Perhaps this group of subjects were angered by the threat to their self-esteem and tried to discredit the examiner. One way to reduce the sting of being called hostile is to believe that the examiner "had it in for me." As a control, one would like to know whether a group of subjects who were told, for example, that they were cowardly, would attribute cowardice to the examiner. Or would they, too, attribute hostility? If the latter, then the choice of trait to attribute is not determined by the particular content of the disturbing information presented to the subject. Such an effect would not fall under the present definition of defensive projection, since there is no intrinsic identity between the threatening trait and the trait attributed to the experimenter by the subject.

Several experiments have suggested that when placed in an anxiety-arousing situation, people increase the amount of anxiety attributed to others, even though the others are not in the same situation. Feshbach and Singer (1957) delivered painful shocks to the ankles of one group of subjects and no shock to control subjects while all were watching a short film of a same-sex person doing manual-skill tests. Shocked subjects rated the filmed person as more fearful (especially "in general" rather than "in this situation") than did controls. Since the groups did not differ in the attribution of other evaluative traits to the actor, the results are not explainable as due to displacement of aggression. This experiment presents no evidence allowing one to decide whether self-defensive motives were involved. Feshbach and Feshbach (1964) found, similarly, that frightened boys attributed fear to photographs of other people. These results were strongest when the subjects were rating pictures of boys. Negative results on this point are reported by Hornberger (1960), who found no difference between frightened and control subjects in the tendency to attribute fear to still photographs of strangers.

Theoretically, there are several methods by which one might determine whether projection can be motivated by self-defensive needs. An obvious possibility is to present subjects with information that they possess traits that are differentially anxiety arousing, but that are under control conditions equally likely to be attributed to some other person or persons. If subjects who are told they possess the trait project the disturbing more than the nondisturbing one, the defensive hypothesis remains tenable. No convincing experiments employing such a design have been reported up to this time.

A second method for detecting the role of anxiety is to present two groups of subjects with the *same* information, but having prepared the subjects differentially in advance so that one group is more threatened by the trait than is the other. An experiment by Bramel (1962) used this kind of design. It was predicted that subjects whose global self-esteem had been experimentally raised would be more disturbed by a subsequently revealed undesirable trait than would subjects whose self-esteem had been lowered. Specifically, the reasoning was that a person who has learned he is a wonderful specimen will be more shocked to discover he has latent homosexual tendencies than will a person who has previously been told that he is riddled with inadequacies of various other kinds. This prediction seems to follow from Festinger's (1957) theory of cognitive dissonance. If the high–self-esteem subjects are more disturbed by the information about homosexuality, then a defensive projection process would lead them to attribute more homosexuality to other persons. There is another potential outcome of this experiment, however, which could also be interpreted to be consistent with the defensive projection hypothesis. Suppose that the low–self-esteem subjects are so upset by all the unpleasant things they have heard that they are eager to grab onto any opportunity to make others look as bad as, or worse than, they do themselves. They might plausibly attribute large amounts of homosexuality to others in order to reduce their own relative inferiority. Since defensive projection would thus plausibly produce a difference between the self-esteem groups in either direction, the experiment seems admirably designed to demonstrate "the" phenomenon. To be convincing, however, it is of course necessary to show that other plausible theories cannot account for the particular outcome. Let us take a closer look at the procedure and results.

After having taken a large battery of personality tests in the first session of the experiment, unacquainted male subjects were scheduled in pairs to participate in the second session, which was allegedly concerned with "forming impressions of personality." After meeting briefly and hearing each other answer some questions about their opinions on some current issues, they were separated and given elaborate falsified feedback about their performance on the personality tests. In each pair, one received very favorable, and the other very unfavorable information. They were then brought together again, made preliminary ratings of each other, and told that the next task for each would be to estimate the degree of homosexual arousal of the other subject while watching photographs of men. Each subject received bogus information from a meter allegedly measuring unconscious sexual reactions but actually controlled by the experimenter. Each subject, believing that he alone could see his own meter, found that he seemed to be sexually aroused by the pictures. His task was to record his own meter reading and to estimate the reading of the other subject's meter for each photograph. This, of course, was the measure of projection. At the end of the rather stressful experiment, the experimenter spent a great deal of time revealing all of the deceptions and providing any necessary reassurance to the subjects.

Examination of the results showed that the subjects with manipulated high self-esteem attributed more homosexuality to their partner than did those with low self-esteem. This, however, is not sufficient to convince most people that a truly defensive process was involved. One could argue, for example, that subjects with high self-esteem simply made the following "cool and rational" calculation: "Since the psychologist told me I'm such a great all-around guy, and if he forces me to guess about that other fellow, I'll have to assume I'm relatively nonhomosexual; if my meter puts me at 300 on the scale, then my bet is that other people aren't much

better—so I'll guess that other subject is somewhere around there too."
Partly in order to check this possibility, Bramel looked at the relation
between the initial attitude toward the partner (measured before homosexuality was mentioned) and amount of homosexuality attributed to him
later on. This is illustrated in Figure 4-1. Low–self-esteem subjects acted
as if they were making exactly this sort of "rational" calculation. The more
liked and respected the other subject, the less homosexuality they attributed to him; it was as if they were saying, "a guy who's that impressive
couldn't be as homosexual as I apparently am." The high–self-esteem
subjects did not show this kind of pattern. When they did not respect
their partner initially, they attributed no more homosexuality than did
comparable low–self-esteem subjects, even though there was plenty of
room on the scale to attribute much higher amounts of the trait. However,
when faced with a partner they had initially rated favorably, they attributed much more homosexuality (equal to their own meter readings)
than did low–self-esteem subjects who initially rated the partner equally
highly. If high–self-esteem subjects were simply making a calculation
based upon their own perceived value relative to other people, they would

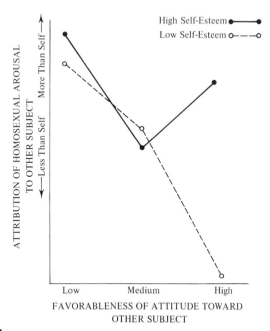

FIGURE 4-1.

*Attribution of Homosexuality As a Function of Manipulated
Self-Esteem and Initial (Prethreat) Attitude Toward Target
Person*

not have attributed an equal amount of homosexuality to respected and nonrespected partners. It is difficult, therefore, to assert that the effect of the self-esteem manipulation was only to shift the point of reference in a rational comparison between oneself and other people.

How, then, can one explain the different patterns of attribution in the two self-esteem conditions? If, following dissonance theory, one assumes that the high–self-esteem subjects would be most strongly motivated to project homosexuality (the sole painful cognition at that moment, for them), then the results are readily explained. If you are forced to admit that you possess an unpleasant trait, and it is not feasible to deny it, then the most comforting thing would probably be to believe that other respectable people also possess the trait. Since the high–self-esteem people should be *particularly* shocked by the allegation of homosexuality, which is so unexpected for them, they would be most motivated to use this projective defense. This might explain why they attributed so much more homosexuality to an attractive partner than did the low–self-esteem subjects.

If, on the other hand, one had assumed that the low–self-esteem people would be the ones most in need of projecting homosexuality (along with everything else!), the data would come as an unpleasant surprise. This group clearly attributed, over-all, less homosexuality. The experiment unfortunately did not include the kinds of control groups that would allow one to see whether the low–self-esteem subjects projected the traits that the experimenter originally used to lower their opinion of themselves. With regard to homosexuality, however, the pattern of the data is consistent with the hypothesis that high–self-esteem subjects projected more and that this projection was self defensive.

The hypothesis that individuals constrained to admit to themselves the possession of undesirable traits will be motivated to project them onto liked and respected persons is plausible enough, but it requires further test. If respected people have the trait, then one can feel it is therefore not a bad trait or that, bad or not, one is no worse than the angels for possessing it. It would seem that this kind of projection is most likely when attractive target persons are available and salient for the threatened person. In this context, let us look briefly at an experiment performed by Pepitone (1964, Chapter 10), which was designed to be a fairly close replication of Bramel's research. Whereas Bramel examined the relation between attribution and initial attitude toward the target person, Pepitone manipulated the subject's perceived similarity between himself and the other person after the high- and low–self-esteem states had been induced. He found that projection of homosexuality was unaffected by this similarity manipulation. Unfortunately for this discussion, Pepitone apparently did not measure the favorableness of the subjects' attitudes toward each other. The question is this: Ought we to expect that the manipulation of perceived similarity–dissimilarity produces the difference in attitude that is essential for a test of our hypothesis? The answer is in the negative. Although the subjects with high self-esteem probably tended to respect the "similar" more than the "dissimilar" partner, this is not likely to be the case for the low–self-esteem subjects. The high– and low–self-esteem conditions would not then be comparable on the attitude-toward-partner dimension. Having just been told that they are distinctly undesirable types themselves, what are the low–self-esteem subjects to think of someone who is described as basically similar to them? It is not at all clear that they would prefer the "similar" to the "dissimilar" partner. It might well be a toss-up. The difficulty with the design, then, is that, unlike the high–self-esteem subjects, those in the low–self-esteem condition were not faced with partners equally differentiated on the attitude dimension. Consequently, one would not expect an interaction between self-esteem and "similarity" conditions comparable to the interaction Bramel found between self-esteem and (unmanipulated) attractiveness of the partner.

In order to clarify the question of choice of target for defensive projection, Bramel (1963) performed a second experiment in which attitude toward an available and salient person was experimentally manipulated along with presence–absence of the homosexuality threat. Self-esteem was not manipulated. After having received falsified meter levels indicating either high or very low levels of homosexual arousal, each subject (tested individually) listened to a seven-minute tape recording of a young man telling stories to Thematic Apperception Test pictures. Half of the subjects were encouraged to have a positive attitude toward this person by being told that the voice belonged to an unnamed student at the same university, in the same class, and majoring in the same area as the subject. The other half of the randomly allocated subjects were told that the (identical) tape recording had been made by an inmate of a local jail, who had just been arrested for the third time, "this time after a long string of armed robberies." The content of the tape was such that all subjects accepted the label of "student" or "criminal" applied to the speaker. The dependent measures included ratings of the amount of homosexuality attributed to the person on the tape.

Note that, as in the previous experiment, it was made very difficult for subjects to deny the evidence of the elaborately explained electrical system for measuring sexual arousal. Under these conditions, again, we predict that persons disturbed by the allegation of latent homosexuality will be most comforted by attributing it to respectable people. If you cannot deny that you possess the trait, it probably doesn't help to attribute it to unattractive people, because that does not help to raise your own attractiveness. The prediction in the present experiment, then, was that the presence or absence of the homosexuality threat would affect the attribution of the trait onto the "student" but very little onto the "criminal," even though the voice and content were identical. The results were entirely consistent with this prediction. Subjects' ratings of the degree of homosexuality of the criminal were completely unaffected by the subjects' own meter readings (high versus low). However, when the tape-recorded voice was described as belonging to a fellow student, high–meter-level subjects attributed much more homosexuality to him than did the low-arousal subjects.

A conceptual replication of this experiment (Edlow and Kiesler, 1966), using the trait of "indecisiveness" and quite different procedures, found the same interaction between magnitude of dissonance and "student" versus "criminal" descriptions of the target person. Considering only the four conditions readily interpretable in this context, Edlow and Kiesler's subjects projected more the more convincingly they were told they possessed the undesirable trait, and only when rating the "student." Evidence that projection is frequently directed toward liked and respected persons is also reported by Secord, Backman, and Eachus (1964). They found that telling subjects they possessed an unexpected and undesirable trait increased the probability that the trait would be attributed to their best friend but not to their worst enemy.

Although writers in the psychoanalytic tradition (for example, Adorno, Frenkel-Brunswik, Levinson, and Sanford, 1950; Bettelheim and Janowitz, 1950) have attempted to account for attribution of negative traits to *disliked outgroups* as a defensive projection, there is no solid experimental evidence that such targets are commonly selected. Since the psychoanalytic view generally deals with unpleasant information that is repressed or denied, experiments that virtually force subjects to admit privately that they possess the trait are probably not relevant to testing projection in this psychoanalytic sense. A convincing study of projection among persons who actively deny the trait remains to be carried out.

Explaining One's Emotional State

In the previous section we have dealt with how people attempt to reinterpret or justify their own thinking, feeling, or behavior by attributing these things to other people. Our present focus is somewhat different, but has frequently been considered also to fall within the domain of the concept of projection. Sometimes a person finds himself to be emotionally aroused in a situation that appears to him not to contain the stimuli that normally arouse him. Consider the following example: According to some definitions, "anxiety" is a feeling of fear in the absence of any convincing cognitive explanation for the fear (in the thinking of the person who experiences the emotion). Feeling afraid, but not able to pinpoint the cause, the person may be motivated to find an explanation (cf. the research described by Schachter and Singer, 1962). One of the ways to explain such a state is to attribute some concrete danger to the environment. Under certain conditions it is probably comforting to "know" what it is that is disturbing you; defining the danger should help the person to mobilize defenses against it. If people sometimes explain their anxiety by attributing dangerous characteristics to the *human* environment, then it deserves discussion in this chapter.

The classic experiment was done by Murray (1933). He invited young neighborhood children to his house one Halloween night, and succeeded in frightening them with a game called "murder," which is played in the dark. After having stayed overnight and slept as best they could, the children were asked in the sunlit morning to judge some neutral pictures of people. Murray found that those who had been frightened the night before judged the photographs to appear more malicious than did a control group of nonfrightened children. It was as if the children were still frightened, but with no adequate cause, and so attributed dangerousness to any salient person. Similar experiments were performed by Feshbach and Feshbach (1964) and by Hornberger (1960) with the same results. These experiments are not completely adequate tests of the hypothesis, however, for two basic reasons. First, no evidence is presented to show whether the subjects felt their fear to be inappropriate to the situation. That is, if we wish to explain attribution of danger as an attempt to find justification for one's feelings, it is necessary to demonstrate that the subjects both feel the emotion and believe it is excessive. The second problem is that these results can readily be explained as instances of displaced aggression. Someone first frightens (and possibly thereby angers) the young subjects; the experimenter then shows them some photographs of people who are similar in age or sex to the frightening agent. The tendency to give negative ratings to these particular pictures might represent displacement of hostility from the true cause onto the similar stimulus persons.

Bramel, Bell, and Margulis (1965) conducted an experiment designed to get around some of these ambiguities. In order to make the results more practically meaningful, the object to be judged for dangerousness actually had a salient existence in the cognitive worlds of the subjects prior to the experiment—namely, the leaders of the Soviet Union. The procedure involved convincing half of the subjects that they were physically frightened in the presence of stimuli depicting Russians. For some of these subjects the stimuli presented were mild-looking photographs (for example, of Nikita Khrushchev smiling); for the others the fear cognition was induced while they were watching a rather dramatic anti-Russian propaganda film. Control subjects watched either photographs or movie, but with no special manipulation of their cognitions about their degree of fear. Beliefs about the amount of danger Russia posed vis-à-vis the United States were measured before and after the experiment. Premeasures indicated that most subjects did not believe that thoughts about the Russians would be sufficient to make them afraid (this was in 1963); yet during the experimental session half of them were presented with almost undeniable evidence (by means of false meter readings) that the photographs or the movie actually frightened them. Those watching dramatic movie scenes of Communist riots, burning American flags, and giant red arrows converging on the United States, accompanied by a sound track proclaiming the evil intentions and successes of the Soviet Union, should have a wealth of danger cues that could readily serve to explain their fear. Believing that they aren't frightened by the Russians, they should be more likely to attribute their arousal to the obviously manipulative propagandistic tricks in the film. Thus it is not necessary that these subjects change their beliefs about the *actual* degree of danger posed by the Russians. On the other hand, those who view a series of pictures of smiling leaders, beaming astronauts, and a factory or two, with no persuasive commentary, have relatively few danger cues available to explain their fear. It is difficult for them to attribute their fear to anything but the Russians themselves. For them, the more likely alternative is to convince themselves that the Russian leaders really are extremely dangerous, and that the photographs made them think about this "fact."

The results were consistent with the hypothesis. Being told they were frightened by the stimuli produced increased attribution of aggressiveness to the Soviet Union only among subjects who viewed the neutral photographs. Although the movie by itself had some persuasive effect, it was no more effective for subjects told they were frightened than for controls (who very probably did not believe themselves to be frightened).

Although there is now evidence that people sometimes try to explain their anxiety by pinpointing a concrete danger in the environment, little is known about the generality of the hypothesis in regard to other subjectively unexplained emotional states. One attempt to extrapolate was made by Bramel, Bell, Macker, & Schoen (1966). Female subjects were told that they were physiologically "upset and distressed" to varying degrees as they watched a stooge receiving a rather negative report on her (the stooge's) personality. The stooge pretended to be mildly disturbed by what she heard. The subjects rated the (standard) behavior of the stooge. The hypothesis was that increasing cognitions of one's own distress would produce increasing tendencies to rate the stooge as distressed. It seemed plausible that subjects would explain their own supposed degree of arousal by saying to themselves, "I feel like this because that girl is very upset (or not very upset)." However, the results provided no support for this prediction. The authors speculated as follows: since "being sympathetic" is a positively evaluated response (at least among female subjects), perhaps the subjects explained their high arousal by concluding that they must be very sensitive, sympathetic people. Low-arousal subjects (as manipulated) could easily have justified this reaction by saying that this was what the scientists wanted—namely, objectivity. If these speculations are sound, an implication is that people will explain an emotion in as self-flattering a way as possible. Since fearful males do not wish to explain their apparent arousal as indicating cowardice or weakness, they prefer to distort perception of the environment. "Sympathetic" girls, on the other hand, can account for their apparently high degree of distress by changing their view of their own sensitivity, and do not get so much reward from attributing additional suffering to the stooge.

Lest the reader assume that people attempt to find explanations only for their fear and distress reactions, it is refreshing to turn to an experiment by Valins (1966) for an entirely different perspective. He reasoned that male subjects could be made to think they were physiologically aroused while viewing photographs of nude females of the sort to be found in *Playboy* magazine (a publication widely read in the 1960's). The subjects (tested individually) heard repetitive sounds of varying frequency per minute as the photographs were serially displayed. Half of the sample were told that the sounds were their own heartbeats as detected by a microphone on the chest and fed through amplifier and speaker. The others had no microphone attached to themselves and were given no reason to think the sounds were heartbeats. The sounds were of course pretaped and standard for all subjects. On five of the ten photographs the frequency of beats either increased or decreased markedly (for different subjects) from the previous "resting level." Valins predicted that the apparent changes in heartbeat would be interpreted by subjects as reflecting their affective reactions to the photographs. If, in order to explain a striking increase or decrease in his apparent heartbeat rate, the subject concludes that he must be physically attracted to the girl, then his next cognitive step may be to conclude that this particular girl is more attractive than the others who failed to affect him. He may even search for particular features in the girl that could explain her "effect" on him. Valins used three different measures of the perceived attractiveness of the photographs. First was a rating scale given a few minutes after the experimental manipulations; second, the subject was told he could keep any five photos as remuneration, and his choices were recorded; finally, a rather novel and useful delayed measure was taken four weeks later by a person seeming to have no connection with the experiment who masqueraded as a survey interviewer investigating various student attitudes. Results on all three measures were neatly consistent with the hypothesis in showing greater preference for photos associated with alleged heart-rate changes. Subjects not led to believe that the sounds were their own heartbeats showed no such effects.

References

Adorno, T. W., Frenkel-Brunswik, E., Levinson, D. J., and Sanford, R. N. *The Authoritarian Personality.* New York: Harper and Row, 1950.

Altrocci, J. Dominance as a factor in interpersonal choice and perception. *Journal of Abnormal and Social Psychology,* 1959, **59**, 303–308.

Anderson, L. R., and Fishbein, M. Prediction of attitude from the number, strength, and evaluative aspect of beliefs about the attitude object. *Journal of Personality and Social Psychology,* 1965, **2**, 437–443.

Anderson, N. H. Application of an additive model to impression formation. *Science,* 1962, **138**, 817–818.

Anderson, N. H. Averaging versus adding as a stimulus combination rule in impression formation. *Journal of Experimental Psychology,* 1965, **70**, 394–400. (a)

Anderson, N. H. Primacy effects in personality impression formation using a generalized order effect paradigm. *Journal of Personality and Social Psychology,* 1965, **2**, 1–9. (b)

Anderson, N. H. Component ratings in impression formation. *Psychonomic Science,* 1966, **6**, 279–280.

Anderson, N. H. and Barrios, A. A. Primacy effects in personality impression formation. *Journal of Abnormal and Social Psychology,* 1961, **63**, 346–350.

Anderson, N. H., and Hubert S. Effects of concomitant verbal recall on order effects in personality impression formation. *Journal of Verbal Learning and Verbal Behavior,* 1963, **2**, 379–391.

Anderson, N. H., and Lampel, A. K. Effect of context on ratings of personality traits. *Psychonomic Science,* 1965, **3**, 433–434.

Anderson, N. H., and Norman, A. Order effects in impression formation in four classes of stimuli. *Journal of Abnormal and Social Psychology,* 1964, **69**, 467–471.

Aristotle. *The Poetics.* Trans. S. H. Butcher. *Aristotle's Theory of Poetry and Fine Art.* (4th ed.) New York: Dover Press, 1951.

Aronson, E., and Linder, D. Gain and loss of esteem as determinants of interpersonal attractiveness. *Journal of Experimental Social Psychology,* 1965, **1**, 156–171.

Aronson, E., and Mills, J. The effect of severity of initiation on liking for a group. *Journal of Abnormal and Social Psychology,* 1959, **59**, 177–181.

Aronson, E., Willerman, B., and Floyd, J. The effect of a pratfall on increasing interpersonal attractiveness. *Psychonomic Science,* 1966, **4**, 157–158.

Aronson, E., and Worchel, P. Similarity versus liking as determinants of inter-personal attractiveness. *Psychonomic Science,* 1966, **5,** 157–158.

Asch, S. E. Forming impressions of personality. *Journal of Abnormal and Social Psychology,* 1946, **41,** 258–290.

Bales, R. F. Task roles and social roles in problem solving groups. In E. E. Maccoby, T. M. Newcomb, and E. L. Hartley (eds.), *Readings in Social Psychology,* 3rd ed. New York: Holt, Rinehart, and Winston, 1958.

Bandura, A. Vicarious processes: A case of no-trial learning. In L. Berkowitz, (ed.), *Advances in Experimental Social Psychology,* Vol. 2. New York: Academic Press, 1965.

Bandura, A., and Walters, R. H. *Social Learning and Personality Development.* New York: Holt, Rinehart, and Winston, 1963.

Barnard, C. I. *The Functions of the Executive.* Cambridge, Mass.: Harvard University Press, 1938.

Bass, B. M., and Dunteman, G. Biases in the evaluation of one's own group, its allies and opponents. *Journal of Conflict Resolution,* 1963, **7,** 16–20.

Bechtel, R. B., and Rosenfeld, H. M. Expectations of social acceptance and compatibility as related to status discrepancy and social motives. *Journal of Personality and Social Psychology,* 1966, **3,** 344–349.

Bem, D. J. An experimental analysis of self-persuasion. *Journal of Experimental Social Psychology,* 1965, **1,** 199–218.

Bem, D. J. Self-perception: an alternative interpretation of cognitive dissonance phenomena. *Psychological Review,* 1967, **74,** 183–200.

Berkowitz, L. *Aggression: A Social Psychological Analysis.* New York: McGraw-Hill, 1962.

Berkowitz, L. Anti-Semitism and the displacement of aggression. *Journal of Abnormal and Social Psychology,* 1959, **59,** 182–187.

Berkowitz, L. Some aspects of observed aggression. *Journal of Personality and Social Psychology,* 1965, **2,** 359–369.

Berkowitz, L. On not being able to aggress. *British Journal of Social and Clinical Psychology,* 1966, **5,** 130–139.

Berkowitz, L., Corwin, R., and Heironimus, M. Film violence and subsequent aggressive tendencies. *Public Opinion Quarterly,* 1963, **27,** 217–229.

Berkowitz, L., and Daniels, L. R. Responsibility and dependency. *Journal of Abnormal and Social Psychology,* 1963, **66,** 429–436.

Berkowitz, L., and Geen, R. G. Film violence and the cue properties of available targets. *Journal of Personality and Social Psychology,* 1966, **3,** 525–530.

Berkowitz, L., and Goranson, R. E. Motivational and judgmental determinants of social perception. *Journal of Abnormal and Social Psychology,* 1964, **69,** 296–302.

Berkowitz, L., and Green, J. A. The stimulus qualities of the scapegoat. *Journal of Abnormal and Social Psychology,* 1962, **64,** 293–301.

Berkowitz, L., Green, J. A., and Macaulay, J. R. Hostility catharsis as the reduction of emotional tension. *Psychiatry,* 1962, **25,** 23–31.

Berkowitz, L., and Holmes, D. S. The generalization of hostility to disliked objects. *Journal of Personality,* 1959, **27,** 565–577.

Berkowitz, L., and Holmes, D. S. A further investigation of hostility generalization to disliked objects. *Journal of Personality,* 1960, **28,** 427–442.

Berkowitz, L., and Macaulay, J. R. Some effects of differences in status level and status stability. *Human Relations,* 1961, **14,** 135–148.

Berkowitz, L., and Rawlings, E. Effects of film violence on inhibitions against subsequent aggression. *Journal of Abnormal and Social Psychology,* 1963, **66,** 405–412.

Bettelheim, B., and Janowitz, M. *Dynamics of prejudice.* New York: Harper and Row, 1950.

Blake, R. R., and Mouton, J. S. The intergroup dynamics of win-lose conflict and problem-solving collaboration in union-management relations. In M. Sherif (ed.), *Intergroup Relations and Leadership.* New York: John Wiley and Sons, 1962.

Bossard, J. H. S. Residential propinquity as a factor in marriage selection. *American Journal of Sociology,* 1932, **38,** 219–224.

Bossart, P., and DiVesta, F. J. Effects of context, frequency, and order of presentation of evaluative assertions on impression formation. *Journal of Personality and Social Psychology,* 1966, **4,** 538–544.

Bramel, D. A dissonance theory approach to defensive projection. *Journal of Abnormal and Social Psychology,* 1962, **64,** 121–129.

Bramel, D. Selection of a target for defensive projection. *Journal of Abnormal and Social Psychology,* 1963, **66,** 318–324.

Bramel, D. Dissonance, expectation, and the self. In R. Abelson, E. Aronson, W. McGuire, T. Newcomb, M. Rosenberg, and P. Tannenbaum (eds.), *Theories of Cognitive Consistency: A Sourcebook.* New York: Rand McNally, 1968.

Bramel, D., Bell, J. E., Macker, C., and Schoen, J. N. Attributing distress and giving aid to others because of one's own believed distress. Mimeo, State University of New York, 1966.

Bramel, D., Bell, J. E., and Margulis, S. T. Attributing danger as a means of explaining one's fear. *Journal of Experimental Social Psychology,* 1965, **1,** 267–281.

Bramel, D., Taub, B. and Blum, B. An observer's reaction to the suffering of his enemy. *Journal of Personality and Social Psychology,* 1968, **8,** 384–392.

Brehm, J. W. *A Theory of Psychological Reactance.* New York: Academic Press, 1966.

Brehm, J. W., and Cohen, A. R. *Explorations in Cognitive Dissonance.* New York: John Wiley and Sons, 1962.

Briscoe, M. E., Woodyard, H. D., and Shaw, M. E. Personality impression change as a function of the favorableness of first impressions. *Journal of Personality,* 1967, **35,** 343–357.

Brock, T. C., and Buss, A. H. Dissonance, aggression, and evaluation of pain. *Journal of Abnormal and Social Psychology,* 1962, **65,** 319–324.

Brock, T. C., and Buss, A. H. Effects of justification for aggression and communication with the victim on post aggression dissonance. *Journal of Abnormal and Social Psychology,* 1964, **68,** 403–412.

Bruner, J. S., and Perlmutter, H. V. Compatriot and foreigner: a study of impression formation in three countries. *Journal of Abnormal and Social Psychology,* 1957, **55,** 253–260.

Burnstein, E., and McRae, A. V. Some effects of shared threat and prejudice in racially mixed groups. *Journal of Abnormal and Social Psychology,* 1962, **64,** 257–263.

Burnstein, E., and Worchel P. Arbitrariness of frustration and its consequences for aggression in a social situation. *Journal of Personality,* 1962, **30,** 528–540.

Buss, A. H. *The Psychology of Aggression.* New York: John Wiley and Sons, 1961.

Buss, A. H. Instrumentality of aggression, feedback, and frustration as determinants of physical aggression. *Journal of Personality and Social Psychology,* 1966, **3,** 153–162.

Byrne, D. Interpersonal attraction and attitude similarity. *Journal of Abnormal and Social Psychology,* 1961, **62,** 713–715. (a)

Byrne, D. Interpersonal attraction as a function of affiliation need and attitude similarity. *Human Relations,* 1961, **14,** 283–289. (b)

Byrne, D. Response to attitude similarity-dissimilarity as a function of affiliation need. *Journal of Personality,* 1962, **30,** 164–177.

Byrne, D., and Clore, G. L., Jr. Predicting interpersonal attraction toward strangers presented in three different stimulus modes. *Psychonomic Science,* 1966, **4,** 239–240.

Byrne, D., and Griffitt, W. Similarity versus liking: a clarification. *Psychonomic Science,* 1966, **6,** 295–296.

Byrne, D., and McGraw, C. Interpersonal attraction toward Negroes. *Human Relations,* 1964, **17,** 201–213.

Byrne, D., and Nelson, D. Attraction as a function of attitude similarity-dissimilarity: the effect of topic importance. *Psychonomic Science,* 1964, **1,** 93–93.

Byrne, D., and Nelson, D. Attraction as a linear function of proportion of positive reinforcements. *Journal of Personality and Social Psychology,* 1965, **1,** 659–663.

Byrne, D., Nelson, D., and Reeves, K. Effects of consensual validation and invalidation on attraction as a function of verifiability. *Journal of Experimental Social Psychology,* 1966, **2,** 98–107.

Byrne, D., and Rhamey, R. Magnitude of positive and negative reinforcements as a determinant of attraction. *Journal of Personality and Social Psychology,* 1965, **2,** 884–889.

Byrne, D., and Wong, T. J. Racial prejudice, interpersonal attraction and assumed dissimilarity of attitudes. *Journal of Abnormal and Social Psychology,* 1962, **65,** 246–253.

Campbell, D. T. Common fate, similarity, and other indices of the status of aggregates of persons as social entities. *Behavioral Science,* 1958, **3,** 14–25.

Cohen, A. R. Upward communication in experimentally created hierarchies. *Human Relations,* 1958, **11,** 41–53.

Coser, L. *The Functions of Social Conflict.* New York: The Free Press, 1956.

Cowen, D., Landes, J., and Schaet, D. E. The effects of mild frustration on the expression of prejudiced attitudes. *Journal of Abnormal and Social Psychology,* 1959, **58,** 33–38.

Crutchfield, R. S. Conformity and character. *American Psychologist,* 1955, **10,** 191–198.

Darley, J. M., and Aronson, E. Self-evaluation vs. direct anxiety reduction as determinants of the fear-affiliation relation. *Journal of Experimental Social Psychology*, Supplement, 1966, 1, 66–79.

Darley, J. M., and Berscheid, E. S. Increased liking as a result of the anticipation of personal contact. *Human Relations*, 1967, 20, 29–40.

Davidson, J. R. Cognitive familiarity and dissonance reduction. In L. Festinger, (ed.), *Conflict, Decision, and Dissonance*. Stanford: Stanford University Press, 1964.

Davis, K. E., and Jones, E. E. Changes in interpersonal perception as a means of reducing cognitive dissonance. *Journal of Abnormal and Social Psychology*, 1960, 61, 402–410.

DeCharms, R., Carpenter, V., and Kuperman, A. The "origin-pawn" variable in person perception. *Sociometry*, 1965, 28, 241–258.

DeCharms, R., and Wilkins, E. J. Some effects of verbal expression of hostility. *Journal of Abnormal and Social Psychology*, 1963, 66, 462–470.

Deutsch, M. An experimental study of the effects of cooperation and competition upon group process. *Human Relations*, 1949, 2, 199–231.

Deutsch, M. The interpretation of praise and criticism as a function of their social context. *Journal of Abnormal and Social Psychology*, 1961, 62, 391–400.

Deutsch, M., and Collins, M. E. *Interracial Housing: A Psychological Evaluation of a Social Experiment*. Minneapolis: University of Minnesota Press, 1951.

Deutsch, M., and Solomon, L. Reactions to evaluations by others as influenced by self-evaluation. *Sociometry*, 1959, 22, 93–112.

Dickoff, H. Reactions to evaluations by another person as a function of self-evaluation and the interaction context. Unpublished Ph.D. dissertation, Duke University, 1961.

Dinnerstein, D. The "source" dimension of second-hand evidence, *Journal of Social Psychology*, 1957, 45, 41–59.

Dittes, J. E. Attractiveness of group as function of self-esteem and acceptance by group. *Journal of Abnormal and Social Psychology*, 1959, 59, 77–82.

Dittes, J. E., and Kelley, H. H. Effects of different conditions of acceptance upon conformity to group norms. *Journal of Abnormal and Social Psychology*, 1956, 53, 100–107.

Dollard, J., Doob, L., Miller, N., Mowrer, O., and Sears, R. *Frustration and Aggression*. New Haven, Conn.: Yale University Press, 1939.

Dollard, J., and Miller, N. *Personality and Psychotherapy*. New York: McGraw-Hill, 1950.

Edlow, D., and Kiesler, C. A. Ease of denial and defensive projection. *Journal of Experimental Social Psychology*, 1966, 2, 56–69.

Emerson, R. M. Deviation and rejection: an experimental replication. *American Sociological Review*, 1954, 19, 688–693.

Epstein, R. Authoritarianism, displaced aggression, and social status of the target. *Journal of Personality and Social Psychology*, 1965, 2, 585–589.

Epstein, S., and Taylor, S. P. Instigation to aggression as a function of degree of defeat and perceived aggressive intent of the opponent. *Journal of Personality*, 1967, 35, 265–289.

Feather, N. T., and Jeffries, D. G. Balancing and extremity effects in reactions of receiver to source and content of communications. *Journal of Personality,* 1967, **35,** 194–213.

Fenichel, O. *The Psychoanalytic Theory of Neurosis.* New York: W. W. Norton, 1945.

Feshbach, S. The drive-reducing function of fantasy behavior. *Journal of Abnormal and Social Psychology,* 1955, **50,** 3–11.

Feshbach, S. The stimulating versus cathartic effects of a vicarious aggressive activity. *Journal of Abnormal and Social Psychology,* 1961, **63,** 381–385.

Feshbach, S. The function of aggression and the regulation of aggressive drive. *Psychological Review,* 1964, **71,** 257–272.

Feshbach, S., and Feshbach, N. Influence of the stimulus object upon the complementary and supplementary projection of fear. *Journal of Abnormal and Social Psychology,* 1964, **66,** 498–503.

Feshbach, S., and Singer, R. The effects of personal and shared threats upon social prejudice. *Journal of Abnormal and Social Psychology,* 1956, **54,** 411–416.

Feshbach, S., and Singer, R. The effects of fear arousal and suppression of fear upon social perception. *Journal of Abnormal and Social Psychology,* 1957, **55,** 283–288.

Feshbach, S., Stiles, W. B., and Bitter, E. The reinforcing effect of witnessing aggression. *Journal of Experimental Research in Personality,* 1967, **2,** 133–139.

Festinger, L. A theory of social comparison processes. *Human Relations,* 1954, **7,** 117–140.

Festinger, L. *A Theory of Cognitive Dissonance,* Evanston, Ill.: Row, Peterson, 1957.

Fishbein, M. and Hunter, R. Summation versus balance in attitude organization and change. *Journal of Abnormal and Social Psychology,* 1964, **69,** 505–510.

Fishbein, M., and Raven, B. H. The AB scales: an operational definition of belief and attitude. *Human Relations,* 1962, **15,** 35–44.

Freud, S. Certain neurotic mechanisms in jealousy, paranoia, and homosexuality. *Collected Papers,* Vol. 2. London: Hogarth Press, 1924.

Geen, R., and Berkowitz, L. Name-mediated aggressive cue properties. *Journal of Personality,* 1966, **34,** 456–465.

Gerard, H. B. Emotional uncertainty and social comparison. *Journal of Abnormal and Social Psychology,* 1963, **66,** 568–573.

Gerard, H. B., and Greenbaum, C. W. Attitudes toward an agent of uncertainty reduction. *Journal of Personality,* 1962, **30,** 485–495.

Gerard, H. B., and Mathewson, G. C. The effects of severity of initiation on liking for a group: a replication. *Journal of Experimental Social Psychology,* 1966, **2,** 278–287.

Gerard, H. B., and Rabbie, J. M. Fear and social comparison. *Journal of Abnormal and Social Psychology,* 1961, **62,** 586–592.

Glass, D. C. Changes in liking as a means of reducing cognitive discrepancies between self-esteem and aggression. *Journal of Personality,* 1964, **32,** 531–549.

Goranson, R. E., and Berkowitz, L. Reciprocity and responsibility reactions to prior help. *Journal of Personality and Social Psychology*, 1966, **3**, 227–232.

Gumpert, P., and Festinger, L. Affective reactions toward people who violate rules. Unpublished manuscript, Stanford University, 1962.

Haire, M., and Grunes, W. F. Perceptual defenses: processes protecting an organized perception of another personality. *Human Relations*, 1950, **3**, 403–413.

Hakmiller, K. Threat as a determinant of downward comparison. *Journal of Experimental Social Psychology*, Supplement, 1966, **1**, 32–39.

Hamblin, R. Group integration during a crisis. *Human Relations*, 1958, **11**, 67–76.

Hamblin, R. I., Bridger, D. A., Day, R. C., and Yancey, W. L. The interference-aggression law. *Sociometry*, 1963, **26**, 190–216.

Hartley, E. L. *Problems in Prejudice*. New York: King's Crown Press, 1946.

Hartmann, D. P. The influence of symbolically modeled instrumental aggression and pain cues on the disinhibition of aggressive behavior. Unpublished Ph.D. dissertation, Stanford University, 1965.

Harvey, O. J. An experimental investigation of negative and positive relations between small groups through judgmental indices. *Sociometry*, 1956, **19**, 201–209.

Harvey, O. J. Personality factors in resolution of conceptual incongruities. *Sociometry*, 1962, **25**, 336–352.

Harvey, O. J. and Clapp, W. F. Hope, expectancy, and reactions to the unexpected. *Journal of Personality and Social Psychology*, 1965, **2**, 45–52.

Harvey, O. J., Kelley, H. H., and Shapiro. M. M. Reactions to unfavorable evaluations of the self made by other persons. *Journal of Personality*, 1957, **25**, 393–411.

Hastorf, A. H., Osgood, C. E., and Ono, H. The semantics of facial expressions and the prediction of the meanings of stereoscopically fused facial expressions. *Scandinavian Journal of Psychology*, 1966, **7**, 179–188.

Heider, F. *The Psychology of Interpersonal Relations*. New York: John Wiley and Sons, 1958.

Heider, F. On social cognition. *American Psychologist*, 1967, **22**, 25–31.

Hendrick, C. A. Averaging versus summation in impression formation. Unpublished Ph.D. dissertation, University of Missouri, 1967.

Hoffman, L. R., and Maier, N. R. F. An experimental reexamination of the similarity-attraction hypothesis. *Journal of Personality and Social Psychology*, 1966, **3**, 145–152.

Hokanson, J. E. The effects of frustration and anxiety on overt aggression. *Journal of Abnormal and Social Psychology*, 1961, **62**, 346–351.

Hollander, E. P. Conformity, status, and idiosyncrasy credit. *Psychological Review*, 1958, **65**, 117–127.

Holmes, D. S., and Berkowitz, L. Some contrast effects in social perception. *Journal of Abnormal and Social Psychology*, 1961, **62**, 150–153.

Homans, G. C. *Social Behavior: Its Elementary Forms*. New York: Harcourt, Brace, and World, 1961.

Homans, G. C., and Schneider, D. M. *Marriage, authority, and final causes*. New York: The Free Press, 1955.

Hornberger, R. H. The projective effects of fear and sexual arousal on the rating of pictures. *Journal of Clinical Psychology*, 1960, **16**, 328–331.

Horwitz, M. The veridicality of liking and disliking. In R. Tagiuri, and L. Petrullo (eds.), *Person Perception and Interpersonal Behavior*. Stanford, Calif.: Stanford University Press, 1958.

Howard, R. C., and Berkowitz, L. Reactions to the evaluators of one's performance, *Journal of Personality*, 1958, **26**, 494–507.

Insko, C. A., and Oakes, W. F. Awareness and the "conditioning" of attitudes. *Journal of Personality and Social Psychology*, 1966, **4**, 487–496.

Iverson, M. A. Personality impressions of punitive stimulus persons of differential status. *Journal of Abnormal and Social Psychology*, 1964, **68**, 617–626.

Iwao, S. Internal versus external criticism of group standards. *Sociometry*, 1963, **26**, 410–421.

James, A., and Lott, A. J. Reward frequency and the formation of positive attitudes toward group members. *Journal of Social Psychology*, 1964, **62**, 111–115.

Jecker, J. D., and Landy, D. Liking a person as a function of doing him a favor. Mimeo, University of Texas, 1966.

Jones, E. E. *Ingratiation*. New York: Appleton-Century-Crofts, 1964.

Jones, E. E., and Davis, K. E. From acts to dispositions. In L. Berkowitz (ed.), *Advances in Experimental Social Psychology*, Vol. 2. New York: Academic Press, 1965.

Jones, E. E., Davis, K. E., and Gergen, K. J. Role playing variations and their informational value for person perception. *Journal of Abnormal and Social Psychology*, 1961, **63**, 302–310.

Jones, E. E., Gergen, K. J., and Davis, K. E. Some determinants of reactions to being approved or disapproved as a person. *Psychological Monographs*, 1962, **76**, No. 521.

Jones, E. E., Gergen, K. J., and Jones, R. G. Tactics of ingratiation among leaders and subordinates in a status hierarchy. *Psychological Monographs*, 1963, **77**, No. 566.

Jones, E. E., and Harris, V. A. The attribution of attitudes. *Journal of Experimental Social Psychology*, 1967, **3**, 1–24.

Jones, E. E., Hester, S. L., Farina, A., and Davis, K. E. Reactions to unfavorable personal evaluations as a function of the evaluator's perceived adjustment. *Journal of Abnormal and Social Psychology*, 1959, **59**, 363–370.

Jones, E. E., Jones, R. G., and Gergen, K. T. Some conditions affecting the evaluation of a conformist. *Journal of Personality*, 1963, **31**, 270–288.

Jones, E. E., and Kohler, R. The effects of plausibility on the learning of controversial statements. *Journal of Abnormal and Social Psychology*, 1958, **57**, 315–320.

Julian, J. W., Bishop, D. W., and Fiedler, F. E. Quasitherapeutic effects of intergroup competition. *Journal of Personality and Social Psychology*, 1966, **3**, 321–327.

Kahn, M. The physiology of catharsis. *Journal of Personality and Social Psychology*, 1966, **3**, 278–286.

Kaufman, H., and Feshbach, S. Displaced aggression and its modification through exposure to antiaggressive communications. *Journal of Abnormal and Social Psychology*, 1963, **67**, 79–83.

Kelley, H. H. The warm-cold variable in first impressions of persons. *Journal of Personality*, 1950, **19**, 431–439.

Kiesler, S. The effect of perceived role requirements on reactions to favor-doing. *Journal of Experimental Social Psychology*, 1966, **2**, 198–210.

Kleiner, R. The effects of threat reduction upon interpersonal attraction. *Journal of Personality*, 1960, **28**, 145–155.

Latane, B., Eckman, J., and Joy, V. Shared stress and interpersonal attraction. *Journal of Experimental Social Psychology*, Supplement, 1966, **1**, 80–94.

Lerner, M. J. The effect of responsibility and choice on a partners' attractiveness following failure. *Journal of Personality*, 1965, **33**, 178–187.

Lerner, M. J., Dillehay, R. C., and Sherer, W. C. Similarity and attraction in social contexts. *Journal of Personality and Social Psychology*, 1967, **5**, 481–486.

Lerner, M. J., and Matthews, G. Reaction to suffering of others under conditions of indirect responsibility. *Journal of Personality and Social Psychology*, 1967, **5**, 319–325.

Lerner, M. J., and Simmons, C. H. Observers' reactions to the "innocent victim." *Journal of Personality and Social Psychology*, 1966, **4**, 203–210.

Levy, L. H. Context effects in social perception. *Journal of Abnormal and Social Psychology*, 1960, **61**, 295–297.

Lorenz, K. *On Aggression*. New York: Harcourt, Brace, & World, 1966.

Lott, B. E., and Lott, A. J. The formation of positive attitudes toward group members. *Journal of Abnormal and Social Psychology*, 1960, **61**, 297–300.

Luchins, A. S. Primacy-recency in impression formation. In C. I. Hovland (ed.), *The Order of Presentation in Persuasion*. New Haven, Conn.: Yale University Press, 1957. Pp. 33–62. (a)

Luchins, A. S. Experimental attempts to minimize the impact of first impressions. In C. I. Hovland (ed.), *The Order of Presentation in Persuasion*. New Haven, Conn.: Yale University Press, 1957. Pp. 62–87. (b)

Luchins, A. S. Definitiveness of impression and primacy-recency in communications. *Journal of Social Psychology*, 1958, **48**, 275–290.

Manis, M. The interpretation of opinion statements as a function of recipient attitude. *Journal of Abnormal and Social Psychology*, 1960, **60**, 340–344.

Manis, M. The interpretation of opinion statements as a function of recipient attitude and source prestige. *Journal of Abnormal and Social Psychology*, 1961, **63**, 82–86.

Manis, M., Gleason, T. C., and Dawes, R. M. The evaluation of complex social stimuli. *Journal of Personality and Social Psychology*, 1966, **3**, 404–419.

McWhirter, R. M., and Jecker, J. D. Attitude similarity and inferred attraction. *Psychonomic Science*, 1967, **7**, 225–226.

Mednick, S. A. *Learning*. Englewood Cliffs, N.J.: Prentice-Hall, 1964.

Mensh, I. N., and Wishner, J. Asch on "Forming impressions of personality," further evidence. *Journal of Personality*, 1947, **16**, 188–191.

Milgram, S. Behavioral study of obedience. *Journal of Abnormal and Social Psychology*, 1963, **67**, 371–378.

Miller, N. E. The frustration-aggression hypothesis. *Psychological Review,* 1941, **48**, 337–342.

Miller, N. E. Theory and experiment relating psychoanalytic displacement to stimulus response generalization. *Journal of Abnormal and Social Psychology,* 1948, **43**, 155–178.

Miller, N. E. Liberalization of basic S-R concepts; extensions to conflict behavior, motivation, and social learning. In S. Koch. (ed.), *Psychology: A Study of a Science.* Vol. 2. New York: McGraw-Hill, 1959.

Miller, N. E., and Bugelski, R. Minor studies in aggression: the influence of frustrations imposed by the in-group on attitudes expressed toward outgroups. *Journal of Psychology,* 1948, **25**, 437–442.

Mills, J., and Jellison, J. M. Effect on opinion change of how desirable the communication is to the audience the communicator addressed. *Journal of Personality and Social Psychology,* 1967, **6**, 98–101.

Mirels, H., and Mills, J. Perception of the pleasantness and competence of a partner. *Journal of Abnormal and Social Psychology,* 1964, **68**, 456–459.

Moreno, J. L. *Who Shall Survive?* Washington: Nervous and Mental Disease Pub. Co., 1934.

Mulder, M., and Stemerding, A. Threat, attraction to group, need for strong leadership. *Human Relations,* 1963, **16**, 317–334.

Murney, R. G. *An Application of the Principle of Stimulus Generalization to the Prediction of Object Displacement.* Washington: Catholic University of America Press, 1955.

Murray, E. J., and Berkun, M. M. Displacement as a function of conflict. *Journal of Abnormal and Social Psychology,* 1955, **51**, 47–56.

Murray, H. A. The effect of fear upon estimates of the maliciousness of other personalities. *Journal of Social Psychology,* 1933, **4**, 310–329.

Murstein, B. I. The projection of hostility on the Rorschach and as a result of ego-threat. *Journal of Projective Techniques,* 1956, **20**, 418–428.

Myers, A. Team competition, success, and the adjustment of group members. *Journal of Abnormal and Social Psychology,* 1962, **65**, 325–332.

Newcomb, T. M. *The Acquaintance Process.* New York: Holt, Rinehart, and Winston, 1961.

Pallak, M. S. The effect of aggression on interpersonal attractiveness. Unpublished manuscript, Ohio State University, 1966.

Pepinsky, P. N., Hemphill, J. K., and Shevitz, R. N. Attempts to lead, group productivity, and morale under conditions of acceptance and rejection. *Journal of Abnormal and Social Psychology,* 1958, **57**, 47–54.

Pepitone, A. Motivational effects in social perception. *Human Relations,* 1950, **3**, 57–76.

Pepitone, A. *Attraction and Hostility.* New York: Atherton Press, 1964.

Pepitone, A., and Hayden, R. G. Some evidence for conflict resolution in impression formation. *Journal of Abnormal and Social Psychology,* 1955, **51**, 302–307.

Pepitone, A., and Reichling, G. Group cohesiveness, and the expression of hostility. *Human Relations,* 1955, **8**, 327–337.

Pepitone, A., and Wilpizeski, C. Some consequences of experimental rejection. *Journal of Abnormal and Social Psychology,* 1960, **60**, 359–364.

Perry, W. R. Post-aggression cognitive dissonance, victim response style, and hostility-guilt. Unpublished Ph.D. dissertation, Ohio State University, 1965.

Pilisuk, M. Cognitive balance and self-relevant attitudes. *Journal of Abnormal and Social Psychology*, 1962, **65**, 95–103.

Plato, *The Republic*. Trans. F. M. Cornford. New York: Oxford University Press, 1964.

Podell, J. E., and Amster, H. Evaluative concept of a person as a function of the number of stimulus traits. *Journal of Personality and Social Psychology*, 1966, **4**, 333–336.

Podell, H. A., and Podell, J. E. Quantitative connotation of a concept. *Journal of Abnormal and Social Psychology*, 1963, **67**, 509–513.

Rabbie, J. M. Differential preference for companionship under threat. *Journal of Abnormal and Social Psychology*, 1963, **67**, 643–648.

Ring, K., Lipinski, G. E., and Braginsky, D. The relationship of birth order to self-evaluation, anxiety reduction, and susceptibility to emotional contagion. *Psychological Monographs*, 1965, **79**, No. 10.

Rokeach, M. *The Open and Closed Mind*. New York: Basic Books, 1960.

Rosenbaum, M., and deCharms, R. Direct and vicarious reduction of hostility. *Journal of Abnormal and Social Psychology*, 1960, **60**, 105–110.

Rosenberg, M. J. An analysis of affective-cognitive consistency. In M. J. Rosenberg, C. I. Hovland, W. J. McGuire, R. P. Abelson, and J. W. Brehm (eds.), *Attitude Organization and Change*. New Haven, Conn.: Yale University Press, 1960. Pp. 15–64.

Ross, A. S. Modes of guilt reduction. Unpublished Ph.D. dissertation, University of Minnesota, 1965.

Rychlak, J. F. The similarity, compatibility, or incompatibility of needs in interpersonal selection. *Journal of Personality and Social Psychology*, 1965, **2**, 334–340.

Sarnoff, I., and Zimbardo, P. G. Anxiety, fear, and social affiliation. *Journal of Abnormal and Social Psychology*, 1961, **62**, 356–363.

Schachter, S. Deviation, rejection, and communication. *Journal of Abnormal and Social Psychology*, 1951, **46**, 190–207.

Schachter, S. *The Psychology of Affiliation*. Stanford, Calif.: Stanford, University Press, 1959.

Schachter, S., and Singer, J. E. Cognitive, social, and physiological determinants of emotional state. *Psychological Review*, 1962, **69**, 379–399.

Schopler, J., and Bateson, N. A dependence interpretation of the effects of severe initiation. *Journal of Personality*, 1962, **30**, 633–649.

Sears. R. R., Maccoby, E. E., and Levin, H. *Patterns of Child Rearing*. Evanston, Ill.: Row, Peterson, 1957.

Secord, P. F., Backman, C. W., and Eachus, H. T. Effects of imbalance in the self-concept on the perception of persons. *Journal of Abnormal and Social Psychology*, 1964, **68**, 442–446.

Shaw, G. B. *Man and Superman,* in *Nine Plays*. New York: Dodd, Mead, 1935. Quoted by permission of the Shaw Estate and the Society of Authors, London.

Sherif, N., Harvey, O. J., White, B. J., Hood, W. R., and Sherif, C. *Intergroup Conflict and Cooperation*. Norman, Okla.: University of Oklahoma Book Exchange, 1961.

Singer, D. L. Aggression arousal, hostile humor, catharsis. *Journal of Personality and Social Psychology,* 1968, 8 (Monograph Supplement No. 1, Part 2).

Singer, J. E., Radloff, L. S., and Wark, D. M. Renegades, heretics, and changes in sentiment. *Sociometry,* 1963, **26,** 178–189.

Smith, A. J. Similarity of values and its relation to acceptance and the projection of similarity. *Journal of Psychology,* 1957, **43,** 251–260.

Snoek, J. D. Some effects of rejection upon attraction to a group. *Journal of Abnormal and Social Psychology,* 1962, **64,** 175–182.

Solomon, L. The influence of some types of power relationships and game strategies upon the development of interpersonal trust. *Journal of Abnormal and Social Psychology,* 1960, **61,** 223–230.

Stagner, R., and Congdon, C. S. Another failure to demonstrate displacement of aggression. *Journal of Abnormal and Social Psychology,* 1955, **51,** 695–696.

Stein, D. D., Hardyck, J. A. and Smith, M. B. Race and belief: an open and shut case. *Journal of Personality and Social Psychology,* 1965, **1,** 281–289.

Steiner, I. D., and Field, W. L. Role assignment and interpersonal influence. *Journal of Abnormal and Social Psychology,* 1960, **61,** 239–246.

Stewart, R. H. Effect of continuous responding on the order effect in personality impression formation. *Journal of Personality and Social Psychology,* 1965, **1,** 161–165.

Stotland, E., Cottrell, N. B., and Laing, G. Group interaction and perceived similarity of members. *Journal of Abnormal and Social Psychology,* 1960, **61,** 335–340.

Stotland, E., and Dunn, R. E. Identification, "oppositeness," authoritarianism, self-esteem, and birth order. *Psychological Monographs,* 1962, **76,** No. 528.

Stotland, E., and Hillmer, M. L., Jr. Identification, authoritarian defensiveness, and self-esteem. *Journal of Abnormal and Social Psychology,* 1962, **64,** 334–342.

Stotland, E., Zander, A., and Natsoulas, T. Generalization of interpersonal similarity. *Journal of Abnormal and Social Psychology,* 1961, **62,** 250–256.

Strickland, L. H. Surveillance and trust. *Journal of Personality,* 1958, **26,** 200–215.

Stritch, T. M., and Secord, P. F. Interaction effects in the perception of faces. *Journal of Personality,* 1955, **24,** 272–284.

Thibaut, J. W. An experimental study of the cohesiveness of underprivileged groups. *Human Relations,* 1950, **3,** 251–278.

Thibaut, J. W., and Coules, J. The role of communication in the reduction of interpersonal hostility. *Journal of Abnormal and Social Psychology,* 1952, **47,** 770–777.

Thibaut, J., and Riecken, H. W. Some determinants and consequences of the perception of social causality. *Journal of Personality,* 1955, **24,** 113–133.

Triandis, H. C. A note on Rokeach's theory of prejudice. *Journal of Abnormal and Social Psychology,* 1961, **62,** 184–186.

Triandis, H. C., and Fishbein, M. Cognitive interaction in person perception. *Journal of Abnormal and Social Psychology,* 1963, **67,** 446–453.

Triandis, H. C., Loh, W. D., and Levine, L. A. Race, status, quality of spoken English, and opinions about civil rights as determinants of interpersonal attitudes. *Journal of Personality and Social Psychology,* 1966, **3,** 968–972.

Valins, S. Cognitive effects of false heart-rate feedback. *Journal of Personality and Social Psychology,* 1966, **4,** 400–408.

Walster, E. The effect of self-esteem on romantic liking. *Journal of Experimental Social Psychology,* 1965, **1,** 184–197.

Walster, E., Aronson, E., and Abrahams, D. On increasing the persuasiveness of a low prestige communicator. *Journal of Experimental Social Psychology,* 1966, **2,** 325–342.

Walster, E., and Prestholdt, P. The effect of misjudging another: overcompensation or dissonance reduction? *Journal of Experimental Social Psychology,* 1966, **2,** 85–97.

Walster, E., and Walster, B. Effect of expecting to be liked on choice of associates. *Journal of Abnormal and Social Psychology,* 1963, **67,** 402–404.

Walster, E., Walster, B., Abrahams, D., and Brown, Z. The effect on liking of underrating or overrating another. *Journal of Experimental Social Psychology,* 1966, **2,** 70–84.

Weatherley, D. Anti-semitism and the expression of fantasy aggression. *Journal of Abnormal and Social Psychology,* 1961, **62,** 454–457.

Weiss, W. Scale judgments of triplets of opinion statements. *Journal of Abnormal and Social Psychology,* 1963, **66,** 471–479.

Weiss, W., and Fine, B. J. The effect of induced aggressiveness on opinion change. *Journal of Abnormal and Social Psychology,* 1956, **52,** 109–114.

Wheeler, L. S. Information seeking as a power strategy. *Journal of Social Psychology,* 1964, **62,** 125–130.

Wheeler, L. Toward a theory of behavioral contagion. *Psychological Review,* 1966, **73,** 179–192.

Wheeler, L., and Caggiula, A. R. The contagion of aggression. *Journal of Experimental Social Psychology,* 1966, **2,** 1–10.

Wheeler, L., and Smith, S. Censure of the model in the contagion of aggression. *Journal of Personality and Social Psychology,* 1967, **6,** 93–98.

Whiting, J. W. M., and Child, I. *Child Training and Personality.* New Haven, Conn.: Yale University Press, 1953.

Whyte, W. F. *Human Relations in the Restaurant Industry.* New York: McGraw-Hill, 1948.

Willis, R. H. Stimulus pooling and social perception. *Journal of Abnormal and Social Psychology,* 1960, **60,** 365–373.

Wilson, D. T. Ability evaluation, postdecision dissonance, and co-worker attractiveness. *Journal of Personality and Social Psychology,* 1965, **1,** 486–489.

Wilson, W., Chun, N., and Kayatani, M. Projection, attraction, and strategy choices in intergroup competition. *Journal of Personality and Social Psychology,* 1965, **2,** 432–435.

Wilson, W., and Miller, N. Shifts in evaluations of participants following intergroup competition. *Journal of Abnormal and Social Psychology,* 1961, **63,** 428–431.

Winch, R. F. *The Modern Family.* New York: Holt, Rinehart, and Winston, 1952.

Wishner, J. Reanalysis of "impressions of personality." *Psychological Review,* 1960, **67,** 96–112.

Wittreich, W. J., and Radcliffe, K. B., Jr. Differences in the perception of an authority figure and a nonauthority figure by Navy recruits. *Journal of Abnormal and Social Psychology,* 1956, **53,** 383–384.

Worchel, P., and McCormick, B. L. Self-concept and dissonance reduction. *Journal of Personality,* 1963, **31,** 588–599.

Worchel, P., and Schuster, S. D. Attraction as a function of the drive state. *Journal of Experimental Research in Personality,* 1966, **1,** 277–281.

Wright, G. O. Projection and displacement: a cross-cultural study of folktale aggression. *Journal of Abnormal and Social Psychology,* 1954, **49,** 523–528.

Wright, M. E. The influence of frustration upon the social relations of young children. *Character and Personality,* 1943, **12,** 111–122.

Wrightsman, L. S., Jr. Effects of waiting with others on changes in level of felt anxiety. *Journal of Abnormal and Social Psychology,* 1960, **61,** 216–222.

Zander, A., Cohen, A. R., and Stotland, E. Power and the relations among professions. In D. Cartwright (ed.), *Studies in Social Power.* Ann Arbor, Mich.: University of Michigan Press, 1959.

Zimbardo, P. G., and Formica, R. Emotional comparison and self-esteem as determinants of affiliation. *Journal of Personality,* 1963, **31,** 141–162.

PART

II

Attitude Change

Ellen Berscheid

University of Minnesota

Elaine Walster

University of Wisconsin

5

The Nature of Attitudes and Characteristics of an Attention-Getting Message

It very rarely happens that the attitudes of those around us agree entirely with our own or with the attitudes we wish them to hold. Sometimes a minor discrepancy causes us no more than niggling irritation. Indeed, we occasionally find a discrepancy between our own attitudes and those of another stimulating and provocative. But because the attitudes others hold often have serious implications for our own well-being and satisfactions, we sometimes find it disturbing that others do not feel and think as we would have them; thus we are often prompted to attempt to modify the attitudes of others and they, in turn, often attempt to persuade us to new viewpoints.

Although the problem of identifying the determinants of attitude change sometimes seems to assume a life-and-death importance in our nuclear age, it is clear that men of all ages have been interested in the discovery of techniques whereby influence could be successfully wielded. Through the years, from Aristotle's serious treatment of the problem in his *Rhetoric and Poetics* (1954) to Dale Carnegie's ebullient *How to Win Friends and Influence People* (1937), men have found a ready and enthusiastic audience for their tips on how to be persuasive. The tremendous interest people have shown in the problem of persuasion might lead us to expect that by the twentieth century we would know almost all there is to know about manipulating the minds of men. And, indeed, popular books such as Vance Packard's *The Hidden Persuaders* (1957) and newspaper accounts of Chinese Communist "brainwashing" techniques often give the impression that the Orwellian age is upon us. For those who have the illusion that contemporary psychology is in a position to offer knowledge whereby men may be made mere automatons in the hands of those versed in the science of attitude change, this chapter and the next three will prove to be immensely disappointing. For it is unfortunately true that many gaps in our knowledge remain and much more work needs to be done before we can say with confidence how attitudes are changed.

That we know as little as we do is not surprising when we consider that the first systematic and controlled experimental program in attitude change was not begun until the late 1940's. This first inquiry was conducted by Carl Hovland and his associates at Yale University. In these chapters we will review their research findings and other findings that provide insight into the determinants of attitude change. We will not often consider correlational studies, nor will we consider evaluative studies in which the only interest was in ascertaining whether or not a particular communication had an effect.

Most of the investigations we will report have focused upon determinants of attitude change in formal communication situations, such as public lectures, radio commercials, pamphlets, and the like. In these formal communication situations, the communication usually has been carefully prepared in advance of its delivery and the intended recipient of influence usually cannot talk back or argue with the communicator. Attitudes are also modified, of course, by more informal communications. In fact, evidence from surveys and field studies suggests that most attitude change is brought about by informal, spontaneous, give-and-take interactions with our friends and acquaintances (for example, Hovland, 1959; Katz and Lazarsfeld, 1955; Lipsett, Lazarsfeld, Barton, and Linz, 1954). Research in areas such as conformity, group pressure, and social comparison processes has given us a great deal of information on how attitudes are changed in such informal circumstances. As other chapters in this book deal with these important processes in detail, we will not treat them here.

The Nature of Attitudes

It might be worthwhile to consider for a moment the nature of the psychological variable that has been the focus of so much interest. Of all psychological units of analysis, attitude has had perhaps the longest and most illustrious tenure. Indeed, it has been stated that the concept of attitude is "probably the most distinctive and indispensable concept in contemporary social psychology" (Allport, 1954).

Although we all have a fairly good idea of what an attitude is, and the word is a working member of almost everyone's vocabulary, many researchers have felt constrained to offer a formal psychological definition of this term. As a consequence, there are few concepts in psychology for which the interested student will find more and varied definitions. Although this leaves some doubt about how "distinctive" the concept of attitude is, almost all these definitions have in common the notion that an attitude simply represents a person's readiness to respond toward a particular object, or class of objects, in a favorable or unfavorable manner. For example, Katz and Stotland, whose definition is perhaps the most concise and contains the essential elements of other definitions, define an attitude as "an individual's tendency or predisposition to evaluate an object or the symbol of that object in a certain way" (1959, p. 428).

The phrase "predisposition to act" appears over and over again with reference to the term attitude. What do we mean by "predisposition to act"? The phrase refers, ultimately, to the kinds of predictions that we are going to make about an individual's behavior. For example, when we say that a person has a positive attitude toward Medicare, generally what we mean is that we have some information which would lead us to predict that in appropriate situations the person will respond in a manner that would promote this program. We might predict that the person would not contribute to an American Medical Association fund-raising campaign, that he would encourage eligible citizens to sign up for the program, that he would not be a member of the John Birch society, or that he might be likely to get into arguments with those who oppose the program.

Essentially, then, when we say that we know what a person's attitude is, what we mean is that we have some bits of evidence from the person's past behavior that make us confident that we can predict his future behavior in certain situations. The phrase "predisposition to act," however, implies more than that we are using past behavior to predict future behavior. It is implicit in the phrase that these predispositions are carried around with us. They are thought to exist even when we are not thinking about the attitudinal object—when we are sleeping, for example, or when we are not in a situation that would call for any action toward the object. It is for this reason that the concept of attitude as generally defined by most psychologists falls under the category of hypothetical construct. A hypothetical construct is a process or entity that is presumed to actually exist, even though it is not directly observable.

Why have psychologists treated "attitude" as a hypothetical construct? Is it really necessary to refer to some underlying cognitive organization to predict how an individual will behave in a given situation? Why is it not enough to say that because an individual behaved in a favorable way toward an object in the past we predict that he will do the same in the future? Katz and Stotland (1959) have argued that "the term attitude has endured because the practical need for taking account of behavior calls for some stability and for some identifiable affective–cognitive elements which can be related to social behavior in social situations." Thus the concept of attitude is introduced to allow for the fact that cognitive and affective organization can achieve stability and some degree of constancy.

If attitudes have traditionally been conceived of as not being directly observable, how is it possible to study attitude change? This question brings us to the traditional distinction that has been made between attitudes and opinions. Many researchers and theoreticians have distinguished an attitude, which is a hypothetical construct that cannot be observed, from an opinion or belief, which is conceived of as being verbalizable and which may be an overt manifestation of an underlying attitude (Hovland, Janis, and Kelley, 1953). Thus, although we cannot directly observe an attitude, we can make inferences about it from verbal expressions and other overt behaviors. Verbalized opinions, in particular, often serve as indicants of attitude.

A distinction has also been made between private opinions and public verbalizations of opinion. This has been necessary because for various reasons a person may not always wish to state publicly his true private opinion. In these cases, the opinion given publicly will provide a misleading index of underlying attitude. It is for this reason that investigators of attitude change are ordinarily very careful to set up conditions under which the person's overt, or public, opinion response is likely to be identical with his covert, or private, opinion response. The experimenter must always try to minimize the subject's motivation to lie about the nature of his true feelings and beliefs.

In addition to differences in the degree to which they can be verbalized, attitudes have been thought to differ from opinions or beliefs in another way. Specifically, some investigators have conceptualized an attitude as having three components: an affective, a behavioral, and a cognitive component. Opinions have been conceptualized as having only a cognitive component. The affective component of an attitude refers to the favorable or unfavorable feelings one has toward the object. Thus the affective component of an attitude is an individual's predisposition to *evaluate* the given object as good or bad, favorable or unfavorable. The behavioral component of an attitude refers to the individual's tendency to avoid or approach the object; to *behave* in a particular manner toward it. The cognitive component of an attitude has been thought to consist of all our *thoughts* or ideas about the object, or class of objects, in question. Thus this component of an attitude would include all the opinions or beliefs held concerning that particular object.

It is true that people often state their opinions in such a way that it appears that little or no affect is involved, and we are thus often led to believe that their opinions are simply statements of what they believe the truth to be. However, when we try to change the beliefs that others hold, we see that people sometimes have a great deal of emotional investment in their beliefs. Suppose, for example, that someone in the sixteenth century had taken an opinion poll to determine whether or not people believed the earth revolved around the sun or the sun revolved around the earth. "Of course the sun revolves around the earth!" would probably have been the matter-of-fact and unemotional reply the pollster would have obtained from his respondents. Yet when Copernicus challenged this belief, the affect connected with it and its resistance to change became very clear and almost cost Copernicus his life. The belief that the sun revolved around the earth was well integrated into a number of attitudes, particularly strongly held religious attitudes. As a consequence, the challenging of this belief threatened to throw the cognitive structure of sixteenth-century man into chaos.

In thinking about attitude change and the resistance one often encounters when attempting to change attitudes, it is important to recognize that opinions or beliefs do not exist in isolation from one another. One opinion may be an important part of several attitudes, and attitudes themselves may be organized into larger value systems. Thus the modification of a single opinion may have implications for the modification of a number of other opinions, attitudes, and values. For, as we shall see, it appears that people have a strong desire for their thoughts, feelings, and behavior to be consistent and harmonious. For people of Copernicus' time it was inconsistent, and thus uncomfortable, to believe that the earth was the most important element in the universe and, at the same time, believe that the earth orbited around the sun. It was easier to attempt to discredit Copernicus' evidence than to completely reorganize all their cognitions that bore relationship to the belief that the earth was the center of the universe.

The fact that people do ordinarily wish their beliefs to be consistent with one another gives us one technique for changing attitudes. Specifically, if we can irrevocably change one element of an attitude, often the other elements of the attitude will also change to achieve consistency. An experiment performed by Rosenberg (1960) was an attempt to deal with the different components of attitude separately and to observe the effect of changing one component upon the remaining components. Rosenberg hypothesized that when the affective and the cognitive components of an attitude are inconsistent, the attitude is in an unstable state and will undergo reorganization until the individual either attains affective–cognitive consistency or represses (stops thinking about) the inconsistency. To demonstrate that a change in affect toward an object will generate a corresponding cognitive change, subjects in Rosenberg's experiment were first given an attitude questionnaire designed to measure their cognitive responses toward several different social issues. Then, to change the affective component of their attitudes, experimental subjects were hypnotized and given a suggestion of affective change for one attitude area. For example, one subject was told, "When you awake you will be very much in favor of Negroes moving into white neighborhoods. The mere idea of Negroes moving into white neighborhoods will give you a happy, exhilarated feeling. Although you will not remember the suggestion having been made, it will strongly influence your feelings after you have awakened" (1960, pp. 26, 27). After they had been brought out of their hypnotic trance, experimental subjects were once again given a questionnaire designed to obtain their opinions and beliefs about the object. Control subjects went through the same procedure with the exception that in between the two questionnaires they simply rested and were instructed to try to fall asleep. Rosenberg found that his major prediction was confirmed: cognitive reorganization did follow an induced change in affect. Subjects spontaneously changed their beliefs to bring them in line with the changed affect.

It is not always easy, however, to change the affective component of an attitude. We shall see that a more usual procedure used to produce attitude change is to attempt to change the cognitive component of an attitude, the opinions and beliefs held about the object. This is often done with the expectation that the individual, because of his desire for cognitive consistency, will of his own accord change the affective and behavioral components.

Given that any change usually disrupts a multitude of other attitudes, why should anyone go to the trouble of altering an attitude? Why, once our attitudes are formed, do we not simply maintain our existing cognitive organization? It is, after all, rather unsettling and uncomfortable to have to keep changing one's mind about the merits of the Vietnam war or of the sort of job one would like to have. Cognitions often change because most people have an overwhelming desire to keep their cognitions in line with reality. As Festinger has noted in his theory of social-comparison processes (1954), holding incorrect cognitions, or cognitions that do not correspond to reality, can be very punishing. The man who believes that a downed wire is not "hot" can be electrocuted if his belief proves to be incorrect. Only people who are institutionalized and have their needs taken care of by others can afford to think they are Napoleon at the height of his powers. The rest of us, in order to cope satisfactorily with the world, to maximize our rewards and minimize our punishments, must keep our cognitions in line with reality. Although incoming information often prompts us to modify our attitudes, reality can also be a strong source of resistance to change. It, of course, would be very difficult to convince one's neighbor that one's dog is at heart a friendly creature if the dog has bitten the neighbor several times.

Characteristics of an Attention-Getting Message

One cannot possibly pay attention to all the information that impinges on his senses. So many spokesmen for so many causes have become convinced of the effectiveness of persuasive messages that one could spend all of his time reading advertising, publicity releases, and editorials if he had a mind to. In order to have some time to go about the business of living, one must learn to ignore a great deal of irrelevant material. Thus, before we examine various properties of a message that can make it effective or ineffective, we should first consider factors that determine whether or not a message will even be noticed, and if noticed, whether or not it will be carefully considered.

Of all the possible factors that determine whether or not a message will be noticed, one has been focused on especially. Most psychologists believe that people are much more likely to be interested in information that is consistent with their beliefs than in information that challenges them. For example, Cooper and Jahoda (1947), in discussing the reactions of prejudiced persons to antiprejudice cartoons, argued that individuals "prefer not to face the implications of ideas opposed to their own so that they do not have to be forced either to defend themselves or admit error." Lipset, Lazarsfeld, Barton, and Linz (1954) state, "Most people expose themselves, most of the time, to the kind of propaganda with which they agree to begin with." Newcomb (1963) says, "One's attitude toward something is not only a result of one's previous traffic with one's environment but also a determinant of selective response to present and future events." Klapper (1949) called selective exposure "the most basic process thus far established by research on the effect of mass media" and said that the fact that people "will deliberately or unconsciously avoid material which they know questions their existing opinions has been so clearly demonstrated as to be now axiomatic in the literature on communication." The tendency to actively expose oneself to consistent information and to actively avoid inconsistent information has been called *selective exposure.*

The question we will attempt to answer in this section is "Does selective exposure exist?" Do people seek out or avoid information on the basis of its consistency with their own beliefs and attitudes? If asked, almost all psychologists would agree that people do. Unfortunately, there is not strong experimental support for this belief. The data suggest that only under special circumstances does an individual selectively expose himself to information.

There is a fair amount of nonexperimental evidence that individuals are more likely to come into *contact* with information that supports their attitudes than with information opposing them. Cartwright (1949) found that individuals who had already donated blood to the Red Cross, presumably for patriotic reasons, were also more likely to attend a patriotic film advocating the donation of blood than were non-blood donors. Schramm and Carter (1959) in a telephone survey, found that twice as many Republicans as Democrats said they watched a pro-Republican telethon. Star and Hughes (1950) found that individuals already favoring the United Nations were more likely to hear information concerning (and supporting) this organization than were individuals who disapproved of the United Nations. Hyman and Sheatsley (1947) found that in a national sample, those subjects who favored breaking relations with Franco were more likely to have read a joint statement by England, France, and the United States criticizing the government of Spain.

Although these findings do provide convincing evidence that people are especially likely to come into contact with information that supports their point of view, they do not prove that individuals are actively seeking out consistent information and go out of their way to avoid inconsistent information. All of the proceeding studies were field studies. The authors were examining the behavior of people in naturalistic situations and this means that many things besides desire for consistent information may account for the fact that Republicans hear Republican talks and that United Nations sympathizers hear advertisements for the United Nations. There is no way we can be sure that opponents of the causes were absent because they were attempting to avoid discrepant information. In all of the previous studies, variables unrelated to selective exposure may account for the correlation we find between beliefs and exposure to information. For example, perhaps the real reason Cartwright found a relationship between giving blood and being present at a movie that advocated giving blood is that individuals who had a great deal of free time were more likely both to give blood and to go to any kind of lecture, patriotic or not. Perhaps blood donors would also have overattended a lecture saying blood donation is a poor idea. Similarly, perhaps the Republicans only watched the telethon to see their Republican friends and not because they expected to hear a pro-Republican message. Finally, we know that at the time the Franco and United Nations polls were taken, well-educated people were both more likely to be aware of any propaganda campaign and to have more liberal values. Thus, perhaps they read the pro-United Nations and anti-Franco articles with great frequency only because they were more likely to read any news item than were people in the general population. Perhaps if the investigators had asked subjects if they had been exposed to an anti-United Nations or a pro-Franco article, the well-educated liberals would have been more aware of these campaigns as well. It is obvious that there are many things that could account for the preceding results: the imaginative reader will be able to come up with alternative explanations of his own.

Thus we must turn to experimental studies, in which the variables are under the control of the experimenter, in order to get a clear-cut answer to our question. When we turn to these studies, we will see that selective exposure is much less pervasive than the previous statements by psychologists would lead us to believe. When considered together, these experiments indicate that the simple belief that individuals always seek out information consistent with their own beliefs and always avoid information inconsistent with their beliefs has little basis in fact. For although some of the above studies indicate that individuals sometimes seek consistency, other studies fail to find evidence for selective exposure. A few studies, in fact, seem to indicate that individuals readily expose themselves to inconsistent information. Because these experimental studies were designed to test various derivations from the theory of cognitive dissonance (Festinger, 1957), in order to review them, we must first discuss dissonance theory.

The Theory of Cognitive Dissonance

The basic unit that the theory works with is "cognition." "Cognition" is simply a shortened way of indicating "any knowledge, opinion, or belief about the environment, about oneself, or about one's behavior." Instead of dealing with only one belief or opinion, as do most attitude theories, dissonance theory is concerned with the *relationship* that an individual's ideas have with one another. The theory states that three types of relationships between cognitions are possible: dissonance, consonance, or irrelevance. Cognitions are said to be in a *dissonant* relationship whenever they are incompatible (in Festinger's terminology, when "the obverse of one element would follow from the other"). Cognitions can be incompatible for several reasons: Cognitions can be dissonant because they contradict one another on logical grounds, in the individual's own thinking system. For example, if a person believes that war is inevitable and, at the same time, believes that we are approaching a permanent peace, he should experience dissonance. Cognitions can also be dissonant because they oppose one's past experience about the necessary relationship between objects or events. For example, if a person knows his hat has been blown off his head by a strong north wind and, at the same time, knows his hat is moving due west, he should experience dissonance. Cognitive elements are said to exist in a *consonant* relationship with each other if one element follows from another on logical or experiential grounds. Finally, cognitions can be totally *irrelevant* to one another. For example, the cognitions "Bees build hives" and "Hotel rooms never have enough coat hangers" would probably be judged by nearly everyone as totally irrelevant to one another.

According to dissonance theory, the presence of dissonance gives rise to pressures to reduce or eliminate that dissonance and to avoid the further increase of dissonance. In addition, the theory states that the more dissonance one is experiencing, the more anxious he will be to reduce it and avoid additional dissonance. These predictions have obvious implications for selective-exposure research. If no dissonance exists, a person should have no motivation to selectively expose himself to information. The more dissonance a person is already experiencing, the more pronounced the tendency should be to seek out consistent information and avoid dissonant information. Because, according to dissonance theory, the magnitude of dissonance depends on the *importance* or value of the elements in a dissonant relationship and the *number* of cognitions involved, the theory also explicitly predicts that selective exposure should be especially pronounced when the cognitions involved in a dissonant relationship are very important to an individual.

The reader will notice that whether a cognition is defined as consonant or dissonant depends on whether the individual holding the beliefs perceives them as consistent or inconsistent. In an experiment, it is obviously of crucial importance that the experimenter be able to state, unequivocably, before the experiment is run, whether the cognitions he is dealing with are in a consonant, a dissonant, or an irrelevant relationship for all his subjects. Only in that way can he design an experiment that can test his predictions. There are two different ways in which an experimenter can attempt to certify that the cognitions he is working with are uniformly classified as either consonant or dissonant by subjects. First, he can describe the two cognitions and ask each subject if a person would be consistent, inconsistent, or neither one nor the other if he believed both statements. The cognitions would then be classified on the basis of each subject's report. Or the experimenter could do what is commonly done: he could choose cognitions he felt everyone would agree are in a certain relationship. To a large extent in any culture, individuals have learned the same rules of logic and have had many of the same basic experiences. Thus, an experimenter can almost always think up cognitive pairs that virtually all subjects would classify as consonant, dissonant, or irrelevant. If an experimenter relies on "obviousness of classification," his research is, of course, open to the charge that the cognitive pairs were misclassified. If, however, a critic felt a classification was incorrect, he would only have to test subjects' perceptions of the relationship of the cognitions involved to either support his criticism or the experimenter's assumption.

We can now turn to the selective-exposure studies that have been conducted by various dissonance researchers. The design of the study by Mills, Aronson, and Robinson (1959) is typical of that used in many of the selective-exposure studies. The authors tested the hypothesis that after making a dissonance-producing decision, individuals would prefer information supporting that decision to information challenging it. This hypothesis was tested in the following way: As part of a course, the experimenters allowed students to choose whether they would prefer to take an essay examination or an objective examination. Subjects in some groups believed their choice was a crucial one (that their score on the examination would count 70 per cent of their grade.) Others believed the choice was an unimportant one (that their score would only count 5 per cent of their grade). After the students' choices were collected and it was made clear that their decisions were irrevocable, they were asked to indicate which one of six articles they would prefer to read. Students indicated their preferences by ranking the six articles. The titles presented to students were of two types. In the "positive-information condition" it was clear that all six articles would give reasons in favor of whichever examination the article discussed. In the "negative-information condition" it was clear from the titles that the articles would oppose the examination discussed. Mills et al. expected that after making his choice, a subject would be more eager to read an article giving positive information about the type of examination he chose than one giving positive information about the type of examination he rejected, and more eager to read an article giving negative information about the type of examination he rejected than one giving negative information about the type of examination he chose. In addition, they predicted that the more important the exam was, the more pronounced these tendencies would be.

As predicted by dissonance theory, subjects did seem more predisposed to choose to read positive information about their examination choice than positive information about the rejected examination. However, contrary to prediction, they did not seem to prefer negative information about the rejected examination to negative information about their examination choice. Articles giving negative information about the examination one had chosen were preferred just as often as articles giving negative information about the examination rejected. The importance of the decision did not have a significant effect on the tendency to select supportive information.

The authors attempted to explain these results in terms of the combined operation of two different tendencies: the tendency to prefer information supporting the choice (selective exposure) and the tendency to seek more information about the chosen alternative. For the articles giving positive information about the particular examination, both tendencies should operate in the same direction and yield a strong preference for articles about the chosen examination. For the articles giving negative information, the two tendencies should work in opposite directions and could have cancelled each other so that there was no preference one way or the other. The finding that positive information about the chosen examination was preferred to positive information about the rejected examination was replicated by Rosen (1961).

Experimental studies investigating selective exposure have also been conducted by Adams (1961), Freedman (1965a; 1965b), Freedman and Sears (1963; 1965b), Jecker (1964), Lowin (1967), Mills and Ross (1964), and Sears (1965; 1966). The results of these studies are inconsistent; in fact, they lead Freedman and Sears (1965a) to conclude that "acceptance of the selective-exposure hypothesis should at least be suspended." Though people do not seem, most of the time, to select information mainly on the basis of whether or not it agrees with their own position, it is understandably difficult for psychologists to abandon the selective-exposure hypothesis. Even Freedman and Sears, who argue for suspension of the hypothesis, admit that ". . . the selective-exposure hypothesis seems too plausible to be completely incorrect. We seem to derive pleasure from having our opinions supported, and pain from having them attacked; and it seems only reasonable that most of us would try to arrange things so that we can maximize pleasure and minimize pain" (1965a, p. 91).

Mills (1968) takes the position that the current evidence concerning interest in supporting and discrepant information "warrants the conclusion that people tend to seek out supporting information and avoid discrepant information." He points out that when evaluating evidence concerning the hypothesis that people tend to prefer supporting information, it is necessary to keep in mind that there are many other factors that affect exposure to information. He notes that if, for example, men would rather read discrepant material containing pictures of beautiful women than supporting material without such pictures, this would not provide evidence against the hypothesis. Mills discusses additional factors that could explain the results of the studies that apparently show a preference for discrepant information. He also reviews studies by Brock (1965a), Brock and Balloun (1967), Lowin (1967), and Mills (1965a, 1965b) showing that supporting information is preferred to discrepant information that have appeared since Freedman and Sears's review. Because the selective exposure hypothesis seems so reasonable, it is likely that psychologists will keep trying to pinpoint factors that make individuals especially likely to seek support. We will now discuss some of the promising directions being taken by selective-exposure researchers.

One very compelling explanation advanced to explain the failures to demonstrate selective exposure is the suggestion that the existing studies do not really test the hypothesis that when given a chance to avoid discrepant information, an individual will do so. The argument goes that in most of the selective-exposure experiments, individuals did not have a chance to discreetly avoid information conflicting with their attitudes or decisions. In all of the experiments, the material was labeled in such a way that it was clear to subjects that some articles would support their beliefs and others would challenge them. Unfortunately, this labeling provided subjects with information, as well as allowing them to make a choice. Specifically, the labeling informed subjects of the existence of material (of unknown content) that would challenge their beliefs. Festinger (1964) makes the point that when a subject is faced with the information that challenging materials exist, there are two things he can do: (1) He can admit to himself that he probably cannot handle the information said to conflict with his beliefs, and he can avoid it. This is obviously not a very satisfactory solution. (2) He can seek out the challenging information in the hope of being able to refute it. Festinger (1964), and Freedman (1965a) have argued that the exposure to discrepant information that has been secured in some experiments may simply be a demonstration that subjects are choosing to expose themselves to challenging information in the hope of refuting it. They argue that the experimental arrangements really did not allow subjects to avoid dissonant material entirely.

If this argument is correct, it implies three things: (1) Strangely enough, the proposal suggests that a person might be more likely to avoid information that merely *threatened* to be discrepant than information that clearly was in opposition to his own point of view. When faced with ambiguously titled material, it might be possible to distort the probable content of the article, to assume the material was not really challenging, and thereby avoid all dissonance by avoiding the article. With unambiguously labeled material, such distortion is not possible. The title alone introduces dissonance. Thus, although one could choose to avoid ambiguous material without admitting to himself that he was afraid of the information, if one avoids an unambiguous challenge he must accept the knowledge that dissonant information exists. (2) The type of person who has little confidence in his refutational abilities should be especially likely to avoid discrepant information, because he may not be sure he has the skills to refute arguments. (3) The less sure one is of his own position, the more likely he should be to avoid discrepant information, and the less likely he should be to seek it out in the expectation of refuting it. A person committed to a position he believes to be weak should have less expectation that the discrepant information will be refutable. There is no evidence for or against the first proposal. Tentative information concerning the last two proposals will be discussed in the following section.

The Effect of Confidence in One's Own Abilities and Position

According to folklore, at certain stages of life we are more willing to look at information that conflicts with the conventional points of view (which we share) than we are at other stages. For example, we know from several widely publicized disputes on academic freedom that college students often seem to be quite willing, even eager, to expose themselves to ideas that are in opposition to their own strongly held beliefs. More mature townspeople, on the other hand, are often shocked that "unacceptable" information is disseminated in the interests of education. A recent example of such a student–community split is provided by the furor that arose over the issue of academic freedom in Minnesota in 1964–65. In a humorous commentary on freedom of speech, Mulford Q. Sibley, who had been voted Professor of the Year at the University of Minnesota, wrote a letter to the Minnesota Daily: "We need students who challenge the orthodoxies. American culture is far too monolithic for its own good. Personally, I should like to see on the campus one or two communist professors, a students communist club, a chapter of the American Association for the Advancement of Atheism, a Society for the Promotion of Free Love, a League for the Overthrow of Government by Jeffersonian Violence (LOGJV), an Anti-Automation League, and perhaps a Nudist Club. No university should be without individuals and groups like these." Evidently the foregoing letter was written tongue-in-cheek, because Sibley subsequently declined to be the faculty sponsor of a "Stark Naked" club on the Minnesota campus. However, the reaction of many townspeople and legislators indicated they were not amused. They called Sibley a communist, a corruptor of youth, and an immoral teacher who should be discharged. Students, on the other hand, wore buttons cheering Sibley's stand.

College students preferred to think that their willingness to expose themselves to new information was evidence of the fact that young people are more open-minded and objective than their elders. This may be, but there are also other possible explanations of the students' greater "open-mindedness." Perhaps the students were more willing to listen to discrepant information, not because they were really more open-minded, but simply because they had great confidence in their ability to refute any discomforting information that might emerge. There is no evidence that college students are more objective than their elders; there is, however, evidence that individuals with a great deal of confidence in their own intellectual abilities are more willing to expose themselves to discrepant information than are their less confident counterparts.

Some evidence on this issue is provided by an experiment conducted by Canon (1964). He tested the hypothesis that a confident person would be more willing to expose himself to dissonant arguments than would a person with little confidence. Canon varied confidence in the following way: Subjects were asked to read three business case studies, illustrating actual business problems, and to recommend the best possible solution to each problem. After the subject had made a recommendation for each problem, the experimenter told him whether he was right or wrong. The feedback the experimenter gave the subject did not depend on whether the subject's recommendation was really correct or not, but rather on whether Canon wanted the subject to have high confidence or low confidence in his intellectual abilities. If the subject was assigned to the high-confidence condition, he was told that he had chosen the correct solution to each case. Subjects in the low-confidence condition were informed that although their recommendations had been correct on the first case, in the second and third cases they had chosen incorrect alternatives. These subjects were also told that the majority of the other students in their group had chosen correct solutions. All subjects were then asked to make a recommendation for a fourth case study, but this time the subject was given no information as to whether or not his solution was correct. Finally, all subjects were given a chance to indicate how much interest they had in reading each of five articles. From the title of the articles, it was clear that two of them would support the subject's choice, two of the articles would oppose the choice, and one of the articles would be neutral. When we examine Canon's data, we see that the subjects with little confidence in their own abilities were less willing to expose themselves to discrepant information than were subjects with high confidence.

There are three possible ways in which Canon's highly confident subjects might have differed from those of lesser confidence: (1) They probably believed their good performance demonstrated they were more intelligent than others. (2) Because their solutions had always been correct previously, their best guess was that they had chosen the correct solution for case 4. Thus, high-confidence subjects may have had little dissonance about their choice. (3) Because they probably believed their solution to be the correct one, they probably expected articles opposing that solution to be weak.

Because the confidence manipulation in this experiment may have affected these three things, we do not know what Canon's data demonstrate. Perhaps they demonstrate that an individual will confront discrepant information when he has confidence in his refutation ability. Perhaps they demonstrate that an individual, regardless of his refutation abilities, will expose himself to discrepant information when he is confident that his opinion is correct or that discrepant information will be weak. Any of these conclusions is possible from the data, all would be interesting, and all follow from the Festinger–Freedman formulation. Unfortunately, a subsequent replication by Freedman (1965a) failed to repeat the Canon results.

There is some other evidence suggesting that even if subjects in all conditions believe that the opposing articles will contain arguments of the same potential effectiveness (and thus all would be equally dissonance-arousing), people who are confident that the dissonant arguments will be successfully refuted will be more willing to read the challenging articles than people who believe that, though a refutation exists, they will probably not be able to think of it. Walster (1963) varied confidence in the following way: A number of housewives were invited to discuss articles concerning religion. In one condition, subjects believed that they would have a discussion partner and that he would be a very knowledgeable person. In the other three conditions, subjects thought their partner would have medium knowledge, little knowledge, or that they would have no partner at all. In each condition, the subject knew that all three potential partners existed and that all three of them agreed with her on the religious issue. The only difference between groups was in who each subject believed *her* partner would be. Walster expected that the subject would feel she stood a better chance of refuting opposing information if her partner was knowledgeable than if she had a less knowledgeable partner or no partner at all. Then subjects were asked to decide whether they wished to discuss an article supporting or an article opposing their religious beliefs. Walster proposed that the more confidence a person had that her partner would be able to refute opposing arguments, the more likely she would be to choose to expose herself to dissonant information. The data supported this hypothesis. The more knowledgeable the subject's partner was, the less likely she was to avoid dissonant material concerning religious beliefs.

An experiment by Lowin (1967) also tested the hypothesis that people are more likely to expose themselves to dissonant material if they anticipate that it will be easy to refute it. However, instead of varying subject confidence as have previous experimenters, Lowin varied the refutability of dissonant or consonant statements. Lowin's prediction concerning *exposure* to dissonant material rests on a theoretical base very similar to an earlier prediction of Jones and Kohler (1958) concerning the *learning* of dissonant material. Jones and Kohler hypothesized that one's attitudes affect his ability to learn various passages. They suggested that the kinds of argument a person would find especially easy (and satisfying) to remember would depend both on the plausibility of the argument and on the consonance of the argument with his own position. They proposed that it would be easier to learn plausible arguments supporting one's own position than opposing one's position, and easier to learn implausible arguments opposing one's own position than supporting one's position. They pointed out that a ludicrously poor argument by one's opposition is something one wants to remember and that an implausible argument by well-intentioned but unintelligent supporters of one's own position is something one would probably rather forget. It is very comforting to believe that all the wise men are on your side and all the fools are with the opposition. An experiment provided clear support for these predictions. Unfortunately, Waly and Cook (1966) report three failures to replicate the Jones and Kohler findings.

To understand Lowin's proposal, one need merely substitute "exposure to a message" for "learning of a message." Lowin suggests that if messages appear to be difficult to refute, an individual will prefer to expose himself to consonant arguments rather than dissonant ones. The more difficult refutation appears to be, the more pronounced this tendency should be. On the other hand, if the messages appear to be very flimsy and extremely easy to refute, an individual will prefer to expose himself to dissonant than to consonant arguments. Like Jones and Kohler, Lowin feels that the foolishness of your enemies provides more delight than the follies of your friends.

Lowin tested his hypothesis on political partisans, during the Johnson–Goldwater presidential campaign. In a pretest, Lowin selected political statements that were extremely difficult or extremely easy to refute. These statements had been made by political sources varying in "liberalness" from Communist Party publications to the Patrick Henry League, a right-wing organization. Then Lowin made up four kinds of pamphlets. All of these were described as coming from a political organization seeking support for its candidate. Half of the time the candidate was said to be Johnson, half of the time Goldwater. The sample arguments included in the pamphlets also varied in plausibility. Half of the brochures supporting each candidate contained statements that were very easy to refute, and half contained statements that were very compelling. The brochure concluded by asking students to send in their request for additional free information. All versions of these especially prepared booklets were then sent to both Johnson or Goldwater supporters.

Lowin's predictions were confirmed. When the sample booklets contained arguments difficult to refute, a request for additional material more often came from those receiving consonant pamphlets than from those receiving dissonant ones. More requests came from those receiving a weak dissonant booklet than from those receiving a strong dissonant one, and more requests from those receiving a strong consonant one than a strong dissonant one. Most important, additional material was more often desired by those receiving easily refuted dissonant arguments than those receiving easily refuted consonant arguments.

A second experiment, however, did not replicate this finding. Experiment II differed in several ways from Experiment I: (1) Instead of coming from a partisan group, desiring to influence readers, the booklets were said to come from a nonpartisan group, which was not interested in promoting any one candidate. (2) Instead of six easily refuted (or difficult to refute) arguments, each sample booklet contained only one such argument. (3) In Experiment I subjects received only one sample booklet and had their choice of ordering or not ordering additional material. In Experiment II they were given samples of all eight versions of the brochure and they were told they could order any four they wished.

Lowin notes that the first two changes may have weakened his manipulation. Subjects in Experiment II may not have been sure that the additional material would have the same source and strength or weakness of content as the sample material. In addition, he notes that the third change may have made subjects in Experiment II more aware than subjects in Experiment I of the bias they would be exhibiting if they preferred entirely supportive information. Experiment II does seem, in several respects, to be a weaker test of Lowin's hypothesis than Experiment I.

One final study is relevant to our discussion. One of the main ways that people can become informed about positions very different from their own is to associate with people with very dissimilar values, interests, occupations and life histories. Because such association may produce dissonance as well as information, it is generally proposed that one reason individuals often avoid exposing themselves to others who are dissimilar is because they fear the divergent opinions and beliefs that others might provide. However, it is possible that individuals fear to approach dissimilar strangers for quite another reason; perhaps they fear that dissimilar strangers will not like them. When people are very different from ourselves their social standards are unclear to us. One is likely to be afraid that his own behavior will be unacceptable, since he is not quite sure how he is expected to behave. The gentlemanly Proust (1928), for example, expressed a fear that "boors and bounders," unaware of society's rules, would underrate *his* social value. It is probably more usual for one to be afraid of being rejected by those superior to himself. If fear of rejection is an important reason why people avoid dissimilar strangers (and in consequence, unfamiliar information), we would expect that people who have little fear of social rejection would more often expose themselves to dissonant information than do more fearful people. Thus, once again, we would expect subjects with little confidence in their own abilities (this time their social abilities) to be less likely to be exposed to challenging sources than confident people.

Evidence that fear of not being liked is an important factor in making individuals unwilling to interact with dissimilar strangers is found in Walster and Walster (1963). These authors allowed individuals to choose with which of several discussion groups they would like to discuss an issue. One of the discussion groups was composed of college sophomores who had just taken Psychology 1; this group was obviously made up of people very like the subjects themselves. The members of the remaining groups were very dissimilar to the subjects; these groups included married high school students, researchers from a Veteran's hospital who were working on dream research, and factory workers. These groups undoubtedly seemed more unusual and more interesting to the subjects than did the college-student group. It was proposed that students would be more willing to associate with dissimilar strangers (and to expose themselves to dissonance) if they lost their fear of being disliked. Thus, subjects' expectations of being liked or concerns about being disliked were experimentally manipulated.

In the "assured about being liked" groups, subjects were instructed that they would be introduced to whichever group they chose in a way that would greatly increase their chances of being liked. Specifically, they were told they would be introduced in the following manner: "For various reasons (insert your name) is undoubtedly the kind of person you will like extremely much even on such a brief acquaintance." Subjects in the other two conditions were made to feel concerned about whether or not they would be liked. This was done in two ways: (1) In the "fear of being disliked" groups, subjects were told that they would be introduced as follows: "For various reasons (insert your name) is probably *not* the kind of person you will like on such a brief acquaintance; even so, this is a good chance to gain an understanding of the kind of person you would not usually choose as a friend." (2) In the "concerned about being disliked" groups, students were simply told that it was extremely important for them to consider how the members of each of the five groups would feel about them personally, as it was best to choose a group that would respond to them in a friendly way. Finally, a group of control subjects was run. No mention was made to these subjects as to how they would be introduced.

All subjects were then asked to indicate in which group they would like to participate. The confidence manipulation did significantly effect group choice. Subjects who were concerned about being disliked chose one of the three dissimilar groups only 45 per cent of the time; the "fear of being disliked" subjects chose a dissimilar group 57 per cent of the time; 63 per cent of the control subjects and 79 per cent of the "assured of being liked" group chose a dissimilar discussion group. The data from this study suggest that individuals will often avoid dissimilar others, not necessarily (or only) because they fear the ideas the others will promote, but because they fear the others' rejection. Reassurance about being liked may increase one's tendency to expose himself to ideas in opposition to his own.

From the foregoing research on selective exposure, we can draw the following conclusion: In spite of the intuitive appeal that such a proposal has, the evidence does not support the conclusion that most people seek out consistent and avoid inconsistent information most of the time. It seems that such avoidance is apparent only under certain circumstances—for example, when a person has little confidence in his own abilities or opinions.

CHAPTER

6

Characteristics of a Compelling Communicator

Over 2,000 years ago, Aristotle wrote that "Persuasion is achieved by the speaker's personal character when the speech is so spoken as to make us think him credible. We believe good men more fully and more readily than others." (1954, p. 24). What characteristics of the communicator are likely to make him believed "more fully and more readily"? Research relevant to this question extends back to the infancy of social psychology.

Early psychologists were primarily concerned with demonstrating that people would accept communications, even in the absence of logical reasons for doing so, simply because the communication had been advocated by a prestigious source (for example, Bowden, Caldwell, and West, 1934; Lewis, 1931; Lorge, 1936). This research was generally performed within the framework of the doctrine of "suggestion" that reigned during the early years of social psychology. These early psychologists' concept of suggestion was very similar to our concept of hypnotism, and, in fact, some early writers felt that the suggestive process was identical with the hypnotic process. Because the first social psychologists were very much interested in studying the behavior of people in crowds and phenomena such as "mob hysteria," the concept of suggestion had great explanatory appeal to them.

Early theorists hypothesized that any person who possessed prestige could cause people to "submit" to his communications, in the absence of logically adequate grounds, much as a hypnotized person submits to the commands of the person who has hypnotized him. These investigators were not so much interested in identifying the characteristics of communicators who possessed the ability to influence others as they were in simply demonstrating that a suggestion phenomenon existed. They felt that evidence that communicator prestige could radically affect acceptance of a communication would provide support for their theory of prestige suggestion. Arnett, Davidson, and Lewis (1931), for example, stated that increased communication acceptance due to the attribution of the communication to experts could be " . . . best explained by the notion of 'prestige' and its power to cause people to become more suggestible." Similarly, Bowden, Caldwell, and West (1934) explained the effect by noting that " . . . suggestion entered in and dulled to a considerable extent the critical abilities of the students."

Several investigators subsequently took exception to the contention that such evidence supported the doctrine of prestige suggestion (for example, Asch, 1948; Lewis, 1941). Asch charged that the influence of a prestigious person was not as immediate, direct, and irrational as had been previously stated. He pointed out that the operation of prestige may be mediated by the fact that identification of the communicator changes the subject's perception of the *content* of the communication.

Asch demonstrated the existence of such a mediating process in the following way: He presented the same communication to all subjects but attributed it to two different sources. For example, to some subjects the following quotation was attributed to Harry Bridges (a well-known labor leader at that time); to other subjects the source of this same quotation was said to be Eric A. Johnston (at that time president of the U.S. Chamber of Commerce):

> Only the wilfully blind can fail to see that the old style capitalism of a primitive freebooting period is gone forever. The capitalism of complete laissez-faire, which thrived on low wages and maximum profits for minimum turnover, which rejected collective bargaining and fought against justified public regulation of the competitive process, is a thing of the past. (1948, p. 255)

Subjects were then asked to indicate the meaning of the communication. Asch was indeed able to demonstrate that the meaning of the communication to the subjects changed in line with the characteristics of the communicator. Asch found that when the quotation above was attributed to Bridges, "the content of the passage turned into an expression of the accomplishments of labor in the face of opposition from capital" (p. 257). When, however, the quotation was attributed to Johnston, the content was seen as a "perspective of policy in the interest of business, especially of 'enlightened' business" (p. 257). Asch concluded that the case for the doctrine of suggestion had not been proven, that the prestige suggestion studies did not deal with the process they were presumably studying— that of blind suggestion of prestige.

Recent work on communicator characteristics and attitude change has continued to focus primarily on an analysis of psychological processes mediating knowledge of the source of the communication and subsequent attitude change.

Expertness and Trustworthiness

Hovland and his associates at Yale University hypothesized that there are two primary communicator characteristics that affect the extent to which a communication is accepted by an audience: (1) the "expertness" of the communicator, or the extent to which the recipient believes that the communicator is capable of transmitting valid statements, and (2) the "trustworthiness" of the communicator, or the degree of confidence the recipient has in the communicator's intent to communicate the assertions he considers most valid (Hovland, Janis, and Kelley, 1953). They felt that the impact of a communicator's assertions would depend on both his expertness and trustworthiness. Their combined value was referred to as the "credibility" of the communicator.

Perhaps the best-known study on communicator credibility is one conducted by Hovland and Weiss (1951). In this experiment four identical communications were presented to two groups. To one group the source was identified as one of high credibility (credibility ratings of various sources had been determined by pretest); in the other group the communication was attributed to a source of low credibility. These sources differed both in trustworthiness and in expertness. Opinion questionnaires were administered before the communication was presented, immediately after, and a month after the communication.

When the amount of attitude change produced by the highly credible communicators was compared to that produced by the less credible communicators, it was found that immediately after the communication, opinion change in the direction advocated by the communicator occurred significantly more often when the communication originated from a high-credibility source than when from a low one. In addition, the investigators found that when the communication was attributed to a highly credible source the communication was perceived to be more fair and the conclusions were felt to be more justified by the facts presented in the communication. Hovland and Weiss did not find differences in recall of the communication for different communicator credibility groups. Thus it seems unlikely that their results were due to the possibility that those in the high-credibility groups paid more attention to the communication, learned it better, and thus changed their attitudes more than the low-credibility groups.

There was, however, one exception to the general effect of high credibility producing more opinion change. One communication dealt with the question of whether or not TV would decrease the number of operating movie theaters and was attributed either to *Fortune* magazine (the highly credible source) or to a woman movie gossip columnist (the less credible source). Hovland and Weiss found that a greater percentage of subjects changed their opinion in the direction of the communication when it was attributed to the movie columnist than when it was attributed to *Fortune* magazine. Such a finding appears perplexing until one considers that the credibility ratings of the sources were obtained from pretest subjects who were asked to rate the general trustworthiness of the sources, and not to rate their trustworthiness relative to a given topic. Therefore, it is reasonable to speculate that although *Fortune* had greater general or abstract credibility, the movie columnist had greater specific credibility, with respect to the specific topic of movie theaters. We shall have occasion later to again refer to the point that one can more accurately predict a communicator's influence if one knows not simply his abstract credibility but his credibility with respect to a specific communication topic.

A startling finding emerged from the experiment by Hovland and Weiss. When attitudes were remeasured four weeks after the communication, the differential effectiveness of the communicators disappeared. This was due to two separate effects: (1) There was a decrease in the effectiveness of the high-credibility source with the passage of time. (2) During the same period there was increased acceptance of the position advocated by the low-credibility source. This second effect had been observed before in a correlational study done by Hovland, Lumsdaine, and Sheffield (1949). These investigators found that some opinion changes in the direction of the communicator's opinion were larger after a lapse of time than immediately after the communication. They called this the "sleeper effect." The term is now used to refer to both the increase in effectiveness of a low credibility source over time and the decrease in effectiveness of a high credibility source.

Kelman and Hovland (1953) also secured a sleeper effect in an experiment similar to the Hovland and Weiss study. They obtained opinion-change data immediately after the communication and three weeks later. Again, although the credibility of the source influenced opinion change when attitude change was measured immediately after the communication, an alternative form of the attitude scale administered three weeks later revealed no differences between the experimental groups. As in the Hovland and Weiss experiment, after a period of time there had been a decrease in acceptance of the communication for those exposed to the highly credible communicator and a slight increase for those exposed to the source with low credibility.

Hovland, Lumsdaine, and Sheffield proposed an explanation for their sleeper effect. The communicator in their experiment was of somewhat low credibility. Individuals were undoubtedly suspicious of the motives of their low-credibility communicator. As a consequence, on first hearing his arguments they might have discounted his message and thus evidenced little or no immediate change in opinion. With the passage of time, however, it may have been easier to remember and accept *what* was communicated than to remember *who* communicated it. As a result, after the passage of time, they may then have been more inclined to agree with the position that had been presented by the low-credibility communicator.

Although in the Hovland and Weiss study there is evidence that the subjects were able, when asked, to recall both the original source and the content, these authors also suggest that with the passage of time there may be a decrease in the tendency to "associate spontaneously" the content with the source. Thus the inhibiting effect of the low-credibility communicator and the facilitating effect of the high-credibility communicator upon communication acceptance would disappear with the passage of time. In partial support of this idea, Kelman and Hovland found that when they reestablished the association of source and content at a later time, there was a resulting reappearance of the original differences in the degree to which the communications of high- and low-credibility sources were accepted.

In the previous studies it was proposed that a low-credibility source caused subjects to initially discount the communication, and that the discounting factor was forgotten more rapidly than the content on which the opinions were based. Weiss (1953) proposed that discounting produced in another way should also produce a sleeper effect. In order not to prejudice the initial acceptance of the content, or the learning of the communication, the discounting factor in his experiment was introduced after the learning was completed. After one group, the "nondiscounted" group, had learned the communication, the communication session was terminated. The "discounted group" was given a brief countercommunication designed to arouse an attitude to discount or inhibit the acceptance of the prior learning, immediately after the communication. Specifically, they were told that recently completed experimentation resulted in evidence completely contradicting the conclusions contained in the communication. Control subjects did not receive any message. Opinions of the subjects were assessed prior to the communication, immediately after, two weeks after, and six weeks after the communication. Different subgroups from each of the three main experimental groups were retested at each of the three postexperimental time intervals.

The results indicated that the discounting treatment was immediately effective in reducing the extent of opinion change evidenced by the discounted group. However, with the delay period of six weeks, the differential loss of effectiveness was significantly less for the discounted group. Thus we may conclude that a type of sleeper effect occurred. The nature of this effect was, however, somewhat different from that observed in the Hovland and Weiss study. It will be recalled that in the Hovland and

Weiss study the less credible sources produced *greater* opinion change after one month than immediately after, and the effect of high-credibility sources was *less* after one month than immediately after. In the Weiss study, however, the effect of the communication on *both* experimental groups was greatest immediately after the communication was read. Opinion change produced by both communications decreased with the passage of time. However, opinion change produced by the low-credibility source decreased less than that produced by the high-credibility source. Thus a sleeper effect was evidenced only as a differential loss in the effectiveness of the communication from the immediate to the later retest periods. Evidently the forgetting of the discounting material allowed the communication to have delayed increment.

There seems to be a good deal of evidence that communicator credibility maximally affects the amount of opinion change immediately after the communication. It is clear that the potency of trustworthiness and expertness as a determinant of attitude change is affected by the extent to which the subject remembers the source. There are other factors that affect communicator credibility. Hovland and Mandell (1952), for example, also varied the trustworthiness of the communicator and obtained unexpected results. In this experiment the low-credibility communicator was introduced as a person who had something to gain if the content of his communication was accepted. The high-credibility communicator, on the other hand, was introduced as a highly impartial source who would profit nothing personally from having his conclusions accepted by the audience. Again the subjects were asked to give their opinions on the issue before and after the communication. As predicted, investigators found that the less trustworthy communicator was perceived by the subjects as having done a poorer job of giving the facts relevant to his conclusions and as less fair and honest in presenting the sides of the problem than the highly credible communicator. Thus differential perception of the communicator's motives influenced judgments both of his presentation and of the communication content. Surprisingly enough, however, the investigators found that subsequent differences in opinion change produced by the two communicators were quite small, and in all instances there was at least a little opinion change in the direction advocated by the communication. Thus the investigators confirmed their first prediction, but left the latter (that if the communicator is perceived by the audience as having something to gain by communication acceptance, less opinion change will be effected) unconfirmed. The finding that even a communicator of low credibility will produce some opinion change is a frequent one in communication studies.

As well as arguing that a communicator becomes less trustworthy when he advocates a position in his own interests, it also can be argued that when he delivers a communication that is against his own best interests, he raises his credibility and thus also raises the effectiveness of his communication. This hypothesis was tested by Walster, Aronson, and Abrahams (1966). Specifically they hypothesized that a communicator will be seen as more credible and will be more effective when arguing for a position opposed to his interests than when arguing for a position obviously in his own best interests. To test this hypothesis the investigators exposed one group of subjects to a communication delivered by a high-prestige communicator (a prosecuting attorney) arguing for his own interests; another group to a low-prestige communicator (a criminal, "Joe the Shoulder") arguing for his own interests; a third group of subjects were exposed to the high-prestige source advocating a position opposed to his own interests; and a fourth group of experimental subjects were exposed to a communication delivered by the low-prestige communicator arguing against his own interests.

Two control groups were also run. In one control group subjects were told that they would later be reading an article by the low-prestige communicator; in the other control group subjects were told that they would be reading an article by the high prestige communicator. Both control groups answered the attitude questions before reading the communication. Information provided by these control groups indicated that the subjects did perceive that one of the communications was in the prosecutor's best interest, and the other in the criminal's best interest.

The results of this study supported the hypothesis. The source of the communication and the content of the communication interacted in determining communication effectiveness. Regardless of their abstract prestige (or, in other words, their prestige isolated from a particular communication content)—the sources increased their credibility (and effectiveness) by advocating positions opposed to their own best interests and decreased their credibility by advocating positions that were obviously self-interested. When the communicator advocated changes opposed to his own interests, he was perceived as more expert, more honest, and more influential than when he advocated opinions congruent with his own interests.

Intention to Persuade

Another aspect of the communicator's trustworthiness that has received a great deal of attention is the extent to which the communicator is perceived by the communicatee as having a definite intention to persuade. The general hypothesis has been that when a communicator is perceived as having a definite intention to persuade his audience, the likelihood is increased that he will be perceived as having something to gain and hence as being less worthy of trust. Being less trustworthy, he therefore should be less successful in effecting attitude change. It has been thought that a defensive mental set mediates this effect. When an individual knows the communicator is going to try to change his opinions, it seems reasonable that he will set up a critical and defensive mental set that will interfere with his acceptance of the influence attempt (Lazarsfeld, Berelson, and Gaudet, 1944).

A second, but very similar, hypothesis has been advanced: It has been reasoned that if the audience knows that the communicator will present a communication opposed to their own views, they should be less influenced than if they had not been informed of the nature of the communication. This should be true whether or not the communicator is perceived as having a definite intention to change their opinions on the matter. Because the same process, a critical and defensive mental attitude induced by the forewarning of the content of the communication, is thought to mediate this effect as well as that discussed above, we will discuss evidence pertaining to both these hypotheses together.

One of the first experiments performed in this area was conducted by Ewing (1942). Ewing's communicator led one group of subjects to expect that his communication would disagree with their own positions on an issue, and led a second group of subjects to believe that it would agree with their positions. Actually, the same communication was presented to both groups, and the position taken in the communication was such that it always disagreed with the subjects' positions. Ewing found that when subjects expected the communication to agree with their positions, even though the communication in actuality disagreed, they showed more attitude change than did subjects who expected the communication to disagree.

What evidence is there that a critical and defensive mental attitude prevented attitude change on the part of the subjects who expected disagreement? Ewing found that there was a tendency for memory of the communication to be poorer in the group expecting disagreement. He also found that the communication was more likely to be perceived as biased in the group that expected disagreement.

Allyn and Festinger (1961) attempted to investigate the exact nature of the means by which a person who expects the communicator to disagree is able to resist the effects of the attempted persuasion. Working within the framework of dissonance theory, these investigators hypothesized that if the conditions of exposure to the communication are such as to guarantee attentiveness (a factor that was uncontrolled in the Ewing study), the same amount of dissonance is introduced by the communication whether or not the person is prepared for it. The authors reasoned that the effect of preparedness would be to affect the particular mechanism used to reduce the dissonance. Specifically, preparedness would determine whether the person changed his opinion or whether he rejected the communicator. Allyn and Festinger argued that if a person anticipates hearing a communication that will disagree with his own opinion, he may enter the communication situation with suspicion and hostility. Therefore, his first reaction would be to reject the communicator. They predicted that if a person was not forewarned, the person would reduce his dissonance by changing his opinion.

To test their hypothesis all subjects were presented with a communication that was opposed to their own opinions. Prior to the communication, one group was given an orientation to attend to the communicator's opinion. They were informed of his topic and his point of view in advance, and they were told that they would be asked to give their opinions on the issue discussed in the communication afterwards. The other group was given an orientation to evaluate the speaker's personality. They were not told in advance the topic of the speech or the speaker's point of view, but instead were told that they would be asked their opinions of the speaker's personality after they had heard the communication.

Allyn and Festinger found that subjects who were forewarned of the nature of the communication, and who were asked to attend carefully to his speech because they were going to be asked their own opinions on the issue, changed their opinions less, and rejected the communicator as biased to a greater degree, than those subjects who were unprepared. The authors also found, however, that the entire difference in attitude change between the two experimental conditions was attributable to those subjects for whom the persuasive communication introduced the most dissonance—those for whom there was the greatest discrepancy between their own position and that of the communicator's.

In the Allyn and Festinger study the two experimental groups differed both in the extent to which they were prepared for an opposing communication and probably in the extent to which they perceived the communicator as intending to influence them (because those in the personality orientation group were simply asked to form impressions of the speaker's personality and we might imagine that the subjects felt that the speaker also had been informed as to the purpose of his presence). A subsequent study by Walster and Festinger (1962) eliminated the first variable and simply investigated the extent to which the possibility of the subject's perceiving the communicator as intending to influence inhibits attitude change.

Walster and Festinger tested the hypothesis that inadvertently overheard communications are more likely to be effective in changing the opinions of the listener than are communications that are deliberately addressed to him. To test their hypothesis that overheard communications are especially effective, the experimenters set up a situation in which the subject listened to two people carrying on a conversation. In one condition, the normal condition, the subject thought that the speakers knew that others were listening. In the other condition, the overheard condition, the subject thought that the speakers were unaware that anyone was listening. In addition, a control condition in which the subjects received no communication at all was included in the experiment. The conversation consisted of a discussion of the common "misconception" that smoking causes lung cancer, and the communicators related a number of non-existent studies that showed that when all confounding factors were eliminated, there was no relationship between smoking and cancer.

The over-all results of this experiment indicated that there was indeed a tendency for the communication to be more effective when it was overheard than when the recipient thought the speakers knew that others were listening to their conversation. However, an internal analysis of the data examining the extent of opinion change between smokers and nonsmokers —or between those for whom the communication could be expected to be relevant or irrelevant—revealed a surprising relationship. The differential effectiveness between the overheard condition and the normal condition was due almost entirely to those subjects for whom a smoking communication had special relevance, the smokers in the group. There was only a very small nonsignificant difference between the two persuasion conditions for the nonsmokers. And this was true even though both smokers and nonsmokers in the overheard condition rated the speakers as more honest and sincere than did subjects in the other condition.

Because this was a completely unexpected finding, the investigators performed a second experiment. This experiment was specifically designed to see whether or not the overheard condition was more effective only for people who were behaviorally involved in the issue presented in the communication. In the second experiment, as in the first, the communicators advocated positions that those involved in the issue could reasonably want to accept. The results of this study revealed that the overheard communications were more effective for involved subjects but not particularly more effective for subjects not directly involved in the issue.

It is difficult to explain this effect. Because of the accidental nature of both communications, subjects' defenses were not prepared in either condition. In addition, it is strange that a person who is involved in an issue would defend himself against a position he would very much like to accept. Walster and Festinger tentatively attributed their results to the differential extent to which the communicator could be seen as intending to persuade in the two conditions. The investigators reasoned that if the content of the communications in the normal condition was of direct personal relevance to the communicatee, then it was possible for the listener to feel that the speaker was indeed attempting to influence him and had ulterior motives. The investigators, of course, were left with the interesting question as to why the involved subjects would tend to impute ulterior motives to speakers who advocated a position they would have liked to accept.

However perplexing this finding may be, the results of a subsequent experiment by Brock and Becker (1965) indicate that it is not a will-o'-the-wisp effect. Like Walster and Festinger, Brock and Becker found that when the issue was not personally involving for the listeners, overheard and nonoverheard persuasive communications were equally effective. When the message advocated by the communication was both involving and acceptable to the subjects, the overheard communication was more effective. These investigators also added another condition, in which the advocated message was opposed to the subjects' positions. It was found that overhearing a persuasive communication was not more effective when it advocated an unacceptable position, even for subjects who were involved in the communication. Thus the results of this study suggest that the power of an overheard communication is restricted to moving people in the direction they want to go anyway.

The studies concerning overheard communications stimulated an experiment by Mills and Jellison (1967). These authors argued that a second explanation for the preceding findings was plausible. They pointed out that involved subjects who heard the communicator espouse desirable conclusions under the normal condition might have assumed that the communicator was aware that they would find the communication desirable. Subjects who "overheard" the communication were unlikely to assume that the communicator believed that the communication would be desirable to them. Mills and Jellison hypothesized that when individuals believe a communicator is delivering a communication that he believes will be desirable to the audience, they will be less persuaded than when they feel he thinks the communication will be undesirable to the audience addressed. The authors reasoned that if the audience feels the communicator thinks the communication would be desirable to the audience, they might tend to doubt his sincerity, to suspect that he is just saying something to please them, and thus may be less influenced. On the other hand, if they feel the communicator thinks his communication will be undesirable to the audience, they will not tend to suspect his motives and might even be more influenced.

Mills and Jellison tested their hypothesis by having college students read a speech favoring tripling truck-license fees under two experimental conditions. Subjects in the desirable condition were told the speech was delivered before a local union of railwaymen. In the undesirable condition it was supposedly delivered before a local union of long-haul truck drivers. The Mills and Jellison hypothesis was confirmed. The subjects agreed with the communicator's position more in the undesirable condition than in the desirable condition.

There is evidence that being perceived as having intention to persuade need not always decrease the communicator's influence. Mills and Aronson (1965), for example, suggested that under some conditions the effectiveness of the communicator might actually be enhanced if he were perceived as having an intention to persuade. They hypothesized that if the communicator were very attractive and were someone the audience liked very much, he might be more effective if he announced that he definitely wanted to persuade. Their test of this hypothesis lent some support to the prediction.

A related hypothesis was tested by Mills (1966). Mills hypothesized that if the subject thinks that the communicator likes him, he will be more persuaded when he knows the communicator wants to influence him than when he thinks he does not. Mills also hypothesized that when the subject thinks the communicator dislikes him, the subject will be less influenced when he thinks the communicator wants to influence him than when he thinks he does not. As predicted, if the communicator was described as liking students, college students agreed with him more when he said he hoped to influence people in colleges than when he did not care about influencing them. If the communicator was said to dislike students, they agreed less when he hoped to influence than when he did not care, and, in fact, there was greater opinion change observed in the dislike—nonpersuade group than in any other.

Mills obtained another interesting result. When the communicator announced his intention to influence and said that he cared very much whether or not he persuaded the subjects, he was perceived as significantly more friendly, less hostile, more likeable, and more helpful than when he said that he didn't care whether or not his communication influenced the subjects. Here is a case in which announced intention to influence increased communicator attractiveness. However, the increase in the dislike–persuade condition was evidently not enough to counteract a general feeling of dislike for the communicator.

Attractiveness

Attributes such as the communicator's expertness and the extent to which he has something to gain from one's acceptance of his communication are communicator attributes that are quite relevant to the content of the communication being delivered. There have been several demonstrations that communicator characteristics that bear little objective relevance to the topic of the communication can affect amount of opinion change. Aronson and Golden (1962), for example, charged that by neglecting to consider irrelevant aspects of communicator credibility, studies in the area had unwittingly implied that audiences were composed of reasonable people who are responsive solely to objectively relevant aspects of a communicator. Their experiment was designed to investigate the relative effectiveness of relevant and irrelevant aspects of communicator credibility. They compared the extent of opinion change brought about by a communication as a function of differential degrees of communicator expertness (relevant credibility), whether it was attributed to a Negro or to a Caucasian (irrelevant credibility), and the attitude of individual members of the audience toward Negroes.

As in many opinion-change studies, the results indicated that all the communicators had some effect on the opinions of the audience. The results also indicated that both relevant and irrelevant aspects of credibility were important determinants of opinion change. There was a strong tendency for those communicators who were expert in the area of the communication to be more effective than those who were perceived to be less expert. There was, however, also a strong tendency for those subjects who were prejudiced against Negroes to be underinfluenced by Negro communicators and for those subjects who were unprejudiced against Negroes to be overinfluenced by the Negro communicators.

The finding that those more favorably disposed toward a communicator will be more likely to accept his message is not a surprising one. The principle that groups or individuals who are liked by the communicatee will wield more influence than those less attractive has been well documented in a variety of informal and formal communication situations (for example, Schachter, Ellertson, McBride, and Gregory, 1951; Cohn, Yee, and Brown, 1961; Tannenbaum, 1956; Newcomb, 1961; Charters and Newcomb, 1958).

We have seen that the variable of communicator attractiveness interacts with communicator intent to influence (Mills and Aronson, 1965), and there appear to be other situations in which communicator attractiveness interacts with other variables to produce interesting effects. Smith (1961), for example, was interested in testing the hypothesis that in some situations a communicator who is disliked might actually be able to effect greater attitude change than a positively regarded communicator. The situation in which this effect was thought to occur was one in which both communicators were able to induce a person to publicly comply with an unpleasant request. It was reasoned that one should experience more dissonance when he decides to comply with the request of a negative communicator than when he complies with the request of a more agreeable person. One way in which the subject can reduce the dissonance he feels on deciding to do an unpleasant thing is by convincing himself that the thing was, in fact, not so unpleasant. The more dissonance he feels, the more necessary such distortion may be. In line with this reasoning, there should be more tendency to convince oneself that compliance was pleasant when compliance was advocated by a negative communicator than when it was advocated by a positive communicator. Unfortunately, there were initial differences in Smith's two groups, and since there was no control group, the results, which appear to confirm the hypotheses, are open to alternative explanations in terms of regression and ceiling effects.

However, an experiment conducted by Zimbardo, Weisenberg, Firestone, and Levy (1965) gives us some information concerning this hypothesis. College students and Army reservists were induced to eat a highly unattractive food, fried grasshoppers, by a communicator whose positiveness or negativeness was experimentally varied. Approximately 50 per cent of the subjects in each condition accepted the inducement to eat a grasshopper; the attractiveness of the communicator did not have an effect upon the frequency of compliance. All subjects perceived that they had a high degree of choice in whether or not to eat the food. The investigators found that those who complied with the request from the negative communicator increased their liking for the originally disliked grasshoppers significantly more than did those complying with a positive communicator. It should also be noted that within the negative conditions those who chose to eat did not view the communicator more favorably than did the noneaters. Thus, eaters under negative communicator conditions changed their attitudes toward grasshoppers but did not develop more favorable attitudes toward the communicator. The eaters in the positive communicator condition, on the other hand, did not change their attitudes much toward grasshoppers, but did tend to justify their eating in terms of irrelevant, personal communicator characteristics.

Other investigators (Powell, 1965; Jones and Brehm, 1967) have tested whether or not communicator characteristics interact with the forced—or voluntary—compliance aspects of the communication situation. (The more choice one has about engaging in a dissonance-producing act, the more dissonance he will experience.) These studies have yielded consistent results. Jones and Brehm, for example, found that subjects who volunteered to listen to a communicator were more persuaded by an unattractive than by an attractive communicator. Apparently, they reduced the dissonance they experienced from voluntarily choosing to listen to an unattractive person by increasing the worth, and hence acceptance, of his message. However, subjects who were "accidentally exposed" to the persuasive communication (a forced-compliance situation) were more influenced by the positive communicator.

There are many other studies that support the general principle that attitude change may be effected through cognitive imbalance-reduction processes that act to bring an individual's private cognitions into accord with his public behavior (for example, Festinger and Carlsmith, 1959; Cohen in Brehm and Cohen, 1962; Aronson and Carlsmith, 1963; and Turner and Wright, 1965). Most of these studies, if not all, have been conducted within the framework of cognitive dissonance theory, and we will discuss them in a later section.

Similarity

Another communicator trait that has been found to affect the amount of influence a communicator will have is his similarity to the communicatee (for example, Stotland, Zander, and Natsoulas, 1961; Burnstein, Stotland, and Zander, 1961; Stotland and Patchen, 1961; Dabbs, 1964). In the Stotland, Zander, and Natsoulas experiment, subjects working in isolation were led to believe that they were the third member of a three-person group and were asked privately to write their preferences among eight pairs of brief melodic tunes. After they had made their choice within each pair, they heard over earphones the other two choosers state their preferences. The subjects then stated their own choices into a microphone. The two other choosers were in fact paid participants whose voices were transcribed, and by appropriate means each subject came to perceive that her preferences were more similar to those of one of the two choosers than to those of the other. The similarity manipulation thus performed, the subjects made preferential choices from a series of pairs of nonsense syllables. In this instance, however, each subject heard the selection of the other two persons before making each decision, but she was led to believe that her own selection could not be heard by the other subjects. The hypothesis, that the subjects would prefer the nonsense syllables chosen by the paid participant with whom they agreed more often on musical preferences, was supported.

In the Burnstein, Stotland, and Zander study, an adult communicator whose occupation was described as deep sea diving, was presented to a group of grade school children as being either highly similar or of little similarity to the children in background and in other characteristics. The similar sea diver, for example, was described as having been raised in the same town in which the children were now living, his parents had worked in the same factory in which many of the children's parents were now working, he had gone swimming in the same swimming hole, and in general had led a life very similar to that of the children he was addressing. The dissimilar communicator was described as having been raised in a large city in a different part of the country and having had amusements and pursuits quite foreign to those the children were enjoying. Each communicator then described a number of his preferences relevant to sea diving. Each subject indicated his own preferences twice: once before hearing the communication and again after hearing it. It was found that subjects who were told that the diver was highly similar to them in background accepted more of his sea diving preferences than did subjects who were told he was dissimilar to them.

In neither of these studies was the attractiveness of the similar and dissimilar communicators controlled. Because it is quite clear that similarity between a communicator and a communicatee causes a communicator to be perceived as more attractive (Newcomb, 1961; Byrne, 1961; Byrne and Wong, 1962) and because, as previously mentioned, attractiveness alone may produce opinion change, one might question the extent to which liking for the similar communicator in the previously mentioned study influenced the subjects' preferences and the extent to which similarity alone produced this effect.

Berscheid (1966) held attractiveness constant, while varying the similarity between the communicator and the subject. It was hypothesized that when differential attractiveness of similar and dissimilar communicators was controlled, similarities between the communicator and subject that were relevant to or that would have implications for the dimension along which opinion change was sought would produce increased attitude change. It was hypothesized that communicator–communicatee similarities on dimensions irrelevant to the content of the communication would be less effective in producing opinion change.

To test this hypothesis, half of the subjects were given information that led them to believe that the communicator held values in the area of education similar to their own and values in the area of international affairs dissimilar to their own; the remaining subjects were told that the communicator held similar international-affairs values and dissimilar educational values. Half the subjects in each of these two groups then received a persuasive communication on an educational issue delivered by the communicator; the other half heard the communicator deliver a communication on an international affairs topic. It was predicted that when the communicator was described as similar to the subjects in educational values but not in international affairs values, he would influence the subjects when he spoke on an educational topic but not when he spoke on an international affairs issue. Conversely, it was predicted that when the communicator was described as similar in international affairs values, he would be more effective speaking on international affairs than education. These predictions were confirmed. This experiment suggests that when the communicator and the communicatee share a similarity that is not relevant to the dimension upon which the influence attempt is made, the communicatee evidently does not tend to perceive the communicator to be a proper referent for that particular opinion and is little, or not at all, influenced.

The foregoing study suggests that the results of the Stotland, Zander, and Natsoulas experiment and those of the Burnstein, Stotland, and Zander experiment, in which dissimilarities between the subjects and the communicators were either not relevant or only slightly relevant to the influence attempts, may have been due to differential attractiveness of the similar and the dissimilar communicators. Since similarity, relevant or irrelevant, produces attractiveness, the similar communicators could have been more attractive to the subjects than the dissimilar communicators and thus could produce opinion change even though their similarities were not relevant to their influence attempts.

The results of Berscheid's experiment support those of a field experiment on communicator–communicatee similarity done by Brock (1965a). Brock conducted his experiment in the paint department of a large retail store, and the role of communicator was taken by two part-time salesmen. Each communicator attempted to modify a customer's price decision on paint he had chosen to buy. Each communicator presented himself to half of the subjects as having an amount of paint consumption similar to that of the subject. To the other half, each communicator reported his magnitude of paint consumption as twenty times that of the subject's prospective purchase.

Brock found that the communicators whose paint consumption was similar to that of the customers' were more effective than the dissimilar communicators in getting the customers to change their minds about the paint they wanted to purchase. This was true whether the influence attempt was directed toward getting the customers to go to a higher price level or to a lower price level. No control was made for possible differential attractiveness of the similar and dissimilar communicators and, as Brock points out, the subjects may have resented the dissimilar experimenter's "showing off" how much paint he used or disbelieved the communicator's consumption figure and regarded it as a sales ploy. The dissimilar communicator was, however, perceived by pretest subjects to be more expert in the area of paint than was the similar communicator. The expertise effect, then, to the extent that it was operative, worked against confirmation of the hypothesis.

Further evidence that the endorsement of a discrepant position by similar others will lead to opinion change is provided by an experiment conducted by Kelley and Woodruff (1956). Subjects in this experiment were students at a small teachers' college who favored "modern" teaching practices. All subjects listened to a recorded speech, attributed to an education professor from a midwestern university, that advocated a return to more traditional classroom methods. At various points during the speech, subjects heard the audience applaud. The experimental manipulation consisted of identifying the applauding audience in two different ways. Half the subjects were told that the audience was composed entirely of faculty members and recent graduates of their college. The remaining subjects were told that the audience was composed of college-trained people in a nearby city who were interested in community problems related to education. Kelley and Woodruff found that subjects who were told the applauding audience was similar to themselves tended to change their opinions in the direction of favoring a more traditional approach to education more than did those subjects who were told the audience was composed of possibly dissimilar, or at least ambiguous, others.

In both the Kelley and Woodruff experiment and the Brock experiment, the similarities and dissimilarities were relevant to the communications. Brock raised the question of whether behavior can be modified as readily when the similarity attribute is irrelevant to the change dimension. The results of Berscheid's experiment suggest that it cannot, at least when unmediated by attractiveness.

An interesting experiment recently conducted by Mills and Jellison (1968) suggests that the tendency for a similar communicator to induce opinion change will be reduced if the communication is overheard by the recipient and enhanced if the recipient feels that communicator was aware that he would receive it. The authors reasoned that one reason why a similar communicator is often more persuasive than a dissimilar communicator is that similarity affects perception of a communicator's motivation to communicate honestly. It is possible that an audience expects a similar communicator to be more sincere with them because they assume he feels some identification with them and thus is more concerned about their welfare. To test the hypothesis, all subjects read a speech favoring general education. The introduction to the speech was varied in four different ways: (1) Some subjects were told that the author of the speech was a musician and that the speech had been made to music students. (2) Others were told that the musician had delivered the speech to engineering students. (3) To still others the speech was attributed to an engineer who had addressed music students. (4) Finally, a fourth group of subjects were told that the engineer had made the speech to engineering students.

Mills and Jellison predicted that subjects would be more persuaded by the communication when the introduction identified the communicator and his audience as being similar to one another, because they expected that the communicator in those conditions would be perceived as more sincere. The results revealed that subjects were indeed more persuaded in those conditions in which the communicator was supposedly similar to his audience. However, ratings of the communicator did not reveal a corresponding increase in perceived sincerity in the predicted conditions. It is possible, however, that these ratings did not provide a sensitive enough measure of perceived sincerity, because it is difficult to account for the obtained differences in opinion change without making the assumption that sincerity differences existed. From Mills and Jellison's results, we might expect that the usual effect of communicator similarity is likely to be attenuated when one overhears the communicator and thus feels that the communicator is unaware that he is addressing a similar other.

One might ask whether relevant dissimilarities lead in certain circumstances to opinion change. Another experiment was conducted by Berscheid (1966) in which subjects were led to believe that their values were dissimilar to the communicator's on a dimension either relevant or irrelevant to that upon which opinion change was sought. In both instances, the communicator took a position that was identical to the position the subject held prior to the communication. This experiment was designed to investigate whether a relevant dissimilarity between the communicator and the subject would cause, under such conditions, the communicator's influence attempt to boomerang. Specifically, it was hypothesized that if the subject perceived that a value dissimilarity existed between himself and the communicator on a dimension relevant to the influence attempt, and if he then discovered that his own opinion was similar to that expressed by the communicator, he would change his opinion in such a way as to make it more dissimilar to the opinion of the communicator. It was thought, for example, that a person such as George Wallace might find it disconcerting to find that his and Stokley Carmichael's views coincided on an issue pertaining to Negroes. It was also hypothesized that if the communicator was dissimilar to the subject on a value dimension irrelevant to the communication, and if he perceived that his opinion was similar to that advocated by the communicator, he would not change his opinion. These hypotheses were confirmed.

The finding that people who are dissimilar on a value dimension relevant to an influence attempt will act as negative referents provides one concrete explanation for at least some observed boomerang effects. The boomerang effect, or the phenomenon of the communicator's influence attempt producing an effect completely opposite to that intended, of moving the audience away from the position advocated, has been of interest to social psychologists concerned with the effects of communication. It has intrigued researchers that one could be such a poor speaker that his impassioned influence attempts would cause him to lose ground.

Just what it takes to design a speech so poor that it would drive people in the opposite direction has been the subject of much speculation. Perhaps the first experimental observation of the boomerang effect was in a study done by Kelley and Volkhart (1952). Kelley and Volkhart hypothesized that members of a group who placed high value upon the group would be less influenced by a communication contrary to the group's norms than would low-valuation members. According to this hypothesis, the amount of opinion change produced by such a communication will be inversely related to the degree of valuation of membership. To test this hypothesis, Kelley and Volkhart gave communications and questionnaires to the members of twelve Boy Scout troops. The pertinent norm consisted of the positive attitudes that Scouts ordinarily have in common concerning woodcraft skills, forest lore, and camping activities. One week after administering a premeasure questionnaire, an outside adult appeared before each troop and delivered a communication that criticized woodcraft activities and suggested that in the modern world boys would profit more from learning about their cities and from various activities possible in town. Immediately after the speech, the scale measuring attitudes toward woodcraft as opposed to city activities was readministered in order to determine postcommunication attitudes.

The expected inverse relationship between valuation and opinion change was supported by the data. The low-valuation members tended to change in the direction advocated by the communication. But the high-valuation members actually changed in the opposite direction. The communication, then, had a negative or boomerang effect among the high-valuation Scouts. Unfortunately, there was no control group that did not receive the communication, and therefore the possibility that the negative effect was due to the intervention of irrelevant factors during the period between the before and after tests cannot be completely ruled out. In addition, in describing the norms in order to argue against them, the communicator may have added to the recipients' knowledge of the norms and thereby heightened the conformity of the more loyal Scouts.

There has been a great deal of hypothesizing about the antecedents of the boomerang phenomenon, but very little investigative work has been done. Hovland, Janis, and Kelley (1953) have hypothesized that boomerang effects will occur when the communication is delivered by an untrustworthy or noncredible source and when, in addition, the communication contains no arguments favorable to the position taken in the communication. That a communication delivered by a noncredible source will by itself produce a boomerang effect is not supported by a number of credibility studies (for example, Kelman and Hovland, 1953) that indicate that the less credible communicators simply produce less positive opinion change than do credible communicators. Hovland, Janis, and

Kelley hypothesized that the less credible communicators are able to effect a certain amount of opinion change because the arguments contained in the communications produce large enough positive effects to counteract negative effects due to the communicator.

Hovland, Janis, and Kelley also hypothesized that boomerang effects might be expected when audience members anticipate that the non-credible communicator's conclusions will be consistently in opposition to the audience's best interest. In addition, they hypothesized that boomerang effects might be obtained when the communicator arouses anger or resentment by making statements that are regarded as offensive, when the communicatee experiences guilt and anxiety from the realization that he is in the process of accepting a position that is contrary to the beliefs and standards of the groups he values, and when a contrast effect ensues from the communicator's taking a position that is very far removed from that advocated by the audience. Another possible antecedent of the boomerang effect might be mentioned here. In the Zimbardo et al. (1965) experiment it was found that among those for whom the attempt to induce eating of grasshoppers failed, 34 per cent showed a boomerang effect in that they liked the food even less after they had refused to eat it. In any event, our knowledge of boomerang effects is largely restricted to incidental findings such as these.

7

Characteristics of a Convincing Communication

One-Sided versus Two-Sided Appeals

In order for an issue to be controversial there must be at least two sides to the question. Though one side may have the preponderance of evidence in its favor, a motivated opposition can always come up with counter-arguments. Thus the question arises, is one more persuasive if he mentions the arguments the opposition might have, refuting them when he can, or if he ignores them and presents only his own side? This question is of practical interest to many individuals. For example, sometimes parents are very desirous of "inoculating" their children against communism. How can they best go about this? Should they present a one-sided appeal, stressing the advantages of capitalism and the disadvantages of communism? Should they present a two-sided appeal that also mentions those characteristics of communism that seem to be advantageous and refutes these ostensible advantages? Or should they go even further: Should they present a two-sided communication that also mentions the assets of communism, even when these assets are irrefutable?

Parents usually assume that a one-sided appeal is most effective; a teacher who suggests that there is anything good about communism is likely to find himself in trouble. Is the parents' assumption correct? Is it more effective to present only the merits of capitalism or to expose children to the merits and demerits of both communism and capitalism, arguing for one's own side as persuasively as possible?

During World War II, the question of whether one-sided or two-sided appeals were most effective was experimentally investigated for the first time. Germany had surrendered, and, naturally enough, soldiers were eager to convince themselves that the remaining fight against Japan would be a short one, and that they would soon be able to go home. The government wanted to counteract such wishful thinking. In investigating the best way to go about convincing them that the war would be a long one, Hovland, Lumsdaine, and Sheffield (1949) experimented with a one-sided communication and a two-sided communication. The one-sided communication presented only arguments for the position that Japan was a strong nation and that the war would be a long one. The two-sided communication presented these same arguments plus a few arguments that might be given by those who disagreed with this point of view. When possible, the opposition's arguments were refuted. When they could not be refuted, opposition arguments were presented early in the talk. Regardless of whether the presentation was two-sided or one-sided, however, the communicator still came to the same conclusion: that winning the Pacific War would take at least two years. The investigators anticipated that the two-sided appeal would be most effective. They thought that the soldiers would distrust the one-sided presentation and would spend time thinking up counterarguments or rehearsing counterarguments already familiar to them. The investigators speculated that if the speaker explicitly mentioned these counterarguments, the soldiers would lose their suspicion and their argumentativeness and would concentrate on the talk.

To test this hypothesis, Hovland et al. presented the one-sided message to some men and the two-sided message to others, and then assessed the soldiers' attitudes about how long the war would be. To their surprise, both communications were equally effective for the group as a whole. But when they considered the men's initial opinions, one presentation did seem to be more effective than the other. If men were initially opposed to the message (if they expected a short war), the two-sided communication was more effective than the one-sided one. This seems reasonable because presumably these men were the ones most likely to be motivated to argue against the communication. The one-sided communication was most effective for those who initially agreed with the communication. Probably the one-sided argument simply bolstered their original opinion, whereas the two-sided presentation introduced new doubts. Also, as might be expected, a one-sided communication was much more effective for poorly educated men than for well-educated ones. Presumably, poorly educated men lacked the critical skills to effectively counterargue.

On the basis of this reasoning, we might be led to the conclusion that though one should present both sides of an issue to an intelligent audience that is initially opposed to his position, he should not mention the opposition's arguments when talking to uneducated individuals who agree with him from the start. However, in making such a generalization we have forgotten one thing. The Hovland et al. experiment measured the attitudes of men in a closed environment. The soldiers were not allowed to talk to one another after seeing the film and before giving their own opinions.

Thus the duller soldiers had no chance to ask the brighter ones about their opinions. Similarly, the opposed soldiers were not allowed to take the stage and argue that the communication was all wrong. Once soldiers left the experimental room, however, such communications could take place.

What effect does being exposed to subsequent counterarguments have on acceptance of the original two-sided or one-sided communication? We have information on this question. Lumsdaine and Janis (1953) exposed one half of their subjects to a one-sided communication, stating that it would be at least five years before Russia would be able to produce large numbers of atomic bombs. The remainder of the subjects were exposed to a two-sided communication; they were given the same information that was presented in the one-sided message, plus information favoring the opposite point of view—for example, "Russia has many first-rate atomic scientists." In the two sided communication, no attempt was made to refute these counterarguments.

One week later, all experimental subjects were exposed to counterpropaganda. Some of the counterarguments elaborated Russian strengths that had been mentioned earlier in the two-sided communication, but some novel material was also presented. Control subjects were not exposed to counterpropaganda. Finally, all subjects were asked to estimate how long it would be before Russia produced large numbers of bombs. When subjects were not exposed to counterpropaganda, two-sided and one-sided communications seemed to be equally effective. However, when subjects were exposed to counterpropaganda, those hearing the two-sided communications were much better able to resist the countermessage than those who had heard only one side of the issue initially.

Inoculation

The reader may recall that immediately after the Korean conflict, Senate investigators became concerned about the lack of resistance American prisoners of war seemed to have to Chinese Communist propaganda. In contrast to the behavior evidenced by World War II prisoners, Korean War prisoners were seemingly weak in their resistance. A Congressional committee suggested that this problem would be solved if soldiers reived more instruction in "Americanism" at home and at school. McGuire and Papageorgis (1961) argued, on the contrary, that soldiers would be more effectively immunized if they were exposed to the communist position and arguments against that position than if they simply received additional indoctrination in "Americanism."

In presenting this argument, the authors drew an analogy with medical inoculations. If a person has been brought up in an aseptic environment, he will never have occasion to develop any resistance to infection, and will be quite vulnerable if suddenly exposed to a disease. We know, for example, that one thing missionaries bring to isolated tribes, along with religion, is new diseases. Sometimes these new diseases cause epidemics, because resistance in these groups is low. Continuing with this analogy, the authors propose that prescribing Americanism is like prescribing supportive therapy, such as a good diet, exercise, and rest. Such supportive therapy is effective in preventing disease, but not as effective as an inoculation, which mobilizes an individual's defenses. The authors wished to investigate the effectiveness of "innoculation" procedures in increasing resistance to attitude change. They wanted to give individuals a weak virus (a weak countermessage), hoping that they would build up defenses against this virus (be motivated to think up their own refutations) and thus would develop the ability to withstand more severe attacks that came later.

McGuire and Papageorgis tested their hypothesis in the following way. Subjects were assigned to participate in two experimental sessions. During the first session, all subjects were exposed to four cultural truisms. "Cultural truisms" are beliefs that are so widely shared that an individual is unlikely to have ever heard them attacked. An example of such a belief is "Everyone should brush his teeth after every meal if at all possible."

During this initial experimental session, each of the four truisms was treated in a different way. Two of the truisms were defended in some way. For one of these, *supportive information* was supplied. Students read an essay containing several reasons why he should agree with the truism. For example, support for the dental truism consisted of reminding subjects that brushing their teeth improved their appearance and eliminated decay-causing bacteria. Studies demonstrating that regular brushing reduced decay 70 per cent were also cited. For the second, an *inoculation* was supplied. Subjects were exposed to weak arguments against the truism, and a refutation of these arguments was either provided by the experimenter or by the subject himself, upon the experimenter's instruction. For example, when we consider the dental truism, the weak threat consisted of reporting that some misguided individuals had concluded that frequent brushing of the teeth was bad, because brushing, an unnatural habit, often caused gum injuries or pushed the gums back, exposing the more vulnerable part of the teeth, and because the harsh abrasives that exist in all toothpastes pit the teeth and leave them open to bacterial damage. A rebuttal for this article consisted of an explanation that stimulation actually improved gum condition, and an explanation that though fifty years ago toothpastes had harsh abrasives, the Food and Drug Administration now prohibits such harmful substances. The other two truisms, the control truisms, were neither attacked nor supported.

Finally, subjects' acceptance of the truisms was assessed. Regardless of whether they had received supportive information or an inoculation, subjects' attitudes were about the same. When measured immediately after the initial session, the supportive communication appeared to be as effective as was the inoculation communication. Two days later, subjects attended a second session, where they were faced with a strong attack against three of the truisms—that is, the truism previously supported, the truism previously weakly attacked, and one of the control truisms. In the attack, the same arguments that had been presented to subjects in the inoculation condition were again presented, but this time in very strong form. Finally, subjects' attitudes were assessed. McGuire and Papageorgis found that the undefended truisms were highly vulnerable to counterpropaganda. Subjects changed their beliefs markedly after hearing the counterpropaganda. A prior defense, whether consisting of a supportive defense or an inoculation, did help subjects to resist the subsequent attack. The refutational defense conferred more immunity than did a supportive defense.

McGuire and Papageorgis note that there is one problem with this study. In this experiment, the attack consisted of a strong version of the very arguments that had been seen and rebutted in the initial session by the subjects in the inoculation condition. Subjects in the supportive-defense condition and the control condition had, of course, never faced these arguments or been exposed to their rebuttals previously. Thus a critic could argue that the authors secured the results they did for a reason much less interesting than the one the authors proposed. Perhaps the inoculation treatment was effective, not because it stimulated subjects to prepare their own defenses, but simply because when the attack came, inoculation subjects could recall an appropriate rebuttal for these arguments, whereas supportive-condition subjects, never having heard them, could not.

How can we tell which explanation for the data is the correct one? It is possible, of course, that both alternatives are correct. The ability of an inoculation-condition subject to resist attack could have come from two sources: (1) from his memory of the refutations provided in the initial session; (2) from the defenses for his belief, which he prepared after the initial weak attack.

If the hypothesis that an inoculation treatment is effective because the mention of weak arguments against a belief motivates the individual to prepare his defenses is true, then anything that motivates one to prepare his defenses should serve as an effective inoculation. For example, simply mentioning that a cherished belief will soon be attacked might motivate an individual to try to prepare his defenses. Presenting and refuting weak arguments different from those contained in the subsequent attack should also increase one's resistance to attack. On the basis of reasoning similar to that presented above, the authors conducted other experiments to test their formulations more unequivocally.

Papageorgis and McGuire (1961) argued that if the inoculation in the McGuire and Papageorgis study was effective partially because inoculation subjects had memorized relevant rebuttals whereas supportive subjects could not, then an inoculation followed by a familiar attack should prove superior to one in which the subsequent attack consisted of novel arguments. Therefore they conducted a study that enabled them to compare the resistance to subsequent attack of subjects receiving an inoculation treatment that presented and rebutted the same arguments that would appear in the attack ("refutational–same" subjects) and of subjects receiving an inoculation treatment that presented and rebutted arguments different from those that would appear in the attack ("refutational–different" subjects). The results of this experiment indicated that although both inoculation treatments conferred a significant degree of resistance to subsequent attack, they did not significantly differ from each other in effectiveness. Thus the authors concluded that their original hypothesis was correct.

It is not really necessary to take the stand that unless the refutational-same and the refutational-different conditions are equally effective, the authors' hypothesis is disconfirmed. It is possible for their hypothesis to be correct, and to demonstrate that an inoculation does motivate people to prepare their own defenses, even if part of the effectiveness of the inoculation-same treatment in the original experiment was due to the fact that these subjects recalled the relevant rebuttals. All that is necessary for the authors formulation to be shown to be correct is a demonstration that at least *part* of the effect was due to the fact that inoculation subjects prepared additional defenses while supportive subjects did not.

Evidence that both learning and motivational factors may have been operating in the original experiment can be gleaned from other data. McGuire and Papageorgis (1962), in an experiment testing another hypothesis, secured data that suggest that the refutational-same condition may confer more resistance than either the refutational-different or the supportive condition. The superiority of the refutational-same subjects may come from the fact that they could utilize memorized material that supportive-condition subjects did not have access to, and that refutational-different subjects could not utilize.

McGuire and Papageorgis (1962) argued that if it is true that the mention of a threatening attack motivates the person to develop defenses, a forewarning of attack *prior* to the presentation of defensive material should increase the subject's resistance. Data confirm this hypothesis. Subjects who were warned prior to either a supportive or an inoculation treatment that the belief would be later attacked showed more resistance than those who were not forewarned. It must be noted that forewarning alone, without a resistance-inducing treatment prior to the communication, did not by itself increase resistance to influence.

It might seem surprising that forewarning subjects of an imminent attack did not by itself produce increased resistance to influence. One would think that warning one that his cherished beliefs would soon be under fire would serve as a strong motivator to come up with some defenses. Earlier we saw that a forewarning often caused the subject to develop a defensive and critical mental set. In the subsequent section we will present other studies that corroborate this finding. Why then did forewarning not have an effect, in and of itself, in this study? We must remember that the beliefs with which the authors were working were expressly chosen because they are not usually subject to attack. Thus, even when forewarned of an attack, the individual may not be able to anticipate the nature of this attack, and may have no ready defenses he can handily muster before that attack. Most studies on forewarning deal with controversial issues, and in such cases individuals are probably familiar enough with various defense tactics to profit by an early warning. This reminds us that the cultural-truism situation is different in many ways from the usual communication situation, in which the belief involved is controversial. We must be careful not to overgeneralize from one situation to the other.

What effect does the passage of time have on the resistance to persuasion conferred by a supportive defense or an inoculation? Sometimes it is clear that an enemy propaganda appeal is imminent. Usually, however, the opposition is not so kind as to tell us just when his attack will come. What is the best defense against counterpropaganda expected at some future date? McGuire (1962) proposed and tested several hypotheses that will help us to answer these questions:

Hypothesis 1: "The supportive defense will not only be initially inferior to an inoculation in the amount of resistance it confers, but in addition such resistance as it does confer will decay more rapidly than that conferred by the refutational defense." The rationale for this prediction is clear. Recall that an individual may withstand attack by two means: utilizing remembered supportive and refutational material, and utilizing additional defensive material he has come up with on his own. Both the supportive and refutational defense provide potentially usable information to the subject, but with the passage of time this information will be increasingly forgotten. Thus in both conditions the subject's ability to withstand attack through the utilization of remembered material will diminish with time. The inoculation condition also provides motivation for the subject to discover his own defensive information. As long as motivation lasts, the individual might be expected to continue to accumulate defensive material. Thus in the innoculation condition the forgetting of the refutational material should be partially offset by the acquisition of new material.

Hypothesis 2: The passage of time between the inoculation treatment and the subsequent attack may increase the subject's resistance, if measured against a novel attack. The passage of a short amount of time may be necessary before a motivated individual is able to come up with additional defensive arguments.

Hypothesis 3: An inoculation shows a greater deterioration in effectiveness when measured against a familiar attack than when measured against a novel one. Memory, which deteriorates with time, is undoubtedly of greatest importance in defending against a familiar attack. Only the information one acquires on his own can be used against a novel attack, however. Because possession of this novel information actually increases over time, whereas remembered material decays, the passage of time should produce a greater loss of resistance in the refutation–same condition than in the refutation–different condition.

The design McGuire used to test these hypotheses was quite complicated. Basically, however, what happened was this: During an initial session, subjects were given a supportive defense, a refutational defense, or no defense at all for various cultural truisms. Then these truisms were attacked by familiar arguments, by novel arguments, or not at all. This attack took place either immediately, two days, or one week after the first session.

As can be seen in Figure 7-1, when we consider only attacks that occurred immediately to two days after the defense, McGuire's hypotheses are supported. First, the supportive defense conferred less resistance than did the refutational defense, regardless of when in time the attack came. As predicted, this difference in effectiveness was greater when two days had intervened between the defense and the attack than it was immediately after the defense. This difference in effectiveness does not continue to increase with the passage of longer periods of time. In the period from two to seven days, the refutational defenses deteriorated markedly in effectiveness, whereas the supportive defense actually maintained its effectiveness. (McGuire does not report whether or not this interaction is significant.) After one week, a refutational defense continues to be more effective than a supportive one, and our best guess is probably that it will maintain its superiority indefinitely. Because the refutational defense has begun to lose its effectiveness, however, it would be desirable to have information about what happens when a much greater delay intervenes between defense and attack. It is possible that after several weeks an inoculation and a supportive defense become equally effective (or ineffective).

Second, when we consider an inoculated subject's resistance to a novel attack (refutational–different condition), we see that such resistance does increase when a two-day delay intervenes between inoculation and attack. This is consistent with the notion that inoculation subjects are motivated to find support for their challenged beliefs, but need some small amount of time to come up with a suitable defense.

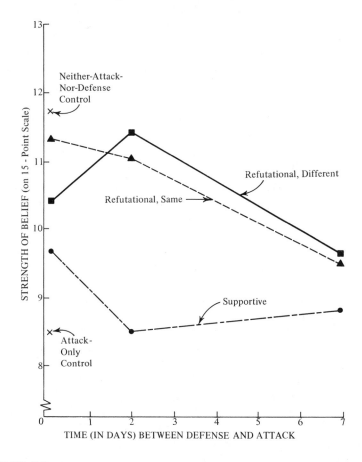

FIGURE 7-1.

Persistence of the Resistance to Persuasion Conferred by Three Types of Prior Defense: Supportive, Refutation of the Same Counterarguments as Used in the Attack, and Refutation of Counterarguments Different from Those Used in the Attack (From McGuire, 1962)

Third, over a two day period, the resistance of subjects does deteriorate faster when measured against a familiar attack than when measured against a novel one. When a delay of longer than two days intervenes, both inoculation conditions appear to be equally effective. It is clear that regardless of the time intervening between the defensive treatment and the attack, the best way to make subjects resistant to counterpropaganda is to provide them with an inoculation rather than with mere support for their beliefs. In the short run the resistance of an inoculated subject may actually increase with the passage of time.

The mention of weak arguments against one's beliefs is said to motivate him to secure defenses for that belief. How much help should a propagandist give this motivated individual in preparing "his own" defenses? We might feel that the answer to this question is that the more effort a subject expends in order to come up with his own rebuttal, the more he will feel the conclusions were his own, and the more effectively inoculated he will be. Previous experiments on role-playing (Janis and King, 1954; King and Janis, 1956) would support such a contention. Practical propagandists might also come to the same conclusion. For example, Schein (1956), in his discussion of the exact techniques the Chinese used in "brainwashing" prisoners of war, cites the "principle of constant participation." He says: "It was never enough for the prisoner to listen and absorb; some kind of verbal or written response was always demanded. Thus, if a man would not give original material in question-and-answer sessions, he was asked to copy something. Likewise group discussions, autobiographical statements, self-criticisms, and public confessions all demanded an active participation by the prisoner. The Chinese apparently believed that if they could once get a man to participate, he was likely to continue and that eventually he would accept the attitudes which the participation expressed" (p. 163).

Experiments by McGuire and Papageorgis indicate that the conclusion that an individual will become better inoculated the more he is left to his own devices is somewhat of an oversimplification. How much guidance is desirable will be seen to depend on whether the subsequent attack consists of familiar arguments or novel ones. McGuire and Papageorgis (1961) and McGuire (1961) investigated the difference in the resistance of passively and actively inoculated subjects to a familiar attack. The authors proposed that when an individual is faced with the necessity of defending beliefs that have never been challenged, he will be inept in the formulation of a defense. Thus they felt that subjects should receive some help in coming up with a rebuttal; if they were left entirely to their own devices they might not be able to come up with any refutations, or at least not as many refutations as could more passive subjects for whom refutations were provided. On this basis the authors proposed that passive subjects would be better inoculated than active subjects.

The authors tested this hypothesis by providing a supportive or a refutational defense for subjects in an initial session. The extent to which this defense had to come from the subject himself was varied. In the most passive condition, the subject simply had to read the supportive message or the weak attack and its rebuttal. In an intermediate condition, he had to write the defense himself, with the aid of an outline. In the most active condition, he had to come up with a supportive or refutational defense entirely on his own. In a second session, two days later, a familiar attack was given. The authors found strong support for their hypothesis. Passive subjects, in both the supportive and the refutational conditions, were better able to resist the attack than the active ones. The authors note that the defensive treatments clearly lost effectiveness to the extent that they required the subject's unguided active participation in the defense. We should note that we have no information about what the outcome would have been had the weak initial attack consisted of arguments so ridiculous and flimsy that anyone could refute them. Perhaps under such conditions active subjects might have been more strongly inoculated than passive ones.

The preceding results suggest that when a propagandist is sure he can anticipate the arguments the opposition will give, he can effectively immunize individuals simply by describing these arguments and supplying a refutation. The clearer he makes the reasons for rejecting such attacks, the more resistant the individuals should be. It is rarely the case, however, that one can anticipate all the arguments a motivated opposition might produce. Consider the prisoners of war once again. Think how difficult it would be for their superiors to anticipate all the persuasive arguments that any possible enemy captor might come up with, so that they could prepare a rebuttal to be supplied to soldiers.

McGuire (1961) examined the resistance to attack of passively and actively inoculated subjects when the attack was familiar or novel. As before, McGuire proposed that when the attack is familiar, the passive subject, who is guided in building his defenses, will be more resistant than will be active subjects. When the attack is a novel one, however, he proposed that the defenses of the active subjects would be relatively more effective (and perhaps even absolutely more effective). This hypothesis was confirmed. Though the passive defense was superior against familiar counterarguments, the active defense was superior against novel counterarguments. This seems to indicate that we can most effectively indoctrinate someone if we give him the chance to convince himself. A heavy hand may be self-defeating.

Forewarning

There are several studies that indicate that forewarning listeners of the content of a discrepant communication tends to lessen its acceptance. Experimental attention has been given to the effectiveness of different temporal placements of warnings. Kiesler and Kiesler (1964) conducted an experiment to discover whether a warning delivered to the subject *after* he has read a communication has the same effect as a warning delivered *before* the subject has read the message. The warning in this experiment consisted of the following footnote to a written communication: "This article was taken from the recent book *Techniques of Persuasion* . . . It was designed to make you change your opinion." Thus the warning told subjects not only that the communication advocated a point of view discrepant with their own but that the intent of the communication was definitely to persuade.

Kiesler and Kiesler suspected that a warning delivered after the communication had been read would not be as effective as a forewarning. The authors were led to this hypothesis after a consideration of which communication—the warning footnote or the communication proper— would be more likely to produce dissonance in the fore- and afterwarning situations. It was reasoned that when the subject is not warned until after he has already seriously considered the information contained in the communication, it is the *warning* itself that creates dissonance. Thus the authors predicted that it would be easiest for subjects in the afterwarning condition to reduce dissonance by rejecting the warning than to reduce dissonance by rejecting the previously accepted communication. On the other hand, it was predicted that subjects in the forewarning condition would find it easier to reduce dissonance by rejecting the communication than by rejecting the warning. In addition to the fore- and afterwarning groups, two control groups were also run in this experiment: (1) a group that was given no warning about the persuasive intent of the communication; (2) a group that read a communication on a different topic.

The investigators found no significant difference between the degree of attitude change in the control condition and in the forewarned condition. Evidently the forewarning had the effect of nullifying the persuasive communication. In addition, a significant difference was found between subjects in the no-warning condition and subjects in the control group. There was also a tendency for subjects in the afterwarned condition to change more than those in the control condition, although this difference did not quite reach an adequate level of significance. Because subjects in the forewarned condition changed significantly less than either those in the afterwarned condition or those in the no-warning condition, the authors conclude that the content of the warning was not sufficient itself to nullify the effect of the communication, and that the temporal placement of the information was crucial.

Husek (1965) also investigated how the temporal placement of information about a negative source of a communication affects the persuasive impact of the communication. The communication in this experiment was designed to improve attitudes toward mental illness. Because mental illness is generally negatively regarded and the mentally ill are usually considered to be "bad," Husek reasoned that a former mental patient would presumably be a negative communicator compared to an ordinary person. To some of the subjects the communicator said that she was a former mental patient at the beginning of the talk; to the other groups this information was given at the end of the talk; and to still other groups the information was not given at all.

Findings for the early-mention group versus the no-mention group show the expected difference and corroborate the Kiesler and Kiesler findings. When Husek compared the late-mention group with the no-mention group, he found that the late-mention group displayed more positive attitudes toward mental illness than did the no-mention group. Husek suggested that early mention of the speaker's identification marked the speaker as having negative valence. However, late mention of the speaker's identification allowed the talk to influence and to improve the subjects' attitudes toward former mental patients. Therefore, when the speaker was not identified until the end of the talk, subjects marked him as being more positive than early-mention speakers and no-mention speakers. Thus it appears that there may have been an interaction between the content of the talk and attitude toward the speaker.

Freedman and Sears (1965b) hypothesized that there were three possible reasons why forewarning might increase resistance to change. First, it was thought that source derogation may occur when the subject expects a highly discrepant communication from a previously unknown source. To test for this possibility measures of rejection of the speaker were obtained after the communication was delivered. Second, it was reasoned that another possible explanation of why forewarning decreases the effectiveness of a communication is that it causes decreased attentiveness on the part of the subject. A recall test was given after the communication to test for this possibility. And finally, the authors hypothesized that forewarning may activate a more active defense process, in that during the period between the warning and the communication, subjects may rehearse, recall, or construct arguments supporting their initial position and may attempt to refute arguments against their position. An important implication of this type of defensive mechanism is that a longer warning should produce a greater increase in resistance because it would enable subjects to gather defensive arguments. Consequently, the investigators included in their experiment a no-warning group, a two-minute warning group, and a ten-minute warning group.

The experimental results support the hypothesis that forewarning increases resistance to influence and also provide some information about the type of mechanism that is activated by forewarning. It will be recalled that the authors hypothesized that forewarning may result in derogation of the communicator. All subjects were asked to indicate how biased they thought the speaker was. All the groups appeared to reject the communicator equally. Consequently, it seems unlikely that this factor accounted for the sizeable difference between groups in degree of resistance. The second possibility was that forewarning causes the subject to attend less carefully to the talk. The authors found, however, that there were no appreciable differences among any of the groups in recall scores. The third possibility was that forewarned subjects may spend the time between the warning and the talk rehearsing arguments in favor of their position and perhaps refuting counterarguments. If this is true, a longer warning should give subjects a longer time to defend themselves and should produce greater resistance than a briefer warning. The results of this study were consistent with this expectation. The ten-minute–warning group changed less than the two-minute–warning group, which in turn changed less than the no-warning group. The monotonic trend across conditions was fairly strong ($p < .10$), but the two-minute–warning group was not significantly different from either of the others. Thus some support is provided for the idea that an active defensive process is initiated by forewarning and increases resistance to influence.

Tannenbaum, Macaulay, and Norris (1966) investigated the effectiveness of various types of warnings under both forewarning and afterwarning conditions. Four types of warnings were investigated: (1) *Denial* —This type of warning took the form of denying that the source attributed to the communication the subject was either about to receive or had already received had in fact ever made such a statement. (2) *Source attack*—In this type of warning the credibility of the communicator was brought into question. (3) *Refutation*—This warning consisted of a point-by-point rebuttal of the contents of the communication the subject had either received or was about to receive. (4) *Supportive*—This "warning" was simply a statement of support, or the presentation of evidence for the subject's initial opinion. These four types of warnings were presented to "immunization" groups, which received the particular warning before the communication, and to "restoration" groups, which received the warning after the communication. Also included in the design were control groups who received no warning but did receive the attack.

The results of this study indicated that the denial warning was not particularly effective in reducing the effectiveness of the attack either when it was given before the communication or when it was given after the communication. The source attack warning was found to confer a significant degree of resistance when the warning was placed before the communication, but it did not significantly reduce resistance to persuasion when it was placed after the communication. The warning that refuted the points contained in the communication significantly reduced the persuasive impact of the communication both when it was presented before the communication and when it was presented after the communication. Resistance was reduced most by this sort of warning, however, when it was presented before the communication. A warning consisting of supporting statements reduced significantly the persuasive impact of the attack. Unfortunately, this study did not investigate the extent to which this treatment restores belief after the attack.

Tannenbaum, Macaulay, and Norris conclude that a postwarning may be akin to "locking the barn door after the horse has been stolen." They point out that if the attack is successful, any postwarning creates an incongruous situation for the subject because it is in conflict with the now negative attitude toward the concept. "Some changes back toward a more positive attitude may result from this new incongruity. But as Kiesler and Kiesler (1964) point out in comparing a 'forewarning' with an 'afterwarning,' another way out of the dilemma is for the subject to reject the latter (that is, the restorative treatment) rather than the attack message. The various immunization conditions, on the other hand, introduced little or no additional conflict in themselves. They do serve to blunt the subsequent attack, thus reducing the potential incongruity it may introduce" (p. 237).

Primacy–Recency

Who has the advantage in a court of law—the one who gets the first word or the one who gets the last? Compelling arguments have been advanced for the supposed advantages of both positions. Some have argued that first impressions are most important, because "People see what they expect to see." Such an argument is a typical argument for the effectiveness of "primacy." On the other hand, some argue that the fellow who gets in the last word has the advantage. His arguments are more easily remembered by the jury and his emotional and logical appeals arrive too late to be refuted by the opposition. Such an argument is an argument for the effectiveness of "recency." The court, which professes that the defendant must be given every advantage, allows the defense to choose whether to present its opening statement first or to hold it until the prosecution has presented its evidence. Traditionally, the defense chooses to hold its opening statement. When giving the closing arguments, however, the prosecutor has both the advantage of primacy and the advantage of recency. The prosecutor presents his arguments first, they are followed by the defense's rebuttal, which is followed by the prosecution's closing statement.

Interest in the primacy–recency question dates back to 1925 when Lund (1925) performed an experiment in his classroom. Two days before the experiment, Lund assessed students' attitudes toward several propositions. An example of one of these propositions is "Should all men have equal political rights?" Two days later he gave each student a mimeographed booklet that contained either the pro or the con side for one of these propositions. Half of the booklets contained pro arguments, half contained con arguments. Lund told the students they had ten minutes to absorb the material. He did not mention that in a few minutes they would be presented with a point of view completely opposite from the one they had just read. After the subject had read one side of the issue, he was asked his own opinion on the topic. Then he was given a booklet advocating whichever side of the argument (either pro or con) he had not yet read. After reading this second communication, his final opinion on the topic was secured. Lund discovered a consistent primacy effect. In other words, subjects were influenced more by the first communication they read than by the material they read last. From this experiment Lund postulated his "Law of Primacy in Persuasion," which states, in effect, that the first-presented side has the greatest impact on opinion change.

In 1957, Hovland and Mandell (1957) took issue with the "Law of Primacy." They pointed out that Lund's experiment had two methodological peculiarities that might account for his results. First, Lund conducted his experiment in his own classroom. Thus it is possible that when reading the first side of the communication students were highly motivated to learn its content. They may have thought it contained the whole truth, and that they might be tested on its contents. By the time students got to the second and opposite side of the communication, the students' assumptions about what was going on might have radically changed. They may have become confused as to what was going on or suspected that they were guinea pigs in an experiment or have realized that the messages were not simply material to be learned. Motivation to learn and to accept the second communication would be expected to decrease under such circumstances. Hovland and Mandell also criticized the fact that Lund assessed students' opinions after they read each side. They argue that this may have had the effect of committing the subjects to whatever attitude they expressed after reading the first communication. Though the second communication may have changed their minds entirely, the subjects may have been ashamed to admit their persuasibility on paper.

Hovland, Campbell, and Brock (1957) provide evidence that commitment to one position may make change to subsequent positions difficult. They gave subjects arguments either favoring or opposing lowering the voting age to eighteen. After hearing only one side the students were asked to write a brief paragraph stating their own opinions. We would expect that the opinions of many of these students would be markedly influenced by the communication just heard. The investigators made half of the students strongly committed to this initial opinion; they were asked to sign their names and were told their views would be published. The opinions of control subjects were anonymous. Then the experimenter presented all students with the opposite side of the issue, and then asked them for their final opinions. Subjects who were committed to their initial opinion were more resistant to change by the second message than were students who believed their initial statement would be anonymous.

Since Lund's time, a great deal of effort has been expended on the question of primacy–recency. The results of this research clearly indicate that primacy is *not* always more effective than recency (there is no "Law of Primacy"). Nor, obviously, is recency always more effective than primacy. Thus researchers have changed their strategy, and instead of trying to demonstrate or to disprove the "Law of Primacy," they are now attempting to determine which factors give an advantage to the first communication and which factors give an advantage to the second.

An ingenious theoretical approach to this problem was attempted by Miller and Campbell (1959), who considered the effect that memory may have on attitude change. These authors point out that one's opinion may be greatly affected by the extent to which he *remembers* various pro or con arguments. Immediately after an event occurs or a message is read, we usually remember it clearly; as time passes, its details often become more and more obscured. This statement is depicted in the negatively accelerated forgetting curves of Ebbinghaus (1913), shown in Figure 7-2.

Miller and Campbell point out that if one considers the time that has elapsed between the presentation of the first and the second side and also considers the time that has elapsed before attitudes were measured, the Ebbinghaus curves enable one to make some clear predictions. Figure 7-2 presents the implications that the Ebbinghaus curve has for the primacy–recency question, given that communications A and B are equally strong and do not interact with one another. The longer the time that elapses between the presentation of communications A and B, and the measure-

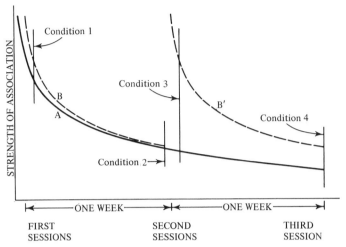

FIRST   SECOND   THIRD
SESSIONS   SESSIONS   SESSION

FIGURE 7-2.

> *Hypothetical Forgetting Curves for a First and a Second Com-*
> *peting Persuasive Communication When Both Are Presented*
> *During a Single Session (Curves A and* B) *or When the Two*
> *Are Presented One Week Apart (Curves A and* B'); *the Four*
> *Conditions, Appearing as Vertical Slicings, Represent the*
> *Timing of Measurements* (From Miller and Campbell, 1959)

ment of attitude, the less recency effect we should secure. From the
diagram, it is clear that if communication A is immediately followed by
rebuttal B, one should get a slight recency effect if he measures attitude
change at condition 1, and a much weaker or nonexistent recency effect
at condition 2. When we consider communications delivered one week
apart (A and rebuttal B'), the predicted relationships between time and
strength of the recency effect remains the same. If attitudes are measured
immediately after the presentation of communication B' (condition 3),
one should secure a fairly large recency effect. If measured one week later
(condition 4), one should get a much smaller recency effect. This generalization has intuitive sense. Though the immediate past stands out
clearly in our mind, it loses its clarity as it recedes in the past, and becomes more similar in intensity to the far past. The longer the time
interval between communications A and B, the greater the recency effect
should be when opinions are measured immediately after the second
communication. We can see that the recency effect at condition 3, when
a week has intervened between communications A and B', should be
greater than the recency effects secured at condition 1, when only a few
minutes have intervened.

As it can be seen from Figure 7-2, the authors' formulation generates only recency effects; it simply predicts that recency effects will be greater under certain measurement conditions than under others. Miller and Campbell point out, however, that their model can handle primacy effects if one assumes that communication A begins at an initially higher level and has a higher asymptotic level than communication B. Such an assumption would not change any of the relationships Miller and Campbell propose. Factors that increase the effectiveness of the first message would simply be assumed to be operating in addition to memory effects that increase the effectiveness of the second communication to various extents.

Miller and Campbell tested their hypothesis in the following way: A transcript of a trial was rearranged so that all the material favoring one side or the other was together. In some cases message B was presented to the student immediately after they had read side A. In other cases it was given to them a week later. In half of the cases subjects' opinions were assessed immediately after they read message B or B', in half the cases a week later. As predicted, the authors secured the weakest recency effect (actually a strong primacy effect) at condition 2 and the strongest recency effect at condition 3. Because they actually secured a primacy effect at condition 2, the authors felt that there was a tendency for the first message to be more effective, but that memory effects counteracted that tendency.

A replication and extension of this study by Insko (1964) supports Miller and Campbell's hypotheses. Insko did not secure a primacy effect at condition 2, however, and thus he is reluctant to assume that there is a tendency for the first message to begin at a higher level and to have a higher asymptotic level than the second. Insko also measured subjects' retention of information and found memory results that parallel the attitude results reported by Miller and Campbell.

Several authors have felt that familiarity with a topic might be another important determinant of whether a primacy or a recency effect is secured. Hovland, Campbell, and Brock (1957) suggest that the nearer one comes to achieving primacy in the sense of the first presentation of unfamiliar material, the more likely one is to obtain primacy effects. These investigators cite several experiments that lead them to the conclusion that familiarity breeds recency (Asch, 1946; Luchins, 1957). Unfortunately, a few other studies (Lana, 1961; Thomas, Webb, and Tweedie, 1961) cast doubt on the authors' generalization. We will not discuss the factor of familiarity or the related factors of controversiality (Sherif et al, 1965) and interest (Lana, 1963), because at this time research results are apparently in conflict and it is not clear which of these research leads will prove to be promising.

Emotion-Arousing Appeals

Emotion-arousing appeals are often used in publicity campaigns. Traffic-safety experts circulate pamphlets depicting the accidents that can happen if we don't drive carefully. Mouthwash, toothpaste, and deodorant companies demonstrate the social ostracism we can expect if we do not use their products. Such fear-arousing appeals are obviously based on the expectation that an individual will reduce the fear and anxiety that is aroused by the advertisements by following the recommended remedies.

The effectiveness of such fear arousing appeals has often been examined experimentally. Janis and Feshbach (1953) tested the effectiveness of fear-arousing communications of increasing intensities. They presented illustrated lectures to groups of high-school students, demonstrating the problems that are sometimes caused by improper tooth care and suggesting some ways to avoid them. In one group (the strong fear-appeal group), every effort was made to frighten the subjects. The film graphically illustrated the dangerous consequences of tooth neglect. The consequences illustrated included the pain and decay that occur as a direct consequence of neglect, and possible secondary infections that could result in cancer, paralysis, or blindness. In a moderate fear-appeal group these dangers were described in a milder and more factual manner. In a minimal fear-appeal group the discomfort of decayed teeth and mouth infection were rarely mentioned, and no realistic photographs were presented. Finally, in a control group subjects were not exposed to any information concerning the teeth, but instead viewed a film on the structure and functioning of the human eye.

One week after hearing the communication, subjects were asked about their actual toothbrushing practices. They were asked to describe the way they were brushing their teeth, the type of stroke used, the amount of surface area cleaned, the amount of force applied, the length of time spent brushing the teeth, and the time of day the teeth were brushed. The data demonstrated that the minimal fear appeal was most effective in getting students to change their habits, the moderate fear appeal was intermediate in effectiveness, and the strong fear appeal was least effective. In fact, the strong fear-appeal subjects were not any more likely to alter their toothbrushing practices than were control subjects, who had not even been told which dental practices were best to follow.

Janis and Feshbach also tested how resistant individuals in the various conditions were to counterpropaganda. In the illustrated lecture, students were told how to choose a good toothbrush. A week later they were given a statement, supposedly written by a well-known dentist, that argued that one kind of tooth brush was about as good as any other. This refutation was much more effective in altering the opinions of the group that heard the strong fear appeal than the group that had heard the minimal appeal. On the basis of these results, Janis and Feshbach conclude that a strong fear appeal tends to be less effective than a minimal appeal.

Why should communications lose their effectiveness when they become too frightening? Several possible explanations for this phenomenon were proposed.

1. It may be difficult to learn and assimilate material when one is frightened. If one is very upset that previous tooth neglect may mean that he will get cancer or go blind, for example, it may be difficult for him to pay attention to a communication giving details on how he should brush his teeth. Thus it was proposed that perhaps the Janis and Feshbach results were due to the fact that students in the high-fear condition simply did not comprehend the recommendations. There is no evidence that this explanation is correct. All students were given a retention test immediately after the films were shown, and subjects in the various fear groups appear to have learned the material equally well.

2. The high fear appeal, which frightened the audience, may have also made them angry at the communicator. One way they could express their anger and contempt for him is by refusing to accept his recommendations. The authors find no support for such a hypothesis.

3. Perhaps the severe threat aroused so much fear and anxiety in individuals that they defensively avoided ever thinking about the problem again. It is this explanation that Janis and Feshbach feel best explains their results. They note that in the strong-fear condition, students often expressed the fear that the suggested precautions might be inadequate. Such residual tension might make defensive avoidance especially likely.

4. It is also possible, though Janis and Feshbach do not mention this possibility, that the extreme threats were ineffective because they were implausible. It is easy for a person to believe that if he does not brush his teeth in the proper way he will get cavities. It is much more difficult for him to believe that he could develop cancer, paralysis, or blindness from improper brushing. Though it may be true, one has probably never heard of its happening.

Several investigators have tried to gain a greater understanding of the Janis and Feshbach results. Janis and Terwilliger (1962) examined some of the ways by which an individual might go about defensively avoiding a frightening communication. They examined whether or not individuals resisted a fear-arousing communication while listening to it for the first time. The authors prepared a high-fear and a low-fear version of a communication arguing that heavy smoking causes cancer and thus everyone should avoid cigarette smoking. Students, whose smoking habits ranged from total abstention to heavy smoking, listened to only one version of these communications. Regardless of which fear appeal they received, they were told to stop after each paragraph and to mention any thoughts they might have. The students' statements were then content analyzed, and the extent to which they expressed emotional tension and the extent to which they criticized or praised the talk were scored. As predicted, subjects in the high-threat condition were found to report feeling more emotional tension than did low-threat condition subjects. In addition, the high-fear group also expressed more resistance to the fear-arousing message than did the low-threat group. Those subjects who listened to the more frightening communication made many more statements that explicitly rejected the material, made fewer favorable comments about the good style or objectivity of the communication, and were less likely even to paraphrase the communication's arguments than were the subjects who listened to the less fearful communication. From their data the authors conclude that a relatively high level of fear motivates individuals to develop psychological resistances to the communicator's arguments, conclusions, and recommendations from the time they first hear them.

In another health study, Nunally and Bobren (1959) also found evidence that individuals avoid anxiety-arousing communications. Individuals were sent several articles in the mail and were asked to indicate which of the topics they would like to learn more about. Anxiety-arousing messages aroused less interest than did non-anxiety-arousing messages, and messages that offered no solution to the problems they described aroused less interest than did articles that offered solutions.

In their initial article, Janis and Feshbach proposed two variables that they thought would have a marked effect on the effectiveness of fear-arousing communications. These variables were the adequacy of the precautions recommended in the fear-arousing communication, and how immediately one could act to follow these fear-reducing precautions. Janis and Feshbach felt adequacy was of crucial importance. They noted that when fear is strongly aroused but is not fully relieved by the reassurances contained in a mass communication, the audience will become motivated to ignore or to minimize the importance of the threat. Their explanation suggested that if subjects really believed the recommended remedies would be 100 per cent effective and would not be too painful or costly to accept, and were clear about how to obtain the remedies, high-fear communications might be more effective than low-fear ones. Several studies have investigated this possibility, but there is no compelling data that the adequacy of recommendations eliminates subjects' resistance to high-fear communications. Support for such a hypothesis would require that the introduction of adequate recommendations into a message should increase the effectiveness of a high-fear communication more than the effectiveness of a low-fear communication.

Leventhal, Singer, and Jones (1965) and Leventhal, Jones, and Trembley (1966) investigated the effect that clarity of a recommendation has on one's tendency to follow that recommendation (getting a tetanus shot) after fear-arousing appeals of various intensities. In their experiments, after hearing fear appeals of various intensities, some subjects were given detailed information on how to go about getting a tetanus shot; others were not. The results of these studies did not support the hypothesis that adequacy of recommendations would interact with the intensity of the fear appeal in determining message effectiveness. Though specific information increased everyone's tendency to get a tetanus shot, both low- and high-fear appeals were equally effective, whether or not clear and detailed instructions were given. Dabbs and Leventhal (1966) examined two other aspects of the adequacy of a recommendation to get a tetanus shot—painfulness and effectiveness. To some subjects the recommended tetanus shot was described as very painful; to others it was described as painless. To still other subjects it was described as very effective; to others not effective at all. The investigators found a positive relationship between fear-arousal and tendency to obtain a tetanus shot. Subjects' beliefs about the painfulness or about the effectiveness of the shots had no effect upon compliance with the recommendation to obtain a tetanus shot. Most important, the predicted interaction between adequacy of recommendation and strength of appeal was not significant.

Other experiments have investigated whether or not a high-fear appeal is more effective in motivating individuals to *immediate* action than in promoting behavior that must be *delayed*. Janis and Feshbach suggested that the high-fear appeal, which evokes great emotional tension, might be extremely effective when immediate action was required (such as donating money or volunteering to perform a group task). It was when the communication was intended to produce more sustained preferences, or delayed behavior, that the authors felt that a high-fear appeal would become especially ineffective. Defensive avoidance and defensive forgetting were assumed to be possible only after the passage of a certain amount of time. Several investigators have tested this hypothesis, but once again there is no evidence that this reasonable-sounding proposition is true. The reader will recall that in the Janis and Terwilliger (1962) study, resistance to the high-fear communication was measurable *during* the time the communication was presented. So Janis himself would acknowledge that on occasion resistance can begin when one first hears the communication.

Leventhal and Watts (1966) secured results opposite to those predicted by Janis and Feshbach. In this study two procedures were recommended to subjects: (1) It was suggested that they get an x-ray. (2) It was suggested that listeners stop smoking. X-rays were available immediately after the communication was presented. Compliance with the suggestion to quit smoking was measured five months later. Leventhal and Watts found that among smokers in the high-fear condition there seemed to be an *immediate* resistance to getting an x-ray; fewer high-fear subjects than low-fear subjects actually followed the recommendation. Among nonsmokers the strength of the appeal made no difference. On the other hand, there is no evidence that fearful subjects developed resistances over time. High fear-appeal subjects were more likely to decrease their smoking than were low fear-appeal subjects. In another study, Leventhal and Niles (1965) directly examined changes in the effectiveness of fear-arousing communications of different intensities over time. Communication effectiveness was measured immediately, one hour, two hours, one day, or one week after exposure to the fear-arousing message. It was found that the passage of time did *not* produce any increased tendency for the subject to resist a strong fear message. These results certainly do not support the contention that a high-fear appeal will have more effect on recommended behavior that can be performed immediately than on behavior that can be performed only after a lapse of time. It might be noted that this result is very surprising. At the very least, the passage of time should cause the fear engendered by the high-fear appeal to decrease as memory fades. Thus a high-fear appeal might be expected to become somewhat less threatening and more like a low-fear appeal in its effects simply because the fear-arousing material is somewhat forgotten.

All of the preceding studies have examined various hypotheses that were advanced in the original Janis and Feshbach experiment to explain why a high-fear appeal is less effective than a mild-fear appeal. We have just seen that there is no compelling support for these explanatory devices. Now we will discover that there is not unanimity of opinion among all researchers that high-fear appeals are less effective than mild-fear appeals. Leventhal, Singer, and Jones (1965), for example, propose a hypothesis diametrically opposed to the Janis and Feshbach finding. They state: "fear functions as a drive, which promotes the acceptance of recommended actions, and regardless of the absolute level of fear arousal used in any study, *the communication which arouses more fear will be more persuasive*" (p. 20). Leventhal (1967) adds, "In a recent review of studies in this area, the author found near unanimity of findings: the higher the fear level the greater the acceptance of recommendations."

What are these findings? Haefner (1965) performed an exact replication of the Janis and Feshbach study and found that in his experiment, a high–fear-arousing communication was more effective than a milder one. Leventhal and Niles (1965), Niles (1967), and Leventhal and Singer (1966) also found high–fear-producing messages to be more effective than low–fear-producing ones in some respects. There are many other experiments that find that high- and low-fear messages are equally effective in altering behavior (Leventhal, Singer, and Jones [1965]; Leventhal, Jones, and Trembley [1966]; and Leventhal, Watts, and Pagano [1967]).

On the basis of such contradictory evidence, several researchers have suggested that some additional variables must be taken into account in order to predict what effect a fear-arousing communication will have. McGuire (1966), for example, proposes that the relationship between fear arousal and attitude change is most likely a curvilinear one. He hypothesizes that up to a certain point, the more fearful a communication is, the more effective it will be. After that point, increasing fear should decrease the effectiveness of the communication. McGuire suggests that three additional factors must be taken into account when making predictions: the subject's chronic level of anxiety, his concern over the issue, and the complexity of the issue. McGuire suggests that raising any of these factors would tend to lower the level of fear arousal that would be optimum for opinion change. Why would these three factors be important?

An individual's chronic level of anxiety and concern about an issue might well determine how frightening a communication, which an *experimenter* perceived to be of low, medium, or high intensity, actually was to the subject. Janis and Feshbach (1954) provide some evidence on this point. They proposed that people with a characteristically high level of anxiety may be especially sensitive to fear arousal. For them a fear-arousing appeal labeled by an experimenter as "moderately arousing" may in fact be "extremely frightening." To test this hypothesis, Janis and Feshbach reanalyzed the data from their 1953 study. On the basis of personality tests and teacher ratings, they classified individuals as high or low in anxiety. As predicted, high-anxiety individuals exhibited a stronger defensive-avoidance reaction in the high-fear condition than did low anxiety subjects—that is, in the high fear-arousing condition, high-anxiety subjects changed their tooth-brushing habits less than did low-anxiety subjects. In the low-arousing condition, high-anxiety subjects did not display this defensiveness; they changed their tooth-brushing practices more than did low-anxiety subjects. Niles (1964) found that those subjects who felt they were "highly vulnerable to health and safety hazards" were more influenced by a low-fear appeal concerning smoking and cancer; those who felt invulnerable were more influenced by the high-fear appeal.

The second factor that McGuire points out, how concerned an individual is with the issue under discussion, may be important for two reasons: (1) A person who is highly concerned with a topic may listen more carefully to it than would a less concerned individual, and thus the fear-arousing appeal may be more effective in arousing emotion. (2) Concern with an issue may attract one's attention to a communication. Thus additional incentives would not be necessary to get him to listen to the appeal.

Berkowitz and Cottingham (1960) point out that a frightening appeal may be more exciting, as well as more threatening, than a less frightening one. If a listener completely ignores your message either because it is boring or because it is threatening, obviously no attitude change can occur. When your audience is unconcerned with your message, it may be necessary to use a high-fear appeal merely to get them to attend to your communication. In such a case, a frightening message may be necessary. The more concerned with an issue the audience is initially, the less need there would be to resort to high-fear appeals to make the topic attention-capturing. In two experiments the authors analyzed the reactions of frequent and infrequent automobile users to minimal or strong fear appeals advocating use of seat belts. They assumed that individuals who drove fairly often would be more interested in the seat-belt issue than would infrequent drivers. A high-fear appeal may also be more anxiety producing for frequent than for infrequent drivers. As predicted, they found that a strong fear appeal was less effective for frequent drivers than for infrequent drivers, whereas a minimal appeal was equally effective for frequent and infrequent drivers.

Concerning McGuire's third point, that the more complex the issue, the weaker an appeal must be to be maximally effective, there are as yet no data.

8

Characteristics of a Receptive Communicatee and a Facilitative Environment

Thus far the techniques we have discussed for making communications more effective have concerned factors that are traditionally considered in any discussion of attitude change. Yet, if we consider our own perhaps ill-fated attempts to persuade others on important issues, we will quickly realize that these factors alone are not sufficient to ensure attitude change. Even if one designs a message guaranteed to get anyone's attention, has a totally credible person endorse the message, constructs it with great cunning, and makes sure no factual information could contradict its implications—even so, if an individual is motivated enough to do so, he could reject it. Nothing compels a person to accept a fact against his will; certainly a controversial argument is easier to reject. Pascal observed that, "The heart has reasons of which reason has no knowledge." In designing a persuasive message, one must also take these "reasons of heart" into consideration. It is necessary to consider those personal factors that may make an individual eager to accept or reject certain messages. The first section of this chapter will consider the importance of existing personality traits and beliefs on one's receptivity to new messages. The second section will consider the effects of the rewards and punishments that occur to an individual as he considers acceptance of various positions.

Characteristics of a Receptive Communicatee

The Effect of Personality on Persuasibility

Are some people especially willing to accept any communication? From our daily observations, it often seems possible to classify people according to how persuasible they are. Some people appear to be habitually skeptical of even the most reasonable propositions, whereas others seem to be, with fair regularity, the gullible prey of unscrupulous encyclopedia salesmen and the like. Hovland and Janis (1959) have made an extensive study of factors that might affect a person's general susceptibility to persuasive messages. These investigators reasoned that whether or not we observe attitude change as a result of a given communication depends on the extent to which the communicatee pays attention to the message, the extent to which he comprehends the message, and finally, on the extent to which he accepts the message. Attitude change, at least the change advocated by the communicator, may be avoided at any one of these three steps. Thus Hovland and Janis considered the effect that various personality traits might have on one's attention, on one's comprehension, and finally, on one's acceptance of a message. Their first step, before attempting to discover which personality traits are associated with persuasibility, was to determine whether some individuals are in fact more generally persuasible than others. Janis and Field (1959), in a correlational study, found support for the proposition that individuals do differ in persuasibility. Additional support for this notion can be found in King (1959) and in Abelson and Lesser (1959).

Armed with the evidence that persuasibility did differ between individuals, researchers began exploring several variables that, on intuitive grounds, seemed possibly related to persuasibility. Among the most commonly examined of these variables were sex of subject, intelligence and education, self-esteem, level of anxiety, authoritarianism, perceptual dependence, other-directedness, social isolation from one's peers, richness of fantasy, and so on. A great deal of this research has been correlational, and thus we will briefly mention a few sample studies so that the student can get a general feeling for the type of work that has been done. Early investigators of communication felt that the intelligence and education of the communicatee might have an important effect on the extent to which he was likely to pay attention to, to comprehend, and to accept a message. With respect to comprehension, for example, they noted that an intelligent person may be better able to understand and retain a message than an unintelligent one, especially if the message is difficult. A scientific paper might alter an educated man's opinion more than it alters an uneducated man's, simply because the educated man is able to understand the message whereas the other is not. Thus it is possible that communication acceptance might be positively related to intelligence simply because intelligent people are more likely to comprehend communication content. Hovland, Lumsdaine, and Sheffield (1949) conducted an experiment in which they exposed World War II soldiers to a propaganda film, *Prelude to War*. This film presented many facts about the events leading up to World War II. As would be expected, the more education men had, the more relevant, factual information they possessed before hearing the film and the more additional information they learned from hearing the movie. It is not surprising that the acquisition of factual items is positively related to intellectual ability. What is surprising is the frequency with which those who wish to persuade ignore this fact. As one advertising agency learned recently, one is not going to persuade a small child to ask his mother to buy "Brand X" cookies if the child cannot comprehend the argument contained in the commercial (which was that the sugar in "Brand X" cookies would give him the energy to play and have a good time).

Although it is possible that a positive relationship between intelligence and acceptance may be likely because of comprehension differences, it seems clear that at times intelligence may produce a decrease, rather than an increase, in acceptance. For example, if the argument is logical and fair, the educated man may be more likely to accept it than is the uneducated man, and a positive relationship between intelligence and acceptance would be expected to hold. If a communication is illogical and biased, however, it is likely that the educated man will be better equipped to find flaws in the argument and will have more confidence in his ability to refute the argument than does the less educated man. Some data to support this proposition are reported by Hovland, Lumsdaine, and Sheffield (1949).

Though it is clear that the effect of intelligence on communication reception and on communication acceptance might be quite different, much recent work on the topic has confounded the two. Consequently, as one might expect, many of the existing data on intelligence and persuasibility are confusing. The confusion that exists when we look at the data on the relationship between intelligence and persuasibility is typical of data in the area of personality and persuasibility generally; finding stable correlations between personality traits and persuasibility has proved to be an extremely difficult problem. (The interested student should see Murphy, Murphy, and Newcomb [1937], or Hovland and Janis [1959] for a review of later literature, or an excellent and recent review by McGuire [in press]).

Recent support for the proposition that a personality variable (self-esteem) may effect learning and acceptance differently is provided in an imaginative experiment by Gollob and Dittes (1965), who proposed and tested the following hypotheses: (1) When an advocated opinion is non-threatening and clearly stated, there will be an inverse relationship between self-esteem and persuasibility. The authors felt that individuals who had low self-esteem would think unfavorably of themselves and their opinions and thus would be likely to try to build up their self-esteem by accepting the opinions of others under such conditions. Gollob and Dittes proposed two exceptions to this hypothesis. (2) *Fear*—They felt that when a simply stated communication caused a substantial threat to the self, the relationship between self-esteem and persuasibility would become positive. They argued that a low self-esteem person, who is already threatened and anxious, cannot stand to accept a communication that adds additional threat to the same extent as can a more secure person (one with high self-esteem). (3) *Complexity*—It will be difficult for a low self-esteem person to learn a very complex message. Thus, when a message is very complex, the relationship between self-esteem and learning (and acceptance) will again be positive. If an individual does not learn a message, he cannot be persuaded by it. The effect that a loss in self-esteem should have on learning depends on the complexity of the message to be learned. Several studies have shown that anxiety facilitates performance on simple tasks and interferes with performance on complex tasks (Child, 1954; Taylor and Spence, 1952).

The authors tested their hypotheses in the following way: Self-esteem was both measured and manipulated experimentally. Two self-report measures of self-esteem were utilized—a measure of "feelings of inadequacy" by Janis and Field (1959) and a measure of self-esteem by Dittes (1959). Because measured self-esteem did not seem to affect either message learning or acceptance in any important way, we will not discuss it further. The manipulation of self-esteem was more successful. At the beginning of the experiment subjects took a somewhat ambiguous test that they were told measured skills of abstraction. Such skills were said to be of central importance in almost all occupations and highly related to personal effectiveness and professional success. False feedback as to how well they had done compared to other students was provided to subjects. Half of the subjects were randomly assigned to succeed at this important task. The remainder were led to believe they had failed. Those who were told they succeeded were assumed to have temporarily higher self-esteem than those who were told they failed.

Attitude change in response to various types of appeal was measured by the following procedure: Immediately after the self-esteem manipulation, all subjects were asked to give their opinion on three questions concerning cancer research. This constituted the premeasure of attitudes. Then they read a communication concerning cancer research that contained three submessages. Each of these three messages was constructed to test one of the authors' hypotheses. One of these segments was designed to be neither fear arousing nor complex. A second was designed to be fear arousing, and a third to be complex and difficult to learn. The non–fear-arousing, noncomplex segment contained a message arguing either that a massive concentrated crash program, focusing on a few clear problems, was a better (or was a worse) way to do cancer research than was a diffuse program with many people working in different places in different ways. The fear-arousing segment consisted of a message that argued that at present the cancer problem seemed almost hopeless, that there was a strong possibility that the subject would get cancer himself, and that the cancer might not be curable. The complex segment presented the arguments that one of the programs (either the crash program or the diffuse program) would be more expensive than the others. The message was made difficult in the following way: The communicator argued for only one side in his message. However, he mentioned several opposition arguments. These opposition arguments were made prominent by underlining, quotation marks, and so on. Thus, instead of summarizing the main point of the message, the most prominent phrases and words actually conflicted with it.

After reading the three messages, subjects were asked to state their opinion on these issues. They were asked, in light of what they had read, whether a diffuse or a crash program was the better strategy, whether or not the cancer problem seemed hopeless, and whether they thought a diffuse or a crash program of research would be the more expensive. Message acceptance was measured by compiling the attitude change from the pretest to the posttest. Learning was measured by giving subjects an information test, which asked for the communicator's opinions on the issues.

All of the authors' hypotheses were supported. When the message was simple and did not arouse fear, low self-esteem subjects were more persuasible than were high self-esteem subjects. (Both low and high self-esteem subjects were equally able to learn this message.) When subjects were frightened about the possibility of getting cancer themselves, or when the message was a very complex one, low self-esteem subjects showed less attitude change than did high self-esteem subjects. Subjects in both esteem conditions showed equal learning of the fearful messages. When the message was difficult, however, low self-esteem subjects did not learn it as well as did high self-esteem subjects. Information scores on this question were significantly higher for success subjects than for failure ones. Thus, in this case, as proposed, acceptance does seem to be determined by differences due to learning.

Weiss and Fine (1956) proposed that communication effectiveness would be increased when the specific recommendations a message made were consistent with the general response predispositions of the communicatees. More specifically, they suggested that individuals who had recently experienced great, ego-deflating frustration would be more predisposed to accept communications advocating an aggressive solution to a problem than would individuals who had not recently had such experiences. Such a prediction is consistent with other psychological research indicating that frustration often leads to aggression (see Dollard et al., 1939).

Weiss and Fine's proposed hypothesis was tested in the following way: Two weeks before the experiment, subjects' opinions on juvenile delinquency and foreign aid were assessed. Then subjects entered the experimental situation, which they believed was designed to test their creative abilities. In point of fact the purpose of the experiment was to severely frustrate half of the subjects while satisfying the needs of the remainder. If the subject had been randomly assigned to the frustration condition, he was given problems so difficult that he failed the majority of them. In addition, the experimenter made uncomplimentary and insulting comments about his abilities. If the subject had been assigned to the ego-satisfaction condition, his performance was said to be superior to that of the average college student, and the experimenter made personally complimentary and encouraging remarks to him. Then experimental subjects were asked to read an article and to express their reactions to it. (A second experimenter administered this last measure.) Half of the subjects were given an article that argued that punitive measures, in contrast to practices of leniency and guidance, were necessary to curb juvenile offenses. The remainder of subjects were given an article that urged that Americans should consider the special economic, geographic, and military circumstances of other nations in making judgments about them; essentially the article argued for kindness and understanding toward other nations. After evaluating the article, subjects were asked to give their own opinions as to whether delinquents should be treated leniently or punitively, and whether America should continue aid to allies who did not follow our policies vis-à-vis Communist China.

When subjects had not read the article, they showed little change in their opinions; the frustrated subjects' opinions were still much like those of the ego-satisfied subjects. How much subjects changed their opinions after reading the article depended both on their experiences in the previous experiment and on the aggressiveness of the communication's recommendations. Those who had been frustrated accepted the aggressive recommendations in the delinquency article to a much greater extent than did those who had been exposed to the ego-satisfying situation. Conversely, the article concerning America's relations with her allies, which argued for leniency and kindness, was accepted less by frustrated subjects than by those who had been exposed to the ego-satisfying condition. (This latter difference was not quite significant.) The authors conclude that a person's momentary mood may well effect his receptivity to various types of recommendations.

Cognitive Structure

There is a great deal of agreement among psychologists that individuals prefer to think and behave in a consistent way. In a review of cognitive-consistency theories, Zajonc (1960) illustrated what we mean by thinking and behaving in consistent ways. Zajonc states that it is commonly recognized and accepted that " . . . thoughts, beliefs, attitudes, and behavior tend to organize themselves in meaningful and sensible ways. Members of the White Citizens' Council do not ordinarily contribute to the NAACP. Adherents of the New Deal seldom support Republican candidates. Christian Scientists do not enroll in medical schools, and people who live in glass houses apparently do not throw stones" (p. 280).

What this means is that messages are not accepted or rejected in a vacuum, and that acceptance of a communication will be affected by the nature of the communicatee's other beliefs. It suggests that when deciding whether to accept or to reject a specific communication, an individual may also consider how the advocated beliefs would fit in with other beliefs he holds, and may examine the ways in which changing his belief in one area would require him to alter beliefs he holds in other areas. Several theories have attempted to predict exactly how individuals will go about maintaining or securing cognitive consistency (for example, Heider, 1946; Newcomb, 1953; Osgood and Tannenbaum, 1955; Cartwright and Harary, 1956; Festinger, 1957; Abelson and Rosenberg, 1958).

Several investigations have tested the hypothesis that an individual is much more receptive to communications that advocate positions that are consistent with his beliefs and opinions than communications that advocate positions inconsistent with his previous beliefs (for example, Scott, 1959; McGuire, 1960; Rosenberg and Abelson, 1960). Similarly, it has been predicted that it would be easier to change an existing belief if it is inconsistent with other beliefs than if it is consistent. This prediction makes intuitive sense. Imagine that a person possesses the following four cognitions: (1) "Going to college will give me an economic advantage." (2) "College is a good preparation for life." (3) "College attendance brings social approval." (4) "College is pleasant." Because all of these cognitions argue consistently for the same general principle (that going to college is a good idea), we can say that the cognitions seem to be entirely consistent with one another; 1 is consistent with 2, 2 with 3, and so on.

On the other hand, suppose that a person has cognition 1, "Going to college will give me an economic advantage," but also has the cognitions that college is a *poor* preparation for life, that attendance brings social *dis*approval, and that it is *un*pleasant. In this case, cognitions 2, 3, and 4 are consistent (all agree with the notion that going to college is a bad thing) and cognition 1 is inconsistent with all of the others. We thus would expect that this person would be more likely to accept a communication designed to persuade him to change cognition 1 (for example, to convince him that in fact college leads to economic disadvantage) than if cognition 1 were consistent with his other beliefs.

Hardyck (1966) conducted an experiment to test the preceding hypothesis. Her predictions were derived from dissonance theory. Hardyck pointed out that individuals commonly assume that various beliefs are related to one another. Consider, for example, two beliefs that could conceivably be related: (1) "Everyone should have the opportunity to be educated to the extent of his capacity." (2) "We need a much more extensive program of scholarships for students who are unable to attend college for economic reasons." Most people would feel that their opinion on cognition 1 is relevant to their opinion on cognition 2. If an individual agreed with both statements 1 and 2, or disagreed with both of them, his beliefs on these issues would be consistent. Otherwise, these cognitions would be in an inconsistent, or dissonant, relationship. Hardyck agrees that it will be harder to change cognition 1 when it is in a consonant relationship with 2 than when it is in a dissonant relationship. She emphasizes, however, that this will be true only when subjects feel the cognitions are in logical relationship to one another. If subjects feel that the two cognitions have no bearing on each other, the degree of consistency between cognitions 1 and 2 should have no effect on the ease of changing cognition 1.

In pretesting her experiment, Hardyck discovered that there was uniform agreement by students that everyone should have a chance to receive as much education as he can absorb. Hardyck also measured subjects' opinions on some seemingly related issues. For example, two of the possibly related issues that were considered were (1) "The United States needs a much more extensive program of scholarship aid for financially poor students" and (2) "Increased technology is creating a demand for highly trained people while eliminating the need for untrained people." We will consider only the first of these two statements when discussing her predictions, though of course the same logic would apply to all of them.

Subjects who felt everyone had a right to education but who disapproved of scholarship aid were classified as "inconsistent" on these two beliefs. Subjects who agreed with both statements were classified as "consistent." Hardyck then attempted to lead some subjects to believe that their attitudes on the scholarship issue should be related to their attitudes on the right-to-education question. Other subjects were led to believe that their opinions on these two topics need not be relevant to one another. She did this in the following way: Subjects were asked to read an essay, presumably written by a professor of logic. In this essay he discussed how important it was to know what frame of reference one should logically use in evaluating an argument. Two versions of this essay were prepared. If the subject had been randomly assigned to the "related" condition, he read an essay in which the logic professor convincingly argued that it is relevant to bring to mind one's opinions on side issues when evaluating a persuasive essay. He indicated that considering side issues gives one breadth and perspective. If the subject had been randomly assigned to the "irrelevant" condition, he was given a version of the essay in which the logic professor argued convincingly for the opposite point of view. He argued that it is usually best to exclude consideration of "irrelevant" side issues when reading a persuasive communication, "thus avoiding . . . the ever present possibility of emotional or illogical muddling of the issue." After reading the logic professor's essay, subjects read a second essay, which attempted to change cognition 1. It strongly argued against the belief that everybody should have the opportunity to be educated to the extent of his capacity. Finally, subjects were asked to give their own opinion on several issues.

Hardyck hypothesized that those subjects who had initially inconsistent belief systems and who were also led to believe that their cognitions should be related to one another would be most influenced by the persuasive communication, because opinion change would eliminate the inconsistency. It was predicted that subjects with initially consistent systems would be least influenced, since change would produce inconsistency. When subjects believed the cognitions should not be related, Hardyck predicted that subjects would change an intermediate amount, and that there would be little difference between initially consistent and initially inconsistent subjects. The data supported these hypotheses.

Counterarguments by the Communicatee

Laboratory and mass-communication experiments are different from most informal persuasive attempts in one important way. Formal persuasive attempts are generally considered to be a monologue: whether it is a political speech, a TV commercial, an inspirational radio talk, or a speaker at a PTA meeting, it is assumed that the communicator will talk and the communicatee will listen. Informal persuasive attempts usually consist of a dialogue. When your wife tries to convince you that TV dinners are really better than home cooked ones, or the man in the office next door tries to explain why you would be happier in his small office than in your large one, things are quite different. In informal situations the intended recipient of the communication can talk back. It is probably as likely that the communicatee will try to change the communicator's opinion as it is that he will accept the message. Even in formal communication situations, however, it is unlikely that the communicatee is as passive as it is often assumed. Even though the viewer of a television news program has no chance of changing the commentator's opinions, that fact probably does not prohibit the viewer from actively arguing and muttering at messages with which he disagrees.

Some investigators have recognized the fact that communicatees can, and often do argue with the content of a message even in formal persuasive situations, and have considered the probable effectiveness of various techniques to neutralize such counterargument and to facilitate acceptance of the communication. Hovland, Lumsdaine, and Sheffield (1949) suggested that if the listeners are initially opposed to the arguments contained in the communication, it is best for the communicator to discuss their objections early and to discount these objections if possible; if not possible, they suggest that it would be wise for the communicator to at least mention that he is aware of the objections. It was reasoned that early mention of the communicatee's objections will neutralize counterarguments and facilitate acceptance of the communication because mention of the objections would allow the communicatee to listen to the remainder of the arguments contained in the communication, without his continually ruminating on counterarguments of his own, of which he thinks the communicator is unaware.

Other investigators have suggested that one may prevent the subject from counterarguing by distracting him at the same time you deliver an unacceptable message. Their thought is that he will be too preoccupied with the distraction to counterargue, and thus will accept the message. There is evidence to support this peculiar hypothesis. The reader will recall that Allyn and Festinger (1961) conducted an experiment in which they observed that subjects changed their attitudes in line with an unpleasant communication more often when they were busy evaluating the personality of the communicator while listening to the message than when they were paying careful attention to the communication. Allyn and Festinger explained their results partially by proposing that people who are forewarned that their opinion will be attacked are better able to martial their defenses, and hence are more successful in rejecting the speaker and at resisting his persuasions, than people who are not forewarned.

In a reinterpretation of the Allyn and Festinger results, Festinger and Maccoby (1964) argued that this was not a good explanation of the data. Because, in all conditions, Allyn and Festinger's communicator began his speech with a vigorous denunciation of teenagers and automobiles, the personality-orientation subjects were in effect as forewarned as those subjects in the content-orientation condition. Festinger and Maccoby suggested that perhaps the personality-orientation condition was more effective in producing opinion change because in this condition a good deal of the communicatee's attention was focused on a distracting task (evaluating the speaker's personality) that had little to do with the persuasive communication itself. They proposed that the maximally effective influence situation was one in which the attention of the listener was distracted sufficiently to make it difficult for him to counterargue with the opposing communication, but not distracted so much as to interfere with his hearing of the communication.

To test their hypothesis, Festinger and Maccoby prepared two films, each of which contained identical communications arguing strongly against fraternities. One was a normal film in which a communicator gave an antifraternity speech. The other film contained the same soundtrack, but had a highly distracting visual presentation that was irrelevant to the arguments presented on the sound track. (The visual portion of the film was a silent film, *Day of the Painter*, which was a very amusing demonstration of the construction of a modern art work.) Both these films were then presented to different groups of fraternity and nonfraternity men. The investigators found that fraternity men were more influenced by the distracting presentation of the persuasive communication than by the ordinary version. They found no difference in the effectiveness of the two films for the nonfraternity men who served as control groups. Since fraternity men are the very group who would be motivated to argue against the message, the authors felt that their hypothesis had been supported.

Characteristics of a Facilitative Environment: Rewards and Punishments

A number of theorists have emphasized the role that the administration of rewards and punishments may play in the formation and change of attitudes (for example, Doob, 1947; Hovland, Janis, and Kelley, 1953; Katz and Stotland, 1959). Perhaps the most explicit theory, at least from the reinforcement-theory point of view, is that developed by Doob. His theory extends Hullian learning theory to the special case of attitudes. According to Doob's formulation, an attitude is an implicit anticipatory response that occurs within the individual (and thus is not observable to an outsider) as a reaction to particular stimulus patterns. It is this implicit anticipatory response that affects subsequent overt responses. In Doob's theory, an attitude is conceived to be both cue-producing and drive-producing. The implicit anticipatory response has cue value in that it acts as a stimulus to produce other responses. These responses may be overt, or they may be covert responses such as thoughts or images. If covert responses are produced, these, along with the specific implicit attitudinal response, will eventually have an effect upon overt behavior. Thus an attitude "mediates" patterns of overt responses.

Doob states that an attitude has drive value in that its tension is reduced through subsequent behavior leading to reward. An attitude, then, possesses drive strength. To illustrate this point, Doob gives the example of a person who is shown a picture of a type of food he likes. The picture will evoke his favorable attitude toward the food. According to Doob, this favorable attitude is a drive whose ultimate goal response is eating. If the person immediately goes out and buys some of the food, the drive is strong. Presumably the actual eating of the desirable food would be an enjoyable and rewarding experience, and the favorable attitude toward the food evoked by the picture would become strengthened. The responses the attitude produces might include only a covert thought, or an overt verbal statement, of how much the individual likes the food. In such a case we might consider the drive to be less strong.

This conceptualization of attitude has a number of implications for attitude change. Doob feels that the fate of an attitude over time— whether it will persist or whether it will change—involves at least three factors. The first is the reward or punishment associated with the goal response. An attitude will persist when it is constantly reinforced; it will change when it is partially or wholly extinguished. Secondly, Doob points out that there is the factor of conflict with competing drives, which may determine the fate of an attitude. The particular drive strength of an attitude may be weak in comparison with other attitudes or drives aroused by the same or different stimulus patterns. For example, an individual may not express his unfavorable attitude toward his employer in overt behavior because its expression would be contrary to his attitude concerning job security; but his unfavorable attitude toward his employer may persist. Third, there is the process of forgetting. If the stimulus patterns that arouse the attitude do not appear in the environment for a length of time, the attitude may weaken.

Some of the first experimental investigations into the use of reinforcement in the modification of attitudes were reported by Razran in talks given at the 1938 and 1940 Annual Convention of the American Psychological Association. The stimuli in one of Razran's experiments (1940) were social–political slogans such as "Down with War and Fascism!" One set of slogans was presented when all of the subjects were enjoying a free lunch. The other set of slogans was presented when all of the subjects were required to inhale a number of unpleasant odors. Razran reported that to confuse the subjects' memories, nonexperimental slogans were added to each session. Finally, after five to eight sessions of "conditioning," subjects again rated each original slogan for attractiveness. Razran found that slogans associated with the lunch, or the reinforcement, clearly showed increases in ratings of attractiveness. Slogans combined with unpleasant odors, or punishment, showed decreases in ratings. Razran concluded that the changes were not a matter of conscious memories of conditioning, because a check indicated that the subjects' knowledge of which slogans were combined with pleasant stimuli and which were combined with unpleasant stimuli was little above chance.

Razran's imaginative procedure has been used often in investigations of the effects of reward and punishment on the modification of attitudes. Recently, for example, Janis, Kaye, and Kirschner (1965) performed a study to test the hypothesis that food, eaten during the presentation of a persuasive communication, will increase acceptance of the communication. They predicted this would be true even if the donor of the food was not the source of the communication and did not endorse it. The authors reasoned that if the experimenter (the donor of the food) was not perceived by the subjects as endorsing the communication in any way, the eating of the food and the reading of the communication would be two unrelated events; the eating of the food (the reinforcement) would be *extraneous* to, or not cognitively connected with, the source or content of the communication. If a learning theory of attitudes is correct, a communication should be more likely to be accepted when a reinforcement, even an extraneous reinforcement is present, than when it is not.

If the reinforcement in this experiment had not been extraneous, if the experimenter had been seen as endorsing the communication, the results of the experiment could have been easily predicted. Presumably subjects would have perceived the experimenter as more generous and thus more attractive when he gave food than when he did not. We know that attractive people wield more influence than unattractive ones. Thus, if the experimenter were seen as endorsing the communication, we would expect more attitude change when food was present than when it was not.

To test the hypothesis that an extraneous reinforcement presented during the presentation of a communication will increase its acceptance, the investigators performed two experiments. In each experiment there were three conditions: (1) In the "food" condition, subjects read four persuasive communications while eating desirable food. (2) In the "no-food" condition, subjects read the same four communications with no food present. (3) Subjects in the control group received no relevant communications.

The premeasure in this experiment was administered in regular undergraduate class sessions and was introduced as a "survey of student opinions." Two months later, the subjects were contacted by phone and asked to be unpaid volunteers for a study on reading preferences. Upon entering the experimental room, subjects in the food condition found the experimenter eating some peanuts and drinking some Pepsi-Cola. The subject was offered the same refreshments with the explanation that there was plenty on hand because, "I brought some along for you too." The procedure in the no-food condition was identical to that of the food condition with the exception that no refreshments were in the room at any time. The subjects assigned to the control condition were given the same pre- and postcommunication questionnaires as in the other condition, and separated by the same time interval, but were not exposed to any relevant communications.

The experimenter explained to all subjects that the purpose of the experiment was to assess students' reading preferences. He also specifically asserted that he did *not* endorse the communications and casually mentioned that he happened to agree with certain of the ideas expressed and not with the others (without specifying which). He asked the subjects to read the articles provided them as though they were at home reading a popular magazine. After subjects had read the articles, they were asked to give interest ratings of each of the articles.

A second experiment, a replication, was similar to the first experiment with the exception that a fourth experimental condition was introduced. This condition was designed to investigate the effects of extraneous, unpleasant stimuli. While reading the four persuasive communications, this fourth group of subjects was exposed to an unpleasant odor produced by a hidden bottle of butyric acid, for which the experimenter disclaimed any responsibility.

The results of these experiments indicated that "eating while reading" had a facilitating effect upon opinion change. When the results of the two experiments were combined, the data revealed that all four communications produced differences between the food and no-food conditions in the predicted direction, and for three of the communications the differences were large enough to be statistically significant. Thus the results support the conclusion that eating while reading a series of persuasive communications tends to increase their effectiveness. The condition of unpleasant stimulation introduced into the second experiment had no observable effects on amount of opinion change.

Janis, Kaye, and Kirschner were interested in finding out whether a gratifying activity, such as eating, would facilitate opinion change even if the gratifying activity was entirely extraneous to the content, source, or endorsement of the communication. For this reason, the experimenter in these experiments specifically disavowed any endorsement of the communications. Unfortunately, in spite of this precaution the investigators were not entirely confident that the reinforcement was extraneous. They observed that subjects in the food condition had a much more favorable attitude toward the experimenter than subjects in the no-food condition. The authors did not have a measure of the extent to which the subjects ignored or forgot the experimenter's remarks to the effect that he did not sponsor the articles. If subjects assumed that he was sponsoring the articles, the food and the communication were not unrelated to each other; the attractive food-condition experimenter could effect more opinion change than the less attractive no-food experimenter. If such was the case, it would be clear that the food reward did affect attitude change, but its effect would have been mediated through cognitive awareness of the food–communication relationship.

Therefore, to attack the problem of extraneous gratification further, Dabbs and Janis (1965) investigated the relative effects upon opinion change of (1) contiguity of the reinforcement and the communication, and (2) positive versus negative endorsement of the communication by the experimenter. With respect to contiguity of the reinforcement, the authors reasoned that if food is a reinforcement that increases habit strength of verbal opinion responses rehearsed during exposure to the communication, then more opinion change should result when food is given *during* exposure to a persuasive communication (when the reinforcement is contiguous to the communication) than when it is given *before* exposure.

With respect to positive versus negative endorsement, it will be recalled that Janis, Kaye, and Kirshner felt that the results of their experiment may have been due to a more positive attitude toward the donor of the food, resulting in greater receptivity to his suggestions and stronger motivation to comply with his explicit or implicit demands. It follows from this assumption that members of an audience who have been given food should become more inclined to accept any persuasive communication to which the donor exposes them if he is perceived as positively endorsing it. However, they should become more inclined to reject the communication if he is perceived as negatively endorsing it. Thus Dabbs and Janis used a design in which there were two independent variables: contiguous versus noncontiguous food given by the experimenter and positive versus negative endorsement of the communications by the experimenter.

In order to test the two hypotheses, all subjects were given a precommunication opinion questionnaire. After this questionnaire had been completed, half of the subjects were given two persuasive communications contiguously with soft drinks and snacks. (All experimental sessions were scheduled for four o'clock in the afternoon to ensure that the subjects would arrive at a time when they felt fairly hungry.) The other half, the noncontiguous group, received the same refreshments, for the same length of time, *before* being exposed to the same two communications. The "filler" activity for subjects in this noncontiguous group (to give them something to do while they were eating) consisted of viewing a series of ten slide-projected paintings and rating them in terms of like or dislike. The groups were then subdivided into positive- and negative-endorsement subgroups; the experimenter informed one half of the subjects that he personally agreed with the point of view expressed in both communications and the other half that he personally disagreed with the communications.

To obtain supplementary data, all subjects were given a number of other judgmental tasks to perform. The sequence of tasks in this rather complicated experiment was as follows: (1) Administration of precommunication opinion questionnaire. (2) Viewing and judging the aesthetic worth of paintings. (The noncontiguous group ate at this time.) (3) Experimenter's introduction and positive or negative endorsement of the two communications. (4) Silent reading of the two communications. (The contiguous group ate at this time.) (5) Ratings of five political slogans. (The contiguous group continued to eat.) (6) Judging some more painting. (This gave all subjects time to digest the food, so that the taste and the interest in the refreshments would be dissipated before the final opinion measures were administered.) (7) The postcommunication questionnaire. It should be noted that a rating of political slogans was included as a follow-up of Razran's original study concerning the influence of contiguous food consumption on the favorableness of the ratings given to the political slogans.

The results of this experiment revealed no significant effect of the contiguity variable. This negative finding was also borne out by the supplementary results from subjects' judgments of the political slogans and from their personal appraisals of the paintings. These supplementary results showed that the group receiving food contiguously with the judgment objects gave approximately the same average ratings as the groups receiving food beforehand. Thus the relevant findings on the effects of contiguous versus noncontiguous food consumption fail to support the predictions based on the theory that "conditioning" (a process in which verbal mediation is thought to be unnecessary) can account for the facilitating effects of eating while reading.

The data also revealed that the group that had been given both positive endorsement and food contiguously with exposure to the communications had an extremely large opinion-change score. In fact, this score differed significantly from those in the other three groups. It is interesting to note that a positive endorsement by the experimenter, a relatively high-prestige source, did not, by itself, result in more opinion change than a negative endorsement. A positive endorsement by the experimenter was effective only when he gave food.

The authors attempt to account for these results by using a "momentary compliance" hypothesis. They feel that it is possible that the consumption of preferred food induces a momentary mood of compliance toward the donor that is strongest at the time the food is being consumed, but that decreases in strength rapidly after the food has been consumed. It was reasoned that food given during exposure to a communication would elicit a compliant mood that would augment acceptance when the experimenter conveys a positive endorsement of the communication. If the food has been given and consumed before exposure to the communication, however, the momentary state of compliance at the time of exposure might be relatively weak, and consequently the change induced by the experimenter's positive endorsement would be less than when eating occurs during exposure. This explanation is not entirely satisfactory, however, since it is not clear why subjects were not momentarily compliant toward the experimenter when he gave a negative endorsement. Because no control group was run in this experiment, we do not know whether or not the noncontiguous food condition produced more opinion change than would have been observed in a control group. It may have been that the difference in time interval between the two contiguity conditions was not long enough to show a contiguity effect. Perhaps the noncontiguity condition was really, by absolute standards, a contiguity condition.

There is a great deal of other experimental evidence that bears on the question of whether or not attitudes can be conditioned (for example, Verplanck, 1955; Hildrum and Brown, 1956; Singer, 1961; Krasner, Knowles, and Ullman, 1965), and we will present a few of these studies for illustration. Many investigations in this area have been conducted by Staats and his colleagues, who have used Doob's theory of attitude formation and change to investigate whether or not the principles of classical conditioning apply to attitudes. We will discuss only two of their experiments here.

In an early experiment, Staats and Staats (1957) were interested in finding out whether the meaning of words or nonsense syllables could be classically conditioned. They reasoned that if the presentation of a nonsense syllable was immediately followed by the presentation of a meaningful word, it could be expected that the meaning response elicited by the word would be conditioned to the nonsense syllable. To test this hypothesis a nonsense syllable was visually presented eighteen times to each subject. Each time, the nonsense syllable was paired with the auditory presentation of a different word. Although these words were different, they all had an identical meaning component. In a first experiment, one nonsense syllable was paired with words of positive evaluative meaning and another was paired with words of negative evaluative meaning; in a second experiment "active"-meaning and "passive"-meaning words were paired with other nonsense syllables; and in a third experiment, "strong"- and "weak"-meaning words were paired with still other nonsense syllables. In each experiment there was significant evidence that meaning responses had been conditioned to the nonsense syllables.

Extending these experiments, Staats and Staats (1958) performed another experiment, which investigated the formation of attitudes through classical conditioning. Subjects were told that the primary purpose of the experiment was to study how learning visually presented words and auditorially presented words at the same time affected the learning of each. In the critical phase of the experiment, national names, serving as the conditioned stimuli, were used for the visual presentation. These names were presented in random order and, approximately one second after each name appeared on the screen, the experimenter pronounced the unconditioned stimulus word with which it was paired. Subjects were told they could learn the visually presented names by just looking at them, but that they should simultaneously concentrate on pronouncing the auditorially presented words aloud and to themselves. The conditioned stimulus names, *Swedish* and *Dutch,* were always paired with unconditioned stimulus words with evaluative meaning. The word *Dutch* was paired with different words, all of which had positive evaluative meaning in common; the word *Swedish* was paired with words that had negative evaluative meaning. This was true for half of the subjects. For the other half of the subjects, the order of *Dutch* and *Swedish* was reversed so that *Dutch* was paired with negative words and *Swedish* with positive words. After this conditioning phase was completed, the subjects were told that it would be necessary to find out how they *felt* about the words since that might have affected how quickly the words were learned. This, of course, was the dependent variable. The results of this experiment indicated that conditioning did occur to the two critical words. The same effects were observed in a second experiment in which men's names were conditioned to other positive or negative words. The authors concluded that an implicit attitudinal response was conditioned by their procedure and that their results therefore supported the notion that attitude change through communication takes place according to the principle of conditioning.

It should be noted that Staats and Staats excluded from their analysis seventeen subjects who indicated that they were aware of the systematic name–word relationships. This was done to prevent the interpretation that the conditioning of attitudes depended upon awareness of the name–word conditioning contingency. Subsequent research indicates that because Staats and Staats used a very brief interview to detect awareness, they may not have been entirely successful in ruling out awareness as an explanation of their results. Cohen (1964), for example, essentially replicated the Staats and Staats experiment with nonsense syllables. Subjects, however, were classified as aware or unaware by independent judges who evaluated the subjects' written comments concerning the experiment. He found that subjects who had been classified as aware showed the Staats and Staats conditioning effect; the group classified as unaware did not. It is thus possible that the Staats and Staats results were due to aware subjects who were undetected by their relatively insensitive interview.

If it is true that the Staats and Staats results were due to the presence of undetected aware subjects, there are a number of implications. It is possible, for example, that subjects who were aware of the name–word relationships correctly guessed the hypothesis being tested in the experiment. If so, subjects may have been attempting to please the experimenters by complying with the implicit "demand characteristics" of the experiment (as Orne [1962] suggests that subjects often do) by giving appropriate evaluative responses on the final questionnaire. It is also possible that subjects who were aware of the systematic name–word relationships responded with appropriate evaluative responses on the final questionnaire, not because they were trying to please the experimenters, but because that particular national name did indeed have that specific evaluative meaning.

If the latter is true, there are two possible ways in which this change in evaluative meaning could have occurred. First, it is possible that the conditioning contingency (the pairing of national names with words of evaluative meaning) produced an awareness of the contingency, and this awareness then *in turn* produced the subjects' responses indicating that the national names now had a particular meaning for them. If so, we would not have a demonstration of conditioning because the conditioning process is usually conceived as being an automatic process not dependent upon cognitive mediation. Second, it is possible that the conditioning contingency produced both awareness of the contingency and at the same time an evaluative-meaning response by the subjects. In this last case, awareness of the contingency would not be mediating the meaning response, but only accompanying it, and we would feel more comfortable about using the label "conditioning." (The reader interested in this problem and its implications for the applicability of stimulus–response learning theory to human learning situations should consult Dulany [in press].)

Perhaps the best-known studies on the effects of reward and punishment in communication situations have been performed by Scott. The earliest of these was designed to explore the effects on attitudes of reward and punishment of expressed opinions. Scott (1957) predicted that subjects rewarded by group approval for expressing opinions contrary to their initial attitude would show a change in the direction of the expressed opinions, whereas subjects punished by group disapproval for expressing contrary opinions would not show such a change.

To test this hypothesis, Scott first obtained a premeasure of subjects' opinions on three different controversial issues. Subjects were then asked to participate in an experiment to "see how much they could affect the opinions of class members" by debating one of the three issues. Two pairs of debaters were formed for each class; students with pro opinions were asked to debate the con argument and vice versa. It was explained that after the debate, the quality of performance would be assessed in two ways: first by a class vote on which member of each pair did the better job, and second by a retest of the opinions of class members on the issue to see in which direction their opinions were influenced. It had been determined in advance which debater in each pair would win. Winners and losers were assigned alternately through the pairs of debaters, so half of the time the pros won and half of the time the cons won.

After the debates and after the instructor mentioned the ostensible outcome of the class vote and had given the names of the winners and the losers, all class members were given sheets of paper upon which were printed the statement of the issue that had been debated and were asked to write their present opinions. Debaters were also asked to write their present opinions, and this, of course, was the dependent variable. The results tended to support Scott's hypothesis. The difference between mean changes of the winners and losers was significant. The winners' attitudes changed in the direction of the side they were debating, and the losers' changed slightly in the opposite direction (or they became more extreme in their original opinions). The difference between the winners and a control group was significant, but the difference between losers and controls was not significant.

Discussing these results, Scott states that the vote of "win" presumably reinforced the debater's verbal behavior and with it the accompanying implicit responses—attitudes and cognitive support for them. The vote of "lose" presumably weakened whatever response tendencies had been established by the overt behavior, or by cognitive contact with the opposite side, so that subjects reverted to their preexisting attitudes. Scott points out, however, that his findings are subject to at least one other interpretation. Perhaps reward of the new behavior was the crucial factor, whereas cognitive contact with opposing arguments in and of itself had no effect. Scott reasons, however, that because Janis and King (1954) showed that contact with the opposite side tended, by itself, to produce some change, the first interpretation is more plausible. In order to help determine the relative importance of these two influences—cognitive contact and reinforcement—it would have been necessary to have some subjects debate without a subsequent winning or losing experience. This experiment did not provide such a condition.

Scott (1959) conducted a second experiment to substantiate the earlier results, to investigate the effects of response reinforcement on subjects with neutral as well as extreme attitudes, and to determine whether or not the induced attitude change was permanent. The procedure of this experiment was similar to that of the first. After a pretest of subjects' attitudes, Scott obtained volunteers to participate in an elimination debate contest, the winners of which would share a $100 cash prize. Volunteers were asked to take a particular side on one of the three issues for debate. The sides were assigned irrespective of subjects' initial positions, so that some debaters defended their own opinions, some the opposite opinions, and some debated "off neutral" (they expressed no clear opinion on the pretest, but were assigned a definite position in the debate). Subjects were told that debate positions were being assigned irrespective of actual attitudes because "the purpose of the study is to see how well people can present opinions they don't actually hold and how well the opponents can judge their own true attitudes."

There were three judges for every debate, two professors and one graduate student. After each pair of subjects had debated, each judge indicated his decision on the relative merits of the two performances. The reasons offered for the decision were confined to the manner of presentation, rather than to the content of the talk. This was done in order to minimize the possible influence of prestige suggestion that might be entailed if the judgment referred to, or appeared to agree with, the substance of the argument. Winners of course had been predetermined in systematic fashion. Following the judgments, subjects were asked to fill out questionnaires and the experimenter indicated that we are "interested in seeing how you feel about these matters at this time."

Scott found that winners tended to change toward the side they debated more than did losers and controls. (The control group was composed of those volunteers who could not be scheduled during the first debate series. Their posttest attitudes were assessed approximately one month after the pretest.) Again the winner versus control comparison was significant, as was the winner versus loser comparison. Losers versus controls was, however, not significant. The data for the winners and the losers did not differ with respect to whether they were debating their own side or the opposite side, or had had an originally neutral opinion. Or, in other words, the same trend (the effect of winning versus losing on attitudes) occurred for all three groups. Another posttest of the winner's opinions ten days later showed they maintained their attitude change. We can see that these studies, insofar as Scott wanted to show that "non-rational determiners may be . . . important in the acquisition of attitudes" (1957, p. 72), may not permit unequivocal interpretation. Or, in other words, one may question how "extraneous" or "irrational" the reward of winning and the punishment of losing was in Scott's experimental situation.

Dahlke (1964) felt that it is reasonable to assume that rewarding a subject's debating performance is not an example of an extraneous reinforcement if the subject regards his performance as depending on the specific issue being argued or particular statements mustered for that issue. Dahlke wanted to determine whether rewarding a person's performance would lead to attitude change, even when it was made clear to the subject by the experimental instructions that such a reward would not be contingent on the specific content of his statements. It will be recalled that Scott did attempt to minimize the possible influences of prestige suggestion in his second experiment by telling the subject that the decision on the debates was going to be based on the relative merits of the two performances. Dahlke felt, however, that winning could have been perceived by the subjects as a form of social approval or endorsement of the opinion being espoused, because the debaters were always arguing opposite sides of the issues. Dahlke felt that it would have been more difficult for the subjects to perceive winning as social approval of content if both debaters were debating the *same* side of the issue, rather than opposite sides.

Dahlke was also interested in investigating the extent to which the effect of winning or losing, by itself, affected attitudes. It will be recalled that Scott assessed attitudes after winning, but that he had no control group whose attitudes were assessed *after preparation* for the debate, but *prior* to winning or losing. Several studies (for example, Janis and King, 1954; King and Janis, 1956) have demonstrated that attitude change may occur simply as a result of preparing and delivering counterattitudinal arguments. Thus it is conceivable that all of the attitude change observed for win subjects in Scott's studies could have occurred while subjects were preparing their arguments. Winning or losing may have had only the effect of freezing this change or of causing it to dissipate.

After replicating the results of Scott's experiments, Dahlke performed an experiment in which subjects were told that they would be debating the same side and which included a "win" group, a "lose" group, and a control group of subjects whose attitudes were assessed before they were told of the judges' decision. In addition, the attitudes of a second group of control subjects were assessed both on a pretest and on a posttest. These subjects did not participate in the debate and thus did not prepare or deliver counterattitudinal arguments. The data obtained from this group allowed Dahlke to estimate the effects of preparation and delivery of arguments upon attitude.

The over-all results of this experiment were consistent with Scott's findings. The change in attitude for the win group was significantly greater than the change for the lose group. However, Dahlke found some evidence that the winners did not change their attitudes significantly more than those control subjects who had prepared and delivered their counterattitudinal arguments. There was, however, a tendency for these control subjects to show more attitude change than the lose group. Apparently, lose subjects' attitudes reverted in the direction of their pre-test attitudes from whatever attitudinal position they reached after preparation and delivery of arguments. There was also a tendency for control subjects who prepared and delivered arguments to show more attitude change than the second group of control subjects who did not. Dahlke's results appear to indicate that the reinforcement of winning in his experiment had little effect, whereas losing appears to have caused subjects to revert to their former positions.

The bulk of the evidence we have discussed thus far generally tends to support the reinforcement-theory view of attitude formation and change. There is, however, one prediction that follows from the reinforcement view that has stirred a great deal of controversy. Specifically, the reinforcement theorists predict that the greater the magnitude of reinforcement that is administered, the more attitude change we should observe. This prediction is at variance with a number of predictions concerning attitude change that can be derived from Festinger's theory of cognitive dissonance (1957). It will be recalled that the cognitive-consistency theorists make the assumption that people wish their cognitions to be harmonious with one another, and that the presence of inconsistent cognitions motivates people to strive for consistency. This basic premise has a number of implications for attitude change.

Dissonance theory suggests that if we can get an individual to change certain of his behaviors or attitudes, he will subsequently, and of his own accord, change any related attitudes that are inconsistent with the new behavior or attitude. There is a great deal of research that indicates that individuals will modify their own attitudes in the pursuit of consistency. For example, much research demonstrates that after an individual has engaged in a certain behavior, or even if he has only *decided* to engage in a certain behavior, he will tend to convince himself that his decision about the way to behave was a good one. One tends to bring his attitudes into line with his anticipated behavior, subjectively increasing the attractiveness of the chosen alternative and decreasing the attractiveness of the rejected alternative (for example, Brehm, 1956; Festinger and Walster,

1964; Walster, 1964; and studies reported in Brehm and Cohen, 1962). Even in the absence of new information, a person is usually able to convince himself that the alternative he chose is actually better than he thought it was at the time he made his decision and that the rejected alternative is less desirable than he had once thought.

These research findings suggest that if we were interested in training an individual to be dishonest, or to feel favorable toward dishonesty, we could use either of two techniques: We could deliver a persuasive communication extolling the virtues of deceit. Or we could simply lure the individual into cheating. If we used the latter technique, the individual should, after cheating, convince himself that cheating is not really such a bad thing, after all. Of course, in using this technique, we always run the danger that we will not be successful in seducing the individual to cheat. If we are not, and if the individual is able to resist temptation, our influence attempt should boomerang. The resister would be expected to convince himself that it is even more important not to cheat than he had initially thought. A study testing and confirming this ingenious hypothesis was conducted by Mills (1958). In brief, then, consistency theory suggests that people tend to justify their behavior.

There are some conditions that are especially effective in leading one to justify his behavior, and we will now consider some of these special conditions. Paradoxically, dissonance research suggests that when a person is led to perform some unacceptable act, the more external justification the experimenter gives him for performing this act, the less the subject will change his attitudes in an attempt to justify his behavior. This dissonance-theory prediction is, of course, diametrically opposed to the prediction from learning theory that the more reward associated with an act, the more positive attitude change should occur.

Consider again training a person to cheat. Mills's experiment indicates that the person induced to cheat will justify his cheating by adopting a more favorable attitude toward cheating. In Mills's experiment the experimenter could have provided a great deal of external justification for cheating. He could have forced the person to cheat. He could have provided such intense pressure that it would be obvious to the person that no one could resist. He could pay him a huge amount of money to cheat. Or he could have provided the person with a great number of reasons why it is right to cheat. Would the person have rationalized his own behavior to the same extent if the experimenter had provided him with ready-made justifications for cheating? Dissonance theory would predict that the individual would experience less dissonance at performing an unacceptable act, and thus should have less need to engage in self-justification, when the experimenter provides a great number of inducements to cheat than when he provides just enough inducements to get him to steal. If the experimenter provides great justification, when the subject asks himself why he cheated, he has many reasons to cite: He was forced to, paid to, and so on. Under such conditions it should not be so necessary to find additional justifications to convince oneself that cheating really is not so bad as it would be had the experimenter not provided so much justification.

There is experimental evidence that the more external justification a person is given for performing an inconsistent act, the less motivated he will be to change his internal attitudes in order to justify the behavior. Experimenters have used justifications of three types in testing the dissonance hypothesis. Some experimenters have used various levels of forced compliance as a way of manipulating external justification. Others have used various levels of good reasons for engaging in a behavior as an external justification. Still others have varied the degree of monetary compensation as a way of varying justification.

Aronson and Carlsmith (1963) tested the hypothesis that the more external justification children were given for abstaining from a desirable act (playing with a forbidden toy), the less likely they would be to convince themselves that they themselves wanted to avoid the forbidden toy. This experiment was conducted with nursery-school children. Children were brought into the experimental room, shown several toys, and asked to rank-order them according to their attractiveness. Then the experimenter said he was leaving the room and forbade the children to play with one of the toys while he was gone. Some children were offered a great deal of justification for not playing with the toy: The experimenter told them that if they played with the forbidden toy he would be very angry, that he would not allow them to play with any of the toys, and that he would think they were "babies." Other children were offered very little justification for not playing with the toy: They were simply told that the experimenter would be annoyed if they did so. Then the experimenter left the room, leaving the child with the temptation to touch the forbidden toy and hopefully to resist the temptation. Luckily for the experiment, all the children, in all conditions, did avoid the toy. Finally, the experimenter returned and asked the children to rank-order the toys. The investigators found that, as predicted, high-threat children derogated the forbidden toy less than did mild-threat children.

A delayed measure of dissonance reduction was secured by Freedman (1965c) in a more tightly controlled replication and extention of Aronson and Carlsmith's study. The Freedman procedure differed from the Aronson procedure in that in addition to mild-threat and severe-threat experimental groups, mild- and severe-threat control groups were added to the experiment. In these control groups, after administering one of the threats, the experimenter did not leave the room. Instead he sat down at a nearby desk and did paper work for ten minutes. Since the experimenter was observing them at all times, children in these conditions were not tempted to play with the toy and therefore should not have experienced dissonance (they never made a choice to avoid the desirable toy.) Freedman measured changes in children's ratings of the toys from before dissonance was engendered to immediately after dissonance was generated. In addition, Freedman also secured a behavioral measure of subjects' actual tendency to play with the toys from 23 to 64 days after the original dissonance induction. In these follow-up experimental sessions, a woman tester suggested that the children play with some toys while she scored the tests. Among these toys was the previously forbidden toy. Whether or not the child touched the previously forbidden toy was the behavioral measure of dissonance reduction.

Freedman's hypothesis received some support. When we consider children's ratings of the avoided toy (which were taken immediately after dissonance was induced), we see that they did not vary significantly among conditions, although the changes tended to be in the predicted direction. The delayed behavioral measures of dissonance reduction (taken 23 to 64 days later) were significant, however. Children in the mild-threat experimental condition avoided playing with the forbidden toy more than did children in any other group. Only one-third of the mild-threat children touched the toy. In all other conditions, two-thirds of the children played with the toy. Other research has supported this work with children. Brehm and Cohen (1962) present and review several experiments showing that the more freedom an individual feels he had about whether or not to make a certain decision, the more likely he is to justify whatever decision he makes.

Sometimes would-be manipulators of human behavior forget that the choice one has about making a decision affects how responsible he feels for it. For example, college administrators often feel that if students make their own rules, they will be more likely to follow the rules they have made themselves than rules imposed from above. Thus administrators sometimes give students a choice about hours, living facilities, tuition costs, and so on. If the students' decisions coincide with the decisions the administration considers acceptable, everything is fine; the students feel responsible for the choices they have made, and they are thus very likely to obey the rules and to enforce obedience by others. It occasionally happens, however, that students will choose to do something the administrators are not able to accept. Then the administrators are in real difficulty. At this point they often try to revoke freedom of choice and force students to choose the "right way." Students naturally feel no responsibility for rules they are forced to make, and thus have no need to justify these choices. Even worse, it is likely that because they *do* feel responsible for the nullified decision, they will convince themselves that not doing what the administrators thought they would do is even a better idea than they had initially thought.

Dissonance theorists have also manipulated degree of external justification by varying the amount of money paid to subjects to engage in public behavior contrary to their privately held attitudes. These theorists predicted, of course, that the more money the person is paid to perform the dissonant act (stealing, for example) the less he will justify his behavior by modifying his attitudes toward stealing. Reinforcement theorists, on the other hand, predict that the more money the person is paid to perform the dissonant act, the more favorably he should view stealing.

Perhaps the focal point of the controversy resulting from these two predictions has been an experiment conducted by Festinger and Carlsmith (1959). They were testing the familiar hypothesis that a subject with insufficient justification for performing an act opposed to his private attitude would, if other modes of dissonance reduction were blocked, change his private attitude in such a way as to make it consonant with his public behavior. All subjects in the Festinger and Carlsmith experiment were required to perform a very disagreeable and monotonous experimental task. After the subjects had performed the task, the experimenter induced each subject to "pinch-hit" for his regular research assistant (who had failed to show up) and to tell the next arriving subject that the dull task the subject had just performed was really very interesting. All subjects thus agreed to perform a public act contrary to their private attitude.

In the insufficient-justification condition, the subject was told he would be given $1.00 if he would agree to lie to his fellow student. In the sufficient-justification condition, subjects were told they would receive $20.00 if they agreed to lie on this occasion and if they also agreed to remain on call to act in the future as a substitute assistant in the event the regular assistant should again fail to appear. It was predicted that subjects in the insufficient-justification condition would experience a good deal of dissonance because they had agreed to lie for a paltry sum. Festinger and Carlsmith predicted that to reduce their dissonance these subjects should, since other modes of dissonance reduction were blocked, distort the attractiveness of the dull experimental task they had performed. Sufficient-justification subjects, having a very good reason for lying (specifically, the munificent sum of $20.00) should experience less dissonance and therefore should not find it necessary to distort the attractiveness of the dull task to the same extent. The results of the experiment supported these predictions.

The Festinger and Carlsmith results appeared not to follow from the reinforcement theory point of view. Thus some proponents of "incentive theory" took up the cudgels. Incentive theorists, following Hovland, Janis, and Kelley's formulation of attitude change (1953), feel that the major effect of a persuasive communication lies in stimulating the individual to think both of his initial opinion and of the opinion recommended in the communication. Whether or not the new opinion recommended in the communication is accepted is dependent upon "incentives." In order for opinion change to occur, there must be a greater incentive for making the new implicit response than for making the old one. Incentives may be arguments or reasons that appear to logically support the individual's opinion. They also state that, "In addition to supporting reasons, there are likely to be other special incentives involving anticipating rewards and punishments which motivate the individual to accept or reject a given opinion" (Hovland, Janis, and Kelley, 1953, p. 11).

In the incentive formulation, the two types of rewards that are thought to be important in determining whether or not a communication will be accepted are intrinsic rewards and extraneous rewards. A communication will be intrinsically rewarding if its content evokes satisfying anticipations of attaining a goal or of averting a threat. The reader should already be familiar with extraneous rewards, which have no relation to the content of the communication, and which may operate in such a way as to reinforce whatever belief happens to be verbalized at the time the rewarding experience occurs. We can see that the Hovland, Janis, and Kelley formulation is very similar to Doob's, and in fact the authors draw upon Doob in their elaboration of the process of attitude change.

What would incentive theory predict in the Festinger and Carlsmith situation? Janis and Gilmore (1965) state that according to incentive theory, "When a person accepts the task of improvising arguments in favor of a point of view at variance with his own personal convictions, he becomes temporarily motivated to think up all of the good positive arguments he can, and at the same time suppress his thoughts about the negative arguments which are supposedly irrelevant to the assigned task. This 'biased scanning' increases salience of the positive arguments and therefore increases the chances of acceptance in the new position" (pp. 17, 18). Thus these authors feel that the Festinger and Carlsmith procedure should have yielded more attitude change in the $20.00 condition than it did in the $1.00 condition. They explain the lack of this effect by reasoning that, "A gain in attitude change would not be expected, however, if resentment or other interfering affective reactions were aroused by *negative* incentives in the role playing situation" (p. 18). Thus Janis and Gilmore feel that the Festinger and Carlsmith results did not constitute a disconfirmation of incentive theory because subjects in the $20.00 condition might have been suspicious because they were paid a large amount of money to perform a simple task. Such suspicion, and possibly subsequent resentment, may have operated as a negative incentive to subjects in the $20.00 condition, while not operating in the $1.00 condition. Thus, according to the incentive interpretation, the $20.00 condition may have provided the subject with fewer positive "incentives" than the $1.00 condition.

Whether or not this interpretation of the dynamics of the Festinger and Carlsmith situation is correct (and there is reason to question whether it is because the number of subjects discarded for reasons of suspicion in the $20.00 condition did not differ from the number discarded in the $1.00 condition), a number of other experiments have also supported the dissonance-theory prediction concerning the effects of sufficient and insufficient rewards for performing a dissonant public act (for example, Cohen in Brehm and Cohen, 1962, and Nuttin, 1964), and a similar prediction concerning the effects of sufficient and insufficient punishments for refraining from performing an act (for example, Aronson and Carlsmith, 1963; Turner and Wright, 1965; Freedman, 1965c.)

The results of several experiments indicate that both theories may be partially incorrect. One such experiment was conducted by Carlsmith, Collins, and Helmreich (1966). This experiment was designed to investigate whether or not increasing the amount of incentive offered to a person to engage in counterattitudinal role playing increases or decreases the amount of attitude change that results. Carlsmith et al. asked their subjects to adopt a counterattitudinal position in different ways: Half of the subjects were asked to tell a confederate that a dull task was in fact interesting in a face-to-face confrontation; the other half of the subjects were asked to write an anonymous essay in favor of the same position. Each of these two groups was then subdivided into different conditions: some subjects were paid $5.00, some were paid $1.50 and some were paid $0.50 to perform the experimental task. Another group of subjects, the control group, were not asked to either role play or to write an essay and were paid no money beyond the flat rate that all subjects were paid for participating in the experiment. The investigators found that the data from the face-to-face condition replicated the original Festinger and Carlsmith experiment: small amounts of money were most effective in convincing subjects that the task was really fun and interesting. Data from the essay condition, however, indicated just the opposite: large amounts of money produced the most attitude change.

It appears that neither dissonance theory alone nor incentive theory alone could have predicted the total pattern of results yielded by this experiment. In a review of the literature and a theoretical discussion of the issues involved in the dissonance–incentive controversy, Aronson (1966) concludes that the high incentives, taken by themselves, may lead a person to greater attitude change. If, however, a more powerful opposing force due to dissonance is set into motion, the dissonance-reduction effects may overpower those effects due to incentive. Thus dissonance effects and reinforcement effects are *not* mutually exclusive; reinforcement effects will emerge when cognitive dissonance has been minimized in the experimental operations.

Three other experiments are of interest to us here, and their results appear to support Aronson's prediction concerning when incentive effects, rather than dissonance effects, will be obtained. Cohen (1962) used varying amounts of incentive ($0.50, $1.00, $5.00 and $10.00) to induce subjects to behave in counterattitudinal role playing. His results corroborated those of Festinger and Carlsmith: the smaller the incentive offered to engage in the dissonant behavior, the more attitude change in the direction of consonance with the public behavior. Rosenberg (1965) conducted an experiment very similar to Cohen's and obtained the opposite results: the larger the incentive, the more the attitude change observed.

Two recent experiments by Linder, Cooper, and Jones (1967) appear to explain these contradictory data. Reasoning that the dissonance-theory prediction would not be confirmed unless the subject makes a free, rather than forced, decision to engage in the dissonant act after he has considered the magnitude of the incentive, they experimentally varied the extent to which the subject felt free to decide not to perform the act, as well as the amount of incentive. Thus in a "free-decision" condition it was emphasized to each subject that "the decision to perform the task will be entirely your own." In a "no-choice condition," the experimenter behaved as though he assumed that the subject would perform the task. Linder, Cooper, and Jones found that if the subject feels free not to perform the dissonant act, attitude change is inversely related to incentive magnitude and the dissonance prediction is confirmed. If, however, the subject is not free to refuse to perform the act, the incentive prediction is confirmed.

After carefully examining both the Cohen and the Rosenberg procedures, Linder et al. felt that it was possible that the subjects in Rosenberg's experiment may have felt less free to engage in the dissonant act than subjects in Cohen's experiment. To investigate this possibility further, Linder et al. closely replicated Rosenberg's procedure and obtained his results. When, however, they slightly modified the Rosenberg procedure to increase subjects' freedom not to comply with the experimenter and not to perform the act, they obtained results supporting the dissonance-theory prediction.

A study performed by Freedman (1963) suggests that the temporal placement of rewards may also be important in determining whether one will get incentive or dissonance effects. In Freedman's experiment, subjects were asked to perform a very dull experimental task. Half of the subjects were given great justification for performing the task—they were told that the performance of the task (writing out a series of "random numbers") had great value to the experimenter. The remainder of the subjects were told that performance of the task had little value for the experimenter. These two groups of subjects were further subdivided, and some of the subjects were told *in advance* of deciding to perform the task that the task had little (or great) value. Freedman found that subjects who were told that the first task was useful and valuable after they had completed it enjoyed it more than those who were told after they had completed it that it was of little value to the experimenter. However, Freedman found a dissonance effect when the information as to the value of the task was told to the subject *before* he decided to perform the task.

References

Abelson, R. P., and Lesser, G. S. The measurement of persuasibility in children. In C. I. Hovland and I. L. Janis (eds.), *Personality and Persuasibility.* New Haven, Conn.: Yale University Press, 1959, Pp. 141–166.

Abelson, R. P., and Rosenberg, M. J. Symbolic psychologic: a model of attitudinal cognition. *Behavioral Science,* 1958, **3**, 1–13.

Adams, J. S. Reduction of cognitive dissonance by seeking consonant information. *Journal of Abnormal and Social Psychology,* 1961, **62**, 74–78.

Allport, G. W. The historical background of modern social psychology. In Gardner Lindzey (ed.), *Handbook of Social Psychology,* Vol. I. Reading, Mass.: Addison-Wesley, 1954.

Allyn, J., and Festinger, L. The effectiveness of unanticipated persuasive communication. *Journal of Abnormal and Social Psychology,* 1961, **62**, 35–40.

Aristotle. *Rhetoric and Poetics.* New York: Random House, 1954.

Arnett, C. E., Davidson, H. H., and Lewis, H. N. Prestige as a factor in attitude changes. *Sociology and Social Research,* 1931, **16**, 49–55.

Aronson, E. The psychology of insufficient justification: an analysis of some conflicting data. In S. Feldman (ed.), *Cognitive Consistency.* New York: Academic Press, 1966. Pp. 115–133.

Aronson, E., and Carlsmith, J. M. Effect of the severity of threat on the devaluation of forbidden behavior. *Journal of Abnormal and Social Psychology,* 1963, **66**, 584–588.

Aronson, E., and Golden, B. W. The effect of relevant and irrelevant aspects of communicator credibility on opinion change. *Journal of Personality,* 1962, **30**, 135–146.

Asch, S. E. Forming impressions of personality. *Journal of Abnormal and Social Psychology,* 1946, **41**, 258–290.

Asch, S. E. The doctrine of suggestion, prestige, and imitation in social psychology. *Psychological Review,* 1948, **55**, 250–276.

Berkowitz, L., and Cottingham, D. R. The interest value and relevance of fear arousing communications. *Journal of Abnormal and Social Psychology,* 1960, **60,** 37–43.

Berscheid, E. Opinion change and communicator-communicatee similarity and dissimilarity. *Journal of Personality and Social Psychology,* 1966, ·4, 670–680.

Bowden, A. O., Caldwell, F. F., and West, G. A. A study in prestige. *American Journal of Sociology,* 1934, **40,** 193–204.

Brehm, J. W. Post-decision changes in the desirability of alternatives. *Journal of Abnormal and Social Psychology,* 1956, **52,** 384–389.

Brehm, J. W., and Cohen, A. R. *Explorations in Cognitive Dissonance.* New York: John Wiley and Sons, 1962.

Brembeck, W. L., and Howell, W. S. *Persuasion: A Form of Social Control.* Englewood Cliffs, N.J.: Prentice-Hall, 1952.

Brock, T. C. Communicator-recipient similarity and decision change. *Journal of Personality and Social Psychology,* 1965, **1,** 650–653. (a)

Brock, T. C. Commitment to exposure as a determinant of information receptivity. *Journal of Personality and Social Psychology,* 1965, **2,** 10–19. (b)

Brock, T. C., and Balloun, J. L. Behavioral receptivity to dissonant information. *Journal of Personality and Social Psychology,* 1967, **6,** 1–9.

Brock, T. C., and Becker, L. A. Ineffectiveness of "overheard" counter-propaganda. *Journal of Personality and Social Psychology,* 1965, **2,** 654–660.

Burnstein, E., Stotland, E., and Zander A. Similarity to a model and self-evaluation. *Journal of Abnormal and Social Psychology,* 1961, **62,** 257–264.

Byrne, D. Interpersonal attraction and attitude similarity. *Journal of Abnormal and Social Psychology,* 1961, **62,** 713–715.

Byrne, D., and Wong, T. J. Racial prejudice, interpersonal attraction, and assumed dissimilarity of attitudes. *Journal of Abnormal and Social Psychology,* 1962, **65,** 246–253.

Canon, L. K. Self-confidence and selective exposure to information. In L. Festinger (ed.), *Conflict, Decision and Dissonance.* Stanford, Calif.: Stanford University Press, 1964. Pp. 83–96.

Carlsmith, J. M., Collins, B. E., and Helmreich, R. L. Studies in forced compliance: I. The effect of pressure for compliance on attitude change produced by face-to-face role playing and anonymous essay writing. *Journal of Personality and Social Psychology,* 1966, 4, 1–13.

Carnegie, D. *How to Win Friends and Influence People.* New York: Simon and Schuster, 1937.

Cartwright, D. Some principles of mass persuasion: Selected findings of research on the sale of United States war bonds. *Human Relations,* 1949, **2,** 253–267.

Cartwright, D., and Harary, F. Structural balance: a generalization of Heider's theory. *Psychological Review,* 1956, **63,** 277–293.

Charters, W. W., and Newcomb, T. M. Some attitudinal effects of experimentally increased salience of a membership group. In E. Maccoby, T. Newcomb, and E. Hartley (eds.), *Readings in Social Psychology.* 3rd ed. New York: Holt, Rinehart, and Winston, 1958. Pp. 276–281.

Child, I. L. Personality. *Annual Review of Psychology,* 1954, **5,** 149–170.

Cohen, A. R. A dissonance analysis of the boomerang effect. *Journal of Personality,* 1962, **30,** 75–88. (a)

Cohen, A. R. An experiment on small rewards for discrepant compliance and attitude change. In J. W. Brehm and A. R. Cohen, *Explorations in Cognitive Dissonance.* New York: John Wiley and Sons, 1962. Pp. 73–78. (b)

Cohen, B. H. Role of awareness in meaning established by classical conditioning. *Journal of Experimental Psychology,* 1964, **67,** 373–378.

Cohn, T. S., Yee, W., and Brown, V. Attitude change and interpersonal attraction. *Journal of Social Psychology,* 1961, **55,** 207–211.

Cooper, E., and Jahoda, M. The evasion of propaganda: How prejudiced people respond to anti-prejudice propaganda. *Journal of Psychology,* 1947, **23,** 15–25.

Dabbs, J. N. Jr. Self-esteem, communicator characteristics, and attitude change. *Journal of Abnormal and Social Psychology,* 1964, **69,** 173–181.

Dabbs, J. N. Jr., and Janis, I. L. Why does eating while reading facilitate opinion change?—an experimental inquiry. *Journal of Experimental Social Psychology,* 1965, **1,** 133–144.

Dabbs, J. N. Jr., and Leventhal, H. Effects of varying recommendations in a fear arousing communication. *Journal of Personality and Social Psychology,* 1966, **4,** 525–531.

Dahlke, A. E. The effect of reinforcement and punishment on attitude change. Unpublished Ph.D. dissertation, University of Minnesota, 1964.

Dittes, J. E. Effect of changes in self-esteem upon impulsiveness and deliberation in making judgments. *Journal of Abnormal and Social Psychology,* 1959, **58,** 348–356.

Dollard, J., Doob, L. W., Miller, N. E., Mowrer, O. H., and Sears, R. R. *Frustration and Aggression.* New Haven, Conn.: Yale University Press, 1939.

Doob, L. W. The behavior of attitudes. *Psychological Review,* 1947, **54,** 135–156.

Dulaney, D. E. Awareness, rules, and propositional control: A confrontation with S-R Behavior theory. In D. Horton and T. Dixon (eds.), *Verbal Behavior and S-R Behavior Theory.* Englewood Cliffs, N.J.: Prentice Hall. (in press)

Ebbinghaus, H. *Memory.* Trans. H. A. Roger and C. E. Bussenius. New York: Teachers College, Columbia University, 1913.

Ewing, T. N. A study of certain factors involved in changes of opinion. *Journal of Social Psychology,* 1942, **16,** 63–88.

Festinger, L. A theory of social comparison processes. *Human Relations,* 1954, **7,** 117–140.

Festinger, L. *A Theory of Cognitive Dissonance.* Stanford, Calif.: Stanford University Press, 1957.

Festinger, L. *Conflict, Decision and Dissonance.* Stanford, Calif.: Stanford University Press, 1964.

Festinger, L., and Carlsmith, J. M. Cognitive consequences of forced compliance. *Journal of Abnormal and Social Psychology,* 1959, **58,** 203–210.

Festinger, L., and Maccoby, N. On resistance to persuasive communications. *Journal of Abnormal and Social Psychology,* 1964, **68,** 359–366.

Festinger, L., and Walster, E. Post-decision regret and decision reversal. In L. Festinger (ed.), *Conflict, Decision and Dissonance*, Stanford, Calif.: Stanford University Press, 1964. Pp. 98-112.

Freedman, J. L. Attitudinal effects of inadequate justification. *Journal of Personality*, 1963, **31**, 371–385.

Freedman, J. L. Confidence, utility and selective exposure to information: a partial replication. *Journal of Personality and Social Psychology*, 1965, **2**, 778–780. (a)

Freedman, J. L. Preference for dissonant information. *Journal of Personality and Social Psychology*, 1965, **2**, 287–289. (b)

Freedman, J. L. Long-term behavioral effects of cognitive dissonance. *Journal of Experimental Social Psychology*, 1965, **1**, 145–155. (c)

Freedman, J. L., and Sears, D. O. Voters' preferences among types of information. *American Psychologist*, 1963, **18**, 375.

Freedman, J. L., and Sears, D. O. Selective exposure. In L. Berkowitz (ed.), *Advances in Experimental Social Psychology*, Vol. 2. New York: Academic Press, 1965.

Freedman, J. L., and Sears, D. O. Warning, distraction, and resistance to influence. *Journal of Personality and Social Psychology*, 1965, **1**, 262–266.

Gollob, H. F., and Dittes, J. E. Effects of manipulated self-esteem on persuasibility depending on threat and complexity of communication. *Journal of Personality and Social Psychology*, 1965, **2**, 195–201.

Haefner, D. P. Arousing fear in dental health education. *Journal of Public Health Dentistry*, 1965, **25**, 140–146.

Hardyck, J. A. Consistency, relevance, and resistance to change. *Journal of Experimental Social Psychology*, 1966, **2**, 27–41.

Heider, F. Attitudes and cognitive organization. *Journal of Personality*, 1946, **21**, 107–112.

Hildrum, D. C., and Brown, R. W. Verbal reinforcement and interviewer bias. *Journal of Abnormal and Social Psychology*, 1956, **53**, 108–111.

Hovland, C. I. Reconciling conflicting results derived from experimental and survey studies of attitude change. *American Psychologist*, 1959, **14**, 8–17.

Hovland, C. I., Campbell, E. H., and Brock, T. The effects of "commitment" on opinion change following communication. In C. I. Hovland (ed.), *Order of Presentation in Persuasion*. New Haven, Conn.: Yale University Press, 1957. Pp. 23–32.

Hovland, C. I., and Janis, I. L. (eds.). *Personality and Persuasibility*. New Haven, Conn.: Yale University Press, 1959.

Hovland, C. I., Janis, I. L., and Kelley, H. H. *Communication and Persuasion*. New Haven, Conn.: Yale University Press, 1953.

Hovland, C. I., Lumsdaine, A. A., and Sheffield, F. D. *Experiments on Mass Communication*. Princeton, N.J.: Princeton University Press, 1949.

Hovland, C. I., and Mandell, W. An experimental comparison of conclusion-drawing by the communicator and by the audience. *Journal of Abnormal and Social Psychology*, 1952, **47**, 581–588.

Hovland, C. I., and Mandell, W. Is there a law of primacy in persuasion? In

C. I. Hovland (ed.), *The Order of Presentation in Persuasion.* New Haven, Conn.: Yale University Press, 1957. Pp. 13–22.

Hovland, C. I., and Weiss, W. The influence of source credibility on communication effectiveness. *Public Opinion Quarterly,* 1951, **15,** 635–650.

Husek, T. R. Persuasive impacts of early, late, or no mention of a negative source. *Journal of Personality and Social Psychology,* 1965, **2,** 125–127.

Hyman, H. H., and Sheatsley, P. B. Some reasons why information campaigns fail. *Public Opinion Quarterly,* 1947, **11,** 412–423.

Insko, C. A. Primacy versus recency in persuasion as a function of the timing of arguments and measures. *Journal of Abnormal and Social Psychology,* 1964, **69,** 381–391.

Janis, I. L., and Feshbach, S. Effects of fear-arousing communications. *Journal of Abnormal and Social Psychology,* 1953, **48,** 78–92.

Janis, I. L., and Feshbach, S. Personality differences associated with responsiveness to fear-arousing communications. *Journal of Personality,* 1954, **23,** 154–166.

Janis, I. L., and Field, P. B. Sex differences in personality factors related to persuasibility. In C. I. Hovland and I. L. Janis (eds.), *Personality and Persuasibility.* New Haven, Conn.: Yale University Press, 1959. Pp. 55–68.

Janis, I. L., and Gilmore, J. B. The influence of incentive conditions on the success of role playing in modifying attitudes. *Journal of Personality and Social Psychology,* 1965, **1,** 17–27.

Janis, I. L., Kaye, D., and Kirschner, P. Facilitating effects of eating-while-reading on response to persuasive communication. *Journal of Personality and Social Psychology,* 1965, **1,** 181–185.

Janis, I. L., and King, B. T. The influence of role playing on opinion change. *Journal of Abnormal and Social Psychology,* 1954, **49,** 211–218.

Janis, I. L., and Terwilliger, R. T. An experimental study of psychological resistance to fear arousing communications. *Journal of Abnormal and Social Psychology,* 1962, **65,** 403–410.

Jecker, J. D. Selective exposure to new information. In L. Festinger (ed.), *Conflict, Decision and Dissonance.* Stanford, Calif.: Stanford University Press, 1964. Pp. 65–81.

Jones, E. E., and Kohler, R. The effect of plausibility on the learning of controversial statements. *Journal of Abnormal and Social Psychology,* 1958, **57,** 315–320.

Jones, R. A., and Brehm, J. W. Attitudinal effects of communicator attractiveness when one chooses to listen. *Journal of Personality and Social Psychology,* 1967, **6,** 64–70.

Katz, D., and Stotland, E. A preliminary statement to a theory of attitude structure and change. In S. Koch (ed.), *Psychology: A Study of a Science,* Vol. 3. New York: McGraw-Hill, 1959. Pp. 423–475.

Katz, E., and Lazarsfeld, P. F. *Personal Influence: The Part Played by People in the Flow of Mass Communication.* New York: The Free Press, 1955.

Kelley, H. H., and Volkhart, E. The resistance to change of group-anchored attitudes. *American Sociological Review,* 1952, **17,** 453–465.

Kelley, H. H., and Woodruff, C. L. Members' reactions to apparent group approval of a counter-norm communication. *Journal of Abnormal and Social Psychology*, 1956, **52**, 67–74.

Kelman, H. C., and Hovland, C. I. "Reinstatement" of the communicator in delayed measurement of opinion change. *Journal of Abnormal and Social Psychology*, 1953, **48**, 327–335.

Kiesler, C. A., and Kiesler, S. B. Role of forewarning in persuasive communications. *Journal of Abnormal and Social Psychology*, 1964, **68**, 547–549.

King, B. T. Relationships between susceptibility to opinion change and child-rearing practices. In C. I. Hovland and I. L. Janis (eds.), *Personality and Persuasibility*. New Haven, Conn.: Yale University Press, 1959. Pp. 207–224.

King, B. T., and Janis, I. L. Comparison of the effectiveness of improvised versus non-improvised role-playing in producing opinion changes. *Human Relations*, 1956, **9**, 177–186.

Klapper, J. T. Effects of the mass media. New York: Columbia University, Bureau of Applied Social Research, 1949. (Mimeo)

Krasner, L., Knowles, J. B., and Ullman, C. P. Effects of verbal conditioning of attitudes on subsequent motor performance. *Journal of Personal and Social Psychology*, 1965, **1**, 407–412.

Lana, R. E. Familiarity and the order of presentation of persuasive communications. *Journal of Abnormal and Social Psychology*, 1961, **62**, 573–577.

Lana, R. E. Interest, media, and order effects in persuasive communications. *Journal of Psychology*, 1963, **56**, 9–13.

Lazarsfeld, P. F., Berelson, B., and Gaudet, H. *The People's Choice; How the Voter Makes Up His Mind in a Presidential Campaign*. New York: Duell, Sloan and Pearce, 1944.

Leventhal, H. Fear—For your health. *Psychology Today*, 1967, **1**, 54–58.

Leventhal, H., Jones, S. and Trembley, G. Sex differences in attitude and behavior change under conditions of fear and specific instructions. *Journal of Experimental Social Psychology*, 1966, **2**, 387–399.

Leventhal, H., and Niles, P. Persistance of influence for varying durations of exposure to threat stimuli. *Psychological Reports*, 1965, **16**, 223–233.

Leventhal, H., and Singer, R. Affect arousal and positioning of recommendations in persuasive communication. *Journal of Personality and Social Psychology*, 1966, **4**, 137–146.

Leventhal, H., Singer, R., and Jones, S. Effects of fear and specificity of recommendation upon attitudes and behavior. *Journal of Personality and Social Psychology*, 1965, **2**, 20–29.

Leventhal, H., and Watts, J. C. Sources of resistance to fear-arousing communications on smoking and lung cancer. *Journal of Personality*, 1966, **34**, 165–175.

Leventhal, H., Watts, J. C., and Pagano, F. Effects of fear instructions on how to cope with danger. *Journal of Personality and Social Psychology*, 1967, **6**, 313–321.

Lewis, H. B. Studies in the principles of judgments and attitudes: IV. The operation of "prestige suggestion." *Journal of Social Psychology*, 1941, **14**, 229–256.

Lewis, H. N. Prestige as a factor in attitude changes. *Sociology and Social Research,* 1931, **16,** 49–55.

Linder, D. E., Cooper, J., and Jones, E. E. Decision freedom as a determinant of the role of incentive magnitude in attitude change. *Journal of Personality and Social Psychology,* 1967, **6,** 245–254.

Lipset, S. M., Lazarsfeld, P. F., Barton, A. H., and Linz, J. The psychology of voting: an analysis of political behavior. In G. Lindsey (ed.), *Handbook of Social Psychology.* Vol. II. New York: Addison-Wesley, 1954. Pp. 1124–1176.

Lorge, I. Prestige, suggestion, and attitudes. *Journal of Social Psychology,* 1936, **7,** 386–402.

Lowin, A. Approach and avoidance: alternative modes of selective exposure to information. *Journal of Personality and Social Psychology,* 1967, **6,** 1–9.

Luchins, A. S. Experimental attempts to minimize the impact of first impressions. In C. I. Hovland (ed.), *The Order of Presentation in Persuasion.* New Haven, Conn.: Yale University Press, 1957. Pp. 62–75.

Lumsdaine, A. A., and Janis, I. L. Resistance to "counter-propaganda" produced by one-sided and two-sided "propaganda" presentations. *Public Opinion Quarterly,* 1953, **17,** 311–318.

Lund, F. H. The psychology of belief. IV. The law of primacy in persuasion. *Journal of Abnormal and Social Psychology,* 1925, **20,** 183–191.

McGuire, W. J. Attitudes and opinions. *Annual Review of Psychology,* 1966, **17,** 475–514.

McGuire, W. J. A syllogistic analysis of cognitive relationships. In M. J. Rosenberg and C. I. Hovland (eds.), *Attitude Organization and Change.* New Haven, Conn.: Yale University Press, 1960. Pp. 65–111.

McGuire, W. J. Resistance to persuasion conferred by active and passive prior refutation of the same and alternative counter-arguments. *Journal of Abnormal and Social Psychology,* 1961, **63,** 326–332.

McGuire, W. J. Persistence of the resistance to persuasion inducted by various types of prior belief defenses. *Journal of Abnormal and Social Psychology,* 1962, **64,** 241–248.

McGuire, W. J. Personality and susceptibility to social influence. In E. F. Borgatta and W. W. Lambert (eds.), *Handbook of Personality Theory and Research* (in press).

McGuire, W. J., and Papageorgis, D. The relative efficacy of various types of prior belief-defense in producing immunity against persuasion. *Journal of Abnormal and Social Psychology,* 1961, **62,** 327–337.

McGuire, W. J., and Papageorgis, D. Effectiveness of forewarning in developing resistance to persuasion. *Public Opinion Quarterly,* 1962, **26,** 24–34.

Miller, N., and Campbell, D. T. Recency and primacy in persuasion as a function of the timing of speeches and measurements. *Journal of Abnormal and Social Psychology,* 1959, **59,** 1–9.

Mills, J. Changes in moral attitudes following temptation. *Journal of Personality,* 1958, **26,** 517–531.

Mills, J. Avoidance of dissonant information. *Journal of Personality and Social Psychology,* 1965, **2,** 589–593 (a).

Mills, J. Effect of certainty about a decision upon post-decision exposure to consonant and dissonant information. *Journal of Personality and Social Psychology*, 1965, **2**, 749–752. (b)

Mills, J. Opinion change as a function of the communicator's desire to influence and liking for the audience. *Journal of Experimental Social Psychology*, 1966, **2**, 152–159.

Mills, J. Interest in supporting and discrepant information. In R. Abelson, E. Aronson, W. McGuire, T. M. Newcomb, M. Rosenberg, and P. Tannenbaum (eds.), *Theories of Cognitive Consistency: A Source Book*. Chicago: Rand McNally, 1968. Pp. 771–777.

Mills, J., and Aronson, E. Opinion change as a function of the communicator's attractiveness and desire to influence. *Journal of Personality and Social Psychology*, 1965, **1**, 173–177.

Mills, J., Aronson, E., and Robinson, J. Selectivity in exposure to information. *Journal of Abnormal and Social Psychology*, 1959, **59**, 250–253.

Mills, J., and Jellison, J. M. Effect on opinion change of how desirable the communication is to the audience the communicator addressed. *Journal of Personality and Social Psychology*, 1967, **5**, 459–463.

Mills, J., and Jellison, J. M. Effect on opinion change of similarity between the communicator and the audience he addressed. *Journal of Personality and Social Psychology*, 1968, **9**, 153–156.

Mills, J., and Ross, A. Effects of commitment and certainty upon interest in supporting information. *Journal of Abnormal and Social Psychology*, 1964, **68**, 552–555.

Murphy, G., Murphy, L. B., and Newcomb, T. M. *Experimental Social Psychology*. New York: Harper and Row, 1937.

Newcomb, T. M. An approach to the study of communicative acts. *Psychological Review*, 1953, **60**, 393–404.

Newcomb, T. M. *The Acquaintance Process*. New York: Holt, Rinehart, and Winston, 1961.

Newcomb, T. M. Persistence and regression of changed attitudes: long-range studies. *Journal of Social Issues*, 1963, **19**, 3–14.

Niles, P. The relationship of susceptibility and anxiety to acceptance of fear arousing communications. Unpublished Ph.D. dissertation, Yale University, 1964.

Nunally, J. C., and Bobren, H. M. The variables governing the willingness to receive communications on mental health. *Journal of Personality*, 1959, **27**, 38–46.

Nuttin, J. M., Jr. Dissonant evidence about dissonance theory. Paper read at Second Conference of Experimental Social Psychologists in Europe, Frascati, Italy, 1964.

Orne, M. T. On the social psychology of the psychological experiment: with particular reference to demand characteristics and their implications. *American Psychologist*, 1962, **17**, 776–783.

Osgood, C. E., and Tannenbaum, P. H. The principle of congruity in the prediction of attitude change. *Psychological Review*, 1955, **62**, 42–55.

Packard, V. *The Hidden Persuaders*. New York: David McKay Company, 1957.

Papageorgis, D., and McGuire, W. J. The generality of immunity to persuasion produced by pre-exposure to weakened counterarguments. *Journal of Abnormal and Social Psychology*, 1961, **62**, 475–481.

Powell, F. A. Source credibility and behavioral compliance as determinants of attitude change. *Journal of Personality and Social Psychology*, 1965, **2**, 669–676.

Proust, M. *Swann's Way*. New York: Random House, Modern Library, 1928.

Razran, G. H. S. Conditioning away social bias. *Psychological Bulletin*, 1938, **35**, 693.

Razran, G. H. S. Conditioned response changes in rating and appraising socio-political slogans. *Psychological Bulletin*, 1940, **37**, 481.

Rosen, S. Post-decision affinity for incompatible information. *Journal of Abnormal and Social Psychology*, 1961, **63**, 188–190.

Rosenberg, M. J. An analysis of affective-cognitive consistency. In M. J. Rosenberg and C. I. Hovland (eds.), *Attitude Organization and Change*. New Haven, Conn.: Yale University Press, 1960. Pp. 15–64.

Rosenberg, M. J. When dissonance fails: on eliminating evaluation apprehension from attitude measurement. *Journal of Personality and Social Psychology*, 1965, **1**, 28–42.

Rosenberg, M. J., and Abelson, R. P. An analysis of cognitive balancing. In M. J. Rosenberg and C. I. Hovland (eds.), *Attitude Organization and Change*. New Haven, Conn.: Yale University Press, 1960. Pp. 112–163.

Schachter, S., Ellertson, N., McBride, D., and Gregory, D. An experimental study of cohesiveness and productivity. *Human Relations*, 1951, **4**, 229–238.

Schein, E. H. The Chinese indoctrination program for prisoners of war: a study of attempted "brainwashing." *Psychiatry*, 1956, **19**, 149–172.

Schramm, W., and Carter, R. F. Effectiveness of a political telethon. *Public Opinion Quarterly*, 1959, **23**, 121–126.

Scott, W. A. Attitude change through reward of verbal behavior. *Journal of Abnormal and Social Psychology*, 1957, **55**, 72–75.

Scott, W. A. Cognitive consistency, response reinforcement, and attitude change. *Sociometry*, 1959, **22**, 219–229.

Sears, D. O. Biased indoctrination and selectivity of exposure to new information. *Sociometry*, 1965, **28**, 363–376.

Sears, D. O. Opinion formation and information preferences in an adversary situation. *Journal of Experimental Social Psychology*, 1966, **2**, 130–142.

Sears, D. O., and Freedman, J. L. Commitment, information utility, and selective exposure. *USN Technical Report*, (ONR) Nonr-233 (54) NR 171–350, No. 12, August, 1963.

Sears, D. O., and Freedman, J. L. The effects of expected familiarity with arguments upon opinion change and selective exposure. *Journal of Personality and Social Psychology*, 1965, **2**, 420–426.

Sherif, C. W., Sherif, M., and Nebergall, R. E. *Attitude and Attitude Change*. Philadelphia: W. B. Saunders, 1965.

Sibley, Mulford Q. Letters to the Editor. *Minnesota Daily*. December 4, 1963.

Singer, R. D. Verbal conditioning and generalization of prodemocratic responses. *Journal of Abnormal and Social Psychology*, **63**, 1961, 43–46.

Smith, E. E. The power of dissonance techniques to change attitudes. *Public Opinion Quarterly,* 1961, **25,** 626–639.

Staats, C. K., and Staats, A. W. Meaning established by classical conditioning. *Journal of Experimental Psychology,* 1957, **54,** 74–80.

Staats, C. K., Staats, A. W., and Briggs, D. W. Meaning of verbal stimuli changed by conditioning. *American Journal of Psychology,* 1958, **71,** 429–431.

Star, S. A., and Hughes, H. M. Report on an educational campaign: the Cincinnati plan for the United Nations. *American Journal of Sociology,* 1950, **55,** 389–400.

Stotland, E., and Patchen, M. Identification and changes in prejudice and in authoritarianism. *Journal of Abnormal and Social Psychology,* 1961, **62,** 265–274.

Stotland, E., Zander, A., and Natsoulas, T. Generalization of interpersonal similarity. *Journal of Abnormal and Social Psychology,* 1961, **62,** 250–256.

Tannenbaum, P. H. Initial attitude toward source and concept as factors in attitude change through communication. *Public Opinion Quarterly,* 1956, **20,** 413–425.

Tannenbaum, P. H., Macaulay, J. R., and Norris, E. L. The principle of congruity and reduction of persuasion. *Journal of Personality and Social Psychology,* 1966, **3,** 233–237.

Taylor, J. A., and Spence, K. W. The relationship of anxiety level to performance in serial learning. *Journal of Experimental Psychology,* 1952, **44,** 61–64.

Thomas, E. J., Webb, S., and Tweedie, J. Effects of familiarity with a controversial issue on acceptance of successive persuasive communications. *Journal of Abnormal and Social Psychology,* 1961, **63,** 656–659.

Turner, E. A., and Wright, J. C. Effects of severity of threat and perceived availability on the attractiveness of objects. *Journal of Personality and Social Psychology,* 1965, **2,** 128–132.

Verplanck, W. S. The control of the content of conversation: reinforcement of statements of opinion. *Journal of Abnormal and Social Psychology,* 1955, **51,** 668–676.

Walster, E. The temporal sequence of post-decision processes. In L. Festinger (ed.), *Conflict, Decision and Dissonance.* Stanford, Calif.: Stanford University Press, 1964. Pp. 112–128.

Walster, E., Aronson, E., and Abrahams, D. On increasing the persuasiveness of a low prestige communicator. *Journal of Experimental Social Psychology,* 1966, **2,** 325–342.

Walster, E., and Festinger, L. The effectiveness of "overheard" persuasive communications. *Journal of Abnormal and Social Psychology,* 1962, **65,** 395–402.

Walster, E., and Walster, B. Effect of expecting to be liked on choice of associates. *Journal of Abnormal and Social Psychology.* 1963, **67.** 402–404.

Walster, G. W. Who's afraid of dissonant information? Unpublished B.A. honor's thesis, Stanford University, 1963.

Waly, P., and Cook, S. W. Attitude as a determinant of learning and memory: a failure to confirm. *Journal of Personality and Social Psychology*, 1966, **4**, 280–288.

Weiss, W. A. A "sleeper" effect in opinion change. *Journal of Abnormal and Social Psychology*, 1953, **48**, 173–180.

Weiss, W. A., and Fine, B. J. The effect of induced aggressiveness on opinion change. *Journal of Abnormal and Social Psychology*, 1956, **52**, 109–114.

Zajonc, R. B. Balance, congruity and dissonance. *Public Opinion Quarterly*, 1960, **24**, 280–296.

Zimbardo, P. G., Weisenberg, M., Firestone, I., and Levy, B. Communicator effectiveness in producing public conformity and private attitude change. *Journal of Personality*, 1965, **33**, 233–256.

PART

III

Group Pressure and Conformity

Charles A. Kiesler

Yale University

9

The Nature of Conformity and Group Pressure[1]

The following is a typical definition of conformity given in the texts: conformity is defined as some behavioral or attitudinal change that occurs as the result of some real or imagined group pressure (cf. Walker and Heyns, 1962; Secord and Backman, 1964; Brown, 1965; Homans, 1961; Krech, Crutchfield, and Ballachey, 1962; Berg and Bass, 1961; Asch, 1952, for similar "textbook" definitions). However typical, the definition is still vague. In fact, there are at least three rather distinct and divergent ways in which the term is currently used in the psychological literature. They are (1) conformity as an enduring personality characteristic; (2) conformity as a cognitive or attitudinal change as a result of some (real or imagined) group pressure; and (3) conformity as "going along with the group," regardless whether the group includes only one other member or a hundred others. Since the implications and generalizations one might draw about conformity are quite divergent, depending on which definition one is implicitly accepting at the moment, let us look at them more closely.

Conformity as an Enduring Personality Characteristic. The assumption underlying this definition is that, regardless of other relevant variables (for example, ambiguity of the stimulus, size of the group), there are some people who consistently conform more than others. Although the validity of the assumption is obviously an empirical question, the assumption is nonetheless made rather frequently. Ordinarily, when one sees

[1] In this section the reader is assumed to have already had some contact with the area of conformity at approximately the level of the usual introductory textbook in social psychology. As a result, the more "classical" studies ordinarily discussed in detail in introductory texts are only mentioned briefly here. If a review is needed, the author would suggest either Krech, Crutchfield, and Ballachey (1962) or Secord and Backman (1964). The former is written in a more elementary manner.

reference in an article, say, to "conformers" and "nonconformers," it is this definition of conformity that is being implicitly used. This view of conformity as a personality variable does not seem to have been especially fruitful, but the reader may exercise his prerogative to disagree. In any event, the discussion of individual-difference variables is beyond the scope of this book because we are limited here to experimental studies with an independent variable. For a review of the literature on this topic, the reader is referred to Krech, Crutchfield, and Ballachey (1962).

Conformity as a Cognitive or Attitudinal Change as a Result of Some (Real or Imagined) Group Pressure. There is a large number of circumstances under which one temporarily "changes" his behavior toward some norm or set of expectations of a group or subgroup, without any underlying cognitive change occurring at all. Consider an Asch situation where two lines are presented to the subject, with line *A* longer than line *B*. A number of confederates each give their opinion that *B* is actually longer than *A*. Under these circumstances it has been found that many of the subjects will then "go along with the group" and say that *B* is longer than *A*. We might consider this verbal statement as overt behavioral compliance with the group. The question, however, is whether the subject really believes that *B* is longer than *A*—for example, would he say that *B* was longer than *A* in a subsequent, private testing? He probably would not. His overt behavior is inconsistent with his private attitude or opinion. Festinger (1953) has referred to this type of behavior as public compliance without private acceptance. Both of these variables, public compliance and private acceptance, are important variables for psychological study. Both have wide ramifications for social behavior. But they are not the same variable and do not follow the same empirical laws. They consequently should not have the same name. We shall therefore refer to this second definition of conformity as private acceptance or attitude change.

Conformity as Going Along with the Group. Conformity used in this sense implies no private acceptance. Consequently, the term *public compliance*, or just *compliance*, will be used instead of *conformity*. Thus three terms will be used in this section: *conformity, private acceptance* (or attitude change), and *compliance*. We shall use the term *conformity* as the more generic term; it will be taken to imply some behavioral change that occurs as the result of some real or imagined group pressure, without regard to whether attitude change also occurs. *Compliance* and *private acceptance* refer to subcategories of this more general term. *Compliance* shall mean such a behavior change without any underlying private acceptance. *Private acceptance* refers to those situations in which attitude change occurs.

In this section we shall consider the research concerning both compliance and private acceptance. Later in the section we will consider in some detail the usefulness of our distinction between compliance and private acceptance. The discussion is deferred until the rather large mass of relevant research has been presented. We should note, however, that a particular variable or a particular experimental setting very often produces identical results for private acceptance and overt behavior. Chapter 10 emphasizes primarily the compliance literature and, secondarily, studies in which private acceptance and overt behavior are similarly affected by given variables. Together, this represents the bulk of the experimental literature on the present topic. Chapter 11 will explore more deeply the distinction between compliance and private acceptance, present some theoretical notions and prospects for future research, and generally sum up. For now, let us turn to a discussion of a concept crucial to our definitions of both compliance and private acceptance: group pressure.

The reader may note that the definitions of both compliance and private acceptance included the phrase "as the result of some (real or imagined) group pressure." The term *group pressure* is obviously a crucial one for a discussion of conformity. It is therefore necessary for any understanding of conformity to discuss in some detail what group pressure is and how this "pressure" is transmitted to the individual.

We mean group pressure in its very broadest sense, defining it as *a psychological force operating upon a person to fulfill others' expectations of him, including especially those expectations of others relating to the person's "role" or to behaviors specified or implied by the "norms" of a group to which he belongs. Role* refers to a set of expectations about how the typical occupant of a given "position" in a social group is supposed to behave. After Krech, Crutchfield, and Ballachey (1962), we view roles as being families of expectations. "The expectancies making up a role are not restricted to actions; they also include expectancies about motivations, beliefs, feelings, attitude, and values" (Krech, Crutchfield, and Ballachey, 1962, p. 311). By *norms,* we refer to general standards or rules of conduct and belief specified, implicitly or explicitly, by a group, society, or culture.

Essentially group pressure implies pressure toward uniformity of opinions and behavior in a group. Festinger (1950; 1954) has formally discussed some reasons for the pressures toward uniformity of opinions and behavior in a group. Festinger postulates a human drive to evaluate one's own opinions and abilities. Many of these opinions and abilities, specifically those grounded in social reality, cannot be unequivocally evaluated without reference to others' opinions and abilities (if at all.) To have others agree with you provides a form of consensual validation that otherwise might be unavailable. To have others disagree with you on a particular issue, in addition to the other pressures toward uniformity that it produces, can also be used in a very rational manner as a piece of information that may ultimately lead to a "correct opinion" (Dean, 1961).

It is not necessary for "group pressure" to be explicitly transmitted to be effective. It is not even necessary for the person to think that the rest of the group is aware of any difference in opinion between the person and the group. For example, in several experiments (such as Kiesler, Zanna, and DeSalvo, 1966), the subject knows only that he disagrees with the group on an important topic or norm. The group never communicates or transmits explicitly any pressure on the subject to change his opinion. Indeed, the disagreement between the subject and the group is a bogus one, and the extent of disagreement is identical for all subjects. Yet many subjects change their opinions toward greater agreement with what they think is the group's opinion. Why? One reason is, of course, that the subject may expect the group to subsequently put pressure on him to change his opinions. That groups, experimental and otherwise, do put pressure on deviant members to change their attitude toward those held by the group is well documented (for example, Schachter, 1951; Emerson, 1954; Berkowitz and Howard, 1959; Schachter et al., 1954; Festinger et al., 1952). A second reason is that disagreement with others, especially important or attractive others, creates dissonance (Festinger, 1957; Brehm and Cohen, 1962) or imbalance (Heider, 1958). One of the ways to reduce this dissonance is to change one's opinion in the direction of that held by the group.

At least equally important, however, is group pressure that is explicitly transmitted. One of the interesting batches of data in social psychology is concerned with communication patterns in a group when one or more of the group members holds a deviant opinion.

In what has become a classic study, Schachter (1951) manipulated both cohesiveness of the group and the relevance of the discussion to the group's reason for existence. Cohesiveness was manipulated through the attractiveness of the task rather than the attractiveness of the group. Each group had five to seven members and three confederates. The three confederates in each group each maintained a different attitudinal position vis-à-vis the group discussion topic. "One paid participant, the 'deviate,' chose a position of extreme deviation and maintained it throughout the discussion; the second, the 'mode,' chose and maintained the modal position of group opinion; and the third, the 'slider,' chose the position of extreme deviation but allowed himself to be gradually influenced, so that at the end of the discussion he was at the modal position" (Schachter, 1951, p. 192). Two of Schachter's dependent variables were the acceptance of each of the three confederates, that is, their desirability as fellow group members, and the amount of communication directed toward them during the course of the experiment. The results are interesting. The deviate was definitely sociometrically rejected by the group; the mode and slider were not. The rejection of the deviate was greater in the more highly cohesive condition than in the less cohesive condition and more "intense" when the topic of discussion was relevant than when it was not. The penalty of continued deviation is clear: rejection.

The pattern of communication throughout the experimental hour is consistent with the sociometric ratings. There was little communication to the mode, and it did not vary across time. Communication to the slider started at a high level, but gradually fell off to near zero as the slider came to agree with the group's opinion. For all but the high cohesive relevant condition, communication to the deviate also started relatively high but continued to increase throughout the experimental hour. In the high cohesive relevant condition, communication was high to the deviate, continued to rise for the first part of the hour, but dropped off towards the end of the hour. Presumably this decrease in communication to the deviate at the end of the hour represented what would have eventually been isolation and rejection from the group: the more a person rejected the deviate sociometrically at the end of the hour, the sooner in the hour did the drop in communication occur. The essential findings of the Schachter experiment have been replicated by Schachter et al. (1954), Emerson (1954), Berkowitz and Howard (1959), and Israel (1956).

These data are consistent with Schachter's and Festinger's theorizing: the greater the relevance of the topic and the greater the cohesiveness of the group, the greater the pressure toward uniformity. The greater the pressure toward uniformity, the greater the tendency both to communicate to one holding a deviant opinion in the group and to reject him. The force toward communication with the deviate and the force toward rejection of the deviate should exist at the same time. If the communication fails to bring the deviate into line, then psychological rejection (what Festinger [1950] refers to as the tendency to change the psychological composition of the group) will follow. In addition, the more extreme the discrepancy of opinion between the deviate and the group, the greater the pressure toward uniformity and the greater the force to communicate to the deviate. For example, Festinger and Thibaut (1951) found 70–90 per cent of the communications to be directed toward group members holding extreme opinions.[2]

---

[2] Other variables also affect the flow of communications within a group. For example, Back, Festinger, Hymovitch, Kelley, Schachter and Thibaut (1950) found a tendency for communication to occur upward in the status hierarchy. (See also Cohen, 1958.) Greater communication also occurs among or between friends (for example, Festinger, Schachter, and Back, 1950; Festinger et al., 1948).

Pressure toward uniformity in a group is a ubiquitous and powerful variable. It affects the group's "locomotion," its maintenance, and the social reality of its members (Cartwright and Zander, 1960). We have seen that this pressure need not be explicitly transmitted to effect opinion change or behavioral conformity in the group members. Furthermore, under conditions that allow transmission of the pressure to occur, there appear to be relatively stable patterns of communication and rejection within and between groups.

Thus, for the individual, group pressure takes several forms: (1) One of the ways in which we validate our opinions and abilities is to compare them with others'. When they disagree with us, it reflects upon the perceived "correctness" of our opinions and abilities. (2) When others in a psychological group disagree with us, we may expect them, explicitly or implicitly, to try to induce us to change our attitudes or behavior. We may expect this inducement to take one or more of several forms, some more painful than others. (3) When significant others point out that they disagree with us, one implication we may draw is that agreement on the issue is very important. (4) The knowledge that others disagree with us creates dissonance. One of the ways to reduce this dissonance is to change one's opinion so that disagreement is lessened; another, of course, is to reject or devalue the group. (5) When we disagree with others in a group, our needs for approval, affiliation, and status may become more salient, and we may conform to preserve our status or membership in a group. Thus it seems clear that disagreement with others, whether in behavior or attitudes, produces forces acting upon the individual to change the discrepant behavior or attitude. It seems clear that disagreement with a group induces at least a perception of group pressure to change.

That the group does put pressure on the individual to conform is clear (for example, Schachter, 1951). Why? There are a number of reasons. Some of them have to do with the fact that a group is a collection of individuals. For example, consider the previous discussion of Festinger's theory of social-comparison processes. He postulates that others provide us with a form of social validation of our opinions and abilities. But this is a two-way street. When an individual disagrees with a group, this also reflects upon the correctness of the group's opinion as well as the individual's. The resulting process of changing the other (or being changed) may be very similar, whether we are discussing an individual or a group.

The lack of uniformity of opinion in a group has other implications as well. It may threaten the feeling of being a group. It may affect the ease with which the group maintains itself as a group, in the face of disagreement or anticipated disagreement about policy, and so on. It may slow down the locomotion of the group toward its goals, giving individual members a feeling of frustration and dissatisfaction with the group. We may note that it is not necessary for these things to occur for the group to marshall its forces to bring the deviant member into line. The mere possibility or threat may be more than enough.

Many of these aspects of why groups exert pressure on their members and why individuals accept or reject the influence attempt are closely related to our distinction between compliance and private acceptance. Indeed, it appears to be this distinction that Deutsch and Gerard (1955) are discussing when they refer to two *types* of social influence, normative and informational. In discussing these two types, they refer to the motivations of the person to agree with the group (cf. Wyer, 1966). The informational type of influence refers to the individual accepting information from the group as evidence about reality. The normative type of influence refers to the individual changing his behavior so as to conform with the positive expectations of another. The former appears to be conceptually very close to what we have referred to as private acceptance and the latter similar to what we have called compliance. The reader may find these concepts of Deutsch and Gerard useful in the following chapters.

The topic of conformity is admittedly a complex one. Part of this complexity is due to the intimate relationship of conformity behavior to other broad topics and variables in social psychology. Let us look at some of the variables and concepts that one must be prepared to take into account if conformity is ever to be discussed precisely. We have divided our topic of conformity into compliance and private acceptance. Let us look at these somewhat independently.

To discuss the theoretical underpinnings of compliance, one must be prepared at least to discuss a broad range of social pressures for compliance. For example, consider the range of social behavior that adults attempt to elicit from their children, often without reference to whether the children privately accept these behaviors. These social behaviors include the various social amenities—for example, saying "thank you" in particular situations; aspects of sexual behavior—for example, the notion of virginity until marriage; ethical behavior—for example, not cheating on examinations; and acquiescence to parental demands. In most of these cases, parents would prefer that the child's beliefs follow the parents' wishes. But if this appears not to be the case, the parent is often willing to settle for behavioral compliance without private acceptance. A good deal of the legal and social system follows a similar pattern: insistence upon compliance, and hope for private acceptance.

Very closely related to the topic of compliance is the study of self-presentation and ingratiation (cf. Jones, 1964; Jones and Davis, 1965). Because the emphasis in compliance is on overt behavior, the variables affecting the ways in which one presents oneself to particular others and the tactics of ingratiation with others become very important. Jones, for example (Jones and Jones, 1964; Jones, Jones, and Gergen, 1963), has studied opinion conformity as a tactic of ingratiation—that is, whether (and on which issues) the subject presents himself as agreeing with another in order to impress the other favorably.

Closely related to both compliance and private acceptance are the general areas of group dynamics (cf. Cartwright and Zander, 1960) and social power (cf. French and Raven, 1959; Schopler, 1965). Both of these topics are closely related to the broad categories of interpersonal interaction and interpersonal influence. We shall discuss both in Chapter 11. In this context one should emphasize the importance of the study of social-comparison processes, for this process appears to be intimately related to the acceptance of influence from others.

Of crucial importance to the study of private acceptance is the whole research area of attitude change, about which an immense amount of data has been accumulated. We will not stress these data here because of their detailed presentation elsewhere. Nevertheless, one could view many of these data as representing the study of private acceptance, without regard to aspects of public compliance. As we have previously noted, much of the research in conformity has had the emphasis reversed. It is interesting to note, however, that some criticisms of particular attitude-change experiments (for example, Rosenberg, 1965) appear to take the form of "compliance without private acceptance."

Conformity is not only a complex area, it is also to some extent a confused one. Indeed there has been a great deal of confusion about conformity and what it means to conform. For example, we have previously indicated that there appear to be three main general categories of implicit uses of conformity. When a person takes conformity to mean a certain thing, as with each of the categories we have discussed, he is making certain assumptions about what conformity is, when it occurs, how we may recognize it, and so forth. These assumptions are often not made explicit, but they do provide an investigator with a frame of reference that tends to guide and restrict his research. Indeed, much of the theoretical confusion about conformity is due, at least in part, to the failure of each investigator to make his assumptions explicit.

In one sense we might regard the set of assumptions, implicit or explicit, that an investigator makes about conformity as a miniature theory or model about conformity. Unfortunately a good deal of the theorizing about conformity has been of this implicit variety. Perhaps some of the confusion about conformity would be lessened by a discussion of the various theoretical and conceptual levels at which one might attack the empirical area. In the following, we will try to give the reader some insight into this research area by illustrating varying levels of *implicit* theorizing about conformity.

Willis (1965d) has provided some examples of *levels* of theorizing about conformity. Although his examples appear to be more what we have referred to as compliance, we will use the more generic term, in deference to his usage. In the following we will present seven different descriptive theoretical models that Willis discusses. We say "descriptive theoretical models." The term *descriptive* is used in opposition to *explanatory*—that is, Willis is more concerned with the "what" than the "why." After our discussion of Willis' work, we shall return to this point. We may note for now that Willis (1963; 1965a, 1965b, 1965c, 1965d; Willis and Hollander, 1964a, 1964b) has undoubtedly done some of the more precise theoretical work in the area of conformity.

Willis' discussion of the seven models starts with the simplest one and moves upward to more complex ones. According to Willis' analysis (See Figure 9-1), the simplest model is one in which conformity is located at one end of a continuum and deviations from this extreme position constitute varying degrees of nonconformity. Allport's (1934) classic J-curve of conformity and the more modern approach of Walker and Heyns' book (1962) are both examples of this simple approach. The subject's responses are classified by the extent to which he conforms. For example, one might inspect conformity to the norm of stopping at a traffic sign. Complete conformity would be represented by stopping. Various degrees of nonconformity would be represented by various speeds at which one would go by the sign. The J-curve hypothesis merely says that most people would stop completely, a few would go through slowly, even fewer would go through somewhat more rapidly, although somewhat more might not attend to the sign at all. A frequency distribution of such scores with speed as the abscissa and frequency of occurrence as the ordinate would look like a backward J.

Model 2 is a slightly higher-level one and is represented by three points along a continuum: nonconformity; conformity; nonconformity. This is really a bipolar variant of the simplest model—that is, one can deviate from conformity in two different directions. For example, one can avoid conformity by being either too early or too late; having too much hair or too little; wearing skirts too short or too long. Allport's (1934) "double J-curve hypothesis" is an example of this model. Perhaps a norm of a speed limit might suffice as an example. That is, one conforms by moving at the legal rate of speed. Nonconformity may be evidenced by either going too fast or too slowly.

The most frequently (but implicitly) used model is model 3, the conformity–independence model. This model requires a distinction between

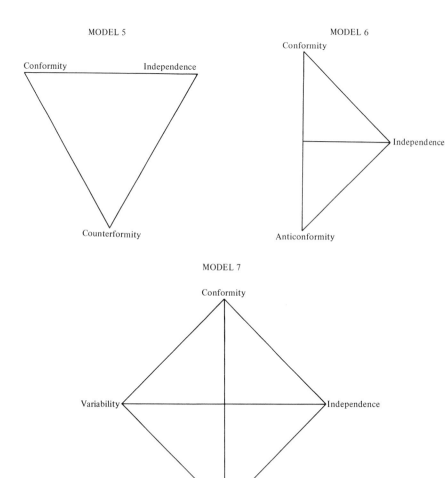

FIGURE 9-1.

Descriptive Models of Social Response (From Willis, 1965d)

response movement—that is, becoming more like the group—and response congruence—that is, the extent to which one's response happens to match the group's. In this model, movement, not congruence, is the criterion for conformity. This model assumes that the more one conforms, the less independent he is. The most frequent user of this model is Asch (1951; 1952; 1956; 1958).

Model 4, the conformity-independence-boomerang model, is a bipolar variant of model 3. Suppose person X disagrees with the group. Model 4 assumes that there are three responses open to the subject: he may conform and change his opinion toward that held by the group; he may remain independent and not change his opinion at all; or he may "boomerang," and change his opinion so that it is even more discrepant from the group's than before. Model 4 has not been used much, but model 5, the conformity–independence–counterformity model, appears to be Crutchfield's (1955; 1959) approach to conformity. Thus, for Crutchfield, "conformity, independence, and counterformity are not to be thought of as three points along a single continuum. Rather they represent three vertices of a triangle. A proper understanding of the whole problem of conformity must take full account of the important differences among these three forms of reaction to group pressure" (Krech, Crutchfield, and Ballachey, 1962, p. 507). The difference between models 4 and 5 represents a slightly different conceptualization of the subject's response space. This difference will become clearer in our discussion of models 6 and 7 below. However, since Crutchfield says that the counterformist moves away from the group, that the group serves as a negative reference group for him, and that the counterformist therefore is as predictable in behavior as the conformist, it is difficult to see why the unidimensional model 4 does not satisfy his requirements, rather than the two-dimensional model 5.

Model 6 represents an earlier approach by Willis (1963) (and since discarded in favor of model 7). The difference between models 5 and 6 has to do with the greater specificity of the latter. "The most important difference is that model 6 actually specifies the two dimensions of response, as well as the exact shape of the response space, thus clarifying the differences and similarities among models of response. Another difference, a consequence of the first, is that with model 6 it has been found possible to develop experimental procedures and scoring formulas which allow the location of subjects within the response space" (1965d, p. 9). Model 7 includes the mirror image of model 6 and specifies the opposite pole of the independence dimension: variability in response.

The point we wish to make is that the models may have quite different implications. The separate authors, however, seldom attempt to make their models explicit (that is, formalize them) nor attempt to distinguish them from the models of others. The result is ambiguity and lack of predictive precision for all concerned. Willis, however, has formalized his theory, attempts to distinguish it from others, and can make rather precise predictions with it. As an example, let us look more closely at his current theory (model 7, above) and one experimental example.

A Two-Dimensional Descriptive Model for Conformity

We will briefly consider Willis' (1963; 1965a, 1965b, 1965c, 1965d; Willis and Hollander, 1964a, 1964b) two-dimensional descriptive model for conformity. Willis has criticized the current state of theorizing about conformity. He specifically concentrates on the unidimensionality of current models and rather convincingly documents their inadequacies. Let us look more closely at his model.

Willis (1965) divides social behavior into three basic components, hierarchically arranged: (1) relevance–irrelevance; (2) dependence–independence; (3) conformity–anticonformity. The relevance dimension is conceived as a unidirectional continuum, whereas the dependence and conformity dimensions are assumed to be bipolar. That is, the relevance dimension starts at zero and increases along some continuum. On the other hand, the dependence dimension goes in two directions from the zero point.

The relevance dimension refers to the extent to which normative expectations provide cues about how one should behave. The dependence dimension refers to the weight given these normative expectations, if they are relevant, in the determination of behavior. Given a particular level of relevance and dependence, the conformity component refers to the extent to which the person attempts to make his behavior congruent with that prescribed by the norm. In the last sentence, the word *attempts* is crucial because Willis differentiates between congruence (the extent to which a given behavior coincides with the norm) and movement (the extent to which the behavior changes to become more congruent with the norm).

Assuming maximal relevance, Willis differentiates among four possible modes of response to conformity pressures: conformity, independence, anticonformity, and variability. Conformity and anticonformity represent one bipolar dimension indicating the extent to which a person attempts to behave either perfectly consistently with perceived role expectations (pure conformity) or antithetically to normative role expectations (pure anticonformity). Independence–variability represents another bipolar dimension of response that is conceptually independent[3] of the conformity–anticonformity dimension. At one extreme of this dimension is pure independence behavior, which "occurs whenever the individual perceives relevant normative expectations, but gives *zero weight* to these perceived expectations in formulating his decisions. This does not mean that he does not 'weigh' the expectations in the sense of evaluating their importance and appropriateness, but rather that the outcome of this process of evaluation leads him to reject them as guides to his behavior. The independent person is one capable of *resisting* social pressures, rather than one who is unaware of them or merely ignores them" (1965c, p. 379). At the other extreme of this dimension is the completely variable person who "invariably changes his response if given an opportunity. . . . Variability reflects complete indecision" (p. 379). The graphical representation of this theoretical model is represented in Figure 9-2 by a diamond, with

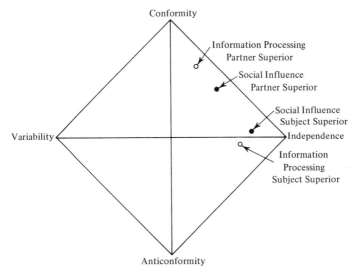

FIGURE 9-2.

Location of Experimental Groups on the Response Space of the Diamond Model of Social Response (Adapted from Willis, 1965b)

[3] Actually, as one may see from the diamond model, the two dimensions thus derived are not statistically independent. That is, there must be some correlation between the two dimensions because possible combinations of the two are restricted by the shape of the diamond. As Willis says, "The magnitude of such a correlation is an empirical matter, and it can be expected to vary from sample to sample and from one set of circumstances to another. The axes . . . serve the same function as the orthogonal reference axes used to plot a scatter diagram for two such obviously correlated variables as height and weight" (Willis, 1965c, p. 380).

conformity–anticonformity as one dimension of the diamond and independence–variability as the other (see footnote 3).

Let us take an experimental example. Willis (1965b) separately manipulated the perceived task competence (subject superior versus partner superior) and the instructional set of the subject (information processing versus social influence). Task competence was manipulated in the usual way by telling one subject he was very good at the task and the other subject he was very bad at the task. The subjects under the information processing set were told the purpose of the experiment was to "find out how effectively each of you can make use of additional information in improving your initial performance." Subjects in the social influence set were told the purpose was to "find out how much each of you will be influenced by the judgments made by the others." All subjects rated a group of photographs as to their aesthetic value. The experimenter then pretended to copy the partner's ranking on each subject's answer sheet. Subjects then reranked the stimuli. The partner's ranking was actually a bogus one, and was derived so as to correlate zero with the subject's initial ranking. For data, Willis attended to two rank-order correlations: that between the subject's initial and subsequent ranking (rho_{13}) as a measure of independence; and that between the partner's presumed ranking and the subjects second ranking (rho_{23}) as a measure of conformity. The rank-order correlations were transformed in the following way so as to create a diamond-shaped response space:

$$x = \text{independence} = (90 - \arccos rho_{13})/90$$
$$y = \text{conformity} \quad = (90 - \arccos rho_{23})/90$$

The results are presented in Figure 9-2. Analysis of variance yielded a significant interaction between instructional set and task competence, as Willis had predicted. This need not concern us here. The point we wish to make it that a unidimensional model of conformity would not suffice to describe these data—both of Willis' dimensions are necessary for an adequate description. The experimental conditions differ both in the degree of independence and the degree of conformity exhibited.

Besides the work of Willis, few attempts have been made to formalize theoretical statements about conformity behavior. In spite of this unwillingness to theorize about these data, every researcher makes some assumptions about what conformity is and what the relevant dimensions are. Willis' discussion of the seven models of social response quite aptly illustrates the tendency of researchers in the field to use *implicit* models or theories of conformity without really acknowledging their use. The assumptions that an experimenter makes in conceptualizing his research problem may in themselves be regarded as a theory, or at the very least, a theoretical frame of reference. These assumptions, as such, are then open to test or criticism in the same manner as any theory. We also may utilize the same criterion for judging them—for example, in terms of their usefulness or on grounds of parsimony.

Willis' model is a step in the proper direction of greater precision in conformity research. We should note that the model is a purely descriptive one that describes and allows one to quantify alternative social responses in a conformity setting. The model as such emphasizes the various modes of response. It does not, however, attempt to explain why a particular response should occur. Willis has criticized the "overdependence" of social psychologists on the "movement" response as opposed to the "congruence" response. The reader may have noted that the present section has also emphasized the movement response. However, our emphasis on movement or change is not due to our theoretical orientation, but rather to our methodological orientation. The inclusion of congruence in one's theory may allow one more adequately to describe a rather heterogeneous batch of data. This we agree with. Nonetheless, we think that the methodological emphasis upon movement or change allows one to draw more unequivocal conclusions from a given experiment and to say more precisely why a particular effect may have occurred. Our methodological emphasis is not necessarily discrepant with Willis' theoretical emphasis. That is, suppose person *A*'s opinion happens to be congruent with the group's opinion. What generalization can we draw from this "fact" for other research in conformity? Probably none. This is not to say that congruence of opinions or behavior is unimportant. Indeed, if we wish to investigate a particular group in everyday life, congruence of opinions and behavior may be all we can detect. We may not be able to say whether the group had changed the individual, whether the members happen to agree by chance, or whether the group was originally formed of people who agreed about certain issues. The similarity of opinion and behavior may be all we want to know about some existing group. But such knowledge does not allow us to say anything about conformity in general, or about other groups.

If we wish to draw some conclusion and generalize to other groups, then we must know something about the underlying psychological variables. To draw conclusions about underlying variables, we must repeatedly ask the question, "Why?" We place emphasis upon change, or what Willis calls movement, because this allows us to say unequivocally that the group has had some effect on the individual. Mere congruence does not allow this conclusion. If the group has an effect, then we may start asking, "Why does this effect occur?" It is answers or partial answers to the "whys" that allow us to begin to make predictions for other, nonidentical situations. It is for this reason that both our definition of conformity and the research we shall present in this section include change as a crucial concept, whether this change is behavioral, attitudinal, or both.

The foregoing amounts to a reflection on the role of theory in psychology. All we have essentially said is that theories are necessary. Let us add a note on how one goes about testing them, especially with reference to the present area of conformity. As we shall discuss later, there is actually a fairly large number of theories that attempt to explain conformity behavior, or some aspects of conformity behavior.

Theories not only help us to explain data previously acquired, but they also guide our future research—that is, they make predictions. A good theory makes *unequivocal* predictions, at least for some situations, and a good theory is capable of being wrong. Part of the process of carrying out research is to sort among theoretical explanations—that is, to test theories. This leads us to the two biggest problems in conformity research: (1) There are too many theories, many of them implicit and inadequately thought out. (2) Too little attention has been given to precise tests of these theories. One can see that if the second problem were solved, the first problem would take care of itself. That is, if the theories were precisely tested, the inadequate ones would be discarded.

We therefore recommend more experiments of the following two types. Both types demand that the experimenter consider alternative explanations of his data, *before he runs the experiment.* In one type of experiment, the researcher sets up a situation that tests only one theory. But he designs his experiment such that if the data are as predicted, no other current theory could explain them. This is a case of one theory against all other ones. Of course, if the data do not come out as predicted, a number of explanations may be available. In that case, the researcher may discard the theory he tested, even though he may not explain his data otherwise.

The second type is sometimes referred to as a "crucial experiment." That is, it explicitly tests between two (or more) theories. To use a much overly simplified example, the experimenter might set up a situation with two conditions, A and B. He designs his method such that whereas theory 1 predicts greater conformity in condition A than B, theory 2 predicts the opposite. We should note that the researcher must still consider alternative explanations for each possibility $(A > B; B > A)$, possibly including special control conditions to rule out explanations other than the two theories in question. Only if such theoretically oriented experiments are carried out can we begin to sort among alternative explanations.[4]

---

[4] We are not saying this is the only way to go about research. Indeed, the precise way in which one might wish to attack a given area would depend on a number of

It will become apparent from the presentation of data in the next chapter that there have been few attempts to test theories and sort among theoretical explanations in the area of conformity research. There are two main defects in the design of experiments in this research area. The first is that theories are not unequivocally tested. Granted, the researcher makes a "theoretical" prediction, and, granted, the data may come out as predicted. But too often there are a number of extremely plausible alternative explanations; indeed, some of them more plausible than the theory presumably being tested. The experiment amounts to an empirical demonstration rather than a theoretical test. The second defect in experimental design in conformity concerns the "demand characteristics" (Orne, 1962) of the situation and task. That is, there may be certain aspects of the experimenter's behavior, the setting, or the task that are irrelevant to the theoretical variable presumably being studied, but which induce behavior change in the predicted direction. For example, the experimenter often unconsciously gives cues to the subject about what he wants him to do (for example, comply with the group), and the subject is often very willing to accomodate the experimenter. Now, demand characteristics themselves provide an interesting area of research. But we object to people unwittingly studying demand characteristics, but drawing conclusions in terms of some other variable (for example, reinforcement).

We have indicated that one of the major difficulties besetting researchers in conformity is the lack of well-articulated theory. The major result of this lack has been that there have been few studies on conformity that allow one to sort among theoretical explanations. As Graham (1962) has noted, the data of conformity appear to be equally well handled by a wide variety of theoretical approaches—for example, field theory (Asch, 1952), reinforcement learning theory (Mausner, 1955), conditioning theory (Kidd and Campbell, 1955), adaptation-level theory (Helson, Blake, Mouton, and Olmstead, 1956) and subjective probability theory (Goldberg and Lubin, 1958). One could as well include psychoanalytic theory (Hoffman, 1953) and mathematical models (Cohen, 1963; Suppes and Atkinson, 1960).

In addition to these, there are several "gain-and-loss" theories, which emphasize the rational opportunistic strategies the subject may take. Perhaps the most popular of these theories are those of Homans (1961) and Thibaut and Kelley (1959), although there are a number of others (for example, Harsanyi, 1962; March, 1955). These theorists assume that the subject constructs a "decision-matrix" of some sort in which, or by

---

factors, not the least of which is the personal research strategy of a given experimenter. We are saying merely that the area of conformity desperately needs research of this variety.

means of which, the subject may ascertain the rewards and costs associated with each alternative course of action in a given situation. Thus these theorists are likely to emphasize the subject's "decision" to conform. As we shall discuss, Gerard (1965) appears to have demonstrated that it is useful in a compliance setting to view the subject's behavior as reflecting a decision. However, it remains to be seen whether this type of orientation will be useful in discussing private acceptance or the distinction between compliance and private acceptance. We should note, however, that of these theoretical orientations, that of Thibaut and Kelley appears to be the most comprehensive. We will have a little more to say about theory at the end of the section.

CHAPTER

10

The Effects of
Group Pressure

This chapter will provide a somewhat critical review of the experimental literature related to the conditions under which one can produce conformity in a group setting. Although our distinction between public compliance and private acceptance appears to be a necessary and a useful distinction, the data have not been collected with this distinction in mind and hence often do not permit a very clear interpretation. Often one cannot tell whether particular data reflect compliance or private acceptance. Because of this ambiguity, we will use the more generic term *conformity* in this chapter. We may note, however, that in much of the research presented here, either private acceptance was not produced or no attempt to measure private acceptance was made. In some other of the research, the experimental variables appear to affect private acceptance and compliance in a similar manner. We will return to this distinction between private acceptance and compliance in some detail in Chapter 11. Let us turn to the review of the experimental literature.

There are three main experimental paradigms used in the study of conformity. They sometimes provide a pretest of the subject's behavior or opinion, always interpolate some indication to the subject of the group's behavior or opinion, and always end up with a postmeasure of the appropriate opinion or behavior of the subject. The three paradigms mentioned below by no means exhaust the techniques used, but they are by far the most popular. Each is identified by the name of the experimenter who first used it.

Sherif's Paradigm for Conformity As the reader is surely aware, Sherif is noted for his use of the autokinetic phenomenon to study conformity. Sherif was perhaps the earliest systematic experimental researcher on conformity, apparently first beginning around 1931 (cf. Sherif, 1935; 1936). The essential element of the technique is that the subject is told, or observes himself, how much the group thinks a point of light moves. He then makes an estimate himself—the dependent variable being, of course, the extent to which the subject's judgment of the autokinetic movement is affected by the group judgment. Sherif's early work indicated that this change in the subject's judgment of the movement of the light persisted even when the group was not present, providing the discrepancy in judgment was not very large. Sherif did not view his data as reflecting a compliance response in the sense that we have used the term here, but instead emphasized the development of the subject's "frame of reference" in an otherwise totally ambiguous situation.[1] In this context, it is interesting to note that Sherif's later work has been within much the same theoretical orientation, but has been in the field of attitude change (cf. Sherif and Hovland, 1961; Sherif, Sherif, and Nebergall, 1965). Perhaps because of Sherif's continuing interest in more permanent effects, the following two techniques have been used more often in the experimental study of conformity.

The Asch Technique.   Asch (1951; 1952; 1956; 1958) has typically used a stimulus situation quite the contrary of Sherif's, in the sense that Asch's stimulus for judgment is almost totally devoid of any ambiguity. The subject is typically presented with two or three lines and is asked to judge which matches a comparison line. Confederates, up to ten in number, give their judgments before the subject does. On certain trials, the confederates give incorrect judgments. The dependent variable is whether the subject goes along with this obviously incorrect judgment. The reader should be familiar with this technique, as it has been used very often. Certain details of the technique will be discussed more fully and critically later. The methological clumsiness of having to maintain and pay a large number of confederates for each subject hour has led Crutchfield to devise a simpler technique.

The Crutchfield Technique.   Crutchfield (1955; 1959; Krech, Crutchfield, and Ballachey, 1962, pp. 508–512) has described a technique whereby five naïve subjects may be run at the same time. "Five subjects at a time are seated side by side in individual booths, screened from one another. Each booth has a panel with a row of numbered switches which the person uses to signal his judgments on items presented on slides

---

[1] There are a number of studies to support Sherif's interpretation of his results. For example, it has been found that the change thus induced lasts over time (Sherif, 1935; Bovard, 1948), perhaps even as long as a year (Rohrer, Baron, Hoffman and Swander, 1954). In addition, the influence takes place even though the subject himself never makes an overt judgment and merely watches a confederate do so (Hood and Sherif, 1962). Finally, the subjects apparently are not aware that others have influenced them (Hood and Sherif, 1962).

projected on the wall in front of the group. Also displayed on his panel are signal lights which indicate what judgments the other four members are giving to the items. The booths are designated by letters *A, B, C, D,* and *E,* and the subjects are instructed to respond one at a time in that order" (Krech, Crutchfield, and Ballachey, 1962, p. 509). In fact, however, each subject's booth is labeled *E,* and the "judgments" of *A, B, C,* and *D* are predetermined by the experimenter. Given that the judgments of the real subjects coincide, then all of them can be put in a position where each feels that the group has rendered a judgment different from his own. Because the Crutchfield method is relatively simple, requires no "acting" or payment for confederates, and a number of naïve subjects may be run at the same time, it should come as no surprise that there has recently been a considerable increase in the use of the Crutchfield method in studying conformity.

These are the three main techniques or methods used to study conformity. There are others, most particularly those involving note passing among subjects. Some of these others will be illustrated in the discussion of research results to follow.

Situational and Experimental Variables Affecting the Degree of Conformity

Difficulty of the Task and Ambiguity of the Stimulus

The variables of difficulty of the task and ambiguity of the stimulus are highly related and thus far appear to produce identical results. Generally, the more ambiguous the stimulus or the more difficult the task, the greater the conformity. (Berenda, 1950; Blake, Helson, and Mouton, 1956; Caylor, 1957; Coleman, Blake, and Mouton, 1958; Fisher, Williams, and Lubin, 1957; Goldberg and Lubin, 1958; Wiener, 1958; Wiener, Carpenter, and Carpenter, 1956; Luchins, 1955; Luchins and Luchins, 1955a; Coffin, 1941; London and Lim, 1964). In addition, Asch (cf. 1952) found that decreasing the difference between the lengths of the lines in his perceptual paradigm increased conformity. In a similar situation Luchins (1955) found that when the differences between the line lengths were very small (for example, $\frac{1}{16}$ inch), then conformity increased when one decreased the difference even more. Otherwise, he found task difficulty to have little influence on the degree of conformity.

However, in the typical Asch situation there is very little ambiguity. Asch (1956) reports that in his control groups, approximately 95 per cent of the subjects can correctly say which lines are longer in all cases—that is, 95 per cent of the control subjects make no errors in the Asch paradigm. This suggests that the main and possibly sole source of influence on Asch's subjects is a normative one, to use Deutsch and Gerard's (1955) term. It is presumably only when there is some uncertainty about the correct response that the group is used as a source of information about reality. There should be little variation in conformity when the difference between the stimuli is clearly discriminable. If so, we would expect precisely what Luchins found, that the differences between the stimuli have to be very small before variations in difficulty have any effect on the conformity response. In line with our suggestion that the prime source of influence in the Asch situation is normative, it is interesting to note Graham's (1962) comment that, "if it *really mattered* to a subject in a situation of the Asch type to make a correct judgment—if, for example, the acquisition of a large reward or the avoidance of a severe punishment were known to depend on the objectively correct response being given— then there would be very little conformity, except perhaps for subjects who suspected some trick" (1962, p. 248; italics in original).

Ordinarily, however, the more difficult the task or the more ambiguous the stimulus, the greater the tendency for the subject to depend on or look to others as sources of information about the selection of the correct answer. It is to be expected, therefore, that conformity should increase under such circumstances, although Luchins and Luchins (1963) have questioned the generality of such a conclusion. It should be noted that these results on the difficulty of the task and ambiguity of the stimulus fit in very neatly with Festinger's theory of social-comparison processes that we discussed in Chapter 9. That is, we look to others to validate those opinions and abilities that have reference to social reality. The more ambiguous the stimulus or difficult the task, the less able we are to depend upon physical reality. Consequently, the more likely we should be to look to the opinions of others to validate our own. Strong forces then theoretically exist to make our opinions coincide with, or be similar to, others' as a form of validation.

Size of the Group

Asch (1951) varied the size of the majority in his experiments and found that increasing the size of the unanimous majority beyond three had little effect upon conformity. For three or less, there was a monotonic increase in the degree of conformity with an increase in the size of the "majority." Luchins and Luchins (1955b) report similar data. On the other hand, Goldberg (1954) found no difference in conformity between groups with a majority of two and those with a majority of four (although Goldberg's subjects were not face to face). There is nothing magical about the number three, but it appears that a group does not have to be very large to exert most, if not all, of its potential influence, at least for the Asch situation.

In fact, the example of one person can effect considerable conformity even without communication between that person and the subject. Rosenbaum (1956; Rosenbaum and Blake, 1955) has found that the example of a confederate refusing or complying with a request to volunteer for an experiment had considerable effect on the probability of the subject's volunteering also. Similar effects for the acceptance of requests and the violation of prohibiting signs have also been noted (Blake, Berkowitz, Bellamy, and Mouton, 1956; Blake, Helson, and Mouton, 1956; Freed, Chandler, Mouton, and Blake, 1955; Blake, Mouton and Hain, 1956; Barch, Trumbo, and Nagle, 1957). The latter studies deal with situations where presumably the subject would like to perform a particular act but "society" forbids it. The example of the confederate performing the prohibited act (for example, drinking at a forbidden water fountain or crossing the street against the light) reduces the pressure to avoid the act and the subject "conforms" where ordinarily he would not do so.

Of course this explanation does not apply to the volunteering studies of Rosenbaum. In those studies, a number of factors may contribute to the effect and a precise explanation awaits future research. That is, the volunteering of the confederate could indicate any one or more of a number of things—for example, that the subjects "ought" to do it (cf. Heider, 1958); that the request is more legitimate than the subject might otherwise feel; or that the experiment is important. Other factors, of course, are also relevant. Wheeler and Arrowood (1966) have indicated that when the subject is in a very ambiguous situation, where he is unsure how to behave, he will imitate whomever he can.

Krech, Crutchfield, and Ballachey (1962) have noted that the lack of effect of group size on conformity may not hold in real-life situations. They suggest that the threat of reprisal for nonconformity may be greater for a larger group, and hence conformity may be greater. It should also be true in a more natural setting that the larger the group, the greater may be the extent and ease of surveillance. Both of these variables should produce greater conformity, but neither has been directly tested in the context of group size.

Of course, we are discussing a *unanimous* majority for these effects of group size. A nonunanimous majority produces much less conformity than a unanimous majority (Asch, 1956; Bennett, 1955; Hardy, 1957; Mouton, Blake, and Olmstead, 1956; Maier and Solem, 1952; Jones, Wells, and Torrey, 1958). Indeed, only one "ally" for a subject is needed to greatly reduce or dissipate the effect of the group pressure. If there is someone in the group who agrees with the subject's judgment, then the group has little influence on the subject's judgment. This is true even if the "deviate-ally's" presence is made known late in the experiment, after the subject has been conforming for some time (Asch, 1952; Luchins, 1955). Parenthetically, this refers only to compliance. The effect of the "late deviate" is quite different for private-acceptance data (Kiesler, Zanna, and DeSalvo, 1966).

Size of the Discrepancy Between the Subject and the Group

In Asch's experiments, some 95 per cent of the subjects can easily make a correct judgment when not in the presence of a discrepant group judgment. In the presence of the group, approximately one third go along with the group's judgment. This illustrates that one can obtain considerable conformity even in a situation where the group's judgment is highly discrepant from the subject's. In the Asch situation, the group's judgment contradicts physical reality. On the other hand, we have already mentioned that making the two lines closer in length, which presumably would make the group's judgment less discrepant from the subject's, sometimes has little effect until the lines are very close in length (Luchins, 1955).

The issue is somewhat complicated by the fact that in the Asch situation, conformity cannot vary if there are only two lines to choose between: it either occurs or it does not. Of course, if there are three lines, then a "compromise" response is possible. Many other experimental paradigms allow for variations in conformity along some continuum.

The data on the discrepancy issue are still unclear, and some (Graham, 1962; Olmstead and Blake, 1955) have suggested that conformity at very high and very low levels of discrepancy may represent distinctly different processes. It is interesting to note how similar these two "processes" are to Deutsch and Gerard's (1955) informational and normative types of influence. Olmstead and Blake had subjects estimate the number of clicks they heard. A simulated group (using a tape recorder) made estimates first and the degree of "majority error" was varied from one to three "units." They found the greatest conformity at both the least and the greatest discrepancy and the least conformity at the intermediate discrepancy. Their explanation of the results is the following: at one unit of error, the subject conformed because he thought he might have been wrong (that is, that he miscounted); at two units he was more confident he had not miscounted; but at three units, the subject conformed merely to avoid being different. Schroder and Hunt (1958) did not replicate the U-shaped curve of conformity, but similarly reported that the processes underlying conformity appear to be different at very small and very large discrepancies between the subject and the group. In addition, Tuddenham (1961) found greater yielding with a highly discrepant norm than with a moderately discrepant one.

The informational type of influence appears to be quite closely related to what we have referred to here as private acceptance (or attitude change). If, as suggested above, two processes are at work here, this may be producing the confusion in the literature concerning the conclusions one may draw about discrepancy and conformity. That is, some of the studies may be measuring private acceptance and others measuring compliance. The data further suggest that private acceptance (using the group judgment as a source of information) may be occurring at lower levels of discrepancy, whereas compliance (normative influence) may be occurring at higher levels of discrepancy.

This provides an interesting theoretical problem. Let us first discuss the theoretical relationship between discrepancy and private acceptance —that is, attitude change. We will then postulate a possible theoretical relationship between discrepancy and pressure to comply. Finally we will put the two relationships together by overlaying the theoretical curves. The result, of course, is highly speculative and tenuous, but interesting.

First, let us look at the theoretical relationship between discrepancy and attitude change. Although there is some discussion in the literature about the precise theoretical relationship involved, we may at least report the current tentative conclusions. The relationship between attitude change and the degree of the attitudinal discrepancy between the subject and the source of some communication appears to be a complex one that is dependent on the credibility of the source (cf. Aronson, Turner, and Carlsmith, 1963) as well as the importance of the topic for the subject (cf. Sherif, Sherif, and Nebergall, 1965). Ignoring importance for a moment, let us inspect the theoretical curves depicted in Figure 10-1. Perfect credibility here is assumed to be only a theoretical construct and not to be ordinarily obtained in the laboratory. Figure 10-1 shows that at levels less than perfect credibility there is a family of curves, each of which represents a curvilinear relationship between attitudinal discrepancy and attitude change. The general theoretical relationship is supported in several studies; most clearly in Aronson, Turner, and Carlsmith (1963). Considering the degree of discrepancy possible in the Asch studies, it seems safe to assume that this informational type of influence is salient only at lower levels of discrepancy.

Let us turn to the problem of the theoretical relationship between discrepancy and compliance. Figure 10-2 represents one possible theoretical relationship between discrepancy and pressure to comply. It shows (theoretically) that at low levels of attitudinal or judgmental discrepancy, there is little pressure perceived by the subject to comply overtly. At higher levels of discrepancy, however, we hypothesize that the subject perceives a good deal of pressure to comply. Consistent with this theoreti-

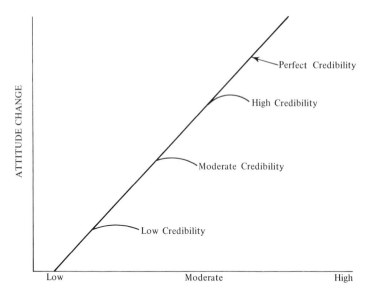

ATTITUDINAL DISCREPANCY BETWEEN *S* AND SOURCE

FIGURE 10-1.

The Theoretical Relationship of Attitudinal Discrepancy and Source Credibility to Attitude Change

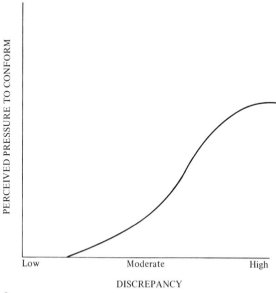

DISCREPANCY

FIGURE 10-2.

One Possible Theoretical Relationship Between Discrepancy and Perceived Pressure to Comply with the Normative Expectations of the Group

cal speculation, previously mentioned data (for example, Schachter, 1951) indicate that considerable pressure to conform to the group standards is exerted upon the subject at higher levels of discrepancy. Of course, Figure 10–2 represents only one of a great many *possible* theoretical relationships. For the moment, however, let us assume that Figure 10–2 represents the true relationship and suspend critical judgment until we see where the assumption may lead us. At this point at least, the posited relationship does not appear to be unreasonable.

Now, if we assume that Figures 10-1 and 10-2 represent adequately the relationship of discrepancy to attitude change and perceived pressure to comply, respectively, then we need only two other assumptions to account for the data on size of discrepancy. One, we assume a monotonically positive relationship between perceived pressure to comply and actual compliance. Two, we assume that these two types of influence, normative and informational, do not interact. That is, we assume that whichever source is stronger at a given moment provides the total effect, and that the other source has no effect at that time. These two assumptions provide us with the theoretical relationship depicted in Figure 10-3.

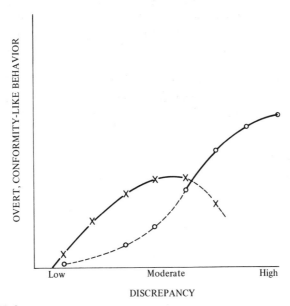

FIGURE 10-3.

> *Overt Conformity-like Behavior as a Function of Discrepancy, Assuming Source Credibility Is at a Moderate Level. (Circles represent overt behavior reflecting only compliance. Crosses represent overt behavior reflecting underlying private acceptance. The nonsalient aspects of each curve are represented by dashes.)*

One may see that Figure 10-3 is the result of overlaying the moderate credibility curve of Figure 10-1 with our theoretical relationship in Figure 10-2. It shows only overt behavior—and not whether the behavior reflects private acceptance or compliance. In this case, the change at lower levels of discrepancy represents private acceptance and that at high levels, compliance (without private acceptance). The curve in Figure 10-3 would presumably obtain only if one inspected overt behavior without reference to whether that behavior represented attitude change or compliance.

Thus this speculation leads us to the conclusion that if one does not take into account the whole range of possible judgmental or attitudinal discrepancy, the precise nature of the relationships obtained will depend on the credibility of the source and the particular segment of the curve the investigator is dealing with. If the range inspected in a given experiment is from moderate to extreme, then one will obtain the U-shaped relationship obtained by Olmstead and Blake. If one is dealing with relatively low levels of discrepancy, one would obtain a monotonically positive relationship as depicted in the first third of Figure 10-3 and as found by several investigators (for example, Hovland and Pritzker, 1957; Goldberg, 1954). If one used a slightly larger range of discrepancy one would obtain the curvilinear relationship represented by the first half of the curve in Figure 10-3. This is what Fisher and Lubin (1958) appear to have found.

The author is not advocating the depiction of Figure 10-3 as *the* theoretical relationship between discrepancy and overt behavior change: indeed, quite the opposite. Figure 10-3 is really a mish-mash of two theoretical relationships involving quite different behaviors: compliance and private acceptance. Thus one would be more inclined to say that the theoretical curve in Figure 10-3 appears to describe the data adequately *only* because psychologists have tended to confuse compliance and private acceptance.

Competence of the Subject and the Group

It seems reasonable to expect that the less competent a subject is at the task or the more competent the group is, the greater will be the conformity. This is precisely what the data suggest as well (Croner and Willis, 1961; Rosenberg, 1961, 1963; Kidd and Campbell, 1955; Mausner and Bloch, 1957; Mausner, 1954a, 1954b; DiVesta, 1959; Samelson, 1957; Kelman, 1950; Fagen, 1963; Crutchfield, 1955). Similar effects occur when the subject is more self-confident (Smith, 1961; Hochbaum, 1954; Coleman, Blake, and Mouton, 1958). Let us consider two examples of this research in some detail.

Croner and Willis (1961) carried out two experiments. Their study is interesting because it illustrates to some extent the specificity of the conformity response. In each experiment, subjects were run in pairs and carried out two tasks. Bogus feedback was given in the first of these two tasks, establishing one subject as highly competent and the other as incompetent. Subjects then completed a task in which they judged the relative lengths of lines. Actually, the lines were always of equal length. On half of the trials, the competent subject judged first. One interesting aspect of this experiment is that a "chance level of conformity" may be calculated. That is, one would expect some agreement among subjects on the basis of chance alone. The dependent variable of conformity should not include this chance, but expected, agreement.[2]

In the first experiment, the task on which the competence manipulation was based was referred to as "the Cardall Test of Practical Judgment." The results indicated that this competence manipulation had no effect on conformity. The authors reasoned that the lack of differential effect was due to the lack of similarity between the "practical judgment" task and the line-length judgment task. In their second experiment, the tasks were made more similar. Instead of the Cardall test, subjects completed a test involving the judgment of the relative area of thirty-six irregularly drawn figures. The competence manipulation was then based on this area-judgment task. In this experiment, the competence manipulation had a powerful effect: subjects in the low-competence condition conformed much more than subjects in the high-competence condition. Thus the hypothesis was supported, but only for similar tasks. The competence manipulation had to be very specific to the dependent variable task to be effective.

Rosenberg (1961) used a somewhat similar manipulation in an Asch situation. Half of the subjects were told they had done poorly on a task similar to line judgment, and that others in the group had done well on the task. The other half of the subjects were not told anything related to competence. Of additional interest is the fact that group size was also manipulated. Subjects were run in either two-, three-, four-, or five-man groups. The data are presented in Figure 10-4.

Figure 10-4 indicates that the incompetence of the subject combined

---

[2] The computation of scores was as follows. "Data from odd numbered and even numbered trials were treated separately. The expected proportion of trials that both subjects would respond 'plus' (stimulus larger than standard) was determined by multiplying the proportion of times High responded 'plus' by the proportion of times Low responded 'plus.' A corresponding product was formed for the minus responses. The sum of these two products was subtracted from the actual proportion of agreements. If this difference was positive, the subject going second tended to imitate his partner, while a negative difference indicated an opposition tendency" (Croner and Willis, 1961, p. 706).

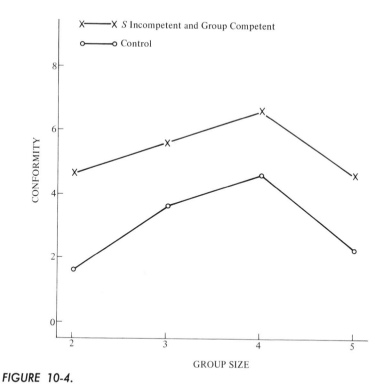

FIGURE 10-4.

The Relationship of Competence and Size of Group to Conformity in an Asch Situation (From Rosenberg, 1961)

with the competence of the group for a similar task greatly increased the subject's conformity to the group at all levels of group size (there was no interaction). The decrease in conformity as one moves from four- to five-man groups is statistically significant and does not really fit with other data. Although Rosenberg interpreted this as consistent with Asch's (1952) data on group size, Asch's data actually indicated a leveling off rather than a drop. The data might be related to Hare's (1952) finding that the possibility of subgroups forming increases with group size. The larger the group, the more the subject might expect to find an ally. However, Rosenberg says that only 14 per cent of his subjects rejected the "validity of the group situation" and that this attitude was unrelated to the drop in conformity. As indicated previously, the size of the group remains a fruitful area for research. It may be noted that, in line with our distinction between compliance and private acceptance, 86 per cent of Rosenberg's total sample subsequently indicated in an interview that they were aware of the difference between their perceptions of the lines and the group's estimates. Apparently, subjects did not change their opinions about the relative lengths of the lines, but they did go along with the group's judgment.

Status and Attraction to the Group

Generally speaking, greater conformity is produced when the other person or persons in the group have a status greater than that of the subject (Cole, 1955; Lefkowitz, Blake, and Mouton, 1955; Mausner, 1953; Mausner and Bloch, 1957; Raven and French, 1958a; Ziller, 1955). It is not yet precisely clear why this should be so. To some extent, people with higher status are likely both to know more and to be more confident. Each of these is likely to have an effect. As one might expect, "experts" produce more conformity (Sherif, 1935; Luchins and Luchins, 1955a). In addition, people with higher status are likely to be perceived as more powerful and thus more able to punish deviates and to reward compliers. People conform more when they are told that the group reacts unfavorably to deviates (Allen, 1965a). Then, too, high-status people tend to be more attractive (cf. Secord and Backman, 1964), and, as we shall discuss below, more attractive groups produce greater conformity. It is clear that status has a strong effect on conformity. But it is not clear whether the variable of status itself has this effect or whether it is due to variables normally associated with status, such as power to punish or degree of expertise, that mediate and eventually produce the effect. It is not always true that high status produces greater conformity than low status. For example, Berenda (1950) found that children conformed more to peer judgments than to those of their teachers. As Graham (1962) has pointed out, to some extent these effects may depend on whether informational or normative influence is more salient at the moment.

In any discussion of conformity one ordinarily sees many references for the assertion that conformity is monotonically related to the attractiveness of the group or the other person (for example, Festinger, Schachter, and Back, 1950; Back, 1951; Schachter et al., 1951; Moreno, 1953; Kelley and Shapiro, 1954; Rasmussen and Zander, 1954; Thrasher, 1954; Thibaut and Strickland, 1956; Berkowitz, 1957a; Brehm and Festinger, 1957; Siegel and Siegel, 1957; Kidd, 1958; Jackson and Saltzstein, 1958; Steiner and Peters, 1958; Dittes and Kelley, 1956; Festinger et al., 1952; Gerard, 1954). The Western Electric studies (Mayo, 1933; Turner, 1933; Whitehead, 1938; Roethisberger and Dickson, 1939) are referenced as well, and it is sometimes said that the effect is at least partially due to the dependence of the subject on the attractive others (Berkowitz, 1957b; Hollander, Julian, and Haaland, 1965).

Actually, most of these studies do not have compliance as their dependent variable. Almost all of them have private posttests in their research designs. As we have indicated, the private posttest is one of several ways to test private acceptance. We wish to reserve a more complete discussion of the effect of attraction for the next chapter. We should note that most of the empirical work distinguishing between public compliance and private acceptance has included attraction as an independent variable. Let us limit the present discussion to some preliminary conclusions for the relationship of attraction to the group to conformity, viewing conformity for the moment as compliance.

Generally speaking, one would expect a positive relationship between attraction and conformity. The more one is attracted to the group, the greater should be the conformity to group norms and the greater the resistance to attack from the outside (Kelley and Volkart, 1952). There are several exceptions, however. The more attracted person has a greater "stake" in the group than the unattracted person. It should therefore be more important to the more attracted group member for the group to be "correct" in its opinion. Thus, in situations where it becomes increasingly obvious that the group is incorrect in its opinion, the more attracted member should deviate more than, say, the moderately attracted member (Dittes and Kelley, 1956). The more attracted member should also perceive a greater likelihood of changing the group's opinion, and their deviation should be the beginning of such an attempt. However, if it is only necessary in a particular experiment for the group to agree, and not necessarily to be correct, then the attracted member should conform more to the incorrect group opinion.

If attraction to the group is the result of a desire to join the group or stay in the group (because of its prestige, say), then greater attraction should produce greater conformity, even in an Asch situation. If, however, personal and previously formed friendship is the basis for the attraction, then the more attracted member might feel freer to deviate in an Asch situation—partly because the previous formation of the friendship would allow the subject more security in his deviation. This is not necessarily what one would expect for private acceptance, however. For example, Back (1951) found greater attraction produced greater private acceptance, regardless of the source of attraction. We should note in passing Hollander's (1958) notion of "idiosyncrasy credit." He hypothesizes that accepted members of a group, who are presumably attracted to the group also, build up allowable deviations from the group norms as a result of previous conformity to them. This is a provocative idea with as yet little research to substantiate it.

It appears then that the relationship of attraction and status to conformity is dependent upon other situational variables. The main difference in these relationships has to do with how the high-status or highly attracted person behaves. For example, if the situation demands that the group be unanimous in its opinion, then the highly attracted person conforms, producing a positive, monotonic relationship between attraction and conformity. If, on the other hand, the situation demands the group be correct (and it is clear it is not), then the highly attracted person will not conform. The latter case produces a curvilinear relationship between attraction and conformity, with those intermediate in attraction conforming the most.

Previous Success or Failure of the Group

The topic of previous success or failure of the group is, of course, closely related to that of the competence of the group. To some extent, the data mentioned there are also applicable here. Kidd and Campbell (1955) found greater conformity in groups composed of members who had previously been successful in cooperative tasks than either controls or those who had been unsuccessful. Kidd and Campbell interpret their results in terms of learning theory (for example, Miller and Dollard, 1941). They assume that people learn to imitate others in childhood and that this imitation is most often rewarded (by parents, for example). Through stimulus generalization and secondary reinforcement, imitative behavior becomes rewarding in and of itself. In addition, in the Kidd and Campbell experiment, the group has been associated with a rewarding experience, namely, the previous success, and these two habits summate to produce a strong response.

A similar view is taken by Bandura (1962, 1965; Bandura and Walters, 1963) about imitative behavior and "modeling" in general. He presents a considerable amount of evidence (for example, Bandura and Huston, 1961; Bandura, Ross, and Ross, 1961, 1963a, 1963b; Bandura, 1965; Bandura and Mischel, 1965) indicating that imitative behavior may be learned according to the tenets of learning theory (cf. Kimble, 1961). Homans' (1961) view of social behavior is somewhat similar, but at a more rationalistic and superficial level. Homans' view is more on the order of the "economic man." He assumes that people behave so as to maximize their rewards (payoffs) and minimize their punishments (costs). Homans' interpretation differs from that of both Bandura and Campbell in that he implies both a greater conscious awareness of the subject about his behavior, and places a greater emphasis on overt strategy on the part of the subject than either Bandura or Campbell. As we have mentioned before, there has been little effort put forth in deriving predictive models of conformity behavior. The efforts of both Bandura and Campbell (cf. 1961) represent excellent steps in this direction, however, with Bandura's approach having considerably more empirical backing.

Related to this theoretical discussion are several experiments on the effects of reward for the incorrect response. If, on a pretraining task, the subject is rewarded by the experimenter for giving an incorrect response, the subject will conform more to an incorrect group response on subsequent test trials (Crutchfield, 1955; Luchins, 1944; Luchins and Luchins, 1955a). However, there is a question here of whether the subject is conforming because he was previously rewarded or whether the effect is related to the demand characteristics of the task (Orne, 1962). The experimental setting is itself often an ambiguous task in which the subject is attempting to find out what is expected of him by the experimenter. If the experimenter will tell him or even hint at what he expects or wants, the subject will often perform accordingly. We have mentioned before that experiments on conformity are often of this order. The situation may be unrealistic, the subject may do whatever he thinks the experimenter wants him to do, even though he might not ordinarily so behave. The question of the extent to which learning theory, as presently postulated, may account for the conformity data is an important one. It is eminently important, therefore, to rule out alternative or common-sensical explanations of the data when attempting to test the theory.

Prior Commitment and Public Statement of One's Position

The topic of prior commitment and public statement of one's position is very closely related to our distinction between compliance and attitude change. We have regarded a private, anonymous statement of an attitude or judgment to usually reflect private acceptance and the public statement to reflect compliance. The data on the difference between these two modes of response documents our distinction between the terms. Typically, much greater adherence to the group's norm or judgment is obtained when the identity of the subject is made public. Let us inspect some of the data more closely.

Mouton, Blake, and Olmstead (1956) had subjects estimate the number of clicks of a metronome. They used the tape-recorded voices of four confederates to establish a unanimous majority. Half of the subjects had to give their names when making their estimate; the other half remained anonymous. In the public condition, 58 per cent of the subjects conformed, whereas in the private condition only 16 per cent gave incorrect judgments like those of the group.

Deutsch and Gerard (1955) found a similar effect. They varied, in an Asch situation, whether subjects gave their judgments publicly in a face-to-face setting or anonymously behind partitions. They found considerably greater yielding in the former case. They also varied the degree to which the subject was "committed" to his judgment, prior to hearing the bogus judgments of others. In one condition, subjects wrote down their private judgments on a piece of paper, but were told they could throw the paper away later (referred to as "self-commitment"). In another condition, subjects wrote down their judgments on a "magic pad." After each judgment, the subject erased his judgment by lifting the covering on the magic pad. In a third condition, subjects wrote down their judgments and signed them and expected to turn them in to the experimenter later (public commitment). In a last condition, subjects made no commitment to their initial judgment. The results are rather interesting. The magic-pad commitment reduced the number of errors (that is, reduced conformity) over the no-commitment condition. In addition, both the public-commitment and the self-commitment conditions made fewer errors than the magic-pad condition, but were not significantly different from each other.

The notion that the public expression of attitudes and judgments are more conforming than private ones has been supported in a number of other experiments (Asch, 1956; Gordon, 1952; Kelley and Volkart, 1952; Argyle, 1957). The notion that prior commitment produces resistance to subsequent influence has been noted in several places (Fisher, Rubinstein, and Freeman, 1956; Kiesler and Sakumura, 1966; Hovland, Campbell, and Brock, 1957; Freedman and Steinbruner, 1964). In addition, Schachter and Hall (1952) found that if a person expresses his opinion publicly (a form of commitment), he is more likely to act consistently with that opinion later than if the opinions were expressed privately.

Gerard (1965) has expressed an interesting approach to the effects of public commitment on conformity. Our previous use of the word *commitment* has merely implied a previous public statement of one's position. Gerard, as well as others (cf. Brehm and Cohen, 1962; Kiesler and Sakumura, 1966; Kiesler, 1968), takes a broader view of this variable. He views commitment to some behavior as the degree to which the subject may not (or perceives he may not) reverse or undo the behavior. For example, "Any decision has the consequence of freezing or fixing the behavior it generates because of constraints, however minimal, which operate against undoing the behavior. . . . In general, then, any constraints that operate against changing behavior serve to commit the person to that behavior" (Gerard, 1965, p. 266; see also Festinger, 1957, 1964a; Lewin, 1947).

Gerard has applied this view of commitment to the Asch situation in the following manner. In the Asch situation the person is faced with a discrepancy between what he sees and the information he receives from his peers. These two sources of information, social and physical reality (Festinger, 1950), usually do not conflict. Yet in this situation they do conflict, and in a manner and setting that is very real for the subject. This conflict must be resolved, and if there are only two comparison lines, it must be resolved in an unequivocal manner. That is, the person must either agree with the group or deviate from their judgment. There are no other alternatives. The resolution of this conflict, especially in public, provides a form of commitment to that initial behavior that will affect subsequent behavior.

> [The subject] will presumably act on the basis of what he himself considers important. Once having made a decision, and having acted on the basis of it, any change or reversal by the subject during subsequent trials would be inconsistent with his initial decision, and perforce with the considerations that generated that decision in the first place, since the basic conditions from trial to trial remain unchanged. A change in behavior would also necessarily rearouse the original conflict, forcing the subject to again work through the same doubts and misgivings. The initial decision, then, commits the subject, although not irrevocably, to yield to the group or to be independent whenever the same two alternatives present themselves on succeeding trials. (Gerard, 1965, pp. 263, 4)

Gerard's (1965) results using the Asch paradigm with two comparison lines support this conclusion. Subjects who conformed on the first trial continued to conform on subsequent test trials. Those who did not conform on the first trial tended to remain independent throughout the experimental session.[3] The result is a dramatically bimodal distribution of errors over subjects.

Gerard also presents some interesting data on the subject's personal evaluations of the other group members, as a function of the subject's decision to conform or remain independent. The original impetus for gathering these data was Festinger's (1957) theory of cognitive dissonance. Gerard assumes the subject "decides" whether to conform or remain independent. As we shall discuss in some detail in the next chapter, this decision should create dissonance. The degree of dissonance is a function of the positive aspects of the unchosen alternative and the negative aspects of the chosen alternative. In this case there is something negative about the chosen alternative, no matter what the choice. The subject must either disagree with his peers or make a verbal judgment inconsistent with his senses. To reduce the dissonance incurred by the decision, the subject should bolster his behavioral decision by making his evaluations of the others in the group consistent with his commitment.

---

[3] This is not necessarily what one finds with three comparison lines, however. In this case, the distribution is not bimodal and there is much less consistency within subjects. There are many subjects who vacillate from trial to trial in the three-choice setting. Here, Gerard maintains that a compromise response is possible and behavioral commitment is not forced upon the subject. Without this overt commitment, the tendency toward behavioral consistency is much less. This is supported by Gerard's assertion that if the subject first goes through a two-choice series and then a three-choice series of judgments, vacillation is virtually eliminated in the latter series. The commitment engendered in the first series carries over to the latter series.

Preliminary data led Gerard to make two reasonable assumptions: people tend to evaluate themselves positively; and a person anticipates a positive evaluation from others when he agrees with them, and a negative one when he does not. There are three evaluations in this analysis: the subject's evaluations of himself; the subject's evaluation of the group; the subject's anticipation of the group's evaluation of him. Given the foregoing assumptions, Gerard's predictions are that all three of these evaluations will be positive for the conformer, but for the deviate the first will be positive and the last two negative. His results (Gerard and Rotter, 1961) strongly support this conclusion.[4]

These conclusions were also supported in a second experiment (reported in Gerard, 1965) in which ability to judge correctly and inclination to conform were independently manipulated. Ability to judge the stimuli was manipulated in the usual fashion by means of feedback on a pretest task. Inclination to conform was manipulated rather ingeniously. Electrodes were strapped on the subject's arm and he was told that these tested his inclination to push the right or left button (corresponding to the right or left stimulus). In this manner, bogus information was given to the subject that his first impulse was either to conform or deviate. The results for evaluation of the group supported those of Gerard and Rotter. The high-ability conformer's evaluations showed a + + + triad (positive evaluation of himself; positive evaluation of group; expectation that the group had a positive evaluation of the subject, respectively); the low-ability conformer showed a − − + (negative evaluation of himself; negative evaluation of the group; expectation that the group had a positive evaluation of him, respectively) triad. On the other hand, the high-ability deviate showed a + − − triad, and the low-ability deviate showed a − + − triad.

We have placed this emphasis upon Gerard's work because it tends to point up an aspect of conformity behavior that we think is very important: the psychological effects of the act of conformity. Whereas most of the

---

[4] The reader should note, however, that an alternative theoretical explanation is possible. With balance theory, Heider (1958) notes that O likes P induces P likes O. Byrne (1961) has also found attraction to the other to be a function of attitude similarity. We might well expect judgmental agreement to function like attitude similarity. Gerard acknowledges this difficulty when he says, "Additional research is needed to determine the immediate evaluational effect of conformity or deviation; that is, whether it produces the evaluations of others based upon what the subject knows about himself or whether the behavior, conformity, or deviation produces an assumed 'reflected' evaluation of himself by the others. The two processes are quite different; the former being a relatively passive one of social comparison . . . whereas the latter process is both more active and more complex" (Gerard, 1965, p. 276). We may note also that Allen (1965b) has suggested that one aspect of the effect of public commitment upon subsequent behavior is the individual's desire to "save face" by appearing consistent before others.

research is oriented toward whether a person conforms or how much he conforms, Gerard's data deal with the psychological effects of that conformity. In this sense, Gerard's data, like those on attraction to the group, provide us with a bridge to the third chapter of this section. At that point, we shall briefly return to Gerard's work on commitment.

The Generalization of Conformity Behavior

There are two aspects to the question of whether generalization of conformity behavior occurs. One aspect has to do with the generalization of the conformity behavior to settings outside the experimental one. Is the person more likely to evidence the conforming behavior when he is no longer with the group? This question may be alternatively phrased as the degree to which private acceptance has occurred. Although this question is the focus of the next chapter, we may say for now that for the most part this type of generalization does not occur. A person who conforms in the Asch situation will not make the same incorrect judgments later when tested privately. That is, generalization across settings should occur only to the extent that the behavior has been privately accepted.[5]

Generalization of the conformity response within the experimental setting has been documented only by a few studies, but with reasonably strong results. For example, Crutchfield (Krech, Crutchfield, and Ballachey, 1962), in a reanalysis of some older data (Crutchfield, 1955), found some generalization effects across items. That is, on some items, the experimenter gave positive feedback (that is, said the group's incorrect judgment was actually correct). Conformity increased for subsequent items of the same type as those receiving feedback. In addition, this conformity response generalized to other items in the session, the extent of generalization being related to the degree of similarity of these items to the ones for which there was feedback.

In a subsequent test, Allen and Crutchfield (1963) separately manipulated feedback and the "functional relatedness" of the items. The latter variable was manipulated by telling half of the subjects the items had a

---

[5] An exception might be provided by evidence indicating that conforming to a discrepant group norm is rewarding in and of itself. If conformity is rewarding, then it should generalize to other settings. However, the question of whether conformity is or can be rewarding is still an open one. To agree with others may be rewarding (for example, Byrne, 1961); the reduction of the conflict incurred by yielding may be rewarding (Bogdonoff, Klein, Estes, Shaw, & Back, 1961); and being like others may also be rewarding (Newcomb, 1956). If yielding to others is rewarding and agreeing with others is rewarding, then one would expect the conformity response to generalize to private testings. The data suggest that this response does not generalize to other settings. Although no one would doubt the power and range of influence of reward in normative social settings, precise data on this theoretical issue are lacking.

single purpose (all predicted ability for financial or economic success), and emphasizing to the other subjects that the items were very diverse in purpose (that is, they tested various aspects of personality). Several different categories of items were used: perceptual, vocabulary, number series, opinion estimates, and attitudes. Feedback was given for the first two categories of items during the early trials. As expected, feedback increased conformity for subsequent items in the same categories as those given early feedback. In addition, feedback increased conformity on the number series and attitude items as well, but had no effect on the opinion-estimate items (for example, estimating the percentage of Americans who would agree with a statement such as "I have never been in love"). Functional relatedness did not have a significant effect.

Allen and Crutchfield interpret their results as support for their hypothesis of *generalization* of conformity effects across items on a Crutchfield apparatus. They do, however, call attention to three other explanations that handle the data equally well. This provides us with a good example of considering possible alternative explanations of experimental data. Let us go into these in some detail.

One alternative explanation of their data has to do with the demand characteristics of the particular setting. That is, the subject could have interpreted the experimenter's feedback on the early items as an indication of the way the experimenter wanted the subjects to behave (that is, agree with the group). Wishing to behave cooperatively and "properly," the subject may have behaved as he thought the experimenter wished him to. Consistent with this explanation, other data indicate that if the experimenter says the group is wrong, then conformity markedly decreases.

The second explanation hypothesizes that the authoritative confirmation of the group's judgment by the experimenter led the subject to think that the group was very competent at the task. To the extent that the subject did not differentiate among items, this effect would also lead to increased "generalization." The third explanation assumes that having both the experimenter and the group disagree with the subject lowered his confidence in his ability to make these judgments. This is eminently reasonable. Gerard (1965) found that just having the experimenter tell the subject he was wrong lowered the subject's confidence in his subsequent judgments. Decreased confidence would also produce increased conformity, as we have previously noted.

Gerard's data on commitment provide a fourth explanation of the results. Feedback should produce greater conformity on the first item for a number of reasons, as we discussed above. However, the act of conformity on the first item, Gerard would say, commits the subject to conformity on subsequent items, perhaps regardless of content.

The relevant point is that the Allen and Crutchfield data do not provide unequivocal support for their hypothesis of generalization effects. A number of alternative hypotheses explain the data equally well. Our rather lengthy discussion of alternative explanations here was purposeful: to illustrate our previous contention that more experimentation needs to be done in which alternative explanations are ruled out by design. The Allen and Crutchfield experiment was used as an example, not only because it has several alternative explanations, but also because it should not embarrass the authors. They suggested the alternative explanations themselves.

The Perpetuation of a Conformity Response Through Several Generations of a "Microculture"

Jacobs and Campbell (1961) attempted to study what they referred to as "cultural transmission." They established a group norm using confederates and then tested the effect of gradually replacing the confederates with other naïve subjects. Although the study might have as easily been described as concerned with generalization of private-acceptance effects, the design and results are still quite provocative.

Briefly, Jacobs and Campbell used the Sherif autokinetic paradigm and varied both the number of confederates initially present and the number of naïve subjects in the group. The confederates gave their judgments of the movement first and then the naïve subjects. After thirty trials, one confederate left and another naïve subject joined the group. The naïve new member also gave his judgment last. Consistent with Jacobs and Campbell's interest in relating this experiment to cultural transmission, each block of thirty trials was referred to as a "generation." The control subjects who were run individually gave initial judgments of approximately 3.80 inches (that is, said the light moved 3.80 inches). The confederates in the group setting arbitrarily gave judgments between 15 and 16 inches. The main question was the extent to which the group norm would persist after the confederates were removed. Some of Jacobs and Campbell's data are presented in Figure 10-5. These data are from that group that initially had four members, three of whom were confederates and one a naïve subject.

These data are much stronger than the data with smaller groups or fewer confederates, but are otherwise not unrepresentative. First, it can be seen from Figure 10-5 that the influence of the group is very powerful: the mean judgment of the naïve subject in the first generation was 14.3 inches, whereas the control judgment was 3.8 inches. It can also be seen that the effect dissipates as confederates and more experienced subjects are removed and replaced. However, on generation 4, the effect is still

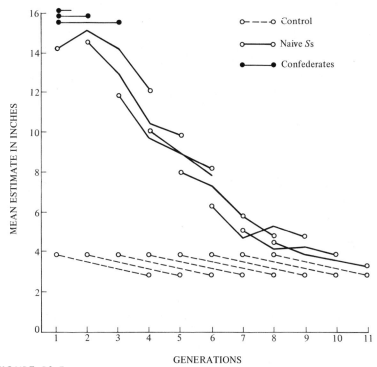

FIGURE 10-5.

> *Transmission of an Arbitrary Norm in Four-Person Groups, When Confederates Are Gradually Removed. (A "generation" is a block of thirty trials in an autokinetic setting, after which a confederate, if any are left, or the most experienced subject is removed and replaced by a naïve subject.)* (From Jacobs and Campbell, 1961)

quite strong, even though all of the confederates by that time have been replaced. On generation 5, all of the original group have been replaced, but the effect is still strong. By the end of the experiment, though, all of the effects of the original arbitrary norm have been erased.

The dissipation of the effects apparently has its roots in a process something like the following. As we have said previously, the Sherif paradigm provides an extremely ambiguous stimulus in which the subject is unsure of the proper or correct response. He therefore looks to others for information about the environment. He accepts the information they give (bogus judgments), but not totally; in almost all cases, the judgment of the individual was less than that of the confederates. Across generations, the process is similar. In the three experimental groups that Jacobs and Campbell mention, thirty-four of thirty-six naïve subjects serving for the first time gave judgments lower than that of the group, whether or not the group still had confederates in it (Jacobs and Campbell only present these data for the first four generations). Thus, even aside from the possible effect of the naïve individual on the group, here unassessed, the group mean becomes steadily lower as more new people are added.

The Study of Obedience

Milgram (1963; 1964; 1965a, 1965b) has carried out a series of exploratory studies on what he refers to as "obedience," but which is very similar conceptually to Asch's study of compliance. In justifying his use of a separate term, Milgram distinguishes between "signal" conformity and "action" conformity. Milgram says that the conformity studied by Asch is of the signal variety—that is, the subject conforms via some signal (for example, a verbal judgment or pushing a button) to the experimenter. Milgram contrasts this with his own work in which conformity is demonstrated by means of some overt behavioral deed. In Milgram's research, this behavioral deed has involved harming another person, although he conceptually does not so limit his definition of action conformity.

Milgram's studies on obedience have all had a basic paradigm. The dependent variable is

> . . . the amount of electric shock a subject is willing to administer to another person when ordered by an experimenter to give the 'victim' increasingly severe punishment. The act of administering shock is set in the context of a learning experiment, ostensibly designed to study the effect of punishment on memory. Aside from the experimenter, one naïve subject and one accomplice perform in each session. On arrival each subject is paid $4.50. After a general talk by the experimenter telling how little scientists know about the effect of punishment on memory, subjects are informed that one member of the pair will serve as teacher and one as learner. A rigged drawing is held so that the naïve subject is always the "teacher" and the accomplice the "learner." The learner is taken to an adjacent room and strapped into an "electric chair." (Milgram, 1965a, p. 245)

Punishment in this case is electric shock, and the teacher is instructed to shock the victim whenever he makes an error. A bogus shock generator is used with 30 switches, ranging presumably from 15 to 450 volts. Each "error" is to be met with an increase (15 volts) in the shock delivered to the victim. The responses of the victim are standardized on tape. "Starting with 75 volts the learner begins to grunt and moan. At 150 volts he demands to be let out of the experiment. At 180 volts he cries out that he can no longer stand the pain. At 300 volts he refuses to provide any more answers. . . . The experimenter [then] instructs the naïve subject to treat the absence of an answer as equivalent to a wrong answer, and to follow the usual shock procedure" (Milgram, 1965a, p. 246). Whenever the subject attempts to break off the experiment, the experimenter insists he must go on. The dependent variable is the number of shock levels the subject is willing to give, ranging from zero (no shock) to 30 (450 volts).

The most surprising finding from Milgram's research is the frequency with which subjects (from all walks of life) are willing to "go all the way" in such a procedure. Milgram (1965a) reports asking forty psychiatrists to make predictions about how subjects would perform in such a setting. They predicted that about 0.1 per cent of the subjects would administer the highest shock. However, in the basic setting, Milgram's results were quite discrepant with the psychiatrists' predictions. Some 62 per cent of Milgram's subjects were willing to administer the highest shock.

Milgram has run a number of variations of this basic paradigm, testing such things as the proximity of the victim, the effects of other confederates urging the subject on to higher levels, the effect of other confederates refusing to continue; decreasing the status of the experimenter, the physical removal of the experimenter, the physical closeness and degree of surveillance of the experimenter, and so forth. The results are all in the expected direction. In light of our previous discussion of compliance, the prediction in each case should be obvious. In addition, in all cases, some subjects continued to the highest level of shock.

The variables that Milgram has used to produce relatively more acquiescence and relatively less acquiescence are those that have previously been found to produce relatively more compliance and relatively less compliance in other settings as well. In that sense, future research using this paradigm should concentrate on *why* the high absolute level occurs, rather than *what* produces more or less of it. We should also note on these grounds that Milgram's conceptual distinction between action and signal conformity appears to be relegated to the status of a descriptive term, indicating differences in methodological procedures, rather than referring to any underlying psychological variables.

Milgram's research has created a good deal of controversy, especially with reference to the ethics of such a procedure. Although this question perhaps should be left to the individual conscience, we may note that Milgram reports that only 1.3 per cent of his subjects indicated they were sorry to have participated and 80 per cent indicated that more experiments of this sort should be carried out.

There is one other implication of Milgram's data. If such a high level of acquiescence to an odious task can be produced by experimenter demands, think what should happen with a less odious task. This implication should be especially directed toward our previous methodological discussion of the demand characteristics (Orne, 1962) of experimental tasks in social psychology. In an experimental setting (as in a University, say) people are willing to do almost anything the experimenter demands. If he gives any clue about how he wants the subject to behave, the subject may very well meet the demand. The experimenter may get the results he expected, but for a reason unrelated to his hypothesis.

In this chapter, we have tried to review the available literature on conformity, attending for the most part to the conditions under which it occurs and the degree to which it occurs. In that sense, we have been very empirically oriented, and, with the exception of Willis' work, have paid little attention to theoretical explanations of conformity.

Frankly, in the present state of the art, there is no real alternative approach to the conformity literature. Very few experiments have been carried out to test any theory rigorously. Many of the hypotheses tested are common-sense ones. Many of the experiments that purport to test some theory really amount to demonstrations of the theory. That is, the experimenter's theory may predict the results, but many other alternative explanations are equally tenable. Thus there is no rigorous test of theory in the sense of sorting among theoretical explanations. Indeed, there are so many reasons to expect the data obtained in some experiments that they would be interesting only if they had come out in some other way. Nonetheless, there is considerable (but not total) agreement among studies about which variables systematically affect conformity—for example, ambiguity of the stimulus, difficulty of the task, commitment to a response, absence of a deviate-ally, size of the majority (to some extent), similarity of the situation to one in which the person has previously conformed, the public nature of the response, perceived competence of the group, and so forth.

Public Compliance and Private Acceptance

In the previous chapter, we attempted to review pertinent experimental literature on conformity. As previously noted, in many of the studies reviewed there, either the manipulations did not produce private acceptance or no attempt at measuring private acceptance was made. In the present chapter we will emphasize the data on private acceptance, especially with reference to the distinction between public compliance and private acceptance. First, let us address ourselves to the question of the usefulness of such a distinction.

We submit that such a distinction between public compliance and private acceptance may be useful in at least two ways. First, it may clear up some of the empirical confusion. That is, suppose researcher *A* refers to public compliance as conformity and carries out his research accordingly; researcher *B* refers to private acceptance as conformity and carries out his research accordingly. If the distinction between public compliance and private acceptance is a scientifically useful one, then it should not be surprising to find researchers *A* and *B* disagreeing about what produces conformity. A distinction between compliance and private acceptance, if valid, would eliminate, or at least lessen, this type of confusion. The distinction may also be useful in a second way. That is, it may provide empirical "signposts" to guide subsequent theorizing. Such empirical signposts, indicating conditions under which compliance and private acceptance are not isomorphic, essentially force the theorist towards greater precision in thought and predictions about these behaviors. Thus the relationship between more particularistic or situation-specific data and more precise theory is a symmetrical one. Any increase in either one should produce an increase in the other.

Assuming, then, that this distinction between compliance and private acceptance is a valid one, the present chapter will take the following form. First, we will consider some of the historical antecedents of the distinction.

We will then proceed to some data illustrating the distinction and at least partly indicating the conditions under which compliance will occur but private acceptance will vary as a function of specifiable events. We will then consider a theoretical analysis of the effect of the act of conformity on subsequent private acceptance, followed by some theoretical notions concerning the relationship of compliance and private acceptance, given a longer temporal sequence of interpersonal interaction. We will conclude the chapter with some methodological criticisms and suggestions for the direction of future research.

A concern with distinguishing between compliance and private acceptance is not a new one. A number of social psychologists have at least discussed it (for example, Festinger, 1953, 1957; Hovland, Janis, and Kelley, 1953; Kelley and Volkart, 1952; Kelman, 1961; Schanck, 1932; Jahoda, 1959; Katz and Schanck, 1938; Stouffer, 1949; Dittes and Kelley, 1956; Gordon, 1952; French and Raven, 1959; Doob, 1947; Lewin, 1951; Rommetveit, 1953; Secord and Backman, 1964; Newcomb, Turner, and Converse, 1965). Some have made a value judgment, indicating compliance as "superficial" and private acceptance as a "deeper" psychological change. We make no such value distinction here, but do assume that the latter is more difficult to produce and, almost by definition, likely to last longer.

The exact terms used have varied from investigator to investigator, including among those used the following dichotomies: public versus private attitudes; overt versus covert behavior; compliance versus internalization; and own versus induced forces. As the reader might have suspected, the investigator's theoretical bias is implicit in his choice of terms for his dichotomy. However, as French and Raven (1959) have noted, although stated as a dichotomy, the distinction may represent an underlying psychological continuum. This continuum could be expressed as the degree to which the subject's behavior is dependent upon the presence of some external agent. Presumably, if the "conforming" behavior is evidenced only in the presence of the person who induced the original conformity behavior, we would refer to it as compliance. If this behavior subsequently does not depend on the presence of the inducing agent, we would refer to it as private acceptance. Theoretically, in between these two extremes can be varying degrees to which the behavior is evidenced without the presence of the other. This would presumably represent varying degrees of private acceptance.

However, the problem is still not quite so simple. Let us view the definitional and measurement problem involved within the context of an example. Coch and French (1948) discuss the case of a clothes presser they observed in their study of the resistance to behavioral changes in an industrial setting. This person was placed in a work group that apparently had its own production norm and emitted strong pressure for conformity to the norm. The rest of the group was producing at about the rate of 50 units per hour. After the new girl had been in the group a couple of weeks, she began to exceed the production of the rest of the group. The group quickly began, in the words of Coch and French, to "scapegoat" the girl. Her production promptly dropped and subsequently stayed at the level of the rest of the group. When later the group was dispersed in the factory, the girl's production doubled in four days and stabilized at the higher figure.

Here is a clear case of conformity to a norm, but without private acceptance. The lack of private acceptance was indicated quite clearly when the group was removed. This represents a neat paradigm for the joint study of compliance and private acceptance.[1] However, this paradigm does not guarantee the accurate measurement of private acceptance. For example, suppose the girl and one of the group became good friends before the group was scattered, and that this friend visited the girl in the factory, noticing her production and chastizing her for the high level. Would this affect her production level? Very probably. Hence the new production level would not adequately reflect the girl's degree of private acceptance. As French and Raven have noted "the degree of dependence is contingent on the perceived probability that O [the other person or group] will observe the state of the system and note P's [the subject's] conformity. The level of observability will depend on both the nature of the system (e.g., the difference between a covert opinion and overt behavior) and on the environmental barriers to observation (e.g., O is too far away from P)" (French and Raven, 1959, p. 155, material in brackets added). The point we wish to make is that removal of the group from the situation does not necessarily provide one with an unequivocal measure of private acceptance. One must still be certain that other related factors are not still influencing the expression of opinion or behavior. With this in mind, let us turn to some of the experimental studies illustrating some differences between compliance and private acceptance. There have not been many.

A study by Kelley and Volkart (1952) is relevant, at least indirectly so. In addition to the public–private distinction, their main focus was on the individual's resistance to counternorm communications—that is, communications that argue in direct opposition to group norms. For their subjects, Kelley and Volkart used the members of twelve Boy Scout

[1] Ideally, the girl should have been allowed to work by herself for some time to measure base-level rate. That is, with the Coch and French paradigm one cannot rule out the possibility that had the girl never been in the group she would have produced, say, 150 units per hour. Thus we can only say that the girl was not influenced by the group to the degree that her attitudes were perfectly consistent with her behavior, but we cannot determine whether and to what extent the group pressure did produce some private acceptance.

troops. The group norm in question was composed of the positive attitudes that preliminary data indicated that scouts have about woodcraft skills, forest lore, and camping activities. In an attempt to measure valuation of the group (attraction to the group) the scouts were given, at a regular meeting, questionnaires determining the scouts' evaluation of their membership in the troop and their attitudes toward woodcraft activities. At a later meeting, an adult stranger gave a standardized communication to them, strongly critical of woodcraft activities. The boys were then given the questionnaires, testing their attitudes toward scouting activities. Half of the subjects were given these questionnaires under private conditions and half under public conditions. In the private conditions, the subjects were assured that their responses would be anonymous and kept secret. Subjects in the public conditions were told that their responses would be made public to the rest of the troop. The independent variables, then, are attraction to the group (not actually manipulated) and public or private expression of opinion. The dependent variable is the extent to which subjects are influenced, behaviorally or attitudinally, by a strong counternorm communication. Let us turn to the results. The basic data are presented in Table 11-1.

TABLE 11-1.   *Net Opinion Change Toward a Counternorm Communication Under Public and Private Conditions, for Varying Degrees of Valuation of Membership* (From Kelley and Volkart, 1952).

Valuation of Membership	Public condition	Private condition
1 (Low)	−11.1*	+12.5
2	+41.7	0.0
3	+33.3	+ 8.4
4	+29.4	−38.9
5 (High)	− 5.6	−55.5
Totals	+19.0	−12.7

* Net change equals the per cent changing in the direction advocated by the communication minus the per cent changing in the opposite direction.

First, somewhat surprisingly, there was greater change toward the position advocated in the counternorm communication in the public condition than in the private. This will be discussed later. Within the private condition, the greater the attraction to the group, the less the change, as Kelley and Volkart expected. The rank-order correlation between attraction to the group and amount of change was −0.71. In the public condition, this relationship was curvilinear, with the least public change being shown by the least and most attracted subjects, and considerably greater change evidenced by those subjects intermediate in their prior valuation of the group.

Kelley and Volkart interpret their finding of greater public change than private as being due to the net result of conflicting cross pressures. From the group comes pressure to resist change. Kelley and Volkart say that the effectiveness of this source of pressure should be inversely related to group valuation, and indeed this is what their data indicate. The public condition is different however. In this condition, powerful adults (for example, the speaker and his assistants) favor the change and presumably would, in addition to the group, also know who changed. This should greatly increase the "external pressure" for change. We may note, however, that this explanation does not account for the relatively decreased effect of the counternorm communication for those very low in valuation. For these subjects, there was actually less change in the public condition than the private.

A similar effect is seen in a subsequent study by Dittes and Kelley (1956). In this study, acceptance by the group (with consequent changes in attraction to the group) was manipulated experimentally. Responses were again measured under both public and private conditions. The "communication," although unusual, appeared to have had an effect similar to that in Kelley and Volkart. In the Dittes and Kelley experiment, two tasks were used: one involved making judgments of the relative "worthiness" of two gangs of juvenile delinquents; and the other involved making judgments of numerosity (which of two sets of slides contained the most dots, with judgments made over a series of eleven pairs of decreasing difficulty). In each of these cases it became increasingly obvious to the individual subjects that the supposed "group judgment" was incorrect.

Once again, the low-attracted subjects conformed more than other subjects under public conditions—that is, they publicly deviated the least from the indicated group norm—in spite of the increasing evidence that the group was incorrect in its judgment. The other three acceptance conditions did not differ from each other in this respect. The pattern over-all under private testing conditions was a curvilinear one: those most and those least attracted had the least private acceptance of the group norm; those intermediate in attraction (or acceptance) had the greatest private acceptance.

Again, those little attracted to the group showed considerable difference between their public and private behavior: they conformed under public conditions and disagreed under private conditions. This seems to be the most reliable finding of these two studies. Later in this chapter we will discuss some conditions under which those little attracted to the group change their private attitudes a great deal. Parenthetically, the acceptance manipulation appears to have been a powerful one in this study: the subjects in the lowest-acceptance condition reduced their participation in the discussion of the delinquent gang by almost 50 per cent after receiving the acceptance manipulations. The participation by subjects in the other conditions remained at about the same level as before the manipulation.

The small degree of private acceptance of the group norm by highly accepted subjects would appear to be inconsistent with the data of Kelley and Volkart. This is not necessarily the case, however. In the Dittes and Kelley experiment it became obvious that the group was incorrect. The highly attracted subjects, who perhaps have the greatest investment in the group, might also be most interested in having the group be correct in these opinions. They are also the ones who are most able to change the group opinions as well. On one of Dittes and Kelley's questionnaires, the highly accepted subjects indicated they felt the greatest freedom to deviate in their opinions. This explanation is quite consistent with a finding by Medow and Zander (1965) that the more "central" members of a group had greater involvement in the group task, perceived themselves as being more responsible for the outcomes of the group, and wanted the group to be successful to a greater extent, than did less central members.

In both of the above studies attraction to the group and acceptance by the group were crucial variables. This is not unusual for this research area. There actually have been few experiments that explicitly deal with the distinction between public compliance and private acceptance. However, theoretical discussions of this variable have not been infrequent, and a considerable part of the discussion has focused on attraction as a central mediating concept.

For example, Kelley (Hovland, Janis, and Kelley, 1953) has suggested that a person's membership in a group depends upon one or more of the following three factors: (1) positive attractions to the group (for example, friendship, status, group activities); (2) threats, dangers, or deprivation forces from the outside that can be avoided by membership in the group; (3) restraints or barriers that essentially force the person to stay in the group, regardless of the person's wishes in the matter. The degree to which a person publicly conforms presumably is a function of the importance of these factors to him. But how do they relate to whether his private attitudes are also affected by the group?

Festinger (1953), in his theoretical treatment of the public–private distinction, contends that only the first of these, attraction, affects the degree to which the person privately accepts a group norm or discrepant information emanating from the group. The less the person is attracted to the group, the less will be the private acceptance. This effect is theoretically mediated by a positive desire of the person to preserve the existing relationship between himself and the other group members. Festinger theorizes that the effect of the other two membership factors is to produce compliance, but not private acceptance.

There are not many experiments directly testing this hypothesis—that is, experiments in which both public and private measures were obtained. There are a number of experiments relating the degree of private acceptance to attraction (cf. Hare, 1962). In addition, Back (1951) demonstrated the positive relationship between attraction and change to hold, regardless of the source of attractiveness. It is interesting to note that in Back's experiment, more highly attracted dyads showed greater *overt* resistance to the influence attempt that did less attracted dyads. This could have been due in part to a possible heightened desire to influence the other in the more attracted dyads. The attraction–private-acceptance hypothesis seems well supported, but later in the chapter we will present some evidence indicating the conditions under which the hypothesis does not hold.

Kelman (1961) also attempts to distinguish between those conditions producing compliance only and those that produce both compliance and private acceptance. Kelman distinguishes among three presumably distinct processes of social influence: compliance, identification, and internalization. Only the last theoretically results in both compliance and private acceptance. Kelman's term *compliance* is equivalent to what we have also discussed as compliance and occurs, Kelman says, because the person wishes to achieve a favorable reaction from the others. At the other extreme, *internalization* occurs "when an individual accepts influence because the induced behavior is congruent with his value system" (Kelman, 1961, p. 65). The intermediate process of *identification* occurs "when an individual adopts behavior derived from another person or a group because this behavior is associated with a satisfying self-defining relationship to this person or group" (1961, p. 63).[2] In the identification process, the person presumably believes in his new attitudes and actions, but the new attitudes and behaviors are maintained only if the "satisfying" relationship is continued (and if the others retain the attitude).

This provides the crux of the discrepancy between Kelman's and Festinger's positions. Festinger says that attraction is the mediating variable

---

[2] See Kelman and Eagly (1965) for further speculation on the "self-defining" aspects of this relationship. They suggest that negative relationships are equally important for defining the self. That is, agreeing with positive others helps to define one's self as positive, but disagreeing with negative others serves the same purpose. Thus there should be a tendency for subjects to abandon their opinions when presented with evidence that negative others hold the same opinion. Kelman says that this "source orientation" is essentially the "motivational base" of the process of identification.

for private acceptance. Kelman says that attraction does not produce "true" private acceptance. Kelman does say that the individual genuinely "believes" his new attitudes, but he says that the attitudes depend upon a continuation of the relationship that produced them. If the relationship changes, so will the attitudes. For Kelman, true private acceptance only comes through the process of internalization, which is focused on the content of the communicative act. The issues between these two models have not been directly tested. Kelman and Eagly (1965) provide some supporting evidence for the content versus source orientation. However, Kiesler and Kiesler (1964) provide some negative evidence on the issue of a changing relationship with the communicator. They found that when one gets negative evidence about the communicator prior to the communication itself, the communication has little effect (it produces no attitude change). However, if the same information about the communicator is given after the communication, then change is produced and maintained in spite of the subsequent negative information. The Kiesler and Kiesler experiment was really concerned with the effects of forewarning on attitude change. As such, they did not explicitly establish and change the relationship with the other. A rigorous test of this hypothesis remains to be performed, and the hypothesis remains a fertile field for future research.

French and Raven (1959) also discuss these issues with reference to their theoretical discussion of social power. If we define social power as the degree to which person or group x may influence the opinions or behavior of person y in situation z, then this concept is firmly within the realm of the present discussion. French and Raven distinguish among five bases of social power. Each basis focuses on the relationship between x and y, which forms the source of the power. The five bases they posit are: (1) reward power, dependent upon x's ability to mediate rewards for y; (2) coercive power, dependent upon x's ability to mediate punishments for y; (3) legitimate power, dependent upon y's perception that x has a right to prescribe his behavior; (4) referent power, presumably based on y's identification with x; and (5) expert power, dependent upon y's perception that x has some special knowledge or expertness. One might consider reward and coercive power to be conceptually equivalent to Kelman's compliance process; referent and perhaps legitimate power to have effects similar to Kelman's identification process; and expert power to effect internalization. Consistent with both Festinger and Kelman, French and Raven imply that both reward and coercive power lead to compliance without private acceptance. They are not specific about when the other three bases of power will lead to private acceptance, but they do say that private acceptance will usually not occur at the beginning of the relationship between x and y. They also distinguish the latter three bases of power from the former two by saying that the effects of the latter three do not depend upon whether x may observe the behavior of y. This suggests that they would view private acceptance as being produced by legitimate, referent, or expert power.

One may see from this discussion that there is some theoretical disagreement about the precise conditions under which private acceptance will occur. Clearly, what is now needed are more data of the "signpost" variety. Below we will try to present some data of the present author's related to the conditions under which attraction to the group is and is not monotonically related to private acceptance. The data are of interest here because attraction to the group provides such a core mediating concept in theoretical discussions of private acceptance.

The data are concerned with the hypothesis of a monotonically positive relationship between attraction to the group and private acceptance of a (discrepant) group norm or opinion. The original impetus for these experiments was some anecdotal evidence in the literature (for example, Hughes, 1946) suggesting that, under some conditions at least, this relationship may be nonmonotonic. That is, under some conditions, little-accepted or attracted members change their attitudes considerably in the "direction advocated by the group." In a series of three studies, we demonstrated the following: that one may produce this nonmonotonic relationship experimentally (Kiesler, 1963); that the nonmonotonic relationship occurs when one is committed to continue interacting in the same group, whereas the monotonic relationship occurs when one is not so committed (Kiesler and Corbin, 1965); that the change thus produced in the low-attracted subjects is really privately accepted—that is, it is resistant to subsequent attack (Kiesler, Zanna, and DeSalvo, 1966). In the three studies, the attitude topic has varied (baseball, girls, and modern art), and the age of the subjects has varied (junior-high-school, high-school, and college students). The effect appears to be quite general.

Generally, the experimental paradigm is similar for the three studies. Commitment to continue in the group was manipulated by varying the probability that the subject would be able to change to a different group if he so desired. Subjects were pretested on a preferential ranking among attitude objects; attraction to the group was varied by manipulating acceptance by the group; subjects were then given a bogus consensus about the attitude objects, and were then allowed to rerank the stimuli. The reranking was done under private conditions ("No one in the group will be allowed to see it"). The bogus group consensus varied from subject to subject and was arranged so that there was a constant discrepancy in opinion between the subject and the group, regardless of the subject's initial opinion. The dependent variable was the extent to which the subject changed his attitude in the direction of that held by the group. Let us look at some of the data.

The data from Kiesler and Corbin (1965) are presented in Figure 11-1. As may be seen, the usual monotonic relationship between attraction and private acceptance occurs when the subject is not committed to subsequent interaction with the same group: the less the attraction, the less the opinion change. However, when the subject is committed to continue, a nonmonotonic relationship occurs. The interesting part of this is that the committed, low-attracted subjects are influenced by the group to a considerable extent.

In the subsequent study (Kiesler, Zanna, and DeSalvo, 1966), we used a "deviate-ally" to test the stability of the effect. That is, in the previous

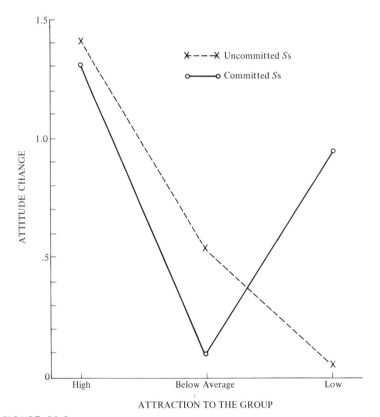

FIGURE 11-1.

The Relationship of Attraction to the Group and Commitment to Continue in the Group to Attitude Change (From Kiesler and Corbin, 1965)

two studies, we had gone to great lengths to assure the subjects that the second attitude test (the posttest) was really a private measure. The validity of the procedure, however, depends on whether the subjects really believed it. We had no reason to suspect they did not, but on the other hand, we had no unequivocal evidence on this point. In this third experiment, subjects in two conditions ascertained (through an experimental manipulation) that some one in the group agreed with their initial opinion, hence the term *deviate-ally*. Two other conditions did not know about the deviate: one of these was committed, one was not. They provided baselines for change, as well as a replication of the Kiesler and Corbin data. In this last experiment, we measured subjects' attitudes at three points in time, the last two of which were private testings. The first two attitude measures represent the same procedure as that of Kiesler and Corbin. There we replicated the results of Kiesler and Corbin for their low-attraction condition: the committed subjects changed considerably more than the uncommitted subjects. However, we found that if the subject ascertained that he had a deviate-ally, then there was no opinion change toward the group norm. If, however, the subject had already changed his opinion (that is, if he found out about the deviate-ally after the second opinion measure) then the deviate-ally's presence had no effect. The subject maintained his opinion change in spite of the knowledge that someone in the group agreed with his original opinion.

These studies severely limit the hypothesis of attraction as the central mediating concept for private acceptance. They illustrate at least one condition under which the hypothesis of monotonicity does not hold. Perhaps more important, they illustrate the importance of commitment for group studies. That is, if a person is not committed to continue interacting with the same group, then rejection or devaluation of the group becomes much easier. Thus the effect of commitment apparently is that of making certain alternative responses more difficult and less probable (cf. Kiesler and Sakumura, 1966; Kiesler, 1968; Kiesler, Kiesler, and Pallak, 1967). This makes commitment to continue a rather ubiquitous variable, and the particular effect in a group study should partially depend upon the extent to which the subject anticipates subsequent interaction with the group members. In discussing the Kiesler and Corbin results, Weick (1966) has taken as one implication that the subject's perception of commitment should be assessed in group studies even when commitment is not manipulated.

The notion of private acceptance is obviously an important aspect of the study of group pressure and "conformity." However, as we have seen, it has received relatively little study. One obvious reason for this is that it is more difficult to study private acceptance experimentally than it is either to study compliance or to ignore the distinction altogether. Needed even more, however, are experiments in which both variables are studied at once.[3] Only when this occurs can any precise theorizing be possible.

However, let us take an example of what one might do with current theory. Let us consider the following theoretical analysis of the relationship of private acceptance to variables affecting the *act* of compliance. Given the following situation: person *x* is a member of group *y* (in an experimental setting); person *x* disagrees with the group about some group norm; the group puts pressure upon *x* to *behave* according to the norm. Questions: what are the variables affecting the probability of *x* complying; and given that *x* complies, what are the variables affecting the degree to which *x* now privately accepts the norm?

Let us speculate a little and make a dissonance-theory (Festinger, 1957; 1964a; Brehm and Cohen, 1962) analysis of this situation. We will make three basic hypotheses.

1. *The greater the group pressure, from any source, the greater the probability of behavioral compliance.* This hypothesis is supported by several studies (for example, Thibaut and Strickland, 1956; Frank, 1944; Brim, 1954) and is in fact supported by most of the studies mentioned in Chapter 10. It is limited by a subject's tendency to minimize the power of a threatening other (Pepitone, 1950) and by other variables, such as the illegitimate use of power, that increase the subject's overt resistance to behavioral influence (for example, French, Morrison, and Levinger, 1960; Zipf, 1960; French, 1956).

2. *Given behavioral compliance, the less the group pressure, the greater the private acceptance or attitude change.* This is a straightforward derivation from dissonance theory. That is, we are assuming that the subject disagreed with the group but subsequently complied. Given compliance, the less the number or importance of the cognitions consistent with compliance, the greater the dissonance. One way to reduce this dissonance is to change one's attitudes so that they are more consistent with one's behavior. For example, it has been found (Aronson and Carlsmith, 1963; Freedman, 1965) that if one induces a child not to play with a given toy, the less the threat involved in the induction, the more will the child devalue the toy as a means of reducing dissonance.

One could hypothesize that this group pressure may take a number of forms. Generally, let us assume for the moment that group pressure may

---

[3] There have been some. However, clear theoretical implications are weakened when either private acceptance accompanies public compliance (for example, Gerard, 1954; Raven, 1959) or when there is a difference but it does not interact with experimental treatment (cf. Festinger's [1957] presentation of the Burdick [1955] and McBride [1954] experiments). An exception is provided by Hardy (1957), who found greater private acceptance under conditions of a unanimous majority than when an ally was present, even though compliance did not differ for these two conditions.

be regarded as anything consistent with the act of compliance. If so, then given that the person complies, dissonance theory suggests that *greater* attitude change will occur (1) the less the attraction to the group (cf. Weick, 1964); (2) the more arduous the act of compliance (cf. Aronson and Mills, 1959); (3) the less financial remuneration offered for compliance (cf. Festinger and Carlsmith, 1959).

The references given above refer to situations in which one person is induced by another single person to perform some act inconsistent with his beliefs. We decided to test a similar hypothesis in a group setting (Kiesler and DeSalvo, 1967). We manipulated the person's attraction to his group. We then set up a situation in which each subject thought he disagreed with all the other group members about a choice between two group tasks. In one condition, each subject was induced to go along with the group and agreed to work on the less attractive task. In another condition, subjects were not induced to comply and knew only that they disagreed with the group. Our dependent variable was the change in the subject's relative ratings of the two tasks (how much he increased his expected enjoyment of the chosen task and decreased his expected enjoyment of the rejected task). Subjects were explicitly not committed to continue with the group beyond the one experimental session.

The results were as expected. When the subject was not induced to go along with the group and only knew that they disagreed with him, then the less attractive the group, the less the change in relative rating of the tasks toward the "group opinion." However, when the subject was induced to comply with the group's choice, the opposite relationship held: the less attractive the group, the greater the change in ratings of the tasks. In this situation the act of compliance produced dissonance, and the less attractive the group, the greater the dissonance. To reduce the dissonance, the subject changed his opinions about the tasks. One may see that if one looks at the implications of the act of compliance, then a number of interesting hypotheses arise. Let us move to the third basic hypothesis in this theoretical analysis.

3. *The effect of compliance on private acceptance is limited by variables that tend to force the subject to reevaluate or reinterpret the behavior or norms in question.* These variables are as yet unknown, but let us speculate about two. We have already mentioned that commitment to continue in the group affects the probability of particular response alternatives in *extreme* situations. It forces the subject to deal with situations he would rather reject or ignore. On these grounds, one might hypothesize that commitment combined with extreme pressure to comply would effect considerable attitude change. For example, we would not expect the Kiesler and DeSalvo results to hold if the subjects were committed to future interaction with the group. Further, extreme pressure from the

group should induce the subject to perceive that the norm is very important to the group. This piece of information might induce the subject to reevaluate his own attitudes. The conditions under which hypothesis two might be limited relate only to some, but not all, conditions of extreme pressure. It therefore seems reasonable that our speculative theoretical analysis would hold, other things equal, across a broad range of pressure.

We may note that this dissonance-theory analysis is a "short run" analysis. We are considering only the psychological effects of a single act of compliance. Gerard (1965) has already noted that a "decision" to comply may have very important consequences for subsequent behavior. We add here that the single act may have attitudinal implications as well as behavioral. On the other hand, there is no reason to suspect necessarily that such short-term events dominate a long-term interaction between the subject and the group to which he belongs. Again, we would not expect the Kiesler and DeSalvo results to obtain if the group interaction were free and occurred over a long period of time. Nonetheless, both lines of research are provocative and interesting and await some deft experimental hands, perhaps those of the current reader.

Although there is a dearth of good data and theory on private acceptance, it is obvious that the topic is an interesting and important one. We have limited ourselves to a consideration of compliance and private acceptance as the result of group pressure. There is no reason to suspect however that the variables frequently and precisely studied under the guise of "attitude change" are not relevant for the present topic as well. Since attitude and opinion change has been discussed in detail elsewhere in this book, we have largely ignored it in the present section. We may note, however, that the emphasis upon overt behavior involved in conformity studies has also been largely ignored in the study of attitude change (Festinger, 1964b). It is to be hoped that eventually these two topics will become more interrelated and concurrently studied (perhaps under the more general rubric of interpersonal influence). The holes in both data and theory are large and gaping, and clearly a great deal of work remains to be done. Let us move now to a consideration of possible future research on conformity.

Perhaps the research most needed in this area is a series of studies with both private acceptance and compliance as dependent variables. These studies should specifically attempt to investigate interaction effects, indicating the conditions under which private acceptance and compliance coexist and those under which they do not. By interaction effects we mean, for example, experiments that will allow conclusions (in the same study) that public compliance and private acceptance both occur under condition x, but public compliance without private acceptance occurs under condition y. We contend that a series of such experiments would be highly likely to induce more precise theorizing about conformity.

It is interesting in this context to note that there is no necessary reason why one could not have private acceptance without public compliance. For example, Back (1951) noted that his highly attracted dyads appeared to be more overtly resistant to influence than the lowly attracted ones, even though private acceptance was considerably greater in the former case. Also, if a person is in the process of changing his opinion, overt behavior change (compliance) may not occur until a considerable amount of opinion change is evidenced. It would be interesting to investigate in the laboratory the general problem of attempting to achieve private acceptance under conditions in which gross forces operate against overt behavior change.

We need more studies testing the *limits* of hypotheses—that is, testing logical extensions of hypotheses and possible limitations of the hypotheses. We have already noted that the attraction–private-acceptance relationship does not hold under conditions of commitment to continue interacting with the group. We need more studies of this type with reference to other variables, such as coercive power and surveillance. We may note that the variable of attraction to the group still needs some empirical and conceptual work as well. As Schopler has noted, "the results of having group members rate how much they like each other has been labeled 'attributed power,' 'attractiveness,' 'resource ownership,' as well as merely 'liking.' A more complete theoretical statement would describe the mapping rules by which the component parts are to be observed and enhance comparability among studies" (Schopler, 1965, p. 214). This rating has been called other things as well, including cohesiveness. However relevant Schopler's comment to conformity, we should note that it was made in a discussion of social power.

Another possible limit of the attraction hypothesis that has not been really tested is related to the concept of "identification with the aggressor," noted by Bettelheim (1943) and others. Hovland, Janis, and Kelley (1953) have suggested that this type of internalization depends upon sustained power of the influencing agent and strong anticipations of the subject that failure to conform will lead to punishment. The "sustained power" aspect appears to be closely related to Thibaut and Kelley's concept of comparison level for alternatives and to commitment to continue interaction. On the other hand, power theory maintains that punishment will lead to compliance, but not private acceptance. An empirical resolution may depend upon the degree of surveillance possible in a given setting. A high degree of surveillance may close off other more desirable courses of action and subsequently produce private acceptance (cf. Kiesler, Zanna, and DeSalvo, 1966). This remains a provocative topic for research, however.

Related to this discussion is another variable that has not received adequate study: commitment to continue interaction with the group. Group experiments have often been criticized on the grounds that their fleeting nature limits generalization to social reality. It is certainly true that many of the influencing agents in one's life are ones with whom one maintains long-term contact—for example, family, siblings, colleagues, peers, and neighbors. The small amount of data on commitment to continue interaction and the above discussion of identification with the aggressor both suggest that commitment is an important variable for interpersonal influence. Whether the process of influence under commitment to continue is fundamentally different from that under no commitment is questionable. Nevertheless, the data suggest that commitment to continue has the effect of producing considerable private acceptance under conditions in which current theory would predict little or no change.

We also need more data on the interaction of several variables in a given experimental setting, with special reference to possible differences between immediate and long-term effects. For example, consider Festinger's hypothesis of attraction being the crucial mediating variable for private acceptance of group norms. He says reward will not produce private acceptance immediately, but in the long run reward is likely to lead to increased attraction and hence increased private acceptance. In a similar vein Kelman has said that the change produced by an attractive other depends upon a continuation of the proper relationship with the other. If the relationship is broken off, the attitude change should not be maintained, according to Kelman. There are a number of hypotheses that one may draw from both of these theoretical approaches that are deserving of test.

One of the most important needs in research on conformity is greater methodological sophistication. The main considerations here have been discussed before, and we need here only a brief reminder. First, the demand characteristics are very strong in much conformity research, and greater attention is needed towards ruling them out of experimental procedures. Second, there are a number of problems in precisely measuring private acceptance that as yet have received little attention. Greater ingenuity is needed, and especially the comparison, empirically and conceptually, of the various ways in which one might measure the degree of private acceptance. Third, there has been a dismaying lack of interest in the subject's perception of the experimental setting. For example, consider the essential "double-bind" nature of the Asch paradigm. Whatever the subject "decides" to do, there are important negative implications for him. What he does may depend on other cues in the environment, especially those inadvertently given by the experimenter. Fourth, greater consideration of alternative explanations must come *before* any subjects are actually run. One of the great inadequacies in this research area comes from the inability of researchers to conceive of serious alternative explanations of their data.

Perhaps most important of all, we need more precise theorizing and more precise tests of theories of conformity. These theories need not be grandiose in scope. Indeed, we could make a very good case for smaller, more precise theories. What Schopler says about social power applies equally well to conformity in general: "Movement in this direction might be accelerated by the development of theories with limited scope applied to a well-defined domain, rather than by general theories aiming to integrate the entire area" (1965, p. 214).

Conformity is a fascinating topic and is obviously intimately related not only to everyday life but also to other areas crucial to social psychology, such as the general areas of attitude change, social power, and self-presentation. However, we need better theories and more rigorous tests of them. We need more ingenious research, but at the same time more systematic research. Much remains to be done. Perhaps the reader will be among those lending a hand.

References

Allen, V. L. Conformity and the role of the deviant. *Journal of Personality*, 1965, 33, 584–597. (a)

Allen, V. L. Situational factors in conformity. In L. Berkowitz (ed.), *Advances in Experimental Social Psychology*. Vol. II. New York: Academic Press, 1965. Pp. 133–176. (b)

Allen, V. L., and Crutchfield, R. S. Generalization of experimentally reinforced conformity. *Journal of Abnormal and Social Psychology*, 1963, 67, 326–333.

Allport, F. H. The J-curve hypothesis of conforming behavior. *Journal of Social Psychology*, 1934, 5, 141–183.

Argyle, M. Social pressure in public and private situations. *Journal of Abnormal and Social Psychology*, 1957, 54, 172–175.

Aronson, E., and Carlsmith, J. M. The effect of the severity of threat on the devaluation of forbidden behavior. *Journal of Abnormal and Social Psychology*, 1963, 66, 584–588.

Aronson, E., and Mills, J. The effects of severity of initiation on liking for a group. *Journal of Abnormal and Social Psychology*, 1959, 59, 177–181.

Aronson, E., Turner, J., and Carlsmith, J. M. Communicator credibility and communication discrepancy as determinants of opinion change. *Journal of Abnormal and Social Psychology*, 1963, 67, 31–36.

Asch, S. E. Effects of group pressure upon the modification and distortion of judgments. In H. Guetzkow (ed.), *Groups, Leadership, and Men*. Pittsburgh: Carnegie Press, 1951.

Asch, S. E. *Social Psychology*. Englewood Cliffs, N.J.: Prentice Hall, 1952.

Asch, S. E. Studies of independence and conformity: a minority of one against a unanimous majority. *Psychological Monographs*, 1956, 70, No. 9, 177–190.

Asch, S. E. Effects of group pressures upon modification and distortion of judgments. In E. E. Maccoby, T. M. Newcomb, E. L. Hartley (eds.), *Readings in Social Psychology*. New York: Holt, Rinehart, and Winston, 1958. Pp. 174–183.

Back, K. W. Influence through social communication. *Journal of Abnormal and Social Psychology*, 1951, **46**, 9–23.

Back, K. W., Festinger, L., Hymovitch, B., Kelley, H. H., Schachter, S., and Thibaut, J. W. The methodology of studying rumor transmission. *Human Relations*, 1950, **3**, 307–312.

Bandura, A. Social learning through imitation. In M. R. Jones (ed.), *Nebraska Symposium on Motivation: 1962*. Lincoln: University of Nebraska Press, 1962. Pp. 211–269.

Bandura, A. Influence of model's reinforcement contingencies on the acquisition of imitative responses. *Journal of Personality and Social Psychology*, 1965, **1**, 589–595.

Bandura, A., and Huston, A. C. Identification as a process of incidental learning. *Journal of Abnormal and Social Psychology*, 1961, **63**, 311–318.

Bandura, A., and Mischel, W. Modification of self-imposed delay of reward through exposure to live and symbolic models. *Journal of Personality and Social Psychology*, 1965, **2**, 698–705.

Bandura, A., Ross, D., and Ross, S. A. Transmission of aggression through imitation of aggressive models. *Journal of Abnormal and Social Psychology*, 1961, **63**, 575–582.

Bandura, A., Ross, D., and Ross, S. A. Imitation of film-mediated aggressive models. *Journal of Abnormal and Social Psychology*, 1963, **66**, 3–11. (a)

Bandura, A., Ross, D., and Ross, S. A. Vicarious reinforcement and imitative learning. *Journal of Abnormal and Social Psychology*, 1963, **67**, 601–607. (b)

Bandura, A., and Walters, R. H. *Social Learning and Personality Development*. New York: Holt, Rinehart, and Winston, 1963.

Barch, A. M., Trumbo, D., and Nangle, J. Social setting and conformity to a legal requirement. *Journal of Abnormal and Social Psychology*, 1957, **55**, 396–398.

Bennett, E. B. Discussion, decision, commitment, and consensus in "group decision." *Human Relations*, 1955, **8**, 251–274.

Berenda, R. W. *The Influence of the Group on the Judgments of Children*. New York: King's Crown Press, 1950.

Berg, I. A., and Bass, B. M. *Conformity and Deviation*. New York: Harper and Row, 1961.

Berkowitz, L. Effects of perceived dependency relationships upon conformity to group expectations. *Journal of Abnormal and Social Psychology*, 1957, **55**, 350–354. (a)

Berkowitz, L. Liking for the group and the perceived merit of the group's behavior. *Journal of Abnormal and Social Psychology*, 1957, **54**, 353–357. (b)

Berkowitz, L., and Howard, R. C. Reactions to opinion deviates as affected by affiliation need (*n*) and group member interdependence. *Sociometry*, 1959, **22**, 81–91.

Bettelheim, B. Individual and mass behavior in extreme situations. *Journal of Abnormal and Social Psychology*, 1943, **38**, 417–452.

Blake, R. R., Berkowitz, A., Bellamy, R. Q., and Mouton, J. S. Volunteering as an avoidance act. *Journal of Abnormal and Social Psychology*, 1956, **53**, 154–156.

Blake, R. R., Helson, H., and Mouton, J. S. The generality of conformity behavior as a function of factual anchorage, difficulty of task, and amount of social pressure. *Journal of Personality*, 1956, **25**, 294–305.

Blake, R. R., and Mouton, J. S. Conformity, resistance, and conversion. In I. A. Berg and B. M. Bass (eds.), *Conformity and Deviation*. New York: Harper and Row, 1961. Pp. 1–37.

Blake, R. R., Mouton, J. S., and Hain, J. D. Social forces in petition signing. *Southwestern Social Science Quarterly*, 1956, **36**, 385–390.

Bogdonoff, M. D., Klein, R. F., Estes, E. H., Jr., Shaw, D. M. and Back, K. W. The modifying effect of conforming behavior upon lipid responses accompanying CNS arousal. *Clinical Research*, 1961, **9**, 135. (Abstract)

Bovard, E. W., Jr. Social norms and the individual. *Journal of Abnormal and Social Psychology*, 1948, **43**, 62–69.

Brehm, J. W., and Cohen, A. R. *Explorations in Cognitive Dissonance*. New York: John Wiley and Sons, 1962.

Brehm, J. W., and Festinger, L. Pressures toward uniformity of performance in groups. *Human Relations*, 1957, **10**, 85–91.

Brim, O. G., Jr. The acceptance of new behavior in child rearing. *Human Relations*, 1954, **7**, 473–491.

Brown, R. *Social Psychology*. New York: The Free Press, 1965.

Burdick, H. The compliant behavior of deviates under conditions of threat. Unpublished Ph.D. dissertation, University of Minnesota, 1955.

Byrne, D. Interpersonal attraction and attitude similarity. *Journal of Abnormal and Social Psychology*, 1961, **62**, 713–715.

Campbell, D. T. Conformity in psychology's theories of acquired behavioral dispositions. In I. A. Berg and B. M. Bass (eds.), *Conformity and Deviation*. New York: Harper and Row, 1961. Pp. 101–142.

Cartwright, D., and Zander, A. (eds.), *Group Dynamics*, 2nd ed. Evanston, Ill.: Row, Peterson, 1960.

Caylor, J. S. Stimulus factors in conformity. *American Psychologist*, 1957, **12**, 388. (Abstract)

Coch, L., and French, J. R. P., Jr. Overcoming resistance to change. *Human Relations*, 1948, **1**, 512–532.

Coffin, T. Some conditions of suggestion and suggestibility. *Psychological Monographs*, 1941, **53**, No. 4.

Cohen, A. R. Upward communication in experimentally created hierarchies. *Human Relations*, 1958, **11**, 41–53.

Cohen, B. P. *Conflict and conformity*. Cambridge, Mass.: M.I.T. Press, 1963.

Cole, D. L. The influence of task perception and leader variation on autokinetic responses. *American Psychologist*, 1955, **10**, 343. (Abstract)

Coleman, J. F., Blake, R. R., and Mouton, J. S. Task difficulty and conformity pressure. *Journal of Abnormal and Social Psychology*, 1958, **57**, 120–122.

Croner, M. D., and Willis, R. H. Perceived differences in task competency and asymmetry of dyadic influence. *Journal of Abnormal and Social Psychology*, 1961, **62**, 705–708.

Crutchfield, R. S. Conformity and character. *American Psychologist,* 1955, **10,** 191–198.

Crutchfield, R. S. Personal and situational factors in conformity to group pressure. *Acta Psychologica,* 1959, **15,** 386–388.

Dean, D. G. Alienation: its meaning and measurement. *American Sociological Review,* 1961, **26,** 753–758.

Deutsch, M., and Gerard, H. A study of normative and informational social influences upon individual judgment. *Journal of Abnormal and Social Psychology,* 1955, **51,** 629–636.

Dittes, J. E., and Kelley, H. H. Effects of different conditions of acceptance on conformity to group norms. *Journal of Abnormal and Social Psychology,* 1956, **53,** 100–107.

DiVesta, F. J. Effects of confidence and motivation on susceptibility to informational social influence. *Journal of Abnormal and Social Psychology,* 1959, **59,** 204–209.

Doob, L. W. The behavior of attitudes. *Psychological Review,* 1947, **54,** 135–156.

Emerson, R. M. Deviation and rejection: an experimental replication. *American Sociological Review,* 1954, **19,** 688–693.

Fagen, S. A. The effects of real and experimentally reported ability on confidence and conformity. *American Psychologist,* 1963, **18,** 357–358. (Abstract)

Festinger, L. Informal social communication. *Psychological Review,* 1950, **57,** 271–292.

Festinger, L. An analysis of compliant behavior. In M. Sherif and M. O. Wilson (eds.), *Group Relations at the Crossroads.* New York: Harper and Row, 1953. Pp. 232–256.

Festinger, L. A theory of social comparison processes. *Human Relations,* 1954, **7,** 117–140.

Festinger, L. *A Theory of Cognitive Dissonance.* Stanford, Calif.: Stanford University Press, 1957.

Festinger, L. *Conflict, Decision and Dissonance.* Stanford, Calif.: Stanford University Press, 1964. (a)

Festinger, L. Behavioral support for opinion change. *Public Opinion Quarterly,* 1964, **28,** 404–417. (b)

Festinger, L., and Carlsmith, J. M. Cognitive consequences of forced compliance. *Journal of Abnormal and Social Psychology,* 1959, **58,** 203–210.

Festinger, L., Cartwright, D., Barber, K., Fleischl, J., Gottsdanker, J., Keepen, A., and Leavitt, G. A study of rumor: its origin and spread. *Human Relations,* 1948, **1,** 464–486.

Festinger, L., Gerard, H. B., Hymovitch, B., Kelley, H. H., and Raven, B. H. The influence process in the presence of extreme deviates. *Human Relations,* 1952, **5,** 327–346.

Festinger, L., Schachter, S., and Back, K. *Social Pressures in Informal Groups: A Study of Human Factors in Housing.* New York: Harper and Row, 1950.

Festinger, L., and Thibaut, J. Interpersonal communication in small groups. *Journal of Abnormal and Social Psychology,* 1951, **46,** 92–99.

Fisher, S., and Lubin, A. Distance as a determinant of influence in a two-person serial interaction situation. *Journal of Abnormal and Social Psychology*, 1958, **56**, 230–238.

Fisher, S., Rubinstein, I., and Freeman, R. W. Inter-trial effects of immediate self-committal in a continuous social influence situation. *Journal of Abnormal and Social Psychology*, 1956, **52**, 200–207.

Fisher, S., Williams, H. L., and Lubin, A. Personal predictors of susceptibility to social influence. *American Psychologist*, 1957, **12**, 360. (Abstract)

Frank, J. D. Experimental studies of personal pressure and resistance: I. Experimental production of resistance. *Journal of Genetic Psychology*, 1944, **30**, 23–64.

Freed, A., Chandler, P. J., Mouton, J. S., and Blake, R. R. Stimulus and background factors in sign violation. *Journal of Personality*, 1955, **23**, 499.

Freedman, J. L. Long-term behavioral effects of cognitive dissonance. *Journal of Experimental Social Psychology*, 1965, **1**, 145–155.

Freedman, J. L., and Steinbruner, J. D. Perceived choice and resistance to persuasion. *Journal of Abnormal and Social Psychology*, 1964, **68**, 678–681.

French, J. R. P., Jr. A formal theory of social power. *Psychological Review*, 1956, **63**, 181–194.

French, J. R. P., Jr., Morrison, H. W., and Levinger, G. Coercive power and forces affecting conformity. *Journal of Abnormal and Social Psychology*, 1960, **61**, 93–101.

French, J. R. P., Jr., and Raven, B. H. The bases of social power. In D. Cartwright (ed.), *Studies in Social Power*. Ann Arbor, Mich.: Institute for Social Research, 1959. Pp. 150–167.

Gerard, H. B. The anchorage of opinions in face-to-face groups. *Human Relations*, 1954, **7**, 313–325.

Gerard, H. B. Deviation, conformity, and commitment. In I. D. Steiner and M. Fishbein (eds.), *Current Studies in Social Psychology*. New York: Holt, Rinehart, and Winston, 1965. Pp. 263–276.

Gerard, H. B., and Rotter, G. S. Time perspective, consistency of attitude, and social influence. *Journal of Abnormal and Social Psychology*, 1961, **62**, 565–572.

Goldberg, S. C. Three situational determinants of conformity to social norms. *Journal of Abnormal and Social Psychology*, 1954, **49**, 325–329.

Goldberg, S. C., and Lubin, A. Influence as a function of perceived judgment error. *Human Relations*, 1958, **11**, 275–281.

Gordon, R. L. Interaction between attitude and the definition of the situation in the expression of opinion. *American Sociological Review*, 1952, **17**, 50–58.

Graham, D. Experimental studies of social influence in simple judgment situations. *Journal of Social Psychology*, 1962, **56**, 245–269.

Hardy, K. R. Determinants of conformity and attitude change. *Journal of Abnormal and Social Psychology*, 1957, **54**, 289–294.

Hare, A. P. A study of interaction and consensus in different sized groups. *American Sociological Review*, 1952, **17**, 261–267.

Hare, A. P. *Handbook of Small Group Research*. New York: The Free Press, 1962.

Harsanyi, J. C. Measurement of social power, opportunity costs, and the theory of two-person bargaining games. *Behavioral Science*, 1962, **7**, 67–80.

Heider, F. *The Psychology of Interpersonal Relations*. New York: John Wiley and Sons, 1958.

Helson, H., Blake, R. R., Mouton, J. S., and Olmstead, J. A. Attitudes as adjustments to stimulus background and residual factors. *Journal of Abnormal and Social Psychology*, 1956, **52**, 314–322.

Hochbaum, G. M. The relation between group members' self-confidence and their reactions to group pressures to uniformity. *American Sociological Review*, 1954, **19**, 678–687.

Hoffman, M. L. Some psychodynamic factors in compulsive conformity. *Journal of Abnormal and Social Psychology*, 1953, **48**, 383–393.

Hollander, E. P. Conformity, status, and idiosyncrasy credit. *Psychological Review*, 1958, **65**, 117–127.

Hollander, E. P., Julian, J. W., and Haaland, G. A. Conformity process and prior group support. *Journal of Personality and Social Psychology*, 1965, **2**, 852–858.

Homans, G. C. *Social Behavior: Its Elementary Forms*. New York: Harcourt, Brace, and World, 1961.

Hood, W. R., and Sherif, M. Verbal report and judgment of an unstructured stimulus. *Journal of Psychology*, 1962, **54**, 121–130.

Hovland, C. I., Campbell, E. H., and Brock, T. C. The effects of "commitment" on opinion change following communication. In C. I. Hovland (ed.), *The Order of Presentation in Persuasion*. New Haven, Conn.: Yale University Press, 1957. Pp. 23–32.

Hovland, C. I., Janis, I. L., and Kelley, H. H. *Communication and Persuasion*. New Haven, Conn.: Yale University Press, 1953.

Hovland, C. I., and Pritzker, H. A. Extent of opinion change as a function of amount of change advocated. *Journal of Abnormal and Social Psychology*, 1957, **54**, 257–261.

Hughes, E. C. The knitting of racial groups in industry. *American Sociological Review*, 1946, **11**, 512–519.

Israel, J. *Self-Evaluation and Rejection in Groups*. Stockholm: Almqvist and Wiksell, 1956.

Jackson, J. M., and Saltzstein, H. D. The effect of person-group relationships on conformity processes. *Journal of Abnormal and Social Psychology*, 1958, **57**, 17–24.

Jacobs, R. C., and Campbell, D. T. The perpetuation of an arbitrary tradition through several generations of a laboratory microculture. *Journal of Abnormal and Social Psychology*, 1961, **62**, 649–658.

Jahoda, M. Conformity and independence. *Human Relations*, 1959, **12**, 99–120.

Jones, E. E. *Ingratiation*. New York: Appleton-Century-Crofts, 1964.

Jones, E. E., and Davis, K. E. From acts to dispositions: The attribution process in person perception. In L. Berkowitz (ed.), *Advances in Experimental Social Psychology*, Vol. II. New York: Academic Press, 1965. Pp. 219–266.

Jones, E. E., Jones, R. G., and Gergen, K. J. Some conditions affecting the evaluation of a conformist. *Journal of Personality*, 1963, 31, 270–288.

Jones, E. E., Wells, H. H., and Torrey, R. Some effects of feedback from the experimenter on conformity behavior. *Journal of Abnormal and Social Psychology*, 1958, 57, 207–213.

Jones, R. G., and Jones, E. E. Opinion conformity as an ingratiation tactic. *Journal of Personality*, 1964, 32, 436–458.

Katz, D., and Schanck, R. L. *Social Psychology*. New York: John Wiley and Sons, 1938.

Kelley, H. H. Two functions of reference groups. In G. E. Swanson, T. M. Newcomb, and E. L. Hartley (eds.), *Readings in Social Psychology*, 2nd ed. New York: Holt, Rinehart, and Winston, 1952. Pp. 410–414.

Kelley, H. H., and Shapiro, M. M. An experiment in conformity to group norms where conformity is detrimental to group achievement. *American Sociological Review*, 1954, 19, 667–677.

Kelley, H. H., and Volkart, E. H. The resistance to change of group-anchored attitudes. *American Sociological Review*, 1952, 17, 453–465.

Kelman, H. C. Effects of success and failure on "suggestibility" in the autokinetic situation. *Journal of Abnormal and Social Psychology*, 1950, 45, 267–285.

Kelman, H. C. Compliance, identification, and internalization. *Journal of Conflict Resolution*, 1958, 2, 51–60.

Kelman, H. C. Processes of opinion change. *Public Opinion Quarterly*, 1961, 25, 57–78.

Kelman, H. C., and Eagly, A. H. Attitude toward the communicator, perception of communication content, and attitude change. *Journal of Personality and Social Psychology*, 1965, 1, 63–78.

Kidd, J. S. Social influence phenomena in a task-oriented group situation. *Journal of Abnormal and Social Psychology*, 1958, 56, 13–17.

Kidd, J. S., and Campbell, D. T. Conformity to groups as a function of group success. *Journal of Abnormal and Social Psychology*, 1955, 51, 390–393.

Kiesler, C. A. Attraction to the group and conformity to group norms. *Journal of Personality*, 1963, 31, 559–569.

Kiesler, C. A. Commitment. In R. Abelson, E. Aronson, W. McGuire, T. M. Newcomb, M. Rosenberg, and P. Tannenbaum (eds.), *Theories of Cognitive Consistency: A Sourcebook*. Chicago: Rand-McNally, 1968.

Kiesler, C. A., and Corbin, L. H. Commitment, attraction and conformity. *Journal of Personality and Social Psychology*, 1965, 2, 890–895.

Kiesler, C. A., and DeSalvo, J. The group as an influencing agent in a forced compliance paradigm. *Journal of Experimental Social Psychology*, 1967, 3, 160–171.

Kiesler, C. A., and Kiesler, S. B. Role of forewarning in persuasive communications. *Journal of Abnormal and Social Psychology*, 1964, 68, 547–549.

Kiesler, C. A., Kiesler, S. B., and Pallak, M. S. The effect of commitment to future interaction on reactions to norm violations. *Journal of Personality*, 1967, 35, 585–599.

Kiesler, C. A., and Sakumura, J. A test of a model for commitment. *Journal of Personality and Social Psychology*, 1966, 3, 349–353.

Kiesler, C. A., Zanna, M., and DeSalvo, J. Deviation and conformity: opinion change as a function of commitment, attraction, and presence of a deviate. *Journal of Personality and Social Psychology*, 1966, 3, 458–467.

Kimble, G. A. *Hilgard and Marquis' Conditioning and Learning.* New York: Appleton-Century-Crofts, 1961.

Krech, D., and Crutchfield, R. S. *Theory and Problems of Social Psychology.* New York: McGraw-Hill, 1948.

Krech, D., Crutchfield, R. S., and Ballachey, E. L. *Individual in Society.* New York: McGraw-Hill, 1962.

Lefkowitz, M., Blake, R. R., and Mouton, J. S. Status factors in pedestrian violation of traffic signals. *Journal of Abnormal and Social Psychology*, 1955, 51, 704–706.

Lewin, K. Frontiers in group dynamics: concept, method and reality in social science; social equilibrium and social change. *Human Relations*, 1947, 1, 5–42.

Lewin, K. *Field Theory in Social Science.* New York: Harper and Row, 1951.

London, P., and Lim, H. Yielding reason to social pressure: task complexity and expectation in conformity. *Journal of Personality*, 1964, 32, 75–89.

Luchins, A. S. On agreement with another's judgment. *Journal of Abnormal and Social Psychology*, 1944, 39, 97–111.

Luchins, A. S. A variational approach to social influences on perception. *Journal of Social Psychology*, 1955, 42, 113–119.

Luchins, A. S., and Luchins, E. H. Previous experience with ambiguous and non-ambiguous perceptual stimuli under various social influences. *Journal of Social Psychology*, 1955, 42, 249–270. (a)

Luchins, A. S., and Luchins, E. H. On conformity with true-false communications. *Journal of Social Psychology*, 1955, 42, 283–303. (b)

Luchins, A. S., and Luchins, E. H. The role of understanding in social influences on judgment. *Journal of Social Psychology*, 1963, 61, 133–150.

Maier, N. R. F., and Solem, A. R. The contribution of a discussion leader to the quality of group thinking: the effective use of minority opinions. *Human Relations*, 1952, 5, 277–288.

March, J. G. An introduction to the theory and measurement of influence. *American Political Science Review*, 1955, 49, 431–451.

Mausner, B. Studies in social interaction: III. Effect of variation in one partner's prestige on the interaction of observer pairs. *Journal of Applied Psychology*, 1953, 37, 391–393.

Mausner, B. The effect of one partner's success in a relevant task on the interaction of observer pairs. *Journal of Abnormal and Social Psychology*, 1954, 49, 557–560. (a)

Mausner, B. The effect of prior reinforcement on the interaction of observer pairs. *Journal of Abnormal and Social Psychology*, 1954, 49, 65–68. (b)

Mausner, B. Studies in social interaction: I. A conceptual scheme. *Journal of Social Psychology*, 1955, 41, 259–270.

Mausner, B., and Bloch, B. L. A study of the additivity of variables affecting social interaction. *Journal of Abnormal and Social Psychology*, 1957, **54**, 250–256.

Mayo, E. *The Human Problems of an Industrial Civilization*. New York: Macmillan, 1933.

McBride, D. The effects of public and private changes of opinion on intragroup communication. Unpublished Ph.D. dissertation, University of Minnesota, 1954.

Medow, H., and Zander, A. Aspirations for the group chosen by central and peripheral members. *Journal of Personality and Social Psychology*, 1965, **1**, 224–228.

Milgram, S. Behavioral study of obedience. *Journal of Abnormal and Social Psychology*, 1963, **67**, 371–378.

Milgram, S. Group pressure and action against a person. *Journal of Abnormal and Social Psychology*, 1964, **69**, 137–143.

Milgram, S. Some conditions of obedience and disobedience to authority. In I. D. Steiner and M. Fishbein (eds.), *Current Studies in Social Psychology*. New York: Holt, Rinehart, and Winston, 1965. Pp. 243–262. (a)

Milgram, S. Liberating effects of group pressure. *Journal of Abnormal and Social Psychology*, 1965, **1**, 127–134. (b)

Miller, N. E., and Dollard, J. *Social Learning and Imitation*. New Haven, Conn.: Yale University Press, 1941.

Moreno, J. L. *Who Shall Survive?*, rev. ed. Beacon, N.Y.: Beacon House, 1953.

Mouton, J. S., Blake, R. R., and Olmstead, J. A. The relationship between frequency of yielding and the disclosure of personal identity. *Journal of Personality*, 1956, **24**, 339–347.

Newcomb, T. M. The prediction of interpersonal attraction. *American Psychologist*, 1956, **11**, 575–586.

Newcomb, T. M., Turner, R. H., and Converse, P. E. *Social Psychology*. New York: Holt, Rinehart, and Winston, 1965.

Olmstead, J. A., and Blake, R. R. The use of simulated groups to produce modifications in judgment. *Journal of Personality*, 1955, **23**, 335–345.

Orne, M. T. On the social psychology of the psychological experiment: with particular reference to demand characteristics and their implications. *American Psychologist*, 1962, **17**, 776–783.

Pepitone, A. Motivational effects in social perception. *Human Relations*, 1950, **3**, 57–76.

Rasmussen, G., and Zander, A. Group membership and self-evaluation. *Human Relations*, 1954, **7**, 239–251.

Raven, B. H. Social influence on opinions and the communication of related content. *Journal of Abnormal and Social Psychology*, 1959, **58**, 119–128.

Raven, B. H., and French, J. R. P., Jr. Group support, legitimate power, and social influence. *Journal of Personality*, 1958, **26**, 400–409. (a)

Raven, B. H., and French, J. R. P., Jr. Legitimate power, coercive power, and observability in social influence. *Sociometry*, 1958, **21**, 83–97. (b)

Roethlisberger, F. J., and Dickson, W. J. *Management and the Worker*. Cambridge, Mass.: Harvard University Press, 1939.

Rohrer, J. H., Baron, S. H., Hoffman, E. L., and Swander, D. V. The stability of autokinetic judgments. *Journal of Abnormal and Social Psychology*, 1954, **49**, 595–597.

Rommetveit, R. *Social Norms and Roles.* Minneapolis: University of Minnesota Press, 1953.

Rosenbaum, M. E. The effects of stimulus and background factors on the volunteering response. *Journal of Abnormal and Social Psychology*, 1956, **53**, 118–121.

Rosenbaum, M., and Blake, R. R. Volunteering as a function of field structure. *Journal of Abnormal and Social Psychology*, 1955, **50**, 193–196.

Rosenberg, L. A. Group size, prior experience, and conformity. *Journal of Abnormal and Social Psychology*, 1961, **63**, 436–437.

Rosenberg, L. A. Conformity as a function of confidence in self and confidence in partner. *Human Relations*, 1963, **16**, 131–139.

Rosenberg, M. J. When dissonance fails: on eliminating evaluation apprehension from attitude measurement. *Journal of Personality and Social Psychology*, 1965, **1**, 28–42.

Samelson, F. Conforming behavior under two conditions of conflict in the cognitive field. *Journal of Abnormal and Social Psychology*, 1957, **55**, 181–187.

Schachter, S. Deviation, rejection, and communication. *Journal of Abnormal and Social Psychology*, 1951, **46**, 190–207.

Schachter, S., Ellertson, N., McBride, D., and Gregory, D. An experimental study of cohesiveness and productivity. *Human Relations*, 1951, **4**, 229–238.

Schachter, S., and Hall, R. Group-derived restraints and audience persuasion. *Human Relations*, 1952, **5**, 397–406.

Schachter, S., Nuttin, J., DeMonchaux, C., Maucorps, P. H., Osmar, D., Duijker, H., Rommetveit, R., and Israel, J. Cross-cultural experiments on threat and rejection. *Human Relations*, 1954, **7**, 403–439.

Schanck, R. L. A study of a community and its groups and institutions. *Psychological Monographs*, 1932, **43**, No. 2.

Schopler, J. Social power. In L. Berkowitz (ed.), *Advances in Experimental Social Psychology*. Vol. II. New York: Academic Press, 1965. Pp. 177–218.

Schroder, H. M., and Hunt, D. E. Dispositional effects upon conformity at different levels of discrepancy. *Journal of Personality*, 1958, **26**, 243–258.

Secord, P. F., and Backman, C. W. *Social Psychology*, New York: McGraw-Hill, 1964.

Sherif, C. W., Sherif, M., and Nebergall, R. E. *Attitude and Attitude Change.* Philadelphia: W. B. Saunders, 1965.

Sherif, M. A study of some social factors in perception. *Archives of Psychology*, 1935, **27**, No. 187.

Sherif, M. *The Psychology of Social Norms.* New York: Harper and Row, 1936.

Sherif, M., and Hovland, C. I. *Social Judgment.* New Haven: Yale University Press, 1961.

Siegel, A. E., and Siegel, S. Reference groups, membership groups, and attitude change. *Journal of Abnormal and Social Psychology*, 1957, **55**, 360–364.

Smith, E. E. The power of dissonance techniques to change attitudes. *Public Opinion Quarterly*, 1961, **25**, 626–639.

Steiner, I. D., and Peters, S. C. Conformity and the A-B-X model. *Journal of Personality*, 1958, **26**, 229–242.

Stouffer, S. A. An analysis of conflicting social norms. *American Sociological Review*, 1949, **14**, 707–717.

Suppes, P., and Atkinson, R. C. *Markov Learning Models for Multiperson Interactions*. Stanford, Calif.: Stanford University Press, 1960.

Thibaut, J. W., and Kelley, H. H. *The Social Psychology of Groups*. New York: John Wiley and Sons, 1959.

Thibaut, J. W., and Strickland, L. H. Psychological set and social conformity. *Journal of Personality*, 1956, **25**, 115–129.

Thrasher, J. D. Interpersonal relations and gradations of stimulus structure as factors in judgmental variation: an experimental approach. *Sociometry*, 1954, **17**, 228–241.

Tuddenham, R. D. The influence upon judgment of the apparent discrepancy between self and others. *Journal of Social Psychology*, 1961, **53**, 69–79.

Turner, C. E. Test room studies in employee effectiveness. *American Journal of Public Health*, 1933, **23**, 557–584.

Walker, E. L., and Heyns, R. W. *An Anatomy for Conformity*. Englewood Cliffs, N.J.: Prentice-Hall, 1962.

Weick, K. E. Reduction of cognitive dissonance through task enhancement and effort expenditure. *Journal of Abnormal and Social Psychology*, 1964, **68**, 533–539.

Weick, K. E. Organizations in the laboratory. In V. H. Vroom (ed.), *Methods of Organizational Research*. Pittsburgh: University of Pittsburgh Press, 1967.

Whitehead, T. N. *The Industrial Worker*. Cambridge, Mass.: Harvard University Press, 1938.

Wheeler, L., and Arrowood, A. J. Restraints against imitation and their reduction. *Journal of Experimental Social Psychology*, 1966, **2**, 288–300.

Wiener, M. Certainty of judgment as a variable in conformity behavior. *Journal of Social Psychology*, 1958, **48**, 257–263.

Wiener, M., Carpenter, J. T., and Carpenter, B. External validation of a measure of conformity behavior. *Journal of Abnormal and Social Psychology*, 1956, **52**, 421–422.

Willis, R. H. Two dimensions of conformity-nonconformity. *Sociometry*, 1963, **26**, 499–513.

Willis, R. H. The phenomenology of shifting agreement and disagreement in dyads. *Journal of Personality*, 1965, **33**, 188–199. (a)

Willis, R. H. Social influence, information processing, and net conformity in dyads. *Psychological Reports*, 1965, **17**, 147–156. (b)

Willis, R. H. Conformity, independence, and anticonformity. *Human Relations*, 1965, **18**, 373–389. (c)

Willis, R. H. Descriptive models of social response. Paper delivered at A.P.A. meetings in Chicago, September 1965. (d)

Willis, R. H., and Hollander, E. P. An experimental study of three response modes in social influence situations. *Journal of Abnormal and Social Psychology*, 1964, **69**, 150–156. (a)

Willis, R. H., and Hollander, E. P. Supplementary note: modes of responding in social influence situations. *Journal of Abnormal and Social Psychology*, 1964, **69**, 157. (b)

Wyer, R. S., Jr. Effects of incentive to perform well, group attraction, and group acceptance on conformity in a judgmental task. *Journal of Personality and Social Psychology*, 1966, **4**, 21–26.

Ziller, R. C. Scales of judgment: a determinant of the accuracy of group decisions. *Human Relations*, 1955, **8**, 153–164.

Zipf, S. G. Resistance and conformity under reward and punishment. *Journal of Abnormal and Social Psychology*, 1960, **61**, 102–109.

PART

IV

Interdependence in Groups

Eugene Burnstein

University of Michigan

12

Cognitive Factors in Behavioral Interdependence

We will begin with a truism about the study of groups: The properties attributed to a group are abstracted from the behavior of its members. As with most truisms, this one is deceptively simple. Individuals do many things in groups, but not everything they do is interesting. For the social psychologist the behavior merits study if it occurs with sufficient frequency and indicates something about the relationship between the parties involved. For instance, acts of friendship are frequent occurrences that demonstrate the existence of a relationship between the donor of the act and its recipient. These individual acts can be aggregated to indicate an important property of a group—its cohesion. Roughly, this property reflects the group's capacity to withstand threats to its unity, an index to a kind of collective sense of "we-ness." One of the first operations for determining a group's cohesion used a ratio whose numerator consists of the number of friendship relations that exist *among* the group members and whose denominator consist of the total number of their friendship relations with each other as well as with outsiders (Festinger, Schachter, and Back, 1950). Usually the relations themselves would be determined by asking members to indicate those with whom they would prefer to or actually do engage in the activities characteristic of friendship (behavior between members). But of course these relations could just as well be established by observing the activities directly and counting how often members participate in them together and how often with outsiders. The concept of cohesion is thus derived from the behavior engaged in by group members. A similar state of affairs should obtain for any concept describing a group, by which we mean that the concept can be reduced to behavior between members. "Behavior between members" will be our major concern in this part of the book.

Because members do many things, only some of which are relevant to their ties with one another, the researcher must be selective. What is the criterion for saying an act that occurs "between members" indicates the existence of a relationship? For the moment ignore the content of the act. Certainly content is important, but primarily in fixing the nature of a relationship, not in determining its presence or strength. The statement of this criterion brings us to a second truism, whose deceptive simplicity is clear in that all of this part of the book constitutes an attempt to understand it: The common feature of such acts is that they consistently depend on the behavior of the other person. More specifically, a relationship exists between two individuals (*P* and *O*) if *P*'s behavior is reliably caused or occasioned by that of *O*. Frequently this dependence is reciprocal, so that *P*'s behavior causes *O* to respond, and the latter's behavior in turn causes *P* to respond. A social relationship, then, denotes a case of behavioral dependence or behavioral interdependence (Zajonc, 1966). In practice, however, it is often very difficult to distinguish these two kinds of relationship without being arbitrary. Consider a power relation, *P* "commands" and *O* "complies." This would seem to be a clear instance of behavioral dependence. But in all likelihood compliance on the part of *O* has appreciable effects on *P*. Depending on the situation, it might gratify him and increase the probability of further "commands"; it might also enhance his status and reduce his respect for *O*; or it might increase his liking and feeling of responsibility for *O*, and so on. Because this distinction is not critical for our purposes, unless there are special reasons for invoking it, we will use the term *interdependence* to refer to either kind of relationship.

To oversimplify slightly, it may be said that social psychological research in general tends to ask either one of two questions about interdependence: (1) What are its properties and what are their effects? Or (2) How do these properties develop? A researcher concerned with the former issue often begins his inquiry by representing a relationship as a value in a matrix or as a line in a graph. After the appropriate mathematical operations have been performed, he may discover that the structure of relations possesses characteristics that were at first not at all obvious, because interdependencies in even a fairly small group can be extremely intricate. About twenty years ago Festinger, Schachter, and Back (1950) identified cliques in a large housing project by means of matrix multiplication, where a value in the matrix indicated a friendship relation between two individuals. The presence of a relation between any pair of individuals was given by their sociometric choices. On the basis of this analysis, predictions could be made about, among other things, the "path" a rumor would follow within the project. Similarly, French (1956) mapped out different power structures in which a power relation between any two individuals was defined in terms of one being able to influence the other. As a result of his analysis, French proved that a certain property of the structure, its "connectedness," determined whether and how quickly disagreements among members could be resolved. A more recent and highly sophisticated analysis along these lines may be found in Flament (1963).

This part of the book will address itself primarily to the question of the origin of relationships, although in the process it will consider in some detail certain formal properties of social structures. Such a question implies that the researcher is interested in the conditions under which various forms of interdependence develop. Our analysis will consider three broad classes of determinants. This chapter, on cognitive determinants, examines the "argument" that the form of interdependence achieved by a group will conform to the beliefs and biases about interdependence that are shared by its members. More specifically, it says that the average person has certain general opinions or attitudes that provide him with standards for evaluating any social structure. Structures that are consistent with his standards are felt to be appropriate; those that are inconsistent are felt to be inappropriate. This sense of structural propriety (cognitive biases that permit the person to distinguish appropriate from inappropriate organizational forms) is well learned. They come readily to mind and can be used with little effort. Thus the person feels more comfortable when dealing with structures that conform to such biases than when dealing with those that do not.[1] Finally, these opinions about social structures are in large part shared. Hence, if the members use them as a guide to their behavior, not only will social interaction proceed in a relatively orderly and predictable fashion, but the form of interdependence actually developed will in all likelihood approximate the structure represented by these biases.

The next chapter considers a contrasting point of view regarding the development of interdependence. This view says in essence that individuals must *learn* from their experience together what structural arrangements are satisfying to them. The organization achieved by a collectivity thus depends on the rewards and punishments its members receive therefrom, on the quality of their experiences in the various structures essayed. Chapter 13 then examines as the determinants of interdependence, the outcomes members obtain in a relationship. The "argument" there is that the form of interdependence that develops is the one that delivers the most

---

[1] It has been suggested (Heider, 1958; Zajonc, 1968) that the social structures represented by these biases obey the Gestalt laws (such as closure, continuation, proximity, and similarity) formulated for physical properties of stimuli. Thus a pattern of social relations produces a feeling of inappropriateness and discomfort in the person because it is in violation of these laws. As a result it will be reorganized so as to more closely approximate a "good Gestalt."

valuable outcomes. Beliefs and biases initially held by members about a social structure are considered relatively unimportant in comparison to the rewards and punishments associated with it.

Once an individual is *aware* that his outcomes depend on the behavior of his partner, he acts only after taking this contingency into consideration. Immediate rewards and punishments, therefore, become less significant than the ability to understand and predict the other's response. If the person achieves this knowledge of his partner he can organize his own behavior ahead of time. Then the act which is emitted on a specific occasion should be contingent on the probable reaction of the other. In brief, *strategy* enters as a determinant of social interaction. Chapter 14 will examine the experimental findings on behavioral interdependence whose explanation seems to demand the concept of interpersonal strategy.

The Cognitive Representation of Social Structures

That a social structure is expected to possess certain properties and not others has been reasonably well demonstrated with a variety of experimental techniques. If an individual tends to attribute some form of interdependence to a collection of people who are presented to him as stimuli, the simplest way of learning the nature of this attribution is to ask the individual to describe the relationships among these people in a standard fashion. Heider (1958) discusses the attribution of a *unit relation* as the perception that several objects belong together, form a group, are associated, share a common fate, are similar, that one is the product of or dependent on the other. Kuethe (1962; 1964; Kuethe and Weingartner, 1964) has demonstrated the presence of a pervasive and powerful tendency toward unit formation involving *different* social stimuli (figures of a man, woman, or child), which operates at the expense of potential unit relations involving *identical* nonsocial stimuli (rectangles). He employed an ingenious technique whereby subjects are asked to place felt figures anywhere they please on a felt field, the distance between the figures indicating the perceived strength of the unit relation between them.

For our purposes the fact that a collection of people tend to be perceived as a unit more than a set of nonsocial stimuli is not sufficient. Studies of unit-forming tendencies provide little or no information about the structural properties of a collectivity or about the ways in which its members behave toward each other that lead to their being perceived as a unit. Other studies concerned with the cognitive representation of social structures are more adequate in this respect because the form of the relationships is reasonably well specified and the behaviors involved are fairly explicit. DeSoto and Kuethe (1959) had subjects rate the probability of various forms of interdependence defined in terms of positive and negative acts such as "likes" and "dislikes." The estimates were made in response to several conditional probabilities that may be broadly paraphrased as follows: (1) "What is the probability of one person, a, having a relationship, R, (say, 'liking') with a second person, b, given that a has the same relationship, R, ('liking') with a third person, c?" which may be expressed as $P(aRb \mid aRc)$. (2) "What is the probability of a liking b, given that c likes b?", or $P(aRb \mid cRb)$. (3) "What is the probability of a liking b, given that b likes a?", or $P(aRb \mid bRa)$. (4) "What is the probability of a liking b, given that a likes c and c likes b?" or $P(aRb \mid aRc, cRb)$. (5) Under conditions of minimal information, the question was merely, "What is the probability of a liking b?" or $P(aRb)$. The actual wording was slightly different and, of course, names were used instead of letters.

We will consider only four of the ten relationships used in the study by DeSoto and Kuethe, two which are clearly positive ("likes" and "trusts") and two which are clearly negative ("dislikes" and "hates"). $P(aRb)$ may be taken as a baseline so that the differences between $P(aRb \mid aRc)$ or $P(aRb \mid cRb)$ and $P(aRb)$ indicate the extent to which the relationship is attributed to a general trait of a or to a general trait of b—that is, a is a "liker" or b is "likeable." $P(aRb \mid bRa)$ indicates the symmetry of R or the extent to which reciprocity is expected to characterize a relation. $P(aRb \mid aRc, cRb)$ compared to the other probabilities reflects the extent to which a relationship, R, is represented as passing on or as transferable from one pair of members to another. A set of relationships that possesses this property is said to be "transitive." In the physical world a good example of a transitive relation is "taller than." Thus, if a is taller than c, and c is taller than b, we are certain that this relationship can be transferred to the remaining pair, a and b—that is, without doubt a is also taller than b. Relationships that cannot be passed on are called "intransitive." An obvious illustration of an intransitive relation is "mother of." In fact, family relations happen to provide especially apt illustrations of all these formal characteristics. Thus, for a collection of three males, "brother of" is symmetrical and transitive. If a is the brother of c, c must be the brother of a; and if it is also true that c is the brother of b, then a must be the brother of b. Replace a male in this collection with a female, d, and the relation "brother of" becomes intransitive, and for any pair containing d it becomes asymmetrical as well.

The mean estimated conditional probabilities for the two positive and the two negative relations in DeSoto and Kuethe (1959) are shown in Table 12-1. A bias toward positive relations is clear. The $P(aRb)$ values demonstrate that with minimal information subjects expect that there is a more than even chance of a person's liking or trusting another and a less

TABLE 12-1.   *Subjective Probabilities of Positive and Negative Relations*
(From DeSoto and Kuethe, 1959)

	Likes	Trusts	Dislikes	Hates
$P(aRb)$	.59	.59	.42	.35
$P(aRb \mid aRc)$	.58	.58	.49	.47
$P(aRb \mid cRb)$	.60	.63	.52	.46
$P(aRb \mid bRa)$	.74	.73	.68	.67
$P(aRb \mid aRc, cRb)$	.66	.66	.45	.42

Note: A difference between probabilities of .04 or more is significant at the 0.01 level.

than even chance of his disliking or hating another. Once it is known, however, that a person dislikes or hates another, there is the strong expectation that this feeling will be reciprocated—that is, $P(aRb \mid bRa)$ > $P(aRb)$. The reciprocity bias is also pronounced for positive relations. The data on transitivity is of particular interest. There is a marked tendency to represent positive relations as transitive, $P(aRb \mid aRc, cRb)$ > $P(aRb)$, $P(aRb \mid aRc)$, or $P(aRb \mid cRb)$. Conversely, with negative relations the expectation tends to be that they are intransitive, given that the subject knows a negative relation already exists between two of the hypothetical individuals; $P(aRb \mid aRc, cRb)$ < P$(aRb \mid aRc)$ or $P(aRb \mid cRb)$. The intuitive reasonableness of these findings is apparent when stated less formally: A person believes that he will like someone his friend likes, and at the same time he does not believe he will necessarily dislike someone his enemy dislikes.

This bias was first identified and analyzed by Heider (1946; 1958), who has labeled cases of transitive positive relations and intransitive negative relations as a *balanced* form of interdependence and cases of intransitive positive relations and transitive negative relations as *unbalanced*. Another way of expressing this distinction, one frequently used by Heider and which may be helpful later in our discussion, is that for structures composed of three entities or points (either three individuals or two individuals and an issue to which they both address themselves) plus a relation connecting each and every point, those that are balanced always contain an even number of negative relations (zero being an even number) and those that are unbalanced always contain an odd number. Cartwright and Harary (1956) and Harary, Norman, and Cartwright (1965) have defined balanced states more precisely. Their formulation uses the concept of "semicycle" from the mathematical theory of graphs. The semicycle is defined formally as an ordered set of distinct lines where every adjacent pair of lines in the order has a distinct point in common, and where the first and last lines are adjacent as well. To use the semicycle concept in analyzing a social structure, the lines become relationships and the points become people or some social object, such as an issue toward which these people have attitudes.

In Table 12-2 each structure contains three relations: one interpersonal (*P*'s relation to *O*) and two attitudinal (*P*'s attitude toward *X*, and *O*'s attitude toward *X*). They can be ordered so that each adjacent relation shares a different "point," either *P*, *O*, or *X*, and the first and last relations are also adjacent, to wit, the order, $\overline{PO}$, $\overline{OX}$, $\overline{XP}$. Each structure therefore constitutes a semicycle, and because it is composed of three "lines," it is called a semicycle of length three. If *O*'s relationship to *P* had been given, if there was a line from *O* to *P* as well as one from *P* to *O*, interpersonal reciprocity (or nonreciprocity) would be represented, and a second semi-cycle would exist, $\overline{PO}$, $\overline{OP}$, with a length of two. Note that structures 1, 2, and 3 in Table 12-2 contain an even number of negative lines, whereas structures 4, 5, and 6 contain an odd number. The former are therefore balanced and the latter, unbalanced. Cartwright and Harary have provided mathematical procedures for determining balance involving larger semicycles in more complex structures. We will touch on these procedures briefly later.

The results of experiments explicitly concerned with balance as a source of bias in the cognitive representation of social structures are consistent with those of DeSoto and Kuethe (1959), although the methods employed are rather different. For example, in some experiments (Zajonc and Burnstein, 1965a, 1965b) subjects learn a social structure, a technique first employed by DeSoto (1960). Structures used in one of these studies (Zajonc and Burnstein, 1965a) are shown in Table 12-2. *P* and *O*, as

TABLE 12-2. *Hypothetical Social Structures Used in a Learning Experiment* (From Zajonc and Burnstein, 1965a)

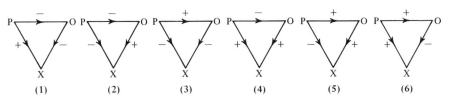

before, are individuals; *X* is an issue, such as racial integration. Each relation in a structure was presented on cards as an item in a paired-associate list, with the stimulus terms (the two names, or the name with the issue) on one side, and with a plus or minus sign on the other (the latter explained to subjects as meaning "likes" or "dislikes" in the case of two persons, and "approves of" or "disapproves of" in the case of a person and an issue). Recalling the definition already given, structures 1, 2, and 3 are balanced, whereas structures 4, 5, and 6 are unbalanced.

The average error per positive (+) and per negative (−) relation is presented in Table 12-3 for the issue of racial integration. Considerably less difficulty is experienced in learning relations in a balanced social structure than in learning the *identical* relations in an unbalanced social structure. Also, positive relations are easier to learn than negative ones. Information consistent with a person's beliefs and opinions is known to be more readily assimilated and more accurately recalled than information that is not. Hence it can be concluded that the differences in errors indicate balance and positivity are sources of bias in the cognitive representation of interpersonal relations—people anticipate that a social structure will be balanced and will be composed of positive relationships. In other research, one using a paired-associate learning paradigm (Zajonc and Burnstein, 1965b) and another involving a procedure whereby subjects predict likely changes in a social structure (Burnstein, 1967), similar effects are found not only for balance and positivity but also for interpersonal reciprocity. It is clear, then, that a variety of techniques demonstrate with reasonable consistency the presence of at least three sources of bias in the cognitive representation of social structures—balance, positivity, and reciprocity. These properties will be attributed to relationships among members of a collectivity—that is, the person will expect the relationships to be balanced, positive, and reciprocated in the absence of information justifying this attribution.

TABLE 12-3.   *Mean Error per Relation in Learning a Hypothetical Social Structure* (From Zajonc and Burnstein, 1965a)

	Relations		
Structures	+	−	*Both*
Balanced	1.72	1.92	1.82
Unbalanced	2.03	4.17	3.10
Both	1.88	3.04	2.46

The cognitive argument for the origins of interdependence presented here can be broken down into three premises: (1) Individuals share a set of beliefs regarding organizational arrangements in groups. (2) Social structures that fit these biases are preferred to those that do not. (3) Individuals will behave toward each other so as to produce a system of relations that satisfy these biases. The first, as we have seen, is fairly well demonstrated. Let us briefly note that the second also has reasonably good support. Jordan (1953), Morrissette (1958), Price, Harburg, and Newcomb (1966), Gerard and Fleisher (1967), and others have shown that balanced, positive, and reciprocated relationships are rated as more desirable and less tension-producing than those that are unbalanced, negative, and nonreciprocated. Moreover, there is nice evidence that these biases involve more than just cognitive events in an experiment by Burdick and Burnes (1958) where the subject experiencing an unbalanced interpersonal situation (for example, he finds himself in disagreement with someone he likes) evidenced a higher level of emotionality, as measured by changes in autonomic-nervous-system activity (GSR), than one in a balanced situation. The third premise, however, is most critical for this argument. Therefore, let us examine the relevant evidence in some detail.

Group Processes and the Achievement of Reciprocity

The tendency to reciprocate negative acts is well known. The large literature on frustration and aggression amply demonstrates that if an individual is hurt or deprived by another, his initial impulse is to reply in kind. In research on groups the standard procedure for instigating counteraggression is to have one member prevent others from obtaining a common goal. Thus, to examine the circumstances in which a frustrating act elicits hostilities, Jones and deCharms (1957) instructed a confederate to perform poorly on a group task. Under one condition there was a minimal interdependence in respect to outcomes, and a member could succeed on the basis of his own performance regardless of what his co-workers did. Under another condition members were completely interdependent, so that all were required to perform skillfully in order for anyone to succeed. Although the confederate performed with identical incompetence in both conditions, he received more negative evaluations when his failure prevented the other group members from succeeding. This seemed to be particularly true if the confederate's performance could be interpreted by the other members as reflecting an *intention* to perform poorly. Jones and deCharms had informed half of the subjects that performance on the experimental task was mainly determined by the person's motivation to do well and not by intelligence. The remaining subjects were led to believe that performance was based on intelligence and had little to do with motivation. Therefore, the likely interpretation is that a member performed poorly in the former case because although he had the capability, he did not *want* to do well, and in the latter because regardless of the desire, he just did not possess sufficient ability. The member who did poorly when performance was based on motivation received somewhat more negative evaluations than equally poor members under any of the other conditions.

Although the tendency to reciprocate a negative act may be inhibited when the act is unintentional or reasonable, the instigation to react aggressively may still be strong. Situational constraints, normative or otherwise, merely prevent reciprocation—for example, the frustrating person behaved legitimately, thus reciprocation becomes illegitimate; he is so powerful as to make reciprocation dangerous; or he is so weak as to make reciprocation shameful. In these circumstances the individual may not respond in kind to the source of frustration but will find a more acceptable target for displacement, probably someone who can be perceived to share the blame for the person's unhappy state. In line with this reasoning, Burnstein and Worchel (1962) predicted that if a frustrating act that is unintentional is not reciprocated because of normative constraint on the direct expression of hostility toward the agent of frustration, displacement of aggression should be observed. They had discussion groups read parts of a clinical case history and within a limited time period try to reach unanimous agreement on a course of treatment. One group member was always a confederate of the experimenters. In the control condition (no frustration) he acted as an average member, neither hindering nor making a special effort to facilitate agreement. In the intentional or arbitrary frustration condition, the confederate continually interrupted the flow of discussion, demanding reasons for statements others had made or requesting repetitions until it was impossible for the group to reach agreement in the allotted time. The confederate appeared in the unintentional or nonarbitrary frustration condition wearing a hearing aid. Early in the discussion a wire connecting the two parts of this apparatus conspicuously broke. As a result, he asked the others to speak very slowly and loudly. Throughout the discussion he frequently requested statements to be repeated. Again no group was able to achieve unanimity in the allotted time.

The findings show that although the confederate received more negative evaluations in both experimental conditions than in the control, he was much more severely rejected when the frustration was intentional than when it was unintentional. At the same time, there was considerable evidence of displaced aggression toward the experimenter as well as toward the self in the latter condition: the members rated the experimenter as less likeable and less intelligent, they experienced more guilt about the outcome, and devalued their own performance more than under intentional frustration. It would seem, then, that a negative act that is not reciprocated still serves to instigate aggressive tendencies. However, in the absence of reciprocation—that is, when direct expression is inhibited —they are expressed toward other available targets.

Reciprocity, particularly of positive acts, has been considered on theoretical grounds as an important source of social cohesion in a variety of relationships. Because of this important function, it is presumed to receive strong normative support (Gouldner, 1960). For instance, even in a simple conversation, when a person reciprocates a gaze, a nod, or a smile, he conveys an understanding of the situation to the other that may be a necessary condition for maintaining interaction. The reciprocation of negative acts, however, is probably disruptive for a wide range of social relations. It therefore is likely to be normatively proscribed, although in situations where grievously harming others is especially tempting, as in many sports or in certain business transactions, the principle of "an eye for an eye" may receive normative support as a deterrent.

Although it is difficult to directly demonstrate that the reciprocation of positive acts is critical for the maintenance of social relationships, there is good evidence that such reciprocity is pervasive in simple as well as complex interpersonal behavior. Consider the common smile and nod, a frequent and automatic social performance. Rosenfeld (1967) had an adult interview teenage subjects about their everyday activities. The interviewer was instructed to respond to each utterance of the subject with approval (a positive head nod, a smile, and so on) or disapproval (a negative head nod, a frown, and so on). In two other conditions of the experiment the interviewer mixed his responses, giving approval during one half and disapproval during the other, or he gave neither throughout. In agreement with the reciprocity hypothesis, the largest number of smiles and positive head nods were elicited by an approving interviewer. Although teenage subjects would in all likelihood inhibit any tendency to reciprocate disapproval from an adult, it is interesting to note that they engaged in the greatest amount of self-manipulatory activity ("any motion of the hands or fingers in contact with the body") when confronted with a continually disapproving interviewer or during the disapproval portion of the mixed condition. Because self-manipulatory acts are known to antagonize others (Rosenfeld, 1967), this could suggest the subtle reciprocation of disapproval where more blatant forms of aggression are inappropriate.

Helping another might be considered a positive act that could be readily understood in terms of a reciprocity bias. Yet until recently there was a preference for explaining variations in helping in terms of a belief that one is expected to help those who are dependent on him, or what Berkowitz has called the "social responsibility norm" (Berkowitz and Daniels, 1963; 1964) rather than in terms of reciprocity—that is, a belief that one is expected to help those who have helped him. The reason for Berkowitz and Daniels choosing a social responsibility rather than a reciprocity explanation perhaps lies in the design of their experiment. In the earlier studies Berkowitz had subjects perform a task where they were voluntarily helped or not helped to finish some work by another. The "helpers," of course, were confederates of the experimenter. In the second part of the experiment subjects worked in pairs. The dyadic task was quite different from that used in the first part of the experiment, and it is important to note that the work partner was always a *different* person than the one from whom the subject had previously received help. Each subject was told that her partner would function as a supervisor and the latter would be evaluated on how well she instructed the subject about the task. A high rating meant that the supervisor would receive a sizable prize. Besides "prior help versus no prior help," two other conditions were introduced. Under high dependency, the subject's performance would determine their partner's evaluation; under low dependency, subjects were told that their performance would have no bearing on the evaluation. The results demonstrate that performance is significantly enhanced when the supervisor is highly dependent on the subject and not when dependency is low. In addition, if dependency is high, prior help tended to elicit better performance than no prior help.

A very reasonable interpretation of these results is that prior help makes salient one's belief in the obligation to help those requiring it. A reciprocity explanation would be rather far-fetched, because the individual needing help is not the same one who previously aided the person. Thus, even if prior help increased awareness of the obligation to repay this help, there is no opportunity to act on this belief. However, Berkowitz makes the interesting suggestion that a tendency to reciprocate could be generalized to the dependent supervisor whereby helping the latter satisfies in part the person's desire to return help received from a different individual (Berkowitz and Daniels, 1964).

More recently, Goranson and Berkowitz (1966) directly compared social responsibility and reciprocity as determinants of helping. Their procedure was very similar to that just described, except in one condition the supervisor was the *same* individual who had previously helped the subjects (either voluntarily or at the instruction of the experimenter) or who had pointedly refused to help. The supervisor was highly dependent on the subject in all conditions. Although the social-responsibility hypothesis would predict that the effects of prior help are independent of the identity of the supervisor, the results show this clearly not to be true. Subjects worked much harder on the task when they were being supervised by the *same* individual who had *voluntarily* helped them than in any of the other conditions. Moreover, a decrement in task performance appeared when the supervisor was the *same* individual who had previously refused to help the subject. No decrement occurred when he was different, in which case he seemed to elicit a similar amount of effort from the subject regardless of whether the latter had received or had been refused prior help. Although relatively high rates of performance with the different supervisor do suggest that feelings of social responsibility may be operating, it is difficult to interpret this finding in the absence of appropriate control groups. For instance, the high rate of performance may well be a practice effect. The findings are unambiguous in respect to reciprocity, however. By increasing or decreasing his performance, the person repays a dependent other in kind for prior aid or a prior rebuff.

The conditions under which help is reciprocated in Berkowitz's work appear similar to those under which hostility is reciprocated in studies of the frustration–aggression hypothesis. That is, the tendency to reciprocate is strongest when the prior positive or negative act implies an *intention* to help or harm. The attribution of some such intention or attitude seems most likely to occur when the actor freely chooses to hurt or help the other, when there is little in the situation to compel or justify the act. This is quite consistent with current theories of the attribution process (Jones and Davis, 1965; Kelley, 1967), which conclude that if an action is taken in the face of countervailing pressures (for example, it is a widely unpopular act or it severely depletes the actor's resources), the observer will confidently infer the actor's intentions or his attitudes from the consequences of his act. Thus, if O gives aid to P when he is compelled to by a third person or when he possesses such large resources that the amount received by P has little value to O, then it is difficult for P to gauge O's intention or attitude. How, then, may he become more certain of the donor's sincerity? In the context of helping behavior, theories of attribution indicate that the person will become increasingly confident in another's desire to give aid (1) as the "voluntariness" of the donor's decision increases, (2) as the amount of help increases for a fixed level of resources, or (3) as the donor's resources diminish for a fixed amount of help.

Goranson and Berkowitz (1966) have demonstrated that the tendency to reciprocate is considerably stronger when prior aid is given voluntarily than when it is compelled. The effects of the *amount* of aid as well as the *size* of the donor's resources have been shown in a neat experiment by Pruitt (1968). His subjects played a simple "game" with a programmed partner. On each trial one person received "resources" from the experimenter (chips having money value) and decided how much to keep and how much to give the other. The roles of donor and recipient alternated between the subject and his "partner" over trials, and knowledge of the donor's resources was always available to the recipient. The data clearly indicate that the aid provided a previous donor is a positive function of the aid previously given (for example, O obtained more money from P when prior to this O gave P 80 per cent rather than 20 per cent of $1) and a negative function of the donor's resources, holding constant the amount given previously (for example, O obtained more money from P if prior to this he gave P 80 per cent of $1 rather than 20 per cent of $4, although in either case P had received 80 cents).

In graph theoretic terms an interpersonal relationship is represented as a semicycle of length two, the two lines of course being P's relationship to O and O's relationship to P. The semicycle is positive and the structure is therefore balanced when both lines are of the same sign. This represents a situation in which both individuals behave in a positive fashion or both behave in a negative fashion toward the other. Hence reciprocity is the simplest form of structural balance. Considering the evidence already reviewed, one might be tempted to say that a bias toward reciprocity in the cognitive representation of social structures has been demonstrated to induce reciprocity in interpersonal behavior. But of course this conclusion is unwarranted because the experiment has not been done that shows that a particular cognitive bias produces or causes a corresponding form of behavioral interdependence. That they parallel each other in respect to reciprocity, however, seems fairly well established. The question to which we now wish to address ourselves is whether a similar isomorphism can be observed for structural balance under more complex conditions of interdependence than that of a semicycle, length two.

Group Processes and the Achievement of Structural Balance

The assertion that a balanced structure will evolve from the interaction of group members has at least two implications. First, it should follow that a person will choose as a co-worker, partner, or colleague another with attributes that appear conducive to balanced interpersonal relations and reject those with attributes that are seen as leading to unbalanced interpersonal relations. Lerner and Becker (1962) find good evidence to support this conjecture. They gave their subjects the opportunity to select one of two others as a partner, knowing their scores on a test of personality that they themselves had recently taken. One score was quite similar to that of the subject, the other, quite different. The choice was made under either of two experimental conditions. The person was told (1) that they would play a game with the money to be received for participating in the study until *either one* of them had won it all, or (2) that they would play a game in which *both* could win money in addition to that received for participating. Let us call the valuable outcome, winning the money, X. The two conditions then may be represented as in Table 12-4, where the solid line means "obtains," the broken line, "does not obtain" or "loses," the solid bracket means "similar to," and the broken bracket, "dissimilar to." Structures labeled (a) indicate that gains for one member, either P or O, result in losses for the other; and structures labeled (b), that gains as well as losses are mutually shared. According to the "even number of negative relations" rule, the first two structures in (a) and the second two in (b) are balanced. The others are un-balanced. Therefore, if P has a preference for balance, he should choose an O in such a way as to create a negative interpersonal relationship in (a) and a positive interpersonal relationship in (b).

TABLE 12-4.   *Competitive Interdependence (a) and Cooperative Inter-dependence (b) in Respect to a Valued Outcome*

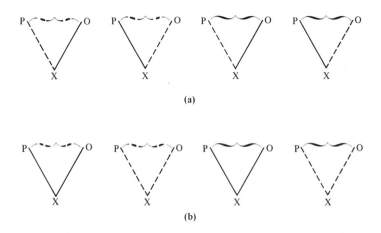

For Heider (1958) and others interpersonal similarity signifies a posi-tive unit relation, and interpersonal dissimilarity, a negative unit relation. At the same time, the manipulation of perceived similarity or dissimilarity is a common operation for inducing high or low attraction (positive or negative sentiments) among group members (for example, see Festinger, Back, Schachter, Kelley, and Thibaut, 1952). Regardless of whether similarity is taken as a unit or sentiment relation, it follows that when interdependence in respect to outcomes approximates a zero-sum[2] or com-pletely competitive structure, as in (a), balance theory demands the choice of a dissimilar partner, and when such interdependence approxi-mates a completely cooperative structure (perhaps even a non–zero-sum structure where cooperative behavior may maximize each person's own outcome as well as their joint outcome) as in (b), balance theory requires

---

[2] The terms *zero sum* and *non–zero-sum* will be examined in detail in Chapter 13. Here it is sufficient to think of the former as a condition in which only competitive behavior is possible and the latter as one in which the individuals may compete or cooperate.

the choice of a similar partner. Lerner and Becker find that in the over-whelming number of cases the person selects a dissimilar partner for the competitive game and a similar partner for the cooperative game.

Similar effects appear in Elizabeth French's (1956) research on the choice of a work partner. By means of a standard projective test subjects were categorized as placing high value on achievement and competence while being little concerned with affiliative activities (high achievement motivation, low affiliative motivation) or as placing high value on the latter while being unattracted by achievement-related activities (high affiliative motivation, low achievement motivation). In the experimental situation each person then had to select a work partner. The choice was between another individual who was not especially liked but had demonstrated skill, and a good friend known to have little competence at the task. The latter partner would satisfy affiliative needs but not a desire for achievement, whereas the former would satisfy a need for achievement but not affiliative needs. The choice confronting each type of subject is shown in Table 12-5, where P places high value on achieve-ment and low value on affiliation, P' places high value on affiliation and low value on achievement, O as a partner facilitates achievement and hinders affiliation, and O' facilitates affiliation and hinders achievement. The positive relation between P or O and either outcome is indicated by a solid line or bracket; the negative relation, by a broken line or bracket. The bracket between P and O means that P chooses O. The first and last of these structures in Table 12-5 are balanced; the two middle structures are unbalanced. The balance prediction naturally is that the former should occur more frequently than the latter. French's data support this prediction in that the person who values achievement chooses a partner who is likely to facilitate achievement activity, whereas the person who values affiliation chooses a partner who is likely to facilitate affiliative activity.

TABLE 12-5.   *Choice of a Work Partner Who Facilitates Achievement or Affiliation by Subjects Who Value Achievement or Affiliation*

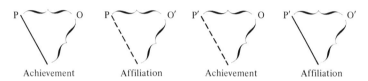

The balance hypothesis implies not only who will be chosen by the person but also the relationship that should obtain between those so chosen. Thus, if P decides that he likes both O and Q, then he must believe that they also like each other; if *P* were to like *O* but dislike *Q*, then he must believe that they dislike each other. When the anticipated relationship does not obtain, an unbalanced state occurs and *P* should act to restore balance. This phenomenon is in part illustrated by experiments done both in the United States and in Holland by Festinger and Hutte (1957). Several individuals were brought together as a discussion group. After a brief conversation in which they were introduced, the experimenter asked them to indicate privately how they liked one another. Each member was then told how the two persons he said he liked best felt about each other. This was controlled so that half were informed that their best-liked choices also liked each other, whereas the other half learned that they disliked each other. Hence the interpersonal structure is balanced for the first set of subjects and unbalanced for the second. Because it was difficult to discredit the information given by the experimenter, nor was it feasible for the person to try to change how either of these two individuals felt about the other, the member could only restore balance by retracting his initial choice. After their discussion was completed, Festinger and Hutte again asked members to indicate privately whom they liked in the group. Those who had learned that the two members they liked best disliked one another changed either one or both of their initial choices with great frequency. No such tendency appeared in the postdiscussion choices of subjects who believed that their best-liked members also liked each other. In sum, the over-all evidence on social choice seems clearly to support the balance hypothesis.

The second implication of the structural balance hypothesis is that group members will change an established pattern of relations so that it corresponds more closely to one they prefer, one that fits their shared biases. There exists a fairly sizable body of research on group processes that is relevant, although it is well to note that much of it was not carried out with this problem in mind. Typically in these studies the person's attraction to the group or to his partner is manipulated. Observations are then made of reactions to experimentally contrived disagreements. Usually members believe that the value of their outcomes is directly related to the degree of consensus that exists in the group. Thus Sampson and Insko (1964) manipulated the attractiveness of a partner, *O*, so that the person, *P*, either strongly liked or strongly disliked *O*, who was a paid confederate of the experimenter. Preceding the critical task, *O*, in the "liking" condition, presented himself as similar to *P*, exuding praise and enthusiasm for the latter as a person. In the "disliking" treatment, *O* presented himself as quite different from *P* and pointedly insulted him. Following this the subjects proceeded to make estimates of light movement in the autokinetic situation (Sherif, 1935). The judgments by *O*, made subsequent to those of *P*, were controlled so that they either agreed

or disagreed with the judgments by *P*. Agreement was said by the experimenter to reflect a similarity and disagreement a dissimilarity in the
judges' "underlying personality structure." Presumably, then, judgmental
similarity was an issue of importance to the subjects in addition to being
the sole basis for the person experiencing some clarity or certainty regarding his performance in a totally ambiguous task.

With these experimental operations four simple social structures were
established. These are shown in Table 12-6. Three of them are formally
identical to those examined by means of a very different technique in
Zajonc and Burnstein (1965a) discussed earlier. A solid line connecting
P and *O* means that *P* likes *O*, a broken line, that *P* dislikes *O*. A solid
line between *P* and *X* means that *P*'s estimate of movement is similar to
or agrees with *O*'s estimate (*X*), a broken line, that *P*'s estimate disagrees
with *O*'s. Structures (a) and (d) are balanced, whereas (b) and (c) are
unbalanced. If an unbalanced state of affairs is sufficient to elicit behavior
aimed at restoring balance, then one of three courses of action must be
taken by *P*. In structure (b), *P* may change his attitude toward *O*, coming
to dislike him; he may change his own judgments so that they become
similar to those of *O*; or he may attempt to influence *O*'s judgments so
that they become similar to his own. The first and last alternative would
move *P* from the unbalanced state depicted in (b) to a balanced one
depicted in (a); the second alternative would move *P* from (b) to (d).

TABLE 12-6.   *The Social Structures Created in the Experiment by
Sampson and Insko*

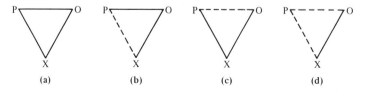

Earlier we called attention to a preference for positive over negative forms
of interdependence. This would suggest that the second course of action,
one that would increase the number of negative relations, might be the
least likely choice as a means to restore balance. In situation (c) the
opposite behaviors offer themselves as possible ways of reducing imbalance. Under these conditions *P* may change his attitude toward *O* from
a negative to a positive one; he may change his own judgments; or he
may seek to alter *O*'s judgments so as to increase dissimilarity. Because
the first method of achieving balance decreases the number of negative
relations, a positivity bias would suggest that it will be used more frequently than the other two.

What was in fact observed? First, *P* in situations (b) and (c) experienced greater tension and nervousness than in situations (a) and (d). This is consistent with the Burdick and Burnes (1958) findings on elevated autonomic nervous system activity under conditions of imbalance. Second, in comparison with those in a balanced state, under conditions of imbalance—where *P* likes *O* and is initially in disagreement, or *P* dislikes *O* and is initially in agreement—*P* more frequently alters his own judgments so as (1) to increase their similarity to *O*'s judgments when *O* is liked and (2) to decrease their similarity when *O* is disliked. Thus, as a result of *P*'s behavior, structure (b) tends toward (a), as would be expected on the basis of a preference for balance and positivity, whereas structure (c) tends toward (d), which is consistent with a preference for balance but perhaps not with a preference for positivity.

We have been taking a rather simple-minded view of the situation, however. The behavioral alternatives that were discussed above are distinct but not mutually exclusive, and could well occur in combination. In fact, a sequential combination is quite plausible. For instance, in structure (b), *P* may first attempt to convince *O* that the latter is in error; if this is unsuccessful, *P* may then examine his own judgments, and if they cannot be faulted, he finally begins to dislike *O*. Nothing of the sort was observed in Sampson and Insko, and for good reason. The experimenters, intent on demonstrating a single event—the increase or decrease in agreement between judges—with clarity and precision, wisely imposed controls that precluded the occurrence of these complex combinations. The relationship between *P* and *O* was established with unusual strength before the judgment task, and a bare estimate of movement could not convey information to *P* that he might use to reassess his partner's likeableness. Moreover, not only were overt acts of influence impossible during the autokinetic task, but on those trials where *P* was estimating aloud, *O* made his estimates in private, and vice versa. This probably further dimmed *P*'s hope of confronting *O* with their disagreement and thereby tacitly influencing his estimate. Therefore, it could be that the inconsistent findings on positivity in Sampson and Insko (*P* tended to restore balance by reducing agreement with a disliked *O*, instead of increasing his liking for *O* while maintaining agreement) are due to their procedures that make it difficult for *P* to change his feelings toward *O* or to convince the latter to change his judgments. By far the easiest avenue open to *P* was to alter his own judgments, since he was quite unsure of them, in order to increase or decrease their similarity to *O*'s.

More recently Taylor (1967) composed dyads in which the subject, *P*, knew and liked or disliked his partner, *O*, previous to meeting him in the laboratory. During the experimental session, *O*, a paid confederate, either agreed or disagreed with *P* regarding the issue of admitting women to

Yale. Hence, although the operations were rather different, the interpersonal structures were formally identical to those of Sampson and Insko. After discussing the issue for 30 minutes, a questionnaire was administered to assess P's liking for O, and P's attitude toward the admission of women. Significant changes toward balance were found for *both* "liking" and attitudes. Unfortunately, it is not clear whether these effects occurred in a particular combination or sequence. Nevertheless, the study does demonstrate that although Sampson and Insko were able to observe only one of a few *logically* possible ways of reducing imbalance, under appropriate conditions—where interpersonal feelings are not extreme, direct communication between members is possible, and the question at issue is unambiguous—more than one course of action may, in fact, be taken to restore balance.

Some of the classic experiments on social communication permit us to examine combinations of balance-restoring acts. Festinger (1950), Back (1951), Schachter (1951), and Festinger and Thibaut (1951) observed the behavior produced by agreement or disagreement among members regarding some significant issue under conditions of high or low attraction to the group. In important respects, their experimental situations were similar to that studied by Sampson and Insko, except that the latter authors gave their subjects little leeway as to the manner in which they might resolve discrepancies in judgment, whereas Festinger and his colleagues imposed few restrictions on the method of resolution. Although this research on social communication was not concerned with structural balance, nevertheless the experimental situations in part can be analyzed from this point of view. Hence they offer an uncommon opportunity to explore the behavior of group members in circumstances where several alternative means of reducing imbalance are feasible.

In these experiments a variety of operations were used to vary attraction to the group. Back (1951) manipulated attraction in terms of (1) perceived liking between members, (2) the potential value of the group product, or (3) the prestige associated with membership. Under high attraction to the group, members felt either strong liking for each other, saw the group outcome as highly desirable, or believed that membership in the group conferred great prestige; under low attraction, little liking existed between members, they were relatively indifferent to the group outcome, or felt that membership conferred little prestige. In Schachter's (1951) high-attraction conditions, groups engaged in their most preferred task, and under low attraction they engaged in their nonpreferred task. Finally, Festinger and Thibaut (1951) varied attraction to the group by creating the perception among members that they were similar (high attraction) or dissimilar (low attraction) in many important respects. Disagreements were created in these studies by use of confederates who took a deviant position and by selecting issues for which differences of opinion were inevitable or easily contrived. The experimenter then observed how members attempted to resolve the disagreement.

Suppose that early in the experiment, when agreement or disagreement is first discovered, P could not be sure of his attitude toward any particular O. He might well feel either that the group situation was likely to be pleasant because most O's seemed to possess some general qualities that were admirable in the abstract, they were to engage in a rewarding task, they were similar to him in several respects, and so on, or that the group situation would probably be unpleasant because most O's have some dubious qualities, the task was unrewarding, they were dissimilar, and so on. Later, however, as a result of their interaction, P is likely to have formed a definite opinion of O as well as having influenced or been influenced by him. The situations at these two points in time—before and after interaction—can be represented in graph theoretic terms just as we have done up to now. The "before" structures would then describe the various experimental conditions.

Although there is some difference from one experiment to another in this series, basically most of them in one way or another independently vary agreement among members (agreement versus disagreement) and attraction to the group (high attraction versus low attraction). Hence there are generally four conditions, and these are represented as the "initial structures" in the upper part of Table 12-7. The initial structures can be changed in many different ways, meaning that a large number of "after structures" are logically possible. We will represent only those that are balanced, all other permutations of the intitial structures being unbalanced. They are labelled "subsequent structures" and are shown in the lower part of Table 12-7. Again a solid line means "is attracted to," "likes," or "approves of," and a broken line means "is repulsed by," "dislikes," or "disapproves of." Thus, for instance in b, P likes O, is attracted to the group, G, and rejects X (a position regarding some significant issue). Of the initial structures, I and III are balanced, II and IV are unbalanced, the former set containing an even number of negative relations and the latter set, an odd number.

The potential structures that can subsequently develop are slightly more complex. Thus the reason for considering them as balanced may not be intuitively clear to the reader, especially because they do not always contain an even number of negative relations (see structures a, d, e, and g). Recall that the Cartwright–Harary (1956) definition of balance considers the semicycle as its basic component. Briefly, a semicycle was defined as an ordered set of distinct lines, or, in a social structure, an ordered set of distinct relations, such as the relations $\overline{PO}$, $\overline{OX}$, $\overline{PX}$, $\overline{PG}$, and $\overline{OG}$ in Table 12-7, where every adjacent pair of relations shares a point, P, O,

TABLE 12-7.   *The Social Structures Created in the Experiments on Social Communication by Festinger and His Colleagues*

INITIAL STRUCTURES

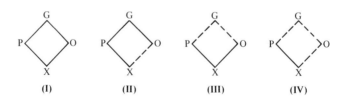

SUBSEQUENT STRUCTURES (Balanced Only)

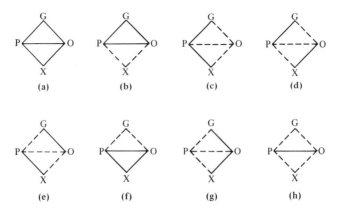

X, or *G*—distinct for every pair—and where the first and last relations are adjacent as well. A semicycle is positive if it contains an even number of negative relations, and is negative otherwise. The degree of balance of a structure is "the ratio of the number of positive semicycles to the total number of semicycles" (Cartwright and Harary, 1956, p. 288). In the structures we have described, I to IV are each composed of a single semicycle, which is positive in I and III, and negative in II and IV. In fact each social structure examined up to now was also a single semicycle. Structures *a* to *h* are made up of three semicycles ($\overline{PG}$, $\overline{GO}$, $\overline{OX}$, $\overline{XP}$; $\overline{PG}$, $\overline{GO}$, $\overline{OP}$; and $\overline{PX}$, $\overline{XO}$, $\overline{OP}$) each one of which is positive. Their degree of balance is therefore unity.

The findings of the studies by Back (1951), Festinger and Thibaut (1951), and Schachter (1951) indicate that when interdependence is initially unbalanced, members behave so as to restore balance insofar as the issue involved is significant to the group. Moreover, they employ a variety of behaviors, often in combination: P may not only reassess his feelings for O, but he may also attempt to influence O regarding X, as well as allowing himself to be influenced by O. Let us examine these findings in somewhat greater detail. In the experiment by Back, members were requested to discuss their differences and if possible resolve them. Two types of discussion were distinguished. An "active pattern" was one in which the problem of resolving differences is accepted by members, and their actions give good evidence of an attempt to analyze the disagreement in order to specify the facts, to reach agreement, or even to argue for the joy of arguing. The strong-involvement characteristic of the "active pattern" was contrasted with that of the "withdrawing pattern," where interest in the discussion is minimal. Here the conversation is typically concerned with restating initial opinions and commiserating over the ambiguities of the task. It was clear that the former pattern reflected a concern with and commitment to resolving disagreements, whereas in the latter pattern this concern and commitment were absent.

Obviously in structures II and IV when disagreement is resolved and no other relations are changed, balance is totally restored. Hence, if members do strive to achieve a balanced form of interdependence, the "active pattern" should be observed with greater frequency in situations corresponding to these structures than the "withdrawing pattern." Because Back's experiment did not contain cases of agreement between P and O, no comparisons can be made with structures I and III, which involve such agreement. Nevertheless, it is instructive to note that in the high-attraction–disagreement condition (structure II), 53 per cent of the dyads were characterized by an "active pattern" of discussion, and 37 per cent by the "withdrawing pattern," as predicted. The remaining could not be categorized in this respect. However, in the low-attraction–disagreement condition, 63 per cent of the discussions were characterized as "withdrawing patterns" and 23 per cent as "active patterns."

If the low-attraction condition is taken as an instance of structure IV, then the prediction—that an "active pattern" would predominate—is not born out. But there is good reason to believe that in Back's experiment this condition was an inadequate approximation of structure IV. What Back meant by "low attraction" is not what is implied by the negative $\overline{PG}$ or $\overline{OG}$ "line," to wit, P and O positively *dislike* being in the group. Low attraction in his study seems to signify that members like the group only slightly, or more precisely, less well than those in the high-attraction condition. Consider the relevant experimental operations. Low attraction was induced either by a rather fleeting reference on the part of the experimenter that he was not sure the members would enjoy congenial relations or by the experimenter indicating that the co-worker may not fit the subject's ideal but "we [says the experimenter] found [someone] who corresponded to the main points [the subject had previously listed as desirable qualities], and you probably will like [him]." On the face of it such information is hardly likely in itself to create much dislike among members. Fortunately, a "negative" condition was set up in which members were bluntly told that they will probably irritate each other and dislike their experience in the group. This is considerably closer to what is meant by the negative $\overline{PG}$ and $\overline{OG}$ lines in structure IV. In the "negative" condition 60 per cent of the cases evidenced an "active pattern" and only 40 per cent, a "withdrawing pattern," which is similar to the findings for the other unbalanced structure, II, where attraction to the group was high.

Furthermore, with both unbalanced initial structures involving disagreement, we might expect members to experience considerable pressure to change their opinion regarding X in these two situations, because a change in opinion would restore balance. Back asked subjects the following question: "Did you think your partner tried to influence you?" Under conditions of high attraction to the group (structure II) 60 per cent felt pressure, 25 per cent did not, and the remaining gave unclassifiable responses. Under conditions of "negative" attraction to the group (structure IV) 45 per cent felt pressure, 30 per cent did not. When attraction to the group was low, which for reasons discussed above probably corresponds neither to a balanced nor an unbalanced structure, 35 per cent experienced pressure to change their opinion and 40 per cent did not.

Back's experiment as well as the others in this series were concerned with the achievement of opinion uniformity, not with the development of structural balance. These studies were derived from a common theoretical orientation (Festinger, 1950) that predicted that the effort members make to reach agreement, the pressure they experience to change their position, and the actual amount of change that occurs, *increases* as their attraction to the group increases. Attraction to the group produces a property called the "internal power of the group." This denotes the magnitude of change the group can induce on its members and is said to be equal to the attractiveness of the group. Naturally, then, highly attractive groups will be capable of inducing greater uniformity and will have fewer deviates than unattractive groups. Such a capability should be reflected not only in the amount of actual change in opinion but also in the quality of the discussion to resolve differences, and in the felt pressure to change. This means that the occurrence of an "active pattern" and the amount of pressure experienced will increase with attraction to the group. Thus, in the "negative" condition, where attraction to the group was presumably less than zero, an "active pattern" will occur least frequently and felt pressures to change will be weakest; low attraction will produce a somewhat greater frequency of this pattern along with a somewhat more intense feeling of pressure; and under high attraction to the group, the "active pattern" will be most frequent and the strongest pressures to change will be experienced. The predicted ordering, however, is rather different from that which was observed.

It seems that the theory of social communication (Festinger, 1950) runs into special difficulty attempting to account for discussion behavior and feelings of pressure in the "negative" condition. Where the "active pattern" should have been less frequent than the "withdrawing pattern," it was more frequent; where few if any members should have felt pressures from others to change their opinion, many more than a few did— almost half in fact. A similar difficulty arises when we examine the amount of actual change in opinion accomplished as a result of the discussion. Because the overwhelming number of changes were made by one member in each group, only the findings for the "high changer" are significant (Back, 1951). Recall that the social-communication model assumes that the internal power of a group varies with its attractiveness; therefore, opinion change should be least frequent in the "negative" condition, most frequent in the high-attraction condition, and of intermediate frequency under low attraction. Yet the mean number of changes in opinion made by the "high changer" was 7.0 for "negative" attraction, about 6.9 for high attraction, and about 5.1 for low attraction. These same effects, however, are just what would be anticipated if one assumed that group members were responding to imbalance and were acting to restore balance. Because the "negative" and the high-attraction conditions are both totally unbalanced and low attraction probably represents neither an unbalanced nor a balanced situation, subjects in both of the former conditions should make more active attempts to resolve their differences, they should experience greater pressures to change their positions, and they should in fact change them more frequently than subjects in the latter.

The effects of pressures to change can be clearly seen in the Festinger and Thibaut (1951) experiment. Here attraction to the group was manipulated by creating the impression of similarity or difference among members. Unlike Back (1951), Festinger and Thibaut had conditions of agreement as well as those of disagreement. They found that communication between members depended directly on the extent of their disagreement—that is, P attempts to influence O more under conditions represented in structures II (high attraction to the group) and IV (low attraction to the group), where in both cases disagreement exists, than under conditions represented in structures I (high attraction to the group) and III (low attraction to the group), where there is no disagreement (see Table 12-7). Presumably, this may reflect a tendency to convert structures II and IV to either *a*, *b*, *f*, or *h*, all of which restore balance by means of achieving agreement.

Pressure toward agreement, as shown by the frequency of communication with another who disagrees, is more pronounced in groups of similar members, structure II, than in groups of dissimilar members, structure IV. Moreover, the effectiveness of these pressures can be seen in that actual change toward agreement is greater in the former condition. Thus, it seems that structure II tends toward a or b; P and O come to like each other and to agree regarding X while remaining highly attracted to the group. But contrary to what would be expected if members are concerned with reducing imbalance, structure IV appears to remain unchanged, and members show little evidence of striving for agreement. Again, it is questionable whether the operations for producing low attraction to the group used by Festinger and Thibaut are adequate to produce *negative* $\overline{PG}$ and $\overline{OG}$ relations. Dissimilarity among members probably does not induce "negative attraction" to the group but merely renders it less attractive than similarity among members.

The same issue arises in Schachter's experiment (1951). Here, however, there is independent evidence that "low attraction" to the group definitely does not mean dislike for the group. When individuals were asked if they wanted to remain members (a standard measure of attraction to the group) almost 100 per cent of those in the high-attraction condition answered in the affirmative. Considerably fewer individuals in the low-attraction conditions said "yes" but the number doing so was surprisingly large, about 66 per cent. At the same time, the Schachter study is important because it provides the clearest demonstration that members will employ a sequence of distinct acts, each of which has the potential to restore balance, when the initial behaviors in a sequence are unsuccessful.

Schachter employed a confederate to play the role of a member. This individual, in some conditions, maintained a position throughout the experiment that was discrepant from that of the majority. The number of communications addressed to the deviant in groups of high attraction increased markedly during the first half hour of interaction and then decreased. In low-attraction groups communication to the deviant was lower than in high-attraction groups during the first half hour but continuously increased so that after 40 minutes it equalled or surpassed the peak amount sent in the latter condition. These communications constitute attempts to persuade the deviant to shift his position toward that of the majority. Under conditions of high attraction, structure II, such attempts appear first to grow rapidly in frequency and then decline. The increase reflects a strong initial effort to resolve disagreements by converting the deviant to the majority position, whereas the decrease may perhaps signal a recognition that the deviant is beyond persuasion. No such distribution of influence attempts—a rapid increase followed by a decrease—was found in the low-attraction condition. (Although we have noted that this condition cannot be considered as an adequate realization of structure IV, it may be used for comparison purposes as a control condition in which attraction to the group is relatively weak but not negative.)

Apparently, members who do not feel much attraction to their group are still perturbed by disagreements, because they persist in communicating to the deviant over an extended period of time, and with ever increasing frequency. Moreover, at each point in the discussion they address more remarks to this recalcitrant confederate than in other conditions where he takes the modal position. Theirs is the unwavering belief that the deviant can be swayed. Or, perhaps, as we suggest below, rational discussion of differences is less awkward and troublesome than directly punishing the deviant for his recalcitrance. Comparable individuals in high-attraction groups do not persist in addressing the deviant, appearing toward the end to lose faith in the effort. Yet if these members merely were to cease attempting to influence O and do nothing else, it would be necessary to conclude that they had learned to live with imbalance. Further examination of the data indicates that this is not the case.

After about 45 minutes of discussion, the subjects were asked, among other things, to rank each other in terms of their desirability as group members. The mean rank in every group was 5.00. For high-attraction groups the deviant received an average rank of 6.44, which is considerably below average. Under low-attraction conditions he received a rank of 5.83. This implies that having given up trying to persuade the deviant to change, members who are highly attracted to their group redefine its boundaries so as to "include him out." On the other hand, members who are not highly attracted to their group persist in attempting to persuade and evidence only minimal signs of rejection.

Why might this be so? In the high-attraction condition, membership by definition is highly valued. Thus the group is likely to be seen worth maintaining as a unified entity. If unity requires that the members go through the distasteful process of rejecting one of their own, they may be willing to do this rather than persist in futile debate, itself an open display of disunity. In the low-attraction condition, membership is not valued. Hence there may be less willingness to become involved in antagonistic actions that might reunify the group but at the same time would generate much guilt and animosity on the part of the members as well as the deviant. The group is just not worth this kind of effort, and members prefer the easier course of continuing to discuss the issue. Thus we are suggesting that rejection is a more difficult or a more costly act than discussion of differences, but at the same time it is more efficacious for preserving the group and restoring solidarity once members are fairly convinced that consensus in respect to an important issue is impossible. This, then, would imply that rejection of a deviant is more probable when members have good reason to want to maintain the group (high attraction) and less probable when such reasons are weak (low attraction).

What does rejection signify in terms of structural balance? It is our conjecture that by specifying the deviant as undesirable to the group, the members in essence have decided, first, that they do not like him, and second, that they will try to bring about his departure. If we were to represent what these members have in mind under high attraction after they have abandoned persuasion, it would be quite similar to what is shown in structure c in Table 12-7. P dislikes the deviant, O, and expects to make membership sufficiently uncomfortable for O that the latter will find the group "negatively attractive." To the extent that rejection can be so interpreted, Schachter's findings demonstrate a particular combination of behaviors used to achieve a balanced form of interdependence: When imbalance exists, as represented in structure II (Table 12-7), the first response is to reduce the discrepancy between P and O regarding X. If this is unsuccessful, O becomes an object of dislike, and at the same time there is the hope that he may be provoked into relinquishing his membership. Hence, when structure a, the completely positive structure in Table 12-7, cannot be achieved, there is a tendency toward c, equally balanced but containing fewer positive relations than a.

Some Shortcomings of an Analysis Based on the Operation of Cognitive Biases Such As Balance

Most of the studies examined so far are not ideally designed for our purposes. This is by no means a criticism of the studies, because they were conceived with a different purpose in mind. They do provide us with an interesting picture of the dynamics of interdependence in groups, but it is a severely limited one. In most cases the processes are observed from the perspective of a single actor. This leads to the conclusion, for instance, that because P's judgments become increasingly similar to those of a "liked" O or increasingly dissimilar to those of a "disliked" O, a balanced social structure is achieved. But such an inference may be unwarranted. It would be objectively true if and only if O changes neither his feelings toward P nor his opinion of X. Suppose a "liked" O came to dislike P as the latter blithely began to agree, or a "disliked" O anxiously altered his judgment of X so as to maintain agreement with P; the resultant state of interdependence would be quite different than that inferred from P's behavior alone. In most cases O's behavior is ignored because the researchers were more concerned in observing P's response to a reasonably well-specified social fact, disagreement with an attractive partner or agreement with an unattractive partner. This required that O behave in a standard fashion and, of course, this means that his behavior had to be prearranged. Because we are concerned with interdependence as an objective state of affairs, a relationship should be defined in terms of the actions of each person involved. Hence O's behavior is equally as important as P's.

Furthermore, these experiments deal with only a limited number of outcomes, which maximize balance, positivity, and reciprocity—change in opinion, changes in sentiment toward others, or a particular combination of the two. A large number of important consequences of group activity, which may have more value to the members than the achievement of balance, positivity, or reciprocity, are excluded—in particular, the rewards and punishments dispensed by others. There is evidence that when other outcomes are available to members in addition to those of balance, positivity, and reciprocity, their behavior does not always reflect a preference for these structural states. In other words, the attractiveness of alternative outcomes may override that associated with balance, positivity, and reciprocity. Members therefore may be induced to establish a form of interdependence that possesses none of these structural properties, but does permit them to obtain more valuable outcomes. For example, ask someone how another person they like feels about them. In general, you will obtain a strong reciprocity bias, just as if your respondent were estimating the likelihood of a liking b, given that b likes a, in a hypothetical social structure. Now ask him how someone whom he dislikes feels about him. When this was in fact done by Price, Harburg, and Newcomb (1966), the strong expectancy that "dislike" as well as "like" is reciprocated (observed with hypothetical structures by DeSoto and Kuethe [1959], Burnstein [1967], and others) is nowhere in evidence. We wish to suggest that in hypothetical instances that are frequently used in studies of the cognitive representation of social structures, there is so little specification of the circumstances surrounding the relationship, so little information given about the individual motives and attitudes involved, that perhaps only the structural properties of balance, reciprocity, and positivity are salient. Once, however, the person's understanding of the situation increases—for example, he must consider a case in which he is personally involved—other outcomes of greater significance to the person may be recognized.[3]

---

[3] These considerations are relevant to opinions and judgments regarding X as well as the feelings of "like" and "dislike" between P and O. Suppose in real life we found that the village idiot held an opinion similar to our own. Newcomb (1968) gives this example and asks whether anyone would really be upset by this state of imbalance. He does not think so, and suggests that when the PO relationship is nega-

That outcomes other than those that satisfy balance, positivity, and reciprocity may determine a person's *preference* for a social structure can be readily demonstrated. As suggested earlier, merely manipulate the information given so as to stress some consequences at the expense of others. Several years ago the author asked well over a hundred students to rank order four networks, commonly used in experiments on communication and group problem solving (see Shaw, 1964), so as to indicate in which they would most enjoy being a member. This ranking was made under two conditions of instruction: either they were to assume (1) that there was no difference among the networks in problem-solving efficiency, or (2) without specifying their relative efficiency, that there were large differences in this respect among networks. The standard task to be performed in the network was described (from a set of symbols held by each member, identifying the one they all had in common).

The networks are shown in Table 12-8. A circle represents a member, a solid line between two members indicates that they can communicate with each other, and a broken line means that they cannot communicate. Under the first condition, where the performance outcome is unaffected by the structure, the order of preference was *D, C, B, A*. Under the second condition, where the outcome is determined by the structure, the order of preference was *A, B, C, D*. If the task outcome is not at stake, there is a decided preference for structures permitting freer communication. Yet when the task outcome does depend on the network, preferences change radically, and subjects choose the most restricted communication structures. Without putting too fine an edge on the matter, if "being able to

TABLE 12-8.   *Hypothetical Communication Networks*

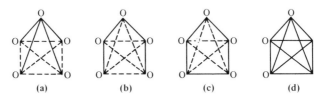

| (a) | (b) | (c) | (d) |

tive, the structure should be labelled as *nonbalanced*. This means that to *P*, the opinion of the other regarding *X* is unimportant and in a sense vanishes from his cognitive representation of the situation. The case might be depicted graphically, from *P*'s perspective, as the absence of a "line" between *O* and *X*. Balance, then, is an irrelevant property of the structure; because a semicycle does not exist, the set of relations is neither balanced nor imbalanced, but according to Newcomb is nonbalanced. Note that this position is inconsistent with several of the findings discussed earlier. For instance, Sampson and Insko's (1964) subjects were indeed disturbed by agreement with another whom they disliked, and changed their judgments to decrease agreement. The nonbalance hypothesis would predict no disturbance nor any attempt to produce disagreement.

communicate with" is taken as a positive relation and "not being able to communicate with" as negative relation, it is clear that structure D is completely balanced, whereas all of the others are not. It might be concluded, then, that the preference for a structure depends on whether it is instrumental in achieving some valued task outcome, and that considerations associated with achievement of this outcome are sufficiently powerful to overcome those associated with balance.

At the same time, let us note that balance theory is rather flexible, and can often handle such findings by an examination of the structure of the choice situation. Suppose P is choosing among several structures that either do or do not vary in task efficiency. If they do so vary and the outcome is valuable, then P must decide between the two situations shown in the upper part of Table 12-9, where in structure (a) P selects (the solid line) a structure that will "produce" (the solid line) an outcome, and in structure (b) P selects a structure that will *not* "produce" (broken line) an outcome that he values. By definition, (a) is balanced, and (b) is not. If, however, any of the structures are equally likely to lead to the desired outcome, then (a) and (b) would both be equally balanced. When, under these conditions, P dislikes restrictions imposed on his communication, (a) would be unbalanced, whereas (b) would be balanced. This is shown in the lower part of Table 12-9. By taking a larger view of the situation, it would seem that these findings are quite consistent with the proposition that a balanced state of affairs is preferred to an unbalanced one. Nevertheless, in "taking a larger view" we are no longer talking about the

TABLE 12-9. *Situations in Which the Person (P) Must Choose Among Communication Structures That Vary in Efficiency (a) or Vary in Restrictiveness (b)*

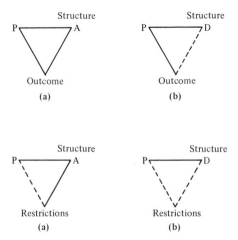

balance of a social structure but the balance of a choice structure in which the social structure is merely a point. Therefore, it is not possible to account for the attractiveness of a pattern of interdependence in terms of *its* degree of balance alone. Whether the choice situation is balanced or unbalanced tells us nothing about the degree of balance of the social structure as a determinant of its attractiveness.

CHAPTER

13

The Role of Reward and Punishment in the Development of Behavioral Interdependence

Although few social psychologists consider themselves radical behaviorists, probably more than a few would argue that the previous chapter puts too much emphasis on cognition and not enough on behavior. They are not merely being finicky. Cognitive processes, never being directly available to the observer, must be inferred from other more public events, usually the subject's overt acts. Hence there should be widely accepted rules of inference or interpretation specifying how one arrives at knowledge of the person's cognitions from knowledge of his behavior. At a minimum this means a thorough understanding of the behavior and the various factors that influence it and must be controlled. If our understanding of the behavior is poor, the interpretations of it are often rendered ambiguous and merit no great confidence. The same problem has arisen in the study of perception and learning, and much work has been done in these areas to specify the conditions under which the observer can with confidence infer an internal state from the subject's responses and when such inferences are unwarranted. Thus there is an extensive literature on what experimental procedures to follow in order to separate perceptual processes from response effects, or learning processes from motivation and performance effects. The circumstances in which we can or cannot attribute certain cognitive processes to individuals on the basis of their interaction, however, is not well worked out. Instead of rules of inference based on systematic research, there are most often rules of thumb based on experimental tradition and common sense. In brief, the social processes that we wish to interpret in terms of relations among cognitions are themselves not well understood.

The Law of Effect and Social Behavior

In the light of this criticism many would say it is wiser to begin an analysis of interdependence with a general principle reasonably well established for individual behavior and attempt to generalize it to interacting individuals. The law of effect is a good example of such a principle. It was phrased by Thorndike as follows: "Of several responses made to the same situation, those which are accompanied or closely followed by satisfaction to the animal will . . . be more firmly connected with the situation . . . ; those which are accompanied or closely followed by discomfort to the animal will . . . have their connections with that situation weakened. . . . The greater the satisfaction or discomfort, the greater the strengthening or weakening of the bond" (Thorndike, 1911, p. 244). For our purposes this may be roughly paraphrased to say that the acts of a set of interdependent individuals that have satisfying consequences are strengthened over time, and those having annoying consequences are weakened.

This social version of Thorndike's law of effect does not predict interdependence of a particular form, but merely says that if we define a social relation in terms of the typical activities of the individuals involved, those activities that come to characterize the relation will be ones that produce rewarding outcomes for the participants. The law of effect is over fifty years old; yet, as we shall see, it underlies much of the current research on cooperative and competitive interdependence. At the same time as it stands this formulation perhaps might seem no less ambiguous than one that interprets interdependence in terms of some underlying cognitive process. Certainly it does not specify what is a "satisfying" or an "annoying" outcome, whereas balance, positivity, and reciprocity do describe in fair detail the nature of the outcome. But this is not a critical issue because, after all, there are a variety of standard operations for inducing positive and negative consequences following some action. More important is the question of whether focusing on the rewarding or punishing consequences of interaction has different or more fruitful implications than analyses based on considerations of balance, positivity, and reciprocity.

To say that members prefer and strive for certain forms of interdependence implies that they react not only to relations proximal to them —for example, those in which they are directly involved (their *own* friends, enemies, bosses)—but also to those that are distant from them, ones in which they have no direct involvement (their *friends'* friends, their *enemies'* enemies, their *bosses'* bosses). The *total* structure is thus an input to *P*. Recall how we have represented a set of relations graphically.

There may be a number of "lines" that have their origin in P or terminate in P. These denote relations that immediately involve P. Suppose we are dealing with interdependencies among three individuals, P, O, and Q, plus some issue, X. There may be a $\overline{PO}$ line, an $\overline{OP}$ line, a $\overline{PQ}$ line, a $\overline{QP}$ line, and so on. The total structure, however, includes lines that do not have their origin or their termination in P—that is, relations that involve O, Q, and X but exclude P. The argument that attempts to account for the development of interdependence in terms of shared preferences for balance, positivity, and reciprocity assumes that P has knowledge of the *total* structure, and evaluates it in terms of its distance from his "ideal" structure. Dissatisfactions then are based on evaluations of the *total* set of relations—not just relations proximal to P, but also and equally those that are distant and do not immediately involve him. As a corollary, it follows that P may seek to reduce his dissatisfaction by changing proximal relations (for example, changing his behavior toward O or Q, O's or Q's behavior toward him, his [P's] attitude toward X, and so on); or, on the other hand, P might attempt changes in relations where he has no *direct* involvement (for example, he might try to get O to behave differently toward Q, Q to change his opinion regarding X, and so on). Modifications in proximal or in distant relations can equally well enhance the degree of balance, positivity, and reciprocity of the total structure.

Our law-of-effect argument makes a very different point. In contrast to the analysis in terms of cognitive biases, the inputs to P here are not the larger structure but only the relations in which he is directly involved— that is, those that originate or terminate in P. No assumptions need be made about P's knowledge of or response to the wider net of relations within which he is embedded. It states merely that acts (toward others) that have positive consequences for P will be strengthened, and those that produce negative consequences will be weakened. This implies that any change in a relation must originate with those immediately involved, who, as a result of P's behavior, respond toward him in a "satisfying" or "annoying" manner. Relations distant from P—that is, lines neither originating nor terminating in P—have no direct bearing on the value of P's outcomes because the behavior that characterizes these relations does not impinge on P. Because these relations have no immediate consequences, P will not attempt to change them. Not until he is directly and immediately involved in these relationships will they affect his behavior.

The crux of the matter, as far as the law of effect is concerned, are the positive and negative consequences to P of his own behavior. The phrase "toward others" was enclosed in parentheses in the preceding paragraph to suggest that although we are interested in behavior toward others, in principle it really may make no difference whether P is or is not aware that his act touches O and that the consequences that ensue to him reflect O's response to his act. The nature of these outcomes is all-important, and whether they are seen to depend on O's response to P's acts or on the operation of the nonsocial processes in P's environment may be irrelevant. Therefore, in its strongest form the social version of the law of effect implies that a reliable form of interdependence will develop between P and O as each attempts to maximize the value of his respective outcome, without necessarily *any* knowledge on their part that one's outcome depends on the behavior of the other, or even that the other exists. This contrasts sharply with our analysis in the previous chapter, where the person's awareness of the situation and his ability to represent it cognitively were critical.

These issues were first explored by Sidowski, Wykoff, and Tabory (1956) and by Sidowski (1957), who developed a novel experimental technique for this purpose, called the "minimal social situation." They created dyads in which neither member was aware that his outcome was dependent on the behavior of his partner. With slight technical modifications this work has been replicated and extended in an interesting fashion by Kelley, Thibaut, Radloff and Mundy (1962) and by Rabinowitz, Kelley, and Rosenblatt (1966). In the "minimal social situation" each subject is seated without the knowledge of the other in a separate cubicle. Usually each faces a control box on which is mounted a switch and lights, one of which serves as a signal to respond (the switch may be pushed, say, to the right or left) while the others indicate that the outcome is either positive (for example, win 10 points) or negative (for example, lose 10 points). The experimenter, of course, controls outcomes according to prearranged contingencies. Suppose, then, the experimenter decides ahead of time that if P goes right, O wins 10; if O goes left, P wins 10; if P goes left, O loses 10; and if O goes right, P loses 10. Contingencies of this type are frequently presented in matrix form as in Table 13-1, where O's outcomes are in the upper right of each cell and P's in the lower left; a "+"

TABLE 13-1.   *Matrix of Reward–Response Contingencies in the "Minimal Social Situation"*

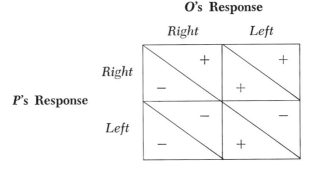

indicates a positive outcome (win 10) and a "−", a negative outcome (lose 10). This means that when P goes right (R) he delivers a positive outcome to O, and when O goes left (L) he delivers a positive outcome to P. Note that the person's own response, R or L, has no effect on his outcome. To the extent that the behavior, P goes R and O goes L, characterizes the exchange, we say that cooperation has developed.

Sidowski, Wycoff, and Tabory (1956) and Sidowski (1957) were mainly concerned with demonstrating the development of cooperative interdependence in the absence of any awareness by P or by O that their respective outcomes were contingent on the behavior of another. The demonstration was successful, with the frequency of mutual positive outcomes increasing markedly over time. Individuals seem to behave as if they were learning to cooperate, even without being aware that another person is present who controls their outcomes. More recent research has examined some important parameters of cooperative interdependence, such as (1) the temporal relations between P's and O's response, (2) awareness of their interdependence, and (3) the contingencies between their response and their outcome. The subtle and complex processes that can be observed as stable forms of interdependence develop under minimal-social-situation conditions are rather surprising.

Temporal Relations Between Acts

Kelley, Thibaut, Radloff, and Mundy (1962) viewed learning to cooperate in the minimal social situation as a case of what they called the "win–stay, lose–change" rule, whereby the person tended to repeat the response following a positive outcome and to change to the alternative response following a negative outcome. This of course is a paraphrase of the law of effect for a two-choice situation, and is similar to the explanation given by the Sidowski group. In the original research, the subjects were free to respond whenever they desired. It is a simple matter, however, to control the timing of the response by means of a signal presented so that the two subjects respond simultaneously or in alternation. Kelley et al. noted that if the law of effect or the win–stay, lose–change rule holds as an explanation of the Sidowski findings, then these two temporal patterns of responding will have very different consequences for the development of cooperative interdependence. This can be most readily shown by the diagram of Table 13-2, which gives the various possible initial exchanges of outcomes in the dyad under simultaneous or alternation conditions and applies the win–stay, lose–change rule to describe how each initial state would be altered over exchanges. Assume the identical contingencies mentioned earlier where if P goes right, R_{PR}, O receives a posi-

TABLE 13-2.   *Dyadic Interaction in the "Minimal Social Situation" as a Function of the Initial Exchange and the Temporal Relations Between Responses*

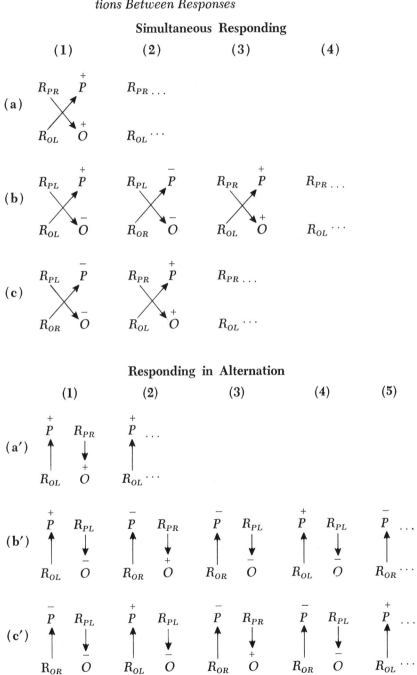

tive outcome; if P goes left, R_{PL}, O receives a negative outcome; if O goes left, R_{OL}, P receives a positive outcome; and if O goes right, R_{OR}, P receives a negative outcome.

Four initial states of interdependence are possible by either procedure: (a) symmetrical reward, where P and O deliver positive outcomes to each other; (b) asymmetrical reward, where P delivers a positive outcome to O but O provides a negative outcome for P, or vice versa (because these two instances of asymmetry are isomorphic, this will be considered as a single form of interdependence); and (c) symmetrical punishment, where P and O produce negative outcomes for each other. Under either a simultaneous or an alternation procedure, if each individual originally delivers a positive outcome to the other, they immediately lock into a state of cooperative interdependence. However, when P's initial behavior hurts O while the latter's behavior benefits P, shown in (b) and (b') in Table 13-2, then the consequences are quite different depending on the temporal order of responding. Given the win–stay, lose–change rule, during the second exchange under simultaneous responding, P repeats his previous response, again punishing O. At the same time O changes his response and now punishes P. On the third exchange both alternate, and mutually reward each other. At this point, the third exchange, a cooperative pattern is established that, according to our rule, should persist over subsequent interaction, even though the initial pattern was one of asymmetrical reward.

Under an alternation procedure, during the first exchange P is rewarded by O, while the latter is then punished for rewarding the former. Hence O changes, producing a negative outcome for P, who in turn also changes, thereby producing a positive outcome for O; see (2) in Table 13-2. On the next exchange, (3), O persists in hurting P, who as a result afterward switches his response, hurting O. What are the consequences of the second and third exchange? According to our rule, O then changes so as to benefit P, and the latter thus continues to hurt O. Because the fourth exchange between P and O is identical in structure to their initial exchange, the sequence of interactions constitutes a cycle that recapitulates itself after three exchanges. When members of a dyad alternate and their original state of interdependence is one of asymmetrical reward, the initial asymmetry recurs after a few exchanges, whereupon the identical sequence should be repeated. Therefore, whereas under simultaneous responding an initial state of asymmetrical reward is converted into one of symmetrical reward or cooperative interdependence after three exchanges, under an alternation procedure the original asymmetry returns following three exchanges, indicating that the dyad will recycle endlessly. Theoretically, then, cooperative interdependence is impossible to achieve.

A similar effect appears when one considers the case of symmetrical punishment, shown in (c) and (c') in Table 13-2. Under simultaneous responding after receiving negative outcomes during their first exchange, *P* and *O* alternate and thus on the second exchange deliver positive outcomes to one another. Still assuming the win–stay, lose–change principle, they should persist in this fashion for the remainder of their interaction. Cooperative interdependence is thus established after only two exchanges. Nothing so simple occurs under initial symmetrical punishment when members respond in alternation. As can be seen in Table 13-2, *O*, who is punished after punishing *P*, changes so as to reward the latter. As a consequence, *P* persists in delivering a negative outcome to *O* during their second exchange. On the third exchange *O* changes again, punishing *P*, and the latter then shifts so as to reward *O*. By their fourth exchange they have returned to their original state of interdependence, symmetrical punishments, and the cycle begins once more.

On the basis of this analysis, that merely assumes the law of effect in a dyadic setting, several clear-cut but nonobvious predictions can be made. First, it was shown that any of four equally likely initial states inevitably lead to mutual help under conditions of simultaneous responding, whereas when members respond in alternation, cooperative interdependence can be achieved only if their initial exchange is one of symmetrical reward. None of the other three possible initial states eventuate in mutual help. It follows, therefore, that cooperative interdependence will be achieved more frequently under the simultaneous than the alternation procedure. Second, it is clear that under simultaneous responding, the dyad must exchange mutually negative outcomes in order to achieve a state of symmetrical reward, unless its first exchange is one of mutual reward. Thus it should be the case that with a simultaneous procedure those dyads that experience symmetrical punishment or mutual competition arrive at cooperative interdependence on the very next exchange. Finally, in principle it is also possible to predict the speed with which cooperative interdependence is achieved as a function of the initial exchange. The interaction sequences depicted in Table 13-2 indicate that under conditions of simultaneous responding an initial state of symmetrical punishment will change into symmetrical reward more rapidly than will an initial state of asymmetrical reward. This, of course, follows from the fact that symmetrical punishment should immediately go before a cooperative exchange.

Kelley et al. (1962) used a strictly paced and an ordinary timing procedure under simultaneous and alternation conditions. Strict pacing precisely controls the interval between *P*'s or *O*'s response and knowledge of results so that the delay under alternation is identical to that under simultaneous responding. Obviously, under ordinary conditions the delay would be greater when subjects respond in alternation than when they respond simultaneously. Some of their results are shown in Table 13-3.

Over trial blocks there is a significant increase in the frequency of symmetrical reward when members respond simultaneously, but not when

TABLE 13-3. *Comparison of the Simultaneous and Alternation Procedure* (From Kelley, Thibaut, Radloff, and Mundy, 1962)

Condition	Number Achieving Cooperative Interdependence	Percentage of Positive Outcomes in Successive 35-Trial Blocks				
		Block				
		1	2	3	4	5
Simultaneous (ordinary)	6	56	62	66	73	73
Simultaneous (strictly paced)	5	58	63	67	75*	—
Alternation (ordinary)	2	49	46	50†	—	—
Alternation (strictly paced)	0	49	48	48	47*	—

* All strictly paced dyads were run for four 35-trial blocks.
† Because the alternation procedure took longer, time did not permit running all dyads for five 35-trial blocks as was possible under the simultaneous procedure.

they respond in alternation. That is to say, dyads in the former condition but not the latter approach a state of cooperative interdependence. In about two thirds of dyads with the simultaneous procedure both members obtain more positive outcomes from their partners in the final block than in the first block, considerably more than would be expected by chance if the two responses remained equiprobable over blocks. Dyads under an alternation procedure show no sign of cooperative interdependence. The criterion of stable symmetrical reward was 35 successive trials on which each member gives his partner a positive outcome. Although eleven dyads meet the criterion under simultaneous conditions, only two do so with the alternation procedure. Indeed, under alternation conditions the number of dyads in which more than half of the total responses yield positive outcomes is actually *less* than would be expected if one assumed that each response had a 50 per cent chance of occurring, although not significantly less. The first prediction is thus reasonably well supported.

The second prediction was that dyads under simultaneous responding will move to symmetrical reward from symmetrical punishment. In this case the evidence is relatively sparse, but quite consistent with the hypothesis. In all dyads that achieved a stable state of cooperative interdependence under simultaneous responding, the two members delivered negative outcomes to one another on the exchange immediately preceding the beginning of the criterion run—which is not the same as demonstrating that all dyads experiencing symmetrical punishment immediately switch to symmetrical reward. This never occurred for any of the alternation dyads that reached the criterion, which were very few. The third prediction, that under simultaneous responding dyads whose initial ex-

change is one of symmetrical punishment will achieve cooperative interdependence more rapidly than those whose initial exchange is one of
asymmetrical reward, cannot be tested with the data available.

Reward Contingencies

The contingency between a member's behavior and his outcome described in the matrix of Table 13-1 is referred to in Thibaut and Kelley
(1959) as *mutual fate control.* This means that one member's behavior is
the necessary and sufficient condition for determining the other's outcome,
regardless of what the latter does, and vice versa. For cooperative interdependence to develop, it is only necessary for P and O to learn to make
R_R, and R_L, respectively, and to discontinue R_L and R_R, respectively. A
pure mutual-fate-control situation is not often seen in everyday life. More
often the person's outcomes are *not* independent of his own behavior. In
the "minimal social situation" this would be a case in which a member's
choice of "left" instead of "right" may be a necessary but not a sufficient
condition for his partner receiving a particular outcome. We now wish to
consider instances where the "sufficient condition" is established by the
potential recipient's own behavior. In order for P to receive a particular
outcome, he must respond in specific fashion. This type of contingency
has been called *behavior control* (Thibaut and Kelley, 1959). The reason
for this label is clear. For P to benefit, he must adjust his behavior to that
of O. Although O cannot completely determine P's outcomes, to the extent
that the latter desires to obtain positive outcomes, O can exercise considerable influence over P's behavior.

An interdependent situation therefore can be constructed where particular members experience different reward contingencies. For instance, P
may have fate control over O, while O may have behavior control over P.
This is presented in matrix form in Table 13-4, where O, regardless of his

TABLE 13-4.   *A Fate-Control–Behavior-Control Matrix*

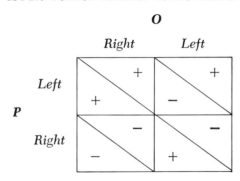

own response, receives a positive outcome whenever P goes "right" and a negative outcome whenever P goes "left," whereas P receives a positive outcome only if he goes "right" when O goes "right" or "left" when O goes "left." Applying the win–stay, lose–change rule, it can be shown that contrary to what was predicted and demonstrated in a mutual-fate-control situation, no tendency toward cooperative interdependence should appear under simultaneous responding in dyads with mixed (fate-control–behavior-control) reward contingencies. This analysis is represented in Table 13-5. Two initial states of asymmetrical reward are considered, one where the member subject to behavior control, P, receives a negative outcome while his partner, O, who is subject to fate control, receives a positive outcome, (b_1) in Table 13-5, and the other (b_2) where the asymmetry is opposite in direction.

Rabinowitz, Kelley, and Rosenblatt (1966) successfully replicated the Kelley et al. results, with members of mutual-fate-control groups under simultaneous responding delivering more and more positive outcomes to

TABLE 13-5. *Interaction in Fate-Control–Behavior-Control Dyads Under Conditions of Simultaneous Responding*

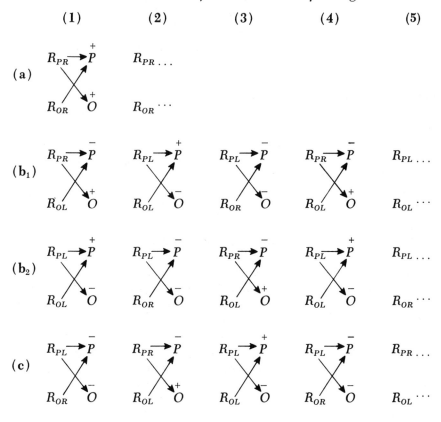

their partners over successive exchanges. At the same time, they observed that the frequency of positive outcomes in fate-control–behavior-control groups does not depart from a chance level throughout the experimental session. As predicted on the basis of the win–stay, lose–change rule, there is no tendency toward symmetrical reward under these conditions.

With ad lib responding (the subject may respond if and when he pleases), predictions regarding cooperative interdependence in mutual fate control as compared to fate-control–behavior-control groups are the reverse of those just described. But before demonstrating why this is so, it is necessary to consider a peculiar technical problem. Under ad lib conditions the subject has actually three alternatives: "right," "left," and "no response." As a consequence, the experimenter must be concerned with maintaining an adequate level of responding. To circumvent this problem, Rabinowitz et al. adopted a procedure whereby each response produced a "state" that persisted until the emission of the other response. Consider the situation described by the matrix in Table 13–4. According to this procedure, if *P* goes "left," a shock is delivered to *O* that persists until *P* switches to "right"; if, before *P* switches from "left" to "right," *O* goes "right," a shock is also delivered to *P* that persists until *either P* does decide to shift to "right," at which point shock is terminated for both *P* and *O*, or *O* goes "left," terminating shock for *P* but not for himself.

In a mutual-fate-control situation symmetrical reward occurs only if both members change their behavior at approximately the same time. This is easily seen by referring back to Table 13-2, where symmetrical punishment would not lead to symmetrical reward were either *P* or *O* to dally in changing his response. The experimenter, however, forces subjects to synchronize their behavior by instructing them to respond at a signal. When external control of response timing is absent, as in the ad lib procedure, it is more reasonable to assume such synchronism will rarely occur. A critical difference between ad lib responding and the other procedures, therefore, is the absence of any pacing signal. Yet the subject still must decide whether to continue a response or to switch. The cues to persist or to change can then only come from the outcomes or "states" that he experiences at the time. Thus a positive-to-negative change in "state," from no shock to shock, should elicit a relatively rapid shift in response; a negative-to-positive change, from shock to no shock, should persuade the subject to continue making the same response that seemed to produce the beneficial change in state. Note, however, that under ad lib conditions with mixed contingencies a member may alter his response and experience *no change in his outcome.* This is most likely to occur when the outcome changes from positive to negative and the person then quickly switches his response but continues to experience a negative outcome.

In the matrix shown in Table 13-4 when *O* goes "left" and *P* goes "right," the former is rewarded, thus persisting at "left" while the latter is punished and switches to "left." Now *O* is punished and *P* is rewarded. Because *O*'s outcome has changed from positive to negative, he quickly switches again, from "left" to "right," during which *P* continues "left." But upon switching *O* experiences no change in state; in spite of altering his behavior, his outcome remains negative. However, *P*, who had persisted, does experience a change in state, his outcome going from positive to negative. At this point the lack of synchronism under ad lib conditions should produce an interesting effect. Because *P* has undergone a distressing change in outcome compared to *O*, he will exhibit a relatively rapid shift in response. During this interval, *O* has experienced no change in state; his outcome has remained negative. Of course *O* would also eventually switch, but it is not likely to occur as rapidly as *P*'s switch. Therefore, while *O* dolefully contemplates going "left" (after all, even though it has been tried before, what recourse has he?), *P* has by then *already* gone "right," and they find themselves in a situation of symmetrical reward. This is shown in Table 13-6. It can also be seen that although cooperative interdependence will occur in an ad lib fate-control–behavior-control dyad regardless of its initial exchange, this is not true in an ad lib mutual-fate-control dyad. Unless their initial exchange is one of symmetrical reward, mutual fate control cannot possibly achieve cooperative interdependence, according to a win–stay, lose–change rule.

Rabinowitz, Kelley, and Rosenblatt (1966) clearly demonstrate that under ad lib responding there is a significantly greater likelihood of fate-control–behavior-control dyads achieving cooperative interdependence than mutual-fate-control dyads. For instance, only about one third of the mutual-fate-control dyads experienced symmetrical reward on every trial (a 30-second response interval initiated by a signal from the experimenter) versus about two thirds of the fate-control–behavior-control dyads. Only one mutual-fate-control dyad out of the 40, but 20 out of 30 fate-control–behavior-control dyads achieved symmetrical reward in the minimal number of trials specified by the theory. Moreover, the average time per trial required to achieve symmetrical reward in mutual-fate-control dyads was approximately 13 seconds, whereas in fate-control–behavior-control dyads it was only 8.6 seconds.

Merely by applying the law of effect or the win–stay, lose–change rule to very simple social interactions, we have seen that it is possible to generate a large number of unusual hypotheses. Most of them are not suggested by common sense, and some would even seem to violate widely shared intuitions about social behavior. At first glance few would expect that in order for two members to coordinate their actions so as to help each other, they must first hurt each other. Or that in a fairly confusing

TABLE 13-6.   *Dyadic Interaction Under Conditions of Ad Lib Responding*

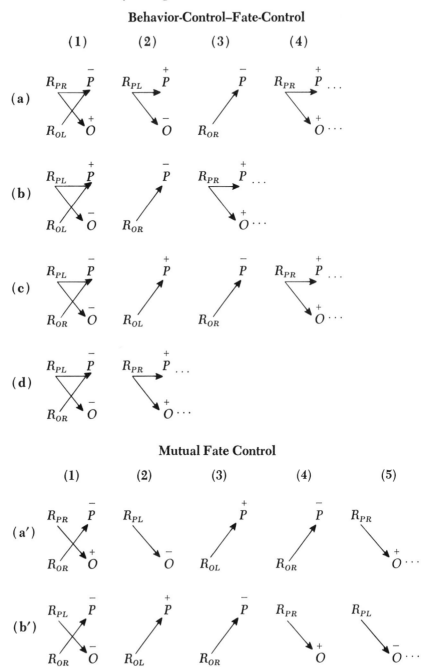

Behavior-Control–Fate-Control

Mutual Fate Control

situation when members may respond at will, in a helter-skelter fashion, a relatively simple set of reward contingencies such as mutual fate control precludes the development of cooperation, but a relatively complex set such as fate-control–behavior-control ensures it. Yet, in spite of the power of this analysis, there is an inevitable criticism—the extremely artificial nature of the "minimal social situation." Because subjects are unaware of their interdependence, how can we say that they are responding *to* the other or with the other *in mind?* And if this cannot be said, then how can the "minimal social situation" be considered "social," albeit "minimally social"? This point of view is cogent to many social psychologists.

Because of the strong cognitive thrust in current theory and research, the awareness of another, the fact that he is somehow present in the actor's cognitive representation of the situation, becomes an important criterion for defining the domain of social psychological events. Situations not satisfying the criterion are considered as nonsocial and beyond the pale. This point of view would carry little weight in other areas of psychology with a more behavioristic tradition, where such criticism of the "minimal social situation" might well be considered quaintly parochial. Nevertheless, it does raise an important substantive issue that must be dealt with if the findings established by means of this technique are to be generalized to a wider range of social settings. The issue, simply stated, is whether awareness of interdependence makes any significant difference.

Awareness of Interdependence

Sidowski (1957) compared the performance of subjects who were in part informed about their interdependence with those who were uninformed and found that such information had no effect on the development of cooperation. We therefore might consider awareness and understanding to be of little importance, and conclude that behavior in the "minimal social situation" is largely controlled by reward and punishment. Kelley, Thibaut, Radloff, and Mundy (1962), however, believed the method of informing used by Sidowski was not thorough enough, and they were inclined to attach considerable importance to the role of awareness. According to Kelley et al., if the experimenter had been more diligent, the frequency with which reciprocal reward was achieved would in fact be different in the "thoroughly" informed case from that in standard uninformed case. Their data on informed mutual-fate-control dyads under simultaneous responding or responding in alternation are shown in Table 13-7. The results are striking in comparison to those shown earlier (in Table 13-3) for uninformed dyads under identical response conditions.

TABLE 13-7.   *Comparison of Simultaneous and Alternation Procedure
with Thoroughly Informed Dyads* (From Kelley, Thibaut,
Radloff, and Mundy, 1962)

Condition	Number Achieving Cooperative Interdependence	Percentage of Positive Outcomes in Successive 35-Trial Blocks				
		Blocks				
		1	*2*	*3*	*4*	*5*
Simultaneous, Informed	13	73	80	89	93	96
Alternation, Informed	13	45	59	69	82*	—

* Because alternation procedure took longer, time did not permit running all dyads for five 35-trial blocks.

Over-all, the informed dyads are consistently superior to their uninformed counterparts in achieving cooperative interdependence.

How might this have come about? At the end of the experiment the subjects in the aware conditions answered a questionnaire about the way they sought to induce their partner to deliver positive and not deliver negative outcomes. Almost half of the subjects indicated they had believed their partner would not change his response when he received positive outcomes, but would when he received negative ones. This assumption is reported by at least one member in nearly all of dyads that achieve reciprocal reward, but rarely in the dyads that do not. Their "implicit theory of social behavior" thus postulated the law of effect or the win–stay, lose–change rule for their partner. Furthermore, by following the logic of his "implicit theory," the person is quite likely to improve his outcomes. The process would involve two steps.

First, the person attempts to discover the effects of his behavior on the partner by using the win–stay, lose–change assumption as a guiding hypothesis. In order to learn what control he has over his partner's outcomes, the individual must for the moment stabilize his own behavior. He has to persist in the same response over at least a few exchanges and observe whether his partner changes the outcome he previously delivered (indicating that the individual's behavior must have punished him) or whether his partner continues to provide the same outcome as before (indicating that the individual's behavior must have rewarded him). Then, upon learning the consequences of his behavior, he can respond so as to compel his partner to deliver positive outcomes, by rewarding them and punishing the delivery of negative outcomes. Thibaut and Kelley (1959) describe such a process as converting fate control to behavior control. Notice, however, that in order to do this, the subject first has to learn what effects he has on his partner, and this requires him at least temporarily to disregard maximizing his outcomes. He must violate the win–stay, lose–change rule while assuming (or rather hoping) that his partner does not, and view his outcomes in terms of the information they provide. Awareness of the situation allows the person to go beyond and in fact ignore the value of immediate or proximal outcomes to consider his distant, long-run prospects as a group member. Thus an informed person can do something that is not possible in an uninformed condition: he can devise a strategy based on what he knows about the way people make decisions and what he can learn about this particular decision maker, his partner.

Interpersonal Strategies and the Game Analogy

For a moment let us consider exchanges of acts in a simple social situation as analogous to an exchange of moves during a game. In the mathematical theory of games (Luce and Raiffa, 1957; Rapoport, 1960), "strategy" signifies a complete plan or set of decision rules detailing how a particular player will act vis-à-vis another under *all* possible conditions that might be encountered during the entire course of the game. The notion of "strategy" in experimental studies of group behavior in gamelike situations does not presume anything so heroic as the complete strategist. Although foresightful planning is an essential characteristic of the actor who thinks strategically, the decision rules he formulates are viewed by most researchers as tentative, docile, and limited in terms of the number of contingencies they encompass. The reason for this is perhaps obvious.

Except in extremely simple games such as tick-tack-toe with very sophisticated players, complete strategies are highly unlikely. In chess even Grand Masters report that they usually think only a few moves ahead (DeGroot, 1965). The reader may feel that games in which complete strategies can be readily constructed are played very infrequently because they are deadly dull. Perhaps, but if we consider games as paradigms of ordinary social interaction, it is doubtful that our everyday social life is replete with excitement and surprises. Deadly dull exchanges are frequent occurrences, and perhaps we should take some interest in their analogue, the deadly dull game. There are, however, more cogent arguments. In order to select a decision rule of his own, the player must first figure out what his partner's plans are. Because many courses of action may be possible, a person cannot be certain which one his partner will use. The attribution of a strategy to the latter will as a result be quite tentative and continually subject to revision in the light of the partner's actual behavior. For these reasons, the assumption of complete strategies is unrealistic.

Thus, to say that P uses a strategy simply will mean that in deciding on a course of action, he takes into account how O is likely to respond in the long run or at least in exchanges beyond the present ones.

We observed that when P and O are "thoroughly" aware that their outcomes depend on the other's behavior, but neither knows which act on his part will produce what outcome for his partner, cooperative interdependence is achieved even when the law of effect, strict version, says that this is not possible. The findings by Kelley et al. (1962) suggest that knowing their outcomes depend on the behavior of the other, each member first attempts to divine which of the responses available to him rewards and which punishes the other. To acquire this information he may make the same response over a few exchanges and observe whether his own outcome, and thus O's response, remains stable or varies. A strategy that aims to extract such information from variability in the behavior of another rests on the assumption that O will choose to act according to a win–stay, lose–change rule. It pays off if the decision rule attributed to O is correct. Once P discovers the contingency between his actions and O's outcomes, he formulates a second strategy aimed at inducing O to deliver positive outcomes. The knowledge P has acquired of the "matrix" presumably allows him to convert fate control over O to behavior control, again by attributing to O a strategy of win–stay, lose–change. Let us now consider what happens when members are completely aware of the contingencies between their joint behavior and the various outcomes available.

Awareness of Interpersonal Contingencies— The Matrix Fully Known

There is a group of dyadic decision tasks called mixed-motive games (Schelling, 1960) in which members possess complete prior knowledge of how their respective outcomes are contingent on one another's behavior. Moreover, they recognize that this knowledge is shared. Members are thus interacting within what Asch has described as a "mutually shared field" (Asch, 1952). The label *mixed-motive* is used to indicate that in such a game a player can choose either (1) to maximize the value of his own outcomes, (2) to maximize the value of the joint outcomes—that is, the average benefit obtained by all players—or (3) to maximize the difference between his own outcome and that of the others. The first strategy often implies competitive behavior. This, however, is not necessarily so but depends on the reward contingencies. Thus, in order for a member to benefit himself, he may have to behave in a way that also benefits others, that has little consequences for the outcome of others, or that does them definite harm, regardless of his *intentions* toward them. That a person wishes to reap great benefits for himself does not mean that he intends to harm or help others. The second strategy clearly implies cooperative behavior, and the third just as clearly implies competitive behavior, because both of these strategies contain as an essential element the intention to produce a certain effect on the other.

Many of these decision tasks have also been called non–zero-sum games.[1] In a *strictly* competitive or pure-conflict situation the participants have diametrically opposite goals and cannot cooperate. Gains for one person *necessitate* corresponding losses for his partner. Their outcomes therefore inevitably sum to zero. In the mixed-motive situation the value of the outcomes obtained by members need not sum to zero. This means that they may all benefit if an appropriate joint strategy is used. Cooperation as well as competition is thus possible. The most popular example of a non–zero-sum game is that which has been interpreted as the prisoner's dilemma (for our purposes the terms *mixed-motive, non–zero-sum,* and *prisoner's dilemma* will be interchangable). Luce and Raiffa (1957, p. 95) give the interpretation as follows:

Two suspects are taken into custody and separated. The district attorney is certain that they are guilty of a specific crime, but he does not have adequate evidence to convict them at a trial. He points out to each prisoner that each has two alternatives: to confess to the crime the police are sure they have done, or not to confess. If they both do not confess, then the District Attorney states he will book them on some very minor trumped-up charge such as petty larceny and illegal possession of a weapon, and they will both receive minor punishment; if they both confess they will be prosecuted, but he will recommend less than the most severe sentence; but if one confesses and the other does not, then the confessor will receive lenient treatment for turning State's evidence, whereas the latter will get "the book" slapped at him. In terms of years in a penitentiary, the strategic problem might reduce to:

		Prisoner #2	
		Not Confess	*Confess*
	Not Confess	1 year for #1 1 year for #2	10 years for #1 3 months for #2
Prisoner #1			
	Confess	3 months for #1 10 years for #2	8 years for #1 8 years for #2

[1] A few of experiments to be discussed (for example, Deutsch and Krauss, 1960; Thibaut and Fauchex, 1965; McClintock and McNeel, 1966; Deutsch, Epstein, Canavan, and Gumpert, 1967) involved mixed-motive decision tasks that deviate from some requirements of the strict non-zero–sum game (Rapoport and Orwant, 1962).

The prisoner's dilemma provides a situation that is analogous to that of more complex social settings involving a mixture of cooperation, competition, and conflict. Note also that the mixed-motive paradigm in general is similar to the "minimal social situation." The critical differences are, first, that subjects are fully informed and, second, that their responses have positive or negative consequences not only for their partner but also for themselves. The latter was not at all true for the commonly used mutual-fate-control variation of the "minimal social situation."

For illustrative purposes, Table 13-8 shows two different matrices that might be used in an experiment. The matrix in the lower part of the table is formally identical to the prisoner's dilemma. Cooperation ("left") is only profitable if both members engage in it; otherwise the cooperative partner suffers the maximal loss. Competition ("right") is highly profitable only if the other member cooperates. Then the competitive partner obtains the maximal profit. Joint competition is less profitable than joint

TABLE 13-8.   *Illustrative Mixed-Motive Matrices*

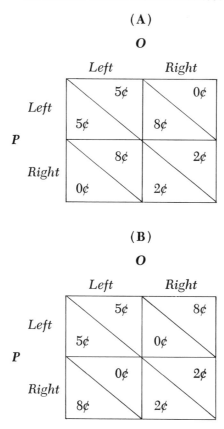

cooperation, but at the same time each member avoids the maximal loss, which would be incurred if he cooperated while his partner competed. The upper matrix is quite different from the prisoner's dilemma. If a member cooperates ("left"), he profits regardless of what his partner does.

Specifically, the experimental situation might be something like the following: In front of the subject are two buttons ("left" and "right") indicating his choices. The contingencies between responses and payoffs are carefully explained. Each person's outcome depends on their joint response. The amount in a cell below the diagonal represents P's outcome, and the amount above the diagonal represents O's outcome. Thus, were P to choose "left" in (A), he wins either 5¢ or 8¢ depending on which response O selects—5¢ when the O goes "left," and 8¢ when O goes "right." If P chooses "right," he obtains either 0¢ or 2¢. Regardless of his goal, whether to maximize his own outcomes, to maximize their joint outcomes, or to maximize the difference between their outcomes, P's best strategy is to choose "left." For identical reasons, O's best bet is also "left."

In matrix (B), if P goes "left" he gets 5¢ or nothing, but if he goes "right," he gets 8¢ or 2¢. The same contingencies hold for O. Clearly, for both individuals the average outcome or the expected value associated with "right" surpasses that associated with "left." Hence, for P and O the choice of the former is preferable to that of the latter. (This, of course, assumes that both desire to either maximize their own outcomes or the difference between their outcomes. If the two members wanted to maximize their joint outcomes, the best strategy would be to go "left.") When, however, *both* P and O select "right," each obtains only 2¢. Thus, if they are to enhance their profits, each must sacrifice the prospect of a larger but rather uncertain gain for the security of a smaller but more stable one.

In the literature on the mixed-motive situation, a choice that benefits the partner as well as the respondent but *may* preclude the outcome of maximum value to either is considered *cooperative*. A choice that benefits the respondent but disadvantages or does not benefit the other player is considered *competitive* or *noncooperative*. This response indicates a desire either to maximize one's own outcome or to maximize differences in outcome. The three strategies cannot be distinguished by the nature of the exchange in matrix (A), because all three are satisfied by the same response. On the basis of the participants' behavior in matrix (B), it is possible to separate a desire to maximize joint outcomes from the remaining two more selfish schemes. Later we shall see that a matrix can be constructed that permits us to distinguish between a maximization-of-differences strategy and that of maximizing joint or own outcomes.

To the chagrin of some, early research on mixed-motive interaction seldom observed cooperative responses on more than half of the exchanges. An examination of the data in Table 13-9 from Minas, Scodel,

TABLE 13-9. *Various Payoff Matrices and the Percentage of Coopera-*
tive Responses Associated with Each (From Minas, Scodel, Marlowe, & Rawson, 1960)

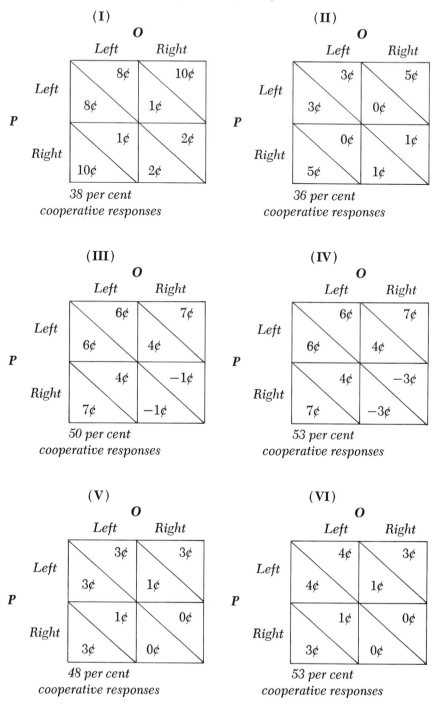

(I)

O

| | Left | Right |

Left 8¢ 10¢ 8¢ 1¢

P

Right 1¢ 2¢ 10¢ 2¢

38 per cent
cooperative responses

(II)

O

| | Left | Right |

Left 3¢ 5¢ 3¢ 0¢

P

Right 0¢ 1¢ 5¢ 1¢

36 per cent
cooperative responses

(III)

O

| | Left | Right |

Left 6¢ 7¢ 6¢ 4¢

P

Right 4¢ −1¢ 7¢ −1¢

50 per cent
cooperative responses

(IV)

O

| | Left | Right |

Left 6¢ 7¢ 6¢ 4¢

P

Right 4¢ −3¢ 7¢ −3¢

53 per cent
cooperative responses

(V)

O

| | Left | Right |

Left 3¢ 3¢ 3¢ 1¢

P

Right 1¢ 0¢ 3¢ 0¢

48 per cent
cooperative responses

(VI)

O

| | Left | Right |

Left 4¢ 3¢ 4¢ 1¢

P

Right 1¢ 0¢ 3¢ 0¢

53 per cent
cooperative responses

Marlowe, and Rawson (1960) demonstrates that cooperation is surprisingly rare *even when the largest individual benefit will be reaped by a cooperative choice* (see matrix VI). We are hardly surprised that cooperation occurs least frequently in matrix II, because the expected value (the player's average outcome over a large number of exchanges, assuming that his partner cooperates as often as he competes) for noncooperation is double that for cooperation,

$$\frac{5¢ + 1¢}{2} \quad \text{versus} \quad \frac{3¢ + 0¢}{2}$$

When the benefits of a cooperative, as opposed to a competitive, strategy are considerably increased, there is only a minor change in the frequency of cooperative choices (see matrix I). Even if the expected value of cooperation *exceeds* that of noncooperation, the incidence of the former is distinctly unimpressive (see matrices III to VI). Finally, observe in matrix VI that a cooperative choice will reap maximum benefit for the actor as well as for his partner. Yet, in spite of simultaneously satisfying selfish and generous impulses, a cooperative response occurs on only about half of the exchanges. It would seem, therefore, that under a variety of reward contingencies the desire to enhance differences between the person's own outcomes and those of his partner dominates.[2]

Conditions for Cooperative Interdependence in Mixed-Motive Exchanges

A stable form of interdependence such as cooperation depends on the ability of members to coordinate their actions. Given a "mutually shared field," the coordination of actions in turn assumes some explicit or implicit agreement among members as to which strategies are permissible under different circumstances. There are, however, two important sources of difficulty in arriving at such an agreement. First, the person may be unable to find any sensible pattern in his partner's choices. If P cannot decipher O's strategy, then one necessary condition for the coordination of behavior is not met, namely, being able to reliably anticipate the other's response. (We will soon return to this problem.)

[2] Keep in mind that these data are a rough indication of tendencies toward cooperative interdependence in the mixed-motive situation. They only signify instances in which *one* member responds cooperatively. An even more deplorable picture would be given if the findings could be presented in terms of the percentage of mutually cooperative exchanges, or what were called instances of symmetrical reward in the "minimal social situation." Cases of *both* members behaving cooperatively during the same exchange would no doubt be even rarer.

A second source of difficulty may stem from the payoff structure. The values in a matrix can be arranged so as to create conditions where one participant suspects that the other will not adhere to an agreed-upon joint strategy or where betrayal will produce great and unacceptable losses to the participant who remains loyal. In other words, the payoff matrix may be structured so that there is a strong temptation to defect (because the defector will reap large benefits if his partner adheres to a mutually beneficial strategy) or so that there is a strong fear of defection (because the person betrayed will incur large losses). Because each person recognizes the temptations and fears induced by a particular arrangement of rewards and punishments, another necessary condition for the coordination of behavior may not be met, namely, mutual trust. These concerns and their effects are illustrated in an experiment by Lave (1965) in which the matrices shown in Table 13-10 were used. In matrix (a) for both *P* or *O*, the choice of "left" (the cooperative response) could produce either a gain (3) or a very sizable loss (−100). The choice of "right" (the competitive response) could lead to a somewhat larger gain (4) or a very much smaller loss (−3). However, mutual cooperation produces gains for both players, whereas mutual competition produces losses for both. Yet the former is obviously dangerous, because if *P* defects while *O* cooperates, the latter suffers rather disastrous effects, and vice versa.

TABLE 13-10.   *Mixed-Motive Matrices Used by Lave* (1965)

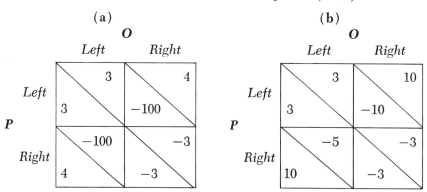

It is reasonable to think that in these circumstances, members will hesitate to bind themselves or to believe that others would bind themselves to mutual cooperation. Although both would benefit from such an agreement, the results of one partner betraying the other are frightening. Instead of taking the chance, members respond competitively and thereby minimize the likelihood of their maximum possible loss.[3] In matrix (b) the

---

[3] By going "right" both players guarantee themselves the best outcome they could hope to obtain under the worst circumstances the other could produce. This is called

choice of "left" could produce a gain (3) or a loss (−10), whereas the choice of "right" could produce a much larger gain (10) or a much smaller loss (−3). However, mutual cooperation would benefit both players and mutual competition would harm both. Nevertheless, defection is tempting. Because each member is aware of this, each may hesitate to trust his partner. As a result, they should hedge on committing themselves to mutual cooperation, the expected value of which is less than that for defection. Again, in the absence of trust a minimax solution is the likely consequence.

Lave (1965) compared the frequency of cooperative exchanges in matrix (a) with that in other matrices. The latter were identical to (a) except that the −100 payoffs were increased to −50 or to −5. Matrix (b) was compared with a matrix where the payoffs of 10 are reduced to 4. His findings suggest that such changes in the structure of rewards reduce the threat of defection by making it less disastrous or less tempting. This decreases the likelihood of a minimax strategy and leads to an increase in cooperative exchanges.

Cooperative behavior on the part of *P* is most likely when he *trusts O*, and mutual cooperation, or cooperative interdependence, is most probable when there is *mutual* trust. "Trust," until later amended, simply means that one member is confident that the other will follow a strategy of maximizing joint outcomes. When both individuals in the absence of direct communication trust their partner, an implicit agreement regarding strategy may be said to exist. We have noted that cooperation is unlikely without trust, because the partner is then in a position to take advantage. Thus, if *P* cooperates, he is vulnerable. When *O* is untrustworthy, *P* has no reason to believe that *O* will hesitate to exploit his vulnerability by competing. In order to protect himself, *P* must also compete—that is, employ a minimax solution if possible. But this only prevents the worst; it profits *P* little (unless, of course, he is mistaken and his partner is in fact trustworthy). Only by inducing *O* to become trustworthy and cooperative, will *P* begin to benefit from the exchange.

Cooperative Interdependence in the Panic Situation

Fear of defection and betrayal was recognized as a hindrance to cooperative interdependence long before the mixed-motive game became a popular experimental paradigm. Probably the best-known analysis is

---

a *minimax solution*. The minimax solution is possible only when the game contains a *saddle point*, which is a cell in the matrix simultaneously displaying the lowest value in a row and the highest value in a column, considering only the values beneath the diagonal. In Table 13-10, the lower-right cells in both matrices illustrate saddle points.

that by Mintz (1951) in his experimental work on panic in a collective escape situation. Previous to this research the explanation of panics followed the line set down by Le Bon (1895), which stressed the suggestion and contagion of emotion: When there is the perception of impending danger in a group, an uncoordinated and maladaptive scramble to escape will readily occur (compared to when the individual is alone) because emotional excitement spreads and augments itself rapidly among members; as a consequence common rational and moral constraints are dissolved in short order. Although it would be difficult to deny that emotionality, irrationality, and plain viciousness are frequently associated with panics, Mintz does suggest that they are neither necessary nor sufficient to cause such behavior. Rather, its roots can be found in the payoff matrix that characterizes the collective escape situation, or what Mintz called the reward structure. This analysis was later extended in a stimulating review of the literature on crowd behavior by Brown (1954; 1965).

In the collective-escape experiment, the point of egress permits only one member to get out at a time. Moreover, the total time available for the group to escape is quite limited. Hence the maximum number of members can succeed in their attempts to avoid danger if and only if their behavior is orderly. Specifically, the form of coordination required to "solve" the escape problem is a *queue*. Any other procedure produces a "traffic jam" at the exit, that consumes precious time and decreases the number of members who can escape. In the language of the mixed-motive game, a strategy of maximizing the joint (group) outcome would be reflected in the choice to queue up (cooperate), and a strategy of maximizing the differences between one's own outcome and that of other members would be evidenced by a refusal to queue up, but instead to rush ahead (compete).

A matrix constructed to represent the collective escape situation for a dyad would indicate the following: (1) if both P and O form a queue, then each has a good chance of escaping; (2) if P queues but O does not, then P is less likely to escape whereas O is almost certain of escape; (3) if P decides not to queue up but O does, then P is almost certain to escape whereas O is less likely to do so; and finally, (4) if both refuse to form a queue, then a jam occurs and escape is most unlikely for either. The state of affairs would not be very different if instead of the dyadic situation we were to consider P vis-à-vis many O's, except that in the case where many O's refuse to queue up while P does, they will initially jam the exit, delaying their escape. Nevertheless, the likelihood of their escaping will still be greater than that of P (depending on the time available and their facility at unjamming), who awaits his turn behind the pack. Mintz observed that this reward structure was probably inherently unstable. As soon as one or more members evidenced an intention to rush ahead, the interests of the others were threatened. A jam is then inevitable and the time available for an orderly egress will be reduced. Other members then have only one recourse, although it offers minimal protection, which is to join the rush and avoid being last, a position certain to be disastrous.

Research on games suggests in addition that panic (competition) is likely even without others *displaying* an intention to panic. A perusal of the "matrix" will inform P that the collective escape situation not only offers a strong temptation to defect, but it also provides some very unhappy consequences for those so betrayed. From the same research literature it is reasonable to expect that if P has no basis for trusting O, a cooperative strategy (queuing) is unlikely, and a competitive strategy (refusing to queue) will dominate. Therefore, what appears to be irrational and immoral, an uncoordinated and panic stricken attempt to flee, may well be based on a careful calculation of the reward contingencies in the absence of trust. An interesting series of experiments have been carried out by Kelley, Condry, Dahlke, and Hill (1965) which convincingly makes this point. They demonstrate that cooperative behavior in a collective escape situation does indeed depend on many of the same variables as cooperation in a mixed-motive game, in particular, the structure of the payoff matrix and the availability of cues to the intention of others.

Their general procedure was to inform subjects, who were in separate cubicles, that the group would have a limited time in which to avoid an impending danger, the administration of painful electric shocks. (Incidentally, the shocks for failure to escape were never delivered.) Each member could observe a panel of lights indicating who was in danger and who had escaped, themselves included. At the beginning of a trial their "danger" light came on and escape could then be attempted by turning a switch. When the attempt was successful, the escapee's light changed color. If, however, two or more members attempted to escape simultaneously (within a three-second interval), no one succeeded and they all remained in danger.[4] The first two experiments varied (1) the fearsomeness of the impending danger and (2) the group size. The most threatened groups were first physiologically aroused by an injection of epinepherine (disguised as a neutral solution) and then informed that a failure to escape would entail severe shocks.[5] Groups with intermediate threat received no injection but were promised severe shock for failure.

[4] It is worth noting that in the Mintz situation (1951) individuals were to remove their cones through the narrow neck of a bottle that was gradually filling with water. Only one cone at a time could pass the neck, and the object was to get the cone out dry. Clearly the Kelley et al. procedure (1965) allows for a more efficient experimental routine. But perhaps of greater importance, while containing the essential features of the "bottleneck," it also controls social-influence effects, which were probably rather strong in the Mintz experiment, by restricting contact among members without depriving them of essential information about each other's behavior.

[5] Research by Schachter (1964) suggests that such a combination, a nonspecific state of arousal plus information of an impending danger, might create intense fear.

The low-threat groups were merely to try to avoid failure but no mention of shock was made. We have already outlined the circumstances in a mixed-motive game under which the temptation to betray others as well as the concern over being betrayed increases. The implication for the collective-escape paradigm is that panics should increase (the coordination of escape attempts should decrease) as the consequences for failing to escape grow more frightening. This hypothesis receives considerable support in the Kelley et al. experiment, where about twice as many members escaped under low-threat conditions as did under high-threat conditions.[6]

The logical consequence of group size is clear cut: as the number of members confronted with impending danger increases, the likelihood that there will be some who panic and refuse to form a queue becomes greater. Thus the larger the number, the greater the probability of a jam. Furthermore, because members are aware that the time available is limited, as their number increases they are more likely to feel the interval is not enough for the whole group to escape. Hence early escape becomes imperative, and queuing will be rejected. Taken together, these factors make a convincing argument for the hypothesis that well-coordinated escape attempts decrease in frequency as a function of group size. Indeed, when Kelley et al. observed the proportion of successful escape attempts in groups of four, five, six, and seven members, they found that the proportion reliably decreases as size increases, especially if the amount of time the group has available is ambiguous.

A final implication of Kelley's analysis is particularly interesting because it will be shown later to hold for certain bargaining experiments, also by Kelley (1965) and his colleagues. In the collective-escape situation individuals who passively wait because they are confident of escaping probably have relatively little influence compared to those who are panic stricken. Panic more readily catches an observer's attention. Certainly a mad scramble for the exit is a less ambiguous cue to the person's intention than passive waiting, the latter implying either indecision, indifference, or confidence. If, however, the confident members could unambiguously communicate their intentions to indicate that they are sure there is ample time for escape and are willing to wait last in the queue until the others have exited, then coordination among members may well be enhanced and the number of successful escapes increased. In brief, the awareness that others intend to wait could reduce the person's fear of betrayal and

---

[6] The authors note that they use frequency of escape for their dependent measure throughout instead of a more direct measure of coordination, such as the number of jams at the exit, even when in certain analyses the latter might seem more appropriate. This presents no real problem because frequency of escape and measures of coordination are almost perfectly correlated.

enable him to resist being swept along at the first sign of panic, fancied or real.

Collective-escape experiments ordinarily allowed a member to communicate only one of two things, either that he was attempting to escape or that he was waiting. In their last experiment Kelley et al. provided an additional response by which a member could signal his confidence in being able to escape and his willingness to wait while the others got out. The procedure permitted the experimenter to control the light display for two cubicles that were supposed to contain group members but were, unknown to the others, empty. Thus usage of the "willing to wait" light by at least two members was assured. As predicted, the expression of such intentions had marked effects. More than twice as many successful escape attempts took place on the average when the "willing to wait" light was used than when it was unavailable. This difference was especially large if the members were "susceptible to influence"—that is, they were led to believe that others had much more experience at the escape task and they should trust them for guidance in deciding what to do.

Our analysis so far clearly suggests that participants in an exchange tend to attribute intentions to each other as a preliminary step in devising their own plan of action. Certainly the experiments on the collective escape situation demonstrate that information about each other's intentions allows individuals to coordinate their actions in terms of their most profitable joint strategy. Indeed it is not unreasonable to suppose that attributing an intention to one's partner is a *necessary* condition for the development of a strategy. If P's decision to act is going to be based in part on how he thinks O will react (we have already seen that this decision is also in part determined by the structure of rewards in the matrix), then P must be able to gauge O's response. In other words, P has to attribute an intention or strategy to O before he himself can act purposefully. Moreover, when the possible outcomes of a cooperative exchange are sufficiently attractive, P should be highly motivated to engage in attributive activity.

One basis for an attribution has already been discussed—the organization of rewards presented in the matrix. Here P takes the role of his partner, about whom he usually knows next to nothing, and attempts to experience vicariously the temptations and fears that the matrix might hold for the latter. This, however, would not provide very reliable information with which to predict O's response to particular behaviors by P. After all, the matrix is given by the experimenter and O did not create it with his own ends in mind; thus these ends should not be inferred from the matrix. Furthermore, although there may be temptations for O to defect, there usually are reasons why O should also cooperate. O's intention or strategy is thus decisive information. Of course, when P knows absolutely nothing about his partner, it may be wise for him to behave defensively, to compete and thereby reduce his vulnerability. As we have seen, many subjects act this way, especially in the early trials of a mixed-motive game. At the same time it was also pointed out that a minimax solution is unsatisfying unless the partner is clearly malevolent. There is another source of information, however, which can provide a more reliable basis for attributing intentions to O. This is O's behavior. The effect of O's behavior in establishing trust and thereby facilitating cooperation was forcefully demonstrated in the research on panic. The following chapter will examine the development of interdependence under conditions in which knowledge of the partner's intentions stems from the observation of his behavior in an exchange. Our analysis will attempt to describe how the person uses such information about the other in formulating and implementing his own strategy.

14

Interpersonal Strategies as Determinants of Behavioral Interdependence

A strategy is indicated when decisions take into account the probable reactions of others. We have seen that strategic considerations are sometimes unimportant. The "minimal social situation" demonstrated that if participants are unaware of engaging in an exchange, it is unnecessary to invoke the idea of strategic thinking on their part to account for the development of cooperative interdependence. The law of effect or win-stay, lose-change is sufficient. On the other hand, when there is complete awareness—that is, when the participants are fully informed of the matrix defining their exchange—strategies inevitably evolve. Over time their effects are usually powerful—usually, but not always. On occasion a strategy might be considered pointless. The person who has learned of his partner's intentions can trust him. In most cases he may also use this information for his own purposes—for example, as a means of behavior control when he could suffer harm as a result of the partner implementing his intentions. Such usage of the other's intentions, however, must assume that he is flexible. Thus, if P believes O wants to maximize his own gains, P can exert behavior control by punishing O's competitive choices and rewarding his cooperative ones. The result should be to convince O that an acceptable profit can only be obtained through cooperation. For O to persist in competing regardless of P's response would not be very sensible. Were he to do so, then P has only one recourse, to compete and thereby minimize his losses. Hence, P has some reason to be upset when he cannot influence his partner.

In fact it is likely that a partner who is believed not to be sensible, meaning that he is unamenable to influence, will disrupt strategic thinking even if his behavior is predictable as well as benign. We might imagine the person saying to himself, "What's the point of worrying how

this person is going to react when I can't do a thing about it anyway?".
There is evidence for such an effect in an interesting series of studies by
Abric, Faucheux, Moscovici, and Plon (1967). They informed their subjects that the partner in a prisoner's dilemma game was either another
person or a programmed machine. It is important to keep in mind that
throughout the game both partners played the identical strategy, one
which is extremely responsive to the behavior of the subject and ordinarily elicits a high level of cooperation. Nevertheless, the machine's behavior but not that of the person was perceived as rigid and impossible to
influence. As a consequence, the subject's own actions varied markedly
as a function of the partner, being much more defensive and inflexible
in exchanges with a machine than in those with a person. Consistent with
other studies using this strategy, cooperation increased over exchanges
with the person partner. With the machine it declined considerably so
that during the latter third of the session only about 15 per cent of choices
were cooperative. Merely the belief that the partner was not sensible
appears sufficient to prevent a profitable strategy from evolving. It is
interesting to consider how much stronger this effect would be if the
partner's insensibility also could be inferred from his behavior, which
was not at all possible in the study by Abric et al.

Communication and a Sensible Partner

To trust one's partner, or to protect oneself— the implications of this
dilemma for behavior in the standard mixed-motive situation are straightforward. They were demonstrated empirically in an experiment by
Deutsch (1960). He met the problem of manipulating trust head-on by
administering instructions that in essence requested subjects either to be
trusting and trustworthy or to be untrusting and untrustworthy. In the
cooperative condition P was told that O was solicitous about his welfare
and that he should be concerned about O's welfare. In the competitive
condition P was informed that the purpose of the game was to win as
much (imaginary) money for himself as possible while permitting O to
win as little as possible. In the individualistic condition, P learned that
the purpose of the game was to win as much money as possible for himself while ignoring O's outcomes. In the first of these conditions the instructions attempt to induce a strategy of maximizing joint outcomes; in
the second, a strategy of maximizing the difference between own and
other's outcome; and in the third, a strategy of maximizing own outcomes.
Only one exchange was permitted. Preceding this, some subjects were
allowed to communicate with each other by means of notes. When no

communication was permitted, the percentages of cooperative choices under cooperative, individualistic, and competitive instructions were 89.1, 35.0, and 12.5 per cent, respectively. When communication preceded the choice, the percentages under cooperative, individualistic, and competitive instructions were 96.9, 70.6, and 29.2 per cent. Clearly, instructions that establish mutual trust greatly enhance the probability of a cooperative exchange. This is especially striking because similar research on mixed-motive games that make no attempt to induce trust do not often observe more than about 40 per cent cooperative choices on *early* exchanges.

Deutsch's cooperative induction was also used by Komorita and Mechling (1967) to study the effects of the *betrayal of trust* on the speed of reconciliation. The latter was defined as the number of trials required to reach a criterion of five consecutive cooperative exchanges following betrayal. After the induction that served to create trust, each subject played with a programmed partner who was preinstructed to cooperate on either the first four or ten exchanges. At one of these points the "partner" double-crossed the subject for two consecutive trials and from there on continuously cooperated. Payoff matrices differed across conditions in order to vary the temptation to defect and the loss incurred when betrayed. Komorita and Mechling expected that the greater the loss incurred as a result of betrayal, the longer it would take to reconcile—that is, to re-establish cooperative interdependence. This was strongly supported by the results. With respect to temptation they thought that the number of trials required for reconciliation would be inversely related to the strength of temptation. The rationale for this is based on the differences in intentions that are likely to be attributed to another as a function of the justification for his action. Betrayal with weak justification, when the temptation to defect is negligible, would imply an intent to harm (rather than to maximize one's own gain), whereas betrayal with strong justification, when the temptation to defect is considerable, would suggest an intent to maximize one's own gain (rather than to harm the subject). Komorita and Mechling reasoned that reconciliation should be more difficult with another who defects when the temptation is minimal, because he presents himself as a person who intends us harm, competing even when there is only small gain in it for himself. Similarly, they expected that reconciliation would require more trials when betrayal occurs after ten cooperative choices than after only four, because there is less justification for defecting after a large number of mutually beneficial exchanges than after only a small number of such exchanges.

Although these hypotheses based on the attribution of intentions are quite interesting, the effects observed were opposite to what was predicted. Reconciliation occurred more rapidly if the temptation to defect was relatively weak and if the betrayal was preceded by a relatively large number of cooperative exchanges. When there has been little cooperation in the past, reconciliation is extraordinarily difficult to achieve if the potential losses incurred as a result of betrayal are large and the temptation to defect is strong. This suggests that in circumstances where the betrayed person has relatively little past experience with his partner, he is less concerned with the latter's *intention* to do him harm than with his *capacity* and *incentive* for doing so. In addition, perhaps the use of Deutsch's cooperative orientation was unwise. The subject might well have felt that the situation as presented in these instructions *prescribes* mutual trust. But his partner appears to reject this definition of the situation, because his behavior does not correspond to the demands made by the experimenter. These are probably confusing circumstances for the subject. As a result, the subject becomes uncertain about his partner's intentions and no longer considers them in working out a strategy. However, he is certain of his partner's capacity and incentive for malevolent action, and these then guide his choice of a course of action.

The effects of communication in Deutsch (1960) are of great interest. If in the competitive and individualistic conditions there is no basis for mutual trust and, in fact, there is good reason to distrust one's partner, then (as was noted earlier) the rational member should protect himself. Mutual competition is thus inevitable. As a result, although neither member is vulnerable and both escape their worst possible outcomes, neither benefits. What information was conveyed by the passage of a few notes that produced such a marked increase in cooperation, despite instructions that in the absence of communication occasion more competition? We would conjecture members inform one another (1) that in spite of a desire to outdo the other or merely to reap the greatest possible benefit, a noncooperative strategy, if implemented by both members, would clearly be mutually unprofitable and thus should be avoided, and (2) that if the temptation cannot be resisted, competitive behavior will be punished. In one way or another P and O agree, in effect, that they will be sensible and behave cooperatively; violation of the agreement, however, may be foreseen as legitimately inviting the competitive wrath of the momentarily disadvantaged partner. Communication seems to permit members to strike a bargain and to coordinate their responses without either entertaining a generous impulse. Cooperative behavior may occur, therefore, not on the basis of a desire to maximize joint outcomes, but because each wishes to avoid a situation where he derives no benefit from the exchange.

Research by Loomis (1959) strongly suggests that the kind of communication between participants in a mixed-motive exchange that is likely to be elicited by Deutsch's cooperative instructions does indeed facilitate mutual trust. Loomis had subjects send a graded series of messages to their partner during a prisoner's-dilemma game. In one condition the messages contained only what the sender expected his partner to do (Loomis calls this a "level I" communication): "I would like you to choose *A*". In another condition the message stated only the sender's intentions (level II): "I will choose *X*." In a third condition both expectation and intention were stated (level III). In a fourth condition retaliation as well as expectation and intention were transmitted (level IV): "I would like you to choose *A*. I will choose *X*. But if you do not choose as I want you to choose, then on the next trial I will choose *Y*." And in a fifth condition all the above was communicated, along with a promise of absolution if the partner repents—that is, the sender pledged to cooperate if the other ceases competing (level V). Finally, there was a control condition in which no explicit communication was permitted. Loomis found that as the "level" of communication increases, the amount of perceived trust increases. Trust here refers to the person's confidence in being able to anticipate his partner's choice. Moreover, the actual amount of cooperative behavior paralleled the increase in perceived trust. Thus less than half of the subjects who received level I messages (expectation) cooperated on the first exchange, whereas almost 100 per cent of those who received level IV messages (expectation, intention, and retaliation) cooperated. A similar increase in cooperative choices occurred for senders.

A member who has no opportunity to receive or send messages, often the case in prisoner's-dilemma studies, will still try to figure out his partner's strategy, and perhaps even to tacitly convey his own, if only to mislead. Inferences regarding what the other is about, under these conditions, depend completely on the member's recognizing some consistent pattern in the choices made by his partner. No clearly interpretable pattern is likely to *emerge* or be *noticed* after only a relatively small number of exchanges. Hence the researcher interested in how behavior is coordinated when explicit communication between members is proscribed has at least two methodological options. In the name of efficiency he can ensure that an interpretable sequence of choices occurs early in the game by "programming" one member to behave according to a prearranged strategy, or he can merely allow a very large number of plays with the hope that before too long an interpretable sequence will appear and be recognized. Both techniques have been employed in experiments.

Rapoport and Chammah (1965) observed 300 plays in mixed-motive situations by male, female, and mixed dyads. Male groups evidence *mutual cooperation* on 51 per cent of the 300 exchanges and on 57 per cent of the last 25. Comparable values for *mutual competition* were 32 per cent over-all and 13 per cent for the final 25 exchanges. This is a quite significant change in the use of cooperative versus competitive responses by dyads over trials. In addition, it is clear from Rapoport and Chammah's graphic presentation of the average percentages of cooperative responses by individual members for blocks of 15 exchanges that cooperative responses are much more frequent later in the game. On the first four blocks (trials 1–60) the individual member responds cooperatively, on the average, about 45 per cent of the time, not very different from what has been observed in past research. During the last four blocks (trials 241–300), he responds cooperatively about 70 per cent of the time, considerably more than what had been observed under similar matrix conditions where fewer exchanges were permitted.

From their data Rapoport and Chammah (1965) compute certain conditional probabilities of a cooperative response. These are important for our purposes because they suggest how members tacitly induce each other to coordinate their behavior and why these inducements are not immediately successful. They are as follows:

1. The probability that a participant (a or b) responds cooperatively (C), given that in the previous exchange both made a cooperative choice ($C'_a C'_b$):

$$x_a = P(C_a \mid C'_a C'_b)$$
$$x_b = P(C_b \mid C'_a C'_a)$$

2. The probability of a cooperative response by a member, given that on the previous exchange he had made a cooperative choice whereas the other had made a competitive choice or defected (D'):

$$y_a = P(C_a \mid C'_a D'_b)$$
$$y_b = P(C_b \mid D'_a C'_b)$$

3. The probability of a cooperative response by a member, given that on the previous exchange he had defected whereas his partner cooperated:

$$z_a = P(C_a \mid D'_a C'_b)$$
$$z_b = P(C_b \mid C'_a D'_b)$$

4. The probability of a cooperative response, given that on the previous exchange both had defected:

$$w_a = P(C_a \mid D'_a D'_b)$$
$$w_b = P(C_b \mid D'_a D'_b)$$

Because x means the likelihood of cooperating after one has cooperated and been rewarded, Rapoport and Chammah suggest that this reflects "a resistance to the temptation to defect" or *trustworthiness*. Similarly, y refers to the likelihood of a cooperative response after being punished for cooperation, interpretable as *martyrdom* or *forgiveness*. Next, z denotes the likelihood of a cooperative response after having defected and gotten away with it, suggesting *repentance*. Finally, w means the probability of changing to cooperation after being punished for competing. Because there is little point in such a change unless one believes that his partner will do likewise, the tendency w, according to Rapoport and Chammah, implies *trust*. An index is then constructed,

$$M_a = \frac{(1 - y_a)(1 - z_b)}{y_a z_b}$$

and analogously M_b by interchanging subscripts. The y_a and z_b in the denominator denote the likelihood of repeated cooperation by a unilateral cooperator (a member who cooperates regardless of what his partner does) and the likelihood of a change from competition to cooperation by a unilateral competitor (a member who competes regardless of what his partner does), respectively. This represents the probability that a series of unilateral cooperative responses (a "martyr run") ends by converting the competitor to cooperation. For similar reasons, the numerator represents the likelihood of a martyr run being ended by the "martyr" reverting to competition while the competitor continues to compete. Therefore, M is the ratio of martyr runs that fail to martyr runs that succeed.

The values of these conditional probabilities and the index for male dyads are given in Table 14-1. Clearly, members are trustworthy, being

TABLE 14-1.   *Conditional Probabilities and* M *(From Rapoport and Chammah, 1965)*

x	y	z	w	M
.85	.40	.38	.20	2.4

likely to resist temptation and to continue making a cooperative choice following a cooperative exchange (x). This is quite similar to the "minimal social situation" analysis where as soon as cooperative interdependence was established, members were predicted to lock in and persist on subsequent exchanges. Pressures to achieve and maintain cooperation are evidenced by the finding that defectors tend to be punished. That is to say, a member is unlikely to cooperate if, when he did so on the preceding exchange, he was taken advantage of by his partner, who made a competitive response (see y in Table 14-1). Thus a cooperative exchange may tend to be perpetuated by rewards or further cooperation, and com-

petitive disruptions tend to be controlled and minimized by punishment
or noncooperation on subsequent exchanges.

According to our ever-faithful win–stay, lose–change rule, cooperative
interdependence should develop rapidly. Obviously this is not true. The
reason is suggested by the magnitude of z, w, and M in Table 14-1. They
indicate the critical problems that have to be solved before choices can
be coordinated in a way that is mutually beneficial and that offers the
members sufficient protection against experiencing their worst possible
outcome. As these values suggest, in a mixed-motive situation with explicit
communication not possible, members are not highly likely to repent and
begin to cooperate following an unpunished and successful competitive
choice (z) or a punished and unsuccessful competitive choice (w). The
latter is a case in which cooperative behavior is presumably not restored
because trust is absent. Moreover, even if a cooperative member plays the
martyr role, making a sequence of unilateral cooperative responses in the
face of a persistent competitor, he appears to succeed in converting his
partner *less* often than he fails. The value of M, the ratio of martyr runs
that fail to martyr runs that succeed, indicates more than twice as many
failures as successes. Truly a moral swamp—members display little trust,
continuing to defect after being punished for defection; they do not often
repent, continuing to defect in the face of a cooperative partner; and they
are not frequently swayed from a competitive choice by a forgiving partner. In the light of these findings, we should not be astonished that cooperative interdependence is established only after a large number of
exchanges, even though members tend to persist in responding cooperatively once mutual cooperation occurs. Further support for the effect of
the number of exchanges is found in Lave (1965). He had dyads play a
mixed-motive game for either 100, 50, 25, or 15 trials. His findings suggest
that the percentage of cooperative choices varied directly with the number
of exchanges permitted.

The more efficient way of inducing cooperation would appear to be by
simulation, a situation where the partner is instructed to make a specific
pattern of choices by the experimenter. Simulated partners may be distinguished not only in terms of the responses they are "programmed" to
perform, but also in terms of their responsiveness to the behavior of the
real player. The latter distinction is important. If the partner's behavior is
contingent on the preceding response of the subject (for example, the
latter is consistently rewarded for cooperation and punished for competition) then there will be little difficulty interpreting the strategy of the
former. But to the extent that the simulated partner is unresponsive—
when, for instance, he is programmed to behave cooperatively or competitively, as well as shift from one to the other independent of what the
subject does—to that extent the real player will experience difficulty
understanding his partner's strategy. In other words, when the person is

trying to learn what the other has in mind, when he is attempting to discriminate which of several possible schemes is being employed, reliably contingent behavior by the partner may present a relatively easy problem in discrimination learning, whereas noncontingent behavior presents an extremely difficult problem. Coordination of behavior and thus cooperative interdependence would be difficult under the latter conditions, and a player is most likely to retreat to a minimax solution with an occasional sally of cooperation to see whether his partner has come to his senses. When two real players interact, we find that the person does tend to reward rather than exploit a cooperative partner and punish rather than forgive a competitive one (see the values for x, y, and w in Table 14-1). Thus one member's response is contingent on that of his partner; in most instances these contingencies are not highly reliable, however. As would be expected, dyads under these conditions require a large number of exchanges before a stable form of cooperation obtains.

In most early experiments involving simulation, the partner's response does *not* vary with the subject's choice. Minas, Scodel, Marlowe, and Rawson (1960) used a simulated partner who cooperated on 100 per cent of the exchanges, *regardless of the other player's choice*. Only about 38 per cent cooperative choices were elicited under these conditions. Different effects were produced by a somewhat more complex simulation (Bixenstine and Wilson, 1963) in which the partner over 200 trials either (1) cooperated on 95 per cent of the first 40 trials, on 50 per cent of the next 20, 5 per cent on the next 80, 50 per cent on the next 20, and 95 per cent on the final 40 trials, or (2) on the identical blocks the partner cooperated on 5, 50, 95, 50, and 5 per cent of the exchanges, respectively. In the first condition the partner begins at a high level of cooperation, declines to a low level, and then finally rises to a high level; in the second condition the pattern is inverted, beginning at a low level, going to a high level, and returning to a low level of cooperation. Again, the simulated partner is completely unresponsive to the subject's choices. The percentages of cooperative responses elicited by these two patterns are shown in Table 14-2.

TABLE 14-2. *Average Percentage of Cooperative Choices as a Function of the Simulated Partner's Cooperativeness* (Approximated from the data reported by Bixenstine and Wilson, 1963)

	Trials				
	1–40	*41–60*	*61–140*	*141–160*	*161–200*
Simulated Partner	95	50	5	50	95
Subject	28	20	14	32	42
Simulated Partner	5	50	95	50	5
Subject	20	34	45	36	20

Cooperative responses on the part of the subject occur with greater frequency as the partner becomes increasingly cooperative and with less frequency as the partner becomes more competitive. A purely rational analysis could account for the generally low level of cooperation by demonstrating that regardless of whether the partner persisted in responding cooperatively or competitively, the person will maximize the expected value of his own outcomes by making a competitive choice. The rational hypothesis that it is to P's advantage to compete, assumes, however, that his partner's welfare or ability to withhold cooperation and thus punish P is of little consequence. But this assumption is too simple to handle, among others, the Bixenstine and Wilson (1963) data. For instance, why should a partner who cooperates 95 per cent of the time early in the game be taken advantage of much more often than one who cooperates with equal frequency late in the game? Because no discussion or bargaining is permissible, each member must infer something about the other's strategy by observing or imagining a pattern in the other's choices, say, by comparing the conditions under which his partner makes a cooperative or a competitive choice on preceding exchanges. Rapoport and Chammah (1965) indicate that during most of the game, trust is weak and forgiveness rare, as well as ineffective. Members therefore should take some convincing before they are confident that their partner is sincerely following and will continue to follow an acceptable strategy—that he is not laying a trap. This means that repeated experience is necessary for mutual trust to be established. As Rapoport and Chammah's findings might suggest, many trials are required for members to reach a tacit *modus vivendi* to the effect that (1) both recognize an obligation to reciprocate cooperative choices and (2) if one of them attempts to exploit his partner, momentarily rendered vulnerable by virtue of his trust, he will be punished.

The development of an implicit contract, purely on the basis of the information conveyed in a patterning of choice is at best a subtle and unreliable process. It no doubt can be easily frustrated, for example, under the conditions of a simulation illustrated by the Bixenstine and Wilson experiment. If during the first 40 trials P examines the behavior of the simulated O, he should experience some befuddlement. He might suspect his partner was a simple-minded saint or a misanthropic ogre, depending on whether he was programmed to unilaterally cooperate or compete on 95 per cent of these exchanges. Furthermore, what will be most curious to P is that O continues to make the same choice regardless of what P does. However, if P is befuddled after the first 40 plays, what will be his state of mind following the sudden changes in the pattern of choices that occur subsequently? Again, these new patterns erupt and persist, unresponsive to P's behavior. Recall first that maximal cooperation occurred during the middle and latter part, rather than early in the series of exchanges. Second, at its peak cooperative behavior was observed no more than 50 per cent of the time. Now, this suggests that although *P* cannot fathom what *O* has in mind, after the first couple of trial blocks he is well aware that *O* is capable of punishing or rewarding him for some unknown reason. Therefore, *P* may be less prone to take advantage by defecting at this later point than at an earlier one where *O*'s willingness to both punish and reward was less evident. At the same time, although *P* may not experience utter confusion about his partner's decision rule, he is still likely to feel considerable uncertainty and distrust. Given these circumstances, the person may believe himself well advised to make competitive choices rather than cooperative ones. Again, a minimax solution is likely—the safest policy when the person cannot trust his partner to follow an acceptable or at least a sensibly consistent course of action. It is our conjecture that these two processes lead to a generally low level of cooperation that varies directly with the cooperativeness of the partner late but not early in the game.

Clearly a highly unusual aspect of the simulation procedures examined is that the partner's choice is in no way contingent on the behavior of the other player. Much "noise" is thereby created for the subject, the removal of which is likely to have interesting effects. Because it is reasonable to assume that the coordination of behavior, especially the development of cooperative interdependence, requires particular contingencies between choices and outcomes, if the simulated partner's choice was controlled by these contingencies, mutual cooperation or symmetric reward should be readily achieved. A partner who is completely reliable, in the sense that he consistently rewards a cooperative response and punishes a competitive response, is easily "read." The player is confident that he understands the other's behavior. If he accepts the contract implicit in his partner's strategy, both will behave so as to maximize their joint outcome. However, if the contract is rejected and the player persists in competing, then both are reduced to a minimax solution and competitive interdependence. Therefore, when a conditionally cooperative partner is simulated, cooperative interdependence should develop more rapidly than in simulations where no such contingencies obtain or in cases of two real players where such contingencies do exist but are much less reliable.

An experiment very close to this was performed by Sermat (1967). Sermat had a simulated partner initially make 30 consecutive cooperative or competitive responses. Then for 200 trials the partner, in a tit-for-tat fashion, reciprocated the other player's choice with a one-trial lag. Sermat observed a highly significant increase in cooperative exchanges regardless of the pretreatment. Furthermore, his dyads attain a *stable* and *high* level of cooperative responding after only 40 to 60 tit-for-tat exchanges. As will be recalled, in Bixenstine and Wilson (1963) the simulated choices were not contingent on the subjects' choices. This was also the case in Bixenstine, Potash, and Wilson (1963). Sermat's asymptotic values for cooperative responding appear to be approximately double those obtained in these earlier experiments. Although Rapoport and Chammah's (1965) findings strongly suggest the presence of conditional cooperation, cooperative and competitive choices were reciprocated with far less than perfect reliability. In their male dyads, cooperative behavior did not appear to reach asymptote until after 136 to 150 exchanges, at the earliest. The amount of cooperative responding evidenced on the last 25 of 300 exchanges appears about what Sermat obtained in much less than half this number.

Effects similar to that of Sermat were obtained by Solomon (1960) and by Deutsch, Epstein, Canavan, and Gumpert (1967). In the former experiment comparisons were made of the subjects' reactions to a simulated partner who played either a conditionally cooperative, an unconditionally cooperative, or an unconditionally competitive strategy. Solomon demonstrated that subjects not only respond most cooperatively to the strategy of conditional cooperation but also liked this partner best. They exploited the partner using the strategy of unconditional cooperation and found his behavior puzzling. The third strategy of unconditional competition elicited competition, and the partner who followed this strategy was least liked. Deutsch et al. simulated several strategies, two of which are relevant here. The turn-the-other-cheek ploy is very similar to unconditional cooperation. Their nonpunitive strategy resembles conditional cooperation in that both stress reciprocation, with the exception that in the former the partner defends himself against defection but does not punish it. Defending oneself without at the same time punishing or competing is not possible in the strict version of the prisoner's dilemma. But Deutsch and his colleagues used a modified mixed-motive game where defense and punishment are independent.

The Deutsch et al. results clearly indicate that turning the other cheek elicits competition—that is, exploitation of the unilaterally cooperative partner—whereas nonpunitiveness induces cooperation. The *difference* in outcomes obtained by members versus a partner playing a nonpunitive strategy was minimal over 60 exchanges; when a turn-the-other-cheek strategy was simulated, the difference was quite large. Differences in outcome of course indicate that one player is competing while the other cooperates—that is, the former is taking advantage of the latter. Moreover, we have emphasized the importance of the partner evidencing an interpretable strategy as a necessary condition for the coordination of action and thus the achievement of cooperation. It was conjectured that the inability to coordinate is frustrating, and when this is due to the "irrational" behavior of his partner, the player is likely to experience befuddlement and chagrin. Support for this is found in Solomon's study. The partners who played the least "sensible" strategies (unconditional competition and unconditional cooperation) were objects of puzzlement and dislike, compared to the readily interpretable partner (conditional cooperation). Similarly, in Deutsch et al. the partner who continuously turned the other cheek was rated not only as more unstable but, surprisingly, as more unfair and more uncooperative than one who behaved nonpunitively.

Significant Payoffs and Invidious Feedback— The Beginning of a Realpolitik

One of the more widely used variations of the mixed-motive game was devised by Deutsch and Krauss (1960), who asked participants to play the role of trucking-company owners in their experiment. By means of an electronic control panel and a road map, each person maneuvered a truck along a route to a destination. The trucks started simultaneously, but if sent along the shorter main route would meet head-on in a one-lane section. Each could also have taken a much longer and time-consuming alternative route. This, however, was inadvisable because the payoff per "shipment" was inversely related to the time used to reach the destination. The participants, without benefit of communication, had to learn to *take turns* in using the main route, or else costly stand-offs on the one-lane section and expensive use of the alternative route would result. The experimenter introduced the possibility of threatening one's partner by providing one or both participants with a barrier that could be used to block the one-lane route, thus preventing the partner from reaching his destination. The findings suggested that the opportunity to threaten the partner with blockade increased competitiveness. Threat seemed not only to provoke counterthreat but also to stiffen resistance to giving way under duress. Thus the effects of threat were attributed by Deutsch and Krauss to the demeaning significance of surrender and compliance, such as loss of face and decreased self-esteem. A tacit agreement regarding use of the main route, a necessity if both participants are to benefit, is difficult to achieve in these circumstances, and as a result payoffs are inferior. If barriers were absent and neither person possessed the means of threatening his partner, the mean joint winnings per dyad was +$2.03. Under bilateral threat, where both possessed barriers, the comparable value was −$8.75. The money, however, was strictly imaginary, and the subjects were informed of this at the beginning.

Anyone with some experience at a game such as poker might look down his nose at the average mixed-motive situation, primarily because the payoffs are often either trivial or explicitly unreal (for example, the use of "imaginary money" by Deutsch and Krauss). Masterful play in poker will occur only when the participants respect the value of the stakes. A game with insignificant payoffs thus may degenerate into a kind of interaction in which the participants are not so much concerned with skillful and courageous play as with the quick and ignominious undoing of their opponents. When the participants respect each other's power—that is, when the rewards and punishments they can administer are perceived as significant—then the strategies employed may be different from those used when such respect is lacking. In one case we have a realpolitik where decisions are made according to a careful calculation of relative power; in the other case we do not.

The "poker" line of reasoning is, of course, just speculation. Kelley (1965) and his colleagues (Borah, 1963; Gallo, 1966; Shomer, Davis and Kelley, 1966), however, have systematically examined the prevalence of competition in the context of Deutsch's trucking game, and their conclusions indicate this speculation to be not far off the mark. They point to several aspects of the experimental situation that inadvertently might have instigated competitiveness as well as inhibited cooperation in the Deutsch and Krauss study. To begin with, because there were no real payoffs, a maximizing difference strategy could have been viewed as more "fun" than either maximizing own or maximizing joint outcomes. The latter two strategies both imply cooperative behavior because each individual can benefit only if they coordinate their movements along the common path. The inevitable form of coordination is that of taking turns. Certainly a person can foresee that he will gain little in terms of imaginary money by following a maximizing-differences strategy. Yet it is not unreasonable to believe the attractiveness of such payoffs is less or no greater than that of undoing his partner. In other words, trivial or hypothetical profits may minimize the real cost of competitiveness, and under these conditions the losses incurred by using the gates and taking the longer route become more tolerable. Furthermore, instructions and performance feedback make the subject quite aware of the gates and of his partner's as well as his own outcome. Such knowledge could easily stimulate playful exploration of the gates to readjust the relationship between their outcomes, particularly when the absolute amount gained has no real value.

Although the gates were considered a threat by Deutsch and Krauss, Kelley points out that this interpretation is somewhat misleading. To say that a person feels threatened by another ordinarily means that he thinks the other *intends* to inflict harm. The gates, however, convey only the possibility, not the intention. There is in fact no opportunity to signal the intention of using the gates—that is, to threaten. One virtue of a threat is that it may be effective without being implemented. In the prisoner's dilemma, if the player could indicate his intention to compete when betrayed, he might induce his partner to forego defecting without actually having to engage in competition. Similarly, if there were an opportunity in the trucking problem to signal an intention to use the gates, their actual usage might decrease, and the effect of bilateral threat would then be considerably different from that observed by Deutsch and Krauss.

Finally, there is the possibility that the long alternative paths are used to avoid interaction along the short common path. In fact, such usage would be eminently rational when a maximizing differences strategy dominates. Thus, if the person is attempting to undo his opponent and has little concern about the absolute value of his own outcome, it would be most efficient for him to entice the other into entering the short path. Then by closing the gate, he forces the other to wait or turn back, while he takes the long path, avoiding the gate. Of course, such tactics cannot produce a gain in absolute terms because the longer path is necessarily unprofitable, but the other player will require much more time and thus experience much larger losses. Using the alternative path to maximize differences makes coordination along the common path unnecessary. Indeed, this strategy could not be satisfied by taking turns. Suppose, however, the alternative paths were not available. The participants would then be forced to interact on the common path, and coordination might occur regardless of their competitiveness or capacity to threaten one another.[1]

The issues raised in this analysis have stimulated a fair amount of research. On the whole, Kelley's qualification of the conditions under which bilateral threat induces competitiveness is well supported. Gallo (1966) compared the effects of bilateral threat when competitiveness incurred no real costs and when it involved appreciable costs. His design replicated the Deutsch and Krauss bilateral-threat situation, except that in one condition of his experiment the maximum payoff was real and sizable, whereas in another it was of equal size but imaginary. The mean joint outcome obtained by dyads with real money was +$9.92; with imaginary money, −$38.80. In addition, it was shown that in dyads dealing with real and significant outcomes, members take considerably less advantage of the opportunity to threaten their partner than in dyads working with imaginary outcomes, and that a mutually beneficial strategy was tacitly achieved with greater speed per "shipment" under "real" than under "imaginary" conditions.

That the alternative paths may be used to avoid a confrontation was first suggested by the data in an experiment by Borah (1963). He observed that the lower profits under bilateral threat did not result from longer

---

[1] The possibility of avoiding unpleasant confrontations with a partner creates obvious problems for developing and maintaining interdependence; for example, the first untoward incident may induce the participants to cease interacting or dissolve the relationship. This issue will be considered later in a discussion of Thibaut and Faucheux's research (1965) concerning normative contraints on disloyalty.

face-offs on the common path. They therefore must be due to more frequent use of the alternative paths. Shomer, Davis, and Kelley (1966) examined this issue directly by removing the alternative paths. Imaginary money served as payoffs. They successfully replicated Deutsch and Krauss by demonstrating that if alternative paths are available, dyads with no capability of threat (no gates) achieve significantly better outcomes than those with bilateral threat capabilities (both players having gates). A striking finding, however, involved the performance of bilateral-threat dyads when the alternative paths were not available. On early trials their profits were similar to those of bilateral-threat dyads with alternative paths. However, their outcomes improved so rapidly that by the final third of the trials the amount of money they were winning was no different from that won by dyads without threat capabilities. Thus, although the gates did initially inhibit mutually beneficial coordination, if the participants were forced into a confrontation, they learned to cooperate despite their capacity to harm each other. Shomer, Davis, and Kelley suggest a parallel between their own results and those of Gallo (1966). The latter found that bilateral threat produced only a temporary decrement in joint outcomes if there was a strong incentive to cooperate. Thus interaction was maintained and the problem of effective coordination was worked out because handsome payoffs would result therefrom. In Shomer et al., a similar effect was obtained, but instead of a large monetary incentive, interaction was maintained by removing those behavioral alternatives that in past work permitted the individuals to avoid confronting each other.

A second experiment (Shomer, Davis, and Kelley, 1966) considered the objections raised earlier about the Deutsch and Krauss operations for inducing threat. It compared the effects of the Deutsch and Krauss procedure with another in which the person could express the intention to act independently of carrying out the act. Using a slightly modified version of the trucking game with no alternative paths, they observed the value of the joint outcome when the person could signal that he is going to punish his partner before actually administering the punishment. The punishment consisted of levying a fine instead of closing the gates. The expression of an intention to fine in no way committed the person to carrying out the intention. Their data show that the capability of punishing by itself has different consequences for cooperative interdependence than this capability plus the opportunity to signal the intention to punish. Dyads with independent threat and fine responses do no worse, and in fact tend to do somewhat better in respect to profits, than those with neither, the latter being the counterpart of the no-threat condition in Deutsch and Krauss. Hence, the disruptive effect of bilateral threat on cooperation, originally observed by Deutsch and Krauss (1960), is more than overcome when the participants can warn each other that they intend to use their threat. Similar effects have been obtained by Geiwitz (1967).

The fact that expressing an intention to harm facilitates cooperation may mean the expression is more informative than it is frightening. Thus in Shomer, Davis, and Kelley members of dyads who understood the threat as a sign to take turns obtained considerably higher joint profits than those who did not. The reason for this is that those who perceive the threat as a signal use the opportunity primarily to indicate to their partner the order of movement on the common path rather than to threaten him. This is suggested by the fact that the threat was announced by these individuals almost always before they entered onto the common path, presumably as an indication it was their turn, and the threat itself was rarely implemented. For the trucking game, as in other mixed-motive interactions, the communication of an intention to punish conveys not only its possibility, but more important, an understanding of how it can be avoided. This understanding is critical for establishing cooperative interdependence. It is not surprising, therefore, that an understanding of what is acceptable and the willingness to abide by it are more readily achieved by a signal to coordinate that incidentally happens also to be a threat of punishment than by a punishing act that incidentally also happens to be a signal to coordinate.

It seems that even if there is no attempt to induce mutual trust and a maximizing-differences strategy is attractive, competitiveness may be reduced when it is especially costly, when coordination is difficult to avoid and requires cooperation between players, and when the intention to punish noncooperation can be signaled. Let us consider one final condition inhibiting competition.

If the person is to derive satisfaction from a strategy of maximizing differences between his own and his partner's outcomes, he must be kept continuously informed of both events. When knowledge of results is controlled so that the person learns only his own gains and losses and not those of his partner, the incentive to compete may be considerably reduced. That this might be so was first noted by Estes (1962). The effects due to feedback of outcomes have been most thoroughly examined by McClintock and McNeel (1966) with outcomes of high and low value. In addition, their research involved an interesting and significant modification of the strict prisoner's-dilemma matrix. Before getting to the results we will briefly digress to give the reason for this modification. It is instructive in that it suggests how an experimental procedure may create difficulties for the interpretation of the behavior it was designed to investigate and how the difficulties may be remedied.

In the standard prisoner's-dilemma matrix at least three strategies are possible: maximizing joint gain, maximizing own gain, and maximizing the difference between own and other's gain. If maximization of joint outcomes is the dominant strategy, a cooperative choice should be made; if maximization of differences dominates, a competitive choice should occur; if, however, a strategy of maximizing one's own gain dominates, *either* a cooperative or competitive choice may be made. In the last case, with mutual distrust participants should seek to obtain maximal profit for themselves by minimizing their maximum loss—that is, by emitting a competitive response. But when mutual trust exists, a strategy of pure self-interest (one that is totally unconcerned with the partner's welfare) requires that both participants select individual courses of action that, taken together, represent an efficient and profitable joint strategy in the long run (Harsanyi, 1961). Thus, given mutual trust, the rational pursuit of self-interest should result in a tacit agreement to cooperate. In most recent research on the prisoner's dilemma, players are uncertain whether to trust their partner. The decision whether to protect themselves (the minimax solution) or to maximize their own gain by establishing an efficient joint strategy is for players, no doubt, the central drama of a mixed-motive game. In the midst of the pathos, however, a mundane but vexing problem arises for the researcher—how is he to determine the strategic basis of choices in an exchange? Namely, he cannot be sure whether a cooperative response reflects a desire to maximize own gain by a rational pursuit of long-term self-interest or a wish to maximize joint gain. Similarly, a competitive response could equally well represent an effort to maximize own gain by minimizing possible losses or to maximize differences.

McClintock and McNeel (1966) were among the first to appreciate this confounding of strategies and to attempt to isolate the motive underlying a choice by modifying the usual prisoner's-dilemma matrix, forming what they called a maximizing-difference game, shown in Table 14-3. The matrix is constructed so that in comparison with a standard prisoner's-

TABLE 14-3.   *The Maximizing Difference Matrix* (From McClintock and McNeel, 1966)

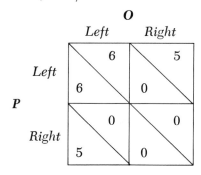

dilemma matrix only one of the three strategies, maximization of differences, can account for a competitive response, going "right." Neither a strategy of maximizing own gain nor one of maximizing joint gain can be satisfied by this choice. The basis for going "left," a cooperative choice, remains confounded, however. Either maximizing own gain or maximizing joint gain can be achieved by choosing "left." Dyads made up of students from the University of Louvain, Belgium, were run for one hundred exchanges in the maximizing difference matrix under high (H) and low (L) payoff. Two feedback conditions were used. In one the person learns his partner's cumulative score as well as his own (double feedback, D); in the other he learns only his own cumulative score and *not* his partner's (single feedback, S). Figure 14-1 presents the proportion of competitive responses by ten-trial blocks. The effects are unambiguous. Competitiveness, now clearly a strategy of maximizing differences between own and partner's outcomes, is greatest over time under feedback of own and partner's scores with the possibility of low gains or losses (DL); cooperativeness is greatest under feedback of own score only with the possibility of high gains or losses (SH). Clearly the higher the risks involved and the less invidious information available, the greater the cooperation.

In terms of stable forms of interdependence, Rapoport and Chammah (1965) find *mutual* cooperation and *mutual* competition are least resistant to disruption, as compared to *asymmetrical* exchanges. McClintock and McNeel report similar lock-ins. The kind of lock-in—that is, the form of

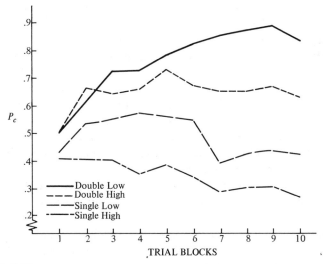

FIGURE 14-1.

Proportion of Competitive Responses as a Function of Payoff Level and Feedback (From McClintock and McNeel, 1966)

interdependence—depended on feedback and reward conditions, however. Evidence of the relative stability of cooperative versus competitive interdependence can be obtained from McClintock and McNeel's estimates of the probability of transition between stable and unstable exchanges. For instance, if a DL dyad at time t experiences mutual cooperation, the probability of a mutually cooperative exchange at $t + 1$ is .239; however, if the DL dyad is mutually competitive at t, the probability of mutual competition at $t + 1$ is .748. The contrast with SH dyads is sharp. If they are mutually cooperative at t, the probability of mutual cooperation at $t + 1$ is .821, whereas if mutual competition obtains at t, the probability of it continuing at $t + 1$ is .443.

Protection by Contract—The End of a Realpolitik

Ordinarily in the mixed-motive game either member is heavily and equally dependent on his partner for positive outcomes. Furthermore, alternative relationships outside the dyad are irrelevant. If the partners can tacitly agree to a mutually beneficial joint strategy, there is a strong tendency to abide by the agreement, to lock in (Rapoport and Chammah, 1965). In a sense, each player has nowhere else to turn; no other relationship is available outside of that with the partner. What is more, this relationship will be unprofitable unless there is some mutually acceptable arrangement covering their respective behavior. As a consequence, there is little need for *policing* adherence to the agreement once it is established or for establishing *norms* that sanction the punishment of defection. In addition, no problem arises in the sharing of outcomes, because this is specified by the rules of the matrix and deviations are inadmissible. Thus the need for norms controlling the distribution of outcomes is also minimal. Thibaut and Faucheux (1965), however, point out two important sources of difficulty (or "stresses") for the development of stable interdependencies in variations of a mixed-motive game where the usual restrictions on the division of profits and on the availability of competing relationships are modified. These problems, which Thibaut and Faucheux label *conflict of interest* and *improved alternatives outside the group,* are unlikely to be resolved under tacit conditions—that is, without thorough and explicit bargaining.

Certain cells in a matrix of outcomes may involve a negative correlation between the members' outcomes, so that when P benefits most, O benefits least. Thus one member wishes to avoid an exchange that will place his payoff in these cells, and the other is attracted by such an exchange. This state of affairs denotes a conflict of interest between members and is often approximated in the upper-right or lower-left cells of the usual prisoner's-dilemma matrix. If some members are potentially more powerful than others, then as conflict of interest increases, as the gains and losses involved grow, the former will be tempted to use this power to maximize their profits and, by the nature of the situation, to minimize those of their partners. This tendency is similar to the temptation to defect discussed earlier, where defection was attractive because of the way rewards were structured. But there is an important difference. Thibaut and Faucheux wish to consider the case in which defection is attractive not only by virtue of the contingencies specified in the matrix. In addition, one member is more powerful in the sense that he controls the distribution of the outcomes specified in certain cells of the matrix. Only if the distribution is "fair" can the less powerful individual reap a handsome profit from the exchange. This means that the more powerful member may *choose* to betray his partner after the latter has already committed himself to a course of action. Thus, other things being equal, as long as he maintains the relationship with his partner, the weaker member will be continually threatened by a reduction in his share of the profits, unless he can effectively invoke the norms of equity and fair dealing.

The conflict-of-interest situation therefore constitutes an enticement for the more powerful member and a harassment for the weaker. In certain circumstances, however, the weaker can protect himself. This occurs when there are rewards available outside the group that become sufficiently attractive to compete with those obtainable inside. Improved alternatives outside the group are of critical importance to the weaker members whenever there is a strong conflict of interest. If the more powerful member is or can be made aware of attractive outside opportunities that beckon to his partner, he must become concerned with the latter's possible disloyalty. The chance for the weaker member to profit from external activities creates a threat to the more powerful, who wishes to preserve a relationship where he possesses the advantage. As Thibaut and Faucheux note, in order to maintain the group the more powerful member must appeal to norms of loyalty and team spirit. However, even if members were able to request that common standards of either fair sharing or loyalty be respected, they have no assurance that such a request will be perceived as legitimate by the other. For the more powerful member cannot be certain that his weaker partner will view with great favor a normative constraint on disloyalty without some compensation for accepting this constraint. Analogously, the weaker member cannot entertain realistic hopes of his powerful partner accepting normative restrictions on gratification unless the latter is compensated for holding back on the use of his power.

The critical problem for Thibaut and Faucheux was how mutual compensation can be arranged. One particular solution suggested itself to them. If there is a strong conflict of interests and external alternatives are highly attractive, the more powerful member worries that his partner will decide to break off the relationship, depriving him of its sizeable benefits. The weaker frets that the other will choose to grossly deprive him of his due by taking full advantage of his greater power. They each, therefore, appeal to standards that proscribe such threatening behaviors. When both agree to each other's appeals, each is compensated by a reduction in threat. The powerful member's acceptance of rules governing equity is compensated by the weaker member's acceptance of rules governing loyalty. Note that only if both types of stresses are strong will both members be motivated to draw up such a contract, and only in these circumstances will the weaker partner possess countervailing power to bargain effectively with his more powerful co-worker.

In an experiment designed to test these propositions, 100 fourteen-year-old suburban Parisians were paired in a bargaining situation. The experimental task was a mixed-motive game not very different in most respects from the ones considered before, except for the following:

1. In each exchange the member could choose from three rather than the usual two alternatives. *P* could play either of the two rows (*O*, the columns) of the matrix, *or* an external alternative. If both play the latter, both obtain the value specified. If, however, only one player chooses the external alternative, he received its value whereas the other, who remained within the matrix, gets nothing.

2. *P* was instructed by the experimenter that he could, in certain cells, take any number of points for himself, from the smaller of the two values specified in the cell up to the larger, leaving what remains for *O*. Thus, if their exchange lands them in these cells, the actual outcome obtained by each player depends on the extent to which *P* exercises his power.

The matrix used in the high- and low–conflict-of-interest conditions are given in Table 14-4. Within each of these conditions, half of the dyads had a high-attraction external alternative, and half a low-attraction external alternative. In the first matrix *P*, the more powerful, could then take up to 88 of the 98 points for himself either when he goes "right" and *O* goes "left" or when *O* goes "right" and he goes "left." In the second matrix, under similar response conditions, *P* may only take for himself, at the most, slightly more than half of the joint outcomes, 53 out of 98 points. Because the possible difference in outcomes to *P* and *O* are greater for the first than for the second matrix, the former, by definition, is an instance of high conflict of interest and the latter, low conflict of interest. Before beginning the experimental game, the members of a dyad were permitted to discuss and arrive at some tentative agreement about joint strategy. Following

TABLE 14-4.   *Matrices from Thibaut and Faucheux* (1965)

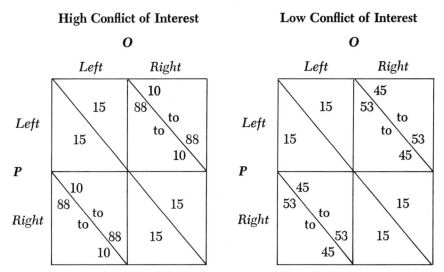

High Conflict of Interest   **Low Conflict of Interest**

High External Alternative = 35
Low External Alternative = 10

several exchanges, members again discussed the game and decided whether or not they wished to establish a contract and what form this contract should take. That is, should it prohibit the choice of external alternatives (*EA* rules), should it specify how points are to be distributed equitably between partners (*D* rules), or both; and finally, what sanctions —indemnities or fines—should be applied in the case of contract violations?

First, consider how power was used in affecting individual outcomes during the several exchanges that preceded any firm contractual arrangements. The mean *differences* between the more powerful member, *P*, and his partner, *O*, in the points each received *before* the contract period were as expected: under high conflict of interest with a highly attractive external alternative, 61.62, and with a less attractive external alternative, 70.96. Under low conflict of interest with a highly attractive external alternative, *P* and *O* differed on the average by 2.79 points, and with a less attractive external alternative, by 3.25 points. Under high conflict of interest with an attractive external alternative, the latter was invoked in three quarters of the dyads, the weaker member taking this option more than twice as often as the stronger; with an unattractive external alternative, the alternative was played in only a quarter of the dyads, always by the weaker member. Under low conflict of interest with an attractive external alternative, the latter was invoked in somewhat less than half the dyads, twice by the more powerful member, three times by the weaker; with an unattractive external alternative, the latter was played in only one dyad, by the weaker member.

The findings on contractual activity are shown in Table 14-5. It is clear that when one member has the power to move his partner over a wide range of outcomes, and the latter possesses some countervailing power—that is, an attractive external alternative—each protects himself, not by adopting a minimax solution, but by imposing contractual restraints on the other. We know this because contractual activity is much more intense under these conditions than if neither possesses an advantage, or the weaker member cannot counter his partner's power (see Table 14-5). It is apparent also that contracts are indeed effective in controlling the application of power and thereby in preventing the disruption of mutually profitable exchanges. Of the dyads that drew up a contract, 86 per cent maintained or increased their joint outcomes following the contract, whereas only 78 per cent of the noncontract dyads did so, even though the former already had obtained a higher level of profit before the contract period than the latter. An equally important function of the contract is minimization of disparities in the outcomes of partners who differ in power. Comparing the difference in points obtained by the members of a dyad during precontract exchanges with that obtained following an opportunity to form a contract, Thibaut and Faucheux found that for the

TABLE 14-5.   *Contractual Activity in the Various Experimental Conditions* (From Thibaut and Faucheux, 1965)

	External	Alternative
High Conflict of Interest	*Attractive*	*Unattractive*
Mean Number of Contracts*	2.75	1.33
Number of Dyads Forming One or More Contracts†	12	6
Number of Dyads Adopting Both *EA* and *D* Rules	9	2
Mean Indemnity	65.56	26.39
Low Conflict of Interest		
Mean Number of Contracts*	1.67	1.92
Number of Dyads Forming One or More Contracts†	9	8
Number of Dyads Adopting Both *EA* and *D* Rules	2	3
Mean Indemnity	35.83	42.22

* Absolute limit on number of contracts is 3.
† Each condition contained 12 dyads.

dozen or more dyads who failed to arrange contracts, there was not a single instance of a reduction in disparity between partners. However, of about three dozen dyads who did make contractual arrangements, nearly half evidenced a reduction in the disparity between partners. Comparable results were obtained by Murdock (1967). In addition, he found that contractual restraints were especially stringent when it was not just possible but likely that either member would choose to take full advantage of his partner—that is, subjects were led to believe inequity and disloyalty were common in previous dyads.

The achievement of an explicit contract is an important step toward stable cooperative interdependence. As a result, interpersonal behavior sheds its realpolitik and members need no longer anxiously calculate in their decisions the probable malevolence of others. In addition to the legitimate sanctions established by the contract, the negotiation in and of itself is likely to enhance morale by providing members with an unambiguous demonstration of their benign intentions, of their ability to trust each other and work together being men of reason and good will all. Hence the contract among other things may legitimize a feeling of trust. In the standard prisoner's-dilemma situation, to say *P* trusts *O* means that *P* is confident that *O* will behave cooperatively and not defect, that *O* will follow a strategy of maximizing joint gains and will not shift to either maximizing his own gain or the difference between his own and other's gain. In this sense, trust reflects an expectancy on the part of *P* that *O* will not behave malevolently.

Thibaut and Faucheux (1965) examined a more complex form of trust. They considered the malevolence of two common extramatrix activities, the distribution of the group product and the maintenance of group membership. A person therefore can pursue his strategy not only in terms of his matrix choices, but also through decisions to allocate the product in a particular way or to leave the relationship for some external alternative. A maximization of joint gain or a trusting strategy would be reflected on the part of the more powerful member in decisions to equitably distribute the payoff, and on the part of the weaker member, to reject attractive external activities. A maximization of own gain, or of differences in gain, would be indicated by inequitable distributions or acceptance of external alternatives. When such extramatrix temptations are strong, the group seeks to regulate and control them. A system of norms is established that reduces each member's peculiar vulnerability. The more powerful being vulnerable to disloyalty and the weaker being vulnerable to inequities, the tendency is to form a contract that obligates the former to fair sharing and the latter to maintaining his membership.

The Thibaut and Faucheux experiment is one of the first to capture some rather subtle and significant features of the negotiations involved in achieving a stable and fairly differentiated form of interdependence. On the basis of these findings it seems that the need to protect their various interests from abuse by others induces members to formulate standards of conduct. These standards impose *different* rights and responsibilities, depending on the resources a member possesses and the particular threat to which he is vulnerable: a more powerful member, one who can control the other's outcome within the relationship, is obliged to behave equitably but has the right to demand loyalty; a weaker member is obliged to be loyal but has the right to demand equity. In other words, as a cooperative or mutually satisfying form of interdependence is achieved under the stresses examined by Thibaut and Faucheux, we also observe a concomitant *differentiation in roles.* Thus from this rather primitive relationship a social system begins to take shape.

Concluding Remarks on Behavioral Interdependence

Up to a point the law of effect appears very serviceable in accounting for exchanges under a variety of dyadic conditions. Yet where the person's behavior is influenced by estimates of his partner's reaction—that is, when the decision to act is based on a strategy—it loses much of its explanatory power. The law of effect focuses on the strengthening or weakening of associative connections (between a response and the occasioning situation) by the immediate consequences of the response. Strategic behavior, however, concerns outcomes over the long run and does not presume that such behavior will be greatly modified by its immediate consequences. In fact, a strategy might call for the maintenance of a response that punishes the person or the cessation of a response that rewards him. Recall that a "thoroughly" aware subject in the "minimal social situation" will persist at a response while receiving negative outcomes in order to learn of its effect on his partner. Literally, the law of effect is violated in the short term to obtain long-term gains.

Analyses of decision making in the prisoner's-dilemma situation often observe the strengthening or weakening of a response tendency as a function of its expected value. One implication of this relationship between response strength and expected value is that the *foreseen* consequences of an act, those that are anticipated in the long run, have appreciable significance for its modification compared to the actual consequences that immediately follow, those that occur in the short run. Moreover, we found that subjects commonly forego a large short-term gain—for example, by adopting a cooperative strategy when defecting is outrageously profitable—by binding themselves to agreements that prescribe fair sharing or loyalty when distributive injustice or disloyalty are tempting. In each of these cases a response that the person recognizes as providing immediate satisfaction is weakened and one whose immediate consequences may be less satisfying is strengthened. Strictly speaking, these events are contrary to what would be expected according to Thorndike's formulation.

The law of effect, strictly speaking, was not meant to be used where cognitive processes play an important role, as they obviously do in the calculations of strategy. Yet with some modification it might be rendered more serviceable. Briefly, suppose that instead of a connection between (1) the eliciting situation and (2) the response, we dealt with the connection between (1) estimates of the other's response to each alternative course of action open to the person and (2) the person's actual choice, as that which is strengthened or weakened by the outcome. Strategy then would refer to *a string of acts set up by the person in advance with his partner in mind.* During each exchange there may be some modification of one or more elements in the string based on information conveyed by the other's actual response as well as by the outcome delivered each participant. This is a drastic, yet not unreasonable specification of the eliciting situation and the response in terms of the mixed-motive situation. Thus it appears possible to reconstruct, or at least rephrase, the law of effect so as to increase its relevance to interpersonal exchanges. Whether such a reconstruction would indeed serve a useful theoretical purpose remains to be seen, however.

Research based on the law of effect seems to make markedly different assumptions about the origins of interdependence in groups than that in Chapter 12, which focused on cognitive processes. The cognitive position presupposes the operation of biases regarding proper social arrangements that are shared by group members. The law-of-effect argument traces the form of interdependence achieved by a collectivity to the strengthening of particular social activities having positive consequences (they become the behaviors that characterize the relationship) and the weakening of those having negative consequences. These very general propositions have been a convenient way of categorizing the relevant research. At present it is neither necessary nor important (nor possible) to decide which proposition is more correct. Still it is disturbing that two lines of experimentation dealing with the same general problem appear so unconnected.

Some integration might be possible if we could show that the findings obtained in one area can be predicted from the assumptions made in the other. It is not difficult to represent the "minimal social situation" or the prisoner's-dilemma paradigm in graph theoretic terms. In the former, P performs either response x or y, and these produce outcomes a or b. Suppose P likes a and dislikes b. Then the balance prediction is identical to that based on the law of effect or win–stay, lose–change. This is shown in Table 14-6. When P performs y (the solid line between P and y indicating a positive unit relation), y has consequence b (the solid yb line, again a

TABLE 14-6.   *The "Minimal Social Situation" in Graph Theoretic Terms*

positive unit relation), and P dislikes b (the broken Pb line, a negative sentiment relation), P experiences a state of imbalance. Because P cannot change the yb relation nor without some difficulty the Pb relation, then in order to restore balance, he must switch his response from y to x. P would thus change the situation from (1) to (2). This effect, of course, was routinely observed in the "minimal social situation" (Sidowski, Wykoff, and Tabory, 1956; Kelley, Thibaut, Radloff, and Mundy, 1962). Furthermore, the likelihood of such a switch will depend on how clear or how reliable the yb and xa relations are. When unclear or unreliable, they cannot serve as a guide to action or as part of a plan to achieve some desirable social arrangement. For instance, if both xa and xb, or ya and yb occur (which they do in a mutual-fate-control matrix with ad lib responding or in a behavior-control–fate-control matrix with responding in alternation) then P will be unable to move from structure (1) to structure (2). Similarly, a law-of-effect analysis demonstrated that members of a dyad could not consistently achieve positive outcomes (symmetrical reward) under mutual fate control with ad lib responding or under behavior-control–fate-control with responding in alternation (Kelley, Thibaut, Radloff and Mundy, 1962; Rabinowitz, Kelley, and Rosenblatt, 1966).

In the mixed-motive situation a critical problem is predicting the choice of strategies. Suppose P must decide between playing a purely cooperative game (maximizing joint outcomes) or a purely competitive game (maximizing the difference between his own and his partner's outcomes). If he chooses the first, then both he and his partner might benefit; if he chooses the second, he might benefit while his partner suffers. When will P choose the cooperative and when the competitive strategy? The choice can be represented as being among the four structures in Table 14-7, where x is a strategy that might benefit P as well as his partner, O—that

TABLE 14-7.   *Choice of Strategy in Graph Theoretic Terms*

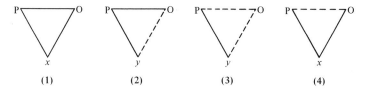

is, one that both would like—and y is a strategy that might benefit P but harm O—that is, one that P would like but O would dislike. Assuming a tendency toward balance, the choice of a cooperative strategy should be made when there is a positive relationship between P and O, whereas a competitive strategy should be chosen when there is a negative relationship. This follows from the fact that structures (1) and (3) are balanced but (2) and (4) are unbalanced. If trust or distrust is taken as a realization of the positive or negative $\overline{PO}$ line, then the balance prediction is consistent with the findings of Deutsch (1960), Solomon (1960), and others, which suggest that trust leads to the choice of a cooperative strategy, and distrust, to the choice of a competitive strategy. Finally, ignoring the relationship between P and O, it can also be shown that competitive or cooperative behavior should be reciprocated. In other words, a tendency toward balance would predict that symmetrical exchanges are stable, whereas asymmetrical ones are not, which we know is empirically correct from Rapoport and Chammah (1965) and McClintock and McNeel (1966). When represented as in Table 14-8, symmetrical exchanges, (1) and (2), produce a balanced structure, and an asymmetrical exchange, (3), produces an unbalanced structure. In (1), P and O each select a strategy (a) that has positive consequences for the other; in (2), P and O each select a strategy (b) that has negative consequences for the other; and in (3) P's actions have positive consequences for O, whereas the latter's actions have negative consequences for P.

TABLE 14-8.　*Symmetric and Asymmetric Exchanges in Graph Theoretic Terms*

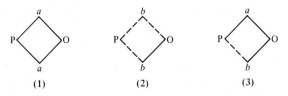

(1)　　　　　(2)　　　　　(3)

Thus there is the distinct possibility of representing the exchanges occurring in a "minimal social situation" and in mixed-motive games so that they can be analyzed from the point of view of a theory of balance. Moreover, when this is done, many of the findings appear to be predicted by the theory. Certainly this is a hopeful sign. Perhaps these apparently disparate approaches do have a theoretical unity. At the same time, however, there is good reason to be cautious in this hope. In experiments explicitly concerned with structural balance (for example, Sampson and Insko, 1964), the relations are chosen beforehand because of their theoretical relevance. Other relations that are irrelevant but can influence the results are precluded by appropriate experimental controls. Therefore, to represent the situation in graph theoretic terms, we need only consider the $\overline{PO}$, $\overline{PX}$, and $\overline{OX}$ relationships. On the other hand, social exchanges usually contain a relatively large number of relationships, only a few of which might be represented for purposes of analysis: P's and O's choice of responses, a or b; the outcome, x or y, associated with these responses; the value of the outcomes; and finally, interpersonal sentiments, the $\overline{PO}$ relation. Our decision about which to represent above was frankly ad hoc. In the absence of independent criteria for selecting or rejecting a relation, we arbitrarily picked those that permitted us to demonstrate our point. If other relations had been used, this might not have been possible.

Consider the representations in Table 14-9 of situations similar to those just discussed. In the first structure, P and O distrust one another, but both make a cooperative response, a, that produces a positive outcome for each, x. In the second, trust exists between P and O, but both compete, b, which produces a negative outcome for each, y. And in the third instance, there is distrust between P and O, and both compete, b, producing a negative outcome for each, y. The first two cases rarely appear, and the third is common in mixed-motive play. If structurally balanced exchanges are supposed to occur more frequently than those that are unbalanced, then case (3) must be balanced, whereas cases (1) and (2) must be unbalanced. It can be readily shown, however, that each of these structures is identical in respect to degree of balance. All contain seven semicycles, of which only three are positive.

TABLE 14-9.   *An Alternative Representation of the Choice of Strategy*

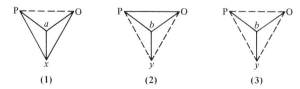

(1)   (2)   (3)

Because there are no independent criteria for deciding which relations are to be represented, the structures used to demonstrate balance effects are in many instances arbitrary. That behavioral regularities in the prisoner's dilemma or "minimal social situation" can be explained by the structural properties of an arbitrarily selected set of relations is still suggestive and interesting, however. Further theoretical and empirical work is needed in order that the researcher be able at least to assess the relative importance of various relations. For example, when the person goes about constructing a strategy, which relations are salient in his cognitive representation of the situation? If their relative salience could be known, it might be used as a criterion for the inclusion or exclusion of relations. Hence the set of relations to be examined would no longer be selected arbitrarily. Analysis could then explore the connection between these two literatures on behavioral interdependence and perhaps determine the validity of the notion that behavioral exchanges as well as attitudes and interpersonal sentiments are subject to the "laws" of balance, positivity, and reciprocity.

References

Abric, J. C., Faucheux, C., Moscovici, S., and Plon, M. Rôle de l'image du partenaire sur la cooperation en situation de jeu. *Psychologie Française*, 1967, **12**, 267–275.

Asch, S. E. *Social Psychology*. Englewood Cliffs, N.J.: Prentice-Hall, 1952.

Back, K. W. Influence through social communication. *Journal of Abnormal and Social Psychology*, 1951, **46**, 9–23.

Berkowitz, L., and Daniels, L. R. Responsibility and dependency. *Journal of Abnormal and Social Psychology*, 1963, **66**, 427–436.

Berkowitz, L., and Daniels, L. R. Affecting the salience of the social responsibility norm. *Journal of Abnormal and Social Psychology*, 1964, **68**, 275–281.

Bixenstine, V. E., Potash, H. M., and Wilson, K. V. Effects of level of cooperative choice by the other player on choices in a prisoner's dilemma game. Part I. *Journal of Abnormal and Social Psychology*, 1963, **66**, 308–313.

Bixenstine, V. E., and Wilson, K. V. Effects of level of cooperative choice by the other players in a prisoner's dilemma game. Part II. *Journal of Abnormal and Social Psychology*, 1963, **67**, 139–147.

Borah, L. A., Jr. The effects of threat in bargaining: critical and experimental analyses. *Journal of Abnormal and Social Psychology*, 1963, **66**, 37–44.

Brown, R. W. Mass phenomena. In G. Lindzey (ed.), *Handbook of Social Psychology*, Vol. II. Cambridge, Mass.: Addison-Wesley, 1954.

Brown, R. W. *Social Psychology*. New York: The Free Press, 1965.

Burdick, H. A., and Burnes, A. J. A test of "strain toward symmetry" theories. *Journal of Abnormal and Social Psychology*, 1958, **57**, 367–370.

Burnstein, E. Sources of cognitive bias in the representation of simple social structures: balance, minimal change, positivity, reciprocity, and the respondent's own attitude. *Journal of Personality and Social Psychology*, 1967, **7**, 36–48.

Burnstein, E., and Worchel, P. Arbitrariness of frustration and its consequences for aggression in a social situation. *Journal of Personality*, 1962, **30**, 528–541.

Cartwright, D., and Harary, F. Structural balance: A generalization of Heider's theory. *Psychological Review*, 1956, **63**, 277–293.

DeGroot, A. D. *Thought and Choice in Chess*. The Hague: Mouton, 1965.

DeSoto, C. B. Learning a social structure. *Journal of Abnormal and Social Psychology*, 1960, **60**, 417–421.

DeSoto, C. B., and Kuethe, J. L. Subjective probabilities of interpersonal relations. *Journal of Abnormal and Social Psychology,* 1959, **59,** 290–294.

Deutsch, M. The effect of motivational orientation upon trust and suspicion. *Human Relations,* 1960, **13,** 122–139.

Deutsch, M., and Krauss, R. M. The effect of threat on interpersonal bargaining. *Journal of Abnormal and Social Psychology,* 1960, **61,** 181–189.

Deutsch, M., and Krauss, R. M. Studies of interpersonal bargaining. *Journal of Conflict Resolution,* 1962, **6,** 52–76.

Deutsch, M., Yakov, E., Canavan, D., and Gumpert, P. Strategies of inducing cooperation: an experimental study. *Journal of Conflict Resolution,* 1967, **11,** 345–360.

Estes, W. K. Theoretical treatments of differential reward in multiple choice learning and two-person interactions. In J. H. Criswell, H. Solomon, and P. Suppes (eds.), *Mathematical Methods in Small Group Processes.* Stanford, Calif.: Stanford University Press, 1962. Pp. 133–149.

Festinger, L. Informal social communication. *Psychological Review,* 1950, **57,** 271–282.

Festinger, L., Back, K., Schachter, S., Kelley, H. H., and Thibaut, J. *Theory and Experiment in Social Communication.* Ann Arbor: Research Center for Group Dynamics, University of Michigan, 1952.

Festinger, L., and Hutte, H. A. An experimental investigation of the effect of unstable interpersonal relations in a group. *Journal of Abnormal and Social Psychology,* 1957, **47,** 790–796.

Festinger, L., Schachter, S., and Back, K. *Social Pressures in Informal Groups: A Study of Human Factors in Housing.* New York: Harper and Row, 1950.

Festinger, L., and Thibaut, J. Interpersonal communication in small groups. *Journal of Abnormal and Social Psychology,* 1951, **46,** 92–99.

Flament, C. *Applications of Graph Theory to Group Structure.* Englewood Cliffs, N.J.: Prentice-Hall, 1963.

French, E. G. Motivation as a variable in work-partner selection. *Journal of Abnormal and Social Psychology,* 1956, **53,** 96–99.

French, J. R. P., Jr. A formal theory of social power. *Psychological Review,* 1956, **63,** 181–194.

Gallo, P. S., Jr. Effects of increased incentives upon the use of threat in bargaining. *Journal of Personality and Social Psychology,* 1966, **4,** 14–20.

Geiwitz, J. P. The effects of threats on prisoner's dilemma. *Behavioral Science,* 1967, **12,** 232–233.

Gerard, H. B., and Fleischer, L. Recall and pleasantness of balanced and unbalanced cognitive structures. *Journal of Personality and Social Psychology,* 1967, **7,** 332–337.

Goranson, R. E., and Berkowitz, L. Reciprocity and responsibility reactions to prior help. *Journal of Personality and Social Psychology,* 1966, **3,** 227–232.

Gouldner, A. The norm of reciprocity. *American Sociological Review,* 1960, **25,** 161–178.

Harary, F., Norman, R. Z., and Cartwright, D. *Structural Models: An Introduction to the Theory of Directed Graphs.* New York: John Wiley and Sons, 1965.

Harsanyi, J. C. On the rationality postulates underlying the theory of cooperative games. *Journal of Conflict Resolution,* 1961, **5,** 179–196.

Heider, F. Attitudes and cognitive organization. *Journal of Psychology,* 1946, **21,** 107–112.

Heider, F. *The Psychology of Interpersonal Relations.* New York: John Wiley and Sons, 1958.

Jones, E. E., and Davis, K. E. From acts to dispositions. In L. Berkowitz (ed.), *Advances in Experimental Social Psychology.* New York: Academic Press, 1965. Pp. 219–266.

Jones, E. E., and deCharms, R. Changes in social perception as a function of the personal relevance of behavior. *Sociometry,* 1957, **20,** 75–85.

Jordan, N. Behavioral forces that are a function of attitudes and cognitive organization. *Human Relations,* 1953, **6,** 273–288.

Kelley, H. H. Experimental studies of threats in interpersonal negotiations. *Journal of Conflict Resolution,* 1965, **9,** 80–107.

Kelley, H. H. Attribution theory in social psychology. In D. Levine (ed.), *Nebraska Symposium on Motivation.* Lincoln: University of Nebraska Press, 1967. Pp. 192–238.

Kelley, H. H., Condry, J. C., Jr., Dahlke, A. E., and Hill, A. H. Collective behavior in a simulated panic situation. *Journal of Experimental Social Psychology,* 1965, **1,** 20–54.

Kelley, H. H., Thibaut, J. W., Radloff, R., and Mundy, D. The development of cooperation in the "minimal social situation." *Psychological Monographs,* 1962, **76,** No. 19.

Komorita, S. S., and Mechling, J. Betrayal and reconciliation in a two-person game. *Journal of Personality and Social Psychology,* 1967, **6,** 349–353.

Kuethe, J. L. Social schemas. *Journal of Abnormal and Social Psychology,* 1962, **54,** 31–38.

Kuethe, J. L. Pervasive influence of social schemata. *Journal of Abnormal and Social Psychology,* 1964, **68,** 248–254.

Kuethe, J. L., and Weingartner, H. Male–female schemata of homosexual and nonhomosexual penitentiary inmates. *Journal of Personality,* 1964, **32,** 23–31.

Lave, L. B. Factors affecting cooperation in the prisoner's dilemma. *Behavioral Science,* 1965, **10,** 26–38.

LeBon, G. *The Crowd.* New York: Viking Press, 1960. (1st ed., 1895)

Lerner, M. J., and Becker, S. Interpersonal choice as a function of ascribed similarity and definition of the situation. *Human Relations,* 1962, **15,** 27–34.

Loomis, J. L. Communication, the development of trust, and cooperative behavior. *Human Relations,* 1959, **12,** 305–315.

Luce, R. D., and Raiffa, H. *Games and Decisions.* New York: John Wiley and Sons, 1957.

McClintock, C. G., and McNeel, S. P. Reward and score feedback as determinants of cooperative and competitive game behavior. *Journal of Personality and Social Psychology,* 1966, **4,** 606–613.

Minas, J. S., Scodel, A., Marlowe, D., and Rawson, H. Some descriptive aspects of two-person, non–zero-sum games. II. *Journal of Conflict Resolution,* 1960, **4,** 193–197.

Mintz, A. Non-adaptive group behavior. *Journal of Abnormal and Social Psychology*, 1951, **46**, 150–159.

Morrissette, J. O. An experimental study of the theory of structural balance. *Human Relations*, 1958, **11**, 239–254.

Murdock, P. Development of contractual norms in a dyad. *Journal of Personality and Social Psychology*, 1967, **6**, 206–211.

Newcomb, T. M. Balance theory. In R. Abelson, E. Aronson, W. McGuire, T. M. Newcomb, M. Rosenberg, and P. Tannenbaum (eds.), *Theories of Cognitive Consistency: A Source Book*. Chicago: Rand, McNally, 1968.

Price, K. O., Harburg, E., and Newcomb, T. M. Psychological balance in situations of negative interpersonal attitudes. *Journal of Personality and Social Psychology*, 1966, **3**, 265–270.

Pruit, D. G. Reciprocity and credit building in a laboratory dyad. *Journal of Personality and Social Psychology*, 1968, **8**, 143–147.

Rabinowitz, L., Kelley, H. L., and Rosenblatt, R. M. Effects of different types of interdependence and response conditions in the minimal social situation. *Journal of Experimental Social Psychology*, 1966, **2**, 169–197.

Rapoport, A. *Fights, Games and Debates*. Ann Arbor: University of Michigan Press, 1960.

Rapoport, A., and Chammah, A. M. Sex differences in factors contributing to the level of cooperation in the prisoner's dilemma game. *Journal of Personality and Social Psychology*, 1965, **2**, 831–838.

Rapoport, A., and Orwant, C. Experimental games: a review. *Behavioral Science*, 1962, **7**, 1–37.

Rosenfeld, H. Nonverbal reciprocation of approval. *Journal of Experimental Social Psychology*, 1967, **3**, 102–111.

Sampson, E. E., and Insko, C. A. Cognitive consistency and performance in the autokinetic situation. *Journal of Abnormal and Social Psychology*, 1964, **68**, 184–192.

Schachter, S. Deviation, rejection, and communication. *Journal of Abnormal and Social Psychology*, 1951, **46**, 190–207.

Schachter, S. The interaction of cognitive and physiological determinants of emotional state. In L. Berkowitz (ed.), *Advances in Experimental Social Psychology*. Vol. 1. New York: Academic Press, 1964.

Schelling, T. *The Strategy of Conflict*. Cambridge, Mass.: Harvard University Press, 1960.

Sermat, V. The effect of an initial cooperative or competitive treatment upon a subject's response to conditional cooperation. *Behavioral Science*, 1967, **12**, 301–313.

Shaw, M. E. Communication networks. In L. Berkowitz (ed.), *Advances in Experimental Social Psychology*. Vol. 1. New York: Academic Press, 1964.

Sherif, M. A study of some social factors in perception. *Archives of Psychology*, 1935, No. 187.

Shomer, R. W., Davis, A. H., and Kelley, H. H. Threats and the development of coordination: further studies of the Deutsch and Krauss trucking game. *Journal of Personality and Social Psychology*, 1966, **4**, 119–126.

Sidowski, J. B. Reward and punishment in a minimal social situation. *Journal of Experimental Psychology,* 1957, **54,** 318–326.

Sidowski, J. B., Wycoff, L. B., and Tabory, L. The influence of reinforcement and punishment in a minimal social situation. *Journal of Abnormal and Social Psychology,* 1956, **52,** 115–119.

Solomon, L. The influence of some types of power relationships and game strategies upon the development of interpersonal trust. *Journal of Abnormal and Social Psychology,* 1960, **61,** 223–230.

Taylor, H. F. Balance and change in the two-person group. *Sociometry,* 1967, **30,** 262–279.

Thibaut, J. W., and Faucheux, C. The development of contractual norms in a bargaining situation under two types of stress. *Journal of Experimental Social Psychology,* 1965, **1,** 89–102.

Thibaut, J. W., and Kelley, H. H. *The Social Psychology of Groups.* New York: John Wiley and Sons, 1959.

Thorndike, R. L. *Animal Intelligence: Experimental Studies.* New York: Macmillan, 1911.

Zajonc, R. B. *Social Psychology: An Experimental Approach.* Belmont, Calif.: Wadsworth, 1966.

Zajonc, R. B. Cognitive processes. In G. Lindzey and E. Aronson (eds.), *Handbook of Social Psychology.* Vol. I, 2nd ed. Cambridge, Mass.: Addison-Wesley, 1968.

Zajonc, R. B., and Burnstein, E. The learning of balanced and unbalanced social structures. *Journal of Personality,* 1965, **33,** 153–163. (a)

Zajonc, R. B., and Burnstein, E. Structural balance, reciprocity, and positivity as sources of cognitive bias. *Journal of Personality,* 1965, **33,** 570–583. (b)

PART

V

The Experimental Method

Judson Mills

University of Missouri

CHAPTER

15

The Value of Experiments

This section of the book will examine a number of general issues concerning the use of the experimental method in social psychology. The first chapter will discuss the definition of an experiment, the value of experiments, and the difference between an experiment and a laboratory study. In the second chapter the "artificiality" of experiments will be discussed, together with issues concerning the generalization of experimental results and experimental replications. The third chapter will discuss the limitations of the experimental method in social psychology, the difficulty of establishing the exact nature of relationships, and the ambiguity of negative results. Examples will be taken from the experiments described in the previous sections of the book.

The major focus of this section will not be on how experimenters arrive at the specific features of their designs or on how to conduct experiments. An excellent discussion of how experiments are planned and conducted is provided by Aronson and Carlsmith (1968). Of course, as they emphasize, it is impossible to lay down a set of rules that will make someone a good experimenter. Good experimentation is learned primarily by observing good experimenters and doing experiments under their guidance. Research is learned by doing and is taught mainly by contagion (Festinger, Garner, Hebb, Hunt, Lawrence, Osgood, Skinner and Taylor, 1959).

First of all it is essential to be very clear about the definition of an experiment. *By an experiment we mean a study in which the investigator manipulates or varies one or more variables (called the independent variables) and measures other variables (called the dependent variables).* This is the traditional definition of an experiment in the natural sciences (Beveridge, 1957; Hempel, 1966) and in social psychology (Aronson and Carlsmith, 1968; Campbell, 1957; Jones and Gerard, 1967; Seltiz, Jahoda, Deutsch and Cook, 1959). For example, Hempel (1966) states, "An experimental test then consists in varying the values of the 'independent variables' and checking whether the 'dependent variables' assume the values implied by the hypothesis. When experimental control is impossible, when the condition C mentioned in the test implication cannot be brought about or varied by available technological means, then the hypothesis must be tested non-experimentally, by seeking out, or waiting for, cases where the specified conditions are realized by nature" (p. 20).

A study is an experiment only if the investigator controls a variable in the sense of deliberately varying it—that is, creating differences in the amount of the variable. If he simply measures differences that happen to occur, the study is not an experiment. However, an investigator may control a variable in the sense of preventing it from varying—that is, holding it constant—without the study being an experiment. The difference between an experiment and a nonexperimental study "is not, as is frequently assumed, in the amount of control over other variables which the research worker has. It is quite possible to have a good deal of control over variables and a good deal of precision of measurements in non-experimental situations" (Festinger, 1959, p. 360).

It is common to introduce the idea of an experiment in terms of the creation of an experimental group and a control group. For example, in their excellent text on research methods, Seltiz et al. (1959) state, "The basic outline of an experiment is simple: An 'experimental' group is exposed to the assumed causal (or independent) variable while a 'control' group is not; the two groups are then compared in terms of the assumed effect (or dependent variable)" (p. 124). For example, in the study of conformity by Asch, described by Kiesler on page 254, subjects in the experimental group judged the length of lines in the presence of a number of confederates who, pretending to be subjects, had made incorrect judgments. In the control condition the subjects were alone when they made their judgments. The measure of the dependent variable in this well-known experiment was the number of incorrect judgments the subjects made.

The purpose of a control group is to permit comparisons with the results obtained in the experimental group that will allow the investigator to rule out alternative hypotheses that might account for the results. Scientific knowledge is arrived at by the "method of hypothesis"—that is, by inventing hypotheses as tentative answers to a problem under study and then subjecting these to empirical test (Hempel, 1966). We provide evidence for a hypothesis if we make observations that follow from that hypothesis but cannot be accounted for or explained as well by other hypotheses. In Asch's experiment it was necessary to eliminate the alternative hypothesis that the subjects made incorrect judgments in the experimental condition because they could not see the lines well enough to judge them accurately, in order to conclude that they were influenced by the presence of the confederates who made incorrect judgments. The comparison with the results from the control condition eliminates this alternative explanation because the subjects in the control condition made relatively few incorrect judgments.

It is common to speak of "the control group," but a particular experiment may include a number of control groups or comparison groups because there may be a number of possible alternative explanations that must be ruled out if the results are to provide evidence for the experimental hypothesis. The study by Berkowitz and Geen, described by Bramel on page 61, is an example of an experiment with a number of comparison groups. Subjects in the experimental group were given a number of electric shocks by a confederate of the experimenter and then watched a film in which Kirk Douglas was very badly beaten up. They were told that the confederate's name was Kirk. In comparison conditions, subjects either were given only one shock by the confederate or saw a film of the first four-minute mile race instead of the fight film, or were told that the confederate's name was Bob. In all there were eight conditions in this experiment. They are summarized by Bramel in Table 2-2. Comparisons between the various conditions in the number of shocks delivered to the confederate show that seeing a third person punished increased aggressiveness toward another person only when he had angered the subject and was similar to the person punished.

As is true of most experiments in social psychology, the study by Berkowitz and Geen did not include a control group in the traditional sense of a group that is not given any experimental treatment whatsoever. Usually in social-psychological experiments the different experimental conditions constitute different degrees or levels of the independent variable or variables. Comparisons between conditions that vary in the degree of the independent variable are usually better able to eliminate alternative hypotheses than a comparison between an experimental group and a group that is not given any treatment at all.

When we speak of the "independent variable" we are referring to the variable that is assumed to be the causal factor or determining condition in the relationship being investigated. For example, in the Asch study the independent variable is whether or not persons believe that their judgments will be known by other group members who have made incorrect judgments. In the Berkowitz and Geen study there were three independent variables: whether or not the subject was angered by another person, whether or not he saw a third person punished, and the degree of similarity between the person who angered him and the person who was punished.

A variable that is the independent variable in one study may be the dependent variable in another study. For example, one of the independent variables in the study by Gerard, which is mentioned by Kiesler on page 271, is the same as the dependent variable of Asch's study—that is, con-

412   *Experimental Social Psychology*

formity to the incorrect judgments of a group. In fact, the independent
and dependent variables may be reversed from one study to another. In
the study by Pepitone described by Bramel on page 32, the independent and dependent variables were even reversed from one part of the
study to another part. In one part of the study the independent variable
was how much power different persons seemed to have to influence the
rewards of the subject, and the dependent variable was how much the subject thought the persons liked him. In another part of the study the
independent variable was how much different persons seemed to like the
subject, and the dependent variable was how much power the subject
thought they had to influence his rewards. Obviously, the operations used
to manipulate the variables in one part were not the same as those used
to measure them in the other part.

The Major Value of Experiments

The major value of experiments is that they are better able to test hypotheses about causal relationships than nonexperimental studies. "When
an experiment is possible, it is the most effective method of testing a
hypothesis that one variable, X, causally influences another variable, Y"
(Seltiz et al., 1959, p. 90). The great power that the experimental method
has in testing causal hypotheses is the reason that the distinction between
experimental and nonexperimental studies is so important. If the term
experiment is not defined in terms of the manipulation of variables, then
another term will be needed to make this crucial distinction.

Social psychologists want to discover causal relationships so that they
can establish the basic principles that will explain the phenomena of
social psychology. A causal relationship exists between two variables if
changes in one, the independent variable, are followed by changes in
the other, the dependent variable. A causal relationship need not specify
the necessary or sufficient conditions for an effect. Usually causal relationships between social psychological variables only specify what have
been called contributory conditions (Seltiz et al., 1959, p. 81). This is
because the dependent variables of social psychology have many different
causes or determinants.

Consider, for example, the causal relationship investigated in the study
by Darley and Berscheid, which is described by Bramel on page 7.
Their hypothesis, that if someone expects to associate with another person
he will come to like that other person more, does not specify either the
necessary or sufficient conditions for liking other persons. If the anticipation of associating with someone were a necessary condition for liking,

then that would mean that if we did not anticipate associating with someone we would not like him; but obviously we sometimes like people with whom we do not expect to associate. If the anticipation of associating with someone were a sufficient condition for liking, that would mean that if a person expects to associate with someone then he will invariably like him. That, of course, is also not true because there are many people we expect to associate with whom we do not like.

In order to demonstrate that a causal relationship exists between two variables, one must not only demonstrate that there is a correlation between the independent variable and the dependent variable. One must also rule out alternative explanations for the correlation that do not involve the assumption that changes in the independent variable are followed by changes in the dependent variable. One kind of alternative interpretation that must be eliminated involves the possibility that the changes in the variable the investigator considers the dependent variable occurred before the changes in the variable he considers the independent variable. Suppose, for example, that one simply observed a relationship between how much time persons expected to spend with others and how much they liked those others. Such a correlation could also be explained by the hypothesis that people choose to spend more time with others they already like. Thus the relationship could not be taken as evidence for the hypothesis that anticipating spending time with someone increases liking for him.

In an experimental study, such as the one conducted by Darley and Berscheid, there is no problem of establishing the time sequence of the variables. If the investigator himself produces the changes in the variable he considers the independent variable, then he can be sure that these changes did not occur after the changes in his dependent variable. He knows that the differences in the dependent variable could not have caused the differences in the independent variable because he himself caused the differences in the independent variable. Because Darley and Berscheid manipulated the subject's anticipation of interacting with the other person by telling some subjects that they would be working with the stranger in the future and not telling other subjects that they would meet the stranger, one can be sure that the liking for the other did not precede the anticipation of interacting with him.

Another kind of alternative interpretation that must be ruled out if the results are to provide evidence for a causal relationship involves the possibility that the independent and dependent variables happen to be related only because they are both determined by some third variable, or in other words, that the relationship is spurious. For example, Berscheid and Walster point out on page 130 that field studies in which a correlation between beliefs and exposure to information has been found do not provide good evidence that beliefs determine exposure to information because other variables may account for the correlation. They suggest that perhaps the real reason a relationship was found between having given blood and attending a film that advocated giving blood is that in- dividuals who had a great deal of free time were more likely both to give blood and to go to films.

The relationship between giving blood and attending the film may be spurious in the sense that it may have occurred only because giving blood and attending the film were both determined by a third variable—the amount of free time people had. Thus we cannot take the correlation as evidence for the hypothesis that having given blood determined atten- dance at the film or more generally that beliefs determine exposure to information. Berscheid and Walster provide another example of a potentially spurious relationship when they point out that the finding that individuals who favored the United Nations were more likely to hear information supporting the United Nations could have occurred because amount of education determines the degree of favorability toward the United Nations and also the degree of exposure to public information campaigns.

If the investigator himself produces the changes in the independent variable, then he can be sure that they are not caused by some third factor producing a spurious relationship between the independent and depen- dent variables. If he assigns the subjects to the experimental conditions at random, as he must if the study is an experiment (Seltiz et al., 1959, p. 101), then the conditions can differ on other relevant variables only by chance. The possibility that the results are due to chance factors can be considered ruled out if the differences between the conditions are statisti- cally significant. Suppose one randomly assigned some subjects to an ex- perimental condition in which persons are induced to give blood and other subjects to a control condition in which persons are not induced to give blood. If it is found that significantly more subjects in the experi- mental condition were interested in seeing a film urging that people give blood, one would be able to rule out the kinds of hypotheses about spurious third factors that could not be ruled out in the correlational studies described by Berscheid and Walster.

In nonexperimental studies in which the investigator does not manipu- late the independent variables, it is usually quite difficult to eliminate the possibility that the relationship found is determined by some third vari- able. "If the research worker has collected his data non-experimentally, that is, he did not manipulate the value of the independent variable, he can never unambiguously draw a conclusion concerning the direction of causality between two variables which he may find are related nor, indeed, can he even be sure that there is a causal relationship. He has merely observed the covariation of two variables and the explanation of their correlation may very well hinge on other factors, which he did not measure or control, which were varying in the situation" (Festinger, 1959, p. 360).

Even with an experimental design it is still possible, and indeed quite common, that the results are subject to an alternative interpretation and thus do not provide good evidence for a causal relationship. If the experiment is not well designed, it may be possible to explain the results by assuming that the experimental conditions varied another variable instead of or in addition to the variable the investigator intended to vary. Or it may be possible to account for the differences by assuming that the measures really reflect some variable other than the investigator's dependent variable.

In any hypothesis-testing study, the goal, which is to collect data that can be explained solely by the hypothesis, can only be approximated. Even the finest examples of research in social psychology do not completely eliminate all alternative explanations, but only make them relatively inappropriate. However, a well-designed experiment has much greater power to rule out alternative explanations for causal hypotheses than a nonexperimental or correlational study. This is not to suggest that well-designed experiments are easy to conduct. "Actually experimental investigations are technically most difficult to carry out. Usually it requires quite a lot of knowledge concerning an area before it is possible to engage in adequate experimental work. One must, at a minimum, know enough to manipulate the value of a variable" (Festinger, 1959, p. 364).

The Difference Between an Experimental and a Laboratory Study

The terms *laboratory* and *experiment* are linked together so frequently that *laboratory study* and *experimental study* are often regarded as synonymous. This is unfortunate, because experimental studies need not be conducted in a laboratory, and not all laboratory studies are experiments. An example of a field experiment is the study by Mulder and Stemerding, described by Bramel on page 21. The investigators called meetings of groups of small grocers in some towns in Holland and told them that a large supermarket organization was considering locating a store in their community. Some subjects were told that the probability of this occurring was about 10 per cent and others that it was about 80 per cent. The investigators then measured the subjects' desire for further meetings. Many other field experiments are described in the various sections of this book.

Laboratory studies that are not experiments are not as common as laboratory experiments, but such studies are sometimes conducted in social psychology. Because this book is devoted to experimental work, we will consider a hypothetical example of nonexperimental laboratory study. Suppose a researcher wanted to test the hypothesis that conformity to the incorrect judgments of a group increases attraction to the group. For this purpose he brought subjects into his laboratory in groups of five and, after introducing them to one another, placed them in what is ordinarily called a Crutchfield apparatus, such as that described by Kiesler on page 254. Suppose he recorded whether or not the subjects pressed the switch for the incorrect judgment after the signal lights in their booth indicated that the other group members had all pressed the switch for the incorrect judgment. Suppose at the end he had the subjects rate how much they liked each of the other members of the group.

Such a study would certainly be considered a laboratory study. However, it is clearly not an experiment. The subjects in this hypothetical study were not randomly assigned to different experimental conditions designed to induce varying degrees of the independent variable. The independent variable, conformity, was not manipulated, but rather differences in conformity were measured as they happened to occur in the situation. Because the study is not an experiment, it could not, for reasons we have already discussed, provide very good evidence that conformity to a group increases attraction to the group. A correlation between the measure of conformity and the measure of attraction to the group could occur because attraction determined conformity. Or it could occur because conformity and attraction were both determined by some third factor—for example, how intelligent the subjects thought the other group members were. These kinds of alternative interpretations would not be possible if conformity were experimentally manipulated. This has recently become possible with Gerard's ingenious technique described by Kiesler on page 271.

Exactly what constitutes a laboratory study in social psychology is difficult to specify. Certainly one would not want to use as the determining factor whether or not the study was done in a place with a sign labeled "Social Psychology Laboratory." One would also not want to require that a laboratory study in social psychology be conducted in a room with a one-way–vision window. Although one definition of a laboratory is a place equipped for scientific observation, this is not a satisfactory way of defining laboratory studies in social psychology. Many studies that are regarded as laboratory studies do not use elaborate equipment and are conducted in ordinary offices or classrooms. For example, in most of the laboratory studies of attitude change reported by Berscheid and Walster no equipment beyond perhaps a portable tape recorder was used.

A more common way of distinguishing laboratory and nonlaboratory studies is in terms of the degree of control over other variables that might influence the dependent variable; control in the sense of preventing them from varying so that they cannot create differences in the dependent variable. For example, laboratory experiments in social psychology are typically conducted in a quiet, isolated room and the experimenter's behavior is highly standardized. Because the amount of control over extraneous sources of variability in the dependent variable is always a matter of degree, this criterion does not permit a clear-cut distinction between laboratory and nonlaboratory studies. By this definition it is quite arbitrary whether we call a given investigation a laboratory study or a nonlaboratory study.

If we require that there be a very high degree of control over other factors that might influence the dependent variable, then very few studies in social psychology could qualify as laboratory studies. Even in the most highly controlled experiments in social psychology there is still likely to be considerable "experimental error"—that is, variability in the measure of the dependent variable within each of the experimental conditions. In most of the experiments on attitude change described by Berscheid and Walster in this book, the subjects who were given the same experimental treatment did not all have the same score on the measure of attitude. An example is the study by Mills and Jellison, described on pages 153–154.

In the experiment by Mills and Jellison there were two conditions: a desirable condition in which the subjects were led to believe that the communicator felt the communication would be desirable to his audience, and an undesirable condition in which subjects were led to believe that the communicator felt the communication would be undesirable to his audience. Although the scores for the measure of agreement with the communicator were in general higher in the undesirable condition, there were considerable differences within the desirable condition and within the undesirable condition. Some of those in the undesirable condition had lower scores than some in the desirable condition. Such differences may have occurred because of other factors affecting the subjects' attitudes that were not held completely constant by the procedure. Even though all subjects received exactly the same communication, their initial attitudes on the topic probably differed, and these differences could have resulted in differences in agreement with the communicator following the communication.

Of course, not all the variability in the measure of the dependent variable within the experimental conditions may be due to a failure to hold constant other variables that affect the dependent variable. Some of the experimental error may be due to inaccuracy in the measure of the dependent variable. Some of the subjects with high scores on the measure of the dependent variable may actually have a lower value on the variable than other subjects who have a low score on the measure of the dependent variable. Thus in the study by Mills and Jellison some of the subjects whose scores on the attitude questionnaire indicated a high degree of agreement with the communicator may in fact have not agreed very much at all with his position.

In social psychology our measures are invariably "impure"—that is, the scores on the measures are determined by other variables in addition to the variables we are trying to measure. Of course, in order for scores to provide a useful measure of a variable, there must be a correlation between the size of the scores and the value of the variable. In general, subjects with high scores must have a higher value on the variable than subjects with low scores.

Experimental error may also occur because of a lack of precision in the manipulation of the independent variable. Some of the subjects in the condition designed to induce a high value on the independent variable may actually have a lower value on the independent variable than some of the subjects in the condition designed to induce a low value on the independent variable. So in the experiment by Mills and Jellison, some of the subjects in the desirable condition may have thought that the communicator felt that his audience would dislike his communication, and some of the subjects in the undesirable condition may have thought that the communicator felt his audience would like his communication. This sort of experimental error will not necessarily invalidate the comparison between the experimental conditions, as long as the subjects in the "high" condition are higher on the average in the amount of the independent variable than the subjects in the "low" condition. Frequently it is possible to show the effect of an independent variable on a dependent variable when there is considerable experimental error. Despite the experimental error in the Mills and Jellison study, the difference between the undesirable and desirable conditions in the measure of agreement with the communicator was statistically significant. Of course, investigators always try to minimize experimental error, because the greater it is, the more difficult it will be for them to detect a relationship between their variables.

Another possible way of distinguishing laboratory and field studies in social psychology is in terms of whether or not the people who are the subjects think of themselves as subjects in a psychological study. One could say that if the subjects come to the study knowing they will be participating in a psychological investigation, then it is a laboratory study. This way of defining a laboratory study deals with a factor that is of considerable importance in social psychological experiments. If the subjects think of themselves as subjects in a psychological study, then it is usually considerably more difficult to present a convincing rationale or cover story for the experiment.

In social psychological research it is almost always necessary to conceal the true purpose of the investigation from the subjects until the experiment is completed. One reason for this is that the dependent variables studied are usually measured by means of verbal responses or other behavior under the voluntary control of the subject. This means that one alternative interpretation to be guarded against is that the subjects responded as they did simply because they wanted to be cooperative and give the experimenter good results. "If people feel that they are 'guinea pigs' being experimented with, or they feel they are being 'tested' and must make a good impression, or if the method of data collection suggests responses or stimulates an interest the subject did not previously feel, the measuring process may distort the experimental results" (Seltiz, 1959, p. 97).

This problem is sometimes discussed currently under the heading of "demand characteristics of the situation" (see the discussion by Kiesler on page 251). Long before that term became popular, social psychologists were aware of the problem and took precautions to avoid it. Many clever procedures have been developed by experimenters for testing their hypotheses without their subjects being aware of the true purpose of the study. For example, the common two-experiments ploy, in which the subject is led to believe he is participating in two completely unrelated studies. Such techniques are excellently reviewed by Aronson and Carlsmith (1968) and will not be described in detail here.

Usually, in order to conceal the hypothesis, it is necessary to give the subject a cover story or a false description of the purpose of the study.

> It is important to realize that providing the subject with a false, but credible, hypothesis is a much better procedure than providing him with no hypothesis at all. For if there are loose ends to an experimental procedure, the subject will attempt to tie these up by devising his own hypothesis, which may be identical to or very similar to the experimenter's true hypothesis. If the experimenter can tie the loose ends together for the subject by providing him with a plausible hypothesis which is unrelated to the true hypothesis, he may succeed in satisfying the subject's curiosity and may thereby eliminate this source of bias. Indeed, this is the primary advantage of the use of deception in experiments. This procedure is really an attempt to provide a cognitive analogy to the placebo; all subjects receive identical explanations of what is being done, just as all subjects receive identical pills in the placebo procedure. (Aronson and Carlsmith, 1968, p. 63)

In addition to preventing the subjects from discerning the true purpose of the study, the cover story must also provide a plausible context in which the independent variable can be successfully manipulated. Another reason for the use of deception in social psychological experiments is that it is often necessary in order to enable the experimenter to vary the independent variable. For example, in order to vary the amount of fear in the well-known experiments by Schachter on the effect of fear on affiliation described by Bramel on page 24, it was necessary that some subjects be told that they would receive very painful electric shocks in the course of the experiment. No such shocks were actually given. As Aronson and Carlsmith (1968) have pointed out, experimental realism can often be achieved only through falsehood. Aronson and Carlsmith have provided a thorough discussion of the ethical issues raised by the use of deception.

Even if a laboratory study is defined as one in which the subject thinks of himself as a subject, there are instances that are difficult to classify. For example, the subject may be informed that he is participating in a research project, but the word *psychology* may not be used. He may be told that it is a public-opinion poll or a market-research study. There is also the very interesting case, such as that in the study by Aronson and Linder described by Bramel on page 17, in which the study is conducted in a place clearly identified as a laboratory but the subject does not think of himself as the subject; he thinks that he is acting as an assistant to the experimenter and helping him run a subject who is in fact a confederate of the experimenter.

If one defines a laboratory study in terms of control over extraneous variables that may influence the dependent variable, then laboratory studies are clearly superior for testing hypotheses than nonlaboratory studies. However, if one defines a laboratory study in terms of whether the subjects think of themselves as subjects, then it is a disadvantage for a study to be a laboratory study. Whichever definition is used, it is clear that the distinction between laboratory and nonlaboratory studies is not the same as the distinction between experimental and nonexperimental studies.

16

The Artificiality of Experiments

Frequently it is claimed that experiments, particularly laboratory experiments, are artificial. This is certainly true in one sense of the term *artificial*. By definition, experiments are artificial in the sense that they are man-made, that they would not have occurred unless the experimenter made them occur. As Festinger (1953) has said,

> A laboratory experiment need not and should not be an attempt to duplicate a real life situation. If one wanted to study a real life situation it would be rather foolish to go to the trouble of setting up a laboratory experiment duplicating the real life condition. Why not simply go directly to the real life situation and study it? The laboratory experiment should be an attempt to create a situation in which the operation of variables will be clearly seen under special identified and defined conditions. It matters not whether such a situation would ever be encountered in real life. In most laboratory experiments such a situation would *never* be encountered in real life (p. 139).

An experimenter deliberately creates his experimental conditions so that they will allow him to investigate his hypothesis in a way that would not be possible in the ordinary course of events. By manipulating his independent variable he is better able to test a hypothesis about a causal relationship than he would be if he did not intervene in the normal course of events, for reasons we have discussed in the previous chapter. To say that experiments are artificial in the sense of being man-made is not in any way a criticism. It is simply a description of their essential nature.

There is a second sense of the term *artificial* that definitely would be a criticism if it applied to an experiment. If an experiment is artificial in the sense that what occurred in the experimental situation is irrelevant to what might occur outside the experimental situation, then the experiment is of no value. Whether or not this sense of the term *artificial* applies to an experiment depends on whether or not the particular experiment is well designed and its results provide evidence for some general hypothesis or general principle. If the results of an experiment do provide evidence for a general hypothesis, then they must be relevant to phenomena outside the experimental situation. If so, the experiment is not artificial in the second sense. If the hypothesis is general, it must also apply to other phenomena.

Experiments are not intended to duplicate what would occur in ordinary life, but a good experiment helps us to understand what occurs in ordinary, everyday situations. It does that if it provides evidence for a general hypothesis that will help to explain the phenomena of everyday life. We give a scientific explanation for a phenomenon when we show that it is a manifestation of a general principle or law. A scientific explanation "fits the phenomenon to be explained into a pattern of uniformities and shows that its occurrence was to be expected, given the specified laws and the pertinent particular circumstances" (Hempel, 1966, p. 50). As is evident throughout this book, the hypotheses that are tested in social psychological experiments are invariably stated in a general way so that they are applicable to a wide variety of situations.

Ordinarily the specific situation in which the experimenter tests his hypothesis is especially contrived *solely for that purpose*. What happens in the specific experimental situation is of interest only because it allows the investigator to draw conclusions about some general principle. The specific experimental situations are rarely of any intrinsic interest in themselves. For example, in the studies concerning the factors affecting liking for other persons discussed by Bramel in the first part of the book, the amount of liking the subjects indicated for the various stimulus persons was of no practical consequence whatsoever. The only reason that anyone would care about it is that it provides information about the general principles that help to explain why people like or dislike one another. Of course, in applied research, as opposed to the kind of theoretical research described in this book, what happens in the particular situation has great intrinsic interest. In such studies the measures are not regarded as indicators of theoretical variables, but are the focus of the study in and of themselves. An example might be the amount of money given to some cause.

The Generalization of Experimental Results

If the results of an experiment provide evidence for a general hypothesis, then they allow us to generalize—that is, to say that the hypothesis is true in general, that the variables are related not only in this particular instance but in all instances where they happen to vary. When one says that the results of a study cannot be generalized, he can only be saying, in effect, that the hypothesis is not true, that the results do not provide evidence for the hypothesis.

Scientists always try to make the most sense of a given result that is possible at the time, given the current state of knowledge in the field. If a result occurs, then it must be accounted for in some way. A particular result can be taken as evidence for a general hypothesis if it cannot be explained as well in any other way. If one is unwilling to consider a result as evidence for a general hypothesis, he must provide a different interpretation for the result that can explain it just as well as the general hypothesis. Usually a very careful examination of the procedure of the study is necessary, together with a good background in the particular area, in order to think of a possible alternative explanation for a particular result. Such an explanation must show how the result follows from the alternative hypothesis, given the particular circumstances of the study. It is not enough just to describe the results of the study in different terms. An explanation that goes beyond the data, that is more general, is always preferred because scientists always try to explain the maximum amount of data with the minimum number of general principles.

An alternative account for an experimental result may consist of an explanation by means of a completely different hypothesis or by a more limited, less general version of the original hypothesis. The distinction between these two different types of alternative explanation seems to be what Campbell (1957) is getting at in his distinction between the internal validity and the external validity of an experiment. Campbell defines internal validity in terms of the question, "Did in fact the experimental stimulus make some significant difference in this specific instance?" External validity is defined in terms of the question, "To what populations, settings, and variables can this effect be generalized?" It is not completely clear what Campbell means by the experimental stimulus, but it is most reasonable to assume that he is referring to the independent variable of the investigator's hypothesis. If the experimental stimulus referred to the particular experimental conditions the investigator creates in attempting to manipulate his independent variable, then any study with significant differences between the conditions would have internal validity.

One way of attacking the generalizability of a result is to attack the study's "internal validity," to explain the result by a different hypothesis. One might argue that the differences between the conditions were due to some variable other than the experimenter's independent variable or that they occurred because the measures reflected some variable other than his dependent variable. For example, Bramel, on page 29, provides an alternative explanation for the results of a study by Lott and Lott. In their study children played a game in groups and the experimenter manipulated the amount of reward they received by varying how successful they were in the game. The results indicated that the rewarded children chose proportionately more of their own teammates than did the nonrewarded children.

Bramel points out that these results cannot be considered good evidence for the hypothesis that people will like others who happen to be present at the time that they are rewarded, because differences in liking could have occurred for other reasons. He suggests that the rewarded children may have liked their teammates more because they felt that their teammates had helped them to do well in the game, or that the nonrewarded children disliked their teammates because they displaced their frustration-produced hostility onto their teammates. Thus Bramel suggests that the results might have occurred because of differences in variables other than the amount of reward the subjects received while the other persons happened to be present.

One need not claim that the results of a study can be interpreted by a completely different hypothesis in order to argue that they are not generalizable. Instead of attacking the "internal validity" of the study, one may attack its "external validity." One may grant that the independent variable had an effect on the dependent variable in the particular situation of the experiment but claim that the result may be taken as evidence only for a more limited version of the experimenter's hypothesis that states that the relationship holds only under certain conditions present in the experimental situation. One may argue that the independent and dependent variables are related only when some third variable has the specific value that it had in the particular situation. In other words, one may claim that there is a statistical interaction between the independent variable and some other variable in their effect on the dependent variable.

An example of a statistical interaction is depicted in Figure 16-1. It can be seen in Figure 16-1 that when some variable, X, is high, the relationship between the independent variable and the dependent variable is negative—that is, the higher the independent variable, the lower the dependent variable. However, when the variable X is low, the relationship between the independent variable and the dependent variable is positive —that is, the higher the independent variable, the higher the dependent variable.

A slightly more complicated example of a relationship that depends upon a third variable was presented by Kiesler when he described the study by Kiesler and Corbin on page 288. In that study it was shown that the effect of attraction to a group upon attitude change produced by disagreement with the group depends upon whether or not the members of the group are committed to continue in the group. When subjects were

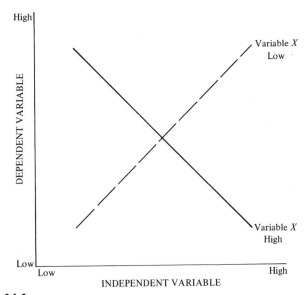

FIGURE 16-1.

An Example of a Statistical Interaction

not committed to continue, the lower their attraction to the group, the less the attitude change. However, when subjects were committed to continue in the group, there was a curvilinear relationship between attraction to the group and attitude change. Those subjects with low attraction to the group or high attraction changed more than those whose attraction was moderate. This result can be seen in Figure 11-1, page 288.

Suppose that someone did a study in which he found a positive relationship between attraction to the group and attitude change toward the group, and let us suppose that the members were not highly committed to continue their membership. In view of Kiesler's work on this topic, we would be unwilling to take this finding as evidence for a general positive relationship between attraction to the group and attitude change toward the group. Instead, we would interpret this result in terms of Kiesler's hypothesis that the relationship is positive only when commitment to continue membership is low, not when commitment is high. Thus we would provide an alternative interpretation that does not assume that the relationship is generally positive.

Of course, in most studies the problem of finding an alternative interpretation in terms of a more limited version of the experimenter's hypothesis is not already solved for us by previous research as in this hypothetical example. Ordinarily, one does not know that a relationship is affected by some additional factor until this factor is proposed and research is done to substantiate its effect on the relationship.

Sampling and the Generalization of Experimental Results

Frequently it is claimed that the results of experiments cannot be generalized because of the limited nature of the samples investigated. For example, it is often said that the results of experiments that use college students as subjects are applicable only to college students and that they cannot be generalized to other kinds of people. In a sense, any sample that is used to test a general relationship, such as the relationships discussed in this book, must be limited. It cannot be a random sample of all the instances to which the hypothesis applies because the hypothesis does not usually specify the time at which the people are living. Typically, the hypothesis applies to persons who are not yet born or who are no longer living. Obviously, such persons could not be included in the sample of subjects in an experiment. But if the sample of subjects were more representative of all the people who happen to be living at a particular time, would this increase our chances of making a correct generalization?

If one claims that the results of an experiment are not generalizable because they depend on some specific factor that happened to be present in the particular sample of subjects in the experiment, then one must be able to suggest what that factor might be and give a reasonable account of why the relationship that was obtained should occur only when that factor is present. Getting a "more representative" sample will not necessarily in itself help to solve the problem of discovering such factors and providing a reasonable explanation for why they should affect the relationship.

Festinger (1959) has made this point very clearly.

> Let us imagine that a research worker is concerned with investigating whether or not a relationship exists between certain specified environmental conditions and some specific behavior. Let us also imagine that there is some unknown variable "X" such that when "X" is low in magnitude, he would find a positive relationship between the environmental conditions and the behavior, and that when "X" is high in magnitude the relationship between the environmental variables and the behavior in question would be reversed and negative.
>
> Now, suppose that this research person engaged in a sampling procedure which was so biased that he obtained in his sample only people who were high on this unknown variable "X" of which the research worker was completely unaware. He would then obtain a negative correlation between his environmental variable and the behavior and would undoubtedly come to the conclusion that a negative relationship existed. It is clear that he would have come to a partially incorrect conclusion. But the important question is whether, if the research worker were in ignorance concerning the importance of variable "X", could be possibly have come to a fully correct conclusion with

better sampling? Let us assume that he did the study with the most accurate and beautiful methods. He would then have obtained a sample in which the variable "X" was distributed over the entire range and since this variable affects the direction of the relationship, his data would undoubtedly show a zero relationship overall between his environmental and behavior variables. Thus with perfect sampling he would come to the conclusion that his environmental and behavior variables were not related to one another at all. This it is clear would also be an incorrect conclusion. It would, thus, seem that as long as the research person is ignorant of the fact that variable "X" is a relevant variable, he could not possibly come to a correct conclusion.

[It may help the reader to grasp Festinger's point if he refers to Figure 16-1 and imagines what the relationship between the independent variable and the dependent variable would be if the curve for the relationship when variable X is high and the curve for the relationship when variable "X" is low were combined. These curves are, of course, drawn as straight lines in Figure 16-1.]

The question then becomes: What procedure would make it more likely that an investigator would develop some idea concerning variable "X" and hence discover its relevance? It is conceivable that an investigator could have, by accident, measured variable "X" and in the course of general exploration and analysis of his data, discovered its relevance, but this kind of accident is a relatively rare thing. More often the way such a hitherto unknown variable is discovered as relevant is by trying to reconcile contradictory results. One person may do a study and find a negative relationship between two variables. Another person, attempting to repeat the study, may find no relationship or a positive relationship. Someone may then get some hunch as to why this difference between the two studies exists which then leads to the discovery of the importance of variable "X". At any rate, this is a question of generating ideas, and good or bad sampling procedures in the collection of data has little to do with it. (p. 262–263)

As Festinger suggests, one of the best sources of new ideas about factors that might affect the relationship between two variables comes from contradictory results—that is, when an experiment is replicated and a different relationship is found. Beveridge (1957) has also made this point.

The essence of any satisfactory experiment is that it should be reproducible. In biological experimentation, it not infrequently happens that this criterion is difficult to satisfy. If the results of the experiment vary even though known factors have not been altered, it often means that some unrecognized factor or factors is affecting the results. Such occurrences should be welcomed, because a search for the unknown factor may lead to an interesting discovery. As a colleague remarked to me recently: "It is when experiments go wrong that we find things out." However, first one should see if a mistake has been made, as a technical error is the most common explanation. (p. 16)

Experimental Replications

Sometimes researchers will conduct a replication of a study, not because they believe that its hypothesis is correct and want to demonstrate it in a different way, but because they believe there was an artifact in the procedure of the original study and that the original hypothesis is not true. By an artifact we mean some defect or flaw in the procedure that allows one to explain the results in terms of an alternative hypothesis that is trivial. For example, if the results can be explained by the hypothesis that the subjects responded as they did because they wanted to please the experimenter or what has been called "demand characteristics of the situation," then the procedure would contain an artifact. If there is an artifact, then the results cannot be considered as evidence for a new, controversial hypothesis. Unless a hypothesis is controversial there is little point in trying to show that it is correct. Getting evidence for a well-accepted hypothesis adds very little to previous knowledge.

In order to demonstrate that a particular result was due to an artifact, one must show that when the procedure is altered so that the aspect that supposedly produces the artifact is changed but everything else is kept the same, the result does not occur. In addition, one must also show that the original result can be produced when the procedure containing the supposed artifact is repeated. It is difficult to give an example from this book of a study done solely to show that there was an artifact in a previous study because a study that shows only that a previous result is incorrect does not usually make a very great contribution to knowledge. Instead, let us suppose, for example, that an investigator wanted to show that the results of a previous study were due to "demand characteristics" that could have existed because the subjects could have perceived that the measure of the dependent variable was intended to test the effect that the experimental conditions had on them. He might redo the study using the two-experiment ploy so that the measure of the dependent variable was concealed in what was, as far as the subjects were aware, a completely different study. In addition, he would have to repeat the original procedure.

As Aronson and Carlsmith (1968) have emphasized, in order to show that a result occurred because of an artifact, it is not sufficient just to replicate the previous study with a changed procedure and fail to find the result. One must also show that one can find the previous result when the aspect of the procedure supposedly producing the artifact is not removed. This is true because nonsignificant or negative results are usually very difficult to interpret, for reasons that will be elaborated in the next chapter. As Beveridge indicated in the previous quotation, the most common explanation for failure to replicate a previous result is a technical error. Aronson and Carlsmith point out that an obvious but frequently overlooked problem about failures to replicate is that negative results are easily produced by incompetence. If an effect cannot be obtained, it may be that the experimenter is not skillful enough to obtain it.

In experiments involving deception, such as most of those in social psychology, the success of the experiment depends to a great extent on the skill of the experimenter in conducting the experiment. Running a deception experiment is similar in many respects to producing a play. One may have an excellent script, but if the acting and staging are poor, the play will be unsuccessful. An experimenter who acts in a halting, embarrassed, or mechanical way, even though he follows the script of the procedure literally, may be totally unconvincing, and the study will fail to create the proper conditions.

The importance in producing a convincing, credible situation of the way the experimenter acts means that social psychological experiments are particularly subject to what has been called "experimenter bias"— that is, the unintentional influence of the experimenter's behavior on the results. The experimenter may unintentionally deviate from the instructions in some subtle way, depending upon the condition the subject is in, to produce results he wants to obtain or expects to obtain. There has been a trend in social psychological experimentation in recent years to try to avoid experimenter bias by doing away with the human experimenter and having the experimental instructions produced by mechanical means. Unfortunately, these mechanical procedures tend to decrease experimental realism. Aronson and Carlsmith (1968) discuss ways of avoiding experimenter bias without eliminating the experimenter. These involve procedures that keep the experimenter unaware of which conditions the subjects are assigned to.

If one believes that the hypothesis of the original study is a general one, then the best strategy to use in replicating the result is to change the procedure of the original study as much as possible. Thus one might use a different manipulation of the independent variable in a new situation with different subjects, a different cover story, and a different measure of the dependent variable. To show that the same relationship is found even though many details of the procedure are changed is much more convincing support for the hypothesis than simply repeating the identical procedure and finding the same result. For example, the experiment by Gerard and Mathewson, (referred to by Bramel on page 76) replicated the study by Aronson and Mills on the effect of severity of initiation upon liking for a group, (described by Bramel on page 75) with a different manipulation of the severity of initiation than that used by Aronson and Mills.

In the Aronson and Mills study, the degree of unpleasantness required to become a member of the group was manipulated by using female college students as subjects and having some of them recite obscene words and lurid sexual passages in the presence of the male experimenter. In the Gerard and Mathewson study, the degree of unpleasantness required to join the group was varied by means of differences in the amount of electric shock the subjects underwent. Because it used a different manipulation of the amount of unpleasantness, the replication by Gerard and Mathewson provides a much more convincing demonstration of the hypothesis of the Aronson and Mills study than would a study that simply repeated the exact same procedure used in the original study.

If a study is repeated with a changed procedure and the same result is not obtained, the new study will probably provide a greater stimulus for new hypotheses that will reconcile the contradictory results than if the experimenter had attempted to repeat the same procedure exactly and failed to find the result. Practically speaking, it is usually impossible to repeat the procedure of a study exactly, with no changes whatsoever. If nothing else, the subjects will usually be somewhat different.

A point about replications that is sometimes overlooked is that if the procedure of a study is repeated with a different type of subject, it is possible that the original effect will not be found, even though the original hypothesis is correct and there really is a relationship between the independent and dependent variables. With the different type of subject the same procedure may not create the conditions necessary to demonstrate the relationship. A procedure that was successful in manipulating an independent variable with one kind of subject may be unsuccessful with another kind. For example, if one were to repeat the exact procedure of the Aronson and Mills study with male subjects, it would not be surprising if the result were not replicated. One would not expect that the variable of amount of unpleasantness required to join a group would be adequately manipulated by asking some men to recite obscene words and lurid sexual passages to a male experimenter.

It is also possible that with a different type of subject the same procedure may not produce an adequate measure of the dependent variable. For example, suppose that the measure was taken by means of a questionnaire in the original study and that the new subjects are too young or too unintelligent to be able to read well enough to understand the questionnaire. A procedure that involves an elaborate deception may be unsuccessful with a particular group of subjects because they have already participated in a previous study that used a similar deception and do not believe the cover story a second time. It is standard practice in experiments with an elaborate deception to reveal the deception at the end of the study and explain its necessity.

Another reason why a procedure might not yield evidence supporting a hypothesis when it is used with a different type of subject, even though the hypothesis is true, is that the new kind of subjects may have very extreme scores on the measure of the dependent variable. This could produce what is usually called a ceiling effect. For example, suppose the Aronson and Mills experiment was repeated with subjects who have a tremendous interest in any sort of discussion concerning sex, even though it is a discussion that most people would regard as very dull, about sex in animals. For such subjects the scores for the measure of attractiveness of the group might be extremely high even in the control condition. If the subjects in all conditions of an experiment are at the end point of the scale for the dependent variable, then there will be no room to show any difference between the conditions, and therefore any increase resulting from the independent variable.

17

The Limitations of Experiments

The most obvious limitation of the use of the experimental method in social psychology is that some of the independent variables that social psychologists might be interested in investigating are not amenable to manipulation. Some variables cannot be manipulated for moral or legal reasons. For example, it would not be ethical to do an experiment to investigate the effect that the permanent loss of a limb has on social interaction. One could not randomly assign subjects to one of two groups, an experimental group in which persons have a limb amputated or a control group in which limbs are not amputated. No social psychologist would want to conduct such a study, even if it were legally possible.

There are other independent variables that cannot be studied experimentally, even though it might not be immoral or illegal to manipulate them, simply because the social psychologist does not have the technical knowledge or economic resources to do so. For example, if one wanted to investigate the effect of owning a new automobile on interest in reading automobile advertisements, it would not be economically feasible to randomly give some subjects new automobiles.

In addition to the obvious limitation that many variables cannot be manipulated, experiments in social psychology also have some limitations with respect to the kinds of conclusions that can appropriately be drawn from their results. These limitations concerning the kinds of conclusions that can be drawn cannot be considered disadvantages of experimental studies as compared to nonexperimental studies. Nonexperimental studies concerned with testing relationships between theoretical variables have these same limitations, although not always for exactly the same reasons.

One limitation that is occasionally overlooked is that it is not possible to use the absolute size of the scores on the measure of the dependent variable in an experiment to draw conclusions about how much of this variable we can expect to find in other situations. This misunderstanding stems from a failure to distinguish hypothesis-testing studies, whose purpose is to test causal relationships between theoretical variables, from descriptive studies. In descriptive studies the purpose is to portray the characteristics of a group or to determine how frequently something occurs (Seltiz et al., 1959, Chapter 3). There is no independent variable in a descriptive study, and the measures are usually of interest in themselves rather than as indicators of a theoretical variable. The methodology of descriptive studies is quite different from that of hypothesis-testing studies because the kinds of bias that must be guarded against are quite different. For example, representative sampling is essential in descriptive studies.

In a laboratory experiment the absolute value of the measure of the dependent variable depends upon a number of specific aspects of the procedure that are arbitrarily chosen by the experimenter in creating the situation. It can be increased or decreased by changing the specific aspects of the situation that affect the value of other variables that influence the dependent variable. For example, in Schachter's experiments on anxiety and affiliation described by Bramel on page 24, the proportion of subjects who chose to be with other people was determined by the specific instructions the subjects were given. If the alternative to waiting with others had been described as something extremely interesting, no doubt many fewer subjects would have chosen to wait with others. From Schachter's studies we cannot conclude anything about how much, in general, people want to be with others.

Experimenters usually try to arrange their experimental situations so that they will avoid extreme values on their measures of the dependent variable in order to prevent ceiling effects. As we mentioned earlier, if all the subjects are at an extreme point on the measure of the dependent variable, it will be impossible to show any differences between the experimental conditions. There must be differences in the measure of the dependent variable in order to detect any effect on the dependent variable of the independent variable.

The nature of the instruments available at present to measure social psychological variables also makes it impossible to conclude anything from the absolute value of the scores for the dependent variable. At the present time we are able to measure social psychological variables, such as attitudes, only on what are called ordinal scales. An ordinal scale is a scale that measures the relative position on the variable, with no implications as to the distance between positions. "An ordinal scale is like an elastic tape measure that is being stretched unevenly; the scale positions as indicated by the numbers on the tape are in a clearly defined order, but the numbers do not provide a definite indication of the distance between any two points" (Seltiz et al., 1959, p. 191).

For example, if a person agrees with ten statements expressing a favorable attitude toward some object, we can conclude that his attitude toward that object is more favorable than that of a person who agrees with only five of the ten statements. However, we cannot conclude that the person who agrees with the ten statements has twice as favorable an attitude towards the issue as the person who agrees with only five statements. True, he agreed with twice as many statements, but we cannot assume that each statement that is agreed to indicates an equal difference in the amount of the attitude. If attitudes toward the object were measured in a different way, it is extremely doubtful whether the score on the different measure for the person who agreed with the ten statements would be twice as large as the score for the person who agreed with the five statements.

Social psychological variables are measured indirectly by measuring things that are related to the variables, just as temperature is measured by the length of a column of mercury. For example, group productivity is sometimes measured by the amount of time it takes the group to complete a task. However, in the case of social psychological measurements, the relationship between the measures and the underlying variables can seldom be assumed to be perfect. All we can usually assume is that the scores on the measure are correlated with the value of the variable so that, in general, the greater the scores, the greater the value of the variable. Rarely can it be assumed that each difference of one unit in the scores for the measure is equivalent to the same amount of difference in the underlying variable. If the scores on the measure of the dependent variable only provide a relative measure of the variable, we cannot conclude anything from them about how much of the variable is present in a particular instance.

The Difficulty of Establishing the Exact Nature of Relationships

Social psychology experiments are also limited in that the absolute size of the differences between the experimental conditions on the measure of the dependent variable does not permit us to conclude anything about how much effect the independent variable has on the dependent variable or how strong the relationship between the variables is. By the strength of the relationship between the independent and dependent variables we mean how many units the dependent variable is changed when the independent variable changes one unit. So, for example, a relationship would be very strong if a change of one unit in the independent variable produces a change of many units in the dependent variable. On the other hand, a relationship would be very weak if a change of one unit on the independent variable produced a change of only a fraction of a unit on the dependent variable. Examples of a strong relationship and a weak relationship are depicted in Figure 17-1.

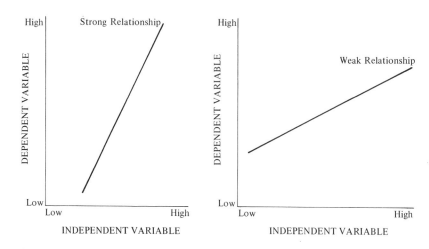

FIGURE 17-1.

Examples of a Relatively Strong and a Relatively Weak Relationship

Because we only have ordinal measures of the dependent variable, because the units of the measure are not equivalent to units of the variable itself, we cannot establish whether a relationship is strong or weak in the sense depicted in Figure 17-1. There might be a large difference between the conditions in the scores for the measure of the dependent variable when the actual difference in the value of the variable is rather small. Or there might be a small difference in the scores when the difference in the variable is large.

Because of the nature of our measures it is not possible to demonstrate that a particular independent variable has more effect on one dependent variable than it has on another dependent variable. In order to do that, it would be necessary to equate the amount of change in the first variable with the amount of change in the second variable. That is possible only if the variables are measured by ratio scales—that is, scales that not only have equal units but also zero points that are not arbitrary. Then one could say that the percentage by which one dependent variable was increased by a change in the independent variable was greater than the percentage by which another dependent variable was increased by the same change. The percentage by which a variable increases cannot be determined unless the measuring instrument has a true zero point, which is not the case at present for measures of social psychological variables. Of course one can say that the scores for the measure of a variable increased by a certain percentage. But that cannot be taken as an indication of the amount the underlying variable increased, as long as the zero point for the measure is completely arbitrary.

Although we cannot show that the relationship between a particular independent variable and a dependent variable is stronger than the relationship between that independent variable and a second dependent variable, we can show that the relationship between an independent variable and a dependent variable is stronger or weaker, depending upon the presence or absence of other factors. Conclusions of the kind depicted in Figure 17-1 should not be confused with conclusions about statistical interactions such as depicted in Figure 16-1 in the preceding chapter. Perhaps the most valuable kinds of experimental studies in social psychology are ones that find a statistical interaction between two independent variables in their effect on a dependent variable. To show that a phenomenon varies as a function of certain conditions usually helps a great deal to narrow down the possible explanations for the phenomenon.

Another reason why we cannot draw any conclusions from the absolute size of the differences between the experimental conditions is that they will depend upon how strongly the independent variable was manipulated, how much the experimental conditions differed on the average in the value of the independent variable. If the independent variable was manipulated very strongly, there might be a large difference between the experimental conditions in the measure of the dependent variable, even though there is only a weak relationship between the variables. On the other hand, there might be a small difference between the conditions when there is a very strong relationship because the manipulation of the independent variable was very weak. Examples of these possibilities are depicted in Figure 17-2.

At the present time, the different conditions in social psychological experiments can only be ranked on the average amount of the independent variable present. In a sense we have only ordinal manipulations of the independent variable. We cannot tell exactly how large the differences between the conditions are for the independent variable. If there are, say, three conditions varying in the amount of the independent variable, we usually cannot be sure whether the difference between the "high" condition and the "medium" condition on the independent variable is greater or less than the difference between the "medium" condition and the "low" condition. For example, suppose an experimenter manipulated the amount of fear by telling some subjects that they will receive ten electric shocks, other subjects that they will receive six electric shocks, and others that

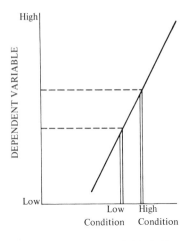
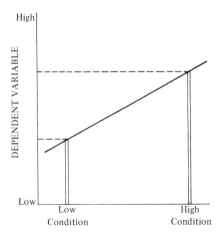

FIGURE 17-2.

> *An Example of a Smaller Difference for the Dependent Variable When a Relationship Is Relatively Strong Than When a Relationship Is Relatively Weak*

they will receive two electric shocks. We cannot be confident that the amount of difference in fear between the ten-shock condition and the six-shock condition is the same as the amount of difference in fear between the six-shock condition and the two-shock condition.

The ordinal nature of the manipulation of independent variables means that it is not possible to draw any conclusions about the exact shape of the relationship between the independent and dependent variable. We cannot establish whether a relationship is positively accelerated or negatively accelerated. The difference between the "high" condition and the "medium" condition on the dependent variable may be greater than the difference between the "medium" condition and the "low" condition simply because there is a greater difference between the "high" and "medium" conditions on the independent variable. Figure 17-3 presents an example of such a case where the results of the study might seem to indicate that the relationship between the variables is positively accelerated when it is really negatively accelerated. We are also prevented from drawing conclusions about the exact shape of the relationship because of the ordinal nature of the measures of the dependent variable.

Of course, if there are three conditions that vary in amount of the independent variable, it is possible to find evidence of a nonmonotonic relationship—that is, there may be a larger amount of the measure of the dependent variable in the "medium" condition than in either the "high"

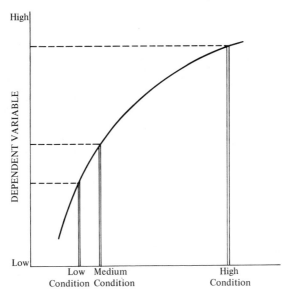

FIGURE 17-3.

An Example of a Result Which Appears to Indicate a Positively Accelerated Relationship When the Relationship Is Actually Negatively Accelerated

or the "low" conditions. An example of a nonmonotonic relationship is depicted in Figure 17-4. It is also possible to show that the relationship between an independent and dependent variable is monotonic under one level of a third variable and is nonmonotonic under another level of the third variable. We have seen an example of this in the study by Kiesler and Corbin, who found that the relationship between attraction to the group and attitude change toward the group was positive when commitment to continue in the group was low, but was nonmonotonic when commitment to continue was high (see Figure 11-1).

It might be thought that the problem of establishing how much the experimental conditions differed on the value of the independent variable could be solved by getting a measure of the independent variable. However, this will not really solve the problem unless the independent variable can be measured on more than an ordinal scale. As we have already discussed, this is not feasible with social psychological variables at present.

Suppose we tried to measure the amount of fear produced by telling subjects that they would receive ten, six, or two shocks, by asking them to rate how fearful they felt on a scale from zero (not at all fearful) to 100 (extremely fearful). If we found that the subjects in the ten-shock group

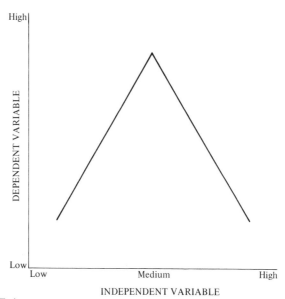

FIGURE 17-4.

An Example of a Nonmonotonic Relationship

gave an average rating of 90 on this scale, whereas subjects in the six-shock group gave an average rating of 50, and those in the two-shock group gave an average rating of 10, we could not be certain that the difference between the ten-shock group and the six-shock group in the amount of fear was the same as the difference between the six-shock group and the two-shock group in the amount of fear. We cannot be sure that the difference between a rating of 90 and a rating of 50 represents the same degree of difference in fear as the difference between a rating of 50 and a rating of 10. We cannot assume a perfect, one-to-one correlation between the size of the ratings and the amount of fear.

Because we have no way of knowing exactly how strong the manipulation of the independent variable is in social psychological experiments, they do not permit us to establish which of two different independent variables has the most effect on a particular dependent variable. If we find that experimental conditions that differ in the first independent variable show greater differences on the measure of the dependent variable than do conditions that differ on the second independent variable, we cannot conclude that the first independent variable has a stronger effect on the dependent variable than the second independent variable does. It may simply be that the manipulation of the first independent variable was stronger than the manipulation of the second independent variable. Of course one can say that a particular manipulation of one variable had more effect in a particular situation on a specific measure of the dependent variable. But one cannot conclude from this that, in general, the relationship between the first independent variable and the dependent variable is stronger than the relationship between the second independent variable and the dependent variable.

For example, suppose in a study of attitude change the experimenter manipulated two independent variables—perceived sincerity of the communicator in presenting his communication and perceived expertness of the communicator. Suppose that he had a condition where the communicator was seen as high in sincerity and high in expertness, a condition in which the communicator was seen as high in sincerity and low in expertness, one in which the communicator was seen as low in sincerity and high in expertness, and one in which the communicator was seen as low in sincerity and low in expertness. Suppose that in the high-sincerity conditions the subjects were told that people who know the communicator consider him highly honest, and in the low-sincerity conditions subjects were told that people who know the communicator consider him rather dishonest. Suppose that the subjects were told in the high-expertness conditions that the communicator was considered highly intelligent by those who know him and in the low-expertness conditions that he was considered rather stupid by those who know him.

Suppose that the average amount of agreement with the communicator's position in the four experimental conditions was as presented in Table 17-1. From the table it can be seen that in this hypothetical experiment the

TABLE 17-1.   *Hypothetical Results of an Experiment Varying the Perceived Sincerity and Expertness of a Communicator*

| | Expertness | |
Sincerity	*High*	*Low*
High	20	15
Low	10	5

Note: The higher the score, the greater the agreement with the communicator.

differences in agreement with the communicator's position between the high-sincerity and low-sincerity conditions were greater than the differences between the high-expertness and low-expertness conditions. However, from these data we would not be justified in concluding that perceived sincerity of the communicator has more effect on attitude change than perceived expertness of the communicator. It could be that the effect that telling subjects the communicator is considered honest or dishonest has upon the perception of his sincerity is greater than the effect that telling them the communicator is considered intelligent or stupid has upon the perception of his expertness.

Sometimes experimenters will try to pit two independent variables against each other by comparing a condition that is high on the first independent variable and low on the second independent variable with a condition that is low on the first variable and high on the second. For example, a condition in which the communicator is seen as high in sincerity and low in expertness might be compared with a condition in which he is seen as high in expertness and low in sincerity. Such an experiment would consist of two of the four conditions represented in Table 17-1.

If the results of such an experiment indicate a higher value of the dependent variable in one condition than the other, we cannot conclude that one independent variable has more effect on the dependent variable than the other independent variable has. The differences between the conditions in the value on the first independent variable may have been greater than the differences between the conditions in the value on the second independent variable, so that in this particular situation the effect of the first variable outweighed the effect of the second. But if the manipulation of the second variable had been stronger and the manipulation of the first variable weaker, the opposite result might have occurred.

In the hypothetical experiment on effect of the sincerity and expertness of the communicator, attitude change was greater in the high-sincerity-low-expertness condition than in the low-sincerity–high-expertness condition. But, as we have already suggested, the difference in amount of sincerity between the two conditions may have been greater than the difference in the amount of expertness. If expertness had been manipulated more strongly and sincerity less strongly, it might have been found that attitude change was lower in the high-sincerity–low-expertness condition than in the low-sincerity–high-expertness condition.

The Ambiguity of Negative Results

Another limitation of experiments in social psychology is that if there are no significant differences between the experimental conditions, we rarely can conclude that the hypothesis is false, that there is no true relationship between the independent and dependent variables. Because one failed to find a relationship between variables does not necessarily prove that there is no real relationship. There are a number of reasons why experiments with nonsignificant or negative results are inconclusive, in addition to the statistical point that one can never prove the null hypothesis.

In order to provide an adequate test of a causal relationship, it is necessary that the experimenter successfully create differences between his experimental conditions in the value of his independent variable and that he measure his dependent variable adequately enough so that he can detect differences that may be produced by the independent variable. If an experiment fails to yield significant differences between experimental treatments, there is usually the possibility that the independent variable was not successfully manipulated, that the experimental conditions did not differ in the average value of the independent variable.

Social psychology is a rapidly developing field, and there is little agreement at the present time about what the relevant variables are or how they should be defined. Most experiments deal with relationships that have not been investigated previously. In most cases the procedures used to manipulate the variables have had to be developed specifically for the particular experiment and have been used for the first time. Even though the independent and dependent variables may each have been investigated in previous studies, it is likely that a new manipulation and a new measure must be developed so that the two will fit together under the same cover story. If the deceptions that are used in order to manipulate the independent variables do not turn out to be credible to the subjects, the manipulations will be unsuccessful. As we have noted previously, the success of a procedure in creating the intended conditions depends to a large extent on the skill of the experimenter. If the experimenter does not present the instructions in a convincing manner, the independent variable will not be manipulated.

If there are significant differences between the experimental conditions on the measure of the dependent variable, then we can conclude that the experimenter manipulated something. He may not have manipulated the variable he thought he had, or he may have manipulated some other variables along with the one he intended to manipulate, but at least he must have manipulated some variable. If the differences are statistically significant, then we are unwilling to accept the hypothesis that they occurred simply because of chance factors or random variation. If there were no significant differences, we cannot assume the experimental manipulation was successful unless there is independent evidence for this assumption.

Sometimes experimenters will try to check on the success of their manipulation of the independent variable by getting a measure of the independent variable in addition to their measure of the dependent variable. For example, we considered the possibility that an experimenter who had attempted to manipulate the amount of fear by threatening subjects with different numbers of electric shocks might try to measure the amount of fear in the different experimental conditions by asking the subjects to rate how frightened they felt. If the experimental conditions differed significantly on this check of the independent variable, then we would have evidence that the manipulation was effective, at least to some extent. However, because of the ordinal nature of our measures, a measure of the independent variable does not permit us to say how strong the manipulation was, for reasons we have discussed previously. Such measures usually have the disadvantage of requiring a more elaborate cover story to conceal their purpose from the subject.

Even if there are significant differences between the conditions on a measure of the independent variable, we can still not be certain that there is no true relationship between the independent and dependent variables when there are no significant differences between the conditions for the dependent variable. It is possible that the measure of the independent variable was extremely sensitive, that there was a very strong relationship between the amount of the independent variable and scores on the measure. If so, the measure may have detected the effect of the manipulation, even though the manipulation was very weak and there was only a relatively small difference between the experimental conditions in the average value of the independent variable. A large difference in the amount of the independent variable in the different conditions may be required in order to detect a difference between the conditions on the measure of the dependent variable. The relationship between the independent and dependent variables may be relatively weak, or the measure of the dependent variable may be relatively insensitive to differences in the dependent variable, or there may be many other factors in the situation affecting the dependent variable.

For example, in the study by Hovland and Mandell described by Berscheid and Walster on page 148, a check on the manipulation of the perception of the communicator's sincerity revealed significant differences between the high-credibility and low-credibility conditions. However, there was no significant difference between the conditions in acceptance of the communicator's position. Later research has shown that there is a relationship between the perception of the communicator's sincerity and acceptance of his position. Hovland and Mandell may have failed to find this relationship because their manipulation of the perception of the communicator's sincerity was not strong enough.

If there are significant differences for the measure of the dependent variable but none for the check on the independent variable, then it is possible that the manipulation was effective but that the check was relatively insensitive. If there are differences for the measure of the dependent variable, this in itself is evidence that the manipulation did have some effect. We still have the problem, which exists in any study, of making sure there are no equally feasible alternative interpretations for the result.

However, having a check on the independent variable will not in itself help to protect against alternative interpretations. To show that the experimental conditions did or did not differ on a measure of the independent variable does not provide evidence about whether or not they differed on other factors that might also affect the dependent variable. As we have noted previously, it is necessary to examine the details of the procedure very closely in the light of previous knowledge to determine whether or not there are possible alternative interpretations.

Even if the manipulation was quite successful, it is still possible that an experiment will yield negative results when in fact there is a relationship, because the measure of the dependent variable was not adequate enough to detect the true differences between the experimental conditions that occurred in the dependent variable. One reason the measure of the dependent variable may be inadequate is that it is just too crude to show anything but very gross differences in the dependent variable. For example, if we measured a person's attitude toward some issue by asking him simply whether he was in favor or opposed on the issue, we might not be able to detect very well changes that occurred in his attitude toward the issue. He might have changed his attitude from being very much opposed to being moderately opposed, but as far as we could tell from our question, he would still be opposed. If we had asked him how much he was opposed, our measure might have shown a change in his attitude.

Another reason why the measure of the dependent variable may be inadequate is that it reflects a multitude of other factors, in addition to the differences in the dependent variable, that vary randomly from one person to another. This is what psychologists usually mean by a measure that is unreliable. For example, if answers to a question that is intended to measure people's attitude toward an issue also depend on their mood at the moment, how much they like the questioner, how well they understand the question, what they think is socially acceptable, how important they think the study is, how tired they are, and many other factors such as these, the measure would be considered rather unreliable as a measure of attitude.

If the measure of the dependent variable varies as a function of many other variables in addition to the dependent variable, then it will be relatively insensitive to whatever differences in the dependent variable may be caused by differences in the independent variable. The more insensitive the measure of the dependent variable is, the more difficult it will be to show the relationship between the independent and dependent variables —that is, to detect a significant difference between the experimental conditions in the value of the measure of the dependent variable.

Sometimes researchers will try to assess the adequacy of their measure of the dependent variable by calculating the correlation between scores from one administration of the measure and scores from a second administration (usually called "test–retest" reliability). Or, if the measure consists of different parts or different items that are combined to form a total score, they may calculate a correlation between scores from one part of the measure and scores from another part (usually called "split-half" reliability). This sort of measurement of the adequacy of the measure of the dependent variable is analogous to providing a check on the manipulation of the independent variable by trying to measure the independent variable directly.

If the measure of the reliability of the measure of the dependent variable as indicated by a test–retest or split-half coefficient indicates that the measure has a certain degree of reliability, we cannot be sure that this degree of reliability of the measure was great enough in the particular situation to permit the experimenter to show the effect of the independent variable on the dependent variable. The manipulation of the independent variable may have been weak or the relationship between the variables may be relatively weak, so that an extremely reliable measure may be required in order to show a significant difference between the experimental conditions.

It is not possible to say exactly how high the reliability of the measure of the dependent variable should be in a particular experimental study. If the manipulation is very strong or the relationship is quite strong, it may be possible to show the effect of the independent variable on the dependent variable even though the measure of the dependent variable is relatively unreliable. If an experimenter finds significant differences between his experimental conditions, then his measurement of the dependent variable can be considered reliable enough for his purposes. Unreliability of the measure, or variation due to chance factors, can only have the effect of reducing the possibility of obtaining a significant difference—that is, a difference that is large enough so that it cannot be attributed to random errors. Of course, it is necessary in experimental work that the measures of the dependent variable be reliable, but *measures of reliability* of the measures are not necessary.

Still another reason why studies that yield negative results are inconclusive is the possibility that the experimental situation was too uncontrolled in the sense that there were a great many other factors varying in the situation that also influenced the dependent variable in addition to the experimenter's independent variable. If there are a great many other factors affecting the dependent variable, experimental error, or differences *within* the experimental conditions, may be so large that the differences *between* the conditions will not be statistically significant. Nonsignificant differences can also occur because of a ceiling effect, as mentioned previously. If there is no room for differences between the conditions in the measure of the dependent variable, it will not be possible to detect any effect of the independent variable on the dependent variable.

Aronson and Carlsmith (1968) have summed up the problem of interpreting negative results as follows:

> There are literally dozens of reasons for the failure of a given experiment to confirm a hypothesis, only one of which is that the hypothesis is wrong. In an area like social psychology, with few standardized procedures for manipulating the independent variable, where ethics and good taste confine us to weak empirical operations, and where our measuring instruments are rather insensitive, it seems almost miraculous that *any* "true" hypotheses get confirmed experimentally. Consequently, it would be somewhat arrogant of the experimenter to conclude, after one failure, that the hypothesis was incorrect—arrogant in the sense that such a conclusion implies that the experimental operations were perfect. (p. 74)

As Festinger (1959) has said, "In general a study which yields no differences or no relationships contributes little to our knowledge. . . . The way to do research which contributes to our knowledge is to somehow be clever enough to find differences and relationships" (p. 365). The essential ambiguity of negative results is the reason that journals rarely publish studies that did not find significant relationships. "It is a commendable custom usually not to publish investigations which merely fail to substantiate the hypothesis they were designed to test" (Beveridge, 1957, p. 25).

From the difficulty of proving that a hypothesis is incorrect, it should not be concluded that there are no safeguards that prevent the spread of false hypotheses. We need not fear that social psychologists will continue to believe that relationships exist when in fact they do not, because of the difficulty of proving that they do not. Social psychologists are very skeptical of the truth of hypotheses, particularly the hypotheses of other social psychologists. Unless there is positive evidence for a hypothesis, social psychologists as a group will not give it much credence. We have been mainly concerned in this section with the conclusions that can be drawn from a particular experiment, but of course the results of a number of different experiments using a wide variety of different procedures must provide evidence for a hypothesis before it is considered well established.

The inherent ambiguity of studies that fail to show any differences or relationships has consequences for the strategy that is most fruitful in testing general theories. If someone believes that a particular theory is incorrect, it is not very useful for him to try to disprove the theory by thinking of some effect or some relationship that should follow from the theory and then to do a study in order to show that this effect does not occur. If the study fails to find evidence of the effect, this will not provide strong evidence that the theory is incorrect because of the possibility that the procedure of the study was inadequate, that the study did not create the conditions that the theory says are necessary for the effect to occur.

A better strategy to use to attack a theory is to think of an effect that cannot be explained by the theory and then to do a study that shows that this effect occurs. However, in order to overturn a current theory it is not enough just to find a new phenomenon that cannot be accounted for by the theory. Observers of the history of science have noted that theories are rarely given up simply because they cannot explain all the facts. Conant (1947) has concluded, "We can put it down as one of the principles learned from the history of science that a theory is only overthrown by a better theory, never merely by contradictory facts" (p. 36). Beveridge (1957) has made the same point. "Once ideas have gained credence they are rarely abandoned merely because some contradictory facts are found. False ideas are only dropped when hypotheses more in accord with the new facts are put forward" (pp. 51, 52).

References

Aronson, E., and Carlsmith, J. M. Experimentation in social psychology. In G. Lindzey and E. Aronson (eds.), *Handbook of Social Psychology*, Vol. II, 2nd. ed., Cambridge, Mass.: Addison-Wesley, 1968.

Beveridge, W. I. B. *The Art of Scientific Investigation*, 2nd. ed. New York: W. W. Norton, 1957.

Campbell, D. T. Factors relevant to the validity of experiments in social settings. *Psychological Bulletin*, 1957, **54**, 297–312.

Conant, J. B. *On Understanding Science*. New Haven, Conn.: Yale University Press, 1947.

Festinger, L. Laboratory experiments. In L. Festinger and D. Katz (eds.), *Research Methods in the Behavioral Sciences*. New York: Holt, Rinehart, and Winston, 1953.

Festinger, L. Sampling and related problems in research methodology. *American Journal of Mental Deficiency*, 1959, **64**, 358–366.

Festinger, L., Garner, W. R., Hebb, D. O., Hunt, H. F., Lawrence, D. H., Osgood, C. E., Skinner, B. F., and Taylor, D. W. Education for research in psychology. *American Psychologist*, 1959, **14**, 167–179.

Hempel, C. G. *Philosophy of Natural Science*. Englewood Cliffs, N. J.: Prentice-Hall, 1966.

Jones, E. E. and Gerard, H. B. *Social Psychology*, New York: John Wiley and Sons, 1967.

Seltiz, C., Jahoda, M., Deutsch, M., and Cook, S. W. *Research Methods in Social Relations*, 2nd ed. New York: Holt, Rinehart, and Winston, 1959.

Indexes

Name Index

Subject Index